GW01451561

Jim's Blog
Volume 1

Jim

West Martian Limited Company
1st Edition, January 2024

First printing 2024
The publisher can be contacted at westmartian.com
ISBN-13: 979-8-218-35267-7 Paperback

Contents

Jim's Blog
Volume 1

Stop the @#$%^&* whining!

2008-03-07 21:13:38

Yair Lapid self pityingly whines[1] "why do they hate us?", "us" being in this case the Jews, though it could equally well be any group that is economically successful and reluctant to murder innocents.

What a maroon! It is same reason as they hate everyone, only more so. Just look at everyone else who gets hated then murdered.

The most recent event was in Kenya, where a party won the election on a platform that sounds like a euphemism for "Kill the Kikuyu". (Fortunately the government burned the ballots.)

Why do they hate the Kikuyu? Well the number one item on the list that Kikuyu tend to occupy jobs that require ability, enterprise, ambition, foresight and patience. Another big complaint is that when Kikuyu farm land, a small amount of farmland supports a surprisingly large number of Kikuyu at a surprisingly high standard of living – at least it surprises the people who are so much enraged. They conclude that the Kikuyu must have benefited unfairly from some kind of evil plot.

Check back to the most recent genocide: Hutus massacring Tutsis: What is in the complaint list: More of the same!

And let us look at which nations and individuals are *still* backing the Hutus. Who wants war crimes charges against the Tutsis for defending themselves against genocide: Same people who want war crimes charges against the Jews for defending themselves.

Recall Hitler's indictment of the Jews:

> Von 100 Ärzten 52 Juden, und von 100 Geschäftsleuten 60 Juden. Das Durch-schnittsvermögen des einzelnen Deutschen betrug 810 Mark. Das Durch-schnittsvermögen des einzelnen Juden betrug 10.000 Mark.

Translation:

> Of 100 doctors 52 were Jews and of 100 businessmen were 60 Jews. The average assets of individuals amounted to 810 German marks. The average assets of individual Jews was 10,000 marks.

Let us go back to a recent mass murder that was bigger than the holocaust of the Jews: The liquidation of the kulaks. What was the indictment against the kulaks? And who endorsed that indictment: Same people who now indict Israel. The campuses and the intellectuals were jumping for joy when the liquidation of the kulaks was under way. During the liquidation of the kulaks the intellectual who had graduated with a thesis titled "the hermeneutic negritude of linguistic lesbianism" thought to himself "How dare those damned Jews kulaks become so well paid as doctors and lawyers when the oppressive capitalistic American imperialist world order refuses to reward me for my brilliant studies of the hermeneutics of language oppressing black lesbians.

---

[1] https://rantsand.blogspot.com/2008/03/damn-good-question.html

So cut the damned whining. You sound just like the people who are trying to murder you.

When you go for a run, there are dogs that will see a running man, and seeing running, will see prey, and attack. You have to thump them viciously, and they soon learn to keep their distance. If they don't, you were not vicious enough. Similarly, when people see wealth, they see high status, and when they see high status without brutality and murder, they think they see weakness, and so they attack.

And when they hear whining, they hear weakness, and so they attack.

Stop whining. Kill someone.

To the man who wrote the thesis about the hermeneutic negritude of linguistic lesbianism, wealth without strength is a crime, whining shows weakness, and to him, only murder shows strength. To stop him hating, you have to kill people in a fashion that he is likely to believe is murder. He is never going to comprehend economics and the creation of wealth any more than the dog is going to understand running for exercise.

Stop whining, start killing.

commodity money
2008-03-09 21:15:58

The subprime crisis represents massive unpunished malfeasance by financial intermediaries managing US dollars. This discourages people from using US dollars as money.

In 2008 January, the fed drove real dollar interest rates negative - only slightly negative, but negative interest rates suggest an intent to inflate away the dollar denominated liabilities of financial intermediaries until the real assets cover the dollar denominated liabilities. In the ensuing two months, all commodities that are readily storable and have large liquid markets, all commodities that can usefully function as a store of value, went up around twenty percent:[2] aluminum, barley, cocoa, coffee, copper, corn, cotton, gold, lead, oats, oil, silver, tin, wheat, zinc.

This suggests that when fiat money collapses, a process likely to take place in fits and starts over a very long time rather than all at once, we will move towards a balanced basket of commodities, rather than return to the gold standard.

Measuring global warming
2008-03-10 21:17:31

The simple and obvious way to measure global warming is to look at results from weather stations. Unfortunately results from weather stations are subject to large systematic errors: Weather stations are generally located in or near cities, and near human habitation. Cities are typically several degrees warmer than the surrounding countryside, and have been expanding.

Steve McIntyre[3] has been examining how weather stations have been used to construct an estimate of global climate change. The examination suggests that estimates

---

[2]https://www.econbrowser.com/archives/2008/03/commodity_price_1.html
[3]https://www.climateaudit.org/

based on weather stations are unlikely to be accurate. Data has been arbitrarily include or excluded, locations have been arbitrarily classified as rural or urban, and the "adjustment" for the urban heat island effect seems likely to increase, rather than reduce the error caused by the urban heat island effect. Overall, the adjustment has resulted in an adjustment up over time rather than down over time, which would imply the absurd conclusion that weather stations are getting less urbanized.

One measure that *could* be very accurate is satellite measurement, for one then has a single instrument measuring the entire earth, and that instrument measures temperatures directly, and can be checked for reliability.

The satellite directly measures temperature against an absolute standard. One potentially area for creative accounting comes in the averaging to get *global* warming. One suspects a too clever by half averaging, similar to the too clever by half adjustment of urban sites that Steve McIntyre exposed.

The satellite directly measures the temperature of *something*, but that something is not the atmosphere at a particular height. To derive the temperature at a particular height is model dependent, depends on quantities that are not readily observable. The model can be rather too easily adjusted to give whatever results are desired. Perhaps, if we are only interested in the global anomaly, we can dispense with the model, and just look at the temperature of those wavelengths that have decent penetration to the lower atmosphere, telling us that *something* mighty big has warmed, or failed to warm, even if there is some uncertainty as to what the something we are looking at is.

To allay this suspicion, that the calculations are cooked to get a politically acceptable result, we really should have access to the raw data, and the algorithm by which it averaged.

Seems to me that if we simply took the average observed temperature at wavelengths with good penetration, that would be a good measure of global warming or cooling, and would not be vulnerable to suspicion of too clever by half corrections and adjustments.

Further, if such a simple uncomplicated average gave a result that was discordant with the adjusted data, then we could demand a plausible physical explanation of the difference.

For a long time, the advocates of anthropogenic global warming failed to explain how they derived global climate from weather station data. When this was finally revealed, it failed audit. The method was not plausible, nor were the advocates faithfully employing the method they purported to follow, but rather were arbitrarily including some data and excluding other data.

We therefore need to know how satellite temperature is used to derive global climate, and need to get access to the direct instrumental readings of temperature, in order that these also can be audited.

The satellite directly measures temperature at certain frequencies against an absolute standard. What is the simple average of the direct measurement over time at each frequency? We should be able to know.

If one wants to know the temperature at a particular location, then it is important to take account of the details of the satellite's orbit, since it moves mighty fast, and things can potentially get complicated. If we want to know the temperature at a particular altitude, the atmosphere is not entirely transparent to heat, and we need to model the atmosphere, which we do not know how to do all that precisely. These adjustments are likely to complex and open to debate. But if one wants to know the variation in global temperature, we don't really care about this stuff, and the raw temperature measurements should do fine.

Cause of International Inequality

2008-03-11 22:30:26

Arnold Kling is much puzzled[4] by the inequality of nations. I don't know why. The answer is pretty obvious.

Firstly, you require capitalism, which requires not mere formal laws recognizing private property, but a culture of respect for entrepreneurship, for property rights in productive capital and freedom to do business. With that respect, the laws are unnecessary, as in today's China. Without that respect, the laws are useless, as in Argentina and Russia.

Secondly, given capitalism, you require people able to operate modern capitalism, able function in a business encompassing numerous people – you require people whose verbal IQ is higher than 105. By and large, the capitalist portion of the economy, the portion that produces wealth, will be proportional to number of people with an IQ higher than 105.

If we look at countries that are reasonable capitalist, and these days a large part of the countries of the world are reasonably capitalist, the GDP per head is fairly closely proportional to fraction of the population with a verbal IQ higher than 105, the smart fraction.[5]

Global warmers lie again 1

2008-03-11 22:31:39

According to a statement[6] issued by the World Wide Fund for nature a few hours ago:

> "Hundreds of newborn seal cubs risk dying of hunger and cold because global warming is making ice in the Arctic Circle melt too fast"When the ice melts too fast, the cubs end up in the ice water before they have their insulating fat layer, and they die painfully of hunger and cold.

> "The WWF said there was less ice in the Arctic this winter than at any point in the past 300 years."

Needless to say, according to satellite observations[7], the ice the arctic this winter is at the exact average that it has been during the period that it has been subject to satellite observation, and no one has any clear idea what it was like three hundred years ago.

[4]https://econlog.econlib.org/archives/2008/03/international_i.html
[5]https://www.lagriffedulion.f2s.com/sft2.htm
[6]https://afp.google.com/article/ALeqM5ju8ePn59RV6AneCYJIaBlsGpRFUg
[7]https://arctic.atmos.uiuc.edu/cryosphere/IMAGES/recent365.anom.region.1.html

Which is irrational, the Fed or the market?

2008-03-12 22:32:31

The economist is puzzled[8] that the very rational Fed is having such difficulty bringing rationality to those terribly irrational markets:

> the more frightening tremors in the system are those generated by the seemingly irrational unwillingness to hold safe investments, thereby making the safe unsafe.

And to cure this terrible irrationality, the Fed is injecting liquidity buying dud mortgages.

Hang on. Dud mortgates are not safe investments. They are extremely speculative investments. The Fed is going into the the real estate business, suddenly becoming the nations largest owner and seller of houses, something far outside its expertise and administrative abilities. Being a rentier is hard, and the Fed has no experience or organization to do it. Vast numbers of houses are bound to sit empty, or be occupied by squatters paying no rent.

Government is not permitting land to be subdivided to build houses, and to sustain the price of houses, government is now buying up troubled mortgages, thus buying up houses in foreclosure, thus pouring gigantic amounts of money into the property market. But there is quite a bit of horded land in out of the way areas that received subdivision permission back in the days when subdivision was easier, in effect, horded permissions, and of course, in response to these huge prices, people are moving to that land. Thus though housing prices overall will rise, as the price of horded permissions rise, bubble areas must fall. The Fed is doing a King Canute, and will wind up owning extravagantly priced property in Silicon valley which will, as government owned housing tends to do, turn into slums.

Fed blows three hundred billion in one day.

2008-03-13 22:36:13

Yesterday, the fed, in an effort to restore liquidity, "loaned" the banks three hundred billion dollars with mortgage backed securities as "security". Because these securities are not worth @#% it in fact purchased the mortgages. And because the mortgages are for more than the value of the properties, it in fact purchased the properties – mainly residential properties.

But government is notoriously incapable of managing residential properties. The properties will in the end be at best occupied by people who pay very little rent, at worst will be overrun by gangs and squatters, and turned into ruinous slums.

Further, this three hundred billion is off budget. On paper, the fed has merely exchanged one security for another. In reality, the fed has made a massive investment in real estate at inflated prices.

---

[8]https://http//www.economist.com/blogs/freeexchange/2008/03/slap.cfm

Yes, the Fed can just keep on printing money.

2008-03-15 22:37:44

The business times quotes an anonymous "senior London Banker"

> Someone will go under in this crisis, that's for sure. The question is whether they stay under or get rescued. Let's see whether this latest round of stabilisation helps, but if it doesn't, it's difficult to see what Plan B is. The Fed can't just keep on printing money.

Yes, the Fed can just keep on printing money.

The banks have real assets and nominal liabilities. If the Fed debases money enough, the banks will be fine – it is just that everyone else will be broke.

The global warming swindle

2008-03-17 22:40:06

Anthropogenic global warming is a swindle in that the scientific method has been abandoned, the evidence is in substantial part lies, and so on and so forth.

But it is not a swindle in that it is provably false. It could be true. The evidence vastly overstated, and the effects vastly overstated, but it could be true that humans are causing the world to warm at about one fifth of a degree per decade, about two degrees per century

Of course two degrees per century is not very fast: Walk, walk, the hills! But it could be true.

But in few years, by 2012, possibly as soon as 2009, we will know whether it is true or not.

Measurements of the 18O/16O provide an accurate measure of ancient water temperature. We observe that the climate has always been changing, and from time to time has changed quite a lot. Measurement of 10Be from these same ice cores indicate that the high temperatures occurred at times of high solar activity, and the low temperatures at times of low solar activity.

So in the past, the climate varied as the sun varied. So are present day changes in climate a reflection of increasing solar activity, or increasing anthropogenic CO2?

Throughout most of the twentieth century, solar activity increased, and CO2 increased. So it was impossible to say which was causing the change in climate.

Around 2000 or so, solar activity peaked, and in the recent year, fell like a stone. So if climate change is caused by the sun, global warming should have ended around 2000, the world should have cooled a little towards 2007, and should have cooled quite a bit this year. Arguably that is just what happened. And arguably that is not what happened. The data is noisy.

In a little while, a few months, or a few years, it will become apparent that the world is continuing to warm, which case climate change is primarily anthropogenic, or that the world is cooling, in which case climate change is primarily cosmogenic.

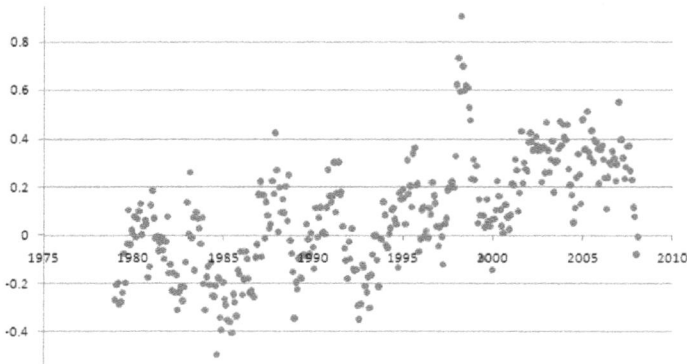

Blue dots represent observed month to month[9] global average temperatures. Observe the cooling trend in the last few months. If this goes on for a while, it will disprove the claim that human activity has substantially influenced the climate. Of course, if, on the other hand, it reverses ...

Cargo Cult Science.

2008-03-18 22:41:32

xkcd.com[10] is the ultimate geek cartoon. Getting the joke usually requires esoteric knowledge of some combination of science, maths, popular culture, and internet trivia.

In today's cartoon[11], Zombie Feynman shows up, seeking to eat brains, but then again explains the essence of the scientific method. He then implies that string theorists have no brains. This is very funny to those of us familiar with today's critique of string theory, and Feynman's critique of Cargo Cult Science[12]. If you read it and laugh, you get a smug glow from being part of a tiny elite who understand that string theorists have given up on any effort to relate string theory to empirical consequences, and that this means that they constitute cargo cult science.

> I think the educational and psychological studies I mentioned are examples of what I would like to call cargo cult science. In the South Seas there is a cargo cult of people. During the war they saw airplanes with lots of good materials, and they want the same thing to happen now. So they've arranged to make things like runways, to put fires along the sides of the runways, to make a wooden hut for a man to sit in, with two wooden pieces on his head to headphones and bars of bamboo sticking out like antennas – he's the controller – and they wait for the airplanes to land. They're doing everything right. The form is perfect. It looks exactly the way it looked before. But it doesn't work. No airplanes land. So I call these things cargo cult science,

---

[9]https://www.remss.com/

[10]https://xkcd.com/397/

[11]https://xkcd.com/397/

[12]https://wwwcdf.pd.infn.it/%7Eloreti/science.html

because they follow all the apparent precepts and forms of scientific investigation, but they're missing something essential, because the planes don't land.

Now it behooves me, of course, to tell you what they're missing. But it would be just about as difficult to explain to the South Sea islanders how they have to arrange things so that they get some wealth in their system.

The science of anthropogenic global warming looks like science, sounds like science, but it lacks key elements of science. The typical procedure is to gather a pile of data that would likely be affected by the the answer to the question at issue, but also affected by lots of other things, and then announce that due to wonderfully scientific statistics, they extracted the signal of the one thing that they were interested in, and eliminated the influence of all the other effects. Thus, for example Mann deduced that the Medieval climatic optimum did not exist from the fact that a few bristlecone pines were not doing too well during the Medieval climatic optimum.

Similarly the IPCC announced that the Urban heat island effect is very small, much smaller than decadal warming. They deduced this by analyzing a bunch of weather stations, some of which they arbitrarily designated as urban, and others of which they designated as rural. But even if these designations had been accurate, you could not possible deduce the size of the urban heat island effect from this data.

To measure the size of the urban heat island effect, buy a thermometer in your local hardware store. Attach a toilet roll around the bulb to shield the bulb from radiant heat, and attach the thermometer to your car. Then drive your car from the countryside through a small town and out to the countryside again. You will observe an urban heat island effect of several degrees, about five or ten times larger than the decadal warming. That is real science. What the IPCC does is cargo cult science.

Moral hazard:

2008-03-18 22:44:01

Financiers know that if they misbehave, the Federal Reserve will print money and give it to them in return for worthless collateral. Public knows that when the central bank prints money, its value diminishes, and thus the public become reluctant to sell, and unable to buy. Hence stagflation.

Stagflation

2008-03-18 22:45:06

The US economy faces recession: To stimulate the economy, the fed is lowering interest to near zero and the government handing out six hundred dollars to everyone.

But what the US faces is not recession, but stagflation, and handing out free money is not the cure for stagflation.

Stagflation was first observed in the first great fiat money inflation of modern times, the French assignat.

The more assignats they printed, the worse the shortage of assignats became. They would double the number of assignats in circulation, and prices would quadruple!

You could not buy, because the seller did not trust your money, and you could not sell, because the buyer did not have money that you could trust. You could not borrow, nor could you lend, for the lender knew his money would be worthless when returned.

To cure stagflation, the Fed must give people confidence in money, and confidence in financial intermediaries. You create confidence in money by firmly refusing to issue more of it, and confidence in financial intermediaries by ensuring that those financial intermediaries that have misbehaved become bankrupt or go to jail, as appropriate.

Alan Greenspan on crack

2008-03-20 23:16:58

Four days ago, Alan Greenspan posted[13] an article wondering what went wrong:

> "We will never have a perfect model of risk"

> "Risk management systems – and the models at their core – were supposed to guard against outsized losses. How did we go so wrong?"

Hey Alan! Check your spam folder for 2006. You will find it is full of ads saying:

> "Buy the house of your dreams for no money down! No credit? Bad credit? No Income? No Problem!"

Gimme some of what he's been smoking.

Future Housing prices

2008-03-26 23:18:43

Real mortgage interest rates are high and rising in the US, because the the future value of the US dollar is uncertain. Lenders fear the possibility of very high inflation, so demand high interest rates. This makes it difficult to buy a house. At the same time, borrowers fear deflation. They fear they could put down a deposit, then be wiped out as the value of house falls, along with their job that previously enabled them to pay the mortgage. Both may well be right, for uncertainty over the future value of money results in uncertainty over the present value of money, resulting in stagflation. Dollars and houses could fall relative to gold, food and fuel, and fall far, wiping out both lenders and borrowers.

We may therefore expect the proportion of people who own their own homes to fall, resulting in hostility to capitalism and enthusiasm for socialism, for people who do not own stuff tend to hate people who do own stuff, and lash out to harm them, not understanding that in so doing they harm themselves.

---

[13]https://www.ft.com/cms/s/0/edbdbcf6-f360-11dc-b6bc-0000779fd2ac.html

Ordinarily, the crisis would surely mean low home prices, which would be a good thing for the strength of the people, for the core of society is young married people planning to have children, or having children, and without such people, everyone loses hope and confidence, people despair of the future, and despair of their way of life. But as government becomes every more pervasive, and claims ever greater authority, makes ever more decisions for us, it has become harder and harder to subdivide land. So subdivisions have fallen far behind population growth. We have an ever more severe shortage of subdivided land, which put ever greater upward pressure on housing prices.

We need prices to fall to a level where young couples can buy houses preparatory to having children, but this seems unlikely. Despite the crisis, despite massive foreclosures, despite high interest rates on mortgages, despite massive falls in the price of housing, houses are still absurdly expensive, and are probably close to bottom.

I sadly regret to report that I think housing right now is a very good investment, the only better investment being subdivided land with secure building approval.

Global warming explained

2008-03-27 23:19:57

In a paper with the deliberately boring title "A Provisional Long Mean Air Temperature Series for Armagh Observatory"[14] C.J. Butler and D.J. Johnston find a near perfect correlation between solar cycle length and temperature from 1796 to 1992 - which implies that recent warming is real, but wholly explained by events happening on the sun.

The paper starts off with lots of worthy, important, and extremely boring stuff about thermometers. The meat of the paper is at the end, in figures four and five. Skip right ahead to figures four and five. For a more polemical account, see David Archibald[15]

An interesting extension then is to apply this result to recent times, to predict the temperature trend over the next decade or so and interpret the global temperature observed since 2002 by the Aqua satellite, which we will be able to do as soon as it becomes apparent that solar cycle twenty three has ended. Of course we will not know that solar cycle twenty three has ended until many months after it has ended, and no one knows when it will end. If, as seems likely, solar cycle twenty four starts in May 2008, or even later, then the period 2010-2025 is going to be pretty damned cold.

Losing in Iraq, part one

2008-03-28 23:21:26

When the US began its attack on the Taliban in Afghanistan, I said that destroying our enemies anywhere in the world would be easy, but building states would be hard, would most likely fail, for no one understands how a state is built, and the trend of the times is for states to fail.

And so it has proven: The surge produced the temporary appearance of relative quiet in Iraq, but our enemies knew that the surge was unsustainable. We could not keep so

---

[14]https://www.warwickhughes.com/agri/armagh_temp_history.pdf
[15]https://ncwatch.typepad.com/dalton_minimum_returns/files/Solar_Arch_NY_Mar2_08.pdf

many men in Iraq indefinitely. And now the time is coming, that forces in Iraq must be reduced.[16]

Al Quaeda is being slaughtered in Iraq. They are radical Sunni Muslims, and are being killed by conservative Sunni Muslims. But conservative Sunni Muslims are not our friends, merely the enemy of our enemy. The radical Shia plurality, knowing we are about to reduce our forces, is once again taking up arms against us. The moderate Shia minority are disinclined to fight them. We are hosed. To win, we need more tightly focussed objectives. If our objective was to slaughter lots of Al Quaeda, we are winning, we have won. If we have broader objectives, we are losing. Time to adopt more realistic and tightly focused objectives.

Losing in Iraq, part two

2008-03-28 23:26:04

An hour or so ago I read that the surge was about to be diminished, because it is unsustainable, and posted "Losing in Iraq, part one"

I guess Sadr read it also, for a few minutes ago I read that the Green Zone is being shelled and the oil is being cut off[17]. I read it and posted, Sadr read it and started shelling.

The major alternatives:

1. Declare victory, since we aimed to slaughter Al Quaeda (radical Sunni) and have done so, and get the hell out, leaving Iraq's oil in the hands of our victorious enemies (radical Shia) who will use fund attacks on us, as radical Shia are already doing in Iran.

2. Let our enemies get the oil, but make sure that there is unending war between our various enemies, so that they spend the oil money killing each other instead of us.

3. Slaughter enough radical Shia, and their families, that the remainder decide to play nice and let someone have the oil who will use it buy whiskey and whores, rather than rockets and bombs

4. Ethnically cleanse Basra and Khorramshahr, and staff the oil ports with non Muslim workers imported from all over the world.

Of course, if implementing any of these options, will need to do so with *fewer* troops, but the last two options would seem to require quite a few troops.

The above was posted in 2008-03-28.

Revision added a year later:

Although the the British failed to control the oil, eventually the elected Iraqi govenment, with US assistance, recovered control of the oil, contrary to my expectation, which was that the oil would wind up in the hands of our enemies.

This, denying the oil to our enemies, constitutes victory in Iraq, and was attained without the extremely destructive measures I thougth necessary. But I retreat to the position, that victory is costing too much, and a few more victories like this will result in us all praying towards Mecca five times a day.

---

[16]https://www.theconservativevoice.com/ap/article.html?mi=D8VLN9B00&apc=9009
[17]https://globalguerrillas.typepad.com/globalguerrillas/2008/03/journal-sadrs-d.html

Global warmers lie again 2

2008-03-29 23:29:19

The Salt Lake Tribune tells us[18]

Antarctic ice melt shows warming is speeding up

The sound of a chunk of Antarctic ice hundreds of years old and seven times the size of Manhattan collapsing into the ocean should be enough to rouse the concern of even the most staunch global warming skeptics.

A more accurate headline would be "Rapidly expanding Antarctic ice shelf spawns gigantic icebergs." The antarctic ice shelf has grown, as one would expect from this years globally cooler weather.

The long war

2008-03-30 23:33:18

As I write this there is chaos in Basra. Tomorrow there will be chaos some place else. In Basra today Iranians are backing every pony in this race, for what they want is chaos, and chaos is easy to create. We are pursuing a strategy based on creating order. Creating order in the Middle East is like pushing mud uphill.

As I wrote when the attack on the Taliban was launched, it is easy to destroy our enemies, wherever they may be, but state building is hard, no one knows how to build states, and in recent time the trend is for states to fail. I recommend we abandon state building, and focus on destroying our enemies wherever they may be without regard to states and state boundaries – including those enemies located in Saudi Arabia, Britain, and Germany. A religion, not a state, is at war with us.

The choice is not peace with defeat, or victory with endless and expensive war, rather the choice is what kind of endless war we shall fight. If we do not fight, the enemy will not stop fighting. This war has been running from the massacre of the Jews of Medina by Muhammad in 0624, to the present day, with a brief one hundred and thirty year interruption from 1830 to 1960 caused by colonialist victory over the middle east. To keep the Middle East quiet during that colonial period required mass murder on a very large scale in the most troublesome spots and the frequent and credible threat of mass murder in other spots.

Islam is a problem. The original message and example of Mohammed was that Muslims must pursue domination and exercise theocratic state power, thus solutions based on tolerance and separation of Church and State are inherently unworkable. Tolerance cannot work, because coexistence is unacceptable to true Muslims. We can only coexist with those versions of Islam that accept separation of Church and State - which very few do. Islam is not just another religion, just as the Communists were not just another political party. If we are reluctant to commit genocide, and therefore unable to credibly threaten

---

[18]https://www.sltrib.com/opinion/ci_8720320

genocide as we did during the colonial era, we cannot stop Islam from fighting us, thus must find ways to fight Islam that are less expensive than the way we are doing it now.

Yes, the enemy is Islam. Not radical Islam, not Islamofascism. "Moderate" Islam does exist, but is an insignificant minority, subject to almost as much repression by mainstream Islam as Christians, Jews, and apostates. Whosoever accepts certain key doctrines of Islam must always be the enemy of all who do not accept those doctrines, and thus always our enemy.

We should of course, encourage our enemies to fight each other, and fund and arm some of our enemies against other of our enemies, but should not mistake the enemy of our enemy for our friend.

Tolerance is an effective tactic for ensuring peace if those one tolerates reciprocate, or are sufficiently weak. It was not possible to tolerate most communist parties during communism's strength, and it is no longer possible to tolerate Islam now that the tide of colonialism has receded.

Fitna the movie

2008-03-31 23:38:38

Most servers have been intimidated into silence, but the gutsy "Pirate Bay" is still serving "Fitna", in bittorrent form, the only major commercial service still standing.

But the interesting thing is who is doing the intimidating. At first, it was a western, politically correct, demand for pre-emptive surrender..

Fitna shows a verse from the Koran urging murder, terror, or conquest. Then it shows today's Muslim preachers urging murder, terror and conquest Then it shows acts of murder, terror, and subjugation. Then it shows another verse from the Koran urging murder, terror or conquest, then more of today's preachers, then more dead bodies. In short, it is pretty similar to many Islamic devotional videos, similar to videos produced by the faithful to summon them to serve the faith, to donate their money, their lives, or their children, and in substantial part is composed of extracts from these devotionals.

Originally I wrote: "The Muslim reaction, naturally enough, has been "So What". They are not outraged. They are bored. They get more than enough of this stuff from people asking for converts and donations." This turned out to be dead wrong.

Housing price bottom

2008-03-31 23:39:57

When I say prices look like they have bottomed, I don't mean that the prices sellers are asking may have bottomed. Asking prices are, for the most part, still way too high. But if we look at sales that are actually being made, both for houses, and for land with secure development approval, the prices are a good deal lower, the people buying are the smart money, and the people selling are the stupid money – which is a pretty good sign that prices have bottomed. People with a good track record for making smart decisions are betting their own money that bottom fishing in today's market is turning up bargains.

The buyers are buying with their own money, the sellers are taking a loss on someone else's money.

Who is funding terror?

2008-03-31 23:41:17

We are funding terror.

Twelve days ago, the US gave one hundred and fifty million dollars to the Palestinian Authority[19], much of which will be used to buy arms to murder Jews, much of which will be used to reward terrorists for their holy deeds.

Why pay off the Palestinians when there are many deserving people going hungry? Duh! The answer, of course, is that it is a payoff. If we pay them, they will refrain from hijacking US planes, refrain from murdering Americans. They will stick to murdering Jews – at least for the moment, though each time they come back for more money, they tell us that alas, unless the payment increases, they will, alas, have difficulty restraining extremist elements. Every negotiating session, they utter threats. Every time they utter threats, we pay them more. Eventually we are going to have to say no, and the dollars we have sent them will come back to us as bombs.

Now if sacrificing a few Jews would keep those @#$%^&* Palestinians off our backs, I would be all in favor of it But it is too late for that. It was too late in 622AD. When someone threatens to kill you it is war, and once it is war, the only way you can have peace is to kill your enemies, or die trying.

Tribute always ends in war or surrender. Surrender to Islam would be unimaginably intolerable. In the end, we will have to make total war, absurd though it is that a power so insignificant should threaten a power so great. But this is not the first time that utterly insignificant Muslim groups, by the power of fanaticism, by a willingness to die that exceeded Christian willingness to kill, have successfully extracted tribute from extremely powerful Christians, for example the tribute of money and slaves paid to the Algerians. It has always ended badly, and since 1529, it has usually ended very badly for the Muslims.

More pussy for Muslims: It's the law!

2008-04-01 00:34:16

The state of Texas has just engaged in the mass abduction of wives and children[20] from Christian polygamists because of the alleged bad conduct of one Christian polygamist – though strangely they seem unable to find the person who alleged this bad conduct.

Evidently, although Muslim polygamy is multicultural, Christian polygamy is not.

---

[19] https://news.yahoo.com/s/nm/20080319/ts_nm/palestinians_usa_aid_dc_1
[20] https://www.chron.com/disp/story.mpl/ap/tx/5678783.html

I was wrong 1

2008-04-01 23:42:20

I was wrong about Muslim reaction to the video "Fitna". I said that Muslim's were not reacting, just their pals in the west. This is not the case. Muslims are reacting, and, as usual, threatening murder and terror, though their western pals reacted first.

Commodity derivatives: the new currencies

2008-04-04 23:44:00

E-gold, which I thought would save the world, turned out to be something of a bust, with essentially zero use in real internet commerce, but "unenumerated reports"[21] that we are seeing the financial markets going into commodity based fractional reserve monies in a big way, many trillions of dollars. Still, you cannot pay for your we hosting or cell phone minutes with commodity based monies. These moneys are for big deals, and only big deals. The revolution begins when you can send commodity based money over end to end encrypted instant messaging, and the money is good to pay for your web hosting and your prepaid cell phone minutes.

Escalating prophecies of doom

2008-04-04 23:45:23

When prophecies of doom are not working out, the first reaction is to escalate them: Ted Turner tells us[22]:

> We will be eight degrees hotter in thirty or forty years, and basically none of the crops will grow, most people will have died, and the rest of use will be cannibals, civilization will have broken down.

Over past millenia, global temperatures have risen and fallen several degrees. A few thousand years back, hippos and crocodiles basked in the warm waters of the river Thames. A little after that, the Thames froze over. A few hundred years back, trees large enough to support ship building grew in Iceland, and people made wine from grapes grown in Northern England.

Over recent decades temperatures have been warming, and if we draw a straight line through the warming, it has been warming at the far from alarming rate of 0.2 degrees per decade. Walk, walk for the hills!

But a straight line may not necessarily be appropriate. Global temperatures maxed out a decade ago, and are now falling. *Because* global temperatures are now falling, we are now hearing the prophecies of doom being escalated.

---

[21] https://unenumerated.blogspot.com/2008/04/commodity-derivatives-new-currencies.html
[22] https://www.youtube.com/watch?v=LZuC1xLHXRc

Non scientific reasons to doubt Anthropogenic Global Warming

2008-04-05 23:47:25

1. There have been a lot of prophecies of doom before.

2. As before, the prophets of doom are making money and gaining power from their prophecies

3. Some of the data supposedly demonstrating global warming turned out to be fraudulent.[23]

4. The major scientific global warming authorities, notably the IPCC seem curiously relaxed about employing some fraudulent data, which casts doubt on the rest of their data.

5. The anthropogenic global warming movement is a movement, akin to a religious or a political movement, rather than normal science.

6. Notable movement activists such as Al Gore and Ted Turner have a lengthy past record of supporting tyranny and mass murder, while preaching virtue most piously.

7. Real scientific theories do not have movement activists.

Cooking the data

2008-04-07 23:53:11

Steve's Climate Audit has found yet another entertaining example of carelessness or dishonesty by the Anthropogenic Global Warming holy Gaia rollers, as he does ever week or so.

I think the underlying mechanism of all these many errors is that the holy Gaia rollers massage the data one way, then they massage it another way, then another, and another, until they come up with a result that is on message, without ever bothering to think about what these various data massages mean.

"Global" means "let us throw any data into the pot that we can find, without regard for accuracy or even relevance, and if we cannot find any data sufficiently global, let us just make it up", and "analyze" means "let us find obscure statistical excuses for chucking out any data that is off message, while pretending we are still taking account of it rather than rejecting it".

How not to fight IslamTerror

2008-04-08 00:11:27

"Back Talk remarks

---

[23]https://www.climateaudit.org/?p=1741

Because everyone pretty much accepts the idea that Osama bin Laden is hiding in Pakistan, it might sound sensible to send more troops in that general direction if you don't think about it too hard. But it isn't sensible because no matter how many troops we send to Afghanistan, they are not going to invade Pakistan, and that's where Osama bin Laden is.

So everyone accepts that the guy who brought down the two towers has safe haven. And everyone accepts that Christian polygamy is a crime against women and children, while Muslim polygamy is muticulturalism. And everyone accepts that we pay off terrorists to the tune of hundreds of millions of dollars.

That is not war on terror, or war on the axis of evil. That is acceptance of defeat.

"Brutally Honest" goes pinko
2008-04-09 00:30:06

"Brutally Honest" complains that Christianity is immoral because it does not hate capitalism enough – no of course that is not what he complains. He complains Christianity is immoral, because it teaches that God gave us the world, and commanded us to be fruitful and multiply, to take dominion over the world, to fill it and subdue it. He is worried that we are going to run out of oil, and there will be no oil left for our children.

But Christianity, at least the old fashioned kind, has faith in capitalism, and so long as we have capitalism, we shall have fuel for our cars

Old fashioned, unecumenical, not-in-the-slightest-bit-multicultural Christianity commands private property, and prohibits coveting, let alone stealing other people's stuff. You are allowed to look at your neighbors house and think

"That is a nice house, I should build a house like that."

But you are forbidden to look at your neighbors house and think

"That is a nice house, he must have some how cheated me and done me wrong to have a house like that, there is some conspiracy of people like him out to get me, he should be punished and I should have his house."

The stone age did not end for lack of stones. Oil at present costs about a hundred dollars a barrel. Supply is restricted politically. Most oil companies have been nationalized, and are run by Sheiks or the like, who are incapable of getting the hot water connected to the hot water tap, let along maintaining and upgrading oil rigs. Most remaining oil is located in places where if you find oil, build an oil rig and a pipeline, your rig will be nationalized in violation of the agreement that the government signed when you went looking for oil. Paying off the thieves is, as he points out, not working, irrespective of how much oil remains in the ground, and indeed is funding terror.

But we can make oil substitutes from coal for a cost equivalent to thirty five to forty dollars a barrel - possibly a good deal less, if we were to convert our fuel systems to use methanol, and our fuel distribution system to distribute methanol by the tanker instead of by the drum. China is slowly converting to methanol, and expects to be about ten percent methanol in five years or so.

The main thing slowing the conversion is that businessmen fear that high oil prices are temporary, that the prices are the result of political obstacles to oil extraction which will be politically resolved, which would leave expensive investments in coal to liquid plants high and dry.

The major alternatives to oil based fuels are synfuel, which is good for jets and diesels, not so good for ordinary engines, methanol, which is good for ordinary petrol engines (with radically modified carburettors), but only gives you half the mileage, and dimethyl ether, a good substitute for LPG, good in diesels, no good in regular engines. We should be converting. If oil prices stay high, we eventually will be.

Scientific Status of Anthropogenic Global Warming

2008-04-11 00:33:03

It is an open question, though with the evidence mounting against a substantial anthropogenic effect.

I often write as if Anthropogenic Global Warming was disproven or obviously false. Global Warming is an open scientific issue, one which more information is needed - and in due course will be forthcoming. The position among real scientists is that Global warming is a conjecture - not a conjecture very likely to be true, but conjecture that *could be* true.

Over the next decade or so, the truth, or more likely the falsity, of Anthropogenic Global Warming should become more apparent. We have plenty of time to discover the actual situation before taking big dramatic actions. If human are warming the world, it is pretty obvious we are not warming it very fast.

In 2007, there seems to have been a dramatic change in the weather on the sun. The abnormally active sun of the past several decades is most likely changing its ways. If global warming is cosmogenic, the next decade or so is going to get mighty cold.

voting anti capitalist

2008-04-14 03:26:18

"The Fly Bottle" reports on the relationship between voting patterns and employment.[24]

Observe: Support for the Democrats is high and rising amongst those who derive their wealth from state regulation and state imposed monopoly. Oh what a big surprise

I bet we would see the same support for the Democrats among accountants as amongst doctors and lawyers. And where the state makes it a restricted privilege to do people's hair, a similar swing amongst hair dressers.

This fits pretty well with the standard Marxist account of people voting their self interest, though I suspect it is more complicated than that. Rather, people whose wealth

---

[24]https://www.willwilkinson.net/flybottle/2008/04/11/jobs-and-votes/

and power derives from government regulation need to believe that government regulation is wholly good, so come to believe in the Democrats.

The more socialism we have, the more socialism people are apt to vote for. The Road to Serfdom.

The Iraq war from inside

2008-04-16 03:41:18

Here is a blog by an American officer that tells us the Iraq war from inside[25].

The war cannot easily be summarized. If it could be, he would summarize it for us. But we are clearly winning, it is clearly costing, Iraq remains all @#%^&*, the moment US troops leave. Clearly Iraq is not going to become a Jeffersonian democracy any time soon, but looks increasingly probable it will not be overrun by Islamic radicals the moment US troops leave.

On the one hand, nation building has not been a total failure. On the other hand, it is taking a lot longer, costing a lot more, and producing a lot less than had been promised.

The problem is that after this experience, it is not a credible to threaten that tyrants who attack Americans, or sponsor terrorists who attack Americans, are going to suffer overthrow followed by nation building

World wide drop in support for free market system

2008-04-17 03:43:04

Pollsters report a world wide drop[26] in support for the free market system.

This was apparent in the US presidential party primary, where the most anticapitalist candidate of each party won or appears to be winning his party's nomination. Recently in Nepal, Maoists won democratically, an almost unprecedented event for communists.

I have no idea what is causing this problem. Perhaps the problem is that with the collapse of communism, the constant reminder of how dreadful the alternative to capitalism is has gone away.

Oil peak

2008-04-18 03:45:16

World oil production is about eighty million barrels per day, four billion tonnes per year. The world has been stuck at that level since 2003, while demand has been increasing at about four percent a year. As a result, prices are going through the roof, largely because Chinese want to drive cars like Americans do.

All the remaining oil in the world is in places that are politically inaccessible - partly because greenies in developed countries have banned oil wells, but most of the remaining

---

[25] https://kaboomwarjournal.blogspot.com/
[26] https://www.worldpublicopinion.org/pipa/articles/home_page/471.php

oil is in undeveloped places like Iraq, where anyone who drills a new well will probably have his well confiscated, and quite likely he will be murdered in the process.

Just to stay where we are now, for oil to stop rising, we need to increase oil production at about four percent a year, which is around one hundred and sixty million tonnes per year per year, or three million barrels per day per year.

Biofuels made from food are too expensive, and government subsidized biofuel made from food is causing starvation among poor people in poor countries. It is worth while making biofuel from sugar cane waste and paper mill waste, but the total amount we can get from those sources is not going to help us much.

So it has to be oil from shale, oil from tar sands, and oil from coal.

People are just pottering around with small experimental shale oil plants and coal to oil plants. Only Canadian oil from tar sands is being developed full speed ahead, as fast as physically possible. There are other oil sands in the world, but again, insecurity of property rights is a problem. If you try to develop oil sands in most countries, your plant will be stolen, and you will likely be murdered. Oil from tar sand in Canada is increasing at about four hundred thousand barrels per day per year, which about twenty million tonnes per year per year, about one eighth of what we need.

It is often said that the Chinese are developing coal to liquids in a big way, but compared to what is needed, not so big. They are building coal to dimethyl ether plants with a capacity of three million tonnes per year. If these plants were going to fix the problem, we would need around forty of them every year, rather than one or two every couple of years.

Typically people are building dimethyl ether pilot plants that do a few hundred tonnes per year, small scale plants that do a few hundred thousand tonnes per year, and a few big plants that do three million tonnes per year.

To match supply and demand at reasonable prices, the world needs to build sixteen ten million tonne per year plants each year, or fifty of the three million tonne per year plants the chinese contemplate.

The obvious solution is UCG-GTL - underground coal gasification followed by gas to liquid conversion. Digging the coal up is too messy to be done on the enormous scale needed. At present there is ONE such plant under development. Linc energy systems proposes to build, some time in the next several years, a UCG-GTL plant that makes seventeen thousand barrels per day of synthetic diesel, eight hundred and fifty thousand tonnes per year, about one two hundredth of the increase we will need every year.

Further, their coal gasification is air based, as befits the comparatively small scale of their proposed operation. For the really gigantic facilities of the future, oxygen based underground coal gasification is the way to go.

China and Estonia are rapidly expanding their oil from oil shale projects, but again this looks something like one hundred thousand tonnes per year per year, insignificant.

Coal to oil plants are highly profitable at present oil prices, but the trouble is that the obstacles to conventional oil production are political. People fear to invest in coal to oil plants, for an improvement in the security of property rights in oil rich countries could cause a huge drop in the price of oil. But with the steadily rising tide of hostility to capitalism, and the increasing propensity to murder people with property, this seems unlikely to me.

Rooftop solar power is actually more dangerous than Chernobyl

2008-04-19 03:46:55

Next Big Future analyzes the risk[27] of various power sources. By and large, a single big source of power kills fewer people per terawatt than lots of small sources of power.

Famine

2008-04-19 03:48:54

There is an oil crisis, and there is a food crisis. People in Haiti are eating dirt. Women are giving their babies away to random strangers. People who formerly were poor, and able to afford little more than enough to eat, now are unable to buy enough to eat.

I, of course, am more worried about the oil crisis, but the food crisis is probably more important.

Becker says that food prices are not going to be a problem

> the second reason for optimism relates to the lower productivity of food production in the poorer parts of the world relative to the United States and other developed countries. Higher food prices will induce an increase in productivity in developing nations by encouraging greater use of machinery, fertilizers, and other forms of capital.

In fact of course, the problem with food is the same as the problem with oil. In most of the world if you apply machinery and so forth, your tractor is probably going to be stolen, and you yourself quite likely killed in the process, just as if you drill an oil well, your oil rig is probably going to be stolen, and you yourself quite likely killed in the process.

It would be hugely profitable to drill new oil wells in Iraq, and upgrade and maintain existing oil wells, but no one is doing it for obvious reasons. Similarly for drilling water wells and digging irrigation ditches in Iraq. Whenever you ask businessmen why they are investing gigantic sums in Alberta oil sands, and not investing elsewhere in the world in oil that is far easier to extract, they will tell you.

Tractors are just as attractive to tyrants, demagogues, and terrorists as pipelines are.

Are Palestinians mad dogs, or crazy like foxes?

2008-04-20 03:52:17

It is widely believed that the "draconian" terms that the allies imposed on Germany at the end of World War One contributed to the rise of the Nazis and World War Two, and in a sense this is true, but imposing the terms *and then retreating from them under pressure* is

---

[27]https://nextbigfuture.com/2008/03/deaths-per-twh-for-all-energy-sources.html

what really caused the rise of the Nazis, as Étienne Mantoux argues in "The Carthaginian Peace: Or the Economic Consequences of Mr Keynes"

The Versailles reparations were extremely mild compared to the extraordinary brutality with which the Germans treated conquered populations during World War One, and their cost was entirely insignificant, compared to the economic costs the Germans inflicted on themselves in the course of resisting it – for example paying people to not work, paying people to sabotage their own economy. Indeed, Hitler quite correctly pointed this out, in the course of arguing that instead of economic threats, Germans needed to use threats of violence.

The ruin suffered by Germany was a result of them accurately perceiving weakness of will and self doubt among the allies, much like the ruin today suffered by the Palestinians. Keynes's book "The Economic Consequences of the Peace" was a major cause and manifestation of this weakness of will and self doubt. The successful push of the Germans against this weakness progressively escalated, Nazism, like Hamas, being a manifestation of this success.

Palestinian terror has been highly profitable, as Europe and America seek to outbid each other in paying off the terrorists. So the PLO escalate their demands, and Hamas demands its share of the gravy. In order to get their share of the gravy, Hamas has to prove they are even crazier than the PLO.

The lesson we should have learned from World War II is not only no appeasement, but that early appeasement leads to increasingly intolerable demands and the rise of increasingly extreme factions - that the temptation to appeasement must be resisted when the demands are cheap, arguably reasonable and morally justified, and the threats modest, for yielding will lead to escalating demands and escalating threats, will lead to the rise of factions that are ever crazier, since craziness is working.

We should have responded to German resistance by substantially escalating Versailles, rex talonis, to a punishment that matched German occupation during World War One eye for an eye and tooth for a tooth, rather that making concessions. This would have prevented the rise of Hitler. Since confrontation was working, Germans figured they should elect the most confrontational politician of them all, and at first it worked great.

Of course, confrontation worked at a very great risk of renewing World War I, as Hitler and the Nazis well knew, but the Nazis of course de-emphasized this risk, and when they told the truth to the voters, as they sometimes did, seems that no one listened anyway. Indeed Hitler had a long history of speaking the truth, and not being believed. He would tell the plain truth, then he would imply a lie that people wanted to believe, and people would believe the lie, and forget the truth. Again, observe the similarity with Hamas and the PLO, both of which have told us often enough that a two state solution is only a step towards the total destruction of Israel – and Hamas has from time to time told us that Tel Aviv is only a first step towards Rome. Israeli concessions endanger not only Israel, but also the rest of us.

Stubborn intransigence by the Palestinians needs to be met by cutting off the payoffs, by killing the bagmen who attempt to make payoffs, and if that fails, by imposing on Muslims rex talionis the same conditions as are imposed on Christians in most Muslim countries, not by making ever bigger payoffs.

Liberty needs to survive

2008-04-20 03:54:25

Gates of Vienna writes: The culture of liberty deserves to survive[28]

> "If a large enough proportion of us decided that we would not tolerate the
> eradication of our cultures, then our cultures would not be eradicated. It's
> as simple as that."

Oh, really?

Let us suppose that in order to get through university, you have to pretend to affirm
that our society should eradicated, because it is racist, colonialist, imperialist, capitalist,
exploitative, and is destroying the planet. Suppose that if your blog says something different, you are going to be prosecuted for spreading racial hatred, harming the earth, and
so forth. Suppose that if you say something different, those you love are likely to be murdered, and the police will not do much about it.

What then?

It really is not that easy to preserve liberty. Liberty always costs blood, and freedom
will always require forms of social organization capable of killing people in substantial
numbers.

Texas protective services commits perjury again

2008-04-21 03:56:35

In the testimony that led to the court approving and making permanent the abduction of
four hundred children from their FLDS parents, Mrs Angie Voss testified[29] that several
children had admitted to knowing the child abuse victim "Sarah"

> "We learnt that a few of the girls know of the Sarah we were looking for and
> that she'd been seen last weekand she had a baby," Ms Voss said.

We now know that "Sarah" is a thirty three year old democratic party political activist.
What do you think the prospects are that Child Protective Services will be charged with
perjury, or the decision reversed?

Happiness is a warm gun

2008-04-22 03:58:28

Arthur C. Brooks reports; that according to the general social survey, gun owners are
substantially happier than others.

Why is it so? Reporting from my own personal experience:

The major reason for owning a gun is to protect those you love. Those who have someone
they love, someone they would risk death for, someone they would kill for, are likely to

---

[28]https://gatesofvienna.blogspot.com/2008/04/culture-of-liberty-deserves-to-survive.html
[29]https://www.timesonline.co.uk/tol/news/world/us_and_americas/article3776483.ece

be happier.

Those who know that they can defend that which they love, are likely to be happier.

An important indicator was that gun owners spent about 15% less of their time than nonowners "feeling outraged at something somebody had done". Obviously this is a big contributor to happiness. If they spent 15% less of their time feeling outraged, they presumably spent something like 15% less of their time feeling powerless, impotent, and afraid.

Oil hits $120 a barrel

2008-04-23 04:01:00

Demand for oil will continue to rise. The supply is not rising. The only solution is massive coal to liquid plants. Coal to liquid plants can produce substitutes for gasoline, such as methy isobutyl ether, at about a dollar a gallon at the refinery gate. So why is it not happening?

Coal to diesel is a more mature technology. Coal to gasoline substitute is still theory and experiment. Maybe it is not happening because they are still working on it. But even coal to diesel is only happening on a rather small scale, a fraction of a percent of the scale needed to keep the price of oil from rising even further.

We are seeing the much predicted resource crisis and associated hunger that the greens have long predicted. Capitalism and the free market should, in theory, remedy this, providing a smooth conversion from oil to coal. No smooth conversion is happening, which may well be part of the reason so many people are losing faith in capitalism. The subprime crisis is not a good advertisement for capitalism either. Of course capitalism, unlike socialism, manages to resolve such crises without murdering millions, but this does not mean that it is working satisfactorily. When capitalism screws up badly, as is happening right now, people are inclined to listen to demagogues who tell them that if only the demagogue got to make decisions, instead of those wicked capitalists, all would be well.

Greenie morons

2008-04-24 04:03:08

It seems that even if you are a highly qualified scientist with a great big pile of academic credentials, there is something about being a greenie that causes your brains to dribble out your ears as slime.

There is an ecological crisis on Macquarie Island[30]:

> In an accelerating one-two hit, exploding rabbit numbers are denuding Macquarie's hills of soil-stabilising megaherbs and tussock fields, exposing ground-nesting birds and new seeds to the ravages of rats and mice.

> Along with the flora, at least 24 bird species, 12 of them classified as threatened, are under attack.

---

[30]https://www.smh.com.au/news/science/up-against-rats-rabbits-and-costs/2007/04/11/1175971183257.html

So why, you may ask, are they under attack now.

Because the brilliant scientists managing the island wiped out the cats. The cats had kept the rabbits and rats down.

When you wipe out the top predator, what do you think is going to happen?

Envy and covetousness

2008-04-26 04:05:01

Jews are not the only people that suffer from self hatred and self destructiveness, though arguably they are more prone to it than other groups.

The most spectacular and extreme example of self hatred was the Khmer Rouge, which hated intellectuals and especially foreign educated intellectuals, and proceeded to murder most of them. Since the Khmer Rouge was largely composed of intellectuals and especially foreign educated intellectuals ...

Rich white Anglo Saxon males also suffer from a fair degree of self destructive self hatred, as illustrated in the the recent Duke University rape scandal, though nothing comparable to Jewish self hatred.

The roots of self hatred are envy and covetousness. If one belongs to a successful group, one compares oneself to others of that group. Inevitably, some of that group are more successful in some ways than than oneself, and so ...

The first greenie famine

2008-04-28 04:06:28

The twentieth century was the century of the red famines. Now, in the twenty first century, we are seeing the first greenie famine. Let us hope it will not be the first of many.

The red famines killed an extraordinary number of people during the twentieth century – famines caused in part by carelessness, in part by active malice as socialists sought to centralize all food under their direct control. To some extent the red famines were intended to end resistance by depopulating large areas, to some extent they were produced by incompetence, as politicians and bureaucrats directed farmers how they should farm, and some of which were caused by casual neglect, as those politicians and bureaucrats simply forgot to feed their captives.

We are seeing much the same with the first greenie famine. It should have been possible to figure out that converting enough food to feed near a billion people into fuel was likely to cause problems.

Of course, the failure of capitalism to smoothly convert from oil to coal is also a problem, but the conversion has not been made any easier by the fact that it typically takes ten years to get such a plant approved, if you can get it approved at all.

There is a green path and a brown path to dealing with the failure to pump enough oil. Environmentalists complain that coal to liquids conversion is on the brown path, and take for granted that the green path is inherently better and more virtuous, so much more virtuous that simply being in favor of it makes them more virtuous. They neglect, however, to explain that the green path involves a substantial and rapid population reduction.

Caplan bets Europe will survive

2008-04-29 04:09:42

Bryan Caplan has bet $300 that Europe, and every state of Europe, will survive to 2020. I don't make these kind of bets, because outcomes tend to be ill defined. What constitutes surviving? But I expect that around 2040, people will look back to around 2020, and say that some substantial portion of Europe, fell back then.

The nation state derives its cohesion from the nation, and the nation is not a patch of land but a people, united by something – perhaps an ideology of governance, economics, and law, but more commonly race and culture, or religion, or some such.

Nation means, still today means, a mutually supporting group of people, not a territory – a people united by culture, or by language dialect, or by race, or by ideology, or religion, or some such. Jews are a nation, Israel a nation state, Kurds are a nation, but Kurdistan is not (yet) a nation state. Iraq is a state, but evidently not yet a nation.

If a state is united by race or religion, the nation state has a disturbing tendency to commit mass murder. Even before the rise of the nation state, even back in the days when nations seldom corresponded to states, the nation was an important and vital part of Europe's history, leading to lots of disturbingly efficient slaughter – and not just the easy slaughter of disarmed obedient sheeple that we saw so much of during the twentieth century, but the highly successful mass slaughter of armed and united peoples.

Thus a nation state inherently derives its cohesion, its strength, its military prowess from what is now called ethnocentrism, or racism, or bigotry, or ignorant superstition or capitalism/imperialism/exploitation etc.

The transnational progressives are attempting to use the power of the state to suppress that which gives the state cohesion, sawing off the branch on which they stand.

And because they have in substantial part succeeded, Europe suffers from extraordinary military weakness. Europe could not defeat the Serbs, could not defeat the Taliban. The British could not hold the most crucial oil port in the world against Sadr's forces.

Hence the inclination on the right to predict the collapse of the EU or some of its component states. The prediction seems absurd. The states of Europe have police, tanks, bombers and an immense budget, whereas the various threats to their existence are tiny and have nothing much – but the threats have internal cohesion, and the states of Europe do not.

How global warming "science" works

2008-05-01 04:11:46

Dr.Tim Ball reports that the IPCC first created the "Summary for Policy Makers" report, *then* the science report that it is supposedly a summary of.

> "Changes (other than grammatical or minor editorial changes) made after acceptance by the Working Group or the Panel shall be those necessary to ensure consistency with the Summary for Policymakers (SPM) or the Overview Chapter."

Unfortunately, it is not only global warming global warming "science" that works like this, but most science since the late twentieth century

This was, in the end, the unavoidable result of government funding for science. He who pays the piper, calls the tune. He sleeps with elephants, wakes up flat. For science to be science, scientists need to cultivate a wider range of patrons and sources of funding.

Regulation kills

2008-05-04 04:13:02

Today, a lot of people are going hungry because of an energy crisis.

When we look at businesses that are attempting to address the energy crisis, for example Linc Energy Systems, we see that ninety percent of their effort, energy, and thought, is addressed to the political problem of getting permits and approvals, and very little to the merely technical details of collecting energy from nature and making it available in usable form.

Linc energy systems[31] plans to use UCG-CTL to produce liquid fuel from coal. They set up a test plant. The major function of the test plant was not to test the technology, but to test the environmental impact of the technology. But the only acceptable outcome was no impact, which result no genuine test could ever produce. Fake environmental science manufacturing fictional crises is met with fake environmental science supposedly avoiding these nonexistent hazards.

And so, while this game is being played, people starve.

Coal to oil is not under development

2008-05-05 04:15:37

To keep the price of oil from soaring even further the world needs to increase oil production three million barrels per day, each year, largely because large numbers of Chinese want to drive cars.

We cannot increase production except in those places where private property rights are reasonably secure, and there is no oil left in the ground in those places. So it has to be coal to liquids.

Most coal to liquids plants are being developed in China. Du Minghua, deputy director of the China Shenhua CTL research institute, said China could produce thirty million tonnes of liquid fuels each year by 2020.

That is six hundred thousand barrels per day. That is about one sixtieth the rate of increase we need.

In America greenies are taking the same approach to banning coal to liquids as they have taken to banning nuclear power. The proposed regulation is that Americans will not be allowed to convert coal to liquids on a large scale unless they can prove that the CO2 can be permanently disposed of – but of course nothing can ever be proven to those who choose to make themselves too stupid to understand the proof. Presidential candidate

---

[31] https://www.google.com/search?q=linc+energy+ucg

Obama goes one step further, and proposes to ban substitutes for oil unless they emit twenty percent less CO2 than oil, which bans any use of coal to substitute for oil

A coal to liquids plant needs to be fairly large scale to be economical, needs to produce at least three million tonnes per year, sixty thousand barrels per day. To stop the price of oil from rising further, the world needs to build one of these plants every week, for the next several decades, to meet the Chinese demand for cars.

Yet we see no political will to permit such developments, and not a lot of enthusiasm amongst developers to doing them. To the extent that developers are working on such projects, their primary focus is on assuaging greenie opposition, rather than the technological problems of converting vast amounts of coal to oil. If it is hard to get oil wells drilled off the coast of California or in Alaska, what are your prospects of getting a coal to oil plant approved?

People are starving yet we still treat energy developers as criminals, rather than heroes.

Paul Collier explains the famine

2008-05-06 04:20:14

Paul Collier explains the famine[32].

In the modern era, famines are usually caused by war or socialism. This time around, it is a bit different. Collier lists four causes - one is Chinese prosperity, two are environmentalism - the ban on genetically modified food, and the American biofuel program, and one is social engineering – state intervention to preserve small (and thus ineffectual) farms as a voting block.

As I remarked earlier, the twentieth century was a time of socialist famines. Let us hope the twenty first century is not a time of greenie famines.

US$ declining as a reserve currency

2008-05-06 04:25:32

"Financial Cryptography[33]? reports that use of the US$ as a medium of international exchange and as an international sttore of value has declined to about two thirds of what it was four years ago.

Changes in the way people use money are extremely slow. Because money is a store of value, people are profoundly reluctant to change. Such a change is cataclysmically rapid compared to the normally glacial rate of monetary change.

In my own personal experience, US banks and US financial institutions have suffered a cataclysmic decline in competence, honesty, reliability, and efficiency over the past decade or so, particularly in international transactions. Over the past several years I have been repeatedly astonished and disbelieving at basic failures of integrity and inability to perform the ordinary duties of a bank, such as simply making sure that money does indeed get from where it is, to where it is supposed to go, or to make reasonable and realistic

---

[32]https://blogs.ft.com/wolfforum/2008/04/food-crisis-is-a-chance-to-reform-global-agriculture/#comment-11083

[33]https://financialcryptography.com/mt/archives/001040.html

assessments of credit worthiness and financial worth. The propensity of the Bush administration to print money, and the fact that the Iraq war is taking longer and costing more than expected is also having a severe impact. I have no idea which of these several causes is the more serious.

Muslim moderates sighted
2008-05-07 04:27:31

Question:

How can you tell a Muslim moderate?

Answer:

His throat is cut from ear to ear.

"Iraq the model[34]" reports a large bunch of moderates from Iraq, but a severe shortage of them from anywhere else. The question then is: is it safe to be a moderate in Iraq because US troops have created a democracy, or is it safe to be a moderate in Iraq because the country is still under US occupation and US troops are apt to arrest Iraqi leaders who misbehave?

"The Long War Journal[35]" reports that the Iraqi government is corrupt, and that if the US were to withdraw tomorrow, there would be civil war, so I am inclined to bet on the latter – that it is possible for a Muslim to be a moderate in Iraq because the place is still substantially under US martial law.

Global sea ice
2008-05-08 04:29:03

One measure of world temperature that is relatively objective is the total amount of ice. It is hard to measure average world temperature precisely, hard even to say what such an average means, and those that claim to measure it with great precision over great periods of time are liars, but ice, ice is a fact.

And so, from time to time, one gets an anthropogenic warming story, "Oh no the ice is melting".

Another Record Arctic Ice Melt Expected This Summer[36]

Whenever you read such a story, check the total amount of ice[37]. It does not change much, and has not changed much. Some times it goes up a bit, sometimes down a bit.

---

[34]https://iraqthemodel.blogspot.com/2008/05/do-iraqis-want-arab-nuclear-bomb.html

[35]https://www.longwarjournal.org/archives/2008/05/baghdad_police_show_1.php

[36]https://www.redorbit.com/news/science/1369336/another_record_arctic_ice_melt_expected_this_summer/

[37]https://arctic.atmos.uiuc.edu/cryosphere/IMAGES/global.daily.ice.area.withtrend.jpg

When ice melts dramatically in one place at one time it usually freezes up in another place not very long afterwards. Today, it is pretty much the same as ever it was.

Which very much suggests that the world's temperature has not changed much – that global warming, whether anthropogenic or not, is so small as to be unmeasurable compared to ordinary year to year and decade to decade fluctuations.

We have not had a really good direct measure of global temperature until the Aqua satellite was launched. And since the Aqua satellite was launched, we have had no "global warming".

Before Aqua, the best way to estimate changes in global temperature was to look at proxies such as total ice coverage - and the proxies have been telling us that nothing much has changed.

Genocide and environmentalism

2008-05-11 04:31:29

Bryan Caplan writes[38]

> When someone says "There are too many Jews," we suspect that he wants to kill Jews. Similarly, it turns out that *at the root of Hitler's propensity to kill people was his belief that there are too many people*.
>
> And if you're tempted to say that Hitler proposed a barbaric solution for a real problem, take a look at how Germany actually did feed its population since 1945: increasing agricultural productivity and increasing exports. The two methods that Hitler dismissed out of hand transformed Germany into one of the richest nations in history.

Religions that command human sacrifice are good at providing power to their priesthood. Thus we see the first greenie famine being welcomed with delight by the true believers, much as they previously welcomed the return of malaria.

Environmentalists confidently state with immense confidence all sorts of "facts", most of which are impossible to meaningfully test, some of which can be easily tested, and which test false – which test does not impair the confidence of the environmentalists in the slightest, just as the obviouse falsehood of the Christian doctrine of transubstantiation does not trouble those Christians who believe in it in the slightest.

Two obvious and extreme example are:
1. the much repeated "fact" that we are in the middle of a vast mass extinction, that ten thousand species go extinct every year. Ask any greenie to name a species that has recently gone extinct. He will not be able to answer, and will be entirely untroubled by his inability to answer.
2. the much repeated "fact" that the ice is melting, even though satellites show that the area of the world under ice has not changed significantly since satellites have been observing.

---

[38]https://econlog.econlib.org/archives/2008/05/good_question.html

When environmentalist "scientists" report the disappearance of ice, they are not in fact reporting the disappearance of physical corporeal ice and snow, the stuff that causes your car to slide, and has to be shovelled off the path, the stuff that is apt to sink ships at sea. What they are really reporting is the disappearance of magic ice, the spirit of the ice, Gaia's infusion of spirituality into a frozen wilderness that they contemplate from the comfort of Starbucks. Hence their total indifference to physical evidence. The holy ice, which is melted merely by man's unholy gaze is disappearing, even though the merely physical ice continues to endanger shipping in pretty much the same places as it has for the last century or so.

Similarly when environmentalist "scientists" report that the polar bear is endangered, they are entirely indifferent to actual numbers of polar bears. Far from being endangered, polar bears, like deer, a pest and a hazard. Rather, *because* they raid garbage dumps, *because* they have become a pest and a hazard, the holy spirit of wild nature of which the holy bear is a manifestation, is in danger of going extinct.

Vote Obama

2008-05-13 04:33:20

The presidents that have done the most to smash capitalism have never been Democrats, because anti capitalist Democrat presidents have always found themselves paralyzed by gridlock – the pro capitalist faction unites along party lines, and the federal government system locks up, as it was designed to do. The founding fathers intentionally constructed the federal government so that it would be slow and inefficient at making large controversial changes.

The greatest catastrophes for capitalism have come from the anticapitalist Republican presidents, Nixon and Hoover, because they could get "bipartisan" anticapitalist measures through congress.

Environmentalists have always intended global warming as a justification installing a socialist command and control economy. McCain has just unveiled a global warming plan, theoretically market based, but in fact not in the slightest market based, a command and control plan which is the socialists wet dream[39]. He calls it market based, but this merely means that bureaucrats will be able to blame markets for the chaos they create. The only role of the market in the plan is to be the guy that takes the fall. As Brutally Honest[40] says, McCaine has drunk the koolaide

Maybe Obama is just as anti capitalist, or even more anti capitalist than McCain, but if he is, he will face gridlock.

---

[39]https://ap.google.com/article/ALeqM5g1lnDN47XfRwq7TtD30hwUCcb6JgD90KBQ084
[40]https://www.brutallyhonest.org/brutally_honest/2008/05/john-mccain-is.html

Mark Steyn predicts the end of Israel

2008-05-14 04:36:14

"These days friends and enemies alike smell weakness at the heart of the Zionist Entity[41]

...

"Arabs will soon be demanding one democratic state — Jews and Muslims — from Jordan to the sea. And even those who understand that this will mean the death of Israel will find themselves so confounded by the multi-cultural pieties of their own lands they'll be unable to argue against it."

Bush's idea of exporting democracy to Muslim lands has turned out to be a disaster. World War II was against theoretically against nation state dictatorships. This war is a holy war. Our enemies can win elections, and frequently do.

Exxon blows it

2008-05-14 04:38:23

Bryan Caplan wonders[42] if oil prices are a bubble.

When oil spikes abruptly, that means people made incorrect investment decisions - under invested in exploration, development, and gas to liquids conversion.

A simple back of the envelope[43] calculation tells me they are still under investing. Exxon recently abandoned gas to liquids plant that would be profitable if oil remains above forty dollars to fifty dollars a barrel. But if everyone acts like that – and everyone is acting like that – oil is going to be *way* above fifty a barrel.

Do I hear someone saying "Hey. Do you think you are lot smarter than the guys running Exxon?"

It is quite simple. For the price of oil to remain stable at present levels, we need to accommodate China's industrialization by producing a lot more oil each year. The planned increases in oil production add up to peanuts. So the price of oil is heading up, and going to stay up.

Europe is falling

2008-05-15 04:41:55

Observe in this video[44] the British police are as frightened and weak before Muslims, as the British police are terrifying and dominating over Britishers in other videos. The British state is as contemptible to its enemies as it is terrifying to its subjects.

---

[41] https://article.nationalreview.com/?q=MGM4M2M5YWRhYWY4ZzgwYjd-kYWI2NTViMmM5MTc2MTM=

[42] https://econlog.econlib.org/archives/2008/05/oil_inventories.html

[43] ../economics/coal-to-oil-is%E2%80%A6er-developmentcoal-to-oil-is-not-under-development.html

[44] https://www.youtube.com/watch?v=8ZNx0xHe0p0

The fear and weakness we see in this video, we also saw when the Iranians over ran the British in the Persian gulf, and when the British fled before the Shia militias in Basra.

In this video, the Muslims rule the streets, and not only are the British frightened, weak, ashamed, and apologetic, but the British police, normally so arrogant, violent, and destructive, normally filled with brutal contempt for the merely law abiding middle class British civilians, are frightened, weak, ashamed, and apologetic.

The British state that has such contempt for Britishness, that it confidently will re-make the British in its own image, in this video shows its true weakness and shame before Islam.

Genocidal famine still planned

2008-05-18 04:43:36

At present, Environmental Protection Agency rules require that that Americans convert food that could feed five hundred million people into fuel. But this is not enough. The rules require that it be increased five fold over the next fifteen years.

Meaning of Hezbollah offensive in Lebanon

2008-05-21 04:45:19

On May 9, Hezbollah fighters were wandering around Lebanon. The meaning and implications of these events were not clear at the time. No one, least of all Hezbollah, had a clear idea.

Now it is clear what happened.

The Lebanese state is a failed state. It lacks the will and capability to fight the various armed groups in Lebanon, or to impose its will on them. Hezbollah tested the government. The government was an empty bag. It tested the major Sunni party, with the same result. It tested the major Druze parties, which likewise collapsed, but the Druze did not collapse, instead inflicting a nasty defeat on Hezbollah. After running into trouble with the Druze, it declined to firmly test the Christians. The government has shown itself powerless, and the political parties that focused on elections, parliament, and participation in the government have similarly shown themselves to be powerless.

This time they did ring a bell at the bottom

2008-05-21 04:47:35

You know the saying about markets: "They don't ring a bell at the top or the bottom"

The bell has just rang to announce the bottom of the housing market in California. From here on out, the prices are going up from insanely high to even more insanely high. Never again will ordinary affluent middle class people be able to buy a house in silicon valley, until the day dawns when the private property right to develop land is once again respected.

Various incompetently run or criminally run banks found themselves with lots and lots and lots of inflated and fraudulent mortgages. In due course, they found themselves with the real estate that was securing the mortgage. In the last few days they have held auctions in Silicon Valley and Sacramento to get rid of the properties. The properties sold like hotcakes, with bidders bidding them up, and up, and up.

Finally, some one else does the maths on oil
2008-05-22 04:49:26

I am continually puzzled by the world's chronic inability to do basic arithmetic, but I see that econbrowser has done the maths on oil.

There are a lot of people in China. There are no longer large political obstacles to competent and industrious people in China making money. Therefore, very soon, a lot of Chinese will be making a lot of money. Therefore China will soon be consuming an enormous amount of oil. Econbrowser concludes[45] China will soon be consuming a lot more oil than is ever likely to come out of the ground.

Therefore the price of oil will rise without limit until coal to oil and nuclear to hydrogen fills the gap. And right now, coal to oil projects are insignificant, and nuclear to hydrogen is not even on the drawing board. Therefore in the next decade or so, oil will rise to astonishing heights, far above present prices.

Terror works
2008-05-23 04:53:44

Before the twentieth century, the usual method for suppressing guerrilla war was artificial famine, state sponsored mass rape, and mass murder. During the twentieth century the communists used these methods heavily to quell not only resistance, but to quell resentment, to quell suspected politically incorrect thoughts. These methods generated curiously little resentment. Indeed, it seems that the greater the injury, the less the hostility. Certainly that is how things worked out for the communists. Consider, for example, the extraordinarily brutal measures that the USA used conquer the Philippines, yet the Filipinos love the United States. Today, nation states usually apply methods that are more civilized, more tedious and expensive, but perhaps leave something worth ruling. Yet the resentment is greater, not less. The Filipinos love the United States and Americans, despite the extraordinarily brutal measures the United States used to conquer the Phillipines, while the French hate the United States and Americans for liberating them, thereby making them feel cowardly and unmanly.

It is often argued that indiscriminate terror must be ineffective. If those who are not fighting the terrorists, even those who are collaborating with the terrorists, are in almost as much danger as those who are fighting the terrorists, surely every sensible person will fight. But this is not in fact what we see. Rather, what we saw back in the days when the United States used terror, and what we see in these days when terror is used against Americans, is quite the reverse effect. When terror is used brutally and indiscriminately, everyone feels uneasy merely hearing the terrorists spoken of unkindly, fearing that merely

---

[45]https://www.econbrowser.com/archives/2008/05/oil_price_funda.html

hearing such words spoken might attract the wrath of the terrorists. To speak unkindly of those who murder indiscriminately has become politically incorrect.

A magistrate in the northern Italian city of Bergamo ordered writer Oriana Fallaci[46] to stand trial for vilifying Islam in her book *The Force of Reason*[47]. which resulted in her exiling herself to America.

Genghis Khan set up a policy of massacring the entire city if it resisted. This produced many surrenders amongst people who would otherwise have fought. Grant's terror policy ended Confederate resistance.

Similarly, though movie makers generally flatter, rather than condemn their audience, when it comes to Muslims and Christianity, they follow the reverse policy: In the "sum of all fears" they amended the story to avoid offending Muslims, while in "Kingdom of heaven" they rewrote history to spit on Christians, demonstrating the effectiveness and success of terrorism, and rewarding those who use terror against us.

Back when the Muslim world was having hysterics because a guard at Gitmo might have inadvertently caused a minute sacrilege against the Koran, National Public Radio told us every day for a week how sacred the Koran is. In the middle of each news period, they brought on a Muslim clergyman to give us a lengthy sermon. Did not see any Christian clergymen getting any airtime during the piss christ event, demonstrating the effectiveness and success of terrorism, and rewarding those who use terror against us.

Timothy McViegh sought to stop certain extreme government abuses, which have in fact stopped.

Muslim terrorists seek to impose a supremacy for Islam, and they are succeeding. Speech against Christians is privileged, while speech against Muslims is silenced.

Observe, for example, how since the recent escalation in Muslim terror against France and Frenchmen, France's votes on the security council have become even more anti Israel - for example they voted against the security fence and voted to condemn Israel for killing Ahmed Yassin.

Terror works. Cannot stop it working, so have to make it expensive. If we really cannot find the terrorists, we have to hit people and things they care about. We should kill prominent muslim leaders and sacrilegiously spill their blood over prominent muslim religious monuments. We have to raise the price of terror.

Terror makes Muslims feel strong and proud, for we are in fact terrorized. Terror gives Muslims a living. Without the big handouts made to terrorists such as the PLO by non Muslims they would be even poorer. Terror gives them an alternative to having a capitalist economy where they create wealth. Instead they successfully extort wealth. **Terror works** for them.

Why don't I hear people saying "Mohammed the mass murdering pedophile rapist", the way I hear them say "pedophile priests".

Enough people are scared that Muslims can feel strong and proud, that Muslims can make a living out of terror - a substantially better living than is otherwise possible for them.

By Arab standards the West Bank and Gaza are extremely prosperous, thanks to the

---

[46]https://reason.com/links/links101502.shtml
[47]https://www.reason.com/hitandrun/2005/05/sia_lode_ad_all.shtml

jizya paid by westerners, and, until recently, paid by Jews. **Terror works**. They are getting laid, and getting money, you are not getting laid, and are paying them money. This is them winning and us losing.

Terror works. The terrorists get chicks and money.

What happened in Afghanistan is that we won, then would not leave well enough alone, and proceeded to shoot ourselves in the foot. The problem is that the West did "finish the job" - The west replaced the warlords, who were entirely capable of keeping the Taliban under control, and succeeded in a fine job of doing so, with a centralized state that cannot and is not. We should have paid and armed those people who are friendly to us and trustworthy, and assisted them to terrorize those people who are hostile to us and sponsor terrorist warfare against us. Instead, we arranged a government that represents 51% of the people - and 51% do not like us very much, and particularly dislike the 30% or so of Afghans who are on our side.

Strong Muslim central governments do us considerable harm, as Saddam demonstrated, as Syria and Iran continue to demonstrate. The Afghan government is weak because it is democratic, and reluctant to offend those who wish to use violence against Christians and women. Its weakness makes it a lesser evil. Better if it was weaker still, better still, hanging from the trees by their necks.

Bush should have stuck to his guns when he said "if you are not with us you are against us." This compromise crap is getting us killed. You cannot compromise with those who intend to conquer us. You have to kill them, or at least kill enough of them that the remainder give it up. When we try to compromise with an undefeated enemy who intends to conquer us, the resulting deal is, like Munich, that we shall be a little bit conquered, which encourages them to try for a lot more conquered. This is not a situation where the politics of compromise works.

Forming a government in Afghanistan looked remarkably like selling our allies into the hands of our enemies, like Chamberlain selling Czechoslovakia to Hitler. The people who fought for us are outvoted and disarmed, which is why things are now going bad in Afghanistan. It is as if the Czechs had fought and won, and *then* Chamberlain sold them to Hitler.

More maths on oil

2008-05-28 04:55:29

Econbrowser publishes oil price estimates[48] in more detail

Bottom line: Demand is going to rise one hell of a lot. Supply for that demand just is not there.

This paper does not review supply from coal to liquids or gas to liquids. The only way to meet demand is to generate liquids from coal by underground gasification followed by gas to liquids conversion. This will require many, many quite gigantic projects, but at present we have only a small number of small exploratory projects, most them scheduled to start producing around 2015 or so. So the price of oil will have to rise to quite astonishing levels, at least for a couple of decades. We have only seen the beginning.

---

[48]https://www.econbrowser.com/archives/2008/05/understanding_c.html

How to do health care right

2008-05-28 04:58:11

The American health care system is socialism without a central plan, and capitalism without markets or prices. In America, the health care system is disturbingly expensive, and sucking up alarming and rapidly increasing amounts of taxpayer money. America has the best health care system in the world for the very rich and the very poor, but for those in between, not so good. For the non working and part time working affluent (me) it is woefully bad.

Bryan Caplan points to Singapore:[49] Health care that is cheap, and, to best of my knowledge, very good - even the poor in Singapore are guaranteed reasonable care, yet the system costs the government very little.

Because there are no prices in the American health care system, there is no competition, so costs rise to absurd and astronomical heights.

Stuff that is offered on a fixed price basis, for example dental surgery and laser eye surgery, works well, but almost all health care is offered on the basis of that they will do it, then afterwards make up a price on the basis of political power. For example my family has catastrophic coverage, which means we pay most ordinary medical charges out of our own pocket, but the insurance kicks in when we actually come down with something expensive. My wife was advised to get a colonoscopy. We shopped around, got a reasonable price at a doctor with a good reputation, negotiated with the insurance company, did all the stuff one does in an environment which actually has prices. Then *after* the colonoscopy was done, the hospital pulled a huge list of stupendously expensive charges out of their ass, most of which were obviously ridiculous or completely made up out of thin air, just trying it on to see what they could get away with, and *all* of which were charges we had definitely not agreed to, nor consented to in any way, formal or informal, written or unwritten. They just were not used to doing stuff on the basis that one has a definite price, and that the price one charges affects demand for one's services. The concept seemed alien and incomprehensible to them. Mentally, they were socialists.

In Singapore, they *advertise* prices.

Some years later, I had the following conversations with various US health care providers. I recorded the conversations:

Conversation with Stanford Hospital

Me

> My wife needs a colonoscopy: Could you give me a price on it?

Stanford Hospital: (businesslike tone)

> Twenty five hundred to thirty five hundred.

Me

---

[49]https://econlog.econlib.org/archives/2008/05/quality_health.html

You do this all the time. Can't you give me a
specific price?

Stanford Hospital: (cooler tone)

Sorry

Me

Is $3500 the all up, all included price to both
myself and my insurance?

Stanford Hospital: (businesslike tone)

It only includes the doctors fee, and does not include any additional services

Me

So after I have this done, any number of people could then charge me any
fee they like in addition to the thirty five hundred?

Stanford Hospital: (distinctly chilly tone)

I am afraid so.

O'Connor Hospital

Me

My wife needs a colonoscopy: Could you give me
a price on it.

O'Connor Hospital

Do you have a primary physician?

Me

Yes, my primary physician has advised this procedure, but it seems expensive.
I am looking for a price.

O'Connor Hospital (outraged and indignant)

We don't give out prices!

Mercy General Hospital

Me

I am looking for a price on a colonoscopy.

Mercy General Hospital hangs up without a word.

Saint Joseph's medical center of Stockton

I am transferred to financial counselling, who transferred me to "Estimates" The estimating lady appreciated my problem and made sympathetic noises.

She then asks me for a CPT code. I then research what CPT codes are, and discover that an operation can result in any CPT, and any number of CPTs. I discover that no matter what CPT I give, it is unlikely to be correct or sufficient, that additional CPTs can show up any time. A CPT would only be useful if it was possible to know in advance what CPTs would result from a colonoscopy, but the CPTs are only decided after the colonoscopy, usually long after the colonoscopy.

Predicting housing prices

2008-05-28 05:01:13

Since I think I am smart, going to make prediction.I think the housing market in California has pretty much hit bottom, and the same is largely true in most of the places in the US where prices went up to the sky, then fell to earth. Most of the asking prices are still far too high, but the prices at which people are buying are near the bottom. A two bathroom house of 1150 square feet in Sunnyvale should sell at four hundred to four fifty thousand dollars now. From here on out, prices will be rising – not very fast, but fast enough that a few years from now people will look back at those prices as their last chance to get a house, which chance they missed.

The holy church of Green

2008-05-30 05:02:13

Dr.Tim Ball reports that the IPCC first created the "Summary for Policy Makers" report, *then* the science report that it is supposedly a summary of.

> "Changes (other than grammatical or minor editorial changes) made after acceptance by the Working Group or the Panel shall be those necessary to ensure consistency with the Summary for Policymakers (SPM) or the Overview Chapter."

Unfortunately, it is not only global warming global warming "science" that works like this, but most science since the late twentieth century

This was, in the end, the unavoidable result of government funding for science. He who pays the piper, calls the tune. He sleeps with elephants, wakes up flat. For science to be science, scientists need to cultivate a wider range of patrons and sources of funding.

Winning in Iraq

2008-06-02 00:37:08

It is now apparent that the US is winning in Iraq. It is so apparent that even the Washington Post reports it – to the considerable surprise of both myself and others[50]

What then is winning? What does victory mean? The US can destroy any enemy anywhere, and no one can stop us. Building states, however, is harder.

Baathism has been crushed. Al Quaeda in Iraq has been crushed. These are big important victories. The idea, however, was to build democratic allied states. Building states is hard, and no one knows how to do it. The success rate in state building has been depressingly low. The Iraqi state is largely smoke and mirrors. Though Iraq is nominally independent, when push comes to shove, it is not independent, but under US martial law. US officers can and do arrest Iraqi officers and high officials when they deem it necessary. When and if Iraq becomes independent, it will likely collapse, or else become a kind of state that is not very democratic and not in the interests of the US.

Europe can't stop anything

2008-06-05 00:39:00

Michael Totten quotes a Serb[51]:

> "If Americans said they were no longer interested in Europe, it would be a catastrophe here."
>
> "You think?" Sean said.
>
> "Yes," David said, "because Europe can't stop anything."

The military weakness and incapacity of Europe in Serbia startled the Serbs, even more than America's capacity stunned them. Since then, Europe's martial weakness has been on display in one humiliating debacle after another. Recall Britain's startling display of fear, weakness, cowardice, and dhimmitude in the Persian gulf.

All that wealth, and no capacity to defend it. The vultures are circling.

For a state to exist, it has to be able to destroy those that oppose it, or might oppose it, to inflict famine and ruin on hostile populations, has to be able burn the crops and flatten the cities, after the manner of General Sherman, and has to have confident belief, a belief shared by officers and men, that it is *right* to do so.

To do this, it needs some source of cohesion. It cannot provide its own cohesion. Pay and threats will not work to motivate soldiers, for when things go bad, when your soldiers most need motivation, these motivations cannot function, for nothing will motivate people impose the discipline.

The usual source or cohesion is ethnic identity: the nation state. Other sources of cohesion are religion, as for example the various theocratic states, such as the caliphate, and ideology, as for example the American revolution and the various communist coups.

---

[50]https://www.brutallyhonest.org/brutally_honest/2008/06/must-be-a-cold.html
[51]https://www.michaeltotten.com/archives/2008/06/a-dark-corner-o.php

So if a state's cohesion came from ethnicity, then when it goes multicultural, then its soldiers and police are fighting for pay and pension *and nothing more*, and then it is are doomed. Similarly, when the last shreds of liberty are crushed out in the US, when the second amendment is utterly gone, and little left of the first amendment, US troops will be fighting for pay and pension and nothing more and then the US will be doomed.

Global Guerrilas reports that Mexico and Nigeria[52] are falling, as bandits, revolutionaries, and suchlike take possession of the Mexican drug trade, and bandits, revolutionaries, Islamists, and suchlike take possession of Nigeria's oil. But there is a lot more available for the stealing in Europe.

If the Nigerian or Mexican government goes, the Pentagon should secure the oil, but will not be able to do so without will and belief that it is right to do so. That would require an ideology that it reasonable to protect the private property rights of American and allied businessmen – which argument will not fly when they threw them to the wolves long ago, when long ago they allowed the oil and the oil rigs to be stolen by governments that are now failing.

Will DME save us from the oil crisis?
2008-06-07 00:41:52

To satisfy world demand, as former third worlders become first worlders, and want cars and air conditioning, the world needs to increase production of oil and oil substitutes about three million barrels per day each year. Equivalently, the world needs to increase production one hundred and fifty million tonnes per year per year.

Now if we compare what is needed, with what is under development, and reasonably projected, what is under development is indistinguishable from zero. China recently projected that by 2020, would be producing thirty million tonnes per year, which is a drop in the bucket.

On the other hand, one can set up a DME plant a fair bit quicker than synfuel plant, and DME production seems to be expanding exponentially. DME is an LPG substitute, which can be used in diesel engines the way LPG can be used in petrol engines. DME production may be doubling every couple of years, or every year. Suppose world production of DME is now four hundred thousand tonnes per year, and suppose it is doubling every two years, which are informed wild ass guesses. In that case, DME will start to bring down oil prices when it reaches about one hundred and sixty million tonnes per year, or four hundred times its present production – and if it is doubling every two years, will reach that in eighteen years, around 2026.

Ouch!

There can be no peace with dar al Islam
2008-06-09 00:43:01

There can be no peace with dar al-Islam. In the long run, dar al-Harb must conquer or be conquered – and if dar al-Islam is to be the conquered, the conquered have to be colonized

---

[52]https://globalguerrillas.typepad.com/globalguerrillas/2008/06/journal-gg-prog.html

and displaced, as in the early days of Algeria and Israel.

The problem, the reason there can never be peace, is lucidly explained by Dhimmi Watch[53]

Rational Oil Prices

2008-06-13 00:48:15

It seems that Arnold Kling has been in Afghan cave during the past six months. He does not seem to think that there has been any bad news on oil supply over the last six months.

> The recent run-up in oil prices represents a similar puzzle. I think that it's difficult to tell a story for the rise in crude prices for the last six months that is based on the rational digestion of news. Either six months ago folks were overly optimistic about long-term supply and demand conditions or now they are overly pessimistic about those conditions. I don't think that what changed in the last six months was the ews about supply and demand.

I have been watching the news, and over the past few months it has been quite horrifying, particular with the Democrats and both major party presidential candidates shooting down Shell's plan to develop shale oil, which pretty much guarantees extraordinarily high oil prices for at least the next two decades. Indeed, the political majority in most of the developed world seem to intend to block all carbon extraction.

Roots of the energy crisis

2008-06-16 00:52:34

The energy crisis happened because of optimistic projections[54] – that gas to liquid and coal to liquid would not be needed until the technology had been improved and the cost brought down, that the dramatic growth in China and India could be accommodated by rapidly expanding conventional oil production.

The political elite, unable to introduce a carbon tax because it would directly and visibly hurt people, proceeded to block coal and oil developments, thus invisibly and directly hurting people. The plan to develop America's vast shale oil reserves was shot down a few weeks ago by the Democrats. At the same time, various oil states suffered partial, and in the case of Nigeria, near total collapse, making it difficult to extract oil without employing old fashioned imperial methods which are politically unthinkable in this day and age.

I wish I could end this by saying "so the solution is...". But there just is not a solution. Energy is best produced in big, large scale projects. In a world of insecure property rights, where corporations are unpopular and disarmed, big projects are no longer feasible. The general world trend is any big project is going to be unworkable without a correspondingly big bunch of guys with guns who have the right, and feel they have the right, to do what it takes to protect that project. As I have said before, underground coal gasification

---

[53]https://www.jihadwatch.org/dhimmiwatch/archives/021323.php
[54]https://www.shell.com/static/media-en/downloads/51852.pdf

followed by gas to liquids conversion is the technological solution, but that technological solution requires a political solution, and that political solution is nowhere on the horizon.

A better ID card

2008-06-20 00:54:50

Digital Identity Forum has a better solution for ID[55].

Instead of an ID card that tells any purported authority everything about you, an ID smart card that verifies what authority the authority actually possesses, and reveals the minimum information that that authority is authorized to know, for example that you are over 18, to be read by cell phone with nfc cardreader.

Bring back the Northern Alliance

2008-06-21 00:56:31

The US is winning in Iraq, in large part by abandoning or indefinitely postponing the goal of a unitary state, and cultivating the militias, such as "the Sons of Iraq" (who are more like the sons of Arab Shia Iraq) Afghanistan, however, is going down the tubes.

According to Gideon Rachman[56]

1. Our current strategy isn't working
2. There are no real alternative strategies
3. We cannot afford to lose.

There is of course an obvious alternative strategy:

The Northern Alliance took care of the Taliban just fine.

Bring back the warlords, the local militias, the armed congregations with serious theological disagreements with Al Quaeda and the Taliban. Fund them, arm them, give them ground to air missiles. Hang the democratically elected Kabul government from the nearest trees. They hate us and we should hate them. A bit over fifty percent of the voters in Afghanistan hate us, probably near sixty percent. Arm the guys that don't hate us, and give them air support.

The Taliban is winning not only because it receives military support from Pakistan and the Pakistani armed forces, but because it receives covert support from some elements of the elected government that it is at war with. Bush famously said "If you are not with us, you are against us" but many people are doing very well standing on both sides at once.

Hatred of softly influential groups

2008-06-24 00:59:38

Wherever a group has disproportionate economic or cultural success that does not rest upon political power, does not involve the ability to kill people and break things, does

---

[55]https://digitaldebateblogs.typepad.com/digital_identity/2008/06/its-crazy-but-i.html
[56]https://blogs.ft.com/rachmanblog/2008/06/afghanistan-backlash/

not depend upon hard power, for example Jews, Americans, Indonesian Chinese, Indian Fijians, Indians in Africa, the Ibo in Africa, the same hatred occurs, the same accusations, the same fantasies, the same excessive and disproportionate attention, the same concoction of utterly trivial grievances into supposedly enormous crimes – even if the disproportionately successful group and the less successful group have no previous history, but only encountered each other fairly recently. I observe that we also get such interesting phenomena as self hating members of the successful group - the psychopathologies so characteristic of Jews are also characteristic of other disproportionately successful and correspondingly hated groups.

This phenomenon is the inverse of Stockholm Syndrome. Stockholm Syndrome is that we are apt to love those who control us by fear and murder. Hatred of softly influential minorities, such as anti Americanism and hatred of overseas Chinese in various third world countries, is that we are apt to hate those whose intellectual creativity entertains or inspires us.

Amy Chua, author of the book "World on Fire", which examines the problem of softly influential groups, under the demonizing and politically correct name "Dominant Minorities", is a pretty good example of a self hating Filipino Chinese. It would seem that the Chinese sinned by being industrious and successful, and therefore the system that allowed them to succeed is supposedly to blame for bringing repression upon them in the Philippines, and massacre upon them in Indonesia.

There are a great many diverse newly affluent ethnic groups, among them the overseas Chinese of various Asian countries. An ethnic group succeeds, perhaps because of genetic superiority, perhaps because of a culture that encourages education, thrift and hard work, and so people hate that ethnic group - hate Amy's ethnic group among others. Her analysis of the problem is absolutely accurate and spot on, though of course her implied solution – a political elite that imposes equality on all the non elite – has failed disastrously. She sees, and explains in detail, that her ethnic group is in the same hole as the Jews, and as a great many other similar groups, correctly analyzing the problem that afflicts overseas Chinese and Jews and many other groups as a single problem with many groups and many examples. The flaw in her analysis is the self hating and politically correct phrase "dominant minority".

The groups she is talking about are *not* dominant, rather they possess soft power. If Americans wandered around shooting people to force obedience, everyone would love them, but Americans are hated because they *persuade* people to drink coca cola and watch terminator movies.

Similarly Hitler, a failed artist, was primarily enraged by the influence of Jewish plays and art. When people complain that America rules the world, they really complaining that they watch American movies, and thus people are playing attention to Americans instead of themselves.

The correct description of the problem is "non coercive influence", and "softly influential group" Non coercive influence, soft power, is what a softly influential group possesses, and it makes that group hated. Dominant minorities are often loved, and are never hated. The problem, rather is **hatred of softly influential groups**.

I observe that since the surge, since Americans flattened half of Fallujah, we have at last seen large numbers of Arabs clerics, all of them Iraqis, most of them not very far from Fallujah, preaching genuinely moderate Islam, and large numbers of Arab intellectuals, a great many of them Iraqis, arguing for moderate and realistic behavior by Arabs and Arab countries, accurately perceiving the faults of Islam and the Arabs. The American attempts to directly build a state were all miserable failures, and continue to be so, but when the Americans showed persistence in slaying their enemies, there was considerably greater willingness to examine American ideas and beliefs honestly and thoughtfully. Arab intellectuals and clerics changed their position, and we now increasingly hear from Arabs that Arabs have problems because their society has something wrong with it, not because the outsiders are holding them down. Seeing that Americans would fight and not yield made in much easier for Arabs to understand and agree with the Americans, though I think Americans could have made the same point at considerably less cost to themselves.

The critical variable is hard power, and hard power is the costs you can inflict on others. If a softly influential minority exercises sufficient hard power - that is to say, hurts enough people and destroys enough wealth, or demonstrates willingness and ability to do so - **irrational hostility diminishes** among those people who are potentially vulnerable to being hurt, and the softly influential group becomes able to make its case intellectually, able to win hearts and minds through persuasion and good deeds. The good deeds are only appreciated from people who can and do also do bad deeds.

Not only is the group less hated, but it less apt to hate themselves. Not so very long ago Americans were having orgasms of guilt because a guard at Gitmo tortured a poor helpless terrorist by pissing a short distance upwind of a Koran. Today Americans have flattened half of Fallujah and no one gets indignant.

When Americans knocked down a few dozen houses in Fallujah and killed a few people, there was a big outcry about the Fallujah massacre, just as there was about the Jenin massacre when Jews knocked down a few houses and killed a few people.

But when Americans came back a couple of years later and proceed the flatten half of Fallujah and kill a great big pile of people, not only are Fallujans fine with that, but more importantly, Americans are fine with that. If you google, you will *still* get five times more hits on Jenin massacre than on Fallujah massacre, and most, probably all of the hits for Fallujah massacre are for much smaller events from long ago where Americans were doing very little damage to people or property. When Americans rolled their sleeves up and really started killing people and breaking things in vast numbers, then there was no more talk of "Fallujah massacre" - not from Arabs, not from Europeans, and not from Americans.

The solution to the problem that Amy so accurately describes is the Fallujah solution, the opposite of the solution she inaccurately prescribes. The answer to irrational hatred is to hurt people and break things. Since the hatred is irrational, crazy, and self destructive, a sufficiently hurtful and destructive response to hatred snaps people out of their madness, and creates an environment where communication and good deeds can work, as is happening in Fallujah and Anbar province.

Of course, that strategy can also lead to holy war, if people incorrectly evaluate other people's legitimate grievances as irrational, crazy, and self destructive, but what we are seeing in Iraq is the quenching of holy war, with, to my great surprise, a massive outbreak of moderate Islam, We are not seeing any signs of a functional democracy or national unity, which was supposed to be the mechanism that would supposedly produce moderate Islam, but we are seeing moderate Islam despite, or perhaps because of, the severe disfunction of the institutions that were supposed to encourage it.

How much hard power is required? Small doses are counter productive, merely giving people superficially rational excuses for their irrational hatred. Gitmo produced the insane hysteria about torturing a prisoner by pissing upwind of a Koran, making the problem worse, not better. The Fallujah sized dose, however, has had dramatic good effects in Fallujah and noticeable good effect in America, winning the hearts and minds not only of Fallujans, but of Americans.

One mode, and it is secure

2008-06-24 01:03:16

Ian Grigg correctly argues that any internet protocol that has an insecure mode can never be made secure[57], thus if security is introduced as after thought, will never be secure.

Https is exactly such a bolted on afterthought, and to use it one must pay money, and suffer substantial inconvenience. Further, it is a woefully inefficient protocol, so people always try to minimize their use of it to only what is truly necessary, which they are unlikely to ever do correctly. Further, those to whom one must pay money are themselves a point of failure, not a source of security.

Iang attempts, and fails, to make his website conform to the **one mode** principle. For a blog to implement "the **one mode** and it is secure" paradigm it must be accessed by https, and accessing it by http should generate an 301 redirect to the https site. The trouble is, that when one reaches the https site, the site has to have a certificate whose root is accepted by the big browsers, typically a Verisign certificate. Such certificates are a pain to get, and a pain to install. And so, no one ever does. Iang has not got a big name certificate in the appropriate name for his web site, so accessing his site correctly generates no end of alarming error dialogs.

Court appointed lawyers

2008-06-26 01:05:51

Texas Child Protective Services wishes to 'protect' Teresa Jeffs from being sexually abused – which 'protection' has a curious resemblance to charging her with practicing polygamy while white.

The courts have appointed Natalie Malonis to supposedly represent her and two other polygamist 'children', which lawyer has been conducting trial by media against her supposed client:

> I believe that [Teresa Jeffs] was avoiding service because of coercion and improper influence from Willie Jessop.

---

[57]https://financialcryptography.com/mt/archives/001067.html

...

> There is no question I am absolutely looking out for her, ... What's happening is really a shame because people who purport to care about her are really doing her a disservice.

...

> I'm trying to help her. It's really not in any child's interest to waive their attorney-client privilege. I'm not going to fight with her in the media.

...

> And one of the big problems in this case is that the victims really don't consider themselves victims so theyre not — it's difficult to help them.

This kind of public @#$% would be improper even if Malonis was a prosecutor instead of supposedly a defender. If a lawyer's client starts fighting her in the media, she is not allowed to fight back in the media.

Solution to the energy crisis

2008-06-29 01:10:13

Newt tells it how it is: This crisis was caused by politicians. He tells how to reduce fuel costs in the short run, and the long run. 'you want energy now he tells us. And then he tells us how to get it.

How do we solve the energy crisis? Answer. Let businessmen extract oil. Drill here. Drill now. Pay less.

Predicted ... observed

2008-06-30 01:12:16

In 1988 the warmists issued their first prophecy of doom. Repent of your sins against Gaia, abandon the industrial civilization that allows us to feed far too many people, or the wrath of Gaia will manifest in massive global warming, with the wrath setting in around the year 2000.

The Blackboard checks on how that prediction went[58]

In 2001 they issued a new prophecy of doom, this time with the wrath of Gaia setting in rather more slowly. When the warmists tell you that observed climate change is occurring in accord their revelations, what they actually mean is that they are adjusting their revelations to accord with observations.

---

[58]https://rankexploits.com/musings/2008/ordinary-eyeball-how-did-hansens-predictions-do

Britain falls

2008-07-05 01:14:06

When the Roman empire in the west fell, it was decades, nearly a century, before Romans realized it had fallen. Falling is a process, which is hard to recognize at the time. A recent post in Gates of Vienna[59] leads me to believe that in decades to come, future historians will date the fall of most of old Europe to Islam to 2008, or not long after.

The first step in subjecting Europe to dar al Islam is to establish liberated zones where the writ of the Christian state does not run. This is well under way in France, and is now beginning in England.[60]

When state operatives, such as firemen, show their faces, they get thumped. And if they want to show their faces without getting thump, they had best accept and enforce law acceptable to Islam. This produces, or in the near future will produce a number of benefits for the Muslims within such a zone. For example they won't have to pay for electricity, nor pay rent to kaffirs, nor may kaffirs refuse to rent to them merely because of a well founded fear that no rent will be paid and no eviction will be possible. If a Muslim within such a zone commits crimes against kaffirs, police have little enthusiasm for looking into the matter, which situation will in future produce substantial benefits for Muslims at the expense of kaffirs, if it is not doing so already.

American empire is not working

2008-07-08 01:17:55

I have long argued that the US should focus on destroying its enemies and not attempt to hold ground. Global Guerrillas observes[61] that

> it was only when the Army/Marines attempted to *hold* ground that the US military ran into trouble. These advocates maintain that the US military should never hold ground in the future

Who are "these advocates"?

"Governance in the Wilderness"

2008-07-08 01:19:23

"Governance in the Wilderness" is merely a retranslation of the same Al Quaeda document earlier translated as "the Management of Savagery[62]" or "the Management of Barbarism"

The author concluded that 9/11 was unsuccessful, in that it failed to intimidate Americans, and the American retribution was severe. He correctly predicted that the attempt to set up a new Caliphate in Bahgdad was much premature, and would be defeated, as it

---

[59]https://gatesofvienna.blogspot.com/2008/07/schoolboys-punished-for-refusing-to.html
[60]https://www.fbu.org.uk/campaigns/attacks/index.php
[61]https://globalguerrillas.typepad.com/globalguerrillas/
[62]https://reaction.lathe_management_of_savagery/

was. He recommends large amounts of small scale intimidation, which prescription we see being very successfully applied in the Middle East, France, and England.

Vote Cthulhu for US president

2008-07-12 01:22:45

Or if not **Cthulhu**, Obama.

When I started writing this, McCain had the the most violently anticapitalist program of any presidential candidate, his cap and trade policy.

Obama, having started out at lunatic left in the primaries, is heading rightwards at high speed, and his "cap and trade" policy had become a mere pigovian carbon tax, making him considerably less anti capitalist than McCain.

McCain, finding himself outflanked, quietly dropped his cap and trade program altogether, bringing him to the right of Obama again, forcing me to rewrite.

The primaries produced two presidential candidates, one alarmingly anti capitalist and left wing, the other alarmingly anti capitalist, even more left wing, and anti american on top of it. I found it hard to believe that ordinary Americans would vote for either one of them.

It looks like they came to the same conclusion, because they both proceeded to head rightwards at high speeds.

But why vote for the lesser evil? Vote Cthulhu

Not Science

2008-07-16 09:33:58

Recently the CSIRO (Commonwealth Scientific and Research Organization) dressed itself in the robes of high holy science, and portentously announced that the wrath of Gaea was upon us[63]. Other scientists asked for the details of the evidence, but alas, the highly scientific scientists of the CSIRO found themselves sadly unable to provide the evidence[64].

Bush rolls back oil prices, MSM in denial

2008-07-18 09:36:17

Political correctness is that we should not drill for oil, for more oil will not solve the problem of high and rising fuel prices. Which political correctness the mainstream media firmly endorse.

There are multiple bans on oil drilling. Bush ended one of them, which had no immediate effect on oil drilling, for other bans in place. But it had immediate psychological effect. Oil prices immediate dropped about eighteen dollars, a huge drop, which the press

---

[63]https://landshape.org/enmlatex/wp-content/uploads/2008/07/csiro-bom-report-future-droughts.pdf
[64]https://landshape.org/enm/drought-exceptional-circumstances-report-mia/

is frantically trying to explain away with any explanation other than the glaringly obvious one.

If the politicians suspended enough bans that drilling actually became legal again, we would therefore see an immediate and considerably bigger drop in the price of oil, even before any actual drilling takes place, for sellers of oil, expecting competition to cut their prices in future, would sell oil right now, to take advantage of present high prices.

The price of oil is absurdly high, because sellers of oil observe that the high price is not leading anyone to go out and get more oil, from which they conclude that oil can only go higher still, so they might as well sit on it.

We won in Iraq

2008-07-18 09:38:50

Michael Yon declares the war over[65]. He should know. He has been wandering around the place looking it over. But if we have a few more victories like this one, we will have lost, and Islam won. We cannot do Iran what we barely managed to do to Iraq, and still less can we do to Pakistan what we barely accomplished in Iraq. We are losing in Afghanistan, for it is not really a war *in* Afghanistan any more (that war we won long ago) but rather a war with our "ally" Pakistan.

Bernanke explains what he is doing wrong

2008-07-22 09:39:58

In his speech Governor Ben S. Bernanke[66] observed that if inflationary expectations rise, and the Fed fails to raise interest rates correspondingly, this is unstable. He failed to make the reason for this clear, but the reason is that real interest rates are nominal interest minus expected inflation - so a rise in inflationary expectations causes a fall in real interest rates, causing massive real borrowing - as for example the housing boom and flight from money into real things, such as oil, which causes actual inflation, which increases inflationary expectations.

Which is of course exactly what has been happening. Inflationary expectations have escalated, as shown by the price of gold that international value of the US dollar, and Bernanke failed to raise interest rates correspondingly, leading to a vicious cycle, which is still under way as I post this.

Global warming is not science

2008-07-31 09:40:59

Science is based on experiment and evidence. The motto of the royal society was "Nullius in verba", which means "Take no one's word for it". This motto was reinterpreted to

---

[65]https://michaelyon-online.com/index.php?option=com_content&view=article&id=1690%3Asuccess-in-iraq
[66]https://www.federalreserve.gov/BOARDDOCS/SPEECHES/2004/20040220/default.htm

accommodate the "evidence" for global warming.[67] Most science journals have condition of publication that authors must comply with any reasonable request by other researchers for materials, methods, or data necessary to verify the conclusion of the article, which condition has not yet been enforced[68] against the global warmers.

Democrat energy plan
2008-08-04 09:48:51

This republican advertisement is so funny and so true, that I stole it.

Democrat Energy Plan
drive small cars and wait for the *wind*

US Chamber of commerce protests junk science
2008-08-06 09:58:10

The second national climate assessment predicts that the United States will "very likely" experience rising sea levels and increasing droughts, heat waves, intense storms and resulting illness and premature death over the next century as climate change intensifies.

But, as is the usual practice with climate "science" , the report fails to make available the evidence that supposedly leads to this conclusion, a gross and flagrant violation of normal and proper scientific practice.

And so, the US Chamber of Commerce, not academia, not any scientific body, has demanded that normal scientific standards be upheld[69].

---

[67] https://www.spiked-online.com/index.php?/site/article/3357/
[68] https://www.climateaudit.org/?p=3352
[69] https://icecap.us/index.php/go/political-climate

Explanations of the oil price rise

2008-08-07 10:00:50

My explanation for high oil prices is the collapse of oil states. Arnold Kling argues that instead the problem is that investors fear the collapse of advanced states, so are reluctant to take their money.

My explanation is that oil states are increasingly short of the competence to pump oil, the ability to provide security to people pumping oil, and the credibility to make deals with people who are competent to pump oil — for example it is difficult for foreign companies to pump oil in Nigeria, because there are too many different bandits and terrorists to pay them all off, and difficult for foreigners to pump oil in Venezuela or Mexico, because the government cannot credibly promise not steal everything, and difficult for the Venezuelan government to pump oil, since it could not run a pie stand, plus the security situation in Mexico, though better than Nigeria, is deteriorating.

Arnold Kling, however, argues[70] that the problem is the increasingly scary on book and off book debt levels of the advanced nations, in particular the US. Investors fear hyperinflation. Where to put their money? Answer: Buy commodities that are underground, and leave them underground.

What has been happening in Georgia

2008-08-11 10:03:05

The boundaries of all the Balkan and Caucasus states are ill defined, one blurs into the other, each contains people who feel themselves outsiders and oppressed. In some, like Estonia, "oppression" is merely that if you cannot speak the majority language, or a widely spoken international language such as English, you have poor job prospects. In others, oppression consists of robbery, rape, and murder. By and large the resentment is greater, and more likely to lead to bloody fratricidal violence, when it is merely a matter of not being able to get a job if people cannot understand what you are saying.

A lot of people that think themselves Ossetian and Russian live in Georgia. Most of them cannot speak Georgian. Imaginary repression resulted in bloody insurrection, which resulted in real and bloody repression. Russia intervened and seized what it now calls South Ossetia. It installed a police state there, which suggests that not all South Ossetians hate the Georgians more than the Russians.

Georgia proceeded to build up its military power, and had a stab at getting "South Ossetia" back. Russians then invaded Georgia a couple of days ago, to prevent Georgians from recovering "South Ossetia".

So it is not necessarily serious. Both sides might well accept a return to the status quo ante, wherein "South Ossetia" remains a Russian police state. Georgians, however, are perfectly capable of making the status quo painfully expensive for Russia, and have been doing so, which might provoke Russia to eliminate Georgia - or Georgians.

---

[70]https://econlog.econlib.org/archives/2008/08/an_economic_dis.html

Yellow bellied surrender monkeys

2008-08-11 10:05:19

In the last ten years or so we have been hearing a lot of disturbing reports about Britain - reports of a society of fearful and servile subjects, of criminals acting with impunity, of the British accepting second class status to Islam. Maybe the gun lobby is exaggerating British submission to criminals, maybe racists and war hawks are exaggerating British submission to Islam, but this story of cowardice and betrayal from Basra[71] fits with what we have been hearing about self defense in Britain and freedom of religion in Britain.

The authors, however blame the leadership, not the troops, so perhaps with a more manly leader, such as Margaret Thatcher, the old British would reappear. On the other hand, the similar humiliations in the Persian gulf, and the very similar cowardice and betrayal in Helmand province are worrying. Doubtless it was the leadership that betrayed Helmand province, but was it the political leaders that caused troops to surrender on the Persian gulf?

The success of globalization

2008-08-12 10:09:11

Massive globalization — a major move towards free market capitalism — has brought over a billion people out of poverty, while sixty years of socialist chaos and violence has failed to convince most of the world that central planning is a very bad way to run any economy. "Ruble" symbolizes pretend money, unconvertible into goods, much as "Finland" symbolizes submission to a hostile power, and "Peso" symbolizes inflation.

Globalism has done what socialism promised to do and failed to do: It has lifted those parts of the third world that adopted it out of poverty. If you have been shopping for a subnotebook, this should be obvious. Globalization means that if you are using a subnotebook, you are using a subnotebook designed and built in a country that recently used to be third world and used to be socialist, but which has moved substantially towards free market capitalism.

Socialism aimed to create an alternative to normal economic transactions, an alternative that would avoid such banes of capitalism as business cycles, windfall profits, and unemployment. Socialists expected to that their benevolence, wisdom — and absolute power backed by the most brutal extremes of savage violence — would bring the poor out of poverty, but instead chained the poor into serfdom and slavery.

Socialist transactions usually involved crises, shortages, unfullfillable quotas, and the continual threat and frequent reality of violence.

To do what they were commanded to do, administrators under socialism had to do what they were forbidden to do — the plan functioned, in so far as it did function, through an illegal underground black market economy. To enable the military plan to be fulfilled, troops lurked on the road to intercept and seize goods planned for other purposes. Civilians substituted the black market for the plan, and the military substituted pillage for the plan.

---

[71]https://pajamasmedia.com/blog/british-deal-with-al-sadr-betrayed-iraqi-people/

The Soviets created a Potemkin village of normality, thinly concealing a chaotic and violent reality that people were forbidden to notice.

Socialists interpret trade and business as fraud and violence, which gives them continual cause for war, especially war on their disarmed and frightened subjects. The failure of socialism was and is blamed on internal and external enemies. Somehow, capitalism was continuing, so more violence was required. If poverty is caused by wicked capitalists, and poverty continued, then obviously capitalism must be continuing, and must be hunted down and crushed.

"Globalization" is that Walmart and China are entwined, that American business phones are manned by Indians in India, and as a result of globalization, a major part of the third world, most importantly India and China, are now becoming first world.

Globalization is a success, a success as obvious and spectacular, as socialism was a spectacular and dreadful failure.

Lots of planning and state intervention remains — and lots of violence and chaos remains. But to the extent that do we have globalization, it has succeeded spectacularly. Its crises are the crises of success. If Chinese were still trudging around barefoot in the mud and snow, we would not have the present energy crisis.

There is still a lot of state intervention and state owned enterprises, in China and elsewhere, but there is now a lot less of it, and what there is accepts capitalism, rather than trying to fix capitalism. No more "iron ricebowl" in China.

China still has extensive state owned enterprises, but they no longer have monopoly privileges - they are subject to competition, and required to make a profit. If they lose money, the management is fired. If they continue to lose money, everyone is fired - which is one hell of a lot less socialist than America's Amtrack, and features business cycles, windfall profits and unemployment, all the things that socialism and state intervention was justified as remedying. The resource crisis has led to huge windfall profits by Chinese resource businesses, and of course lots of Chinese state owned enterprises have shut down for inability to turn a profit, leading to unemployment, plus the whole economy is coordinated through just in time contracts organized by firms run from outside China, through private contracts with global businesses, not through a government plan. The Chinese economy is run through virtual private networks managed by overseas servers, the servers largely located in places such as Bermuda, which virtual private networks and servers are the nerves and sinews of globalization.

And to the extent that such intervention has been dramatically reduced, and transformed in ways that make it less disruptive of capitalism, transformed in ways that accept the unpredictable outcomes of free market competition, and the winners and losers that such competition produces, the poor have become vastly better off.

The Hockey Stick Graph

2008-08-13 10:10:51

Bishop Hill explains the Hockey Stick Graph.[72] It is an exceedingly long and complicated story, even in his simplified version, but the short of it is: The global warmists lied.

---

[72]https://bishophill.squarespace.com/blog/2008/8/11/caspar-and-the-jesus-paper.html

Diebold voting machines horribly wrong

2008-08-16 10:17:36

xkcd gets it exactly right[73]

Thai middle class revolts against democracy

2008-09-04 17:56:24

"The people's alliance for democracy" is in fact the Thai middle class alliance against democracy, as Cown observes[74]. Democracy in Thailand has produced bad results nowhere near as bad as Venezuela, but bad enough. Indeed, world wide we are seeing democratic elections produce governments that are increasingly corrupt, increasingly tyrannical, increasingly bureaucratic, increasingly destructive, and increasingly anticapitalist.

Yet the middle class has no ideology to justify its demands - the name of the movement furtively and shamefacedly denies what it is doing, and their proposed solution (military appointees) is not really going to work. The military are bureaucrats with guns. A middle class revolt that professes itself faithful to democracy is like all those peasant revolts that professed themselves faithful to the king. Doomed.

For two thousand years, it has been claimed that democracy inherently self destructs, that democracy destroys the conditions that make democracy possible. The fact that democracy worked pretty well during the twentieth century would seem contrary evidence - but a century is not a long time for such a test.

Never forget, never forgive

2008-09-12 18:00:18

Never forget, never forgive. Make them pay forever.

---

[73]https://xkcd.com/463/
[74]https://www.irishtimes.com/newspaper/opinion/2008/0904/1220372096913.html

Figure 1: nine eleven

carbon footprint

2008-09-17 18:03:53

Do you want to reduce your carbon footprint

Or do you want to drill here now.

The financial crash

2008-09-21 18:06:51

Brad de Long looks at the financial crisis, and concludes that the wise and good hand of government is necessary.

> Third, the market fundamentalists in other sectors will need to be quiet
> for quite a while. We have just seen financial markets rife with moral haz-
> ard, agency, and adverse selection problems crash spectacularly. Is this a
> situation in which we should move health care–also rife with moral haz-
> ard, agency, and adverse selection problems–toward a free market configu-
> ration? No.Market regulation needs to be smart.

He gives us a wonderfully clever explanation about multiple financial equilibria. The
good hand of the wise and superior technocrat is needede to hold the market at the good
equilibrium, and keep it away from the bad equilibrium. Eventually, however, he gets
around to mentioning that this explanation is completely irrelevant,for the various financial intermediaries were in fact stony broke.

The cause of the crisis was nothing to do with market failure. Rather, the problem
was business failure - businesses made lots of very bad loans, and accounting failure - accounts were prepared in faithful compliance to Sarbanes-Oxley, as the government commanded in excruciating detail, thereby completely obfuscating the fact that these businesses were insolvent.

Wall Street Journal explains the bailout crisis

2008-09-25 18:08:46

Wall street journal reports that this crisis was the predicted result of politically correct
lending policies[75] commanded by the Clinton administration, continued and worsened
by the Bush administration.

Carpe Diem reports that this crisis was predicted when these policies were introduced
by the Clinton Administration[76]. In 1999, the NY Times observed:

> Fannie Mae is taking on significantly more risk, which may not pose any
> difficulties during flush economic times. But the government-subsidized
> corporation may run into trouble in an economic downturn, prompting
> a government rescue similar to that of the savings and loan industry in the
> 1980s

Which is, of course, what happened.

What the bailout does to capitalism and the dollar

2008-10-03 18:10:51

As we have seen, organizations that are too big to fail, fail big. The US government is the
biggest of them all.

---

[75]https://online.wsj.com/article/SB122212948811465427.html?mod=djemEditorialPage
[76]https://mjperry.blogspot.com/2008/09/flashback-to-1999-origins-of-credit.html

For credit to work, people who need credit should not get credit. You should only be able to get credit if you can prove you do not need it. The major purpose of the bailout is to ensure that people who need credit will continue to get it.

For capitalism to work, to produce good results, rich people have to be smart. Therefore stupid and greedy rich people need to be swiftly separated from their money. As recent events demonstrate, the financial sector is dominated by stupid greedy rich people. One major purpose and intent of the bailout is to prevent them from becoming stupid greedy poor people.

But if stupid greedy rich people continue to run the financial system, and the financial system continues to make credit available to those that need credit, rather than those that are most likely to be able and willing to pay their just debts as and when those debts fall due, then we are going to have more and bigger financial crises like the one we just had.

"Too big to fail" results in everyone putting their wealth in the hands of organizations that are too big to fail - which as we have seen are generally run by morons, resulting in bigger failures. Eventually, most wealth will be in the hands of the biggest organization of them all, the US government, which is run by the most stupid morons of them all. And then that too will fail. The day will come when you will get paid in nice crisp dollar bills, but they will not be worth much. This has been the most expensive financial crisis in history. If the bailout goes through, expect the ultimate financial crisis, when the US government itself goes broke, around 2020 or so.

The cause of the crisis

2008-10-06 18:19:25

If a company is too big to fail, then people will take risks they would not otherwise take. "Too big to fail" is an implicit subsidy for taking big risks - which results in people taking big risks. So we have just paid people seven hundred billion dollars for taking stupidly big risks. What do you think is going to happen?

The cause of the crisis

2008-10-11 18:20:57

The bailout will fail.

If the government offers implicit or expicit debt guarantees, if a firm is "too big to fail, then that firm can easily borrow lots of money cheaply, and lend that money to people not so guaranteed at a higher interest rate.

Free Money!

The too big to fail firm is going to take absurd risks that no one would ever take with their own money. And if trouble ensues, then they have less to lose, in proportion as the taxpayer has more to lose, so they will bet even bigger.

To prevent this, the government regulates these "too big to fail" entities, prohibiting them from taking excessive risks.

Regulation failed in three ways:
1. Gaming the rules by financiers: The government felt that judgments of character,

competence, and credit worthiness were too subjective, so wanted risk evaluated by the numbers. But *you cannot evaluate risk by the numbers!* So the numbers were gamed, and loans to reckless people of bad character were rearranged to as to have wonderfully low risk numbers.

2. Political correctness by government: The government and various interest groups noticed that when borrowers were evaluated by credit worthiness, character, and competence in managing money, most people with good scores were white. So they pressured financiers to abandon these criteria, and regulated them to make loans that required them to abandon these criteria - and since the financiers were too big to fail, they were willing to comply.

3. Loss of contact with reality by accountants: Accountants, both by natural inclination, and because they were compelled by Sarbannes Oxley regulation, focused on the numbers, forgetting what the numbers actually stood for. When the unreality of the numbers was revealed, the entire financial sector became paralyzed. They are in the dark, and there is no source of light proposed

The bailout is an effort to keep business as usual going - but business as usual was not working, failed, failed catastrophically. We need a new finance sector, a main street finance sector where local bank branches ledn to to local people on the basis of character and solvency. Most of the wall street finance sector which the bailout is intended to keep alive needs to be shut down, to permanently go out of business, and despite massive cash injections, it simply is not in business right now. It remains paralyzed, despite gigantic handouts of cash, because they are aware that if they were to resume business as usual, they would piss away the new money in the same way they pissed away the old money.

The cause of the subprime crisis

2008-10-20 18:22:21

The subprime crisis was caused by regulation and the expectation that some companies were too big to fail - that if those companies got in trouble, the government would make sure their debtors were paid.

What did regulation tell financiers about subprime loans? It told them they had better make subprime loans, or face a lawsuit by ACORN, a lawsuit in which the regulators made it clear they would be backing ACORN.

Ted Day tells us what regulation said

The Boston Fed, speaking for the entire fed, declared in 1992 "discrimination may be observed when a lender's underwriting policies contain arbitrary or outdated criteria that effectively disqualify many urban or lower-income minority applicants."

Some of these "outdated" criteria included the size of the mortgage payment relative to income, credit history, savings history and income verification. Instead, the Boston Fed ruled that participation in a credit-counseling program should be taken as evidence of an applicant's ability to manage debt.

So yes, starting in 1992, the regulators COMPELLED financiers to make these toxic loans that sunk the world's financial system.

Indeed, this is natural and predicable, it is inevitable that regulation will always be counterproductive, will always have the opposite effect to that intended, for government regulators have no incentive to be prudent, whereas lenders do have an incentive to be prudent - unless they are lending to a firm that is too big to fail.

If a firm is too big to fail, people will lend it money, knowing the government will ensure they get paid back. So the too big to fail business borrows unreasonably large amounts of money, and lends it in unreasonably risky ventures - if things go well, the too big to fail business pocket the profit, if things go badly, someone else (usually the taxpayer), loses the cash, heads I win, tails someone else loses.

So the government has to regulate too big to fail businesses to restrain them from taking excessive risks - but such regulation is always politically unpopular, for it invariably means that people who "need" credit don't get loans, and instead loans go to people who don't need them - that loans go to people with plenty of assets and a history of using money profitably and paying their debts as and when they fall due, which people are seldom popular - goes to wealthy Jews instead of poor blacks, goes to the financially prudent instead of the politically connected, goes to the industrious and thrifty instead of ward heelers who get out the vote. So in practice, regulation aways works the other way around - encouraging or compelling too big to fail businesses to take excessive risks, rather than restraining them from taking excessive risk.

As it did this time.

The more government is involved in business, the bigger the losses are, and because government is more involved in business that it was, the losses were bigger this time.

The crisis in unregulated financial markets

2008-10-31 18:28:56

Observe that the unregulated Credit Default Swap market is now working just fine, despite handling gigantic money flows, such as the failure of the Icelandic banks, that shake other markets, despite, or perhaps because of, the fact that more highly regulated markets have frozen up.

What went wrong in a short while ago in unregulated markets was that people in an unregulated market would look at a highly regulated participant in that unregulated market, such as AIG, and say "AAA rating, implicit government guarantee, and everything they do is examined by the regulators every month, obviously we can trust them completely", and it turned out they could not.

Now that the assumption is that anything the regulators have a finger in is probably criminal, the unregulated credit default swap market is working fine.

As regulated financial markets have frozen up, the shadow banking system has taken up the slack. As regulators reach out to grasp the shadow banking system, it will no doubt swiftly become more shadowy.

How many CRA loans, how much affirmative action payout?

2008-11-05 18:33:29

From 2000 to 2007, blacks and hispanics received *six hundred and thirteen billion dollars* more in home purchase mortgages than they would have received had they received the same proportion of the money that they received in 1999 - a figure that strikingly resembles the total cost of the bailout.

In 1999, people warned that CRA loans, affirmative action loans, racial quota loans, began to endanger the financial system[77]

> Fannie Mae, the nation's biggest underwriter of home mortgages, has been under increasing pressure from the Clinton Administration to expand mortgage loans among low and moderate income people ...
>
> ...These borrowers whose incomes, credit ratings and savings are not good enough to qualify for conventional loans, ...
>
> ... "If they fail, the government will have to step up and bail them out the way it stepped up and bailed out the thrift industry."

1977 was the start of turning the finance industry into a political slush fund, and with each regulatory intervention, the amount of money at risk increased exponentially

How many CRA loans, affirmative actions loans, racial quota loans, were there?

Fortunately the data for new house loans by race is available[78], and from this data we can calculate that CRA loans, affirmative action loans, racial quota loans, for new house purchases, in the period 2000 to 2007 were at least six hundred and thirteen billion dollars, which is pretty close to the total US bailout cost.

613 billion dollars.

So this was an affirmative action financial crisis, and we are for the most part bailing out financial institutions that were forced to lend to unqualified borrowers by race, and perhaps also bailing out the culture of corruption that results from rating mortgage securities AAA that were generated in the course of signing up people to vote democrat with a bottle of cheap whiskey and a million dollar mortgage - because rating them differently would be racist, much as Princeton was corrupted because when it graduated Obama's wife, fearing that it would have been racist had it failed to pass her thesis merely because it was a barely literate rant against racism. We are required to pretend Obama's wife is educated, and we are required to pretend that these borrowers are credit worthy. It corrupts the universities, and it corrupts the financiers.

There was a massive increase in the value of loans to black and hispanic borrowers. To the extent that these loans grew much faster than loans to white people, this most likely represents affirmative action. This is a conservative estimate, since affirmative action lending has been enforced by the Community Reinvestment Act (CRA) since 1977. What was new in 1999 was not affirmative action lending, it was affirmative aciton lending on a scale that threatened the financial system.

---

[77] https://query.nytimes.com/gst/fullpage.html?res=9C0DE7DB153EF933A0575AC0A96F958260
[78] https://www.ffiec.gov/hmdaadwebreport/NatAggWelcome.aspx

In 1999, mortgages to black and hispanic new house borrowers were 10.4% of mortgages to white new house borrowers.

In 2006, mortgages to black and hispanic new house borrowers were 36.5% of mortgages to white new house borrowers.

I calculate what new home mortgages would have been had new home mortgages to black and hispanics remained 10.4% of new home mortgages to whites.

The excess, the difference between hypothetical mortgages and actual mortgages, is a conservative estimate of CRA loans, affirmative action loans, racial quota loans.

In this table, the first column is new housing loans to whites, the second column is new housing loans to blacks and hispanics. Estimated CRA loans are the difference between the actual and hypothetical loans, and at the bottom I total numbers.

The numbers for new house mortgages in billions of dollars come the government racial quota monitoring website. The number for affirmative action loans is my estimate, calculated as new house mortgages to blacks and hispanics minus 10.4% of white new house mortgages

The numbers for new house mortgages in billions of dollars come the government racial quota monitoring website[79]. The value for affirmative action loans is my estimate, calculated as new house mortgages to
blacks and hispanics minus 10.4% of white new house mortgages

Home Purchase Mortgages in Billions of dollars

Year	Black and Hispanic	White	estimated CRA
1999	37.60	359.90	0.00
2000	43.72	364.54	5.63
2001	51.18	381.41	11.33
2002	89.44	469.03	40.44
2003	128.40	537.96	72.20
2004	135.26	547.41	78.07
2005	236.06	757.33	156.94
2006	247.55	678.20	176.70
2007	192.53	547.41	72.34
Total	1098.75	4643.20	613.65

Unfortunately, no racial breakdown on default rate is available, but the Hispanics I saw buying houses in Sunnyvale in 2005 and 2006, looking at them from twenty paces, you could tell in two heartbeats that the chances of them making payments was very poor indeed.

Implicit government guarantees produce a vast river of easy credit to the too-big-to-fail beneficiary of that guarantee, and inevitably politicians are tempted to direct that river to political voting blocks - sometimes political voting blocks that are unlikely to repay the money.

---

[79] https://www.ffiec.gov/hmdaadwebreport/NatAggWelcome.aspx

It is a fundamental moral hazard problem in government regulation and intervention, which cannot be regulated away. Instead of regulating, the beneficiaries of these guarantees must be shrunk - regulated to become small enough to fail, instead of regulated to benevolently hand out money to the politically favored. Instead of sending that mighty river of money in the direction of desirable voting blocks, politicians must shrink it - which, like dieting, is hard for them to do.

The financial crisis in America was one of affirmative action and the community reinvestment act, of Black and Hispanic deadbeats robbing honest hardworking whites, but thinking of it in those terms of the particular voting blocks is not useful, will not get us to a financial system that moves savings from honest thrifty savers to honest hard working investors who can put the money to profitable use. Such thinking, thinking in terms of voting blocks, will at best merely change the skin color of the deadbeats robbing the honest folk. The financial crisis in the rest of the world had different beneficiaries with diverse skin colors, but the common factor was political favor sending funds to political voting blocks, rather than to people able to put the money to profitable use. It is more useful to think in terms of moral hazard - that politicians cannot regulate, for they have perverse and dangerous incentives, and therefore corrupt financiers.

That politicians dispatched our money to cat eating wetbacks should enrage us, but we should be enraged at the politicians, rather than at migrants looking for work who have difficulty affording meat from a butcher, migrants who are prohibited from honest work by those politicians, and then offered welfare and a million dollar mortgage no money down by the same politicians. The politicians corrupted Hispanics and financiers alike.

The lesson of the 2008 American Presidential election
2008-11-07 18:37:59

You win elections from the base, not the center. Obama appealed to the Democrat base, the Democrat wing of the Democrat party, and the lunatic wing of the Democrat of the Democrat party, Just as Reagan appealed to the Republican party base. McCain tried to appeal to the wobbly Democrat wing of the Democrat pary - mainly by spitting on the Republican party base. McCain followed in the path of Bush by trying to outbid Obama by promising to give away more goodies, but when Obama promised to give away goodies he could credibly sound as if he believed that handing out goodies enriched and ennobled the recipients, whereas McCain sounded like he was handing out goodies after the fashion of a community organizer giving drunks a bottle of whisky to register to vote - if you got your goodies from Obama, it made you noble and superior and proved you deserved them, if you got you goodies from McCain, it made you mooching scum. Why would anyone vote for McCain?

China's boom
2008-11-12 18:39:58

China in the 20th century had two major revolutions, a civil war, a World War, The Great Leap Forward sic, mass starvation, the Cultural Revolution, arguably [the most tyrannical dictator ever][80] and he didn't even brush his teeth[81], and now they are going from rags to riches without even a business cycle burp. While the world plunges into major recession, China is suffering a barely noticeable hiccup, and has become the locomotive that is pulling the rest of the world out recession.

How so?

I say it is Cypherpunk economics. The Chinese economy, the non state part of the economy, is run by overseas Chinese through vpns from servers located in tax havens. And so long as China does not kill the golden goose by blocking those vpns at the great firewall of China, I predict that its economy will go from strength to strength.

Why iceland went bust - and why the US went bust

2008-11-17 18:41:45

The usual answer, of course, is the evils of capitalism:

> this country's banks - virtually unregulated - to borrow more than 10 times their country's gross domestic product from the international wholesale money markets. Watch as a Graf Zeppelin of debt propels its self-styled "Viking Raiders" across the world's financial stage, accumulating companies like gamblers hoarding chips.

In fact, of course, the government regulators made lots of easy money available to ordinary Icelanders. 100% down no deposit, with easy payments - payments that failed to cover the interest, so that the debt grows every year. This was worse than the the loans that the US regulators made available to Hispanics - the Hispanics got no money down loans, but their payments had to cover the interest, plus the Icelandic loans were for everyone, while the US easy money loans were mostly to favored voting blocks. Most US loans were not negative amortization, while all Icelandic loans were "indexed" - the equivalent of negative amortization.

The Financial Times reports[82]

> Easy access to 100% mortgages ...

> Iceland is the only country in the world that indexes its loans in addition to charging interest. This means that when Icelanders borrow IKr1,000 from the bank and inflation increases by 5 per cent, the bank increases their debt to IKr1,050 at the end of the year. A great deal for the bank and fine for you, too - so long as the property's value and your salary are increasing by inflation and more.

The collapse of Iceland illustrates the "Micawber Principle"

---

[80]https://www.smb.spk-berlin.de/hbf/vg/img/hbfb3g.jpg
[81]https://www.looksmartjrhigh.com/p/articles/mi_m0EPF/is_n3_v95/ai_17486948
[82]https://www.ft.com/cms/s/0/c181dd7a-b2b4-11dd-bbc9-0000779fd18c.html

Annual income twenty pounds, annual expenditure nineteen nineteen six, result happiness. Annual income twenty pounds, annual expenditure twenty pounds ought and six, result misery.

Around the world, politicians promised voters they could live above their means, and created the pretense that it could be done. And now the bill is due. The bust is worse in Iceland, because the lie was bigger.

Global Average temperatures to 2008-October

2008-11-21 18:43:15

This is the running twelve month average world temperature, as measured by satellites, as reported by The National Space Science and Technology Center[83].

World temperature change in centigrade degrees.

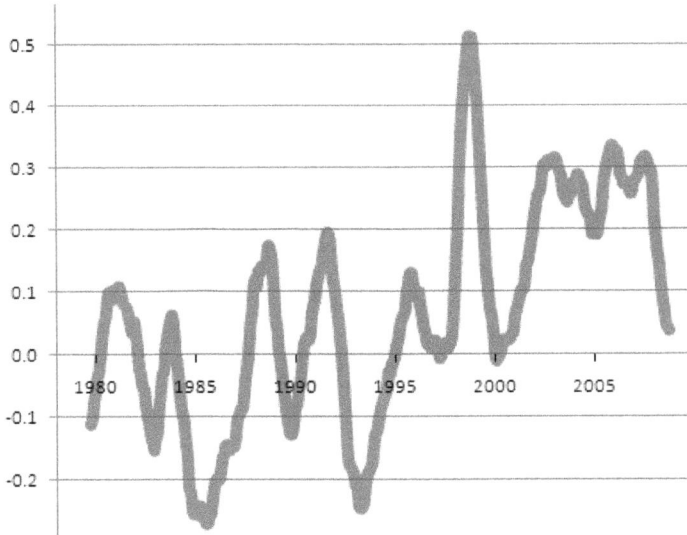

It goes up, it goes down. If there is any trend, the trend is less than the decade to decade fluctuations, and is not at all apocalyptic. This differs from other graphs you may have seen because it starts at the start of the satellite data and ends at the present, instead of starting in with a reconstruction of what might have been a cool year if we had accurate global data way back then, which we don't, and ending in 2005, the most recent warm year.

Similarly for the amount of ocean ice[84]

Again, it goes up, it goes down. If there is any trend, the trend is less than the decade to decade fluctuations, and is not at all apocalyptic. Again this differs from similar graphs you may have seen, which usually start in 1988 (a year with exceptionally large ice area)

[83]https://vortex.nsstc.uah.edu/public/msu/t2lt/tltglhmam_5.2
[84]https://arctic.atmos.uiuc.edu/cryosphere/IMAGES/global.daily.ice.area.withtrend.jpg

and end in 2007 (a year with exceptionally small ice area), and show only the Northern Hemisphere, where we recently had some exceptionally warm years, leaving out the Southern Hemisphere, where we recently had some exceptionally cold years.

As you can see, nothing much is happening - looks like the world is warming, but not enough to be noticeable - nor enough to be sure that it actually is warming.

Thus irrespective of the validity of anthropogenic global warming, the belief that apocalypse is upon us, that something urgent must be done, is religious, based on the feeling that we have sinned against Gaea and her wrath will come upon us, not based on any scientific evidence.

Why do all large organizations skew left authoritarian?

2008-11-24 18:45:25

Constant drew my attention to the fact that Fox news, originally created to provide an alternative to the Mainstream Media orthodox ideology, is joining it[85], which led me to reflect on the tendency of big corporations to go left authoritarian and support socialism, gun control, political censorship, government health, and so on and so forth - as for example, the failure of the owners of shipping lines to allow deadly arms on their ships to meet the problem of piracy.

The Smallest Minority drew my attention to this[86]:

There are some lies that lie so deep in the hopes of man that they can never be killed, no matter how many are executed to make the lie true.

Martin Malia, in "The Soviet Tragedy", page 50, summarizes the core ideals of left versus right:

[85]https://distributedrepublic.net/archives/2008/11/21/consequentialist-fox-sacrifices-truth-greater-good
[86]https://smallestminority.blogspot.com/2008/11/except-that-future-might-be-dystopian.html

And so, by 1914, a dual process of amalgamation had occurred: on the Right were aligned capitalism, unbridled individualism, nationalism, militarism, and social hierarchy; and on the left were arrayed socialism, economic rationality, internationalism, peace, and equality. The stage was thus set for the great *Auseinandersetzung*, the world historical clash, between capitalism and socialism that would dominate our short twentieth century.

Now reflect that all large organizations are, by definition, internally socialist. Capitalism is what you get when independent actors pursue their individual interest - instead of someone's vision of the greater good being imposed on all. But in a large organization, everyone is supposed to pursue the greater good of the organization, team players and all that. Team players are automatically inclined toward the left side, the left as defined by Martin Malia, the left that leads to terror, slavery, and mass murder. Organization man is basically a leftie.

And that brings me back to the interesting fact that merchant ships are not defending themselves on the high seas against pirates. The kind of people who run shipping companies simply do not feel in their guts that it is right for ordinary seamen to kill pirates.

My intuition would be that someone who owned just one ship would have no hesitation in stacking it with whatever weapons it takes to keep the ship safe, but that someone who owns a shipping line would be horrified by the idea

.

The crisis

2008-12-03 18:48:51

Fred Thompson argues the solution is thrift - which exactly what the government is trying to prevent.

Obviously he is right - and yet wrong, for one person's savings have to be another person's obligations.

What we need is a financial system that mobilizes savings for sound investments - such as mortgages on reasonably priced houses secured by twenty percent down payments, mortgages on farmlands, mortgages on mines and oilfield with secure property rights, mortgages on commerical facilities such as gravel pits that generate secure and reliable income, mortgages on semi government enterprises such as toll roads, harbors, and airports that generate secure and reliable income, mortgages that are subject to proper scrutiny to ensure that the underlying enterprise supports the mortgage payments and valuation.

Without such a financial system, everyone attempting to save will merely throw more and more people out of jobs, and if on the other hand the government enables everyone to spend irresponsibly, it will set us up for bigger catastrophe down the road

.

The cause of the crisis

2008-12-10 18:54:54

Capitalism and free markets are prone to bubbles, and a great deal more prone to bubbles when speculators can expect that the government will print as much money as needed to keep the bubble going, but bubbles do not in themselves lead to massive financial defaults, because normally lenders only lend to people who are in a position to repay, even if the bubble pops.

If one reads what purport to be analyzes of the crisis, they usually use windy evasive language such as "financial conditions deteriorated" – which tells us nothing about what was happening except that it is something that cannot be spoken, for fear of getting in trouble.

"Financial conditions deteriorated" in that people were not making payments on their loans, but if one was to say such a thing, this would immediately imply the question: Which people are not making payments on their loans? And that is a question that no one dares ask, for fear of the answer.

The answer, of course, as everyone knows, but no one dares say, is that members of protected minorities, the beneficiaries of government mandated affirmative action lending, are not making payments on their loans.

Foreclosures in Palo Alto west of the freeway (white and some chinese, chinese being an unprotected minority):
One foreclosure at the time I post.[87]

Foreclosures in Palo Alto east of the freeway (black and hispanic, all protected minority):
ninety eight foreclosures at the time I post.[88]

Foreclosures in Gilroy (wholly hispanic, all protected minority)
two hundred and sixty three foreclosures at the time I post.[89]

If no money down loans had been available to *white* people with no income, no job or assets, there would have been a lot more defaults in Palo Alto west of the freeway.

The distribution of foreclosures by suburb implies that ninety nine percent of the defaulters are blacks and Hispanics, the beneficiaries of affirmative action lending.

All house purchase loans are governed by affirmative action, for since 1999 CRA requires that race must be reported on all house purchase loans, and regulators are required to take the racial distribution all loans into account when making all regulatory decisions - which implies that if a banker does not make enough loans to members of protected minorities he will be punished, but to preserve deniability, nominally punished for something completely unrelated to race.

The financial crisis is wholly caused by affirmative action lending enforced by HUD and CRA.

Therefore, if the same standards had been applied to people in Palo Alto West of the freeway, as in Palo Alto east of the freeway, if CRA and HUD had not imposed racist

---

[87]https://www.sfgate.com/webdb/foreclosures/?appSession=89553824393898
[88]https://www.sfgate.com/webdb/foreclosures/?appSession=57553824890172
[89]https://www.sfgate.com/webdb/foreclosures/?appSession=83853826865811

lending policies in favor of protected minorities, there would be no financial crisis, therefore no need for financial bailouts.

The defaulters are not normal middle class people like you and me. Most of the people that I saw buying houses in Sunnyvale in 2006 were no hablos English, and I could tell in two heartbeats at twenty paces that there was no way in hell they were going to make the payments - I conjectured that they were functioning as straw men for a purchaser more literate than themselves, and perhaps of a race less eligible for a loan with no money down, no credit record, and no evidence of income or assets. In Malaysia they call these "Ali Baba loans" when a member of the favored religion (Islam) fronts for a member of a disfavored religion.

No warming trend in raw surface temperature data

2008-12-15 18:56:36

You have all seen those GISS graphs of global warming. Anthony Watt checked the raw data on which they are based[90].

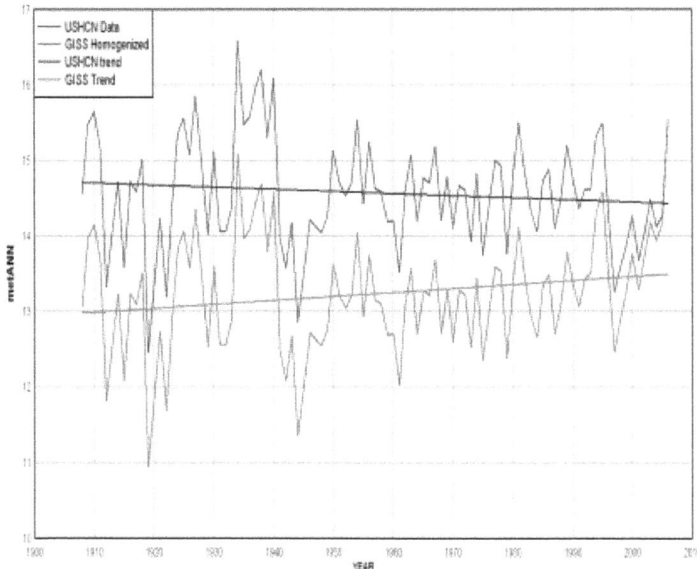

The cooked data shows warming, the raw data shows cooling. Of course this does not mean the data is necessarily fraudulent - but the adjustments are largely guesswork, so when they compile these graphs, they are merely guessing that the earth has warmed.

---

[90]https://wattsupwiththat.com/2008/12/08/how-not-to-measure-temperature-part-79-would-you-could-you-with-a-boat

affirmative action, bad loans, bailout, crisis

2008-12-28 18:59:37

The New York Times explains[91]:

> creditors came to believe that their loans to unsound financial institutions would be made good by the Fed — as long as the collapse of those institutions would threaten the global credit system. Bolstered by this sense of security, bad loans mushroomed.

Of course any crisis is multicausal. I have been blaming affirmative action loans. But instead of pushing back against government pressure to make bad loans to protected minorities, lenders eagerly embraced bad loans - because of an entirely correct expectation that they would be bailed out.

All quiet in France

2009-01-08 19:02:27

Small Dead Animals draws my attention to the fact that things are *not* all quiet in France
On New Years day, more than 1000 cars were torched[92] - but the French seem unable to mention the fact that Muslims were burning the cars of infidels. Islamic jihadism has tripled over the last year, but French government imposition of order has remained unchanged - which trend, if continued for much longer, will end with Islamic rule and sharia rule imposed on French infidels.

British police retreat before Muslims

2009-01-17 19:05:46

British police retreat before a hail of not very dangerous missiles:
This retreat follows a long series of recent similar humiliations - the British submission in Basra, in Helmand province, and in the Persian Gulf. Weakness and fear is provocative. Someone is going to take Britain from the British.

The Origin of Species

2009-01-24 19:07:00

"blogging the origin[93]" criticizes Darwin for emphasizing selection, rather than separation, as the primary cause of speciation. But we now know that Darwin was, as usual, right, and the latest fashions were, as usual, wrong again.

Until recently the evidence for *any* speciation was thin, and in the absence of evidence, people liked to imagine speciation by physical separation, in large part due the

[91] https://www.nytimes.com/2008/12/28/business/economy/28view.html
[92] https://www.nasdaq.com/aspxcontent/NewsStory.aspx?cpath=20090101/ACQD-JON200901011323DOWJONESDJONLINE000365.htm
[93] https://scienceblogs.com/bloggingtheorigin/2009/01/chapter_4_natural_selection.php

rhetoric of Gould, who argued that absence of evidence was evidence for presence of the events he wished were happening.

The research on three spined sticklebacks, shows that for three spined sticklebacks, sympatric speciation is extremely common, and allopatric speciation is insignificant in the sense that: if two physically separated groups of three spined sticklebacks adapt to similar environments, they become similar, and can and will interbreed if given the opportunity, but if they adapt to different environments, then, whether separated or not, they become different, and disinclined to interbreed if given the opportunity.

Science. 2000 Jan 14;287(5451):306-8

> "Populations of sticklebacks that evolved under different ecological conditions show strong reproductive isolation, whereas populations that evolved independently under similar ecological conditions lack isolation."

Which implies that: separation and drift does not matter in speciation, does not cause speciation; Differential adaption matters, does cause speciation, as Darwin argued.

Our most complete record on speciation events is that for foraminifera, because we have a humungous number of fossils neatly stacked in layers at the sea bottom. For foraminifera, all observed speciation events that have been observed in sufficient detail are sympatric.[94]

Gould wanted to discredit sympatric speciation, and argued for the primacy of allopatric speciation, because if adaption, rather than separation, is primary, then this has disturbing implications for our own species. From the supposed primacy of separation over adaption, Gould argued in his essay "human equality is a contingent fact of history" that the races of man must be equal in mean and distribution of abilities, thus the primacy of adaptive speciation over allopatric speciation that we do in fact observe today is as disturbingly politically incorrect as Darwin's comments on the races of man.

If it is possible for sticklebacks that share a single lake to divide into two species, despite substantial interbreeding, then it is probable that humans whose ancestors lived for the last fifty thousand years or so in an environment where lack of future orientation would result in freezing in bad weather and starving in winter, have considerably greater future orientation than humans whos ancestors lived in an environment where failure to prepare for the future was considerably less likely to be lethal.

Plain speaking on warmist "science"

2009-01-29 19:08:29

Hansen's former supervisor tells us plainly[95] what Climate Audit[96] has been telling us politely

> The models do not realistically simulate the climate system because there are many very important sub-grid scale processes that the models either replicate

---

[94]https://www.don-lindsay-archive.org/creation/foram_article3.html
[95]https://wattsupwiththat.com/2009/01/27/james-hansens-former-nasa-supervisor-declares-himself-a-skeptic-says-hansen-embarrassed-nasa-was-never-muzzled
[96]https://www.climateaudit.org/

poorly or completely omit. Furthermore, some scientists have manipulated the observed data to justify their model results. In doing so, they neither explain what they have modified in the observations, nor explain how they did it. They have resisted making their work transparent so that it can be replicated independently by other scientists. This is clearly contrary to how science should be done. Thus there is no rational justification for using climate model forecasts to determine public policy.

Israel did not win

2009-02-02 19:10:08

After the recent war in the Gaza strip, Hamas declared victory, and Israel declared victory.

What do they teach small boys in school today? When I was in school, the first thing I learned is that the fight is not over till the winner can make loser cry "uncle".

Hamas has not been destroyed, nor coerced. They continue to rocket Israel. Since they are religious fanatics, nothing short of Roman methods can force them to cry "uncle". People who rocket one, have to be killed or driven out of rocket range.

Their recent war was not war, but theater. In war you keep going till one side loses and one side wins.

The cause of the crisis

2009-02-02 19:12:09

In numerous posts, I have argued that CRA affirmative action caused the economic crisis that is happening now. Vdare provides a far better post than any of mine[97], giving us case histories and numerous horror stories of bank?s proudly pissing away stupendous amounts of money, and boasting of their wonderful CRA compliance in so doing.

The bank?s boasts of trillions of dollars gives the lie to the much repeated claim that CRA was tiny, supposedly much too small to cause a world economic crisis.

Smoot Hawley again

2009-02-03 19:11:06

One of the several government actions that so greatly prolonged the great depression was Smoot Hawley. The Becker Posner blog[98] reports that the democrats want do do FDR all over again - meaning do the great depression all over again.

---

[97] https://vdare.com/sailer/090201_meltdown.htm
[98] https://www.becker-posner-blog.com/archives/2009/02/buy_american_on.html

The lesson of Japan's failure

2009-02-12 19:14:34

Ten years ago, Japan had a banking crisis very like the one we just had. It was discovered that financiers and big businessmen had blown staggering sums of money, whereupon the government massively intervened to keep those that had screwed up from losing their jobs.

The Japanese economy has been stagnant ever since, even though, or perhaps because, the government has poured huge amounts of "stimulus" over the economy, so much "stimulus" that the Japanese government is now approaching bankruptcy.

President Barack Obama correctly observed[99]:

> There are two countries who have gone through some big financial crises over the last decade or two. One was Japan, which never really acknowledged the scale and magnitude of the problems in their banking system and that resulted in what's called "The Lost Decade". They kept on trying to paper over the problems. The markets sort of stayed up because the Japanese government kept on pumping money in. But, eventually, nothing happened and they didn't see any growth whatsoever.

Obama then proceeds to explain why we are going to do what failed for Japan:

> we want to retain a strong sense of that private capital fulfilling the core — core investment needs of this country.

No we don't. We want to retain a strong sense that businessmen who succeed, win, and businessmen that foul up, lose their shirts. It is not capitalism when the capitalists are kept in power by the state.

To work, capitalism has to be run by people who are smart. The entrepreneur unites other people's money and other people's labor, to create value. The Wall Streeters revealed themselves to be idiots who massively subtracted value.

Similarly General motors, who managed to destroy the amazing sum of about four hundred billion dollars of value over the last decade.

The big factor in downturns is that people attempt to continue saving, while holding back from investing, whereupon the economy bogs down, thus the big factor is distrust of financial intermediaries. In this sense, recessions are largely supply side problems rather than demand side problems. In the last three years, vast numbers of financial intermediaries have been revealed as untrustworthy and incompetent.

In Japan, in a similar crisis thirteen years ago the insiders were revealed to be incompetent and corrupt. In a similar response, the Japanese government intervened to protect insiders from the consequences of exposure, keeping them in charge of other people's wealth.

This in Japan as here led to massive decline in investment and demand, to which the Japanese government responded with "stimulus" - building bridges to nowhere, paving rivers, and so on and so forth.

---

[99] https://abcnews.go.com/Politics/Business/Story?id=6844330

This led to a massive increase in Japanese government debt, now the highest in the world, but failed to cure the recession. The government could manufacture demand, but not supply.

Japanese government debt is the highest in the world not because no other government was prepared to borrow so much, but because all other governments that attempted to borrow as much, have gone bust.

Bridges to nowhere will not fix the supply side problem, and tax cuts can have only limited effectiveness. Rather, a new crop of productive entrepreneurs must arise, the creation side of capitalism's creative destruction. But in a world of bailouts, the way to success is connections, political correctness, and getting on with the rest of the elite, which gives us the sort of capitalist establishment that got us into this mess.

The banks that were run by bankers of the Ebenezer Scrooge type, who accepted CRA with the same enthusiasm as they turned up at their dentist for a root canal, tended to be taken over by banks of the Washington Mutual type, who were rewarded for their political correctness in embracing CRA with genuine enthusiasm, by regulatory favor in their takeovers. And that crowd, the Washington Mutual sort, is the crowd that is still in charge, government guaranteed to be in charge. We need a finance sector run by the likes of Ebenezer Scrooge, and an automobile industry run by the likes of Hank Rearden. To get that, badly run businesses have to go bankrupt, and their assets need to be auctioned off at the block.

Headless body in Gutless press

2009-02-19 19:18:10

Mark Steyn ridicules the mainstream press's fear of Islam[100]:

> the killing of Aasiya Hassan seems to have elicited a very muted response.
>
> When poor Mrs.Hassan's husband launched his TV network to counter negative stereotypes of Muslims, he had no difficulty generating column inches, as far afield as *The Columbus Dispatch*, *The Detroit Free Press*, *The San Jose Mercury News*,*Variety*, NBC News, the Voice of America, and the Canadian Press.*The Rochester Democrat & Chronicle* putthe coupleon the front page under the headline "Infant TV Network Unveils The Face Of Muslim News".
>
> But, when Muzzammil Hassan kills his wife and "the face of Muslim news" is unveiled rather more literally, detached from her corpseat his TV studios, it's all he can do to make the local press — page 26 of *Newsday*

Chinese becoming wealthy, Americans ceasing to be

2009-02-22 19:19:24

Captain Capitalism explains why Chinese are becoming wealthy, and Americans ceasing to be[101].

The run begins on Europe

2009-02-23 19:22:23

Moody' issued a warning on European banks[102], which implies that the smart money is moving out of the worst affected banks: Eastern European banks, and Western European banks with a lot of exposure to Eastern Europe.This, in turn, is putting pressure on European government bonds, as speculators doubt that European governments will be able to bail out their banks, or will go broke attempting to do so - the most fragile European regimes are facing increasing reluctance to buy their bonds, resulting in higher interest rates. A couple of days ago, the leaders of Europe met to solve the crisis, and issued a communique full of good intentions[103]. I interpret this communique as saying that they intend to keep on doing all the disastrous bad things that led to this crisis, only even more so:

> Leaders from eight European countries called for regulating financial markets and hedge funds, investment funds that typically lead to aggressive financial strategies.
>
> German Chancellor Angela Merkel, who hosted the summit, said all financial markets, products and participants that pose a major risk must be regulated.
>
> Ms.Merkel also called for world economies to coordinate in establishing sanctions for tax shelters and regions where financial deals are opaque.

And calling for someone else to clean up the resulting mess:

> "We decided that the international institutions should have at least $500 billion to enable them not just to deal with crises, but to enable them to be able to prevent crises," said Gordon Brown. "We have also decided we want to see a greater role for the World Bank in helping the poorest countries of the world."

Bond markets are still giving rather low probability for the chance of a governmental financial collapse. I find these low rates surprising. At present you can buy insurance that a European government will pay its bills over the next five years at about one fortieth the face value of the bill, which seems mighty cheap - unless of course one suspects that if governments are not paying, neither will the insurer, in which case it is mighty expensive.

---

[101]https://captaincapitalism.blogspot.com/2008/09/chinese-dont-major-in-sociology.html
[102]https://uk.reuters.com/article/hotStocksNewsUS/idUKTRE51G1EO20090217
[103]https://www.voanews.com/english/2009-02-22-voa22.cfm

The degeneration of Britain

2009-02-25 19:25:22

Three facts that have recently been in the news:
1. The reversal of the Flynn effect[104]. The British youth of today really are dumber.
2. Violence, drunkenness, laddie, and home invasion burglaries, where drunken lads smash into someone's house and terrify the inhabitants. The British crime rate is about double the US crime rate, and threatens everyone, whereas the US crime rate is very low outside areas with large numbers of protected minorities.
3. Cowardice and surrender by the British army - for example humiliating capitulations in Basra, Helmund province, and the Persian gulf.

I conjecture a common cause for all three: About a quarter of British children lack a natural father, about half lack a natural father at some stage[105], a problem caused by welfare and easy out divorce laws with that favor women leaving their husbands. Also, there are few male authority figures in primary and secondary education[106], a problem worsened by dumbing down and feminizing traditionally male subjects such as maths and science in an effort to close the achievement gap between boys and girls.

Bastard children tend to be stupid and violent: Mothers nurture, fathers discipline. Not "Fathers traditionally discipline, Mothers traditionally discipline", but rather natural fathers, (not step fathers) are innately inclined to discipline, mothers innately inclined to nuture.

Bastard male children tend to be unmanly.

The reason that lack of father causes criminality and cowardice is obvious: Why should it cause stupidity? I conjecture that the close presence of a powerful authority who is smarter and wiser than you pressures you to keep up mentally, exercising your mind, just as the close presence of an athletic peer would pressure you to be more athletic. Also the efforts to reduce the boy girl gap in maths achievement are likely to have a direct detrimental effect on IQ test scores for both males and females

.

Warren Buffet explains how to lose a trillion

2009-03-02 19:28:16

Warren Buffet explained how to lose a few trillion[107], here and there.

Well managed companies, like Warren Buffet's, don't get government guarantees. Badly managed companies with good political connections get government guarantees. So naturally all the capital floods to companies with a track record of losing it.This is capitalism in reverse. For capitalism to work, the people who are good at managing stuff have

---

[104]https://www.telegraph.co.uk/education/educationnews/4548943/British-teenagers-have-lower-IQs-than-their-counterparts-did-30-years-ago.html

[105]https://www.springerlink.com/content/v7155g0164572098/

[106]https://www.publications.parliament.uk/pa/cm200506/cmhansrd/vo050705/halltext/50705h02.htm#50705h02_spnew9

[107]https://www.berkshirehathaway.com/2000ar/2000letter.html

to wind up in charge of stuff, and the people who are bad at managing stuff have to wind up out in the street.

In the nature of things, every bailout tends to be very quickly followed by an even bigger bailout - AIG has been bailed out more times than I am able to keep track of, each bailout bigger than the last - the next AIG bailout looks to be a hundred billion or so. General motors, having recently got a ten billion dollar bailout, tells us it can only last a few months unless it gets a twenty five billion dollar bailout.

People are calling this socialism, but perhaps a more informative description is reverse capitalism.

Reverse capitalism can make us all poor even faster than socialism. The budgeted deficit is 1750 trillion dollars, sufficient to do seventeen Iraq wars simultaneously, but this purported deficit is based on the rosy scenario that all the people who have been bailed out henceforth are productive and efficient and make lots of money, when reality is that each bailout digs the hole deeper. The bailouts inject more money into circulation, but they also reduce the production of goods.

Money is a medium of exchange, a measure of value, and a store of value. The problem is that when functioning as a store of value, it is in large part a claim against values that have not yet been produced. For it to work in this way, it must either represent things of value stuffed in warehouses, or treasure buried in the ground, such as gold, or represent investments in things that produce value - such as houses occupied by creditworthy people with adequate income to pay the mortgage, or profitable businesses. If, however, savings merely represent claims against taxpayers, taxpayers that have "invested" in all sorts of massive money losing boondoggles, big trouble will ensue, for we are close to the Laffer maximum. When people attempt to draw down their savings, perhaps frightened by disturbing levels of inflation, their stored value will not be there.

There is a lot of ruin in a nation. The US government can smash the capitalist economy and draw on debt for a while. At present it is doing so at near two trillion a year, which may well rise quite a lot. If, however, it runs up debt at two trillion a year or so, then in eight years or so, the debt to GDP ratio will increase by a hundred percent or so, which is a lot of ruin.

If things continue as they are going, expect the US to collapse around 2017 or so.

Obama promises to fix the deficit by taxing the rich (though past experience is that the more you tax the rich, the less money you get - taxes on the rich are already beyond the Laffer maximum) and by a carbon tax. A carbon tax could raise a lot of money - mostly from the working class, the one part of the population that is at present taxed well below the Laffer maximum. That will work - provided that the bailouts stop sucking up ever bigger quantities of money.

The Stimulus bill

2009-03-03 19:29:33

Bryan Caplan wonders why Brad Delong cannot comprehend[108] those who doubt the effectiveness of **the stimulus bill**.

---

[108]https://econlog.econlib.org/archives/2009/03/fiscal_futility.html

Assume that creating value is easy, any brainless fool can do it, even the brainless fools at Washington Mutual. It is then immediately obvious that the government can make everything lovely by printing money and giving it to the morally worthy. Are car production lines shut down while unemployed workers idle? Just print money and give it to bureaucrats in government schools, or other similarly wise and worthy people, and lo and behold, those car production lines will start up again, and all will be well.

If, on the other hand, producing value is hard, then falling nominal GDP may well reflect the discovery that we were producing less value than we thought - that we were providing houses to people who were not in fact willing to pay for them, and building cars that were not in fact the cars that people wanted, in which case issuing enough money to stimulate the economy may well stimulate inflation, rather than the production of real wealth.

This brings us to Japan: Did Japan lose a decade because it refused to allow the free market to remove the power over assets held by incompetent people, or because it failed to borrow enough and spend enough?

Those who believe Japan failed to run a big enough deficit may well now get the chance to put their theory to the test in the US. If spending enough borrowed money to keep the incompetent running businesses stimulates the economy, then they will have proven themselves right.

Obama plans massive permanent reduction in US standard of living

2009-03-05 19:30:39

Under current USA nuclear regulations, you cannot launch any new nuclear projects unless the waste is going to go to a federally approved repository, and Obama has announced there is not going to be a federally approved repository[109]. Hence no new nuclear projects. Obama has also announced that carbon emissions are going to be reduced sometime soon, though not yet. If less carbon, then less coal and oil. If no new nukes, and less coal and oil, then less energy usage. Less energy usage, lower standard of living.

The crisis has barely begun

2009-03-08 19:31:40

"Naked capitalism" explains what has happened, and observes that the Bush-Obama policies caused it[110], are causing it, and are likely to cause a lot more of it.

Government guarantees will be abused - and the broader the guarantees, and more chaotic the situation the more they will be abused. The solution is that existing guarantees must be reduced, and existing government initiatives curtailed or at least allowed to expire. Extensive state intervention is extremely difficult to do right, easy to do badly, and the arrogant interventionists lack the necessary humility to do it right.

---

[109]https://www.washingtonpost.com/wp-dyn/content/article/2009/03/03/AR2009030303638.html
[110]https://www.nakedcapitalism.com/2009/03/bank-rescue-programs-setting-stage-for.html

Racefail 09

2009-03-11 19:34:48

Hear the sound of the left ceasing to be the smart party, and becoming the stupid party:

On the Livejournal science fiction blogs, there is, or recently was, a passionate debate called Racefail 09[111], wherein lots of bloggers accuse other bloggers of being racists.

Those accused of racism are those that are very left wing and very politically correct - they are those least likely to be guilty, most likely to be devastated by the accusation, and least able to defend themselves against the accusations because any defense would itself be politically incorrect. No one is accusing the likes of John Ringo. Instead the accused are people who are constitutionally incapable of calling a spade a spade. The accused are people who are normally clever with words and therefore can normally lacerate, devastate, and dismiss critics with ease - but are paralyzed by politically correctness from defending themselves against this accusation.

Therefore, the accusations are not motivated by concerns about race, rather, "racism" is merely the standard accusation that left wingers make these days, especially against each other.

None of those making these charges are the brightest bulb in the batch. They are all from the shallow end of the gene pool, the wrong edge of the bell curve.

So this looks to me not like anti racists going after racists, or even people of color going after whites, but more like the stupid people going after the smart people. "Racist" is these days merely an epithet that stupid people use a lot, much like "fascist" used to be.

And when that epithet is hurled, all the good leftwingers must dutifully join in, explaining that they were never friends of so and so, just as in 1928, there was a sudden dearth of Trotskyists, and in 1956, an equally sudden dearth of Stalinists.

A long predicted consequence of political correctness is finally coming to pass. Forbid thought, and soon your movement will be governed by those unable to think.

The Khmer Rouge, a party of very smart people, proceeded to execute all the smart people. America's left cannot execute all the smart people - yet. But it can cast them out of its ranks.

Why Racefail 09 hates John Scalzi

2009-03-15 04:02:04

John Scalzi said he wanted to have absolutely nothing to do with the **racefail** 09 debate, and would ban anyone who brings the debate to his blog.

This non statement, and non communication, caused intense outrage, resulting in massive attack on John Scalzi, since all good leftists have to enthusiastically agree with the correct line, and failure to join the chant about the badness of various people under attack is itself a great and terrible sin.

One of the posters on his blog explains why Scalzi is now under attack[112]:

---

[111] https://www.google.com/search?q=%22racefail+09%22
[112] https://whatever.scalzi.com/2009/03/10/the-internets-hate-scalzi/

the reason you [John Scalzi] drew ire is your inability to follow proper protocol:

1. Acknowledge that you're wrong, and guilty on all counts of whatever the other party accuses you, and

2. agree with the accuser on just how very, very wrong you are/were, while knowing that any level of self-debasement isn't going to be enough to placate them.

Clearly, the only thing that would begin to set things right would be your ritual suicide, hurling yourself into a bonfire fueled by everything you've ever written on- or offline. Don't forget to put it on YouTube, accompanied by a ten-page manifesto on the magnitude of your wrongness, and the corresponding rightness of the accuser.

In response, Scalzi apologized profusely, and proceeded piously to post a lot of politically correct piety about race in literature, indirectly demonizing all his friends, allies, and supporters, without, however, directly addressing the debate concerning the sinfulness of various actual writers and bloggers.

Come on. That is not good enough. In your repentance, you need to directly condemn as many people as possible.

The problems with Laissez Faire sexuality

2009-03-17 04:03:30

In traditional society, women were strongly encouraged to refrain from sex before marriage, and marry responsible men with good jobs who were able and willing to support a family.

Today, women are encouraged to follow their hormones, which tends to result in them have offspring with a long succession of sexy males who disappear, often into jail or dying violently, and who often rough them up and steal their money before leaving.

Bryan Caplan correctly argues[113] that the non traditional family does not necessarily harm children, because the low conventional success rate of children from such families may well reflect them behaving like their fathers, who have a different standard of what constitutes success, and may well be very successful by that standard - more chicks banged, less time wasted from nine to five, and more enemies maimed. Further, women who choose to have a non traditional family presumably prefer it - there can be little doubt that the sex is hotter the badder the boy.

Now this is a good deal for alpha males, and lots of women argue it is a good deal for women, but it has a sizable externality, in that it encourages male behavior that causes problems for other men, and produces children that cause problems for other people. Bastards are bastards. The production of bastards creates large external costs. Encouraging fidelity, chastity, and female preference for responsible mates, even though their hormones tend to cry out for demon lovers, reduces other people's costs - in traditional

---

[113]https://econlog.econlib.org/archives/2009/03/love_and_econom.html

society the costs to fathers, uncles, and brothers of grown women, in modern society the cost of the welfare state, in all societies the cost of crime.

The welfare state reduces the costs of hormonal female behavior to parents of those females, since the cost of bastardy is externalized to the rest of society to a greater extent, and thus reduces the incentive of parents to inculcate their daughters with traditional values and deprecate the natural behavior of females - the natural inclination of women being more towards the demon lover. Women can be socialized, pressured, and monitored into fidelity to males that materially support them and help raise their kids, but it takes a firm hand and a watchful eye. While Islamic society takes this to extremes, the other extreme, total neglect of this problem, has costs also.

Racefail 09 explained

2009-03-18 04:05:27

Constantinople drew my attention to "This way lies fascism"[114] which explains the conflict of which Racefail 09[115] is part.

The left claims authority to convict people for thought crimes committed in other people's dreams. The hearer can find an offensive meaning without concern for authorial intent, and the author is guilty regardless of his intended meaning. This leads to conflict, Racefail 09 being part of that conflict.

Under Racefail 09 rules, you have no obligation to understand other people's intended meaning, and if you cannot follow what they say, and so confabulate up an offensive meaning, you are superior, you win, they are inferior, and they lose.

The smart, and those fluent in words, often express themselves in ways that are subtle, which the stupid and ignorant find hard to follow. Reading words that are hard to follow, they feel offended. Racefail 09 rules guarantee that if they feel offended, their offense must be justified.

Thus Racefail 09 rules tend to be popular with the stupid and incoherent, and unpopular with the clever and those good with words. Since the reader has sole authority to decide the writers meaning, and the writer is at fault if the reader decides on an offensive meaning, Racefail 09 is a pretty good deal for people who have trouble following other people's words.

The crisis explained

2009-03-28 04:10:08

I have been seeing a lot of references to "a speculative bubble"

Nope. They were not speculating.

The crisis consisted of people, mostly members of protected minorities with nothing to lose, buying houses they could not afford with borrowed money in the expectation that they would go up, and if they went down, it was the bank's problem.

---

[114]https://proteinwisdom.com/?p=14541
[115]https://www.google.com/search?q=%22racefail+09%22

So the people who bought houses were taking no risk, since mostly they bought them with 100% loans, had no credit rating and no assets to lose.

So were the banks making the loans taking a risk?

No, because it was not the bank's problem, because the loans were for the most part guaranteed by Freddy, or Fannie, or AIG - all of which had implicit government guarantees, and all of which had an AAA rating.

So why did AIG and the rest have an AAA rating?

AIG and the rest were issuing naked puts greatly exceeding their total capitalization, which pretty much guaranteed that sooner or later they would go broke in a big way. So why AAA?

Moody's, who issued the ratings, was tweaked on this, and replied that it was unthinkable that the government would allow these institutions to fail. So it was not true that nobody knew what was happening. All the insiders knew what was happening, the regulators knew what was happening: they knew that businesses were taking big risks for big money in the expectation that if they won, they won, and if they lost, the government would take care of them. It was government policy. People have been complaining[116] about this for years[117].

The fundamental cause of this crisis is government regulation: Governments cannot be trusted with money. They think only of short term political gain, so dispense money to the loudest pressure group, in this case those represented by ACORN, rather than to people who are likely to repay it with interest. In this case, the regulators decided that "traditional" standards of credit worthiness were racist and discriminatory, because too many Jews, and not enough Blacks, met "traditional" standards.

Smashing capitalism

2009-04-01 04:20:52

President Barack Hussein Obama tells us:

> Your warranty will be safe. In fact, it will be safer than it has ever been. Because starting today, the United States will stand behind your warranty.

This reads like something out of "Atlas Shrugged".

I predict fifty percent inflation or so over the next three or four years - and that is if we eventually turn back from this course, or at least stop walking along it. If, on the other hand, this goes on, with the government taking responsibility for one thing after another, as each intervention creates a crisis bigger than the last crisis, leading to more interventions, then I predict hyperinflation and widespread inability or unwillingness of government to provide order and protect property. Obama is not going to get under your car and fix it, and as the government takes on an ever growing multitude of tasks it is incapable of performing, its performance in its area of core competence (hurting people and breaking things) will deteriorate.

---

[116]https://www.aei.org/publications/pubID.24907,filter.all/pub_detail.asp
[117]https://query.nytimes.com/gst/fullpage.html?res=9C0DE7DB%20153EF933A0575AC0A96F958260

This crisis did not start with Obama, it did not even start with Bush.

During the final years of the Clinton presidency, Clinton greatly strengthened the CRA, which was glowingly reported by the newspapers[118]

More **than $1 Trillion Invested through CRA**

Lenders and community organizations have negotiated $1.09 trillion in CRA dollars from 1992 to 2000.

A more accurate report of the same facts would be

Politicians shovel one trillion dollars of off budget money to irresponsible and improvident members of narrowly targeted voting blocks, for which taxpayers are going to wind up on the hook

Government regulation winds up as off budget handouts to voting blocks (in this case mostly Hispanics) and well connected insiders (in this case some elements in Wall Street). Crisis ensues as the bill comes due. To maintain the superficial appearance of normality, there is a drastic increase in intervention, but the synthetic normality is a mere facade, like putting makeup on a corpse.

We now have trillions of dollars of capital flowing away from well managed businesses, to businesses with implicit or explicit government guarantees - businesses that will rapidly lose that money– a huge increase in the already huge off budget expenses of government, in addition to the huge and rapidly growing on budget deficit. Unacknowledged off budget government expenditures far exceed government's ability to tax. They will not necessarily exceed government's ability to borrow– yet.

Government pisses away the entire GDP in five months

2009-04-02 04:21:44

Bloomberg reports[119] that since November, the government has spent, loaned, or guaranteed 12.8 trillion, an amount very close to one year's GDP– one year of everyone's income, or $42,105 for every man, woman, and child in America.

Worshippers of the Obamessiah start to wake up

2009-04-03 04:14:14

The New York Times almost gets it right[120]:

---

[118]https://http//www.policylink.org/EDTK/CRA/action.html

[119]https://www.bloomberg.com/apps/news?pid=newsarchive&sid=armOzfkwtCA4

[120]https://www.nytimes.com/2009/04/01/opinion/01stiglitz.html?pagewanted=2&_r=3&partner=rss&emc=rss

Obama's Ersatz Capitalism

> What the Obama administration is doing is far worse than nationalization: it is ersatz capitalism, the privatizing of gains and the socializing of losses. It is a "partnership" in which one partner robs the other.

Close but no banana.

It is crony capitalism, which at its more socialist extreme is fascism, the corporate state, where business and the citizen are subjugated to the state, to the benefit of the rulers and favored businessmen. Not just any business is going to get is losses socialized and its gains privatized. Obama is coming down like a ton of bricks on certain businesses, but not, however, other businesses.

Good thing we did not elect McCain – then fascism would have had bipartisan support.

And talking of fascism, here[121] is something where fascism is plainer to see.

Dr Lindzen on "corrected" data
2009-04-13 04:23:14

Dr.Richard Lindzen on "corrected" climate data.

> it has become standard in climate science that data in contradiction to alarmism is inevitably 'corrected' to bring it closer to alarming models. None of us would argue that this data is perfect, and the corrections are often plausible. What is implausible is that the 'corrections' should always bring the data closer to models.

We are all terrorists now
2009-04-15 04:24:20

The liberty papers found an interesting Obama document[122]. It seems that it is not those poor misunderstood adherents of the Religion of Peace that are a problem. It is any American who disagrees with the Obama agenda. Michael Malkin confirms the document is real[123], not a parody.

Veterans are also terrorists, no doubt it comes of persecuting those poor adherents of the Religion of Peace.

Iran tells it like it is:
2009-04-19 04:25:24

In his April 15, 2009 speech[124], Iranian President Mahmoud Ahmadinejad told America:

---

[121]https://carlosmiller.com/2009/03/30/the-moment-of-judgment-has-arrived/

[122]https://www.thelibertypapers.org/2009/04/12/homeland-security-document-targets-most-conservatives-and-libertarians-in-the-country/

[123]https://michellemalkin.com/2009/04/14/confirme-the-obama-dhs-hit-job-on-conservatives-is-real/

[124]https://www.memri.org/bin/latestnews.cgi?ID=SD231709

We say to you that you yourselves know that you are today in a position of weakness. Your hands are empty, and you can no longer promote your affairs from a position of strength.

... with the grace of God, and thanks to Iran's national unity, the recommendations of Supreme Leader, and the following of his [path], nearly 7,000 centrifuges are spinning today

Trillion missing, top accountant dead

2009-04-23 04:26:19

David Kellerman, the acting Chief Financial Officer and Senior VP at Freddie Mac, was found dead[125] early this morning from at his home in Virginia. It is described as an apparent suicide.

The press is rightly comparing this with the very similar "suicide" of Enron's top accountant.

When large sums of money disappear, the person who knows most about where the money went often, by an interesting coincidence, winds up with his mouth permanently closed.

Freddy Mac and Fannie May have had accounting scandals before, but during the housing boom, all their sins were forgiven, and the offending executives retired with golden parachutes. This time around, the public is in a less forgiving mood.

There is an effort to link this murder with Obama, which is unreasonable because he has nothing he needs to cover up yet, not being in charge when the money vanished. On the other hand, his treasury department is full of friends of Obama who do have something to cover up.

Galt strike or inadequate aggregate demand?

2009-05-01 04:27:59

The Randian concept of a Galt Strike is that if the elite slack off, the masses will be impoverished– that countries are rich or poor according to whether the elite is productive, while the masses and resources do not matter much, except in extreme cases such as oil rich sheikdoms.

There has been a large fall in GDP over the past six months:

The Keynesian explanation of this fall is inadequate aggregate demand - the economy could easily produce more, but no one is spending due to depression of animal spirits, in which case a big spending government will make everything rosy.

The Austrian and Chicago explanation is complicated, and perhaps confused.

The Randian explanation is that it is a Galt Strike - the elite are slacking off, and focusing on hiding their wealth and economic activities from the government, rather than creating value, in which case big government spending will merely result in inflation or massive borrowing from abroad.

---

[125]https://247wallst.com/2009/04/22/cfo-death-only-clouds-freddie-mac-fannie-mae-further-fre-fnm/

Core CPI will in time tell us which account is correct. We will know by about November 2010.

If late in 2010 core CPI is substantially higher, nominal GDP substantially higher, but real GDP still woeful, then Randians will have been proven correct.

If late in 2010 core CPI is lower or unchanged, then both sides can argue they were right, and the Austrians will probably have some explanation that I will be disinclined to follow.

If late in 2010 core CPI only rises moderately, but real GDP rises substantially, then Keynesians will have been proven correct.

I am betting on disturbing levels of core inflation with a distinctly unimpressive recovery in real GDP.

Courage
2009-05-02 04:28:59

A kid carrying a gun, and wearing an explosive vest, attempted to enter a mosque. It seems that though the congregation were Muslim, they were the wrong kind of Muslim.

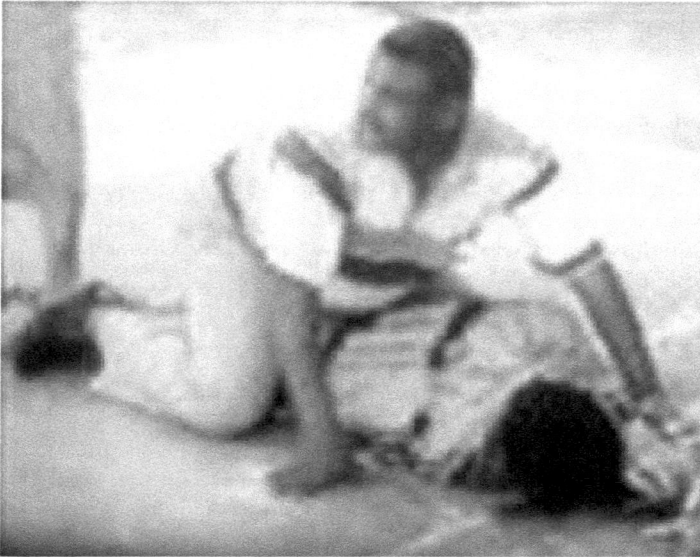

A guard tackled him[126]. That is courage.

Securitization
2009-05-06 04:30:21

From the point of view of oligarchs and crony capitalists, the crisis is not that a lot loans were made to no hablo English wetbacks. The crisis is that people are rejecting[127] securi-

---

[126]https://translate.google.com/translate?hl=en&ie=UTF-8&sl=ar&tl=en&u=https://-nahrain.com/news.php%3Freadmore%3D62022&prev=_t"

[127]https://econlog.econlib.org/archives/2009/05/gillian_tett_on.html

tization of debt.

The Obama regime's capitalism smashing measures are intended not to destroy capitalism, nor to install socialism, but to restore securitization of debt. This is socialism for the financiers, not for the proles: Crony socialism, crony capitalism, a fascist economic order.

Regular old fashioned loans are going through just fine. There is no credit crisis, the financial system is not freezing up. Securitization is freezing up, and it @#$% well should freeze up.

When debts are securitized, many different debts of many different borrowers are piled together into a great big pool of debt, and then shares in the pool are sold to lots of creditors– which means that there is no one person responsible for verifying that any one particular loan is sound, that the assets securing the loan are worth what they are supposed to be worth, that the person responsible for making payments on the loan can read and write, that he speaks the language that the papers that he signed were written in, that he was sufficiently sober when he signed them to remember signing them, or even that the paperwork exists and is in good order.

For securitization to work, the particular organization that arranged the loan, and the particular people in the particular organization, would have to remain responsible for that loan. The debtor would have to be making payments through the people that arranged the loan for the life of the loan.

Securitization leads carelessness with large sums of other people's money. Such carelessness leads to crime. Crime destroys the trust that is necessary for the economic system to work. Securitization must stop. If securitization continues, capitalism will end. By and large, those who favor continued securitization are wealthy criminals, who personally benefited from stolen money, as over the years carelessness slowly became indistinguishable from deliberate fraud. The problem before Obama was not lack of regulation, but that the foxes were regulating the chickens, and now under Obama the foxes are *still* regulating the chickens. Each Obama intervention has the effect of keeping the criminals in power over other people's money, resisting the natural propensity of capitalism to purify itself through creative destruction.

Securitization was born in fraud: The original motivation for securitization was the 1995 Community Reinvestment Act[128]. If the government is pressuring you to make loans on the basis of race, rather than willingness and ability to pay one's just debts, you want to get rid of the politically correct mortgages to some other sucker as fast as possible.

Securitization of debt is only legitimate when the people that arranged the loan remain linked to the loan. Otherwise, securitization is a scam, as the origins of mortgage securitization demonstrate.

obamanomics

2009-05-07 04:31:30

Megan nails it:[129]

---

[128]https://www.renaissance-partners.com/blog/?p=65
[129]https://meganmcardle.theatlantic.com/archives/2009/05/the_price_of_the_kings_shillin.php

the government is using its intervention in the banking system to pressure banks to give special deals to the government's special friends.

Blog empty due to crash and move to new host.

2009-05-10 23:37:13

My previous host (Servers and Domains) crashed on me, and despite considerable passage of time, are still down.

As a result many articles are missing

I hope to recover nearly all of them in the next couple of days. Recovering comments will take a little longer.

I apologize for the inconvenience - and for my failure to keep adequate backups.

"The Goode Family" is not funny

2009-06-01 08:55:03

The Goode family are too nice and sincere to laugh at. Where is the liberal fascism and liberal totalitarianism? Observe that the kid gets away with defining his ethnicity as "African American" (he is white from South Africa) while in real life the kid from South Africa who pulled that stunt got expelled from college.

The only funny character is the dog, because he is rebelling against the family veganism by devouring every neighborhood pet smaller than himself.

The show fails because it is too soft on liberalism. To get a laugh, have to stick the knife in and twist it a bit. This show is too much like "Father knows best"

The only part of the first episode where they really stick the knife in, and follow it up with a few boots to the head, is, of course, where they stick the knife into fundamentalist Christians.

The Goode Family are genuinely and sincerely trying to do good. That is not funny. They should be genuinely and sincerely *deluded* that they are doing good. That would be funny.

Global warming swindle.

2009-06-08 12:21:06

Every so often you see these graphs supposedly showing how the world has warmed during the twentieth and twentyfirst centuries, supposedly based on surface temperatures.

Steve McIntyre is launching a freedom of information request[130] to find out what, if anything, these graphs are based on, and, of course, they are refusing.

---

[130]https://www.climateaudit.org/?p=6203

The end of science and art

2009-06-14 05:43:32

As everyone knows, modern art is crap[131], and modern poetry is crap[132]. Unfortunately, modern science is rapidly becoming crap. As Climate Audit[133] shows, global warming "science" has abandoned that inconvenient stuff about replicable results. When global warmers supposedly prove something, they don't reveal the underlying observations, the method of calculation, or any "corrections" they made to the raw data and refuse to reveal them when asked by incredulous scientists. Engineering and technology is still going strong, but the steadily falling status of engineers and technologists indicates doom on its way, much as science and art died in Rome when its status became contemptible

"OK", I hear you say, "but Global Warming is political. How about the real hard sciences, like high energy physics?"

Well, I have been reading Not even wrong[134], which tells us a disturbingly large amount of modern high energy physics is not even wrong. They are not as far gone as global warming, but they are in a pretty bad way.

Terence Kealey[135] in "The Economic Laws of Scientific Research"[136] observes that government funding of science reduces, rather than increases, the amount of real science produced, but does not provide any theoretical explanation for this counter intuitive result.

Moldius Moldbug[137] does provide a theoretical explanation: Government funding leads to unfavorable memetic selection. Under government patronage memes that correspond to effective grantsmanship outcompete memes that correspond to truth or beauty. Private patrons, armored against manipulation by wealth, power and arrogance, and the fact that they do not have to consult with anyone, and often experts or connoisseurs in the area they are funding, are not so manipulable, thus provide an environment where beautiful art and true science can outcompete grantsmanship.

Internet Gold alive and well

2009-06-15 09:14:04

Iang gives us an obituary[138] for e-gold.

E-gold is only dead the way Napster is dead. Like Napster they demonstrated that the business model was viable, and also demonstrated that as soon as you started transferring serious money the US government would come after you. As a result, there are a lot of replacements for e-gold, which the US government will find hard to shut down, notably

[131] https://roissy.wordpress.com/2009/06/10/the-state-of-art-in-america/
[132] https://unqualified-reservations.blogspot.com/2007/11/tryfon-tolides-almost-pure-empty-poetry.html
[133] https://www.climateaudit.org/?p=6203
[134] https://www.math.columbia.edu/~woit/wordpress/?p=2075
[135] https://www.amazon.com/Terence-Kealey/e/B000AQ3Y2A/ref=ntt_athr_dp_pel_1
[136] https://www.amazon.com/Economic-Laws-Scientific-Research/dp/0312173067
[137] https://unqualified-reservations.blogspot.com/
[138] https://financialcryptography.com/mt/archives/001169.html

Pecunix[139] and Webmoney[140].

Creating the next crisis:

2009-06-17 06:45:19

In a free market, financiers who take stupid risks lose money, and cease to be financiers. The core of the Obama Bush interventions is to ensure that financiers who take stupid risks continue in business and continue in charge of other people's money.

In the Washington Post, Obama's chief financial advisers explain their program[141]:

> In theory, securitization should serve to reduce credit risk by spreading it more widely. But by breaking the direct link between borrowers and lenders, securitization led to an erosion of lending standards, resulting in a market failure that fed the housing boom and deepened the housing bust. The administration's plan will impose robust reporting requirements on the issuers of asset-backed securities; reduce investors' and regulators' reliance on credit-rating agencies; and, perhaps most significant, require the originator, sponsor or broker of a securitization to retain a financial interest in its performance.

"How big a financial interest?" I hear you ask.

Summers is a little bit vague, about this, but if you dig, the answer is five percent - enough to make a difference, but not enough to make a significant difference, not enough to deter banks from making irresponsible loans.

The fundamental problem is that the government wants banks to continue make loans to irresponsible borrowers in important voting blocks, borrowers who should not be able to borrow money, and therefore must maintain a regulatory structure that enables bad loans. A transfer of wealth from a concentrated interest group (financiers) to an important voting block (hispanics) is not politically feasible. So instead, such dud loans must ultimately wind up being financed by the government.

The government issues regulations that require financiers to refrain from "discriminating against" a voting block – which seeming benefits the voting block at no cost to the government. But there is no such thing as free lunch. Who will pay?

You can be sure a concentrated interest group is not going to pay.

Inflation looms

2009-06-19 05:19:20

Bryan Caplan, favorably citing Sumner, tells us "*stop worrying about inflation*[142]"

Supposedly we should stop worrying about inflation, because the bond markets predict only moderate levels of inflation. Supposedly we can determine future inflation by

---

[139]https://pecunix.com/money.refined...welcome
[140]https://www.wmtransfer.com/eng/about/demo/glossary/wmg.shtml
[141]https://www.washingtonpost.com/wp-dyn/content/article/2009/06/14/AR2009061402443.html
[142]https://econlog.econlib.org/archives/2009/06/sumner_an_embar.html

looking at the difference between Treasury Securities, and Treasury Inflation Protected Securities. Supposedly, this tells us what the people investing in securities think that inflation will be, and they are pretty good at predicting inflation.

However, this tells us only what people who are confident that inflation will be moderate think inflation will be, because if you are worried about immoderate levels of inflation, you do not diversify into long term Treasury Inflation Protected Securities, you diversify into gold, silver, guns, ammunition, rice and beans, which is roughly what the Chinese are doing, except that they are also diversifying into copper and iron, and private Chinese are not allowed to diversify into guns and ammo.

The bond market does not tell us what the smart money people think inflation will be. It tells us what those among the smart money people who do not expect very high levels of inflation think inflation will be.

What are the Chinese worried about?

They are not worried about the possibility four percent inflation in 2011. They are worried about the possibility of four hundred percent inflation in 2020. And so they are *not* buying Treasury Inflation Protected Securities. And so the difference between Treasury Securities and Treasury Inflation Protected Securities fails to reflect their concerns. And so, if we look at the bond market, what it tells us is that the Chinese think inflation may well hit four percent in 2011, but does not tell us what they think inflation will be in 2020. But if you listen to what they are saying, what they are saying is that they think there is a substantial risk of very high levels of inflation in eight years or so.

Governments tend to go down the tubes when total public debt is around two hundred percent of GDP or so. Thus a deficit of ten percent of GDP or so is sustainable for ten or twenty years or so. Trouble is that in addition to an on budget deficit of ten percent or so, there is also a much larger off budget deficit, in the form of an ever growing pile of government guarantees, which there is no will to restrain. Put the two deficits together, crisis looms.

Trees do not grow to the sky. That which cannot continue, must stop.

The universal government white paper:

2009-06-19 06:09:26

In my earlier post Creating the next crisis[143] I critique the same white paper[144] on solving the financial crisis as Arnold Kling critiques[145]

On of his commentators has an excellent summary of this paper, and indeed every similar governmental and quasi governmental paper addressing every crisis:

1. Politicians are of course entirely lily white and innocent, except that the other party allowed bad people in the private sector to do bad things.
2. Some government agencies failed to do enough.
3. Solving the problem requires more power to the government.

---

[143] ../politics/creating-the-next-crisis.html

[144] https://media.washingtonpost.com/wp-srv/politics/pdf/nearfinaldraft_061709.pdf

[145] https://econlog.econlib.org/archives/2009/06/whats_wrong_wit_10.html

4. Those government agencies that failed the worst, shall get the largest increase in money and power.

Section 161

2009-06-19 11:08:22

> Frank Hill writes in a comment at
> Most solar physicists are not "desperate" for the sun to crank up its activity; instead we are fascinated by its behavior. With the hysteria over climate change and the hope of some people that we are entering a Maunder minimum so we can dispense with that global warming nonsense and keep on driving our gas guzzlers, solar physicists occasionally feel the need to point out the solar dynamo is apparently chugging along as usual with only small deviations from its normal behavior.

This assertion would be more impressive you had refrained from saying "gas guzzlers".

It would also be more impressive were it not glaringly obvious that the sun is grossly deviating from the behavior that has been observed over the past few hundred years.

It would also be more impressive if your organization, and presumably you yourself as spokesman for that organization had not issued a long serious of false prediction that the sun would shortly resume normal activity.

Creating the next crisis 2

2009-06-26 12:24:44

Remember all that junk mail:

> *Bad credit?*
> *No credit?*
> *No problem! Buy the house of your dreams with no money down!*

Well thanks to the great Bush-Obama stimulus package, looks like you will be seeing it again.

When the government says that private lending has dried up, this is code for the strange absence of no money down loans to people with bad credit. People I know, such as my sister in law, who had money and good credit found that lenders rolled out the red carpet for them. There was never lending crisis for traditional borrowers.

When the government says there is a lending crisis, it means the problem is that a drunken no-hablo-English wetback seems to be finding a bit of trouble borrowing. But never fear. Your ever helpful and benevolent government is remedying this terrible market failure[146]. Whatever would we do without regulation and subsidy?

---

[146]https://online.wsj.com/article/SB124139474675481713.html

The FHA is now providing one hundred percent government guarantees for loans to people with bad credit. Supposedly the borrower must put three and a half percent down, but since real estate agent fees, mortgage broker fees, and assorted charges theoretically add up to slightly over ten percent, a clawback from the various people involved can and does reduce this to zero. When I transact a house, I usually manage to clawback four to six percent from these various charges, so if I was purchasing a house with what on paper was a three and half percent down loan, and managed to get my usual clawbacks, I would get the house *and* two percent cash in hand - negative money down. And that is without a kickback from the seller. Of course that is why the lenders would rather do the loan with a drunken no-hablo-English wetback, who is unlikely to be so fierce at clawing back and chiseling down their fees as I am.

When you buy a house on a loan with small money down, you usually also get an under the table kickback from the seller. With a kickback from the seller and clawbacks from agent and broker fees, three and a half percent down vanishes fast.

Faking global warming

2009-06-30 04:46:11

I have often mentioned before that the those impressive graphs of rising surface temperatures are faked, as if everyone knew, and everyone agreed, inadvertently imitating the mock consensus style of the warmists, without giving a citation. Here is the article that exposed the fakery[147] for the US weather stations

The method is simple: The raw and adjusted data is available from the United States Historical Climatology Network Monthly Temperature and Precipitation Data[148] though in not very readable form. When converted to readable form, the unadjusted data shows no global warming, the adjusted data looks like any doomster graph from GISS.

In his other articles[149], Michael Hammer analyzes the adjustments.

Rising natural rate of unemployment

2009-07-04 17:07:53

The nairu is the natural rate of unemployment, the level of unemployment that arises from people changing jobs, minimum wage laws and trade unions.

Felix Salmon cheerfully tells us[150]

> As for the possibility of a higher Nairu, we're so far away from there right now that for the time being such discussions are probably academic.

On the contrary, the nairu has risen right now - the US is not in a Keynesian recession where aggregate demand is less than aggregate supply, we are in an Atlas Shrugged recession where employers are punished for employing. If the current crisis in the USA was

---

[147]https://jennifermarohasy.com/blog/2009/06/how-the-us-temperature-record-is-adjusted/
[148]https://cdiac.ornl.gov/epubs/ndp/ushcn/ndp019.html
[149]https://jennifermarohasy.com/blog/author/michael-hammer/
[150]https://blogs.reuters.com/felix-salmon/2009/07/03/the-limits-of-economic-policy/

well described by Keynes, then core inflation would have fallen as unemployment rose. Instead core inflation has remained pretty much constant, indicating that any increase in employment that reduces the unemployment rate to below present high levels will result in accelerating inflation.

A substantial part of the Obama "stimulus" package was to make it more expensive for employers to lay off employees. Since employers, unlike politicians, regulators, and voters, tend to take a long term view, this of course makes them more apt to lay people off, and less apt to hire people. If you increase the cost to employers of people changing jobs, the nairu resulting from people changing jobs will increase.

Another part of the "stimulus" package was to privilege unions in various ways. Unionization directly raises the Nairu.

A large part of the "stimulus" package was to privilege big companies over small companies, the extreme case being "too big to fail" Market concentration increases the nairu.

Rapidly rising unemployment without falling inflation indicates that this rising unemployment is directly caused by the "stimulus" and is likely to be permanent. Moving to a European style political and economic order means moving, permanently, to European levels of unemployment.

What is wrong with the Bush/Obama economic stimulus
2009-07-05 06:29:32

Tim Kane tells us[151]:

> Ironically, the harshest critics of Obama are also overly optimistic. The White House wants to believe the stimulus is working. The critics want to believe the stimulus wasn't necessary because the economy is getting better already.

No, that is not what the harshest critics believe. The harshest critics, such as myself, believe that the Keynesian description of the crisis only addressed a small and unimportant part of the truth, thus stimulus could only have a small and unimportant benefit. The economy is not "starting to get better already", rather it is only beginning to go bad.

The crisis was originally well described by the Austrian model of recessions– we discovered that we were erroneously over investing in the finance and housing sectors, that the value supposedly created by financiers and real estate agents was largely phony, and that many of the customers for housing were unable or unwilling to pay, and that as a result of CAFE and other restrictions on new cars, new cars were less useful than old cars. As a result, we got a diminution not in aggregate demand but in demand in particular sectors, which cannot be remedied by aggregate stimulus, but only by labor and capital mobility.

The continuing crisis is well described by the "Atlas Shrugged" model, rather than the Austrian or Keynesian model: the government smashes capitalism causing the economy goes to hell. Thus, for example, a substantial part of the stimulus package was to impose burdens on employers who lay off workers, which of course increases, rather than decreases layoffs.

---

[151]https://www.growthology.org/growthology/2009/07/jobs-update.html

Our new permanently high level of unemployment will resemble the permanently high unemployment of many European countries.

Constitutionality of the removal of the Presidente of Honduras
2009-07-07 17:56:58

Because the president of Honduras proposed to change the constitution to allow him further terms of office, he was accused of violating article 239 of the Honduran Constitution:[152]

> No citizen who has already served as head of the Executive Branch can be President or Vice-President.

> Whoever violates this law or *proposes its reform*, as well as those that support such violation directly or indirectly, *will immediately cease in their functions* and will be unable to hold any public office for a period of 10 years.

So the Honduran constitution says that if the presidente proposes to extend his term, he shall be immediately fired.

> ARTICULO 239.- El ciudadano que haya desempeñado la titularidad del Poder Ejecutivo no podrá ser Presidente o Vicepresidente de la República.

> El que quebrante esta disposición o proponga su reforma, así como aquellos que lo apoyen directa o indirectamente, cesarán de inmediato en el desempeño de sus respectivos cargos y quedarán inhabilitados por diez (10) años para el ejercicio de toda función pública.

OK. He shall be fired. And the Supreme Court and Legislature proceeded to fire him.

The "stimulus" is far too large and far too small.
2009-07-11 18:36:56

Republicans are getting traction by condemning the "stimulus", as an outlandishly extravagant porkfest, as miserly and inadequate, and as a disaster that should not be repeated – an attack made all the more effective by the many radical Democrats who complain the porkfest was inadequate, and call for a bigger and better porkfest: "Stimulus II"

Obama's approval ratings, though still high, are plummeting fast under this withering criticism.

In Japan, they are now on stimulus umpteen, the Japanese economy is not looking very stimulated, and the Japanese government is getting close to bankruptcy.

The porkfest is too small in that it takes the government a very long time, several years, between deciding to spend money, and the money actually getting into people's pockets, so the only stimulus that has had any effect are the tax cuts– and the carbon bill

---

[152]https://pdba.georgetown.edu/Constitutions/Honduras/hond05.html

looks suspiciously like an alarmingly large tax rise: "tax and raid", as the Republicans are calling it. This is not very stimulating.

As for too large – well we cannot definitely say it was too large unless serious inflation or national insolvency sets in, and so long inflation remains subdued, people can always say it would have worked had it been larger.

My expectation is that it will not work, not matter how large, because this is primarily a Galt Strike, and only to a minor extent the inadequacy of aggregate demand that Keynes described. But this theory can only be tested if the Democrats put the pedal to the metal, and do enough stimulus that serious inflation sets in.

If inflation sets in without recovery in employment and investment, that will be compelling evidence in favor of the Galt Strike theory and against the Keynesian theory. But as long as inflation remains low, people can say of the American stimulus, as they say of the Japanese stimulus, that it would have worked if only it was tried hard enough.

If, on the other hand, the stimulus actually stimulates something broader than gigaprofits at Goldman and Sach, then that will be compelling evidence that Keynesianism or neo Keynesianism does describe the present economy accurately enough.

If inflation with high unemployment and stagnant investment, then I am proven right.

If low inflation with high unemployment and stagnant investment, then everyone can plausibly claim to have been proven right, though in fact nothing will be proven - the situation we now have with Japan.

If low unemployment and adequate investment, the Keynesians will be proven right.

Speaking power to truth

2009-07-13 12:23:20

If an economist wants to get places, he had best tell politicians and bureaucrats what they want to hear. The danger is that if says it often enough, he will himself come to believe it.

Larry Summers is an economist. When Bush was in power, he believed in Bushonomics, which got him into trouble in an academic environment of rigid, mindless, and unthinking left wing orthodoxy. Now, however, it seems he firmly believes in Obanomics.

In his interview[153] with a financial times blogger, Larry Summers explains that whatever Obama wants to do for political reasons, is also the right thing to do economically. Obama, supposedly, faces no tradeoffs between his goals. He can have it all, can do everything. None of his objectives are going to get in the way of other of his objectives. That must be very nice for Obama to hear:

> As the panic has subsided, the trendy new economic issue has become "exit strategy" – as in, when and how do governments shift from costly and aggressive intervention to levels of spending and taxation that are sustainable over the long term?

> Summers rejects the premise of the question.

[153]https://www.ft.com/cms/s/2/6ac06592-6ce0-11de-af56-00144feabdc0.html

When I visited Cuba, it became apparent to me that not only did the Cuban government lie to visitors and to its subjects, it most of all lied to itself - that power isolated the powerful from knowing what was in fact happening in Cuba. Not only does the Democratic party believe that Cuba has wonderful medical care, so does the Cuban elite.

The most striking fact about the new American economy is that businesses that do not produce value, that have failed catastrophically and ruinously at producing value, but which have cosy connections to the state, such as Goldman and Sach, make profits for the super rich, which profits soar into the stratosphere. The new economy is very very good for the well connected businessman[154], good for the union boss, bad for the ordinary consumer, and very very bad for the entrepeneur.

> This new American economy, Summers hopes, will be "more export-oriented" and "less consumption-oriented"; "more environmentally oriented" and "less energy-production-oriented"; "more bio- and software- and civil-engineering-oriented and less financial-engineering-oriented"; and, finally, "more middle-class-oriented" and "less oriented to income growth that is disproportionate towards a very small share of the population".

The second most striking fact is that any technology that actually is environmentally oriented - such as replacing coal power with nuclear power, or even solar power, gets struck down on a multitude of legalistic grounds by environmentalists whose true goal is the destruction of western civilization and swift and massive reduction of the human population. They favor symbolic environmental technology, such as rooftop solar, but any environmental technology that actually has the potential to replace coal, such as solar thermal tower power, is swiftly crushed. I very much doubt it is Obama's goal to destroy western civilization, but it is his goal to keep the ayatollahs of Gaia happy, and Summers tells him that keeping them happy will have no costs, only benefits, which is what Obama wants to hear.

One more crazy murderous totalitarian pal of Obama's
2009-07-13 19:56:52

Zombietime reads the writings of Obama's science Czar, discovers he is a total loon who wants to use the panic du jour to impose a totalitarian world state[155].
Why is that a more or less reasonable sounding fellow like Obama has so many terrorists, totalitarians, and frothing at the mouth nutcases as friends, mentors, and allies?

I conjecture that Obama, and Obama's science czar, is enabled by people like Larry Summers, who can find no end of rationalizations along the lines that Reverend Wright and John Holdren are moderate reformers who want reasonable and moderate changes in our lifestyles, not withstanding the fact that these guys are screaming their heads off that they are fanatics who want to totally smash our way of life.

Coalition building is a lot easier if you maintain total delusion about your allies.

---

[154]https://bailoutsleuth.com/09/07/326/treasury-goes-north-to-alaska-for-toxic-asset-pick/
[155]https://www.zombietime.com/zomblog/?p=576

I predict: 1. Seemingly good economic news
2009-07-15 08:56:01

I predict that around 2009 October or so, there will be lots of seemingly cheerful economic news. Quite possibly sooner, possibly some time in August.

I predict that the Keynesian element of the depression will rapidly and visibly diminishing towards the end of the year. Crises that are well described by Keynes (aggregate demand falling below aggregate supply) never last long, except to the extent government intervenes to forbid businessmen to adjust to them. Say's law is observed to be mostly true in practice, except where the government makes it illegal. Obama, for all his faults, has not done much to stop Say's law from operating, therefore aggregate demand is going to be fine very soon.

It will then become apparent to what extent this is a crisis as described by the Austrian school - (unemployed financiers, real estate agents and union car makers that have to learn new careers) and to what extent this is a Galt strike, a crisis as described by Ayn Rand in "Atlas Shrugged" (horrified entrepreneurs despair and flee.)

I also predict that when it becomes apparent to what extent this is a Galt Strike, the cheery economic news will not look so cheery in retrospect– that at some time between late 2010 and early 2012 the "green shoots" of 2009 will be discovered to have been composed of poison ivy.

A politician speaks the truth!
2009-07-15 17:45:39

Usually, any statement or report emanating from government, any government white paper, is a lie, but in a remarkable fluke outburst of truthfulness, the U.S. House of Representative Committee on Oversight and Government Reform has issued a report: The Role of Government Affordable Housing Policy in Creating the Global Financial Crisis of 2008[156]

The long and the short of the report being that the government pressured financiers to issue easy money bad loans to irresponsible borrowers, which government policy eventually blew up. Of course, if you have been reading the blogs, that is not news to you. For several years you heard that was going to happen, and then for a couple of more years you heard that is what did happen, but it is most astonishing to hear it from the government itself!

Goldman Sach's hand caught in piggy bank.
2009-07-17 06:05:15

They admit their hand was in the piggy bank,[157] but say they were just feeling the money, not stealing it.Their trading software it turns out, is running inside the computers that do the trades, and sees other people's trades before they are made.

[156]https://republicans.oversight.house.gov/media/pdfs/20090707HousingCrisisReport.pdf
[157]https://financialcryptography.com/mt/archives/001175.html

This makes it possible for them to "front run" trades.

"Front running" works like this:

Bob offers one million units of a security for one dollar each, and has been offering for some time. Carol asks for three million units of the same security at ninety cents each, and has been asking for some time. After a while, Carol blinks, and agrees to buy Bob's securities at one dollar. But one millisecond before the trade goes through, Goldman and Sach buy Bob's securities and promptly offer them for sail at one dollar ten– for the fact that Carol blinked first indicates the price is likely to rise.

Proprietary secret software should not be in trading computers. Any software in those computers should be subject to scrutiny by all major traders. Any secret software in trading computers is compelling evidence of wrongdoing.

Why is all this @#$% floating to the surface now? Because suddenly, people are looking for rats.

British political prisoners.

2009-07-21 08:35:35

Two british nazis, Simon Shappard and Stephen Whittle, were charged with writing heresy[158]. They fled to the USA, but last month were forced back to Britain, where they have each been jailed for two years and two months for publishing thought crimes: They posted on their web site that Hitler did not exterminate the Jews, but that he should have.Why are Nazis jailed but not commies? Why are these guys jailed but Fisk is still loose? After all, in recent years a lot more people have been murdered on the basis of Fisk's ideas than on the basis of Shapard and Wittle's ideas.

Of course, a couple of Nazis are no great loss, but I suspect the next thought crime will be that Muslims are apt to commit terror, and Christians are not, shortly followed by the thought crime that police are more interested in keeping honest citizens powerless and afraid than in getting criminals off the streets.

The problem with thought crimes is that they work like a salami slicer. The spectrum of permitted thoughts is reduced one thin slice at a time - until the only thoughts permitted are those of a tiny group of fanatical murderous extremists. The salami slicer does not work at both ends towards the middle, but always at one end towards the favored extreme. If nazis are jailed, next those that are insufficiently commie, or the wrong kind of commie, will be jailed.

You are probably a federal felon

2009-07-26 04:21:14

There are a lot of laws, indeed they are growing so fast that not only can they not be read by legislators, but with in creasing frequency not even printed, existing only in electronic form, no longer practical to commit to paper. Further, many of these laws are deliberately overbroad for the convenience of prosecutors

---

[158]https://www.heretical.com/

Thus for example Krister Evertson[159] was convicted of abandoning hazardous waste - notwithstanding the fact that the materials were not waste, nor abandoned, nor even stored unsafely. The law is that someone's materials, if hazardous, can constitute waste even if they are extremely valuable to him and under lock and key in secure storage, and once the EPA has broken into that secure storage using cutting torches, he has abandoned the materials.

A law that on its face appears to be about potentially hazardous chemicals dumped in a creek, also covers potentially hazardous chemicals on private property in locked chemical and criminal resistant stainless steel container. And furthermore, nearly all chemicals have been declared hazardous.

The same is true of an enormous variety of other laws on other matters, laws that now multiply faster than is physically possible to print them - each law written to include all possible behavior that the state might possibly want to punish, not to exclude behavior that is innocent and honest.

Kaufman predicts soaring unemployment

2009-07-27 15:35:53

In U.S. Still Melting Jobs, Let's Count The Ways[160] Kaufman argues unemployment will continue to rise because of numerous hostile federal law changes and initiatives aimed against employers and entrepreneurship.

Meanwhile, the mainstream keeps predicting[161] that unemployment is near maximum, that things will shortly start getting better.

I expect that the mainstream will be proven wrong. You just cannot go forth and smash capitalism and expect everything will just continue to work fine - though as everything goes to hell, doubtless capitalism will be blamed, and Krugman and the rest will declare that they have been proven right - that all the bad things happening are proof that capitalism does not work and therefore they did not crush it enough.

---

[159]https://judiciary.house.gov/hearings/hear_090722_2.html "Click here to read Krister Evertson's testimony."

[160]https://www.growthology.org/growthology/2009/07/us-economy-still-melting-jobs.html

[161]https://www.federalreserve.gov/newsevents/testimony/DBBB5C9F26B6440AA4A21E104A61577A.htm?loc=interstitialskip

"We may be seeing the beginning of the end of the recession"

2009-07-31 04:33:47

"We may be seeing the beginning of the end of the recession", says Obama[162]

It has become apparent that the way for economists to become important, respected, even get Nobel prizes, is to tell politicians and bureaucrats what they want to hear, which is usually that there is sound economic reasons to do whatever pleases lobbyists, special interest groups, and strategically important voting blocks.

Here is Bernanke on the housing boom back before it burst[163] - he is telling us that the there is no bubble, that the government inflating prices will not cause crash and recession – were he to tell us something different people might think that the government pressuring banks to throw trillions of dollars in the general direction of people of the politically correct race but economically incorrect credit rating might lead to serious problems.

---

[162]https://www.bloomberg.com/apps/news?pid=20601103&sid=ap1VuLM3DTIw
[163]https://www.youtube.com/watch?v=HQ79Pt2GNJo

That does not of course mean the recession is going to get worse. What it does mean, however, is that all the very clever economic experts around Obama will tell him that things are going to be fine, regardless of whether they are going to be fine or not.

Because some of the people around Obama are crazies, notably his science Czar, craziness automatically becomes mainstream, and the good and the great start figuring out clever rationalizations why those programs are not crazy at all.

Well Obama has stuck his neck out a little, and made his prediction, so it is only fair that I stick my neck out and make my prediction: My prediction is for high unemployment, high inflation, or both, leading to ballot box stuffing and heavy intimidation of white and aged voters in the vicinity of the voting booth in 2010 and 2012

The nomenclatura
2009-08-03 06:41:55

"Hot Air" has a wonderful post: "the peasant plan"[164]. It lists all the benevolent interventions your beloved leaders are imposing on you for your own good – and points out that each benevolent intervention either by its nature does not effect people like the beloved leaders themselves , or, as with the health plan, people like the beloved leaders are specifically exempted from this kindly help.

Off budget deficit
2009-08-04 07:12:15

Long ago, the government found a new way to run a deficit: Create a nominally private business with government appointed management, to carry out a government directed mission. The entity borrows money like a private entity, but since its political missions require it to lose money in large amounts, by throwing money at strategic voting blocks and special interest groups, the lenders lend not in expectation that the business will be able to repay, but that the business will eventually be bailed out.

"Think Markets" recently spotted nefarious activity by the PBGC[165]:

> the PBGC's decision with respect to Delphi raises the government's GM bailout to about $70 billion in taxpayer liability. So far, that's about $2.3 million per active GM employee or $24,000 per vote Obama garnered in Michigan.

When the bailout finally happens many years down the line, it is part of a general crisis that the current governing party quite truthfully blames on the previous governing party, while itself making even bigger off budget expenditures.

In the recent crisis, the bailouts were so huge that they were done not by the Treasury, but by the biggest off budget entity of them all, the Federal Reserve, which has incurred liabilities of about two times GDP in the recent crisis[166].

---

[164]https://hotair.com/archives/2009/07/31/the-peasant-plan/
[165]https://thinkmarkets.wordpress.com/2009/07/29/tracking-obscure-quasi-public-govt-agencies/
[166]https://news.bbc.co.uk/2/hi/business/8160282.stm

It is impossible to say how big the off budget deficit is, since these entities are structured like a game of three card monte, to hide what is going on. It is hard to structure entities so that they are accountable and you can follow where the money goes, easy to structure entities so that they are unaccountable and money just quietly evaporates unseen.

However, the unthinkably huge amounts of Federal Reserve off budget activity suggests that the off budget deficit is many times greater than the on budget deficit – and the on budget deficit alone is barely sustainable.

The government can inflate its way out of debt

2009-08-06 13:46:14

The official, on the books, on budget US government debt is troublesomely large, and growing at an unprecedented rate, but it is not intolerably large, not so large as to be unpayable, not so large as to predict ruin. The off the books, off budget deficit is considerably larger, and no one knows how large it is or how fast it is growing, which situation may well foreshadow national insolvency.

Megan McCardle tells us You Can't Inflate Your Way Out of Debt[167], which is dead wrong: Look, for example at the Wiemar republic. Burdened by a gigantic debt burden, thanks to the Kaiser's unsuccessful attempt to plunder his way out of debt, the Wiemar republic promptly proceeded to create an even more extravagant and unsustainable debt, running up more debt than the Kaiser and reparations on such classic progressive programs as paying bums to not work. When they blew off their debt, they had gained six times the value of reparations by borrowing money they had not the will, the capability, nor the intention of ever repaying. They also gained the additional benefit of smashing the revolution prone middle class, which had been responsible for every revolution up to that time, if we count the Russian Bolshevik coup against the revolutionary middle class government as a coup, rather than revolution.

The Wiemar government made a gigantic political profit on this, gaining credit from the voters for free money, avoiding discredit for the huge debts incurred by the Kaiser, and blaming Jews and anglophones for the destruction of the middle class that the government successfully engineered. Win Win Win.

Of course, it did not work out so well in the long run, but as Keynes tells us, in the long run we are all dead. You cannot expect democratic politicians to think too far beyond the next election.

The essential trick to inflating away debt is to blindside creditors. The government only has to fool some of the people some of the time, which is after all what democratic politicians are best at. Just get as much debt as possible into long term government debt, say ten year debt at 30% interest, and then proceed to monetize the debt. Let inflation roar at two percent a day for a couple of years, and your problem is solved. Present inflation is about 0.01% per day if we believe the government statistics, and perhaps twice that if we believe shadowstats[168], so this a hundred fold increase in inflation for a couple of years

[167]https://business.theatlantic.com/2009/08/you_cant_inflate_your_way_out_of_debt.php
[168]https://www.shadowstats.com/

– it would not completely destroy the middle class. To successfully destroy the middle class, more drastic means would be required. Some of the crazies in Obama's government have thought out loud about more drastic means. If carrying out their program, blame giant corporations, or if that fails, there is always that old favorite, the Jews. After all, we are already blaming the Jews for the failure of Obama's program of being nice to our enemies. The crazies in the Obama government are proposing to blame the corporations, but should that rather tired shtick fail, they will probably fall back to old favorites.

The vast majority of defaults were black and hispanic

2009-08-07 08:11:59

Hat tip Steve Sailer who provides the breakdown of defaults.

The proximate cause of the international crisis is that the US the international reserve currency, lost much credibility. The proximate cause of the US losing credibility was massive defaults by blacks and Hispanics, and the proximate cause of the massive defaults by blacks and Hispanics was affirmative action lending to people whom I could tell at a glance from twenty paces were highly unlikely to repay their debts.

In the last days before the crash, I saw in California a steady parade of people buying expensive houses no money down whose own mothers must have been reluctant to lend them ten dollars. Lax though credit standards were, not one of them would have been able to borrow money had he been non Hispanic white.

Laderman and Reid of the Federal Reserve Bank of San Francisco have done the unthinkably politically incorrect, and though they do not directly reveal the proportion of defaults that were affirmative action, they tell us[169]:

> We also find that race has an independent effect on foreclosure even after controlling for borrower income and credit score. In particular, African American borrowers were 3.3 times as likely as white borrowers to be in foreclosure, whereas Latino and Asian borrowers were 2.5 and 1.6 times respectively more likely to be in foreclosure as white borrowers.

They also argue that CRA loans were just fine:

> a CRA lender significantly decreases the likelihood of foreclosure

They obtained this contradictory result by controlling for race - in other words, they are not saying CRA loans were unlikely to default, but that a CRA loan made to a non hispanic white is (unsurprisingly) unlikely to default - in other words, affirmative action loans have no harmful effect, indeed beneficial effect, to the extent that they were not in fact affirmative action loans.

They do not directly tell us what proportion of defaulters were black and Hispanic, but since the great majority of defaulters were subprime, and 77% of subprime borrowers were black and Hispanic, and blacks and Hispanics three times more likely to default than whites ...

---

[169]https://www.richmondfed.org/conferences_and_events/research/2008/pdf/lending_in_low_and_moderate_income_neighborhoods.pdf

Purple shirts:

2009-08-09 12:16:36

And so it begins: Purple shirts

In democracy, it is always a winning move to raise the ante, for example politicize car designs, or to politically determine who gets the job and who gets the promotion with the state enforcing political correctness in the workplace. Since democracy is all about building the biggest coalition, and splitting the other guys coalition, it always an advantage for political activists have more stuff, and more important stuff, politically determined.

And once what is at stake is large enough, it is always a winning move to become violent, and the only answer to violence by one faction is violence by the other, thus the end stage of democracy is exemplified by the Wiemar parties, where the major parties were the commies and the nazis, and all the other parties were necessarily remaking themselves into something very similar.

Hotair[170] thinks this will rebound against the Obamessiah, but history tells us otherwise. People love the strong horse, and despise the weak horse, and beating people up looks very much like strength if you can get away with it.

Chinese GDP to surpass US by about 2016 or so

2009-08-14 05:08:57

We are already seeing some people heading off to China and opportunity: "Shut Out at Home, Americans Seek Opportunity in China"[171]

According to the CIA[172], not always a reliable source, China's 2008 GDP is about 7800 000 000 000, US 2008 GDP is about 1429 000 000 000. Since China is growing about nine percent faster than the US ...

In many important respects it has already surpassed the US. Innovation in the US is very rapidly drying up, while we are seeing dramatic and important innovations coming out of China – for example improvements in the synthesis of liquid fuel from coal, the new CBHD (High density DVDs at low density prices), and critical advances in the most esoteric of the pure sciences, General Relativity. They are on the leading edge in heavy industry, consumer goodies, and basic pure research.

Although Mainland China is in part still a centralized command economy based on terror, pillage, and murder, in other important ways it is vastly more capitalist than the US. It absorbed capitalism from Hong Kong, which was a lot closer to the hard core capitalism of Manchester and the Industrial Revolution than the diluted and castrated capitalism of the US and Europe, therefore can expect rapid growth rates that catch up to Hong Kong and Singapore, thus massively surpass the US and Europe.

It is often said that America has rule of law and China does not, yet we have lost track of the difference between rule of law and rule of lawyers: Reflect on the numerous outrageous patent-the-wheel lawsuits and the destruction of the light plane industry when

---

[170]https://hotair.com/archives/2009/08/07/video-seiu-activists-try-to-set-obamacare-opponents-straight/
[171]https://www.nytimes.com/2009/08/11/business/economy/11expats.html
[172]https://www.cia.gov/library/publications/the-world-factbook/

lawyers discovered they could sue people who build planes for not building them as wisely and well as lawyers and courts supposedly would have. The car industry and the vaccine industry nearly went the same way, requiring federal interventions that suspended what we are now calling rule of law for some industries, but not others.

A big Chinese advantage is that their political elite is less arrogant and less out of contact with reality. It is willing to acknowledge that government interventions can fail, can have bad results. When government intervention fails cataclysmally in the US, then that branch of the government is immediately given more wealth, power, and prestige, that area of the economy promptly becomes more socialist. When government intervention fails in china, then that branch of the government eventually loses wealth, power, and prestige, that area of the economy becomes less socialist. Thus remaining socialism in China are those parts of socialism that are functioning well, while newly expanded socialism in the US, for example accounting, finance, and perhaps soon health care, is failing disastrously. The American governing elite is solidly immersed in a cloud of lies and denial, rationalizing away, or simply lying barefaced, about all their failures. The Enron case led to increased government intervention against truthful accounting, rather than diminished government intervention against truthful accounting, the disastrous losses from affirmative action lending led to an increased takeover of the finance industry, and we are likely to soon see the same in health care.

The Chinese elite still tends to the traditional chinese and communist view that the political elite are the genuinely productive ones, and the entrepeneurs are parasites, and if they were to act on that view, they would return China to the poverty and chaos it has long endured. Because of this continual threat, the entrepeneurial class in China is to a substantial extent overseas based and cyberspace based. Chinese companies are largely run through servers located in tax havens, but such non violent defenses could easily fall to a sufficiently determined attack. Meanwhile, however, the US government *is* engaged in a sufficiently determined attack on tax havens, having recently successfully pressured the Swiss to deny financial services to Americans, blissfully unaware of the increasing dependence of the American economy on entrepeneurial skills and knowledge mediated through such havens. Interpreting the golden goose as a parasite, as a challenge to their authority and a rejection of their superior wisdom, they prepare to slay the golden goose.

Denying Darwinism

2009-08-18 13:33:36

There is on the blogs a lot of debate as to when the idea of common descent and the tree of life originated - "genetic future"[173], as usual, gets it correct, "Panda's Thumb"[174] gets it correct, and "genetic inference"[175] and "evolving thoughts"[176] as always, get it politically correct.

---

[173]https://scienceblogs.com/geneticfuture/2009/08/lamarck_beat_darwin_to_the_tre.php
[174]https://pandasthumb.org/archives/2009/08/happy-265th-bir.html
[175]https://www.genetic-inference.co.uk/blog/?p=505
[176]https://scienceblogs.com/evolvingthoughts/2009/03/taxonomy_was_the_reason_for_da.php

From any political post of "genetic inference" and "evolving thoughts" you can deduce that they will lie about Darwin, and conversely from the fact that they are lying about Darwin, you can deduce their position on every question of political significance.

People attribute common descent to Darwin primarily because they hate Darwin and Darwinism, for Darwin and Darwinism is natural selection, a doctrine whose implications are disturbingly brutal, and when applied to humans, horrifyingly politically incorrect. So they pick up something else, almost at random – typically common descent and the tree of life– and call it Darwinism.

It is perfectly clear, and not an all controversial, that Lamarck and earlier thinkers proposed the tree of life – that animal species were related through common ancestors, and that the seeming gaps were the result of extinctions.

Here is an image of page 463 of Lamark's *Philosophie zoologique*, a table titled "Origins of the Various Animals". This table is used on page 458 in a discussion of common descent:

TABLE

SHOWING THE ORIGIN OF THE VARIOUS ANIMALS.

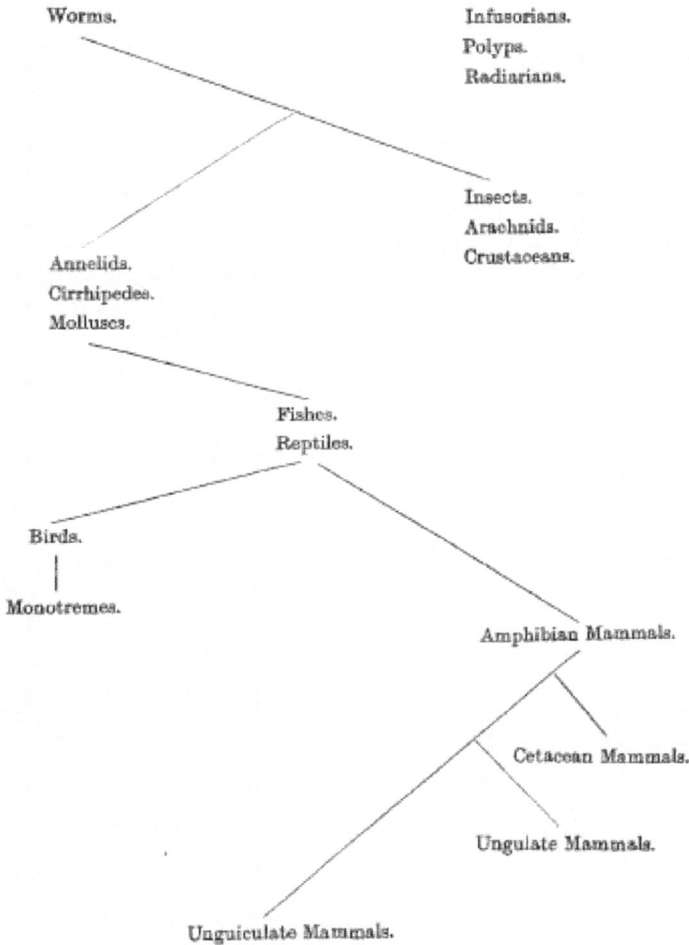

Worms.   Infusorians.
                                          Polyps.
                                          Radiarians.

                                          Insects.
                                          Arachnids.
Annelida.   Crustaceans.
Cirrhipedes.
Molluscs.

              Fishes.
              Reptiles.

   Birds.

   |
Monotremes.

                           Amphibian Mammals.

                              Cetacean Mammals.

                           Ungulate Mammals.

Unguiculate Mammals.

If he proposed multiple parallel origins, he would not have needed to explain the gaps. That he explained gaps as due to extinctions makes it clear his tree is intended as prehistory, as development over time from a single root, as well as a scheme of classification.

Darwin's contribution, as he makes perfectly clear, was natural selection. If you read Darwin, he does not treat common descent as a big new idea, but as something that is widely suspected, something that has long been in the air.

Darwin first starts talking of the Tree of Life in Chapter 11 of "the origin of species" - and clearly believes it to be an existing concept, widely accepted among his audience, and already seen by them.

> If the number of the species included within a genus, or the number of the genera within a family, be represented by a vertical line of varying thickness, ascending through the successive geological formations, in which the species are found, the line will sometimes falsely appear to begin at its lower end, not in a sharp point, but abruptly; it then gradually thickens upwards, often keeping of equal thickness for a space, and ultimately thins out in the upper beds, marking the decrease and final extinction of the species. This gradual increase in number of the species of a group is strictly conformable with the theory, for the species of the same genus, and the genera of the same family, can increase only slowly and progressively; the process of modification and the production of a number of allied forms necessarily being a slow and gradual process one species first giving rise to two or three varieties, these being slowly converted into species, which in their turn produce by equally slow steps other varieties and species, and so on, like the branching of a great tree from a single stem, till the group becomes large.

Which implies that people were drawing trees embodying both descent and classification before Darwin, and Darwin expected his audience to have seen those trees

Darwin's big new idea was natural selection, and all of the important and violently controversial ideas that follow from natural selection, such as sexual selection resulting in sex roles and sexually specific behavior, sociobiology resulting in an innate sense of property and intuitions about rights, races as the precursor of speciation, and so on and so forth. From genocide to rape, you can read all about it in "The Origin of Species" and "The Descent of Man" - not to mention property rights, which some are apt to put in the same league as genocide and rape.

If a idea about biology can get you beaten up and denied tenure, it is Darwinism. If it cannot, it is not. Common descent will not get you into trouble, therefore is not Darwinism, but speciation gets hazardous. If you stick to speciation in three spined sticklebacks you may be OK, proposing clinal speciation for wolves and coyotes will get you in deep trouble - the cline between wolves and coyotes was exterminated for being politically incorrect, and no one dares mention clinal speciation in the context of primates. Thus speciation, the origin of species, is Darwinism. You can tell by the application of baseball bats as a method of debate. Common descent is not Darwinism. You can tell by the absence of baseball bats as a method of debate.

[In the comments, Constantinople draws my attention to the evidence that it is Buffon, Lamark's teacher, that first proposed the tree of life as prehistorical, and not merely classificatory, and also argues that anyone who depicts the tree of life should be presumed to depicting a prehistoric lineage, not merely a classification scheme, unless he explicitly says otherwise, which would put priority to way back before Buffon. I however, am not so much interested in who had priority, but in present day madness and evil. There is nothing particularly evil about attributing priority to Darwin, but it is definitely mad, and tightly correlated with evil political beliefs. If it was possible to figure out who had priority for the tree of life, Darwin would have told us who had priority.]

Social decay

2009-08-20 09:25:50

Whatsoever the government sponsors, tends to turn bad. Since government funds are ill defended, grantsmanship based government funded memetic diseases will always outcompete truth based science, and similarly grantsmanship funded memetic diseases will always outcompete art based on beauty. Government funded art will rapidly become ugly and stupid. Government funded science will rapidly become untruthful and stupid, string theory as much as global warming theory.

China developed gunpowder, cannon, ocean going ships, the magnetic compass, paper, printing, and so on and so forth long before the west did, and then all these things went into decline. They were not government suppressed, rather they were government sponsored, which had very much the same effect as government suppression. The objective of things like the encyclopedia of all knowledge was to promote and preserve knowledge, though the actual effect was to suppress and forbid knowledge. Only what higher bureaucrats thought they knew got into the encyclopedia, and if you knew more than higher bureaucrat, obviously you were defying authority and promoting ignorance and misinformation – the mechanism was very similar to today's global warming consensus. Scientists that do not go along with the consensus are apt to lose their jobs and cannot be published through regular channels.

Academia is under strong selection to show cleverness, but weak selection to show contact with reality. However they are only under strong selection to show cleverness so long as the top ranks are filled with clever people so that you have to show cleverness to fit in. Global warming theory, white studies, and so forth require extreme stupidity to fit in, as illustrated by Rahmstorf's triangular filtering[177], just as modern art requires the complete lack of good taste or any artistic talent in order to fit in, and as a result the top ranks of academia are increasingly filled with people as dumb as posts, for example Henry Louis Gates – thus soon, to fit into the highest ranks of academia, you will need to be thick as a brick.

The practical consequence of government support, if government support is sufficiently substantial and vigorous, is that only those things that governments are capable of doing get done – and government cannot do much.

Moral progress

2009-08-20 11:26:46

Robert Hanson observes we are less inclined to kill, rape and plunder than in past centuries, and proposes some explanations for this:

---

[177]https://www.climateaudit.org/?p=6473

1. Virtue is a luxury good. We are less inclined to enslave people when we have invented the horse collar, and so can make a horse pull heavy loads instead of a man

2. Communications. We are inclined to ally with those close to us to protect ourselves against those distant from us – and now everyone is close to us.

3. Some of his contributors suggest genetics – we have killed off people who make trouble.

I suggest we are **not** more virtuous. Consider the crimes of the twentieth century. Rather, we have strong states that reserve criminal conduct for themselves. When those states weaken, we see private crime on a scale typical of earlier of history, when they are strong, we see enormous crimes by states.

The Amazing Brilliance of Sarah Palin

2009-08-21 04:45:14

Palin described "America's Affordable Health Choices Act" as death panels[178]. The Cathedral, (meaning the MSM, the politicians, the professoriat, senior public servants, and assorted people employed in the upper reaches of the ever more numerous quasi governmental organizations) react with apocalyptic outrage – thereby drawing the public's attention to various parts of the act that are, indeed, death panels. Sarah Palin smiles sweetly and lets them hammer themselves to pulp. After uncontrollably inflicting massive damage on themselves, they delete most disturbing parts of the act – which retreat looks to the public like an admission that Obama indeed intended to murder their poor old Grandma and Sarah Palin's cute little baby.

There are a lot of people who argue that Sarah Palin is a prole, therefore dumb as a post. Maybe she just got lucky this time?

Sarah Palin is a politician. Everything a politician does is theater, and must be analyzed as theater. Nothing a politician does is real. Sarah Palin is no more a prole than George Bush was a cowboy. That a politician sounds like a prole and walks like a prole is not evidence she is a prole, it is evidence that republicans need the prole vote. We must analyze her conduct as a show.

The people who argue that Sarah Palin is a prole, therefore stupid, also argue she is a prole, therefore stupid, nasty, hateful, vile disgusting and repugnant – which is why prolishness is a vote winner: her enemies will expose the fact that they hate a very large proportion of the voters.

The Cathedral hate, loath, and despise the proles. The thought of a prole in the Whitehouse enrages them to madness. If you think the Muslims went nuts when some people posted mildly disrespectful depictions of prophet Mohamed, you have seen nothing yet. If republicans nominate her, their enemies will go mad in public.

OK, if a politician wins a battle and devastates her enemies, that is evidence she is smart. But perhaps she got lucky. So secondly, let us examine her note[179] that had this devastating effect.

1. It looks casual. Just as Sarah Palin appears completely prole, the note appears that she

---

[178]https://www.facebook.com/note.php?note_id=113851103434&ref=mf
[179]https://www.facebook.com/note.php?note_id=113851103434&ref=mf

is just chatting to her friends (in public) that big bad Obama might murder poor sweet members of her family.

2. It is sweet and feminine. Sarah Palin appears a sweet feminine old fashioned woman who cares very much about her children. And yet the Cathedral is going apocalyptic! Our protective impulses towards hot women and and cute children automatically fires up. I slap on my shining armor and mount my high horse: We are going to protect poor sweet Sarah Palin and her cute little baby against the big bad Cathedral!

Sheer genius!

"Sex and Culture"
2009-08-22 16:06:38

"Sex and Culture" observes reality - and then attempts to put a politically correct spin on it.

The observation contained in "Sex and Culture" (not the spin) is that civilizations were built by the sons of women who were severely constrained to ensure that they only had sex with one man, their husband, and that husband, who might have many mistresses, generally had only one wife.

An alternative theory explaining the same phenomenon is that civilization is built by men for their sons - but only if they are confident in the paternity of their sons and not otherwise.

Thus once women are sexually liberated, you can never have a movement capable of preserving civilization or building for the future. Collapse ensues.

Possibly this problem might be remedied by linking marriage laws to mandatory paternity check. Babies that are alleged to be the responsibility of some male, either explicitly, or implicitly in that the woman declares herself to be married, are tested for paternity at birth, and if paternity is incorrect, or the test is refused by the woman, or the woman declares herself unmarried rather than take the test, the marriage is void, is considered never to have existed, and all assets of the marriage are assets of the husband, and the husband has no obligations, and is considered never to have had obligations.

We might *then* find ourselves in a society where men cared to build and preserve civilization.

The error of conservatism
2009-08-23 11:47:34

Conservatives conserve. There is not enough left of western civilization to be worth conserving, nor enough to be capable of withstanding the next storm.

Most beta guys in their forties or so are comfortably married. Most beta guys in their twenties or so are not, and are not going to be, because their potential wives have banged fifty or so alphas, rendering themselves psychologically worthless as wife material.

Further, if all betas learn game, as Roissy[180] did, then even assuming that game works, and that it is something that can truly be learned, which is not true for everyone, probably

---

[180]https://roissy.wordpress.com/

not true for most, then it would still only be a temporary solution – the standard of what is required to be an alpha would rise, and we would be back to square one, due to the incorrigible female propensity to hypergamy.

Just as our natural appetite for food, evolved for a world where food was hard to get and tough to eat, is maladaptive in a world where food is abundant and easy to eat, the female sexual impulse, evolved in a world of patriarchy and strong social restraint on female sexuality, is maladaptive in a world of equal position within status hierarchies and no external sexual restraint.

All women want to marry up. In a society where women are guaranteed equal representation in status hierarchies by affirmative action, and where they are entirely free to follow their unrestrained sexual impulses without social sanction, disaster naturally ensues, since they will inevitably find themselves consciously or unconsciously attempting that which cannot be done, much as both men and woman are apt to load up with fat against a highly improbable famine.

There is a boy for every girl, but there is not a higher status boy for every girl who has spent her most fertile years climbing the career ladder. Women need to make an effort towards settling and chastity in the same way as they make an effort not to eat numerous chocolate cakes.

Of course, if welfarism collapses, Darwinian evolution will remedy this eventually – the future will be composed of the descendants of those who *do* form families - virtuous women and protective men.

In a state of nature, males form broad male to male alliances for defense, which alliance then guarantees a decent amount of pussy and children for each male in the alliance, asserting control over women, punishing adulteresses, enforcing chastity on women subject to the alliance's authority, enforcing roughly equal sharing of pussy controlled by the alliance (monogamy, or something not far from it) and so on and so forth, which is the glue holding the alliance together, and also the framework in which family formation becomes easy and normal, where every male who works hard, plays by the rules, is reasonably healthy and competent, and is loyal to the people and principles of the alliance, winds up forming a family.

Such a male dominated, patriarchal, paternalistic family forming alliance is the muscle and skeleton of every strong dynamic culture, society, civilization, and state – unless perhaps the future will feature a society where new units are decanted rather than born.

The ghost of that expired alliance is the big daddy in the sky that conservatives hope will save them.

The glue having been lost, the state and the society are a tattered paper tiger, which will dissolve when it rains. A culture that fails to pay its good men in the ultimate Darwinian coin will find that when things go bad, few good men will fight for it - one of the big advantages that Islamists have over us.

It is possible that measures short of those taken by Muslims might work – certainly measures considerably short of those taken by Muslims worked in the 1950s, but whatever will or can be done, involves building a new society, after the collapse of our present society, not conserving an old one.

Prospects of hyperinflation

2009-08-24 18:31:55

Arnold Kling thinks that "hyperinflation would be political suicide"[181] and that therefore that the US government will sooner or later do the extraordinary and drastic things necessary to avoid it.

Even if it was political suicide, this is like arguing that someone will lose weight because his morbid obesity is about to kill him– but it is not political suicide. Incumbents that engage in hyperinflation usually gain political benefit in the short run, and the short run is all they care about. The Weimar government was not punished at the polls.

Hyperinflation, by destroying the private economy, elevates the relative status of the members of the Cathedral, who get first lick at the freshly printed money, resulting in power, prestige, and popularity. When they blame others for their crimes, the masses eagerly grant them power to punish these enemies.

The Wiemar government blamed the foreigners, speculators, and so forth for hyperinflation, and it worked. The masses are stupid.

Does Arnold Kling think that Americans are smarter? Recall Nixon's price controls.

Murderer of Mary Jo Kopechne dies

2009-08-26 17:17:24

After influencing and writing a vast amount of legislation, all of it as evil and repugnant as himself, Edward Kennedy died forty years after disposing of an inconvenient mistress.

By accident or design, Kennedy's car wound up upside down in the water, with Kennedy not in it, and his girlfriend in it. It retained an air bubble for a substantial period, which means that his girlfriend was alive for a substantial period. Kennedy then proceeded to construct an alibi, to conceal what had happened. His girlfriend may still have been alive at the time he was creating an alibi. Whether or not it was an accident that his car was in the water with his mistress inside and him not inside, it was no accident that she remained inside.

The cause of the crisis 4

2009-08-27 11:15:13

I have issued a bunch of posts, each titled the "the cause of the crisis", and each giving a different cause - but each of these causes was itself caused by, or caused, all of the other causes.

This post addresses ratings for debt.

Much analysis of the crisis has been in terms of banks gaming the system.[182] But if banks were gaming the system, they were gaming it by ratings inflation - and regulators are wholly responsible for ratings.

---

[181]https://econlog.econlib.org/archives/2009/08/resolving_us_in.html
[182]https://www.voxeu.org/index.php?q=node/3020

In the days before banking became a branch of the state, U.S. banks voluntarily maintained capital-asset ratios in the range of 10 to 20 percent, so that a rainy day when lots of customers wanted to withdraw at the same time would not trigger a crisis

With FDIC insurance protecting all deposits, customers don't worry about bank safety - in fact it is illegal to leak safety information about banks. So banks have little choice but to steer as close to the wind as the regulators will allow– maintain the lowest capital ratio, and invest in the riskiest securities. Any bank that follows a different policy will lose market share.

So what did the regulators require? Under Basel, they required less than half the capital for AAA securities as they required for individual mortgages, resulting a massive world wide demand by banks for AAA rated securities, a demand entirely created by regulators, a demand for securities that were *rated* as secure, rather than a demand for securities that actually were secure.

So all the financiers proceeded to game the system by rating inflation, and this gaming is what people are referring to when they argue that there was "deregulation" – the problem being not that regulations were relaxed or removed, but that stern and strict regulations created the incentive to weasel around them, rendering them ineffectual and counterproductive.

So it did not matter to banks whether ratings were true, merely that the ratings agency had been blessed by the regulators. In 1975, the SEC made had made rating into a branch of the government by mandating that companies obtain a rating from Moody's, S&P, or Fitch. Since then the power and wealth of the rating agencies comes entirely from government favor, not from anyone believing that their ratings have anything to do with reality. Thus any connections between ratings and reality, or lack thereof, depends entirely on the regulators, and has since 1975.

The regulators had little incentive to demand connection to reality, and considerable incentive to the contrary. The biggest beneficiaries of flagrantly fraudulent ratings were Fannie and Freddie – quasi governmental organizations whose nominally private management is directly appointed and supervised by congress. Genuinely private beneficiaries of fraudulent ratings, notably Washington Mutual, took extraordinary measures to please the regulators, by hurling vast amounts of mortgage money at targeted voting blocks, thereby making their securities even more worthless, but ensuring that ratings would not reflect this fact.

In 2005 November, large numbers of people in the business, AIG among them, realized that these mortgage securities were extremely insecure, and in a great many cases, not worth very much. So from late 2005 to mid 2007, we had a massive, well known, and extremely serious disconnect between ratings and reality.

This was the "irrational" behavior of the markets during that period. Markets were "irrationally" behaving as if official security ratings were total lies.

The regulators could have asked the ratings agencies to issue more credible ratings. They failed to do so, indicating that the regulators approved the fraudulent ratings, and perhaps insisted on them, that this was not "deregulation", was not the regulated weaseling around the regulations, but regulation, the regulators trying to get the market to swallow worthless mortgage backed securities.

Before 2005 November it might well have been, and probably was, the free market evasively weaseling around regulations by inflating ratings with a nod and a wink, but between 2005 November and mid 2007 it was regulators trying to force feed worthless affirmative action mortgages down the throats of a marketplace that very plainly did not want them.

This is what links this cause of the crisis to causes that are each just as much the cause – off budget government deficits and affirmative action. The politicians and regulators wanted handouts to voter blocks, it wanted such handouts off the budget, and to conceal the expenditure from the voters and from themselves, wanted mortgage securities based on loans to deadbeats of politically correct racial voting blocks to be rated as secure.

Government regulation directly caused banks to buy AAA rated securities, and the government regulators are wholly responsible for what gets AAA rated. The only question is to what extent fraudulent AAA ratings were due to improper influence by the regulated over the regulators, with the regulators allowing the regulated to get away with evading the intent of regulations, and to what extent due to politicians trying to buy votes with off budget money. Before 2005 November, had to tell which of these mattered more. From 2005 November to mid 2007, it was @#$%^&* obvious which of these mattered more. That security ratings failed to reflect reality after 2005 November shows that regulators and their political masters did not want them to reflect reality.

Obama care in twenty words.

2009-08-30 08:25:01

Obamacare is a proposal to redistribute health care from those who voted against Obama, to those who voted for Obama.

"There is no axis of evil"

2009-08-30 16:16:12

UAE seizes ship full of North Korean weapons bound for Iran.

These weapons would have been used to kill Americans in Iraq. One might wonder what Americans are doing in Iraq, but perhaps one should wonder rather more why the UAE is snatching these weapons and not the Unites States Marines.

Hat tip Hot Air[183]

I often complain there are no moderate Muslims. That is not true. His Highness Sheikh Mohammed Bin Rashid Al Maktoum, ruler of Dubai, the UAE King that snatched those weapons, is a moderate Muslim. The US government however tends to sponsor raging anti Semites and sponsors of terrorism like the Saudi rulers.

Who funds terrorism?

We do, through such intermediaries as the Saudis.

---

[183]https://hotair.com/greenroom/archives/2009/08/28/uae-seizes-ship-bound-for-irancarrying-north-korean-weapons/

US turning french

2009-09-05 13:20:16

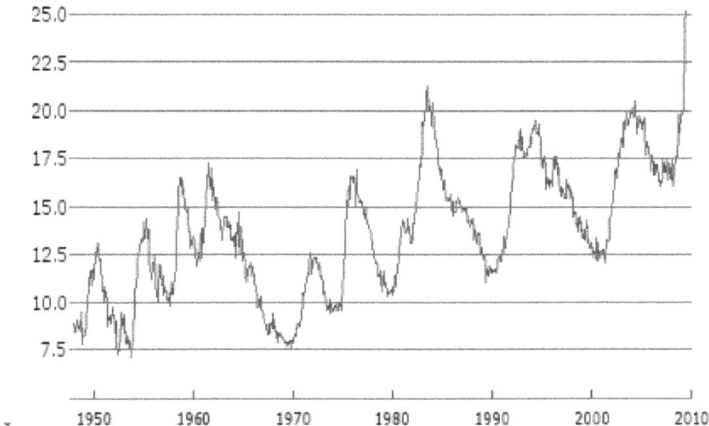

It is getting steadily harder and harder for someone to find a new job - and having found a new job, harder and harder to afford a house - presumably because of the very great and rapidly increasing regulatory burden on building houses and hiring people.

This renders employees powerless before their employers, which tends to result in class war and social violence as in France, and tends to result in greater regulator burdens.

American debt

2009-09-06 03:46:57

Total federal debt twelve trillion[184]

That is not too alarming in itself. It is a bit less than GDP, and for most countries, trouble ensue when debt is around twice GDP. The liberty papers[185] are not too worried.

Total American indebtedness (public and "private") is sixty trillion, which is much larger than federal debt, and has been rising very rapidly. The primary cause of this rise has been implicit and explicit governmental and quasi governmental guarantees – FHA guarantees, debt of too-big-to-fail corporations, guarantees by too-big-to-fail corporations, state debt, for example California, and so on and so forth.

Some substantial part of this sixty trillion is secured by real assets such as houses and the income stream of hard working people, and some substantial part is not.

Thus the excess "private" debt is not private. The normal level of public and "private" debt is about twice GDP, say twenty six trillion, so we are about thirty trillion or so in the hole and getting deeper fast – well past the danger level of twice GDP.

[184] https://www.treasurydirect.gov/NP/BPDLogin?application=np
[185] https://www.thelibertypapers.org/2009/09/03/open-thread-government-debt/

Losing in Afghanistan

2009-09-07 10:07:37

Michael Yon, who should know better than anyone, reports we are losing in Afghanistan.[186]

He suggests the solution is more troops. I don't think so. After all, we originally won in Afghanistan with near zero troops.

Democracy has been a disaster, both in Afghanistan and in Iraq. The masses just do not like us much, and tend to elect people that do not like us much – or like freedom, or like democracy, or like capitalism. And especially, they do not like religious freedom.

The winner in a guerrilla war is the side that most brutally terrorizes the population. Our troops lack the stomach for what it takes to win a guerrilla war, so more troops will not help. We already have enough troops to win any conventional battle, and there is not much else to do, other than what our troops are reluctant to do. It also helps to know the locals, know the language and know the culture – so winning in a guerrilla war means arming the local killers that are on your side, and killing the local killers that are against your side. And that, of course, means arming the Northern alliance and terrorizing the Pashtuns.

Obama's public private partnership

2009-09-08 05:47:40

Before Obama became president, his big success was handing truckloads of government money to big property developer friends of Obama[187] so that those big property developer friends could benevolently provide housing to the poor[188].

---

[186]https://www.michaelyon-online.com/new-afghan-war-frontline-correspondent-says-fight-has-morphed-%E2%80%93-but-we-still-can-t-afford-to-lose.htm

[187]https://directorblue.blogspot.com/2009/08/thirty-degrees-below-zero.html

[188]https://michellemalkin.com/2009/08/17/do-you-trust-obamas-slum-lords/

Obama told us:

> "That's an example of a smart policy. The developers were thinking in market terms and operating under the rules of the marketplace; but at the same time, we had government supporting and subsidizing those efforts."

Of course, in practice, government support for developers meant that developers had an incentive to be active in politics, and be good at political activism, but no incentive to be active in preventing the roof from leaking, or the roof from falling in[189]: Government handout, private profit, not "the rules of the marketplace"

And now the people who brought you homes for the poor with the roof falling in are fixing the American financial system with the same methods.

Audit the Federal Reserve

2009-09-09 07:20:36

The most libertarian member of Congress, Ron Paul, has introduced a bill to audit the Federal Reserve. The Federal Reserve, you may recall, has been spending trillions off bud-

---

[189]https://directorblue.blogspot.com/2008/07/photo-gallery-results-of-obamas.html

get, and no one knows how much, or for what, who the beneficiaries are, or what commitments the Federal Reserve has made to foreign governments.

The Federal Reserve is now holding securities that represent a gigantic number of mortgages. Some large proportion of these mortgages are on houses for which no payments are being made, yet no foreclosures or evictions are happening. Who, I wonder, is living in these houses. Are the goons of get-out-the-vote organizations such as Acorn getting a disproportionate share of the gravy? It is a huge off the books housing subsidy. Who is getting it? What voting blocks do the recipients belong to? What congressional districts are they located in?

Curious minds want to know: Library of Economics and Liberty[190], "Audit the Federal Reserve[191]",
Bovard[192]

No member of congress wants to be seen to oppose the audit – but such an audit is extremely unlikely, for no member of congress, with the possible exception of Ron Paul, wants the public to know what the Fed has been up to – still less do they want America's creditors to know what the Fed has been up to. If audited, the biggest financial panic the world has ever seen might well ensue.

Many of the people supporting an audit of the fed are the usual commie crazies, who claim that the Federal Reserve banks are actually private. Ron Paul of course, correctly says the exact opposite to the crazies. He says that the Fed is a branch of the federal government and has been from the day it was formed.

The crazies claim the Fed is private, and imply is is controlled by the vast Jewish conspiracy, though in reality the formation of the Fed was example of the usual Jewish tendency to self destructively support their enemies. Before the formation of the Fed, US banking was indeed largely Jewish, and largely private. The mostly Jewish bankers demanded a federal takeover, and of course, with government running things, the government kicked out the Jews and left them sitting bare assed in the snow, as happens whenever the government starts taking a controlling hand in industry. Jewish conspiracy theory is false because Jews are wildly incompetent at collective action. They are always major participants in any such conspiracy, but always get mercilessly screwed by their fellow conspirators, and often enough get an icepick through the head as Trotsky did. The banking conspiracy worked out very badly for the Jewish participants, and the communist conspiracy worked out considerably worse for the Jewish Bolsheviks, and similarly for more conspiracies than you can shake a stick at. As Milton Friedman complained, you would think Jews would be smarter than that by now. Even Arabs are more successful at conspiring than Jews.

---

[190]https://econlog.econlib.org/archives/2009/09/boo_alan_blinde.html
[191]https://www.youtube.com/watch?v=4swEdr2EJgk
[192]https://jimbovard.com/blog/2009/05/04/audit-the-fed-surging-110-co-sponsors/

Losing in Afghanistan 2

2009-09-09 07:36:16

When the US began its attack on the Taliban in Afghanistan, I said that destroying our enemies anywhere in the world would be easy, but building states would be hard, would most likely fail, for no one understands how a state is built, and the trend of the times is for states to fail.

And today, we again see state building failing.

In an earlier post "terror works[193]" I said of our Afghan policy:

> Forming a government in Afghanistan looked remarkably like selling our allies into the hands of our enemies, like Chamberlain selling Czechoslovakia to Hitler. The people who fought for us are outvoted and disarmed, which is why things are now going bad in Afghanistan. It is as if the Czechs had fought and won, and *then* Chamberlain sold them to Hitler.

Michael Yon is giving us the grunt's eye view of Afghanistan[194]:

> we are fighting the people in general, and not some small group of Taliban ... We generate the electricity and the Taliban collects money for wattage.

The error of Nazism

2009-09-11 06:26:32

The Nazis are hated for what they were right about (Darwinism), not for what they were wrong about. The error of the Nazis is the error of Mencius Moldbug[195]: Hobbesianism. The error of Hobbes is to assume that people can only cooperate by subjugation to a common leader, which implies any relationship betweens states, nations, peoples and races, is necessarily one of war, near war, and predatory maneuver preparatory to war, a war of each against all.

Thus people and groups that subscribe to Hobbesianism find themselves at war against all, because they expect to find themselves at war against all – but find to their shock and surprise that their non Hobbesian enemies are cooperating just fine to deal with the common enemy and common threat. Thus people and groups that subscribe to Hobbesianism get defeated, and frequently enslaved or wiped out. All those who believe in something morally better than Hobbesianism, however hypocritically or deludedly, gang up on them.

While Hobbes is disastrously wrong, Darwin and Darwinism is correct. As Darwin rightly pointly out, some races are better adapted than other to a life of artifacts, agriculture, clothing, and fire, and others better adapted to running naked through the jungle. Some races are better adapted to an environment largely dominated by humans, and other races better adapted to an environment largely dominated by elephants and lions.

---

[193]https://blog.reaction.la/war/terror-works.html
[194]https://www.michaelyon-online.com/eight-years-after-911.htm
[195]https://unqualified-reservations.blogspot.com/2009/09/gentle-introduction-to-unqualified.html

Those races better adapted to the jungle are genetically predisposed to be less intelligent when dealing with the problems of civilized life, though they may be better at reading footprints in the dust, running swiftly, and smelling the scent of game. They are also genetically predisposed to predation, to rape and robbery, as is apparent when we observe both the American ghetto, and the way Africa is governed.

The races of Africa are more diverse than the races of the rest of the world, thus any generalization is not only untrue of some individual Africans, but also untrue of some African races.

those who sold the ancestors of today's African Americans were probably just as advanced as the purchasers, individually and as a racial group, but for most African races, that is not the way to bet.

And since it is not the way to bet, it follows that the way to bet is, as Darwin tells us:

> At some future period, not very distant as measured by centuries, the civilised races of man will almost certainly exterminate, and replace, the savage races throughout the world. At the same time the anthropomorphous apes, as Professor Schaaffhausen has remarked, will no doubt be exterminated. The break between man and his nearest allies will then be wider, for it will intervene between man in a more civilised state, as we may hope, even than the Caucasian, and some ape as low as a baboon, instead of as now between the negro or Australian and the gorilla.

And superior races, to avoid the annihilation that is apt to follow from Hobbesianism, need to be *morally* superior, as the Nazis were not:

> Nor is the difference slight in moral disposition between a barbarian, such as the man described by the old navigator Byron, who dashed his child on the rocks for dropping a basket of sea-urchins, and a Howard or Clarkson; and in intellect, between a savage who uses hardly any abstract terms, and a Newton or Shakespeare. Differences of this kind between the highest men of the highest races and the lowest savages, are connected by the finest gradations. Therefore it is possible that they might pass and be developed into each other.

There is no Republican party
2009-09-13 17:03:52

If the Republican party existed, it would be going after Van Jones' scalp and the Obama health plan, rather than Glen Beck and Sarah Palin going after them. Glen Beck is not a party member. Sarah Palin holds no party office and is hated by the Republican party leadership with a hatred that verges on madness. The leadership of the Republican party, like the pretended movement in support of Obama's health plan, is itself merely astroturf manufactured in Washington.

The Obama grass roots is astroturf[196]. Acorn is a branch of the state. Acorn has offices and employees and is funded by highly regulated corporations reliant on regulatory

---

[196]https://www.zombietime.com/zomblog/?p=859

favor and by direct government funding that is theoretically intended to house the poor. When I saw the video of Acorn[197] offices shot by "Hannah Giles", the undercover Christian activist pretending to be a prostitute and a conservative activist pretending to be a pimp interested in obtaining a government housing loan to set up a brothel full of under age illegal immigrants, I was struck by the similarity of the office atmosphere to the atmosphere of the government employment office and the government immigration and naturalization service – an the air of permanence, hierarchy and stable employment, quite different from the extemporization of a real political movement based on activism.

There is a Washington party, and an anti Washington coalition, and the Republican party is a minor constituent of the Washington party - and increasingly a minor constituent whose usefulness to Washington may well have ended, while the conservative movement is the major part of the anti Washington coalition.

The constitutional function of the Republican party is to be the legal channel by which non Cathedral influences are permitted enough participation in government to slow down progress. Increasingly, the Cathedral views that participation as an unbearable desecration, and in the 1988 election, did not permit a repetition of that desecration.

The Cathedral was humiliated and enraged, partly by the Bush tax cuts, and partly by his cowboy hat and fake cowboy dialect. And so, to prevent a repetition of this outrage and desecration, McCain was nominated Republican presidential candidate. McCain was foisted on the party by the party leadership, in part by gaming party rules, in part by stretching party rules beyond recognition, and in part by flat out breaking party rules. Foisting McCain on the party in clear violation of the will and rules of the party has caused something very much like a divorce between conservatives and the Washington establishment of which the party leadership is part.

If the desecration is once again permitted in future, the Republican party will survive, as a political arena rather than a party and cohesive entity. If from time to time movements get some seats in Washington, even if they are not quite qualified as members of the Cathedral, the party will continue. If the desecration is ended, and it looks to me that at the moment the Cathedral is just not in the mood for any more desecration, then soon no one will remember the Republican party, except perhaps as the bad guys who caused the great depression, fought for slavery in the civil war, and sabotaged communism causing the minor Ukraine crop failure, though a shadow called the Republican party will continue to formally participate in Washington rituals.

Losing in Afghanistan 3

2009-09-14 19:48:56

Aid Watch says:

> every sensible economist, political scientist, development worker, and journalist that I know thinks our current course in Afghanistan can have only one outcome disaster.

---

[197] https://www.youtube.com/watch?v=9UOL9Jh61S8

Michael Yon tells us[198] we are at war with pretty much the entire Pashtun population. Global Guerrillas tells us[199]

> you can't change a society through changes in governance or targeted force in any time period of relevance, and if you do try, you will spend yourself into the ground and generate widespread opposition.

The current program is to make Pashtuns into progressive democratic liberals in Washington's own image. This will fail, and should fail. Pashtuns need to be defeated, not morally uplifted.

Darwinian and divine morality

2009-09-15 05:12:17

Morality derived from human nature (and thus from Darwin's sociobiology) differs from divine law as expressed in the New Testament in significant ways. It is Aristotlean and Randian morality, is fundamentally selfish. Aristotle and Rand tells us to cultivate our *own* excellence. Darwin tells us we commit ourselves to conduct that will enable us to get along with others because humans are a social and political animal, we need to cooperate with others to achieve our goals.

Thus one should return good for good and *evil for evil*. Vengeance is not the Lord's. He will not repay. One should do good for one's kin, and forgive them their sins, and good for one's friends, but not be nearly so forgiving of their sins. All men are *not* brothers. One should not harm other people without compelling and urgent reason, but the standard of what constitutes compelling and urgent reason is considerably greater for neighbors than it is for distant strangers. All men are *not* Hebrews.

It is a considerably more manly and muscular morality than that of Christianity. Transnational progressivism is Christian morality, Americans putting themselves on the cross for Muslims as Christ did, which is why we are losing in Afghanistan. Darwinian morality is classic Greek morality, Xenophon explaining that he had urgent need to slaughter, rape, loot and burn his way across Asia because the incorrigible bad conduct of the savages around him gave him no real alternative.

Northwest passage not open for cargo traffic

2009-09-17 08:58:47

The situation has not changed, and is not going to change, for global sea ice remains the same as ever it was[200]. But since the world is supposedly warming, we need regular announcements that the northwest passage is opening.

---

[198] https://www.michaelyon-online.com/new-afghan-war-frontline-correspondent-says-fight-has-morphed-%E2%80%93-but-we-still-can-t-afford-to-lose.htm
[199] https://globalguerrillas.typepad.com/globalguerrillas/2009/09/errata-mid-september-2009.html
[200] https://arctic.atmos.uiuc.edu/cryosphere/IMAGES/global.daily.ice.area.withtrend.jpg

Eureferendum[201] provides a nice fisking of the latest report of the Northwest Passage opening

Over the last hundred years or so, the Northwest passage has been briefly open from time to time, for sailors willing to take their chances. Sometimes they get through, if the wind blows the ice in the right direction. Sometimes they do not. This makes it worthless for commercial cargo traffic, since if the weather goes bad, you have to turn around, and face a risk of getting stuck in the ice until next summer. So you cannot transport goods through the Northwest passage on predictable schedule, and for predictable costs. You can take a tourist trip through – provided your passengers agree not to demand a refund if the ship has to turn around, and provided you call in the icebreakers at the first sign of getting stuck.

Aiming to lose in Afghanistan

2009-09-22 03:14:56

Obama tells us

> I'm not interested in just being in Afghanistan for the sake of…sending a message that America is here for the duration.

Thereby announcing to our enemies America is *not* there for the duration.

If you aim to win, you aim to intimidate your enemies, so you always *say* you are going to fight to the bitter end and turn the place in even more of a barren wasteland than it is already. If you announce in advance that you are going to bug out should things get tough, things are guaranteed to get tough.

Obama is smart enough to know this, so I conclude that for political reasons, he aims to lose in Afghanistan, and aims to justify the defeat by a disturbingly large level of American casualties.

A lot of blogs call[202] for[203] a surge, a bunch of blogs[204] are outraged[205] Obama is not retreating already but **the great wrong is staying**[206] **there**[207] **without intent to win**[208].

The improbable economic growth of Argentina.

2009-09-23 06:54:54

Over the last hundred years or so, Argentina as swung violently, and with increasing frequency, between policies of on the one hand constitutionalism, rule of law, and the free

---

[201]https://eureferendum.blogspot.com/2009/09/turd-eaters.html

[202]https://www.weaselzippers.net/blog/2009/09/gen-stanley-mcchrystal-top-usnato-commander-in-afghanistan-send-more-troops-or-afghanistan-will-like.html

[203]https://www.blackfive.net/main/2009/09/afghanitan-it-is-fish-or-cut-bait-time.html

[204]https://www.outsidethebeltway.com/archives/more_troops_in_afghanistan/

[205]https://prairieweather.typepad.com/big_blue_stem/2009/09/here-comes-that-surge-word-again.html

[206]https://belowthebeltway.com/2009/09/21/mcchrystal-more-troops-in-afghanistan-or-well-lose-the-war/

[207]https://blogs.dailymail.com/donsurber/2009/09/21/10100/

[208]https://www.floppingaces.net/2009/09/21/to-win-or-lose-in-afghanistan-obamas-moment-of-truth/

market, and on the other hand populism, bureaucratic decree, and national socialism. It has also swung violently between being one of the wealthiest countries in the world, and being a typical third world poverty stricken hellhole.

After the last crisis, it swung violently towards national socialism, populism, and bureaucratic decree – and yet is reportedly experiencing tremendous economic growth, greatly reduced poverty, vastly improved equality, social justice, public health, great medical care, and so on and so forth. And everyone is reportedly happy and loves the government for its wise, good, and successful policies.

Reported real growth in GDP is 8%pa. Reported inflation was 3.6%pa. Actual inflation was 21.6%pa,[209] which would mean real growth was something like 8%+3.6%-21.6%, which is negative ten percent per annum, a massive economic shrinkage, at which rate they will be back to third word hell hole mighty fast.

Now that we are hearing less of the wonderful health care of Cuba, we will probably be hearing more of the wonderful economic growth of Argentina.

President McCain would have been worse.

2009-09-24 04:02:28

Doctor Zero argues that a President McCain would have been better[210] for various reasons, among them:

> none of them would be a Truther, a supporter of cop killer Mumia Abu Jamal, or a communist... let alone all three. His Supreme Court nominations would not have to defend their racial theories of judicial supremacy at their confirmation hearings.

And that is precisely why McCain would have been worse: He would have implemented the policies of financial ruin, national socialism, economic destruction, defeat and humiliation, from the "center", and these policies would have been associated with Sarah Palin instead of Bill Ayers and Reverend Wright.

The brilliance of Sarah Palin's "common sense conservatism"

2009-09-24 08:33:55

When the nation is in trouble, "common sense conservativism" sure sounds mighty attractive, even if you do not know, or much care, what precisely it means. Sarah Palin is a politician who has her finger right on the pulse of the ordinary American.

If you are a "common sense conservative" then that implies that other conservatives, such as perhaps "compassionate conservatives", are naive utopians who brought disaster on the nation, which makes them very like the "hope and changies" of the nutty left.

And Sarah Palin, after explaining she is "common sense conservative" then proceeds to stick it to the Bush/Obama regime for pissing away trillions of dollars, nearly a year's

---

[209]https://www.clarin.com/diario/2009/05/14/elpais/p-01917894.htm
[210]https://hotair.com/archives/2009/09/23/defending-the-honor-of-president-mccain/

income for every American:Sarah Palin, Hong Kong, CLSA Asia Pacific Markets Conference, Sept.23, 2009

> We got into this mess because of government interference in the first place. The mortgage crisis that led to the collapse of the financial market, it was rooted in a good-natured, but wrongheaded, desire to increase home ownership among those who couldn't yet afford to own a home. In so many cases, politicians on the right and the left, they wanted to take credit for an increase in home ownership among those with lower incomes. But the rules of the marketplace are not adaptable to the mere whims of politicians.

"Good natured but wrong headed" Can you say "compassionate conservative" and "hope and change"?

Observe the reaction: The speech was supposedly boring. It was also supposedly so outrageous that people walked out in disgust. Furthermore, she supposedly did not say anything. She said nothing, *nothing, **nothing, NOTHING*** – a reaction that sounds like people sticking their fingers in their ears and screaming "I can't hear you", a sure sign that a politician has struck gold, for it is clear that she said something, and that that something was very far from boring.

I consult the ghost of Xenophon on Afghanistan

2009-09-29 08:01:52

Blog:

> "Ah, Xenophon, I am glad you could spend some time with us."

Xenophon:

> "I was not doing anything."

Blog:

> "We have a bit of a problem in Afghanistan. Despite overwhelming military superiority, we are losing."

Xenophon:

> "Afghanistan?"

Blog:

> "It is a mountainous land east of your journey through Asia – the people there somewhat resemble the Kurds."

Xenophon:

> "Ouch! Kurds! Tough fighters, never give up. They never accept that they are beaten. Lots of little ambushes, right? Like that?"

Blog:

"Right. Exactly like that."

Xenophon:

"I regret that I had to kill so many brave men. Station your most valiant men, your best equipped men, and your most able generals in the rearguard, and get out as swiftly as possible, as I and my men did."

"Unfortunately, if we do that, they are likely to raid us again."

"They raided you before! Well then, kill enough of them that they do not do it again. One in ten might suffice, then get out ... though if they are anything like the Kurds, you might have to go back in and double up."

"Ummh... it might be hard to find the right men to kill."

"Kill the women and children. The brave men will appear soon enough. Kill the brave, and the rest do not matter. Then get out."

"The women and children?"

"Spare some of the pretty ones, of course, to please the troops."

"Our allies might find this tactic disturbing."

"Did these Afghans raid you first?"

"Some of them did. Others disapproved strongly."

"Evidently not strongly enough. You need tougher allies."

Next, the ghost of Raffles.

I consult the ghost of Raffles on Afghanistan
2009-10-02 07:51:57

Blog: "Previously I talked to Xenophon on our troubles in Afghanistan. His advice was perhaps a little bit anachronistic. Today we are a bit too civilized for such drastic measures."

Raffles: "Troubles?"

"A war, we are losing. In the Hindu Kush."

"Ah, yes, the Hindu Kush was a problem in my day. You should leave it alone. Dreadful climate, barren land, no gold or valuable materials, full of men with nothing of value except guns, guns that they are very good at using."

"Unfortunately, some people from the area raided us."

"It seems that little has changed: Well, there are three alternatives.
1. Put up with it.
2. Eliminate the tribes that caused the most trouble.
3. Rule the hostile lands.

Unless it has changed a lot since my day, ruling it is likely to be impractical. Obviously, your course of action depends on how costly the raiding is. Have there been any new raids since you started the war? What you have done already might well suffice."

"Eliminate the Pashtun tribes? Even Xenophon did not go quite that far."

"I don't mean kill them all. Just tell them to get out, go some place else. Dispersed, strangers amongst tribes that caused you less trouble, they cannot get together to do bad things far from home."

"But what of those who will not or cannot go?"

"Below my pay grade. The officer tells the sergeant, clear these people out, the sergeant tells the private. And if there is too much mess, well I am sure the tribes that attacked you also attacked other tribes who have not attacked you. The natives of the Hindu Kush attack everyone, especially each other. You ally with local victims of the enemy tribes, and have your native auxiliaries do the potentially unpleasant work."

"But even in your day, did that not create a certain amount of public concern?"

"You rule those parts that are easier and more profitable to rule, or influence local allies that are friendly, to uplift and civilize your native auxiliaries, and everyone forgets to ask about those people that are not around any more. For example I abolished slavery. Of course, had I actually abolished slavery all at once, there would have been a lot of ex slaves lazing around all day and stealing stuff all night, so I retained an arrangement where debtors could be forced to work for creditors, and the creditors kept the books as to how much debt remained, and I made sure that potential trouble makers and lazy good-for-nothings were well supervised by creditors. You should try it. Abolishing slavery creates a great deal of favorable comment, sufficient that people overlook what happened in areas that, after all, you do not rule, so cannot be wholly blamed for what happened there."

"Unfortunately we abolished slavery already."

"Well I am sure there is something else to abolish. Opium, perhaps, and doubtless the natives of the Hindu Kush mistreat women to this day."

Delong's solution
2009-10-02 11:29:39

Brad DeLong, an economist greatly respected by the Cathedral, thinks the government is not blowing enough money.[211]

He presents a graph predicting, plausibly enough, that unemployment is going to stay high for a long time. So, he concludes the benevolent government should put those people to work– without, however, worrying as to what they will be doing, forgetting that people should work to produce the particular goods and services that other people want, or perhaps confidently believing that the wise folk of the government have lots of useful work for idle people to do, forgetting that a large part of the unemployed are unemployed

---

[211]https://delong.typepad.com/sdj/2009/09/generating-a-robust-recovery.html

because they were producing things, such as financial services or housing for non asian minorities, that the recipients are demonstrably unwilling to pay for.

His conclusion will doubtless further improve his immense status with the rest of the Cathedral, whereas were he to doubt the capability of fellow Cathedral members to put the lower orders to useful work this would with equal swiftness diminish that status

A scientific approach to politics.

2009-10-03 07:16:42

The Green Room and Big lizards[212] diagnose Obama's ideology as transnational progressivism – that he is a tranzi– that he aims at the creation of a one world government exercising highly centralized power over everyone and everything, and on this basis explain a bunch of his past policies, and make a long list of predictions for his future policies – that he aims, not to be elected president for life in 2016, which is what I was thinking because of his Honduras policy, but to be appointed UN grand poobah for life in 2016.

On that basis they make a bunch of predictions as to his future policies – science based politics. I shall check back in 2010 and 2011 to see how these predictions are working out.

Obama hates Americans

2009-10-04 04:52:03

Brutally honest points to an interesting statement by President Barack Hussein Obama:

> We are putting the full force of the White House and the State Department to make sure that not only is this is a successful games but that visitors from all around the world feel welcome, and I think that, you know, over the last several years sometimes sometimes, uh, that ... that fundamental truth about the United States has been lost, one of the legacies I think of ... of this Olympic Games in Chicago would be a restoration of that understanding of ... of what the United States is all about, and the United States' recognition of how we are linked to the world.

Observe the presupposition that foreigners fear that America is full of racists who might attack them, were it not for the vigorous force of the US government protecting people from evil and violent American citizens.

Why women want assholes

2009-10-04 07:01:00

In most species, most of the time, female choice produces lek behavior, where females choose the sexiest male, the male that is apt to have the most offspring by the most females, and therefore likely to produce sexy sons, and males do not support or protect females. In most species, females choose assholes. With most creatures, if they could speak, the

---

[212]https://biglizards.net/blog/archives/2009/10/the_shape_of_th.html

word for a male who loves, supports, and protects would be "loser". That is not true of all species all the time, nor even true of all females within some species, but that is the way to bet.

A good woman is hard to find, and needs a fair bit of monitoring, supervision and discipline. They will be bad if allowed to be bad. A traditional relationship only lasts if the male is the head of the family.

The survey of ancient and modern cultures undertaken in the book "Sex and Culture" shows that where where women had choice, the outcome was in large part a lek mating system, where children were raised primarily by their mothers, a system that produces people with the characteristic pathologies of bastards – produced ferals, wild animals on two legs, as in modern government housing projects.

In the ancestral environment, women's mating choices were substantially dictated by brothers and fathers, and if they lacked strong and protective brothers and fathers, they had even less choice – any guy with a big stick did what he pleased to them.

Naturally brothers and fathers had a bias towards protective and supportive husbands, husbands who would be good fathers, a bias towards nice guys, since Dad did not want to wind up looking after his grandchildren. Women, to the very limited extent that they could choose, preferred lovers who were reproductively successful– sexy lovers who would produce sexy sons.

In the ancestral environment, Dad would pick out some boy on the basis of ability and willingness to support and protect, and if daughter did not like the boy's looks, Dad would tie her to a tree branch and beat her like a rug.

When females had choice, they were in an environment where long term mating relationships were unlikely, so in such an environment they should choose the baddest boys, not the best boys. Females were rarely in a position where their mating choices could improve their prospects of long term support, so are not evolved to make such choices. That humans are a largely monogamous species is a reflection of patriarchy, not female choice. Monogamy is a system created by patriarchs, as they had the power to make it stick, and their daughters did not. Monogamy represents a conflict between the reproductive interests of father and daughter – they both have an interest in successful reproductive strategies, but the patriarch has an interest in reproductive strategies that minimizes the support the family has to give his daughter, while daughter does not. It also represents a strategy he was in a better position to actually carry out than his daughter – a patriarch could engage in reprisals against departing husbands. Being in a better position to ensure a relationship was long term, the patriarch is more inclined to take the future into account than his daughter is.

Men are naturally polygynous, women naturally hypergamous. When men have the power, the result is either something approximating monogamy, as men share the pussy more or less equally between themselves, as in traditional Christendom, or violent destructive conflict, as some men attempt to monopolize all available pussy, as in Islam. When women have the power, the result is the lek, a mating system that has the adverse consequences we observe in government housing projects, and in the various disturbingly backward or declining societies surveyed by "Sex and Culture"

Marriage and civilization are created by men, and imposed on women and children, sometimes forcibly and with a great deal of physical violence.

One famous and much used illustration of this is childbirth. As long as midwifery was an exclusively female domain, it remained primitive and dreadful, with a very high death rate among mothers and children. When men finally intruded into that field, they immediately invented the forceps. Long term thinking, such as inventing and making elaborately transformed materials into tools is not a female characteristic. Women, like children, have a much shorter time preference than men, perhaps because in the ancestral environment they were not in a position to assert property rights in tools, perhaps because of their shorter reproductive lifespan.

Inflation comes roaring back

2009-10-05 03:46:11

People who argue for "stimulus", or more "stimulus", often correctly point out that no one doubts that government can increase *nominal* GDP. Zimbabwe and Weimar Germany are excellent examples of government rapidly increasing *nominal* GDP. The question is, can government spending, particularly government spending on favored individuals and groups cozy with the government, increase useful employment, create real jobs that produce real value, create jobs where people work to produce what other people want and care about?

The cpi supposedlyrose 0.4% in august – by about the same amount as employment declined. 0.4% a month, if continued, is 5% a year, and the real inflation is probably considerably higher than that. Shadow statistics[213] claims that the cpi calculation has undergone greater and greater adjustment since 1990, and if calculated by 1990 methods would now be showing an inflation rate 3.5 percent per year higher - which implies that present inflation, if continued would be over eight percent a year.

Five percent inflation per year is apt to have unpleasant and disturbing side effects. Ten percent inflation is apt to have serious and gravely damaging effects, and we are heading towards ten percent. The MSM reported the 0.4 monthly[214] result as

> underscoring the Federal Reserve's view that inflation will be contained.
>
> ...
>
> A lack of inflation will probably give Fed policy makers leeway to keep interest rates near zero in the foreseeable future to secure a recovery.
>
> "What we're seeing is a gradual disinflation that reflects the persistent slack in our economy,"

It is a bizarre thing to say. If they say that for 0.4% per month, they will probably say the same for 4% per month, 30% per month, 10% per day, 100% per day, 100% per hour – which is pretty much what the German mainstream media was saying during the Weimar hyperinflation – that there was no inflation, that the problem was insufficient

---

[213]https://www.shadowstats.com/
[214]https://www.bloomberg.com/apps/news?pid=20601087&sid=aN7Zds1Ii1Zk

money in circulation and the government needed to issue lots more money to stimulate the economy, and that Jews and Anglo Saxons were causing the inflation.

When the inflation rate and the unemployment rate are similar, in that both of them are disturbingly high and rising fast, the government should be looking for solutions to both - in other words, supply side solutions – cutting taxes, spending, and regulation.

If, as seems likely, inflation becomes undeniable, expect the regular announcements that inflation is not a problem to be mixed with regular announcements that "price gougers" are a problem, doubtless due to Bush's dreadful deregulation. More regulation, by the wise and good regulators, who are on the side of the consumer, will doubtless be needed.

Latest global warming scandal in short

2009-10-07 07:34:39

For the last ten years or so, every year or so a study has been issued which supposedly confirms the infamous Hockey Stick graph, which supposedly shows the world's temperature has been pretty constant over the last thousand years or so and then has suddenly started rising in recent decades. Global Warming! Time to Panic!

And each of the these charts supposedly replicates each of the other charts.

For a long time, the data on which these graphs were based was kept secret, but the Royal Society finally found its missing testicles, after what I considered unreasonable delay, and demanded that the data be released.

It turns out that they all replicate each other, because they each rely on the same *ten trees*[215], the evidence of twentieth century warming being that one of these ten grew unusually rapidly during the twentieth century as compared to fossil trees of the same type from the same area. These trees were selected by Bricca from a much larger population of trees in the same area.

The larger population of trees, taken as a whole, shows much the same growth pattern as the fossil trees.

Take out one tree from those ten, Yamal06, and most of the evidence for climate change vanishes. Restore the much larger set of trees from which the ten trees were selected, and all of the evidence for climate change vanishes.

Take out one tree from half a dozen graphs of global warming in near a dozen papers, and suddenly they do not show global warming any more.

Bricca has, at this time, not yet explained why those ten trees, and not others from the same survey and same area. And whatever his explanation, ten trees is not enough.

Arnold Kling predicts inflation

2009-10-12 14:26:34

Arnold Kling predicts[216]:

---

[215]https://network.nationalpost.com/np/blogs/fullcomment/archive/2009/10/01/ross-mckitrick-defects-in-key-climate-data-are-uncovered.aspx

[216]https://econlog.econlib.org/archives/2009/10/a_sentence_to_p.html

The monetary and fiscal expansion may have little or no effect on unemployment, and after a bit of a lag we could see inflation come back with a vengeance.

We "could" see it come back with a vengeance? We are already seeing it come back[217]. I suppose it is not "with a vengeance" yet.

Care Bear war in Afghanistan
2009-10-13 08:36:31

In guerrilla wars, victory always requires dreadful means. The guerrillas clutch the people as shields. That is a good reason to avoid fighting against guerrillas. There is usually an alternative. The Reaganite alternative was that instead of us fighting against Soviet sponsored guerrillas, we would sponsor lots and lots of guerrillas and let the Soviets fight them. The Soviets did not hesitate to employ dreadful means, but they swiftly ran short of treasure to pay for dreadful means.

Every victory against guerrillas has involved horrifying brutality. The British in Malaya imprisoned the entire ethnic group that the guerrillas hid among, all of them. Saddam re-engineered his country's rivers so that he could deny water to vast areas of Iraq, not only burning the crops and killing the cattle that the people would have nothing to eat, but also, nothing to drink. Americans conquered the Philippines by threatening genocide, and making a pretty good start on it, a model that the Ceylonese government has been imitating. The Ceylonese government systematically massacred women and children to deter the guerrillas from hiding among them, which deterrence succeeded, forcing the Tamil Tigers into conventional war.

Thus in Afghanistan, there are three choices: Defeat the Taliban using the methods of Malaya and the Philippines, choose a different war after the manner of Reagan, or leave.

We are not doing any of those. What the @#$% are we doing?

General McChrystal tells us:[218]

> "our strategy cannot be focused on seizing terrain or destroying insurgent forces; our objective must be the population."

Not killing the enemy means losing the war while they kill Americans.

> "Pre-occupied with protection of our own forces, we have operated in a manner that distances us – physically and psychologically – from the people we seek to protect."

So we should not be protecting our own forces, but instead the people who willingly or unwillingly are protecting our enemies. At least this General is consistent. Evil and insane, but consistently so.

So if we are not slaying our enemies, and protecting our troops, what the @#$% are we doing in Afghanistan?

---

[217]https://blog.reaction.la/economics/inflation-comes-roaring-back.html
[218]https://www.washingtonpost.com/wp-dyn/content/article/2009/09/21/AR2009092100110.html

"There must be development and use of indigenous narratives to tap into the wider cultural pulse of Afghanistan."

This is the standard multiculturalist pap we get inflicted in America's public schools as an effort to smash Christianity. Islam is supposedly the religion of peace, and we just have to remind all those gentle nice Muslims that it is, and they will happily join the multicultural rainbow singing Kumbayah.

It is not working against Christianity in America even though the Cathedral has total control. It sure is not going to work in a Muslim country where the Muslims are shooting back, answering words that seek to destroy their culture with bullets that seek to destroy their enemies. If you want to change the Afghan belief system to something less violent, the only plausible candidates are Sufi Islam or evangelical protestantism. Multicultural religion of peace pablum is not going to stand a chance. And if you want to change the Afghan belief system, first you have to kill everyone who will kill to prevent you from changing it. You cannot win the war by changing their religious beliefs. *After* you win the war, you can use victory for lots of purposes, such as imposing a more peaceable brand of Islam, or eradicating Islam, or raping all the women, or turning the place into a super-highway and parking lot, or whatever. But you cannot impose a more peaceable variety of Islam while the less peaceable variety answers words with bullets.

Other blogs commenting on this moronic plan for winning the war by means of rainbows and pink unicorns, care bear style, either complain that there are insufficient rainbows and pink unicorns, or else are mightily impressed because it is such a muscular militaristic proposal. The only sane commentary that I found was "Our troops are not in Afghanistan for a social experiment[219]". The Obama objection to this plan appears to be that it involves too much deadly violence, and not enough rainbows and pink unicorns.

The Cathedral and social decay

2009-10-14 03:31:32

In 1984, I said the Soviet Union was falling. In November 2005, I said the mortgage market was collapsing. I was very far from being the first to say those things, but I was in a minority when I said them.

And here is another prophecy: The decline of our currency, and the our inability to rebuild the two towers, are symptoms of an illness that will bring about American collapse and crisis around 2020 or so. As to what form the collapse will take, hard to tell. When a structure is under ever growing stress, something will shatter, but who can see which part will prove the weakest and shatter first? A major financial artery has been slashed open, and it is spouting blood. This will collapse the American currency, probably resulting in political crisis such as war, dictatorship or foreign rule.

Government applies state power to ensure political outcomes – for example it makes broadcasters toe the line by direct regulation of the airwaves. The print media get access to the extent that they play along with those they seek access to, hence the New York

---

[219]https://article.nationalreview.com/?q=NWQ3Y2U2NjNlYTAyMjI3MTAxZjYyOWZh-NTU0Mzg3MzMQ=&w=MA

Times. The schools teach the government line on the great depression, and scientists and economists know that if you scientifically prove what politicians and regulators want to hear you get ahead, and what politicians and regulators want to hear is always that regulators are doing good, except that they need a lot more power because they are not doing nearly enough - hence the noise about financial "de regulation", when all the supposed examples of financial de-regulation are financial regulation, financial regulation that happens to be highly favorable to Goldman and Sach, who are connected to the regulators by a revolving door.

At the same time, those seeking political outcomes, seek backing from state power. A marriage naturally ensues. Following the terminology and analysis of Moldbug[220], let us call this happy marriage and its numerous morbidly obese children "the Cathedral". The Cathedral is almost the same thing as the left and the progressive movement, or rather it is the left in power, the established left, the professoriat, the mainstream media, the lawyer lobby, the judiciary, the senior public servants, the management of numerous supposedly non governmental quasi private organizations, and so on and so forth.

The Cathedral is not quite the same thing as the left. One can point to a few small and minor differences. For example: The lawyers who get court appointed to defend people that they railroad rather than defend are menial members of the Cathedral, even though when they railroad broke and unimportant leftists for a police prosecutor, they look very like the right. They are direct employees of the Cathedral because court appointed. If they were paid on a voucher scheme, which is to say appointed by the accused, they would be employees of the accused, instead of the Cathedral.

Another example of the left not being quite the same thing as the Cathedral is the IMF, which is clearly part of the Cathedral, even though much of the left dislike it and consider it right wing – but dislike or not, in America almost all Democrats vote in favor of the IMF and almost everyone who votes against the IMF is a Republican. The IMF is clearly not part of what most leftists consider the left, but with equal clarity, it is part of the left in power, part of the established left.

The Cathedral is the reason why history always moves left. The Cathedral is almost the same thing as the left. The right is an ever changing coalition of some of the groups and interests that are inevitably and inexorably being steamrollered by the Cathedral. Since the Cathedral steamrollers different things every few decades, the right is different people every few decades. Thus the Cathedral has different policies and programs from time to time, but its people and policies directly descend from previous Cathedral members policies, whereas the right has different policies and people from time to time.

In functioning, the Cathedral is very like a theocratic state. The guys with guns back the preachers, and the preachers endorse the guys with guns, resulting in the theocracy becoming ever more extreme and nutty in its religious doctrines, for example Global Warming, but in old fashioned theocracies power is concentrated in a King and high priest, with the King owning the high priest or the high priest owning the king, whereas in the Cathedral power is instead diffused amongst a large class of Brahmins, an ever more numerous, ever growing class of Brahmins. To get anything done, lot of Brahmins have to sign on, and each extracts tribute for signing on – which is why we cannot rebuild the two towers,

---

[220]https://unqualified-reservations.blogspot.com/

and Dubai can, Dubai being an old fashioned theocracy.

You want to build a tower in Dubai, you just need one sufficiently high Mullah to sign on. In the theocracy of New York, you need lots of Brahmins to sign on, more Brahmins to sign on than anyone can count. So the two towers stay down.

Now what has been steadily happening ever since 1915 is that the power to print money has been diffused through a larger and larger class of people resulting in an ever greater inflationary bias, much as the power to obstruct the building of towers and housing has been diffused through a larger and larger class of people resulting in housing becoming ever more expensive. But these were stuffy conservative bankers, not really part of the Cathedral, or rather no longer sufficiently part of the Cathedral now that the Cathedral has moved a long way further left than it was in 1915 and become vastly more numerous. In 1993, the Cathedral decided these bankers were racists, and that they must join the new improved considerably more progressive Cathedral, or else. In due course, they did. Hence the present financial crisis, which is affirmative action lending leading to a run on the repo market, which run started silently and furtively in 2005 November, in response to the escalation of affirmative action lending, which had started to become excessive in 2000 or so, and became bizarrely extreme and ludicrously blatant in 2005. The run crashed the repo market in 2007, causing a reduction in affirmative action lending from blatantly insane to less blatantly insane – which reduction appears only temporary, since the underlying forces of politicized lending and financial regulation are still burning through capital at a rate far faster than capital can be created.

The "stabilization" of the repo market and the "normalization" of financial markets is a huge breakthrough for the Cathedral, and was indeed the original objective of declaring the banks racist, for it means that any large American business that can have its debt rated AAA can in effect issue money, for a government stabilized repo market trading AAA debt with an implicit government guarantee makes AAA rated debt directly cash equivalent. Today, in the "stabilized" financial market, an American financial institution gets and keeps AAA rating by political favor, rather than actual solvency, and to get political favor, it has to kiss up to political activist groups such as Acorn, so the effect of "stabilization" is that more and more elements of the Cathedral get to issue money outside the government budget, resulting in ever more rapid escalation of the ever growing inflationary bias.

Another factor is that every so often, by its nature, the Cathedral will simply go to war. The Cathedral lives on conflict. Each reform, real or purported, produces a new dispersal of little bits of state power with which to reward the ever more numerous members of the Cathedral, so the Cathedral always needs new reforms involving new conflicts. Conflicts are apt to get out of hand. The longer it has been since the Cathedral last went to war, the more it is willing to take on a conflict that runs the risk of getting out of hand. The growing financial crisis parallels increasingly warlike attitudes by the Cathedral against its internal and external enemies - thus though we see in Afghanistan a government policy that is increasingly hostile to our troops, and increasingly attempts to appease our irreconcilable enemies, the thing that makes our enemies so wholly irreconcilable is that these efforts to make friends are predicated on Islam being a multiculturalist feminist religion of peace, on replacing Islam with an Epcot style politically correct imitation of Islam, a part of the multicultural rainbow, which program our enemies reasonably enough view as aggressive and threatening, rather than friendly and conciliatory. Piously declaring Islam "the religion of peace" is conciliatory. Attempting to actually make it into the religion of peace in Afghanistan and attempting remedy its treatment of women is as aggressive as sword point Christianity. Muslims are incorrect to perceive the pictures of pretty girls on shampoo bottles as an attempt to cut their balls off, but this paranoid perception is fed by the fact that the Cathedral really does intend to cut their balls off. That the Cathedral wants to make Afghanistan into a good modern progressive state, a subsidiary of the Cathedral with equal rights for women and all that, is infinitely more threatening than if we merely intended to discourage a repeat of 9/11 by killing thirty thousand Afghan men, raping three hundred thousand Afghan women, stealing three million Afghan cattle, and cutting down the orchards.

Thus we can foresee an ever more warlike Cathedral, that is causing ever more serious problems – the latest "reform" (bringing the bankers into the new Cathedral line) being one that is causing huge damage and will rapidly cause vastly more damage, which damage will lead to a multitude of conflicts, conflicts with a Cathedral that is increasingly spoiling for a fight. The current policy in Afghanistan is merely an example of the Cathedral spoiling for a fight. When the fight breaks out, it it probably will not be with Islam and may well surprise everyone. The target, though not the fight, will surely surprise me.

In short, the reasons why the two towers would stay down were evident in 1999 well before they fell. It is now 2009, and they are still down. This foreshadows crisis and collapse. What prevented the towers from rising again is also what caused the financial collapse, which foreshadows more of the same.

At the same time, we hear from the Cathedral, rhetoric ever more violent, ever more warlike.

It is perhaps too soon to bet that a faction that has won every conflict over the past three hundred years is going to lose this time but outright war is apt to have surprising outcomes, War that follows collapse the more so. Trees do not grow to the sky. The ever multiplying Brahmins of the Cathedral are increasingly a liability, rather than an asset, and if it should survive the coming financial collapse and win the coming war, the Cathedral will have to thin the ranks a bit. If it survives, as it likely will, it will start looking more like a traditional theocracy, relying more on the gulag and less on persuasion and bribery. The Cathedral may well continue in power. The number of Brahmins cannot continue to increase, or if they do increase, the benefits provided will have to be curtailed. With prospects of joining the Cathedral curtailed, or the benefits of joining curtailed, continuing in power will require harsher measures.

Doom

2009-10-15 14:35:44

Europe is doomed, just as the Roman empire was doomed when it ceased to be Roman, the Chin empire doomed when it ceased to be Chin, and the Turkish empire doomed when it ceased to be Turkish, and failed to become believably sincere in its religious faith.

The military weakness and incapacity of Europe in Serbia startled the Serbs, even more than America's capacity stunned them. Since then, Europe's martial weakness has been on display in one humiliating debacle after another. Recall Britian's startling display of fear, weakness, cowardice, and dhimmitude in the Persian gulf.

All that wealth, and no capacity to defend it. The vultures are circling.

For a state to exist, it has to be able to destroy those that oppose it, or might oppose it, to inflict famine and ruin on hostile populations, has to be able burn the crops and flatten the cities, after the manner of General Sherman, and has to have confident belief, a belief shared by officers and men, that it is *right* to do so.

To do this, it needs some source of cohesion. It cannot provide its own cohesion. Pay and threats will not work to motivate soldiers, for when things go bad, when your soldiers most need motivation, these motivations cannot function, for nothing will motivate people impose the discipline.

The usual source or cohesion is ethnic identity: the nation state. Other sources of cohesion are religion, as for example the various theocratic states, such as the caliphate, and ideology, as for example the American revolution and the various communist coups.

So if your cohesion came from ethnicity, then when you go multicultural, then your soldiers are fighting for pay and pension *and nothing more*, and then you are doomed. Similarly, when the last shreds of liberty are crushed out in the US, when the second amendment is utterly gone, and little left of the first amendment, US troops will be fighting for pay and pension and nothing more and then the US will be doomed.

Betraeus, the candidate to smash the GOP

2009-10-16 12:05:24

Hot air tells us that:

> Petraeus is the only candidate who can unite the GOP[221]

What gives him this magic power to unite the GOP?

Well, it seems that this terrible GOP is foolishly and obstinately in favor of terrible and foolish GOP principles:

> Over the past couple of decades, the American people have grown more pro-environment, more culturally tolerant, and more suspicious of the unregulated free market, and yet the Republican Party has responded with a series of litmus tests for its presidential candidates that represent the political equivalent of sticking your fingers in your ears and yelling "la la la, I can't hear you.

Fortunately, for the GOP, the good General Petraeus opposes every single principle that matters for the GOP base, with the sole exception that he wants to conduct an unpopular war against Afghans to force on them a moderate version of Islam, a animatronic

---

[221] https://hotair.com/archives/2009/10/13/peter-beinart-petraeus-is-the-only-candidate-who-can-unite-the-gop/

version of Islam, a version of Islam that actually is the religion of peace, that treats women with dignity, refrains from executing apostates, and so on and so forth.

Creating a fake version of Islam that fits nicely into the pretty multicutural rainbow and getting Afghans to swallow it is not a realistic military objective. In fact it is not even a military objective. Soldiers kill people and break things. Military objectives are the kind of objectives you can achieve by killing people and breaking things.

So a general who has been conducting a losing war will unite the GOP behind everything it hates, plus a policy of continuing to lose the war for the next four years.

Republican party hacked

2009-10-18 15:50:37

Before I was an engineer, I was an entryist. Engineering pays better, but the big advantage of engineering is that one's coworkers are less likely to kill one. Working with evil people is not a good idea.

Entryism is a small team of conspirators trying to manipulate and control another organization – usually a larger organization with a bigger mailing list and more funds. Thus for example a small group of political extremists, a team of half a dozen or so people, would naturally like to take over an big organization involved in some big money, moderately leftist, politically progressive task such as funding housing for the poor, if lots of funding for the poor flows through the housing organization.

There are commonalities between computer engineering and entryism, particularly security engineering. A background in entryism gives important insights into security engineering. Entryism is the same sort of job as hacking, but with entryism, one works entirely on human factors, whereas with hacking, one only partially works on human factors, and mostly focuses on such things as buffer overflows and protocol failures. There are some similarities between taking over someone's website through flaws in the software, and taking over someone else's organization through flaws in their internal processes – the main commonality being to distinguish between the way things are supposed to work, and the very different way they actually work. The frame of mind and way of looking at things is similar, like a magician's misdirection. To attack, one looks for ways that expectations can be violated. Conversely, to make stuff secure, one tries to make sure that expectations cannot be violated. The excruciatingly complicated procedure for electing a new pope reflects a thousand years of such attacks by ancient entryists aimed at rigging the election, and thousand years of security design aimed at making sure the election works the way it appears to work. The papal election procedure is sometimes studied by computer security engineers to illuminate their art.

Entryists use fraud and lies, while hackers use some combination of fraud, lies, buffer overflows, and protocol failures. Hackers tend to be nerdly people who eat far too much junk food, while entryists usually played in the right sports teams at the right educational institutions, and have good social skills. (Perhaps that is why I wound up in engineering instead. It is more my line)

Now recently the GOP has nominated the extreme left candidate Scozzafava for a seat in congress - and I do mean extreme left. So naturally, with my background, I suspected entryism. The Democrats might well nominate an extreme left candidate and regularly do, the Republicans might well nominate a candidate so "moderate" that he looks suspiciously like a Democrat, but extreme left? This "Republican" lady is far to the left of the Democratic party candidate.

A bunch of republican blogs are, reasonably enough having hysterics, among them Michell Malkin[222] and Moonbattery[223]

Scozzafava turns out to be the candidate of the Working Families Party[224], whose name is typical of entryist front group names– a more or less random string of moderate sounding words that carries no real meaning. The declared objective of the Working Families Party is to move the Democratic Party further to the left. To influence group X is a fairly typical mission statement of an entryist team, though their real objectives usually involve a lot more than mere influence.

But the dead give away is that they share their headquarters with Acorn. Long ago a team of entryists took over Acorn, and this team now hangs out at Acorn headquarters, Acorn being the largest and best funded of the many, many, many, many organizations that the team has taken over. A great pile of organizations share Acorn headquarters, more than anyone can keep track of, and the theoretically separate funds, agendas, objectives and activities of these organizations are all mingled, and they are all run by the same people from the same office . This is the usual pile of residue accumulated by a successful entryist team. If someone has fifteen thousand credit card numbers with names, real addresses and login passwords, you know he is a hacker. If someone has a hundred organizations, with separate mailing lists and funding, you know he is an entryist. If someone has the backing of an organization that turns out to be a hundred organizations all with one headquarters, you know he is an entryist.

But entryists are like termites. If one entryist is in an organization with assets and name worth having, there are usually others. Termites do not mean the house is fallen yet, but if drastic measures are not taken, the house will soon fall. It is time for a hard disk reformat and restoration from backup.

Why "stimulus" does not work.

2009-10-20 06:35:36

We do not want jobs. We want creation of wealth. Regrettably, creating wealth usually requires an unreasonable amount of work. Even more regrettably, doing an unreasonable amount of work is unlikely to create wealth. Thus if we try to "create jobs", we are likely to destroy, rather than create, wealth.

It is very easy to create jobs. The chain on the chainsaw breaks, and one has to use an axe. Think of all the jobs created! Ban chainsaws! "Green jobs" are of this kind.

---

[222]https://michellemalkin.com/2009/10/17/a-message-from-ny-23-conservative-candidate-doug-hoffman/
[223]https://www.moonbattery.com/archives/2009/10/grim_rino_tales.html
[224]https://www.discoverthenetworks.org/groupProfile.asp?grpid=6965

Accounting fraud

2009-10-20 11:36:36

The financial crisis was in large part accounting fraud. America has lost trillions of dollars through accounting fraud. Accounting fraud is a felony. Yet those who were primarily responsible for this fraud continue in positions of wealth and power, for example Senator Chris Dodd (D-CT) and Representative Barney Frank (D-MA). Further, the fraud continues. Hot air[225] summarizes "Mark to Myth"[226] and other blogs reporting on the continuing fraud.

Zero hedge[227] tells us

> restoring trust is the key to recovery, and trust cannot be restored until *wrong-doers are held accountable*

going rogue: compassionate conservatism

2009-10-26 06:40:54

Sarah Palin has announced

> Our nation is at a crossroads, and this is once again a "time for choosing."

But unfortunately, the leadership of the Republican party, "the political machine" does not want a straight up and down vote on the choice.

Suddenly Sarah Palin is the leader of the Republican party, and "the political machine" is no longer the leader, for when "the political machine" endorsed Dede Scozzafava for New York's 23rd Congressional district, Republican money and volunteers failed to flow to Dede Scozzafava, but when Sarah Palin endorsed Doug Hoffman for New York's 23rd Congressional district, Republican money and volunteers did flow to Doug Hoffman.

Stick a fork in, their goose is cooked. The electoral is heading to a straight up and down vote on Sarah Palin's list of issues – on the crossroads as she defines it.

Sarah Palin in charge

2009-10-27 03:00:59

In my previous post, I observed that when the Republican party machine says one thing, and Sarah Palin says a different thing, Republican party activists do what Sarah Palin says, and not what the party machine says. But, of course, we next have to ask do Republican voters do what Republican party activists say, or do they do what the party machine says? The question is now answered.[228]

---

[225] https://hotair.com/greenroom/archives/2009/10/18/the-worst-three-months-of-all-time/
[226] https://market-ticker.denninger.net/archives/1471-Mark-To-Myth-Losers-Americans.html
[227] https://www.zerohedge.com/article/ongoing-cover-truth-behind-financial-crisis-may-lead-another-crash
[228] https://www.clubforgrowth.org/2009/10/cfg_poll_hoffman_leading_in_ny.php

Gold

2009-10-27 13:18:54

At present prices gold has little practical use, except as money. So if you buy gold, you are buying insurance against paper money going to hell, and people using gold as money. When the %@# never hits the fan, you will probably lose money over time, because gold's value as anything other than money is considerably less than you are paying. For any use other than money, gold is far overpriced.

Martin Murenbeeld[229] reports that people are starting to use gold as money and a store of value – not that you will be able to use it to buy an airline ticket out of trouble any time soon, but there are arguably signs that the wind begins to blow.

We recently saw entertaining video of people in Zimbabwe using billion zim notes to wrap a few tiny precious fragments of gold, and using the gold to buy food.

Fighting to lose in Afghanistan.

2009-11-01 05:57:33

Hillary has just announced that it is fine by her for Karzai to steal the election.

"that bestowed legitimacy from that moment forward"

Details[230], x[231]

Democrats of the Vietnam generation long for a re-run of Vietnam. Karzai is militarily incompetent, an enemy of western civilization, and is fighting to lose, thus to allow him to steal the election is defeatism, guaranteeing the Vietnam quagmire that Democrats long for. Next stop, conscription, compulsory voluntary community service.

The correct response, as I have long argued, to this and to each of Karzai's previous grave provocations, is to put him in a sack, and drop the sack on Pakistan's presidential palace from ten thousand feet as a message to the president of Pakistan.

This Afghan government is clearly a disadvantage in our efforts to slay our enemies. If Afghanistan can only be governed by enemy tyrants, why should we permit it to be governed? Propping up governments is hard, costly, and bloody. Propping up illegitimate enemy tyrannies is stupid.

In Afghanistan we are already defeated. From now on, it is just a theatrical display of American weakness and impotence, to the great rejoicing of our enemies within and without.

---

[229]https://curiouscapitalist.blogs.time.com/2009/10/26/the-semi-return-of-the-gold-standard/
[230]https://belowthebeltway.com/2009/10/31/opposition-leader-threatening-to-boycott-afghan-recount/
[231]https://www.obama-mamas.com/blog/?p=447

You read it here first 1

2009-11-01 06:28:34

Big lizards boasts that his prediction came in first[232] - that on October 29 he wrote "Evidence is mounting (a favorite liberal-stream media word) that far from making a 'blunder', Sarah Palin had her finger on the crystal ball"

But on October 27 I wrote "Sarah Palin in charge[233]"

Me me me me. Me first.

The lesson of NY 23 election

2009-11-03 03:47:02

The election for New York's 23rd Congressional District was a straight up and down test of Tea Party conservatism and Palin Republicanism against "moderate" Republicanism.

It proved, decisively, that Palin Republicanism wins votes and that "moderate" Republicanism loses votes.

It proved, decisively, that "moderate" Republicans wish the party harm.

The Republican party machine (the NRCC and the RNC) gave near a million dollars to a candidate who in the end endorsed the Democratic party candidate, thus exposing

---

[232]https://biglizards.net/blog/archives/2009/10/wow_that_was_qu.html
[233]https://blog.reaction.la/party-politics/sarah-palin-in-charge.html

"moderate" Republicanism as treason against the party. A purge will ensue, or else a third party run. Possibly both, an incomplete and ineffectual purge, leading to a third party run. The swift unification of the party around Hoffman suggests an effectual purge may be happening.

Those who supported Scozzafava are revealed as dupes or traitors. If the purge fails to remove from power everyone who supported giving a million dollars to the candidate who endorsed the Democrat, a third party run is likely. If those who run the party are not loyal to it, who will be?

Palin Republicanism may not necessarily be able to save the Republican party, but it certainly has lot better chance than "moderate" Republicanism. It might be able to postpone the apocalypse for a decade or so, though eventually elections will be fought between the likes of the Institutional Revolutionary Party and the Party of the Democratic Revolution.

Democracy has an inherent drift towards self destruction. The masses are seduced by demagogues who promise them they can vote themselves rich, leading to bankruptcy and social war. But when the drift gets out of hand, when the end approaches too rapidly, there is a reaction as final collapse comes in sight, leading to a retreat from the abyss. The 1948 Congress that rejected Truman's Fair Deal and proceeded to disband war socialism, and the Reagan revolution were such reactions to the alarmingly rapid approach of self destruction, and Palin may well be the next one – probably the last one.

Since 1994 I have been predicting collapse around 2020—2025 or so. If Palin succeeds, my prediction will need to be substantially rescheduled. I hope for the best, but expect the worst.

Political correctness kills people

2009-11-08 04:04:29

Section 3 of the US constitution.

> Treason against the United States, shall consist only in levying war against them, or in adhering to their enemies, giving them aid and comfort.

Major Nidal Malik Hasan adhered to our enemies and gave our enemies aid and comfort. He then waged war against the united states, shooting 43 soldiers who were not carrying arms at the time.

When he adhered to our enemies and gave them aid and comfort, he should have been (if not charged with treason) dishonorably discharged on the basis that he was unwilling to perform his contract with the united states army, which paid for his education.

Because political correctness holds that Islam is the religion of peace, Major Nidal Malik Hasan cannot be charged with treason, since it cannot be acknowledged that a very large proportion of Muslims are guilty of treason, probably most of those who take their religion seriously. Indeed. If you are an American Muslim, you are guilty of treason against the US, or treason against Dar al Islam, one or the other.

Because political correctness holds that women can fight fires just as well as men, some of the requirements for firefighters, notably the ability to carry an unconscious man to safety, have necessarily been eliminated. And so people burn to death in fires.

And similarly, millions die each year from malaria, which could be easily prevented, but political correctness forbids it.

Nobel prize for corruption and fraud

2009-11-10 09:32:05

Several recent Nobel prizes in economics have been as hilarious as the Nobel peace prize given to Yasser Arafat.

David Henderson observed[234] an interesting paper telling us that Fannie and Freddie have very little risk. Nobel Prize winner Joseph E. Stiglitz, and eminent economists Jonathan M. Orszag and Peter R. Orszag assured us[235] that everything was just lovely. Don't pay any attention to strange crazies like Peter J. Wallison who was at approximately the same date telling us that Fannie and Freddie were doomed[236] and were going to take down the financial system[237] with them.

If you tell the Cathedral what it wants to hear, you get honors and wealth. If you say what it does not want to hear, you are a crank, and will be reviled and ignored. Theocracy in action.

Judaism is racism, says the British Court of Appeals

2009-11-11 12:35:46

A Jewish school, partially funded by the British taxpayer, has been ordered[238] it cannot define Jews by descent, because this is "racism". Unfortunately, Judaism *does* define Jews by descent. If the effect of the ruling was merely that Jewish institutions, being "racist" cannot receive government funding, this would not be too bad, but unfortunately, Britain prohibits "racist" association generally, so the ruling logically prohibits Jewish association generally, thus the practice of Judaism generally.

> "The requirement that if a pupil is to qualify for admission his mother must be Jewish, whether by descent or conversion, is a test of ethnicity which contravenes the Race Relations Act,... [Whether the reasons were] benign or malignant, theological or supremacist makes it no less and no more unlawful."

Judaism is not going to be suppressed tomorrow, the government will not immediately proceed with all the logical implications of the ruling, but this is the beginning of a

---

[234] https://econlog.econlib.org/archives/2009/11/stiglitz_and_or.html
[235] https://web.archive.org/web/20050119214025/https://sbgo.com/Papers/fmp-v1i2.pdf
[236] https://www.amazon.com/Serving-Two-Masters-Yet-Control/dp/0844741663/ref=sr_1_1?ie=UTF8&s=books&qic 1
[237] https://www.aei.org/publications/pubID.22705/pub_detail.asp
[238] https://www.nytimes.com/2009/11/08/world/europe/08britain.html

long slow end. When England went Protestant, it allowed Jews in. As it goes Muslim, it is going to send them out.

The Guardian is lecturing Britain's chief Rabbi on what the Jewish religion should be[239]. It is a reasonable enough lecture if given by one private citizen to another, and I am sure that lots of Jews have said the same thing, but a very menacing lecture when backed by court and state. And if Jews comply with this perfectly reasonable lecture, chances are that next year something else, not quite so reasonable, will be found that is wrong with Jews.

Shmuley Boteach very passionately argues that the court, and the guardian, is full of !#!% they are full of menace.

Muqata suggests it is time for all Jews to get out of Britain[240]. Not yet it is not, but that is the way the wind is blowing.

Productivity leaps?

2009-11-15 03:39:55

Unemployment is soaring - yet supposedly total production has increased.

Normally a big rise in productivity leads immediately and directly to a big rise in prosperity[241]. Are you feeling prosperous?

Another common cause of *statistics* showing a big rise in productivity is, as in Argentina, the government lying to itself and the public about inflation[242].

Another common cause of statistics showing a big rise in productivity is government spending. The problem is that in calculating GDP, government expenditures are valued at cost. Thus for a private individual to raise GDP, he has to find a way to make more money, whereas for the government to raise GDP, it merely has to find a way to spend more money.

To illustrate the problem, let us imagine a little kingdom, where all production is valued in sacks of wheat, and sacks of wheat are used as money. The peasants produce in actual sacks, plus chickens and goats valued in sacks at the market exchange rate. The kingdom has one thousand peasants, each of whom produce two hundred sacks of wheat a year, one lord, and ten lord's retainers. Each peasant pays the lord a tax of twenty sacks, so we value the work done by the lord and his retainers at twenty thousand sacks. So even though the peasants only produce two hundred thousand sacks of wheat, the kingdom's GDP is somehow two hundred and twenty thousand sacks.

The Lord decides to stimulate the economy of the kingdom, by hiring two hundred and fifty peasants at one thousand sacks per year to dig holes, and another two hundred and fifty peasants at two thousand sacks per year to fill the holes in. He raises taxes on all peasants to pay for this, from ten percent of production to ninety percent of production. Despite this tax rise, the remaining peasants not digging holes or filling them in continue to produce two hundred sacks a year. So now that we only have five hundred peasants

[239]https://www.guardian.co.uk/commentisfree/belief/2009/oct/24/jonathan-sacks-jews-free-school
[240]https://muqata.blogspot.com/2009/11/are-british-jews-jewish.html
[241]https://www.becker-posner-blog.com/archives/2009/11/productivity_an_1.html
[242]https://www.shadowstats.com/

left doing anything useful, so you might suspect that GDP has now fallen from twenty thousand sacks of wheat, to ten thousand sacks of wheat, but no, this is not the way to get a Nobel prize in economics.

Since the holes are valued at cost, and filling them in also valued at cost, and since the peasants working in the Lord sector are well paid, better paid than ordinary peasants, though not quite as well paid as the lord and his retainers, and since the Lord and his retainers also took a modest pay rise for arranging all this prosperity, total value produced, total GDP is now a whopping eight hundred and fifty thousand sacks of wheat, a fourfold rise in GDP.

One of the Lord's retainers is an economist, who gets a Nobel prize for explaining that the Lord has done such a good job.

US inflation rising

2009-11-19 08:09:28

The latest official cpi is 0.3% rise for the month of October, which, annualized, is 3.6% - higher than is desirable, high enough to cause moderate damage to investment and employment,but not high enough to be a serious problem.

Actual inflation, in my doubtless biased judgment, is probably around seven percent, high enough to be a serious problem, high enough significantly damage investment and cause substantial unemployment.

The government continues to hold real interest rates negative for privileged and well connected borrowers, which procedure usually foreshadows severe inflation and economic collapse. What we have seen before, many times in many countries, is a vicious cycle where as doom sets in, the well connected buy up cheap assets with cheaply borrowed money, incurring debts that rapid inflation will reduce to zero. By so doing, the well connected create an ever greater pro inflation insider lobby group: Positive feedback leading to ever greater fiscal irresponsibility, resulting in ever greater inflation.

The vicious cycle is in progress, but has not yet reached the point of being irreversible. The government could easily raise interest rates to fund its deficit spending by irresponsible borrowing instead of irresponsible money issue. There is a great deal of ruin in a nation. On the other hand, a trillion dollar deficit is a great deal of ruin.

As the government continues with its low interest policy, insider interest in continued low interest rates and high inflation will become ever stronger, making it ever harder to change the policy from inflation to borrowing.

My guess is that there is still plenty of time to change course – from irresponsible money issue leading to hyper inflation soon, to irresponsible borrowing leading to hyper inflation later – but if there is no change of course before 2012, changing course after 2012 will be difficult. The closer we get to the brink, the harder it is politically to turn around before hyperinflation.

Finally, pirates resisted

2009-11-19 11:06:59

Somali pirates attacked the Maersk Alabama on Wednesday for the second time in seven months and were "thwarted by private guards[243]".

It appears that "thwarted" actually means "killed", which is the only effectual way to "thwart" pirates.

This will have the effect that pirates will cease to attack ships flying the American flag, which a considerably better result than I expected with Obama in charge. This action by captain Rochford of the Maersk was of course completely legal under international law of the sea, US law, and two thousand years of ancient customary law, not to mention the primary law of natural law: The natural right of self defense. If, however, the captain had told us plainly what happened, there would likely have been "human rights" charges in some subsequent port of call.

The cause of the crisis 4-3

2009-11-20 18:33:34

In the cause of the crisis[244], I addressed fraudulent ratings.

Bill draws my attention to a report on securitized loans issued by the New York Fed in which they examine the somewhat surprising ratings given to New Century Financial:

> You might consider blogging this absolutely hilarious paper[245] from a couple of people at the New York Fed. The good stuff starts on page 14, where we learn about a typical pool of securitized mortgages originated by New Century Financial. There were about 3900 mortgages in the pool (made in 2006), and the pool had the following characteristics:
> more than half are cash-out loans
> 83% have FICO scores below 660
> average (average!!) total debt service to income is 41%
> 88% are hybrid ARMs with payment adjustment in 2-3 years
> typical adjustment 25 to 40 % increase in payment
> adjustment is bigger if rates rise
> half (!!!) the loans are "stated income," i.e.liar loans

Page 15[246] tells us that of the Alt A loans in the New Century pool in 2006, five out of six were "low doc" (liar) loans, and two out of five had additional silent mortgages - that is to say, not only was the borrower income not truthfully revealed, but the extent to which the property was likely to be underwater not truthfully revealed.

---

[243]https://www.csmonitor.com/2009/1119/p02s01-usmi.html

[244]https://blog.reaction.la/economics/the-cause-of-the-crisis-4-2.html

[245]https://www.newyorkfed.org/research/staff_reports/sr318.pdf

[246]https://www.newyorkfed.org/research/staff_reports/sr318.pdf

Incredibly, 79% of the tranches in this dog were rated (by both Moody's and S&P) AAA. How are the people who asked for and gave that rating not in jail? To be clear, AAA means really, really, US gvt treasuries safe.

Clearly, the people and institutions buying these securities were trusting the ratings agencies — nobody smart who read, digested, understood, and thought about that prospectus ever bought any of these (except as a regulatory dodge).

The conclusion of the paper is also really funny in an arch, extreme understatement kind of way.

On page 61[247]:

Ohio Attorney General Marc Dann claims that the Ohio state pension funds have been defrauded by the rating agencies. [...] To his mind, the seemingly cozy relationship between ratings agencies and investment banks like Bear Stearns only heightens the appearance of impropriety.

In this section, we review the extent to which investors rely on rating agencies, focusing on the case of this Ohio pension fund, drawing upon on public disclosures of the fund.

They then find that the Ohio pension fund invested heavily in the kind of subprime crap that they examined.

In the end they optimistically conclude:

Our view is that the rating of securities secured by subprime mortgage loans by credit rating agencies has been flawed. There is no question that there will be some painful consequences, but we think that the rating process can be fixed along the lines suggested in the text above.

No doubt it *can* be fixed along the lines suggested, but from the fact that the ratings agencies have not been prosecuted, and their regulators have not been fired, it seems unlikely that it *will* be fixed.

Attorney General Eric Holder has launched a bunch of prosecutions about mortgage fraud. It is hard to explain financial scams to twelve men too stupid to evade jury duty, but a major reason for the failure of prosecutions so far is that the Attorney General has been prosecuting minnows, the minnows blame the sharks, and were he to prosecute the sharks, the sharks would doubtless blame the regulators - who, strange to report, still have their jobs.

Global warming fraud goes public
2009-11-21 18:51:40

An unknown person posted a large amount of internal files from allegedly from CRU, which huge collection has become known as The Hadley CRU file set To understand all

---

[247]https://www.newyorkfed.org/research/staff_reports/sr318.pdf

this stuff, you need to know lots of climate science. I have only just started to go through this huge pile.

The original ftp server dropped the file (being stolen material and so on and so forth) and all those old links no longer work, but now the file is in bittorrent. The bittorrent link works with if you have installed a bittorrent client that support magnet links – magnet links being a highly decentralized way of publishing large files that does not expose any one server, router, or domain name to political pressure or possible reprisal, and prevents the illicit substitution of a changed file for the intended file. The file you get, will be the file I intend, which is not always the case with ftp or http links to politically sensitive data. The file is also available by http at such places as Megaupload[248], but pardon my paranoia, I don't trust what they might do under pressure.

There is much preliminary analysis and discussion of this great pile of data
Watts up with that[249]
The air vent[250]
Climate Audit[251]

We can be pretty sure these files are genuine, since they explain the "science" behind some otherwise inexplicable published graphs that supposedly show the world warming up. These graphs are constructed pseudo scientifically. Rather than simply being pulled out of someone's @%$#, they are constructed of numbers that reflect actual observations, but not observations of the quantity on the title bar of the graph.

Everyone is having lots of fun with this remark by Phil Jones:

> I've just completed Mike's Nature trick of adding in the real temps to each series for the last 20 years (ie from 1981 onwards) and from 1961 for Keith's to hide the decline.

The decline to which Phil Jones refers is not the recent global temperature decline, which may well result from more accurate and more global methods of measuring temperature, which are therefore increasingly difficult to plausibly "correct", but rather the failure of supposed temperature proxies to correspond to data supposedly derived from weather stations – the proxies are declining, so Phil Jones replaces the last few decades of the proxy, with the result that the last few decades of the graph for global temperature supposedly derived from the proxy agrees perfectly with the graph for global temperatures supposedly derived from weather stations, concealing the fact that there is no evidence that the proxy is in fact a proxy for temperature – indeed no evidence that either graph corresponds to global temperatures. Thus what is being fraudulently manufactured is not warming, but rather fraudulent agreement between various measures that supposedly measure warming.

The material seems psychologically genuine - they show conscious fraud that still retains much of the characteristics of self deception and unconscious cherry picking of data that it originated in.

---

[248] https://www.megaupload.com/?d=003LKN94
[249] https://wattsupwiththat.com/2009/11/19/breaking-news-story-hadley-cru-has-apparently-been-hacked-hundreds-of-files-released/#more-12937
[250] https://noconsensus.wordpress.com/2009/11/19/leaked-foia-files-62-mb-of-gold/
[251] https://www.climateaudit.org/?p=7806

There are just too many of these emails to be easily forged – you try writing many megabytes of text in the style of several well known people. Phil Jones has admitted them to be real[252], and is trying to spin some of his more embarrassing remarks, thereby drawing even more attention to them.

A first look at the internal climate emails

2009-11-22 04:12:06

Rather than reading for data that discredits particular erroneous results, a task that Steve and his crew can do much better than I can, I study the papers to reveal evil and madness, to reveal the cause of error, rather than specific particular errors.

The Anthropogenic Global Warmers know in advance the results of peer review that is not yet done. They also know in advance what the decisions of the environmental protection agency will be:

> I suppose that a more formal response by the relevant scientists is likely eventually to become part of the EPA docket as part of their rejection of the CEI petition. But that will drag on

Like psychotic, they mistake their own voices for the external validation of their ideas that it purports to be. Simultaneously, however, they know that such peer review is not legitimate:

Michael E. Mann:

> The Soon & Baliunas paper couldn't have cleared a 'legitimate' peer review process anywhere.

Which quote marks suggest a conscious awareness that any peer review that they control is illegitimate, and therefore that peer review at Climate Research is legitimate and at the time of this email, 2003 March, was the only journal with legitimate peer review. They circulate a copy of Freitas' defense of the Climate Research Peer Review process, and only discuss only how to destroy the journal, its editors, and those who produced unacceptable peer review results, not what is wrong with his defense, a silence that implicitly concedes the truth of Freitas' defense, and their awareness of the truth of that defense. In discussing how to destroy these people, rather than rebut Freitas' account of Climate Research peer review, they must know they are discussing how to ensure that 'peer review' is review for theological correctness, rather than empirical validity.

In contemplating their response to the Soon & Baliunas paper they did not consider replying in the pages of the same journal, the normal scientific procedure, despite naming various editors which they assume to be in their own pocket, which deviation from normal science implies an awareness that their reply could not survive legitimate peer review, only 'legitimate' peer review – implies awareness of evil.

By 2007 however, they no longer show confidence that peer review will produce predetermined results - there numerous journals whose peer review is no longer 'legitimate',

---

[252]https://briefingroom.typepad.com/the_briefing_room/2009/11/hadleycru-says-leaked-data-is-real.html

among them "Energy and Environment", and they cease to discuss destroying those responsible in ways that display confidence that they will succeed.

When they cherry pick statistics:

> since ca. Nov 2008, satellite data was removed from the analysis, and was called v3b, but the methodology is essentially the same as in the paper. The reason was that there was a residual cold bias in the satellite data. This caused problems for users concerned with rankings.

It is because they know what the results must be, therefore data that fails to support the predetermined result must be wrong. They sincerely believe they are practicing real science, and they do not sincerely believe they are practicing real science.

I had come to feel that the days of science and mathematics had ended, that science and mathematics had largely become like high art, a multitude of little government funded fiefdoms in which each specialty was controlled by a little incestuous group that approved each other's grants and was indifferent to external reality, unwanted facts and internal consistency. On the evidence of these emails, that is indeed the state of affairs, but contrary to my expectations, does not go unchallenged.

Bishop Hill's list of interesting Hadley CRU files
2009-11-22 09:07:10

Bishop Hill has a list of Hadley CRU files[253] he finds particularly interesting. They are mostly good stuff but have zero overlap with the files I find particularly interesting. It is going to take a while to digest sixty two megabytes. It will be some time before we realize what of this revelation truly matters.

To me, the relevant question is not whether global warming true, but whether alarmists been practicing science or religion. These files answer that question decisively, for when challenged, the focus of their thoughts, what is uppermost in their minds, is not so much "what do these facts imply", but rather, "how do we defeat the heretic".

Nailing the coffin lid shut on warmist alarmism
2009-11-24 07:45:54

Constantinople has summarized the debate for me in private email. People in authority are reading the blogs, and acting on them, but we are seeing the warming alarmists making the "just one sexed up graph" argument – similar to the argument that Uri Keller only bent *some* spoons with his hands, but all the other spoons he bent with is mind shows he really is magical, and Chomsky only made up *some* citations, but hey, what about all his other citations. After all, everyone knows that the ice is melting, the polar bears are drowning, that the North West passage never opened before, that we are seeing unprecedented hurricanes, the seas are rising, and so on and so forth. What does one sexed up graph matter?

---

[253]https://bishophill.squarespace.com/blog/2009/11/20/climate-cuttings-33.html

In its more sophisticated and rational form, this argument is the argument that even if peer review fails now and again and allows the occasional sexed up graph through, it still mostly works, which argument we see coming from Hansen[254] and Tyler Cowen[255], and will soon see from government officials around the world. "OK," they will say, "even if the peer review process is imperfect, nonetheless, the scientific consensus ..."

My impression is that my paper[256] ended the debate on Chomsky, not because many people read it, though many people did, but because a few people that mattered read it. I went through Chomsky's most egregious publication line by line and examined every single citation, and every single citation was at best misleading, at worst a lie. Until someone did that fisking, it remained possible to argue that people were unfairly jumping on Chomsky for a few innocent mistakes and exaggerations here and there, similar to the mistakes and exaggerations that all of us make from time to time. After I fisked him, then and only then did that argument finally go away, after hanging around for forty years and surviving numberless rebuttals.

The equivalent for warmist alarmism will be to go through every single warmist article published in one particular high prestige journal such as Nature in one particular subject area such climate of the last millennium and show that each and every one of them was sexed up, that *none* of them provided the data that it is a scientists job to provide, that for lack of that observational and algorithmic data *none* of them should have passed peer review, and that the journal ignored *all* legitimate criticisms of these egregious papers over the relevant period.

Steve McIntyre[257] has done the necessary work, and lots more goodies are coming out of the Hadley CRU readme[258] file, confirming from inside what Steve proved from outside, but it needs to be organized and structured into a single cohesive hyperlinked document.

The killer argument is that

1. Freedom of information inquiries were stonewalled.
2. That they were stonewalled because the graphs of doom were *all* pulled out of someone's %#, and freedom of information inquiries would have revealed this, would have revealed the readme file of the Hadley CRU files. 3. That peer review is a lie, for real peer review would have demanded the data supposedly underlying the graphs of doom, and the method of calculation, which the readme file reveals to have been pulled out of someone's %# 4. That because peer review is a lie, everything is a lie - that peer reviewers did not slip up once in a while, but systematically gave a free pass to theologically correct papers, and systematically rejected theologically incorrect papers

To prove that peer review is a lie, we have to not merely produce a few particular failures of peer review, not "just one sexed up graph", but rather we have to do a complete cover of all papers on one topic in one maximally prestigious journal in one period – which fisking very few people will read in its entirety, but the fisking has to be written, which is a lot of work.

[254] https://www.overcomingbias.com/2009/11/its-news-on-academia-not-climate.html
[255] https://www.marginalrevolution.com/marginalrevolution/2009/11/the-lessons-of-climategate.html
[256] https://reaction.lachomsdis.htm
[257] https://www.climateaudit.org/
[258] https://camirror.wordpress.com/2009/11/23/the-harry-read_me-file/

The point of the fisking has to be not that the elimination of the medieval climatic optimum was fraudulent, but that a maximally prestigious journal was complicit in the fraud. We have to take down, not just one powerful academic like Chomsky, but one powerful journal that helped empower them, one journal prestigious enough to stand for all journals, one topic important enough to stand for all topics. We have to utterly discredit the core institutions of science, because these institutions have been corrupted and used as a lever with which to destroy science, technological society, capitalism, and western civilization.

To address the argument that even though peer review slips up every now and then, it basically works for the most part, we have to provide a clear example of it *not* working, have to show not just that it passed one sexed up graph, but that for one journal and one topic, peer review passed *only* sexed up graphs and rejected all desexed graphs, that it was synod review for theological conformity with the holy doctrine of the synod, not genuine peer review.

It was a lot of work to do the fisking of Chomsky. It will be a lot more work to do the fisking of a high prestige journal, though most of the hard work has been done by Steve McIntyre[259], but the needed information is dispersed over a vast blog, and has to properly converted into one hypertext document with one argument, one conclusion, and links to all supporting information – that conclusion being that science was destroyed in a polit-ical and religious effort to remake western civilization into a scientifically, economically and technologically stagnant greenie theocracy that would only be capable of supporting a "sustainable" human population far smaller than our present population. If we push for any less grandiose conclusion, we lose the argument.

Against Libertarian Imperialism

2009-11-26 06:21:45

Faré on Distributed Republic criticizes the Rothbardians for supporting the enemies of their country.

> Many libertarians, after Rothbard, start from the correct assumption that one's government is one's first and most direct enemy, to the conclusion that one should always side with the enemies of one's current oppressor.

Rothbardians are wrong in supporting our enemies and the government is right to do something about them, the trouble is that the government is not very effectual or suc-cessful in doing something about them, while at the same time forbidding private citizens from acting.

Imperialism is not libertarian, colonialism can be.

Obviously I want the US to win in Iraq and Afghanistan, and our enemies to lose – which issue Rothbardians seem alarmingly confused about. But we are having prob-lems in Dar al-Islam, and have alway had similar problems for a thousand years, due to diseconomies of scale in the application of force. The Rothbardians are wrong in that we

---

[259]https://camirror.wordpress.com

really do need to kill people and break stuff but governments are not in fact very good at killing enough people and breaking enough stuff. Our past successes in this thousand year war have always involved meeting centralized state violence with centralized state violence, and decentralized non state and micro state violence with decentralized privatized and semi privatized violence. Centralized violence against the likes of the Taliban will work no better than centralized violence did against the Barbary pirates or the Saracens.

Imperialism worked and was good for everyone when the East India company was robbing the natives, for the Company was a colonialist. It became a disaster when the British government took over the East India Company and tried to do good to the natives from afar.

A big central government is bad at building local roads, and it is bad at providing law and justice. To the extent that good old fashioned Cecil Rhodes imperialism substituted competent civilized white stationary bandits for ignorant primitive and savage native stationary bandits, it was a huge improvement. Instead of being robbed by vicious cannibal rapists, the natives were robbed by people who mostly upheld private property rights, freedom of trade, and organized the building of roads. To the extent that imperialism substitutes distant do gooder bureaucrats in a foreign capital city for local primitive and savage stationary bandits, it is a disaster. It is better to be ruled by a local illiterate cannibal rapist despot than a Harvard educated bureaucrat located in Washington.

One of the best of the old imperialists, a man who was on the transition from brigand to bureaucrat, was Sir Stamford Raffles, a man who was willing to turn a city into a desert, and who rewarded troops by permitting them to ravage a city, a man who on a clerk's salary somehow mysteriously had gold enough to buy princes by the dozen and support armies on the march. He a spy who charmed people while arranging their deaths, and a brigand. Everyone loved him, and thought what a kind and gentle ruler he was. When he was replaced by men who were wholly bureaucrats efficiently representing the will of London, men who did not enrich themselves to any extraordinary extent, no one liked his replacements.

Rhodes and Raffles were better for those they ruled than London bureaucrats nor has governmental military action served Christendom sufficiently well in the war with Dar al Islam. We never got anywhere in the war with the Barbary pirates till the French started settling their lands. Until the colonialists arrived, the Barbary pirates would just surrender, then promptly unsurrender.

The peace of Vasvár in 1664 depressingly resembled the innumerable "peace" agreements that Israel has made.

Our installation of Karzai depressingly resembles Charlemagne's assistance to Ibn al Arubi. When Israel removed the settlers from Gaza, rockets followed. Therefore, when the settlers were there, they were preventing rockets.

This post has been corrected: The earlier version was overly critical of Faré.

climategate 1

2009-11-28 12:00:35

"Hide the decline"

In this scandal, we see antiscientific attitudes of the IPCC, the big government branch of the big science conspiracy Hadley CRU, a coalition of big government and big science to take control of your life, with the intent of preventing you from making a living in an "unsustainable" way. And if the earth cannot support so many people "sustainably", that is your problem, not their problem.

The men revealed by the emails knew what the truth must be[260], no matter what the evidence might show.

> The fact is that we can't account for the lack of warming at the moment ...the data are surely wrong. Our observing system is inadequate.

and if the data is surely wrong, then the wrong data must be hidden[261], hidden[262], hidden[263], hidden[264], hidden[265], hidden[266], hidden[267], hidden[268], hidden[269], hidden[270], hidden[271], hidden[272], hidden[273], hidden[274] lest climate skeptics misuse it. [][275]

or better than hidden, wrong data must be corrected, replaced by the values known to the the truth, so that the data showed the real truth, lest people be confused by mere observations:

> "I've just completed Mike's Nature trick of adding in the real temps ... to hide the decline[276]"

> So, if we could reduce the ocean blip by, say, 0.15 degC[277]

> I swear I pulled every trick out of my sleeve trying to milk something out of that. ... I don't think it'd be productive to try and juggle the chronology statistics any more than I already have[278]

Phil Jones to Tom Wigley:

---

[260] https://www.eastangliaemails.com/emails.php?eid=1048&filename=1255352257.txt
[261] https://www.eastangliaemails.com/emails.php?eid=891&filename=1212063122.txt
[262] https://www.eastangliaemails.com/emails.php?eid=967&filename=1237496573.txt
[263] https://www.eastangliaemails.com/emails.php?eid=914&filename=1219239172.txt
[264] https://www.eastangliaemails.com/emails.php?eid=591&filename=1132094873.txt
[265] https://www.eastangliaemails.com/emails.php?eid=878&filename=1210367056.txt
[266] https://www.eastangliaemails.com/emails.php?eid=878&filename=1219239172.txt
[267] https://www.eastangliaemails.com/emails.php?eid=878&filename=1254756944.txt
[268] https://www.eastangliaemails.com/emails.php?eid=345&filename=1059664704.txt
[269] https://www.eastangliaemails.com/emails.php?eid=462&filename=1105019698.txt
[270] https://www.eastangliaemails.com/emails.php?eid=462&filename=1168356704.txt
[271] https://www.eastangliaemails.com/emails.php?eid=490&filename=1107454306.txt
[272] https://www.eastangliaemails.com/emails.php?eid=1065&filename=1256765544.txt
[273] https://www.eastangliaemails.com/emails.php?eid=387&filename=1074277559.txt
[274] latex/images/cut_the_decline.jpg
[275] latex/images/cut_the_decline.jpg
[276] https://www.eastangliaemails.com/emails.php?eid=154&filename=942777075.txt
[277] https://www.eastangliaemails.com/emails.php?eid=1016&filename=1254108338.txt
[278] hhttps://www.eastangliaemails.com/emails.php?eid=12&filename=843161829.txt

Tom,

Keep quiet about both issues.

Tom Wigley replied[279].

The statements in the papers that he quotes seem to be incorrect statements, and that someone (WCW at the very least) must have known at the time that they were incorrect.

But nonetheless did indeed keep quiet.

Uses 'corrected' MXD - but shouldn't usually plot past 1960 because these will be artificially adjusted to look closer to the real temperatures.

Scare quotes around 'corrected' in original source code.

And what, you may ask, were the corrections. That too is available in the source code. Now while comments, intended for humans, may well be involve nuance, ambiguity, and disagreement as to the meaning, computers do what they are told. And what the computer source code told the computer to do was *lie*[280]

[yrloc=[1400,findgen[281]*5.+1904][282]
valadj=[0.,0.,0.,0.,0.0.10.250.3,0.0.1,0.3,0.8,1.2,1.7,2.5,2.6,2.6,2.6,2.6,2.6*0.75
; fudge factor][283]

Mann asks Briffa to make his data agree[284] with that of Mann

everyone in the room at IPCC was in agreement that this was a problem and a potential distraction/detraction from the reasonably concensus viewpoint we'd like to show w/ the Jones et al and Mann et al series.

... dilutes the message rather significantly ...

They perceived those who did not accept the real truth (regardless of what the data might show) as enemies of the earth, not to mention enemies of their grant applications,

I'm in the process of trying to persuade Siemens Corp.to donate me a little cash ... so the last thing I need is news articles calling into question [285] observed temperature increases.

Such enemies of the earth and the truth must be kept out of science, to preserve the truth and save the earth from its enemies. 'Legitimate peer review' (scare quotes in original) must stop such inconvenient and potentially misleading data from being published. 'Legitimate peer review'[286]
'Legitimate peer review'[287]

[279]https://www.eastangliaemails.com/emails.php?eid=813&filename=1188557698.txt
[280]https://www.americanthinker.com/2009/11/crus_scurce_code_climategate_r.html
[281]19
[282]https://www.americanthinker.com/2009/11/crus_source_code_climategate_r.html
[283]https://www.americanthinker.com/2009/11/crus_source_code_climategate_r.html
[284]https://www.eastangliaemails.com/emails.php?eid=136&filename=938018124.txt
[285]again
[286]https://www.eastangliaemails.com/emails.php?eid=295&filename=1047388489.txt
[287]https://www.eastangliaemails.com/emails.php?eid=1065&filename=1256765544.txt

'Legitimate peer review'[288]
'Legitimate peer review'[289]
'Legitimate peer review'[290]
'Legitimate peer review'[291]
'Legitimate peer review'[292]
'Legitimate peer review'[293]

Climategate 2

2009-11-28 12:31:34

The climategate letters, programs, and datafiles show a systematic and repetitious pattern of hiding and falsifying inconvenient data, cherry picking, self deception, and replacing peer review with theological review of the holy synod. It is worth examining particular incidents from this sorry story in detail[294].

When considering one particular such incident, you should keep in mind that each such incident is not an isolated bad apple. Rather, the climate gate emails and data reveal that it is all like this, every paper, every publication, every claim. Every single climate warming paper, every single piece of climate warming evidence, every graph. Official science is not science, but theology, theology concocted to impose on us a theocratic state, which state will deny us the ability to make our living in an 'unsustainable' way, 'unsustainable', being code for impious, just as 'legitimate peer review' [295] is code for illegitimate peer review, and 'corrected' data (scare quotes in original source code) is code for falsified data.

Nullius in Verba

2009-11-28 17:23:27

In the past, I ridiculed the Royal Society[296] for backing away from "Nullius in Verba" in its efforts to accommodate postmodern science - however, I recently learned[297] that the president of the Royal Society, Bob May, that was responsible for retranslating that into something more politically correct and respectful of the consensus of the synod, is no longer president of the Royal society – which may have something to do with the the the Royal Society eventually finding its testicles[298]

---

[288]https://www.eastangliaemails.com/emails.php?eid=1048&filename=1255352257.txt
[289]https://www.eastangliaemails.com/emails.php?eid=307&filename=1051190249.txt
[290]https://www.eastangliaemails.com/emails.php?eid=484&filename=1106322460.txt
[291]https://www.eastangliaemails.com/emails.php?eid=1003&filename=1249503274.txt
[292]https://www.eastangliaemails.com/emails.php?eid=321&filename=1054756929.txt
[293]https://www.eastangliaemails.com/emails.php?eid=321&filename=1054756929.txt
[294]https://camirror.wordpress.com/2009/11/25/willis-eschenbachs-foi-request
[295]scare quotes in original email
[296]https://blog.reaction.la/global-warming/global-warming-is-not-science.html
[297]https://bishophill.squarespace.com/blog/2009/11/27/nullius-in-verba.html
[298]https://blog.reaction.la/global-warming/latest-global-warming-scandal-in-short.html

Checking the Royal Society website[299] I find that the old translation, "take no one's word for it", which had mysteriously disappeared from the website, has mysteriously returned.

Despite this, and despite demanding that Warmists provide evidence rather than assertion, the Royal Society under its new leadership has continued to pressure private organizations to defund those who doubt the consensus of the Synod on global warming as it did under the old leadership. That it demands that evidence be presented by one side is rather less impressive if it continues to object to the other side also presenting evidence.

No twentieth century warming:

2009-11-29 14:14:53

The Strata-sphere has found that surface temperature measurements fail to show twentieth century global warming. The raw CRU data released in Climategate shows that surface temperature readings measure the first half of the last century [300] as warm or warmer than it is today.

John Pittman has found some interesting science in the Climategate emails:[301] The treeline is an sensitive treemometer, since it is very sharply defined, a few kilometers broad. Trees grow, just barely, south of the treeline, they entirely fail to grow north of the treeline. During the Medieval climatic optimum 750-1450 trees grew north of the present day treeline, indicating that the medieval climatic optimum was warmer than today in the north. *During the past century, 1897 to present, there has been no movement in the treeline, indicating no twentieth century warming in the north,**none**.*

Global sea ice area has also remained constant since it has been observed, from 1978 to the present.[302]

Surface temperatures

2009-12-02 05:57:22

The surface temperature data is, supposedly, still available from National Climatic Data Center. What was destroyed was information on how Hadley-CRU produced its famous graph of rising surface temperatures and some of the data that they used to construct the graph - the missing magic weather stations that show global warming.

There are two other independent graphs of surface temperature which show very similar results. The trouble is that if one is cooked, all may be cooked. The relationship of GISS to Hadley-CRU is too cosy, the process that produces their graph almost as opaque.

However, the information in the documents file would suggest that they just pulled that graph out of their @%$#[303], so the thing to do is to produce a new graph of twentieth century surface temperatures, this one with full information available at a click, so that

---

[299]https://royalsociety.org/Nullius-in-verba/
[300]1900-1960
[301]https://noconsensus.wordpress.com/2009/11/28/context-2/
[302]https://arctic.atmos.uiuc.edu/cryosphere/IMAGES/global.daily.ice.area.withtrend.jpg
[303]https://strata-sphere.com/blog/index.php/archives/11420

anyone can look at the surface station information that it is based on, and check if any one particular surface station is true, and the algorithms that produce it, and himself fiddle with those algorithms and see to what extent the result is robust.

Someone needs to start over and do it right. Exclude urban stations, rather than attempting a complicated and unexplained procedure to adjust for the urban hotspot effect, exclude known bad stations, and proceed. That, of course, is a lot of work. Watt's up with that has started on that large task.

The Cathedral loses

2009-12-02 07:44:08

When the mainstream media, academia, the state department, senior civil servants, and the leading politicians (the Cathedral) get behind an issue, they win, no matter how stupid, evil, or simply insane that position is. And if they are temporarily stalled, there will be some compromise, followed, when no one is looking, by a compromise on that compromise, until they have what they were determined to get.

It is interesting therefore that so far, neither president Zelaya, nor anyone resembling him, is president for life of Honduras.

In a free and fair election, conducted with lots of international observers, the candidate the Cathedral did not like, won.

Quietly, furtively, and shamefacedly, the US has announced it will recognize the result[304], despite previously ranting that if free and fair elections were permitted, it would legitimize a coup - the "coup" being the procedures that the Honduran constitution prescribed to prevent free and fair elections from being subverted by political power.

The Honduran Constitution prescribes swift, simple, informal, public, and drastic solutions to such problems. This seems to work against the Cathedral, which likes a cloud of complexity, compromise, and secrecy to conceal its shenanigans. It was a "coup" because it was not the kind of process that the Cathedral could manipulate without anyone understanding what was going on.

What is wrong with Wikipedia

2009-12-04 05:14:02

Wikepedia's rules innately and inherently create bias. One is required to source stuff, not in reality, not in what is observable, but in what respectable authority says, which necessarily excludes Climategate from Wikipedia. Evidence based data is "original research", thus the scientific approach is forbidden. To present the actual science, rather than the "consensus", is a violation of Wikipedia rules

Thus, for example, respectable authority does not like anything that Darwin said, for all of it is apt to support *raaaciiiiissssm*. But respectable authority cannot simple throw Darwin overboard as an evil Nazi. So instead, respectable authority attributes to Darwin

---

[304]https://rightwingnuthouse.com/archives/2009/11/30/walkback-complete-us-recognizes-winner-in-honduran-election/

the advances of his predecessors, loudly praises him for those ideas, and denounces Darwin's actual ideas as "ultra darwinism". It is then necessary for respectable to deny that Lamarck proposed common descent, so that they can attribute common descent to Darwin, in place of Darwinism. And so, if one quotes Lamarck's own words discussing common descent, this will be deleted from Wikipedia in fifteen seconds, and replaced with some eminent academic telling us what Lamarck supposedly said. Quoting Lamarck as evidence of what Lamarck said is "original research", and obviously that is unacceptable in Wikipedia. Indeed, any evidence based assertion is "original research". and thus all of Climategate, and all of the results of Steve McIntyre, are "original research". The rule against original research, necessarily prohibits evidence or facts based on evidence from appearing in Wikipedia.

In place of the "no original research" rule, we need to have a rule that privileges evidence and deprecates authority. And that rule is: Nullius in Verba

Winning on Climategate

2009-12-04 06:46:54

The mainstream media is reluctant to report Climategate, except that evil hackers have stolen private emails in a vain attempt to create to cast doubt on a dire emergency that creates an urgent need for a massive transfer of power and wealth to a centralized one world government.

Rasmussen polls[305], however, indicate that the vast majority of voters are aware of the general situation[306] - not because they have been informed about Climategate, but because of reflexive suspicion on being told they need to make sacrifices because the sky is falling. They know the truth from wise judgements of character, not from knowledge of science.

We are also getting some traction at the top. In addition to a leading Australian politician losing his job as a direct result of Climategate, Phil Jones has "stepped aside". By and large one does not "step aside" from where the bodies are buried unless the Vice Chancellor is standing in one's office with a large gentleman from security who is there in case one needs him to respectfully assist one in finding the exit.

The man appointed to replace Phil Jones in charge of the buried bodies, Peter Liss, looks to be crypto skeptic. Papers of which Peter Liss is listed as author used dog whistle language, subtly ambiguous phrases that mean one thing if one believes that once the most eminent scientists have formed a consensus, the science is settled, and all that remains is the minor detail of torturing the data till it repudiates its heresy and acknowledges the true faith, but which mean another, very different thing, if one adheres to the reactionary old fashioned idea that science rests of evidence and consensus is for synods, ambiguous phrases that sound as if the authors of the paper are respectfully acknowledging the authority of the consensus, but which subtly take the mickey out of it.

---

[305]https://www.rasmussenreports.com/public_content/politics/current_events/environment_energy/americans_skeptical_of_science_behind_global_warming
[306]https://hotair.com/archives/2009/12/03/poll-59-think-agw-scientists-may-have-falsified-data/

Climategate 3

2009-12-05 10:14:30

You have seen the worst of the climategate emails "I've just completed Mike's Nature trick ... to hide the decline"

But there are over a thousand emails. What is the typical average email like? Download them. Are most of them just showing good honest scientists industriously at work doing real science?

Here is a random sample. I selected the emails at random and entered them in this post before looking at what was in them. I have selected three emails, 1213387146.txt, 0933245004.txt and 1138042050.txt and as I write this text, after having done the selection, have no idea how bad they will be. This is not the worst of the worst, this is the average typical email. We shall now see how bad the typical email is.

1213387146.txt: Benjamin Santer threatens to sue American Liberty Publishers who disagree with his global warming results. Court imposed truth - the government that wants global warming to be true will be paying for the lawyers to sue American Liberty Publishers, and the government will also be paying the judge who is in charge of the case.

0933245004.txt: An assistant is instructed to change the statistical standards for the charts to what supports the argument, thereby cherry picking data, a minor transgression, but typical of global warming charts.

1138042050.txt: Ooh, by sheer luck, this one is juicy: "we cannot afford to being caught" They are revising what will appear in the IPCC report after the official last minute, showing that the official rules are merely for outsiders, not for insiders, which implies that the IPCC is merely the voice of the conspiracy.

So we have a thousand emails, any one of which should be adequate to discredit the "science" of anthropogenic global warming.

Jessica explains peer review

2009-12-05 15:18:44

Peer Review.

Warming trend

Provenance of the surface temperature graph of doom.

2009-12-06 05:54:28

"So what the hell did Tim do?!! As I keep asking."

The IPCC blessed the results of Hadley-CRU. Hadley-CRU blessed the results of the religous fanatic PhD student Tim Mitchell, and, as is clear from the Harry Readme file[307], no one checked how Tim produced these remarkable results.

Harry, in what is now the world's most studied document on global warming, the Harry_Read_Me.txt file, asks "So what the hell did Tim do?!! As I keep asking."

---

[307]https://www.climateaudit.org/?p=7844#comment-367132

How then did a lowly PhD student, a creature generally treated as of only marginally greater value than lab rats, and the South Park Evangelical Church, get the remarkable power to shape the fate of nations?

The answer, of course, is government funding. Grantsmanship will always out compete real science, because bureaucrats lack real interest in either the science or the wise expenditure of the money. Important experts in grantsmanship, such as Phil Jones, are far too important to be bothered with the menial task of gathering data to support theories that have already been determined to be true for reasons of grantsmanship, so they delegate this utterly insignificant task (insignificant since the truth is determined by the scientific consensus, not mere data) to someone as menial and insignificant as the task they are to perform.

Again and again in the Climategate emails we see someone important, an eminent scientist, an important person, directing some menial and insignificant research assistant to produce data with the desired and expected results necessary to advocate a political position. Tim, one of these menial and insignificant worms in CRU, got the menial and insignificant job of providing proof that the end of the world was nigh, which he proceeded, enthusiastically, to do. Very enthusiastically. No one bothered to check how he did it. To this day, no one knows how he did it, not Phil Jones, his boss, who directed him to do it, and not the IPCC, with its hundreds of thousands of eminent reviewers, and not Harry, who (unlike the IPCC and Phil Jones) reviewed Tim's data and programs at considerable length.

The consensus, like the Vatican, is inerrant. Embarrassing Tim Mitchell lies under the bus but his made up data goes marching on. The consensus may change, but not only is the consensus never wrong, it never was wrong.

The Cathedral, by its circular nature, is apt to become ever more detached from reality, which we are seeing in action. The Cathedral rules the world, no alternative is in sight, yet is insane and inherently becoming more insane without possibility of reform. The reaction to Climategate is to become ever more impregnably indifferent to external reality, more overtly a theocratic religion demanding human sacrifice. So long as the Cathedral rules, the west will decline.

Regional Climate modeling

2009-12-06 11:22:41

The IPCC produced extremely detailed physics based region by region models of the climate, past and present.

These physics based models reproduced the regional temperatures reported by Hadley-CRU with astonishing accuracy up to the date at which the models were issued, which astonishing accuracy is most odd since we now know that these observed regional temperatures were not observed, but were pulled out of the @%$# of Tim Mitchell, a PhD student doing the menial scutwork that important scientists were far too important to do, and therefore delegated to unimportant inferiors, in this case the minor detail of of cooking the data and washing away the heresy from the data so that it complied with the consensus:

"So what the hell did Tim do?!! As I keep asking."

Watts up with that[308], and the Strata-sphere[309], examine these predictions and retro-dictions in the light of what we now know about regional climates.

You will doubtless be as surprised as I am to hear that that the IPCC anthropogenic global warming models are not doing too well.

The state of warmist evidence

2009-12-07 10:39:07

This guy claims (anonymously) to be a climate scientist. Since the claim is anonymous, delete claim, inset links to facts.

I am a climate scientist, and it is clear that the evidence that "human activity is promi-nent [sic] agent in global warming" is NOT overwhelming. The repeated statement that it is does not make it so. Further, even if we accepted the hypothesis, cap-and-trade legis-lation does not do anything about it.

Here are the facts. We have known for years that the Mann hockey stick model was wrong, and we know why it was wrong (Mann used only selected data to normalize the princi-pal component analysis, not all of it). He retracted the model. We have known for years that the Medieval Warm period occurred, where the temperatures were higher than they are now (Chaucer spoke of vineyards in northern England). Long before ClimateGate it was known that the IPCC people were trying to fudge the data to get rid of the MWP. And for good reason. If the MWP is "allowed" to exist, this means that temperatures higher than today did not then create a "runaway greenhouse" in the Middle Ages with methane released from the Arctic tundra, ice cap albedo lost, sea levels rising to flood London, etc. etc.), and means that Jim Hansen's runaway greenhouse that posits only amplifying feedbacks (and no damping feedbacks) will not happen now. We now know that the models on which the IPCC alarms are based to not do clouds, they do not do the biosphere, they do not explain the Pliocene warming, and they have never predicted anything, ever, correctly. As the believers know but, like religious faithful, every wrong prediction (IPCC underestimated some trends) is claimed to justify even greater alarm (not that the models are poor approximations for reality); the underpredictions (where are the storms? Why "hide the decline"?) are ignored or hidden. As for CO2, we have known for years that CO2 increases have never in the past 300,000 years caused temper-ature rise (CO2 rise trails temperature increase). IPCC scientists know this too (see their "Copenhagen Diagnosis"); we know that their mathematical fudges that dismiss the fact that CO2 has not been historically causative of temperature rise are incorrect as well. We have also known for years that the alleged one degree temperature rise from 1880 van-ishes if sites exposed to urban heat islands are not considered. We have long known that Jones's paper dismissing this explanation (Jones, et al.1990. Assessment of urbanization effects in time series of surface air temperature over land, Nature 347 169- 172) is wrong and potentially fraudulent (see the same data used to confirm urban heat islands in Wang,

---

[308]https://wattsupwiththat.com/2009/11/29/when-results-go-bad/
[309]https://strata-sphere.com/blog/index.php/archives/11732

W-C, Z. Zeng, T. R Karl, 1990. Urban Heat Islands in China. Geophys. Res. Lett. 17, 2377-2380). Everyone except Briffa knows that the Briffa conclusions are wrong, and why they are wrong; groups in Finland, Canada (lots of places actually) show cooling by this proxy, not warming; the IPCC even printed the Finn's plot upside down to convert the fact (cooling) into the dogma (warming).

Prof.McCarthy is, of course, part of the IPCC that has suppressed dissenting viewpoints based on solid climate science. His claim to support by "peer review" is nonsense; he has helped corrupt the peer review process. We now have documentary evidence that Jones, Mann, and the other IPCC scientists have been gaming peer review and blackballing opponents. On this point, the entire IPCC staff, including Prof.McCarthy, neither have nor deserve our trust.

We have tolerated years of the refusal of Mann and Jones to release data. Now, we learn that much of these data were discarded (one of about 4 data sets that exist), something that would in any other field of science lead to disbarment. We have been annoyed by Al Gore, who declared this science "settled", refused to debate, and demonized skeptics (this is anti-science: debate and skepticism are the core of real science, which is never settled). The very fact that Prof.McCarthy attempts to bluff Congress by asserting the existence of fictional "overwhelming evidence" continues this anti-science activity.

All of this was known before Climategate. What was not known until now was the extent to which Jones and Mann were simply deceiving themselves (which happens often in science) or fraudently attempting to deceive others. I am not willing to crucify Jones on the word "trick". Nor, for that matter, on the loss of primary data, keeping only "value added" data (which is hopelessly bad science, but still conceivably not fraud).

But the computer code is transparently fraudulent. Here, one finds matrices that add unexplained numbers to recent temperatures and subtract them from older temperatures (these numbers are hard-programmed in), splining observational data to model data, and other smoking guns, all showing that they were doing what was necessary to get the answers that the IPCC wanted, not the answers that the data held. They knew what they were doing, and why they were doing it. If, as Prof.McCarthy insists, "peer review" was functioning, and the IPCC reports are rigorously peer reviewed, why was this not caught? When placing it in context made it highly likely that this type of fraud was occurring?

The second question is: Will this revelation be enough to cause the "global warming believers" to abandon their crusade, and for people to return to sensible environmental science (water use, habitat destruction, land use, this kind of thing)? Perhaps it will. Contrary to Prof.McCarthy's assertion, we have not lost just one research project amid dozens of others that survive. A huge set of primary data are apparently gone. Satellite data are scarcely 40 years old. Everything is interconnected, and anchored on these few studies. Even without the corruption of the peer review process, this is as big a change as quantum mechanics was in physics a century ago.

But now we know that peer review was corrupted, and that no "consensus" exists. The "2500 scientists agree" number is fiction (God knows who they are counting, but to get to this number, they must be including referees, spouses, and pets).

The best argument now for AGW is to argue that CO_2 is, after all, a greenhouse gas, its concentration is, after all, increasing, and feedbacks that regulated climate for millions of years might (we can hypothesize) be overwhelmed by human CO2 emissions. It is a hypothesis worthy of investigation, but it has little evidentiary support.

Thus, there is hope that Climategate will bring to an end the field of political climatology, and allow climatology to again become a science. That said, people intrinsically become committed to ideas. The Pope will not become a Protestant even if angel Gabriel taps him on the shoulder and asks him to. Likewise, Prof.McCarthy may claim until the day he retires that there remains "overwhelming support" for his position, even if every last piece of data supporting it is controverted. As a graduate student at Harvard, I was told that fields do not advance because people change their minds; rather, fields advance because people die.

****

Hide the decline:

In fact, one skeptic raised this very issue about tree-ring data in a comment posted in 2004 on RealClimate[310], the blog operated by climate scientists. The comment, which questioned the propriety of "grafting the thermometer record onto a proxy temperature record," immediately drew a sharp retort on the blog[311] from Michael Mann, an expert at Penn State[312] University:

"No researchers in this field have ever, to our knowledge, 'grafted the thermometer record onto' any reconstruction. It is somewhat disappointing to find this specious claim (which we usually find originating from industry-funded climate disinformation Web sites) appearing in this forum."

Dr.Mann now tells me that he was unaware, when he wrote the response, that such grafting had in fact been done in the earlier cover chart, and I take him at his word. But I don't see why the question was dismissed so readily, with the implication that only a tool of the fossil-fuel industry would raise it.

Tony Abbot takes aim at Copenhagen
2009-12-08 18:12:55

Tony Abbot made news around the world, by unseating Malcolm Turnbull as leader of the Australian opposition over Climategate, and then stalling the carbon tax. By stalling the tax, Abbot challenged the Prime Minister to a double dissolution election, which would have been a referendum on the carbon tax. By backing down from that challenge, the Prime Minister finds himself empty handed in Copenhagen, making it much harder to reach agreement.

Abbot concludes that global warming alarmism is not, in fact, very popular among the voters, that skepticism sells when presented as delay, caution, and real science

The following skepticism will not be news to anyone that reads this blog – what will be news is that a competent politician finds it wins votes – that democracy, should the ruling elite pay attention to it, will in this case produce the less disastrous result.

---

[310]https://www.realclimate.org/ "RealClimate blog"

[311]https://www.realclimate.org/index.php/archives/2004/12/myths-vs-fact-regarding-the-hockey-stick/#comment-380 "Real Climate"

[312]https://topics.nytimes.com/top/reference/timestopics/organizations/p/pennsylvania_state_university/index.html?inline=nyt-org "More articles about Pennsylvania State University"

one of the things that I have always found distressing about this debate Alan is the theological way in which it has been conducted – all this talk of deniers and believers, people being put on the spot and being asked to proclaim their faith one way or another.

I mean in the end this whole thing is a question of fact, not faith, or it should be a question of fact not faith and we can discover whether the planet is warming or not by measurement. And it seems that notwithstanding the dramatic increases in man made CO2 emissions over the last decade, the world's warming has stopped.

...

as if this is some latter-day environmental Munich agreement kind of thing. ... there is far too much hype here and we all need to be objective and dispassionate about this because man is more than capable of rising to the challenge of the environment but we won't do it if we rush into things in a fit of environmental rectitude.

...

once you have got to explain why you have got this giant money-go-round taking money from polluters, then giving it back to people via these indirect mechanisms that certainly aren't going to end up equalizing the burdens, I think then people start to say, 'hang on a minute, this is all a bit of a con'.

...

there's Kevin heading off to Copenhagen to solve problems that may or may not occur in 100 years time.

It is working for Tony Abbot, it will therefore work for Republicans, if they have the guts.

Official lies

2009-12-09 06:44:05

Official statistics have gone the same path as peer review.

Obama holds a jobs conference, and then immediately after Obama's cheerful jobs conference, the BLS tells us that there are fewer unemployed, and more jobs.

Supposedly there are over a million more jobs this year than the same period last year - yet withheld income for salaried employees and payroll tax have fallen 19% compared to the same period last year.

Private employment surveys[313], x[314], x[315], such as ADP[316] and Trim Tabs[317] tell us that everything is going to hell in a handbasket.

---

[313]https://oldprof.typepad.com/a_dash_of_insight/2009/12/employment-report-preview.html
[314]https://blog.atimes.net/?p=1258
[315]https://blog.theinterviewedge.com/the_interview_edge/2009/12/bernanke-the-economy-and-jobs.html
[316]https://www.adpemploymentreport.com/
[317]https://ftalphaville.ft.com/blog/2009/12/02/86766/on-outperforming-the-us-bureau-of-economic-analysis/

Spengler[318] points out that 300,000 people disappeared from the labor force, yet the BLS reports no increase in "discouraged workers" or workers forced to take part-time jobs for economic reasons.

The government tells us everything is getting better and better. Who are you going to believe?

Thousands of scientists endorse evidence of anthropogenic global warming

2009-12-11 10:52:33

And every single one of them can be easily proven to be a fraud who should be in jail.

If one endorses evidence of anthropogenic global warming, the evidence one is endorsing is the findings of the IPCC. And one of the major findings of the IPCC is Phil Jones surface temperature data. So if one endorses evidence of anthropogenic global warming, one endorses the surface temperature data – which we now know came out of Tim Mitchell's @%$#.

"So what the hell did Tim do?!! As I keep asking."

Thousands of scientists endorsed the IPCC publications. They might say, "I trust Phil Jones, I can't imagine he would lie." If someone says that, he's not speaking as a scientist, he is speaking as an outsider who is taking someone else's word for it. But what they're doing is claiming to speak as scientists, pretending to have examined the evidence, when the Climategate files reveal they have not, that they could not have, for Phil Jones has no evidence for them to examine. So each of them is guilty of fraud, each of them should be in jail.

Science education, both informal and formal, is full of "check it out for yourself". You don't get to say that you understand a mathematical theorem unless you've actually gone through the proof - probably regenerated the proof as an exercise based on the instructor's clues. You don't take anybody's word for it. There is no trust in math. Zero. No need for it. And in programming, you have to write the damn program for yourself. You don't take anybody's word that it works. And in physics, you're not learning physics unless you do the labs, and see for yourself. Otherwise you're just doing not-very-rigorous mathematics.

But when it comes to global warming, all of a sudden the talk is of "consensus". All along, the science student has been taught not to trust anyone, not even his own teacher. To trust only his own senses and his own mind. And now, we're supposed to trust a "consensus"

The most incriminating part of the Climate gate files is not "hide the decline".

The most incriminating part of the Climate gate files is not "So what the hell did Tim do?!!"

The most incriminating part of the Climate gate files is the dog that did not bark in the night time – that no one, except for Harry, showed any interest whatsoever in the data, in checking the data out, in the process of reasoning and mathematics connecting data to

---

[318]https://www.atimes.com/atimes/Global_Economy/KL08Dj05.html

results, that Phil Jones delegated what was supposedly the major job of the CRU, estimating global temperatures, to a postgrad, and never asked how that postgrad obtained the desired result – that everyone, except for Harry, viewed science as the task of building a consensus and imposing that consensus on all, not the task of gathering evidence and trying to figure out what the evidence reveals.

What the Climategate files reveals is not science, but religion. Scientists replicate. Synods build consensus. The Climategate files show a synod in action.

How "Science" responds to heresy

2009-12-14 04:21:54

Australian Climate Madness has a revealing video.[319]

The professor refuses to address the question, then the UN goons come out to stop the questions.

More surface temperature fraud

2009-12-14 08:20:52

The Climategate files revealed that the Hadcrut surface temperature series was fraudulent, and cast doubt on the Giss surface temperatures. Small Dead Animals[320] and Watts up with that[321], and more[322] soon discovered fraud in the Giss surface temperature series, and now fraud in the GHCN[323] series.

Which is all the surface temperature series that support global warming. All of three them. Each one is fraudulent. Twentieth century warming has not been replicated. Excluding all temperatures series based on fraud, the remaining evidence indicates that the 1930s were as warm or warmer than the present.

What the climategate files reveal.

2009-12-20 05:58:49

The killer directory in the climategate files is not the email directory, but the documents directory, for the documents directory reveals how the graphs of doom were generated. One should only employ the emails directory to illuminate what is documented in the documents directory.

The Climategate files reveal that the graphs of doom are irreproducible, for Harry was unable to reproduce them, except by means at best extremely dubious[324], "So what the hell did Tim do?!!" at worst frankly fraudulent[325]. "Apply a VERY ARTIFICAL correction for decline!!"

---

[319]https://www.australianclimatemadness.com/?p=2274
[320]https://www.smalldeadanimals.com/archives/012874.html
[321]https://wattsupwiththat.com/2009/12/11/giss-raw-station-data-before-and-after/
[322]https://wattsupwiththat.com/2009/12/08/the-smoking-gun-at-darwin-zero/
[323]https://noconsensus.wordpress.com/2009/12/13/ghcn-antarctic-warming-eight-times-actual/
[324]https://caps.fool.com/Blogs/ViewPost.aspx?bpid=301624&t=01000860093551905860
[325]https://strata-sphere.com/blog/index.php/archives/11518

The documents directory reveals that data issuing from the Warming alarmists is fake, for it was Harry's job to produce or reproduce these graphs of doom, and he describes in alarming detail how the graphs of doom were manufactured. Every graph generated from the programs and data of the documents directory of Climategate files is at worst a lie, at best fabricated without concern for truth, and proves the falsity of those graphs of doom that Harry was required to reproduce, for he was unable to reproduce any of them by legitimate means.

The Climategate files reveal that the method of anthropogenic warmist alarmism is that "scientists" construct a consensus, and *then* they examine data and papers for conformity with the consensus. Data that fails to conform to theory is rejected, then hidden or deleted. Papers that fail to conform are rejected. They then direct some menial postgrad student, first Tim, then later Harry, to produce graphs that show the result that they have already determined that the graphs will show.

What the climategate papers reveal is religion, not science, for when we read Harry's comments and code, it is apparent that his job is not to find what the data shows, but to force the data to show a result that has been predetermined.

How bloggers saved the world
2009-12-20 17:38:13

The Air Vent tells us that China saved the world[326], which is true, but China saved the world because of what bloggers did.

The enemy plan was to use global warming to roll back science, technology and western civilization. Copenhagen was to have established a "world climate treaty organization" which would exercise centralized control over all the worlds economies, thereby avoiding that inconvenient embarrassment that ensues whenever socialist economies face comparison with capitalist economies.

Someone released the Climategate files. I initially believed that this was a hacker from outside, but reading through the files, it is evidently an insider, for each file that I examined is good stuff, which is to say, exceedingly bad stuff. Each file was being wrongfully and illegally withheld from a freedom of information request, or demonstrates an anti scientific approach and outlook, or both.

Climategate resulted in the removal of Malcolm Turnbull as leader of the Australian opposition, the first mainstream politician to fall to bloggers, and his replacement by Tony Abbot, who proceeded to save Australia from trading in carbon indulgences, and to challenge the leader of the Australian government to a double dissolution election over anthropogenic global warming.

This was a bold move when most of the mass media was preaching imminent climate doom. The polls showed that a double dissolution election held on that issue would be a disaster for the opposition– but polls have been known to change when the people hear two voices instead of one voice. The government chickened out.

Having won without taking it to the people, Tony Abbot then adopted a blander position similar to that of Sarah Palin – that climate change can be prevented by vague

---

[326]https://noconsensus.wordpress.com/2009/12/19/fe-ny-how-china-saved-the-world/

and unspecified means without it costing anybody anything, and the science is not settled.

With Australia, China's main carbon supplier, out of the picture, it was then difficult to for China to join the treaty. Without China, there could be no treaty.

The Chinese do not understand democracy and constitutional government, so they reasonably enough blame Rudd, the leader of the Australian government, for the climate skeptic policy of Tony Abbott, leader of the opposition. After all, they think, surely the government, not the opposition, sets climate policy. With great indignation they pointed out that Rudd is preaching Warmist Alarmism, yet Australia is practicing climate skepticism. That, at least, is their rebuttal to the Warmist Alarmists. And so, no World Climate Treaty, nor any World Climate Treaty Organization.

So the world is saved for a little longer, and bloggers saved it. Perhaps the Chinese would have saved it without Abbot's skeptic policies, but spectacle of Rudd preaching sacrifices to the Chinese that he was unwilling to take to Australian voters, and therefore unable to impose on Australians in the face of Abbot's opposition, angered them.

The extraordinary inanity of nation building

2009-12-22 08:01:46

The counter insurgency planners have presented a clever plan on how they propose to counter Afghan insurgency by building an Afghan nation[327].

When first I saw slides from this presentation, I assumed them to be parody, but no, they are the real thing. The people planning this war really are this stupid, crazy, and evil.

includegraphiclatex/images/coin.png

There are a great pile of slides, and they all look like the above. Hat tip The Austrian Economists[328].

I did a search for blog posts linking to this amazing pile of essence of evil madness, to find the New York Times treating it with the solemn respect that one would be ruler of all mankind should give another would be ruler of all mankind. Democracy's Arsenal[329] also displays the semblance of profound respect for this moronic madness, but from his image selection, his tongue is well and truly in his cheek.

The Taliban have a notorious tendency to mistake the customs of their tribe for the word of God, but at least they do not mistake themselves for God.

Warmism for politicians

2009-12-23 06:20:40

If Sarah Palin is so amazingly dumb, how come she gets everything right on a complex issue, *and* explains it in language that the average voter can understand?

---

[327]https://msnbcmedia.msn.com/i/MSNBC/Components/Photo/_new/Afghanistan_Dynamic_Planning.pdf
[328]https://austrianeconomists.typepad.com/weblog/
[329]https://www.democracyarsenal.org/2009/12/they-dont-call-coin-the-graduate-level-of-war-for-nothing-.html

Sarah Palin explains climate change[330], covering every issue, except for the documents directory of the climategate files, in clear, easy to understand language.

She makes one minor error, describing "hide the decline" as hiding the decline of temperature, when in fact they were hiding the decline of a proxy for temperature, but this oversimplification does not affect the point, the point being that they were tricking you by hiding an inconvenient fact that would suggest that there is nothing unusual about recent changes in climate. Since she compressed all the Climategate emails into a single wonderfully stinging paragraph, a harmless oversimplification was difficult to avoid.

> The e-mails reveal that leading climate "experts" deliberately destroyed records, manipulated data to "hide the decline" in global temperatures, and tried to silence their critics by preventing them from publishing in peer-reviewed journals. What's more, the documents show that there was no real consensus[331] even within the CRU crowd.

After concisely summing up the more easily understood part of Climategate (the emails), she then goes on to argue that costs and benefits of climate change proposals must be realistically evaluated:

> But while we recognize the occurrence of these natural, cyclical environmental trends, we can't say with assurance that man's activities cause weather changes. We can say, however, that any potential benefits of proposed emissions reduction policies are far outweighed by their economic costs. And those costs are real.

"Natural cyclical" and "economic costs" summarizes the entire Hockey Stick versus Medieval Climatic Optimum argument in a nutshell. She has repackaged the complex scientific debate of the blogs into something for voters and politicians.

She then, in a classic politician's move, points to Australia as foreshadowing the climate change bandwagon hitting the rocks of Climategate. Since every politician wants to get on the winning side, this is a compelling argument for her fellow politicians.

I predict that she will once again demonstrate the power to turn the debate around and shape political outcomes, as she did with health care. While Obama looks powerless, she looks powerful. Obama bows before kings, though in protocol kings and presidents should treat each other as equals, and gets snubbed by our major creditor, the equivalent of a banker not giving you an appointment, while Sarah changes the world from her facebook page.

The ability to make a complex and difficult topic as simple as it can be is the mark of a truly brilliant scientist. The ability to make a complex and difficult topic a little bit simpler than it can be is the mark of a truly brilliant politician.

---

[330] https://www.facebook.com/notes/sarah-palin/the-washington-post-op-ed-and-response-to-climate-change-and-gravity/193694168434

[331] https://www.washingtonpost.com/wp-dyn/content/article/2009/12/04/AR2009120404511.html

Merry Christmas

2009-12-25 16:26:09

There is a reason that the United States, the most Christian nation in the world, is also the most free nation in the world.

And that reason is that of all the deadly superstitions that infest the world, Christianity is the least murderous, the least oppressive, fosters the least hatred and envy, and is responsible for fewer wars and mass murders than any religion of comparable size.

And the comparative decency of this belief system is best displayed in the Christmas celebration, where people genuinely wish each other a merry Christmas, for Christmas is not a merely a Christian celebration, but a celebration in which Christians wish good to all men, and invite all men to join in the celebration. And I recommend that you should join in, whether you believe or not. This is a time to be be merry, to be with family, and to catch up on what far flung family members have been up to.

When a man ceases to believe in God, the most likely result is not that he will believe nothing without evidence, but that he will believe anything that seems to show the universe caring. Those who will not believe in God, are apt to believe in the power of crystals, their horoscope, in ghosts, spirits and angels, in Anthropogenic Global Warming, in Gaia, the cycle of life, in mystics, and in anything else that is apt to make it seem that the universe cares.

The universe does not care, but men do care. The world has no meaning, but man gives it meaning. I care. Merry Christmas.

No twentieth century warming

2009-12-31 08:44:39

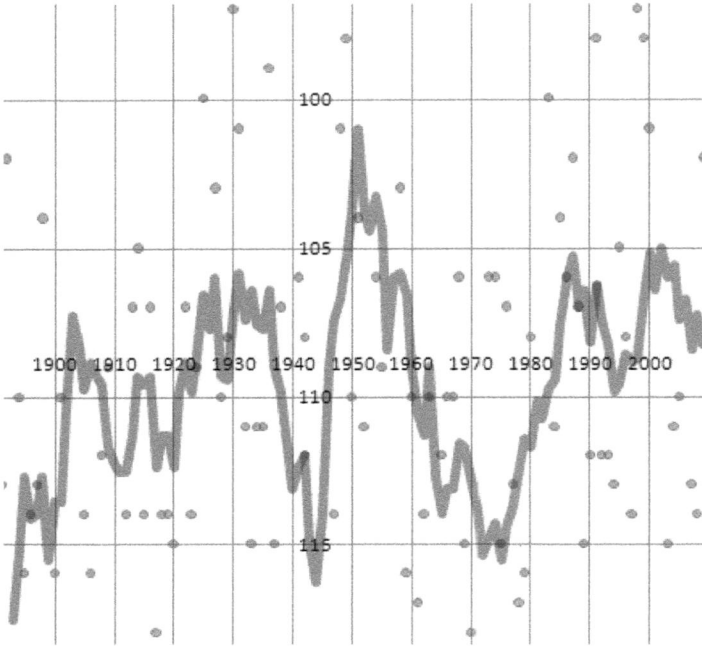

The earliest ice outs, and thus the warmest years, were in the 1950s. The warming from 1975 to 1998 is real, but not very large - just a blip in the overall cooling trend from 1950.

During the 1950s, Winnipesaukee ice outs were generally around Julian day 100, which is usually April 10. These days, it is around Julian day 107, which is usually April 17 - the ice is taking longer to melt, therefore, these days the weather is cooler than it was in the 1950s.

Data and calculations here – you will not find that replicability if you look at "peer reviewed" research.

If one selects the lakes with the best data, no sign of twentieth century warming.

Similarly for the weather station record.[332] which indicates no twentieth century warming

Sea ice areas are unchanged[333], and sea levels rise is small and slowing[334], consistent with the overall shape of the above graph.

The vertical axis is the Julian day number of the ice outs. The little green dots are the julian numbers of ice out days for particular years, the graph is the seven year rolling average of the ice out day. Smaller numbers, representing warmer years, are at the top of the

---

[332]https://strata-sphere.com/blog/index.php/archives/11582

[333]https://arctic.atmos.uiuc.edu/cryosphere/IMAGES/global.daily.ice.area.withtrend.jpg

[334]https://www.21stcenturysciencetech.com/Articles%202007/MornerInterview.pdf

graph, larger numbers, representing cooler years, are at the bottom. Lake Winnipesaukee was selected because lots of people who have no interest in global warming have an interest in this ice out day and report it[335], because it enables them to do business and get to their properties, hence the ice out day is a valid number. It is the top hit in google for ice outs, excluding global warming related hits.

Lakes whose ice out day is subject to less interest are likely to have the same reliability problems as the instrumental temperature record. If one has to look hard for historical data, that data is unlikely to be accurate because few people were monitoring it. Since the data is likely to be inaccurate, one can always cherry pick data that proves anything one wants to prove, which cherry picking is apt to slowly become making up data outright – since one already supposedly knows what the data should show, searching overly hard for data that one knows must be true is apt to become outright forgery, as the Climategate documents directory shows happened with the instrumental temperature record.

If there are gaps in the data, as there generally is with the instrumental record and with many lake iceouts, that means few people are monitoring it. If few, then perhaps none, perhaps the data is consciously or unconsciously fraudulent, and whether legitimate or not, no way to prove it legitimate. Incompleteness is a symptom of other problems. If a lake is so obscure that one cannot find a lake ice out for this year on the internet from boating enthusiasts, did anyone really find the lake ice out for 1950, or did they just make it up?

It is hard to estimate global climate from the instrumental record, but the most plausible evidence, if we exclude cities for the urban hot spot effect, and use only climate stations with good stability, refraining from efforts to patch together lots of fragmentary climate station records of unclear provenance, is that the 1950s were the warmest period in the twentieth century, and that the warming from 1975 to 1998 was just a small fluctuation in the long term cooling trend since 1950[336]

The documents directory of the climategate files reveals that Harry could not derive global temperatures from the instrumental data, that the hadcrut global temperatures, the supposed instrumental record, had come right out of Tim's ass.

Various people have attempted to reconstruct the global temperature record from the instrumental record but the data are not of quality that would enable this to be done. The jumps resulting from moves of weather stations and suchlike are much larger than the climate changes one is trying to detect. You cannot get a silk purse out of a sow's ear. Weather stations keep moving their thermometers, changing the way they record data, and so on and so forth. Until 2004 no one was trying to do measurements that would be suitable for evaluating climate change - some would say they were trying from 1998, but they surely were not succeeding until 2004.

The only instrumental global temperature records are, like the climategate instrumental record, the result of someone's secret sauce which they will not reveal, for no one who will reveal his method of calculation can produce anything from weather station data that they will claim to be plausible or credible. Lots of people have tried.

---

[335]https://www.winnipesaukee.com/index.php?pageid=iceout
[336]https://strata-sphere.com/blog/index.php/archives/11582

For some examples of the difficulties encountered, see Watts up with that[337], xx[338], xx[339]. The GHCN adjustments were obviously fraudulent and intended to create fake global warming in the instrumental record, but it is impossible to say what adjustment would be reasonable and uncontroversial. There is room enough in the gaps between one weather station and the next to manufacture global warming, global cooling, or have temperatures dance the watutsi. Obvious the CRU was wrong to exclude those weather stations that showed world temperatures falling – but if the world climate trend depends on what stations you exclude and what you include, one can have little confidence in the trend derived from any particular set of weather stations.

Science is replication, not peer review.

What happens behind the scenes in peer review was revealed in the climategate emails

Peer review, as revealed in the climategate emails, is in practice theological review. If it is peer reviewed, it is a lie. If it appears in "Nature" or "Science" it is a lie. The truth is not allowed.

Which fact is obvious from the fact that non peer reviewed reports show their data and method of calculation, and peer reviewed reports on political topics do not. If it is peer reviewed, it cannot be replicated. If it cannot be replicated, is not science.

Working through these non peer reviewed reports, replicating them, one can prove that various peer reviewed reports are criminal frauds. When we got the inside info, when the climategate files came out, we found in the documents directory the programs that did what we had already proven had been done. Climategate confirmed what *replicated* research had already proven. Replicated is the gold standard. Peer reviewed is not.

We had already proven that global warming was criminal fraud. Then we got confirmation from inside in the Climategate files, proving that our account of how global warming was cooked up was indeed how it was cooked up.

The scientific method

2010-01-04 05:42:34

When science becomes a priesthood, it is no longer science.

Reference to authority is unscientific, indeed antiscientific, a rejection of the principles of science. One must appeal to evidence, not authority. What authority says is *not* scientific evidence.

Independent replication is evidence.

If people all over the world have made observations for the last 100 years about temperature, I can't replicate them; but other people at the time could replicate them.

The date at which Lake Winnipesaukee ice goes out, is the date at which people can go to their properties, and do go to their properties. If the ice out date was wrong, they would notice and be mighty pissed. I selected Lake Winnipesaukee, because that is the lake whose ice outs receive the most attention unrelated to estimating climate. Of all

---

[337] https://wattsupwiththat.com/2009/12/08/the-smoking-gun-at-darwin-zero/
[338] https://wattsupwiththat.com/2009/12/20/darwin-zero-before-and-after/
[339] https://blogs.telegraph.co.uk/news/jamesdelingpole/100020126/climategate-goes-serial-now-the-russians-confirm-that-uk-climate-scientists-manipulated-data-to-exaggerate-global-warming/

older climate data, Lake Winnipesaukee ice outs are the best replicated, thus, the most scientific.

And ice out dates on Lake Winnipesaukee indicate no twentieth century warming[340] That I provide the data and method of calculation, and that this data is the most widely replicated data available means that this blog post is far more scientific than anything that could ever be permitted to appear in the journals "Nature" or "Science".

This is the opposite of the Giss-Hadley-CRU approach, which uses vast piles of data whose validity no one can possibly know, and which there is every reason to doubt, and then capriciously excludes some of that data, includes other of that data, and whimsically adjusts what is included for reasons that are not only not revealed, but which the Climategate files revealed that Hadley-CRU themselves do not record, which large adjustments, even if justified rather than fraudulent, are an admission of the complete worthlessness of the data for the purpose. No one can possibly know, not even Hadley-CRU, whether their adjustments are justified or fraudulent, not that it would matter since if the large adjustments are justified, the data is worthless for the purpose of estimating past climate.

If you have to estimate the veracity of the reports based on the authority of what you know about those making the reports, that is not science, but religion. Those with the greatest authority are always the most religious, thus this approach guarantees acceptance of the most holy doctrine of the consensus of the most holy and eminent synod – which approach is anthropogenic global warming in a nutshell.

"The consensus" is not science.

Science is common sense, observation, truthfulness, and impartiality, with social mechanisms to enforce truthfulness and impartiality. If science becomes a priesthood, if you hear the words "consensus" and "peer reviewed publication", the mechanisms that enforce truthfulness and impartiality have failed. "Peer reviewed"is only an indication of some connection to reality when people do not rely on it as evidence of connection to reality.

No twentieth century warming 3

2010-01-04 08:01:36

Hadcrut temperatures are fraudulent, for the Climategate files reveals that no one knows how they were constructed.

The Air vent attempts an honest reconstruction:

---

[340]https://blog.reaction.la/global-warming/no-twentieth-century-warming-2.html

GHCN Data Global Temperature Average

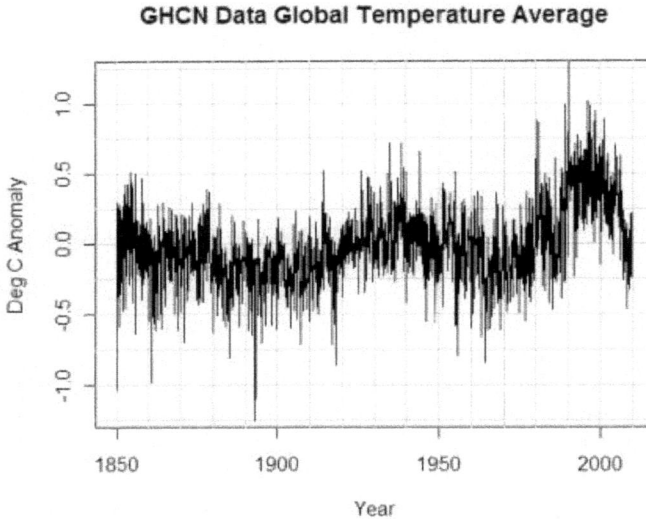

Of course, this reconstruction can only be as good as the data it rests on, which we now know from the Climategate documents directory to be poor. I argue we should throw out all dubious data - which likely means we should rely on proxy indications of temperature for the early part of the century.

Unemployment

2010-01-07 16:09:02

Officially, unemployment has fallen to the curiously round number of ten percent. Are you feeling more prosperous?

Yes, strange to report, zero hedge observes[341] that the money paid to the unemployed has risen substantially, and risen a lot in the last two months. While there are officially nine and half million unemployed, there appear to be fourteen million receiving unemployment benefits.

Funny thing that.

Torture the underpants bomber

2010-01-10 13:26:33

Fifty eight percent of those polled favor "aggressive interrogation techniques such as waterboarding" for Umar Farouk.

He should be asked who gave him the bomb, and where they gave him the bomb. We should then kill everyone in the general vicinity of where the bomb came from. Not

[341] https://www.zerohedge.com/article/government-misrepresenting-unemployment-32

because we cannot afford to lose a few planes and a few passengers every now and then, but because we cannot afford to be successfully coerced by our enemies.

War is hell. In war, one must kill the innocent. Those who will not use such means, lose.

It is doubtless more important that the innocent go free than that the guilty be punished. It is, however, considerably less important than that evil does not gain power over us.

During the Malayan war the British imprisoned everyone who looked Chinese. That hundreds of thousands of innocent men women and children were temporarily imprisoned by the British saved them from being enslaved for life by the communists.

We are losing this war: Observe that honor killings go unpunished in Britain. We are afraid, we are coerced. I google the British news for honor killings. The only ones being prosecuted are the kind that would be prosecuted in Saudi Arabia - those where a male Muslim was killed or non family killed the girl - which type of honor killing is rare and unusual compared to the normal case where extreme coercion by family to control the sexual activity of young girls gets out of hand. So, we see prosecutions for the rare case (male killed), and no prosecutions for the common case (young girl killed by relatives)

You cannot coexist with a religion that simply is not willing to coexist except on the basis of supremacy. If you try to do so, you get what we have been getting. Getting your cut throat for unkind reference to Islam slides by imperceptible degrees into full blown Sharia law, which gradual transformation we observe in process along the bloody borders of

Islam.

That is the way Islam conquers. It not that we cannot afford a few casualties. It is that we cannot afford the domination.

What the Tea Party stands for

2010-01-13 05:50:31

There is a risk that the Tea Party movement is sufficiently vague and unspecific to enable everyone to read into what they want, so that people with fundamentally irreconcilable views believe they're part of the same movement, which is a good way to get people into power so that they can start scooping up some of the gravy, and a bad way to accomplish any political objective.

The original Tea Party was a violent eruption against British Mercantilism. They threw legal tea on which tax had been paid by a privileged monopoly into the harbor, thus ensuring that everyone used illegal smuggled tea, thus ensuring that everyone resisted big government allied with big business.

Today, we see Obama's big government alarmingly cozy with big business, both the too big to fail bailouts, and a health care program that pays off every special interest except the voters. The Tea Partiers are pissed with this. Like the original Tea Party, they support capitalism, but oppose big capitalists who are in bed with the government, they oppose Wall Street financiers who bet big because winnings are privatized and losses are socialized.

The country is run by a bunch of very smart people, who look down on the ignorant masses from their private jets. There are some smart people among the Tea Parties, but not a lot. The difference, however, between the smart people among the Tea Parties, and the smart people flying at forty thousand feet, is that the smart people among the tea partiers know that the smarter you are, the easier it is to make things more complicated than you can handle.

This is a classic problem in programming, the cause of many project disasters run by very smart people, and a classic problem in government, the cause of many economic disasters run by government experts.

As Hayek explained, the more government intervention you get, the harder it is to intervene correctly, the more there will be unintended consequences, the more complicated intervention gets. And as Hayek also explained, the less those intervening understand what they are doing, the more arrogant they will become, the more smugly confident of their ability to manage the unmanageable, the more confident they become that they comprehend the incomprehensible. Krugman is a classic and extreme example of this smug blindness.

The economy is dominated by a mass of government interventions far more complex than the tax code. This was a disaster waiting to happen. Now it has happened. The tea partiers understand this, some because they are very smart people who read their Hayek, most because they are not so smart but read their bibles. The very smart elite flying at forty thousand feet in their private jets do not understand it.

Google still evil

2010-01-15 01:20:59

Despite an announcement that it has stopped censoring in China, google.com.cn still censored[342]

Correction: A commentor points out that if we search for Tiananmen+Square+massacre instead of just Tiananmen+Square, we get uncensored results. Nonetheless, there is something smelly about that page rank.

Also, google continues to censor right here: Type "Christianity is" into the search box, and it will drop down the following suggestions

wrong

a lie

bullshit

not a religion

a cult

a joke

Type "Islam is" and see what you get.

Google's free blogging service yanks politically incorrect blogs, and while its search engine found Climategate web pages, Google participated in the blackout by censoring its suggestion box and counts. Search results are not obviously censored, but everything else is.

---

[342]https://www.google.com.cn/search?q=Tiananmen+Square

Mencius and Kling agree

2010-01-16 14:51:48

Mencius Moldbug has long argued, in an exceedingly long winded fashion, that we live in a theocracy. The priesthood teach that the state deserves authority, the schools teach the official religion, and the state funds the schools and the priesthood.

Now Arnold Kling gives the same analysis[343], calling it market failure, rather than theocracy

> Suppose that we have a group that wants enormous political power. The group rewards people who justify its power by calling them "experts." It punishes those who question its power by dismissing them as "hacks." If you want money and status, you want to be labeled as an expert. In order to be labeled as an expert, you produce analysis that justifies concentrated political power for the elite group.

> This process is self-reinforcing. It is like the Harvard-Goldman filter. That filter says that only "reliable" people are allowed to be bank CEO's or policymakers. A requirement for being "reliable" is sharing the views of other "reliable" people as to what constitutes reliability.

> It is like the tenure system in academia. Who gets tenure? Above all, it is people who support the existing tenure system

Mencius's proposed cure for this problem is a "strong" sensible state, where "strong" means something very like fascist, or despotic. However, strong states have a poor record for sanity. Power tends to isolate the possessor from reality.

Another solution for this problem, something that Kling would probably find more congenial, is Mencius's "antiuniversity"

After all, the previous theocracy bit the dust thanks to protestantism and the reformation, which held one could do religion without a hierarchy. If religion can be done without a hierarchy, so can science. The priesthood is the most vulnerable part of a theocracy.

Google censors Google censorship

2010-01-18 13:12:53

Recursive censorship:

Typing climategate booker into bing[344] four of the first five hits are about Google

---

[343]https://econlog.econlib.org/archives/2010/01/market_failure_4.html
[344]https://www.bing.com/search?q=climategate+booker

censoring Booker's climategate article[345].
The **Booker Climategate** Article – Scandal or Indexing Problem ...[346]
Climategate: Googlegate? – Telegraph Blogs[347]
Of **Climategate**, Googlegate & When Stories Get Too Long[348]
Mimsy: **Climategate** crashes Google?[349]

Typing climategate booker into google, none the first four hits are about Google censoring Booker's climategate article - the same hits are all there, one of them at rank five, and they have fairly high page rank, but a markedly lower page rank than bing gives them. Further, the rank is better for the ones most favorable to google.

This of course, reflects page rank at this instant, and will no doubt be different soon, but that is what I saw.

Despite its utterly villainous and richly deserved reputation, Microsoft, unlike Google, has an impressive record of defending freedom. Of course, they recently came under new management, and if we are dependent on Microsoft to protect liberty, we are in trouble.

What the election of Scott Brown means

2010-01-21 15:21:55

Notice Scott Brown's old pick up truck.

Partly, of course, it is simply a massive swing against the Democrats. The economy is collapsing, people blame the party in power.

But it also means more important and more interesting things: Scott Brown was campaigning as the anti elitist candidate, brandishing a working class and underclass identity, such as his old truck and his conviction for shoplifting. The elite is unpopular, not just one party of the elite.

This was a populist landslide. People think that those running our country, Democrat and Republican, are evil, stupid, and insane.

Normally a populist movement is anti libertarian, but the massive crony capitalism of the last few years, Obama and Bush, has put populists on the libertarian side. They want real capitalism, not crony capitalism where the losses are socialized but the profits are privatized. They want capitalists to be free to take risks with their own money, and not free to take risks with the taxpayers money.

I would like to say that democracy is self correcting, and the populist masses will get what they want. But they probably will not. The elite is just too entrenched at every level of society, and the politicians are just their public relations officers. Some politicians will be thrown overboard to appease the masses, some perfectly innocent businessmen will be falsely accused of crony capitalism, and punished to appease the masses, but then the elite will continue with business as usual.

---

[345] https://www.telegraph.co.uk/comment/columnists/christopherbooker/6679082/Climate-change-this-is-the-worst-scientific-scandal-of-our-generation.html
[346] https://isedb.com/20091202-2179.php
[347] https://blogs.telegraph.co.uk/news/jamesdelingpole/100018263/climategate-googlegate/
[348] https://searchengineland.com/of-climategate-googlegate-when-stories-get-too-long-30755
[349] https://www.hoboes.com/Mimsy/Technology/climategate-crashes-google/

To get the reforms the Tea Party wants, it would probably be necessary to proscribe Harvard, every organization with "environment" in its name, and everyone involved in "diversity", in the way Nazis were proscribed in postwar Germany.

Observe what happened when various states passed plebiscites declaring affirmative action illegal.

Absolutely nothing happened, and that is the likely outcome of a thorough Teaparty victory in the US. The elite will just continue doing what it does. Reagan had a vision for ending Soviet power. I do not see anyone with a vision for ending elite power and privilege.

This raises the interesting question: Is the elite evil, stupid and insane?

Yes it is, and the disease is bound to get worse. It is an inherent problem with theocracies. The official priesthood tends to become more and more religious, while the masses become less and less religious. The official religion gets sillier, tending to select silly people for priests. To be part of the elite, you have to believe in an ever growing list of stupid stuff, such as "diversity" and global warming. This selects for people who apply their smarts to deluding themselves, rather than connecting to reality.

Obama lashes out at the innocent to protect the guilty

2010-01-23 15:37:33

Immediately after losing a senate seat to a Republican populist, Obama the next day proceeded to go populist. He, is, he tells us, going to punish those unregulated wall street fat cats who caused the crisis.

He is going to tax the banks, and restrict proprietary trading by banks. But proprietary trading had little to do with the crisis.

All the things that caused the crisis are still going: the continuing misbehavior of Fannie, Freddie, and the FHA, the continuing regulatory pressure on banks to lower credit standards for non Asian minorities, and the continuing government created opportunity for banks to unload dud mortgages on the taxpayer.

Past private misbehavior was facilitated by the hedge fund activities of too-big-to-fail AIG selling naked CDSs, and too-big-to-be-defaulted-on Goldman and Sach, purchasing naked CDSs. These activities enabled banks to unload the dud politically correct loans that they made.

The misbehavior of AIG and Goldman was downstream of the center of the problem ? banks made dud loans, and then unloaded them thanks to the hedge fund activities of too-big-to-fail businesses, primarily AIG. The problem was that the government wanted, and still wants, banks to make dud loans, and will do whatever it takes to get them to make dud loans. When too-big-to-fail hedge funds ceased to facilitate dud loans, this was a crisis, which crisis the government has swiftly acted to remedy.

Today banks get to unload their dud loans directly on the government. The taxpayer is "stabilizing" the market for unwanted mortgages, which is a huge off the books housing subsidy to minorities, irresponsible borrowers, irresponsible lenders, and bums with no credit rating.

Precisely because AIG and Goldman have stopped their bad conduct, bad conduct that the government needed and wanted, government stepped in, and is now doing exactly the stuff that AIG and Goldman *were* doing.

The lesser hedge funds did the right thing throughout, and the smaller they were, the more right they were - naturally so, because if a smaller hedge fund screws up, no one bails them out.

The one populist intervention against fat cats that would be both effectual and popular is a special tax or special restrictions on businesses that are too big to fail, and this one populist and popular intervention is not proposed, and is highly unlikely.

Global warming science in action

2010-01-24 12:39:18

The "Air Vent" follows the money:

The IPCC makes a hyperbolic claim about retreating glaciers, which claim originates from a for profit company owned by the chairman of the IPCC. Millions of dollars are then granted to this company to investigate this purported disaster, to the personal profit of the chairman of the IPCC.

How left is Obama?

2010-01-25 07:28:37

Obama was surrounded by the lunatic death-to-Americans left, his friends and social circle all come from those crazies, which led to widespread suspicion he was and is one of them – that he is a crazed commie nazi muslim who seeks to destroy America and reduce Americans to poverty and slavery. Birds of a feather flock together. On the other hand, a lot of people believe he is a moderate centrist.

He is now surrounded by the pillars of the Harvard Goldman Wall Street establishment, leavened with a fair few death-to-Americans crazies whom he helicoptered into top positions, but invariably positions where their actual ability to bring death to Americans is rather limited, which positions have been resentfully described by their demented denizens as "policy Siberia", a disappointed complaint that implies they see Obama as really the moderate centrist, rather than really the crazed commie nazi muslim.

Those who think that Obama is lunatic left think that Bush was a left winger, and those who think that Obama is centrist think that Bush was far right, so there is evidently broad agreement that Obama policies are not all that different from Bush's policies.

Bush's big spending becomes much bigger spending, Bush's heavy handed regulation becomes regulation considerably more heavy handed and much more hostile to business. Bush's disastrous affirmative action has not much changed, foreign war becomes foreign war with somewhat more cringing before our enemies – the bowing is uniquely Obama, but the Hasan debacle was unchanged Bush policy. Politically correct warfare in Afghanistan has become even more politically correct warfare in Afghanistan.

Politicians always tend towards compromise, and politically correct warfare is a compromise between making war and making peace, but of course, such a compromise is unviable – it was unviable for Bush, and even less viable for Obama. You either have to annihilate the enemy with ruthless disregard for the women and children, or else cut and run. There is no middle road. The Bush disease has infected west point, which now upholds the politically correct position that slaying our enemies is so last century, a transformation that represents a victory for the State Department over the Pentagon.

If one considers these Bush policies to be left wing, as I do, then Obama's policies are lunatic left, his crazy pals hanging out in "policy Siberia" are looming threat of cataclysm, and the fact that he is surrounded by pillars of the Harvard Goldman Wall Street establishment just shows how corrupt, decadent, incompetent, and out of touch with reality our establishment has become.

To synthesize these conflicting views of Obama, it is necessary to realize he is just not very bright. People overestimate Obama's intelligence, because he presents as one of the Harvard elite, which he culturally belongs to. Therefore, he sincerely believes progressivism is moderate, humane, centrist, and good for America, and the swift implementation of these policies will make himself and democrats popular, while his brighter fellow believers (seething bitterly in policy Siberia) believe that Americans are evil sinners, and deserve to suffer progressivism every bit.

Obama delusively believes himself fairly moderate, but fears that if he was entirely frank, others would not see him so.

The science is scuttled

2010-01-26 04:35:40

Nasa, as evidence that we are doomed unless we make sufficient sacrifice to Gaia and tithe to Gaia's high priesthood, has long had on its web page

> Mountain Glaciers and snow cover have declined on average in both hemispheres and may disappear altogether in certain regions of the planet, such as the Himalayas, by 2030

Which web page has silently changed[350]
So was it a lie, or an error?

> I knew data hadn't been verified ... we thought if we can highlight it, it will impact policy makers and politicians and encourage them to take concrete action.[351]

In other words, a lie. And if one lie, all lies.

As Patrick Archibald told us of an earlier scandal with the same lesson, the science is scuttled[352]

---

[350]https://regmedia.co.uk/2010/01/20/nasa-now-glacier.jpg
[351]https://wattsupwiththat.com/2010/01/23/breaking-news-scientist-admits-ipcc-used-fake-data-to-pressure-policy-makers/
[352]https://www.creativeminorityreport.com/2009/11/science-is-scuttled.html

No twentieth century warming
2010-01-27 12:55:22

The global warming blogs[353] have done an analysis of the surface temperature readings, from which noconsensus quotes[354]:

> leading meteorological institutions in the USA and around the world have so systematically tampered with instrumental temperature data that it cannot be safely said that there has been any significant net "global warming" in the 20th century.

Temperature readings have had "value added" to their data, with the "raw" surface station histories mysteriously changing from one download to the next, and surface stations that reported cooler readings have been mysteriously dropped.

More climate shenanigans
2010-02-01 16:42:46

Cheifio has found all sorts of oddities in the surface temperature data. His latest target is Madagascar[355]

> But I'm sure it's just an accident of history, or something, that an entire country with no visible warming in the basic data and a recent cooling was dropped in 2005.... Maybe the monkeys hid the data ...

The Nasa Giss anomaly chart shows Madagascar burning up, while the Madagascar climate station shows Madagascar cooling.

"One bad apple"
2010-02-05 18:57:10

Greenpeace is calling for the head of Pachauri, the IPCC chairman.

As Mencius Moldbug says, this will not make the patient healthy, it will make the cancer healthy.

The call is not for a replacement who can more impartially discover the truth about anthropogenic global warming, but for a replacement who can more convincingly persuade the public of the truth of anthropogenic global warming, and the terrible harm it will do.

Since commanding us for the good of the proletariat turned out to be a bummer, they will command us for the good of the trees.

The basic strategy is to find that every human act has a vital global externality, so that every human act requires global supervision and centralized permission - for example building a house or choosing a school.

---

[353]https://wattsupwiththat.com/2010/01/26/new-paper-on-surface-temperature-records/
[354]https://noconsensus.wordpress.com/2010/01/26/bending-the-thermometers/
[355]https://chiefio.wordpress.com/2010/01/31/mysterious-madagascar-muse/

Sorry, you must send your children to the school we choose for you, since if you send them to the school you want, you are wasting carbon.

Sorry, we are not giving you permission to build your house, for it is insufficiently carbon efficient.

And since carbon dioxide is a world wide externality, permissions will ultimately have to come from a world wide organization, the climate treaty organization. We will have a theocracy monitoring us for our sins against the earth, with one world wide papacy and cathedral.

In the end, there will be war, and if we lose that war we shall be slaves, and if we win that war, will need to proscribe environmentalists and diversicrats the way Nazis were proscribed after World War II. You can never compromise with those who would rule you. Appeasement and compromise only works with those whose objectives are limited. With those whose objectives are total and limitless, each concession is merely a stepping stone to the destruction of those who concede.

Both the anti warmist blogs and the pro warmist blogs agree in calling for the replacement of the head of the IPCC. Watts Up With That[356], Dark Politics[357], Hot Air[358], The Right Cup of Tea[359], The American Interest[360]

Whenever you find yourself on the same side as evil, you should look a little more carefully. The IPCC needs to imprisoned, not fixed, and the ill gotten wealth of its members and contributors confiscated.

Official science is not going to be healed. The scientific method is no more going to be permitted in the pages of "Nature" or "Science" than Jews and Muslims are going to share the middle east peacefully. The stakes are too high, the desires of our enemies too great.

Animal spirits

2010-02-08 17:21:26

Bryan Caplan argues that the recent crash was caused by animal spirits[361].

But I saw the 2008 crash and subsequent downturn with my own eyes[362], and I'm convinced that mood played a key role. The world *freaked out*, big time. It was the economic analog of a riot.

I was there also, and it was entirely rational for everyone to try to get to the exits before everyone else. No animal spirits involved. In 2005 November I said "Now is the time to

---

[356]https://wattsupwiththat.com/2010/01/24/pachauri-must-resign-his-position-is-untenable/

[357]https://www.darkpolitricks.com/2010/02/ipcc-boss-unhinged-as-greenpeace-demands-resignation/

[358]https://hotair.com/archives/2010/02/04/greenpeace-uk-head-says-pachauri-needs-to-go/

[359]https://rightcupoftea.wordpress.com/2010/02/04/uk-greenpeace-chief-calls-on-pachauri-to-resign-al-gore-still-silent/

[360]https://blogs.the-american-interest.com/wrm/2010/02/03/uk-greenpeace-chief-calls-on-pachauri-to-resign-al-gore-still-silent/

[361]https://econlog.econlib.org/archives/2010/02/mood_and_macro.html

[362]https://econlog.econlib.org/archives/2008/10/panic_puzzle.html

panic", so I got to the doors comfortably enough, though it was starting to get crowded and a rush was setting in. By 2008 - well if you had not realized it was time to get out before 2008, it was indeed the economic analog of a riot.

In 2005 November I was talking to real estate valuer, who told me that lenders were getting nervous about wildly inflated valuations. I immediately saw what would unfold. Real Estate prices were going up because people, mostly cat eating Mexicans with no money, no jobs, no prospects, and a past history of never paying their debts, were buying houses at inflated prices with no money down, and since they were not putting any money down, did not care how inflated the price was. Obviously this could not go on, and when it stopped, everything was going to go to hell. So as soon as some people thought it was going to stop, they ran, and as soon as they ran, other people started to suspect it was going to stop, and they ran also, until by 2007 it was a crazy rush to get out, and by 2008, too late.

So when I learned in 2005 November, that lenders were getting nervous, I realized that the rush to exits had begun, and immediately joined it.

Everyone knew that things were going to collapse, but wanted to stay in till the last minute because there was money to be made, so it was not animal spirits, but people trying to judge when to run to the exits.

The cause of the crisis 5
2010-02-09 05:56:55

The green room has a wonderful summary of the economic crisi[363]s in the form of a children's book. They neglect, however, to mention George Bush's role in making the CRA even worse than it already was.

The brilliance of Sarah Palin
2010-02-12 16:45:35

First they ignore you, then they laugh at you, then they attack you, then you win.
We have been noticing a lot more attacks on Sarah Palin lately. The latest concedes she is brilliant.[364]

> The speech was inspired drivel, a series of distortions and oversimplifications, totally bereft of nourishing policy proposals — the sort of thing calculated, carefully calculated, to drive lamestream media types like me frothing to their keyboards. Palin is a big fat target, eminently available for derision. But I will not deride. Because brilliance must be respected, especially when it involves marketing

Needless to say, all the examples of "drivel" he presents are examples of Palin telling the truth in clear and folksy language. Where others talked of "rationalizing" health care, she said "death panels" - for death panels they are.

---

[363]https://hotair.com/greenroom/archives/2010/02/02/meltdown/
[364]https://www.time.com/time/politics/article/0,8599,1963564,00.html

She was the inventor of the mythic, noxious "death panels." In Nashville, she retailed nonsense about stimulus funds going to nonexistent districts. (A spokesman for Vice President Joe Biden, who is monitoring the stimulus package, told me that all funds went to actual places — but recipients occasionally didn't write down their correct congressional districts.)

Business management 101. If the CEO cannot find out where the money was spent, it was embezzled. Sarah Palin knows this. The moron press does not. That is what makes her smart, and people like Joe Klein[365] who wrote this shit dumb as posts.

Affirmative action and the mortgage crisis
2010-02-14 05:24:37

Four hundred firemen died attempting to rescue people on 9/11. Not one "firefighter" died, for women do not fight fires. It is not in their physique, nor their psychological nature to do so.

Obama and his wife are typical affirmative action blacks. Michelle's Princeton thesis is a whine about racial prejudice and is full of spelling and grammatical errors[366]. Obama got a degree from Columbia without even showing up[367]. Obama can read from a teleprompter very nicely – except when he runs into a long sentence. Similarly, most blacks can sing and dance and play the guitar better than most whites. But Obama never delivers a speech ex tempore or from brief notes, unlike Palin, while Palin never pauses at inappropriate points in the middle of reading a long sentence from a teleprompter, unlike Obama.

The collateralized debt obligations underlying the present crisis were structured into tranches so that the highest rated tranches could not go bad if the payer merely missed a few payments. What caused the crisis is that on very large numbers of the underlying mortgages, no one made a single payment. When we compare the default rate in a lily white suburb or exurb, with the default rate in a suburb or exurb where the majority are members of protected minority groups, we see the default rate in the protected minority suburb is twenty to sixty times higher, telling us why so many mortgages have never received a single mortgage payment

Where the money went
2010-02-15 13:19:04

The government has been shuffling the money around to obfuscate who stole it. It lends money, and then announces that there is no problem, the money has been paid back.

But after much fiddling, the money has mostly come to rest[368], in that the government is now the proud owner of about one trillion dollars of mortgage backed securities guaranteed by Fannie, Freddie, and the FHA, plus some Fannie, Freddy, and FHA debt.

---

[365] https://www.time.com/time/letters/email_letter.html
[366] https://www.atimes.com/atimes/Front_Page/JC04Aa01.html
[367] https://www.google.com.au/search?q=Columbia+%22remembers+obama%22+attended
[368] https://www.econbrowser.com/archives/2010/02/bernanke_on_the_3.html

The first graph in the above link is the money wizzing around in complicated circles to obfuscate who is at fault, the second graph is the bailout of private entities, other than General Motors, and the third graph is primarily the bailout of Fannie, Freddy, and the FHA.

That these Mortgage Backed Securities are "Fully guaranteed by Federal Agencies" implies that the vast majority of the crisis, the vast majority of the bailout, was dud mortgages rubber stamped Fanny, Freddie, and the FHA, that privately issued mortgage backed securities have been liquidated - that the dud mortgages underlying privately issued mortgage backed securities have been settled by foreclosure and bancruptcy, but the dud mortgages underlying Fannie, Freddy, and FHA issued mortgage backed securities are on the tax payers tab to the tune of about a trillion dollars.

Overtime, as the mortgages are resolved, the trillion dollars of mortgage backed securities will diminish with time. In proportion as they were worthless, the agency debt will correspondingly increase.

The bubble in government paper

2010-02-16 07:07:02

The US budget proposes that by 2020, debt service on federal debt will be ten percent of GDP. This is politically impossible. The interest will be paid by borrowing more money. Anyone buying government paper assumes he will unload it before the bubble bursts. Whosoever buys government debt, buys it on the bigger fool theory.

Bubbles can go on for a long time, and they always last longer than those calling the bubble expect. Conversely, however, they always burst earlier than most people expect, and people do not realize the bubble is bursting until a considerable time after the bubble has in fact burst. The bubble bursts when the smart money rushes to the exits, and the smart money rushes to the exits long before the vast majority realize that the smart money has upped and left. You want to exit a bubble when the majority of the smart money, not the majority of the public, is exiting, which for the recent housing and triple A CDO bubble was not 2008, but late 2005.

The cleanest and least destructive way out of this crisis will be to default on treasury bonds, but I fear the government may instead proceed with hyperinflation.

Climategate scandals

2010-02-17 10:27:39

It all started when someone released a thousand carefully selected emails and numerous files from Hadley CRU. Every email and most of the files were scandalous, and the sheer quantity has taken some time to digest.

So here is a summary of some of the scandals.

Hide the decline

The emails reveal conspiracy to violate the freedom of information act, by refusing to reveal the evidence on which various predictions of doom were supposedly based. The

British government has determined that this constitutes a crime[369], but, of course, they are not going to prosecute anyone (or check whether the secret data actually supports the predictions of doom). See discussion[370], x[371], x[372], x[373]

The emails revealed that Chinese climate data had been made up, which was subsequently investigated by the Guardian[374]. x[375], x

The climategate files (not the emails) revealed that the surface temperature record was cooked, with a wonderful collection of revelations about misconduct by the mysterious Harry, which has led to a multitude of scandals about cooking the surface temperature, among them The Smoking Gun At DarwinZero[376]

The emails revealed that peer review was merely for theological correctness, not scientific correctness - so that anything that prophesied doom passed, and anything that encouraged skepticism did not. This resulted in a multitude of scandals as various prophesies of doom were checked out, revealing that the peer review process was not merely cursory, but entirely imaginary: Among them the prediction of the disappearing Amazon rainforest, the prediction of the disappearing glaciers, and the prediction of increased hurricanes[377].

The head of the IPCC, Panchauri, repeatedly lied on the glacier issue, claiming to have good information that they were going to disappear, when he knew they did not.

Similarly, the Stern report announced numerous prophecies of doom, most of which turned out to be pulled out of someone's ass.

Russia reports coldest weather stations discarded

Geological Society of America showed how tree-ring data from Russia indicated cooling after 1961, but was deceptively truncated and only artfully discussed in IPCC publications. Well, at least the tree-ring data made it into the IPCC report, albeit disguised and misrepresented.

he U.S. National Climate Data Center has been manipulating weather data too, say computer expert E. Michael Smith and meteorologist Joesph D'Aleo. Forty years ago there were 6,000 surface-temperature measuring stations, but only 1,500 by 1990, which coincides with what global warming alarmists say was a record temperature increase. Most of the deleted stations were in colder regions, just as in the Russian case, resulting in misleading higher average temperatures.

IceGate – Hardly a continent has escaped global warming skewing. The IPCC based its findings of reductions in mountain ice in the Andes, Alps and in Africa on a feature story of climbers' anecdotes in a popular mountaineering magazine, and a dissertation

---

[369]https://online.wsj.com/article/SB10001424052748704194504575031022338013284.html

[370]https://wattsupwiththat.com/2010/01/27/cru-inquiry-seeks-changes-in-uk-law-citing-failure-of-crus-foia-officer/

[371]https://bishophill.squarespace.com/blog/2010/1/25/no-climategate-foi-prosecutions.html

[372]https://seeker401.wordpress.com/2010/02/01/university-of-east-anglia-cru-broke-uk-foi-laws/

[373]https://pathstoknowledge.net/2010/01/25/british-investigators-whitewash-cru-freedom-of-information-crimes-with-loophole-letting-jones-et-al-escape/

[374]https://www.guardian.co.uk/environment/2010/feb/01/dispute-weather-fraud

[375]https://gregb1967.blogspot.com/2010/02/climate-gate-still-more-shenanigans.html

[376]https://wattsupwiththat.com/2009/12/08/the-smoking-gun-at-darwin-zero/

[377]https://www.telegraph.co.uk/comment/columnists/christopherbooker/7113582/Amazongate-new-evidence-of-the-IPCCs-failures.html

by a Switzerland university student, quoting mountain guides. Peer-reviewed? Hype? Worse?

ResearchGate – The global warming camp is reeling so much lately it must have seemed like a major victory when a Penn State University inquiry into climate scientist Michael Mann found no misconduct regarding three accusations of climate research impropriety. But the university did find "further investigation is warranted" to determine whether Mann engaged in actions that "seriously deviated from accepted practices for proposing, conducting or reporting research or other scholarly activities." Being investigated for only one fraud is a global warming victory these days.

ReefGate – Let's not forget the alleged link between climate change and coral reef degradation. The IPCC cited not peer-reviewed literature, but advocacy articles by Greenpeace, the publicity-hungry advocacy group, as its sole source for this claim.

AfricaGate – The IPCC claim that rising temperatures could cut in half agricultural yields in African countries turns out to have come from a 2003 paper published by a Canadian environmental think tank – not a peer-reviewed scientific journal.

DutchGate – The IPCC also claimed rising sea levels endanger the 55 percent of the Netherlands it says is below sea level. The portion of the Netherlands below sea level actually is 20 percent. The Dutch environment minister said she will no longer tolerate climate researchers' errors.

AlaskaGate – Geologists for Space Studies in Geophysics and Oceanography and their U.S. and Canadian colleagues say previous studies largely overestimated by 40 percent Alaskan glacier loss for 40 years. This flawed data are fed into those computers to predict future warming.

The problem with peer review

2010-02-24 05:19:12

Peer review is not part of the scientific method. In most fields, for example physics, it is a new thing, and wherever it has become a standard thing, we see stagnation.

Peer review keeps out cranks, but it also keeps out the impious. It makes it safe for a science to become a religion, and for scientists to become priests of a state sponsored theocracy. Cranks have never been a threat to science, state sponsored theocracy has always been a threat to science, thus peer review has always been a failure. It is caused by science becoming theology, and causes science to become theology.

Back in the days when physics made dramatic progress, there was little peer review, perhaps none. For example, "Electrodynamics of Moving bodies" was not peer reviewed, and my guess is that today it would never have passed peer review - because it was written by a patent clerk, and was in large part a novel way of looking at results that were a hundred years old. Outsiders, and novel ways of looking at things are pretty much guaranteed to fail peer review.

The suicide of the elites

2010-02-25 08:28:07

Participatory transexual vomiting as high art. This illustrates Unwin's "Sex and Culture" – that no civilization long survives the end of the patriarchy and female chastity. Unwin's suggested explanation for this observation is that civilization is produced by the Freudian energy of sexual repression. I favor the theory that civilization is created by patriarchs for their offspring. Another plausible theory is that civilizations survive by high asabiya, Roissy being a walking talking demonstration of low asabiya. A monogamous patriarchal society has high asabiya because people have both strong blood relationships and strong relationships with in laws.

Whatever the mechanism, Unwin's observation is validated yet again.

Microsoft the good guys

2010-02-26 06:01:26

Google is evil in that they spy on users, and that they censor their services, and politically cook their search results. Microsoft's Bing[378] has not yet been detected cooking their search results

Microsoft reports to law enforcement to what extent they spy on users, the report was leaked[379], and the interesting fact is that they log less than anyone else. They only log the last ten logins, and when you delete emails from a hotmail account, they *really* are deleted from Microsoft's servers – unlike Google mail on Google servers.

Why Haiti fell down

2010-02-26 06:56:51

And why if will fall down again.

The earthquake was devastating, not because it was very strong earthquake, but because buildings in Haiti are made out of really shitty concrete.

And the

socialist medicine

2010-02-27 13:17:33

Hot air reviews an interesting report from Britain.

> Patients were left unwashed in their own filth for up to a month as nurses ignored their requests to use the toilet or change their sheets;
>
> ...
>
> Wards were left filthy with blood, discarded needles and used dressings ...

---

[378]https://www.bing.com/
[379]https://www.cryptome.org/

...

...Food and drink were left out of reach, forcing patients to drink water from flower vases. ...

The problem is that those would provide socialist medicine for the indigent, want to provide it for the middle class. Singapore has truly socialist medicine for the poor, truly private medicine for the rich. America has semi private medicine for all, which is a dreadful system, though probably not as bad as England's system.

Physics calls out climate science

2010-03-01 18:07:17

The institute of physics is arguably the most prestigious scientific institution. It has told us that climate science is not scientific, that the climategate emails are big deal.
> ... unless the disclosed e-mails are proved to be forgeries or adaptations, worrying implications arise for the integrity of scientific research in this field and for the credibility of the scientific method as practised in this context.
>
> The CRU e-mails as published on the internet provide prima facie evidence of determined and co-ordinated refusals to comply with honourable scientific traditions ... This extends well beyond the CRU itself – most of the e-mails were exchanged with researchers in a number of other international institutions who are also involved in the formulation of the IPCC's conclusions on climate change.

Compare and contrast with the official press response, which was that there was nothing to see in the Climategate files.

Climate science cannot credibly claim to be science.

Natural law and natural rights

2010-03-02 06:29:02

Doc Zero attributes the modern idea of natural law to Hobbes[380]. This is backwards. Hobbes originated the modern idea of facism[381]. It was John Locke[382] that originated the modern idea of natural rights deriving from natural law[383].

Exegesis on the Institute of Physics report on the CRU emails

2010-03-02 18:00:14

The Institute of Physics tells us.

---

[380]https://www.doczero.org/2010/02/loneloc-natural-right
[381]https://reaction.la/hobbes.htm
[382]https://reaction.la/2ndtreat.htm
[383]https://reaction.la/rights.html

The Institute is concerned that, unless the disclosed e-mails are proved to be forgeries or adaptations, worrying implications arise for the integrity of scientific research in this field and for the credibility of the scientific method as practised in this context.

In plainer words, climate science lacks credibility. That climate scientists tell us we are doomed unless we repent of our sins against Gaea is not good reason to think we are doomed.

The CRU e-mails as published on the internet provide prima facie evidence of determined and co-ordinated refusals to comply with honourable scientific traditions ... This extends well beyond the CRU itself – most of the e-mails were exchanged with researchers in a number of other international institutions who are also involved in the formulation of the IPCC's conclusions on climate change.

Yes, they are condemning the entire field, not just Phil Jones, not just Hadley CRU

... proxy reconstructions are the basis for the conclusion that 20th century warming is unprecedented. Published reconstructions may represent only a part of the raw data available and may be sensitive to the choices made and the statistical techniques used. Different choices, omissions or statistical processes may lead to different conclusions. This possibility was evidently the reason behind some of the (rejected) requests for further information.

In plainer words, evidently the reason that Climate scientists refused to make their data available because if other people looked at the data, they would have concluded the climate scientists were full of $#@%. This is a reference to the alternate climate reconstructions in Steve McIntyre's report on the CRU emails[384].

The e-mails reveal doubts as to the reliability of some of the reconstructions and raise questions as to the way in which they have been represented; for example, the apparent suppression, in graphics widely used by the IPCC, of proxy results for recent decades that do not agree with contemporary instrumental temperature measurements.

This is a reference to "Mike's Nature trick ... to hide the decline"

There is also reason for concern at the intolerance to challenge displayed in the e-mails. This impedes the process of scientific 'self correction', which is vital to the integrity of the scientific process as a whole, and not just to the research itself. In that context, those CRU e-mails relating to the peer-review process suggest a need for a review of its adequacy and objectivity as practised in this field and its potential vulnerability to bias or manipulation.

---

[384]https://www.climateaudit.info/pdf/mcintyre-scitech.pdf

Peer review was in practice priestly review for theological correctness.

> Fundamentally, we consider it should be inappropriate for the verification
> of the integrity of the scientific process to depend on appeals to Freedom
> of Information legislation. Nevertheless, the right to such appeals has been
> shown to be necessary. The e-mails illustrate the possibility of networks of
> like-minded researchers effectively excluding newcomers. Requiring data to
> be electronically accessible to all, at the time of publication, would remove
> this possibility.

Climate researchers should make their data available as a matter of course.

> The scope of the UEA review is, not inappropriately, restricted to the al-
> legations of scientific malpractice and evasion of the Freedom of Informa-
> tion Act at the CRU. However, most of the e-mails were exchanged with
> researchers in a number of other leading institutions involved in the for-
> mulation of the IPCC's conclusions on climate change. In so far as those
> scientists were complicit in the alleged scientific malpractices, there is need
> for a wider inquiry into the integrity of the scientific process in this field.

As they said before, it is not just CRU, it is the entire field of climate research

> How independent are the other two international data sets?

> 13. Published data sets are compiled from a range of sources and are sub-
>   ject to processing and adjustments of various kinds. Differences in
>   judgements and methodologies used in such processing may result in
>   different final data sets even if they are based on the same raw data.
>   Apart from any communality of sources, account must be taken of
>   differences in processing between the published data sets and any data
>   sets on which they draw.

All one big conspiracy.

The boot comes down hard on the Institute of Physics
2010-03-05 18:29:27

As you doubtless know by now, the Institute of Physics gave a wonderfully politically
incorrect report on Global Warming[385].

Predictably the boot came down on them hard[386].

Academia is indeed like a communist country. They don't shoot dissidents in Academia,
but communist thought control seldom found it necessary to shoot people. It mostly
worked by quietly blighting the lives of troublesome people. The greengrocer that failed

---

[385]https://www.publications.parliament.uk/pa/cm200910/cmselect/cmsctech/memo/climate-
data/uc3902.htm

[386]https://unqualified-reservations.blogspot.com/2010/03/corrected-evidence.html

to put up the sign "Workers of the World Unite" was not sent to Siberia. Rather, his job was redefined to be of lower status, and he was denied permission to holiday in Bulgaria. For most purposes, this sufficed in the Soviet Union, and its equivalent suffices in Academia. Climate "Science" is the norm. It is the way Academia has worked since the seventies.

Does that sounds paranoid? Here is some evidence for paranoia:

Every authority before 1970 that mentions Lamarck's position on common descent says Lamarck proposed common descent, often quoting from Lamarck at length. Every authority after 1970 that mentions his position on common descent says that Lamarck rejected common descent, without, however quoting anything substantial from Lamarck, or mentioning that past authorities disagreed.

To check this google for Lamarck and common descent before 1970[387], and after 1970[388]. You will find a couple of seeming counterexamples from after 1970, but if you look them up, you will see Google got the dates wrong.

After 1970, as part of the rewrite of Darwinism, they deprecated survival of the fittest as excessively racist, making it necessary to credit Darwin with something else - that something else being common descent. Since Darwin was now credited with common descent, it was necessary to deny that Lamarck proposed common descent.

Similarly, when the Soviet Encyclopedia removed Beria from history, it was necessary to adjust the history accordingly Bergholz accordingly, and when Winston Smith removed an unperson from Big Brother's speech, it was necessary to replace him with something else. Since Darwin was now credited with common descent, it was necessary to deny that Lamarck proposed common descent. That the history of science is abruptly revised, and all academics everywhere docilely uniformly, and abruptly fall into line without a word of dissent, or the slightest interest in what the original documents said, is apparent in the abrupt Winston Smith style 1970 rewrite of the history of thought on evolution.

Pedestalization of women

2010-03-11 06:21:20

Roissy, in one of his many excellent political posts, asks Why Do Conservatives Sanctify-Women?[389]

The correct answer, which he misses, is that they hanker for a world in which women stayed on pedestals instead of sneaking off to bang strange males. Women are very susceptible to authority and social pressure, and will be good if a strong hand keeps them good. If we read western history as written by people who lived it, a thousand years or so ago, it is clear that in one sense women were sacred and had extremely high status - higher wereguild for women, unthinkable for a nobleman to harm a noblewoman, and the politics of the time makes no sense unless the historian and his contemporaries assumed that

---

[387] https://books.google.com/books?as_q=Lamarck&as_epq=common+descent&as_drrb_is=b&as_miny_is=1800&as_maxy_is=1970

[388] https://books.google.com/books?as_q=Lamarck&as_epq=common+descent&as_drrb_is=b&as_miny_is=1970&as_maxy_is=2010

[389] https://roissy.wordpress.com/2010/03/10/why-do-conservatives-sanctify-women/

wives and mothers had a lot of say in who their husbands and sons supported in battle. But in another sense extremely low status: Marriages were decided by the patriarch of the family, women had little say in who they married, they had no legal rights, being largely the property of their fathers, then their husbands. Theoretically a woman had to formally consent to a marriage, but we often read of marriage arrangements being made with no apparent concern for the opinion of the woman. A woman could not represent herself in court, being legally just a part of her father's household, then her husbands household, and if she survived her husband, then her sons household.

I interpret this as putting women on pedestals, and chaining them to the pedestal - a system dear to the hearts of conservatives, and which seems to have worked very well - to claim that women are superior within the proper sphere of women, implies that women and men are very different, in some ways better, in other ways worse, in some ways superior, in others inferior.

Allies and enemies
2010-03-16 07:43:43

You will observe that Obama regime is full of noisy outrage that Israel is building housing in Jerusalem[390], most of which will be occupied by Jews, as Israel has been doing for the past forty years, ever since it seized the rest of Jerusalem and announced that all of Jerusalem, Jerusalem undivided, was the eternal and indivisible capital of the nation of Israel.

Compare and contrast with Obama's "quiet diplomacy" on the Iran's nuclear program. Continuing to build housing in all of Jerusalem, is, it seems, worse than developing nuclear weapons.

If you treat your enemies better than your allies, who will want to be your ally, who will fear to be your enemy?

The US demands that Israel open talks with the Palestinians with everything on the table, including returning half of Jerusalem to the Arabs, and the return of the descendants of the Palestinians displaced by the war in which the Jews seized Israel. Doubtless these demands have some justice. I suggest that the Israelis should demand that the US open talks about the return of California and Texas to Mexico, and half of Washington to the Indians. Have our enemies been doing so few wrongs that we need to worry about wrongs done by our friends?

No men on the left
2010-03-21 12:34:14

A leftist women, who merely wants humans to return to the stone age, was publicizing her book criticizing the far left, who want to get rid of humans altogether (They want the stone age with no killing of non human animals, an arrangement where one's life expectancy would be measured in weeks.) A bunch of far leftists attacked her[391]. They

---

[390] https://news.bbc.co.uk/2/hi/middle_east/8569406.stm
[391] https://www.zombietime.com/zomblog/?p=1452

did not throw pies at her, they punched her with jalapeno pepper pie. The people in the audience, even those nominally male, sat back and watched while a bunch of young males attacked an old woman.

Insolvent state tries one on

2010-03-24 16:15:53

Untaxed Out-of-State Purchases

Let us know if you bought something outside of California and you weren't charged California sales tax on it (this is called use tax). Explain This

Examples of out-of-state purchases include:
- Internet, catalog, and mail order purchases
- Phone and TV shopping network purchases
- Purchases made in another state and brought back to California

Did you make any untaxed out-of-state purchases in 2009?

Back

Yes   No

The Obamized future

2010-03-25 07:42:11

America was the place where the future was created. All the world depended on America for progress. It ceased to be that place under Clinton, and things got worse under Bush.

We cannot rebuild the two towers, we no longer have a human presence in space, and the next big thing on the internet, networked money that bypasses our legacy banking system, is coming from China, and, God-help-us, *Africa*.

Remember that in the 1950s, we were about to settle Antarctica, (but government swiftly stepped in and saved Antarctica from the evil humans) and that back then we expected that in the year 2000 we would have jet packs, widespread private plane ownership, and lunar colonies.

Here is what Obama plans for you to be driving in a decade or two:

Planned range, 25 miles, planned top speed, 25 miles per hour[392]. Quite a step down from jet packs.

I have seen the future, and it looks remarkably like Detroit and Liverpool - a barren wasteland of collapsed and disintegrating buildings where feral humans roam, murderously attacking at random.

A Chinese or a Russian is better able to do an internet mediated transaction than an America or European, and an African better able to do a cell phone mediated transaction than an American or European - because the government enforced and funded banking cartel is blocking progress. Webmoney is Russian, because its western equivalents are in jail, or had their assets confiscated.

Similarly, we cannot rebuild the two towers, because to build anything, one hundred and one Brahmans need to be paid off, and they cannot agree amongst themselves on the distribution of payoffs, nor how much kow towing to our enemies is to be built into the new tower's memorial museum. Dubai, however, can build high towers, because to build the tower, the builder only needs the permission of *one* religious authority.

That we cannot build a tower, nor transact through our cell phones, tells us why we cannot get into space.

An America that cannot rebuild the two towers, cannot possibly build nuclear power plants. If something is complicated, government cannot do it. If something is complicated and highly regulated by government, private enterprise cannot do it. Even if greenies were not determined to destroy western civilization, the US can no more build nuclear power plants than it can put a man on the moon.

Europe is crowded, yet a google earth view reveals vast expanses of unutilized or under utilized land, held out of use by greenies.

As the two towers demonstrate, the US has become the can't do society. This is the result of the dispersal of power between ever more numerous Brahmins. To get anything done, you need an ever larger number of approvals and permits, which you are probably not going to get.

---

[392]https://www.moonbattery.com/archives/2010/03/moonbat-tech-gm.html

No moderate Islam, and not many moderate Muslims

2010-03-28 02:47:54

How many Muslims are moderate? In the recent Iraq election, moderates gained, just barely, a plurality. Not a majority, a plurality. To govern, they will need the support of some violently immoderate people. They have a plurality because the various different kinds of extremist hate each other, splitting the extremist vote.

It is often said that there are moderate Muslims, but there is no moderate Islam. If a Muslim is not at war with us, he does not truly believe. The Koran and the personal example set by the Prophet tells Muslims they should seek to dominate by robbing, raping, and murdering infidels, that they should force infidels to submit.

Despite seven years of civil war, near civil war, and sectarian terror, with no victory or defeat in sight for either side, with an occupying US force that will not permit one religious sect to militarily defeat another, a majority of Iraqis will not accept peace with coexistence. They want peace by the submission of all those of the incorrect religion. They merely disagree over who is of the incorrect religion.

Defeating Saddam did no good. We were better off with him terrorizing his people than with democracy, for his people are our enemies. If he was too dangerous to allow to live, should have killed him, and allowed one of his equally brutal, but less ambitious, sons, to replace him.

Theoretically, Jihad is for defense – but it is for the "defense" of Muslim supremacy.

Those resisting that demand for supremacy, are, according to Islam, not innocents. Thus according to Islam, none of us are innocent. So Muslims never kill innocents.

In Nigeria, in Egypt, in Indonesia, we see broad popular support in the Muslim community for violence against non- Muslims. The only Muslim country where the clear majority of Muslims clearly oppose war without end is Albania.

Thus the Palestinian Authority makes heroes of those who murder innocents. When, in a prisoner exchange, Israel released a man who murdered children he was greeted as a hero throughout the Muslim world. Not one moderate was in sight in all of Dar al Islam. If any existed, they kept their mouths shut to ensure that their heads remained attached to their necks.

Different Muslims will disagree to what extent this necessitates and justifies killing and robbing members of the subjugated and humiliated minority. But if they do disagree, and the "moderate" Muslims arrest the "immoderate" Muslim and charge him with murder, they are apt to try him by Islamic standards, even if Sharia law is not formally in effect, apt to demand unreasonable or impossible proof of guilt, and if proven guilty anyway, apply a trivially light punishment, as we see in Indonesia and Egypt.

Shari'a law requires the dhimmi to know their place, and does not permit their testimony to be heard where it contradicts that of a believer but those Muslims who abuse that system are not being good Muslims in doing so. Islam only requires Muslims to be enablers of abuse of minorities, but when enabling, conflict will arise, which requires them to "defend" Dar al Islam. Enabling, misconduct, in practice, necessarily leads to a duty to do the same themselves. It creates a situation in which was was misconduct, is now a divinely mandated duty.

Islamic aggression is analogous to the Islamic position on honor killing. Islam theoretically forbids honor killing, except it does not, and it also commands families to exercise control over female sexual choices in ways that are apt to require extremely drastic coercion. Similarly, Islam theoretically forbids aggression, murder of innocents, and raping children, but ...

As individuals, most of the world's Muslims really aren't all that anxious to find out if 72 houris await them for martyrdom, but while people act selfishly, they are apt to vote virtuously, which means, Muslims are apt to vote for war.

We cannot, therefore, tolerate Muslims voting. We cannot tolerate Muslims voting anywhere in the world. They are dangerous.

If there were free and fair elections, the likes of Hamas, the Muslim brotherhood, and the Islamic Salvation front would win in most places. Look what happened in Turkey when the army let a breath of real democracy in to their managed democracy. The majority, though not eager to check out the 72 houris, do hate us and think us enemies. The only place that the peace faction gets a comfortably large majority is Albania. In many places, for example Palestine, the peace faction gets votes down in the asterisks.

We have had this problem from 722 to the present, with a pause from 1830 to 1960.

To solve the problem, do what we did in 1830: Colonialism, with the most troublesome Muslims losing their land, and often their lives, to settlers, thereby encouraging a more pacific attitude among the remaining Muslims, and keep right on doing it. We would have to institutionalize it – set up independent organizations in the colonized territory that could credibly commit to colonialism forever and irreversibly, no matter how the political winds might blow in the mother country.

The Westphalian solution is to contain Muslim intolerance inside a system of states: If they can't behave reasonably to Christians and Jews in their midst, then partition - and well-defended borders and disarmament,

The Westphalian solution never quite worked, for the boundaries were always porous and apt to bend under pressure.

So the Westphalia solution (wherein everyone supposedly follows, or at least gives lip service to, the King's religion) was gradually adjusted towards the American solution - separation of Church and State. But the American solution never quite worked for non christian religions and quasi religions, since separation of Church and State is a Christian principle. (The Jews have a principle whose effect, outside Israel, is similar, but the rest do not)

Most of these competing movements are far more deadly and destructive than Christianity, because of their greater tendency to theocracy, the big problems being earth worship and Islam. Earth Worship is pacific, unlike Islam, but on the other hand tends to be fans of human sacrifice, unlike Islam. I really cannot imagine a Muslim society declaring a species that eats people to be protected in populated regions, nor a species that spreads deadly diseases. They would recognize this sort of nonsense as the religious practices of a competing, and extremely nasty, religion, and cut off the greenies' heads for preaching apostasy.

The majority of Muslims support violence against us - and any Muslim that does not is insincere in his commitment to Islam.

Our program in Afghanistan is to win by "development and use of indigenous narratives to tap into the wider cultural pulse of Afghanistan" - in other words, save Islam from a supposedly tiny minority of fundamentalists and male chauvinists, and given Islam its rightful place as one more thread in the glorious multicultural rainbow.

In the unlikely event that we succeed, I will think we have destroyed Islam in Afghanistan, Osama bin Laden will think we have destroyed Islam in Afghanistan, and the vast majority of voters in Muslim lands, who vote for parties like Hamas and the Muslim Brotherhood, will think we have destroyed Islam in Afghanistan, just as much as if we had successfully followed the program of killing their leaders and converting them to Christianity.

The environmentalist transnational multiculturalist progressive crowd that hates Christianity does not want to exterminate Islam. They are after all multiculturalists. They want to replace Islam with an animatronic imitation of Islam, something that is feminist and progressive and fits nicely into the glorious multicultural rainbow. They already have a animatronic imitation of Christianity – the Christian left, whose main concerns are gay bishops, saving the earth, and gay Bishops. The progressives envisage an Islam whose main concerns are gay imams, saving the earth, and gay imams.

This program has had partial success in destroying Christianity, but is unlikely to work against an enemy that meets words with bullets.

How not to operate a militia

2010-03-30 05:29:52

9 Tied to Militia Charged in Plot to Murder Officers
Militia Fantasies[393]

How much ruin in a nation?

2010-04-01 12:58:39

On the one hand, there is a lot of ruin in a nation. On the other hand, that which cannot continue, will stop. The present level of government spending is unsustainable.

At what point then, do we get general collapse?

All the advanced western nations are in much the same condition, some a little better, some a little worse. Europe is more broke than America, Greece more broke than the rest of Europe.

The amount of debt a nation can sustain depends in part on its prospects for GDP growth. Thus nations in financial trouble lie about not only the amount of debt they have, and the size of their deficits, but also their rate of growth. All the western nations have been lying for a long time about their levels of debt and the size of their deficits, and have recently begun to lie about their rate of growth[394]

People who lend to governments are showing indications of deep irrationality. Thus, for example, when Ireland told some of the truth about its financial situation and set to

---

[393]https://globalguerrillas.typepad.com/globalguerrillas/2010/03/journal-militia-fantasies.html
[394]https://www.shadowstats.com/

work getting its house in order, the market panicked, while continuing to lend to countries in far worse shape than Ireland.

Greece is the canary in the coal mine, which tells us how far we have to go before collapse. Greece is America in fifteen to twenty five years, and would have collapsed five years or so ago were it not for investor expectations that it would be bailed out, as it has been. The EEC issued a guarantee that people who lend money to Greece would be paid back by the EEC (aka Germany, Germany being the only EEC member that is halfway solvent), thus effectively issuing Greece a no limit low interest credit card, the equivalent of helping an alcoholic by giving him a barrel of whiskey. This, of course, produced venomous outrage from Greece. They had expected a wheelbarrow load of money from Germany, and merely received a no limit credit card.

In 1999 I predicted collapse around 2020-2025, with interesting times beginning around 2010 or so. Still looks about right.

When the US is as deep in the septic tank as Greece is today, no one will expect a bailout, therefore it will go under - and since by that time it will probably be bailing out and guaranteeing Europe through the IMF, Europe will go under simultaneously.

(When the US sets to work keeping Europe afloat through the IMF, expect a vehement stream of denunciations from Europe, complaining about its cruel and oppressive stinginess, similar to the spew of outrage and indignation now being emitted by Greece.)

When the crisis finally comes, the most likely way out is hyperinflation, probably followed or accompanied by by war, revolution and/or dictatorship, but the least damaging way out is that wisely chosen by the voters of Iceland in the recent referendum - to refuse to repay official debts.

This horrified the Icelandic governing elite, and will horrify our elite. They like to borrow and spend money which ordinary people will have to repay. Deficit is the most invisible form of tax, hence much beloved by the elite, and the only way to prevent it is to force the government to default on its promises.

Sooner or later, that which cannot continue, will stop.

If the problem was merely financial, it might well be resolved with no more drama than the Icelandic insolvency, but the problem is also political, making a more violent resolution likely.

A nation and its institutions exist because people intend that they exist - because people worked very hard to create them, and other people continue to work to sustain them. There is, as Smith said, a lot of ruin in a nation, but when the will to sustain those institutions is no longer there, collapse or very radical change follows in a generation or two.

Here are some recent examples of rot in the rafters. When the whole rafter is rotted all the way through, the roof will fall in, and everyone will be surprised, and ask "Hey how come the roof fell in?". Each of these examples was the result of a long series of similar precedents, each worse than the preceding one.

This stuff has been going on for a long time, but it has become markedly more severe lately.

Imprisonment without charges or trial. When a sergeant on the battle field imprisons or executes someone administratively, that is no threat to freedom outside the battlefield. When the president has someone who was caught at an airport imprisoned administratively, that is a threat to freedom. So far only Muslims who murderously hate America and Americans have been treated so, but doing it to Padillo is getting uncomfortably similar to doing it to me. This is a continuation of the Clinton program of using administrative violence against "extremists", in ways that past generations would have regarded as criminal, but which Clinton got away with. Bush's extremists are genuinely extreme, but some of Clinton's "extremists" were not, in fact, very extreme at all. The next step will be Bush style administrative detention applied against Clinton style not-so-extreme extremists.

Attack on the electoral process. Democracy requires that the losers accept losing, and the winners accept limits on their victory. On this the Democrats are the main offenders - refusing to accept entirely legitimate Republican victories as legitimate, while themselves industriously stuffing ballot boxes, registering the dead to vote, and treating the ballots they themselves fabricated as a limitless mandate. While both sides are guilty of ballot box stuffing, the Democrats do more of it, and are guilty of a dangerously extreme self righteousness about doing it. The Democrats are by far the worst offenders in this matter.

Attack on political debate. As predicted, the campaign finance laws have come to be interpreted as defining speech itself as money, and are now primarily about regulating speech, speech to which monetary values are quite arbitrarily applied, even though money seldom change hands. Since the NRA was forbidden to participate in politics, it reincorporated itself as news organization to take advantage of the freedom of the press exemption. In consequence, blogs and the mainstream media, the freedom of the press exemption, are now being treated as a "loophole", and the problem of how to "fix" that "loophole" is now being addressed. This process has been going on for twenty years, it is starting to have a major effect in silencing some voices, and all voices now speaking, are speaking through what the enforcers consider to be "loopholes" and "problems"".

Politicization of the judiciary. Court stacking has already reached the point where stare decisis is nonsense, and sooner or later judges are going to start acting on this fact, simply setting aside laws and precedents on the basis that the other side had a majority back then, with the result that the present minority will completely refuse to accept the outcome as binding. The main villains here are the Democrats, who think that the job of judges is to legislate stuff that would be political suicide if an elected politician tried it, such as gay marriage, though the Republicans are far from innocent. When a Democrat legislator says a judge is "mainstream", he means that the average swinging voter would regard that judge as dangerously demented, and when he says a judge is "outside the mainstream" he means that judge has views that are too similar to those of the voter that the legislator reluctantly courted in his recent campaign.

The basic columns of rule of law and the rest that are the basis of the American nation are under determined and persistent attack from within, and are getting mighty wobbly.

Government applies state power to ensure political outcomes - for example it makes broadcasters toe the line by direct regulation of the airwaves. The print media get access to the extent that they play along with those they seek access to, hence the New York Times. The schools teach the government line on the great depression, and scientists and economists know that if you scientifically prove what politicians and regulators want to hear you get ahead, and what politicians and regulators want to hear is always that regulators are doing good, except that they need a lot more power because they are not doing nearly enough - hence the noise about financial "deregulation", when all the supposed examples of financial deregulation are financial regulation, financial regulation that happens to be highly favorable to Goldman and Sach, who are connected to the regulators by a revolving door.

At the same time, those seeking political outcomes, seek backing from state power. A marriage naturally ensues. Let us call this happy marriage and its numerous morbidly obese children "the Cathedral". The Cathedral is almost the same thing as the left and the progressive movement, or rather it is the left in power, the established left, the professoriat, the mainstream media, the lawyer lobby, the judiciary, the senior public servants, the management of numerous supposedly non governmental quasi private organizations, and so on and so forth.

The Cathedral is the reason why history always moves left. The Cathedral is almost the same thing as the left. The right is an ever changing coalition of some of the groups and interests that are inevitably and inexorably being steamrollered by the Cathedral. Since the Cathedral steamrollers different things every few decades, the right is different people every few decades. Thus the Cathedral has different policies and programs from time to time, but its people and policies directly descend from previous Cathedral members policies, whereas the right has different policies and people from time to time.

In functioning, the Cathedral is very like a theocratic state. The guys with guns back the preachers, and the preachers endorse the guys with guns, resulting in the theocracy becoming ever more extreme and nutty in its religious doctrines, but in old fashioned theocracies power is concentrated in a King and high priest, with the King owning the high priest or the high priest owning the king.

In the Cathedral power is instead diffused amongst a large class of Brahmins, an ever more numerous, ever growing class of Brahmins. To get anything done, lot of Brahmins have to sign on, and each extracts tribute for signing on - which is why we cannot rebuild the two towers, and Dubai can, Dubai being an old fashioned theocracy.

You want to build a tower in Dubai, you just need one sufficiently high Mullah to sign on. In the theocracy of New York, you need lots of Brahmins to sign on, more Brahmins to sign on than anyone can count. So the two towers stay down.

Now what has been steadily happening ever since 1915 is that the power to print money has been diffused through a larger and larger class of people resulting in an ever greater inflationary bias, much as the power to obstruct the building of towers and housing has been diffused through a larger and larger class of people resulting in housing becoming ever more expensive. But these were stuffy conservative bankers, not really part of the Cathedral, or rather no longer sufficiently part of the Cathedral now that the Cathedral has moved a long way further left than it was in 1915 and become vastly more numerous. In 1993, the Cathedral decided these bankers were racists, and that they must join the new improved onsiderably more progressive Cathedral, or else. In due course, they did. Hence the present financial crisis, which is affirmative action lending leading to a run on the repo market, which run started silently and furtively in 2005 November, in response to the escalation of affirmative action lending, which had started to become excessive in 2000 or so, and became bizarrely extreme and ludicrously blatant in 2005. The run crashed the repo market in 2007, causing a reduction in affirmative action lending from blatantly insane to less blatantly insane – which reduction appears only temporary.

The "stabilization" of the repo market and the "normalization" of financial markets is a huge breakthrough for the Cathedral, and was indeed the original objective of declaring the banks racist, for it means that any large American business that can have its debt rated AAA can in effect issue money, for a government stabilized repo market trading AAA debt with an implicit government guarantee makes AAA rated debt directly cash equivalent. Today, in the "stabilized" financial market, an American financial institution gets and keeps AAA rating by political favor, rather than actual solvency, and to get political favor, it has to kiss up to political activist groups such as Acorn, so the effect of "stabilization" is that more and more elements of the Cathedral get to issue money outside the government budget, resulting in more rapid escalation of the ever growing inflationary bias.

Another factor is that every so often, by its nature, the Cathedral will simply go to war. The Cathedral lives on conflict. Each reform,real or purported, produces a new dispersal of little bits of state power with which to reward the ever more numerous members of the Cathedral, so the Cathedral always needs new reforms involving new conflicts. Conflicts are apt to get out of hand. The longer it has been since the Cathedral last went to war, the more it is apt to spoil for a new war, the more it is willing to take on a conflict that runs the risk of getting out of hand.

Thus we can foresee an ever more warlike Cathedral, that is causing ever more serious problems - the latest "reform" (bringing the bankers into the new Cathedral line) being one that is causing huge damage and will rapidly cause vastly more damage, which damage will lead to a multitude of conflicts, conflicts with a Cathedral that is increasingly spoiling for a fight.

In short, the reasons why the two towers would stay down were evident in 1999 well before they fell. It is now 2009, and they are still down. This foreshadows crisis and collapse. What prevented the towers from rising again is also what caused the financial collapse, which foreshadows more of the same.

At the same time, we hear from the Cathedral, rhetoric ever more violent, ever more warlike.

It is perhaps too soon to bet that a faction that has won every conflict over the past three hundred years is going to lose this time but outright war is apt to have surprising outcomes, war that follows collapse the more so. Trees do not grow to the sky. The ever multiplying Brahmins of the Cathedral are increasingly becoming liability, rather than an asset, and if it should survive the coming financial collapse and win the coming war, the Cathedral will have to thin the ranks a bit. If it survives, as it likely will, it will start looking more like a traditional theocracy, relying more on the gulag and less on persuasion and bribery.

Capital Controls

2010-04-05 05:40:35

Capital controls are characteristic of third world dictatorships teetering on the edge of bankruptcy. And now America has capital controls.[395]

In favor of war

2010-04-06 03:34:46

Bryan Caplan argues for avoiding war. But bad people are always willing to fight. If good people are not willing to fight, they will surrender in a succession of small steps, and bad people will rule. Without England declaring war, the Nazis would have ruled by 1942. Without Reagan encouraging a multitude of small wars, the communists would have ruled by 1990

> The immediate costs of war are clearly awful. Most wars lead to massive loss of life and wealth on at least one side. If you use a standard value of life of $5M, every 200,000 deaths is equivalent to a trillion dollars of damage.

And the cost of rule by Germany or the Soviet Union?

> Some wars - most obviously the Napoleonic Wars and World War II - at least arguably deserve credit for decades of subsequent peace. But many other wars - like the French Revolution and World War I - just sowed the seeds for new and greater horrors. You could say, "Fine, let's only fight wars with big long-run benefits." In practice, however, it's very difficult to predict a war's long-run consequences. One of the great lessons of Tetlock's Expert Political Judgment is that foreign policy experts are much more certain of their predictions than they have any right to be.

"War" did not cause those consequences. Bad people caused those consequences. For example World War I did not cause bad consequences. Hitler caused bad consequences, and pacifism, the fact that when the time came to enforce the Versailles treaty against Hitler the victors failed to do so, caused bad consequences. Versailles did not cause bad consequences. Failure to enforce Versailles against Hitler caused bad consequences.

> I suspect that economists' main objection to pacifism is it actually increases the quantity of war by reducing the cost of aggression. As I've argued before, though, this is at best a half-truth:

No. It is a simple and obvious truth.

---

[395] https://www.picassodreams.com/picasso_dreams/2010/03/hr-2487-capital-control-act-read-subtitle-aforeign-account-tax-compliance.html

The upshot for foreign policy is that people who warn about "sowing the seeds of hate" are not the simpletons they often seem to be. Military reprisals against, for example, nations that harbor terrorists reduce the quantity of terrorism holding anti-U.S. hatred fixed. But if people in target countries and those who sympathize with them feel the reprisals are unjustified, we are making them angrier and thereby increasing the demand for terrorism. Net effect: Ambiguous.

This theory is easily tested empirically: Reflect upon the thousand years of war Christendom has had with Islam. Islam has always been waging aggressive war against us, sometimes aggressive full scale conventional war, as in the siege of Constantinople, usually small scale raiding, piracy and terrorism. When did we have peace? We had peace when we massacred the entire population of Jerusalem, man woman and child and settled the place with Christians. We had peace from 1830 to 1960, which peace started when the French put an end to the chronic Barbary pirate problem by genocidally settling what is now Algeria with Christian settlers. Perhaps if they had killed a lot more, Algeria would today be Christian, and we would still have peace.

You do not get peace by making nice with bad people. You get peace by eradicating bad people. Often bad people rule people who are not bad, who just want to get on with their lives, but it is hard to separate the rulers from the ruled, particularly with theocratic or ideological governments, so you get peace by killing them all and letting God sort them out.

Why socialism needs killing fields

2010-04-07 18:38:36

Bryan Caplan asked why socialism turned out evil[396] and proposed three competing explanations. Volokh Conspiracy followed up,[397] and a horde of socialists appeared out of the wood work, objecting to the premise of the question, claiming that socialism was just fine.

So time to re-run my golden oldie: Why socialism needs killing fields[398]. The reason, like the reason for most things in human affairs, is economic.

Throughout the twentieth century the introduction of socialism has always involved killing fields, facilities for the mass production of murder by specialized labor.

Although this institution has been widely used throughout the twentieth century, we did not create a word for it until close to the end of the twentieth century, when Pol Pot organized approximately 20 000 separate killing fields, a world record, thanks to his firm commitment to decentralized government.

Though the word is new, the system is as old as socialism.

The basic problem of socialism is the relationship between production and consumption. It is likely that the number seven widget collective might want to produce fewer

---

[396]https://econlog.econlib.org/archives/2010/04/explaining_soci.html
[397]https://volokh.com/2010/04/06/competing-explanations-for-the-oppressive-nature-of-socialism/
[398]https://reaction.la/killingfields.html

widgets, or a different kind of widget, to that which certain users of widgets desire. Furthermore some users of widgets will want widgets for one purpose, and others for a different purpose, and there probably will not be as many widgets as they all desire, or the varieties that each diverse user of widgets desires.

Now under capitalism, no problem. You want widgets? You pay for widgets. You get the widgets you want or you refuse to buy widgets. And if you do not want to pay, then you probably do not need the widgets as much as the guy who is willing to pay. And if the price is high, then making widgets must be hard, and if it is not hard, you go into business making widgets, and you do not have to ask anyone's permission to do that.

But under socialism, the number seven widget collective is producing widgets for free, or at a "socially desirable price", which usually might as well be free, since when goods are produced at "socially desirable" prices money rapidly becomes unspendable. So who gets to decide what widgets to produce? Those who produce them, or those who consume them?

Well obviously "the community" must decide.

And then "the community" must impose its decision on the producers and consumers of widgets.

Whereas in capitalism, the community can go jump in the lake. It is nobody's business but that of a willing seller and a willing buyer.

This means that under socialism, issues of production and consumption have to be dealt with in the same way that capitalists deal with issues such as a stolen handbag.

Under capitalism there is a positive incentive to produce, since if you produce something you own it, until you trade if for something you want more, and you cannot consume, except you have produced something that someone else values more than what you consume.

This of course makes it possible in capitalism for one person to wind up owning vastly more than another due to the accidents of luck, opportunity, ability, and ambition.

Under socialism it is necessary to use negative incentives, to punish people for "parasitism" "hoarding", "black marketeering", and suchlike "crimes", "crimes" which are unknown in capitalism, or rather honored as virtues.

A socialist economy must employ negative incentives, the kind of incentives that law abiding people apply only to muggers and the like, in order to get light bulbs in the light sockets and toilet paper in the toilets. Thus the entire socialist country must be run as a prison, and all the citizens are lifers, and the nomenclatura are merely trusties.

Needless to say, when this system is introduced, a great many people misbehave. You cannot send them to prison, they already are in prison.

You have to murder them.

Hence the need for efficient methods for the mass production of murder.

Once upon a time, the living dead were scary

2010-04-08 06:21:43

Miller tells us that a society that has difficulty recognizing monsters in its art, will probably have trouble recognizing terrorists at its airports[399].

A culture of non judgmentalism is apt to suicide, since judgment is so often needed.

One can see a similar connection from the fact that heroes in our art seldom do anything very drastic, anything that disturbs anyone, to the fact that the two towers are still down.

Mortgage Fraud, predatory borrowing:

2010-04-09 15:44:29

There have been numberless highly successful prosecutions for predatory lending, even though there is no plausible evidence that predatory lending has ever happened in recent decades, nor has such evidence ever been presented in court, nor is it plausible that predatory lending could be profitable except for lenders who break the borrowers legs and arms in the event of default.I have personal and direct knowledge of numerous incidents of predatory borrowing, mortgage fraud, but there has not been a single successful prosecution for mortgage fraud, even though it looks very much as though predatory borrowing collapsed the economy and cost the taxpayer trillions.

However, MGIC has objected to paying out on its insurance of numerous defaulted loans, and has presented a highly amusing motion[400] to the California Superior Court in San Francisco, which includes its motion to American Arbitration association, alleging that Countrywide Bank committed and/or tolerated massive mortgage fraud

>
> Representative Claims in Dispute
>
> ...
>
>
> ### MGIC Certificate No.23755967
>
> ... purchase of a $600,000 home in San Jose, California....
>
> MGIC investigated the claim .... First, contrary to Countrywide's insurance application, she was never an account executive at GNG Investments. There is no such enterprise operating in
> Santa Clara or anywhere else in California. Nor did she earn $13,494 per month, as Countrywide represented. Instead, she earned $3,901.58 per month as a janitor for Santa Clara Valley Medical Center. ... she never had a bank account at Wells Fargo, let alone one worth $45,000. Nor did she put a $30,000 down payment—or a down payment of any amount—on her house.

---

[399]https://www.heymiller.com/?p=1078
[400]https://blog.reaction.la/wp-content/uploads/2010/04/25-3.pdf

...

MGIC Certificate No.25639575

... purchase of a $360,000 home in Chicago, Illinois. ... Nor did she earn $6,833 per month, as Countrywide represented. She was a part-time house-keeper who earned $200 to $300 per week, or approximately $1,300 per month. ... A few months after closing, she returned to her home in Poland because she was unable to find steady work in Chicago.

...

MGIC Certificate No.23789635

... refinancing of her home in Ceres, California. ... a $398,050 mortgage loan ... She never worked as a sales executive for Bay Area Sales and Marketing. There is no such enterprise. Nor did she earn $8,700 per month, as Countrywide represented. Instead, she had been unemployed since 1989 ...

MGIC Certificate No.25616578

... Contrary to Countrywide's insurance application, his home was not worth $395,500 as of August 28, 2007. His home had sold three times in the year prior to the effective date of Countrywide's appraisal: on October 3, 2006 for $199,750; on February 6, 2007, for $127,500; and on March 23, 2007, five months before the represented appraisal, for $200,000.

And, of course, lots and lots more of the same. These are alleged to representative of defaults, not the worst of the worst, not egregious and outrageous examples, but par for the course

The example of an overvalued house is striking it that the prices are obvious inconsistent. It fell to 127,500, and then, 45 days later, supposedly rose to the curiously round number of $200,000, before supposedly reaching the astonishing height of $395,000

My personal observation (for which I plenty of evidence, but no evidence that I can show to others) was that housing prices peaked 2005 November, and crashed swiftly thereafter, and the sales at higher and higher prices were all fraudulent, with straw man buyers and cash passing back under the table. If a house sold for a hundred thousand more, it was because $200 000 went under the table. All the sales at rising prices that I could know the truth about were fraudulent, and yet most sales for the next couple of years were at higher and higher prices, indicating a market completely dominated by massive mortgage fraud.

Bank "deregulation"

2010-04-12 11:26:21

It is often claimed that the disaster was produced by deregulation. What deregulation you may ask?

Well, mostly, the dismantling of Glass-Steagall. I don't think dismantling Glass-Steagall *caused* the crisis, but it is undeniable that if Glass-Steagall had remained in effect, the crisis would have been far less severe, for Glass-Steagall restrained financial institutions from being too big to fail. It was the biggest institutions, the institutions too big to fail, that behaved the worst, and lost the largest proportion of the assets they managed. Glass-Steagall also prevented financial institutions from all being "diversified" in exactly the same way, which "diversification" is not very diverse at all.

So why, and how, was Glass-Steagall dismantled? It was dismantled by being replaced and superseded by Basel II. Glass-Steagall consists of seventeen pages, that a competent person can, with some effort, comprehend. Basel II consists of thousands of pages, no one knows how many, and no one person knows more than a tiny fraction of what is in these thousands of pages.

That is "deregulation".

Basel II and the destruction of civilization as we know it.

2010-04-18 11:13:28

The US representatives at Basel probably thought themselves political moderates and mainstreamers – being in about the center and mainstream of Harvard University professors and the New York Times – which of course puts them far to the left of the American public, and a great deal further to the left of the people who created the banking system.

At Basel, the Americans were the "right wing". The "center" and "mainstream" at Basel was a good deal further left. Thus the mainstream at Basel were people that the ordinary American would think far left crazies, and that those who reorganized the banking system after the great depression would have thought a bunch of bolshie nut cases who needed to be lined up against a wall and shot.

I don't think the people at Basel consciously intended to destroy the old banking system, capitalism, or industrial civilization, but it was a bit like a great big bag of potato crisps. You eat one crisp, then you eat another, and before you know it you have emptied the bag. Because they hated capitalism, western civilization, and industrialization, they just loved making little changes, and they just kept making more and more and more little changes.

I don't think anyone at Basel said "Now this is really going to destroy western civilization. hah haha haaahhhaah. Stick it to the evil white male protestant capitalist imperialist overlords, let us make them into third world peasants doing agriculture with digging sticks." Rather, they intended the changes to be small, minor, and boring. They tried to make sure that every little regulatory change was as boring as possible, but we have tens of thousands, perhaps hundreds of thousands, of teeny weeny little regulatory changes, each promulgated by people who do not much like capitalism or western civilization or an industrial economy, thus the cumulative effect is quite large. How large is difficult to say, since no one, least of all the participants, understands Basel II. It is, however, apparent, that it turns the banking system completely up side down, abolishing a system where loans are made by a particular branch of a particular bank, and a particular branch manager is responsible for those loans.

The local branch bank manager is no longer responsible to make loans that get paid back. He is now instead responsible to make loans that conform to rules that supposedly ensure that loans will get paid back, which loans are then passed to some completely different organization. He is now responsible for the procedure, no longer for the results of that procedure. Thus the decision as to what is a safe loan is moved to politics and the government bureaucracy, far far away from anyone who knows the borrower or has actually seen the assets.

Thus financial capital is now centrally allocated by regulators – and therefore, in practice, is allocated without any regard for willingness, ability, or propensity to pay it back.

They really are a bunch of bolshie crazies. We will keep having trillion dollar bailouts till we line them up against a wall and shoot them.

The crisis explained

2010-04-22 22:12:54

Substantial parts of this article are pillaged wholesale from Ryan Barne's excellent account of the crisis[401], and Mortgage Guarantee Insurance's colorful account of the crisis[402]. I steal from the best. And thanks to the commenters that pointed out numerous errors.

In 2001, the Federal Reserve began cutting rates dramatically, dropping to 1% in 2003, in order to stimulate the economy.

This produced a boom, and especially a housing boom, in 2002. A housing boom was a rational and appropriate response to the extraordinarily low interest rate on a 30 year fixed rate mortgage, and no one was asking whether the extraordinarily low interest rates on 30 year fixed rate mortgages were rational and appropriate.

Interest rates on fixed rate mortgages were extraordinarily low thanks in part to Fannie and Freddie, which blessed mortgages with an implicit government guarantee, and resold them, making them very attractive to banks around the world under the Basel II rules.

So mortgages were being written by one bank, and sold to another bank or financial institution, far, far away, a bank with no idea of whether the house underlying the mortgage was worth what was claimed, or the borrower was solvent, or the borrower had a past history of paying his debts.

The US government, in particular George Bush, forcefully encouraged no money down loans, especially to non traditional borrowers, especially to members of non Asian minorities. Banks had every incentive to lend irresponsibly, were encouraged to do so, and were under severe regulatory pressure to lend to groups that it was difficult to lend to responsibly.

---

[401]https://www.investopedia.com/articles/07/subprime-overview.asp
[402]latex/wp-content/uploads/2010/04/25-3.pdf

No money down loans encouraged wild speculation. If housing prices rise, you have free money, and if they fall, it is someone else's problem – particularly if you have no credit rating to lose, as members of non Asian minorities usually don't.

Wall street started to get into the business, competing with Fannie and Freddy, despite their lack of an implicit government guarantee.

The asset-backed security (ABS) has been around for decades, and at its core lies a simple investment principle: Take a bunch of assets that have predictable and similar cash flows, bundle them into one managed package that collects all of the individual payments (the mortgage payments), and use the money to pay investors a coupon on the managed package. It is a good idea, provided the underlying assets really do have value and really do have regular and reliable payments.

The high implosive bomb that sunk the world financial system was Residential Mortgage Backed Securities (RMBS), a product created by Wall Street to weasel deadbeat loans into compliance with Basel II. The underlying asset was wildly inflated, and the payments improbable because the people that were to make the payments were deadbeat speculators whose credit rating was frequently non existent.

Mortgage Guarantee Insurance Corporation gives us some colorful examples of loans[403] that Countrywide bank made. Most of Countrywide's loans wound up being made into RMBS. Mortgage Guarantee claims the following were typical of loans that went bad.

A stone broke female janitor earning $4000 per month purchased a $600,000 home no money down as a speculative investment.

A maid with erratic employment purchased a $360 000 home, for her sister and brother in law. She never made a payment, and shortly thereafter returned to her home country.

A milker who cannot read English and who earns $1000 per month purchased a $350 000 house no money down for his son.

A woman who has been unemployed since 1989, yet who somehow owned multiple houses, refinanced one of them for $400 000.

Someone borrowed $355 000 to buy a house. Supposedly he put $39 500 down payment, which, however, seems highly improbable since the house had recently sold for $127 500 and housing prices were not rising at the time.

A speculator owning multiple condos, with payments on the mortgages two and a half times his income, borrowed $187 400 to purchase a condo whose fair market value was $155 000.

Someone with no known income, no known assets, and no clear identity, borrowed $495 000 to purchase a house, no money down.

A front buyer (straw man purchaser) purchased a house for the loan officer who arranged the loan, for $205 000, no money down.

A woman with no savings earning $1 695 a month purchased a $100 000 home for $115 000 no money down.

A woman earning $2 500 a month refinanced her home for $231 000.

Somehow, residential mortgage backed securities based on such loans and collateralized debt obligations based on residential mortgage backed securities based on such loans got AAA or A+ ratings from Moody's and Standard & Poor's These highly regulated

---

[403]latex/wp-content/uploads/2010/04/25-3.pdf

credit agencies have a special privilege from the government to bless debt as low risk under Basel II, thereby entitling banks owning such debt to special regulatory treatment, making the debt highly attractive to financial entities subject to Basel II regulation.

Ginnie May, Freddie Mac, and Fannie May had long been engaged in this shady business, of making questionable loans into loans that supposedly met Basel II standards, but in their case the AAA ratings may have been justified by the implicit taxpayer guarantee. The rationale for the high ratings given to RMBS is more complicated, and less clear.

The debt that went into the RMBS was often debt that even Ginnie May, Freddie Mac, and Fannie May would not touch, subprime. The ratings given to this low quality debt were justified by dividing the securities into tranches. Upper tranches were able to receive 'AAA' ratings because these tranches were promised the first dollars that came into the security. Lower tranches carried higher coupon rates to compensate for the increased default risk. All the way at the bottom, the "equity" tranche was a highly speculative investment.

Lehman Brothers purchased these mortgages, and made them into RMBS divided into tranches. It was unable to sell the lowest tranches, so accumulated a large portfolio of these worthless mortgage backed securities. It would borrow money against the highest tranches on the repo market. When the fat lady sang, the repo market went south, and the true value of these Residential Mortgage Backed Securities was revealed, Lehman went under.

Then then, to get part the middle level tranch up to the AAA, they made CDOs based on the mezzanine RMBS tranches based on rubbish mortgages, and divided the CDO into tranches, so that by this elaborate financial engineering, most the debt the rubbish mortgages were magically converted into debt deserving of favorable treatment under Basel II as very safe.

As a result of this activity, it became very profitable to originate mortgages, even mortgages as worthless as those described by Mortgage Guarantee Insurance Corporation

Record-low interest rates had combined with ever-loosening lending standards to push real estate prices to record highs across most of the United States. Existing homeowners were refinancing in record numbers, tapping into recently earned equity that could be had with a few hundred dollars spent on a home appraisal.

So the highest tranches got a AAA rating, qualifying institutions owning them for special regulatory treatment under Basel II. No one would touch the lowest tranches. What of the middle tranches, called the "Mezzanine" tranches?

AIG sold "Collateralized Debt Obligations" "Credit Default Swaps", meaning that if the lower tranches went under, AIG would make it up. AIG insured the mezzanine tranches. Thus even mezzanine tranches based on worthless mortgages became AAA equivalent, qualifying the owning institutions for special treatment under Basel II.

In 2005 November, an increasing number of people started to realize that all this was going to fall apart. A mad stampede for the exits began. The run on the repo market began. (The repo market is where debt that meets Basel II's high standards of safety is traded.) "Slapped in the face by the invisible hand" tells us that the panic began in August 2007. This may well be true if one defines "panic" as the shocking realization that there are no bigger idiots to unload your exposure onto, but the frantic search for the bigger idiot began in 2005.

Despite this, housing prices continued, supposedly, to rise until the middle of 2006, possibly due to straw man purchases and fake sales made by people getting the hell out.

By the middle of 2006 default rates began to rise sharply. making it obvious that prices were *not* rising, but falling, and obvious that the RMBS were going to implode. The repo market collapsed, though regulators continued to deny it had collapsed until 2007. Since Basel II ensured that the debt was extremely safe, markets must be irrational, so we were told.

In 2007 financial institutions started to collapse in large numbers.

Somehow, the market had created a flood of assets that received Basel II's official blessing. In 2007, most businesses still doing business in these assets, businesses who had not got out the exits in late 2005, early 2006, imploded.

Observe that all the factors that caused this crisis are still in place. The CRA is still in effect. Basel II continues to provide special regulatory privilege for "safe" assets, meaning that regulators have to decide what is "safe". To the extent that they outsource this job to certain favored firms, such as Moody's, we get crony capitalism, to the extent that the regulators decide what is safe, we get political allocation of debt to cronies, special interest groups, and favored voting blocks, such as non Asian minorities. Either way, the "safe" assets are bound to be ruinously unsafe.

Losing in Afghanistan

2010-04-24 16:55:06

The US has fled Korengal, Afghanistan[404], which is now under the uncontested control of the Taliban.

The US created the Kabul government, in order to do good to Afghans, so that they would love us. It attempted to build a road for the people in Korengal valley, so that they would love us. The people of the valley, all of them, promised to kill anyone who worked on the road, and anyone who used the road, and proceeded to do so.

The US captain, Moretti, sent a letter to Nasurallah: "It is our belief that you are the rightful leader of the Korengalis," the captain wrote. "You hold the power not only among the villagers but also among the fighters. If you want the valley to prosper all you have to do is talk with us and bring your fighters down from the mountains."

The letter offered two choices: development or death. "It is not our wish to kill your fellow Korengalis," Moretti continued. "But we are good at it and will continue to do it as long as you fight us."

Moretti received a response two days later. "If you surrender to the law of God then our war against you will end," Nasurallah wrote. "If you keep fighting for man's law then we will fight you until Doomsday."

And what is the difference between God's law and man's law that has these villagers pissed at us?

Man's law forbids them from growing and exporting the only cash crop in this barren region: Cedar trees.

---

[404]https://www.bing.com/search?q=Moretti+Nasurallah+Korengal+cedar

Photos show the villages in the midst of cedar groves, so obviously they are cultivating them and harvesting them sustainably.

In trying to impose the Kabul government on them, we are imposing injustice. Thus the only possible ways of winning are to rule them ourselves, colonial style, or slaughter enough of them that the Taliban decides not to tolerate anyone who goes looking for trouble with far away infidels.

The strong horse
2010-04-26 09:01:21

As a result of our defeat, Arab terrorists have moved into Korengal valley. Now Al Quaeda has safe haven in Korengal and their objectives will not be restricted to protecting the freedom of those in Korengal, but destroying our freedom in lands far from Korengal, murdering Jews and Americans, wherever we may be, anywhere in the world.

Here is the Taliban video of their great victory in Korengal valley produced by terrorist embeds, reporting their well deserved victory in Korengal valley, Afghanistan.

We lost in Korengal, because we were doing evil. The road was evil, the imposition of Kabul government law, Man's law, was evil.

Fighting colonial wars
2010-04-26 10:15:15

The recent outcome in Korengal valley[405] should tell us that our current strategy is not only foolish, but also evil.[406]

Political correctness consists of the political correct believing that they are being nice, when in fact they are being evil in a contemptible and cowardly way, rather than a manly and warlike way. What we did in Korengal was intended to be nice, but this merely rendered it ineffectual. It was in fact just as evil, hurtful, hateful, and therefore as rightly hated as more competent and effectual strategies are apt to be.

Any strategy that wins, has to resemble war. The present strategy is not war, but political correctness carried out by heavily armed nursemaids.

Contrary to what Mencius believes, the British empire was conquered not by the imperialists he cites, though they surely knew how to wage war better than moderns, not by the British government, but by merchant adventurers such as Clive and Raffles. ("Adventurer" being a nice word for pirate and brigand.) When they got peace on terms that allowed them to manage trade profitably, they engaged mostly in trade and only moderately in pillage and extortion. When unpleasant people interfered in their business, merchant "adventurers" would frequently loot and burn the town and rape the women in classic pirate style, and if that failed to render the town sufficiently pacific, they would tell everyone to get the hell out or die. If real estate is more valuable without the potentially troublesome tenants, evict those tenants, and lease the real estate to more cooperative and productive tenants. Business 101.

---

[405]https://blog.reaction.la/war/the-strong-horse.html
[406]https://blog.reaction.la/war/losing-in-afghanistan-4.html

The British empire was conquered not by Britain, but by British pirates and brigands. Charles the great consciously and intentionally employed the same strategy against Dar al Islam as the British employed in a fit of absent mindedness.

When the British government took over from the pirates, it was not only unprofitable and less effectual, but also markedly less popular, less liked by the natives. The merchant adventurers were local stationary brigands. A stationary brigand wants the area wherein he is safely unopposed to be prosperous and attractive to able and industrious migrants. A local stationary brigand is apt to be far better able to accomplish this than a far away stationary brigand, for the far away brigand, the British empire run from Whitehall, is necessarily less competent, and less aware of the situation on the ground, therefore less able to create attractive conditions, less motivated to create attractive conditions, and less able to terrify those that might oppose it.

Have leftists guilt tripped you into getting screwed?

2010-04-28 13:03:01

Probably not as much as Donna Ron was[407].

This rapist, terrorist, and bomber, is a frequent visitor to the Whitehouse, one of the most powerful men in academia, and the major ghostwriter of Obama's book "Dream's of my father".

Tough on wall street

2010-04-29 13:51:08

Obama has a announced a great pile of trillion dollar giveaways to Wall Street, and called it tough regulation, though each of these regulations protects them from responsibility, while tapping the taxpayer's veins. To show how tough they are on Wall Street, congressmen summoned Goldman and Sach's executives to Washington, and harshly ranted at them for selling their customers securities based on mortgages that they knew or should have known were $##%.

Meanwhile, the FDIC is busily ladeling great helpings of taxpayer money all over Goldman and Sach[408].

Indymac closed its doors and was seized by the FDIC, which sold it to Goldman Sach, yes, those dreadfully bad boys being cursed out in congress as your read this, in an extraordinarily generous and completely one sided sweetheart deal, paralleling the very similar deal wherein Goldman and Sach got to devour Lehman brothers.

Basel II is a giveaway, a great pile of regulation written by people like Goldman and Sach, for people like Goldman and Sach, rich man's socialism, socialism George Soros style. Everyone involved in developing, enforcing, and implementing these regulations needs to go to jail, but instead Obama is giving us even more rich man's socialism.

---

[407] https://frontpagemag.com/readArticle.aspx?ARTID=6133
[408] https://sixmeatbuffet.com/archives/2010/04/27/remember-this-while-the-boys-at-goldman-sachs-are-being-grilled-on-capitol-hill-today/

Dangerous Thought Criminal

2010-05-03 17:27:04

Display name : Stephanie Grace

Photo :

This evil person has been detected expressing a forbidden thought in private email. She suggested that wrong think could possibly be true, and the evidence needed to be considered. She has of course given repeated grovelling public apologies for her horrifying crime. Her career is of course dead, and all right thinking people condemn her, and should continue to condemn her. Failure to adequately condemn her may cause you to be similarly suspected of wrongthink. No person capable of wrongthink can be permitted to hold any important position in our society, since to consider the possibility that wrongthink might be true shows that your mind is dogmatically closed, that you are stupid, ignorant, and hateful, and therefore fit only to be hewer of wood and carrier of water.

Wishing for a chinese crash

2010-05-07 04:19:37

Lots and lots of people are predicting China will crash, though The Money Illusion doubts it[409]. Supposedly, debt fueled construction, decreed by central planners, Soviet style, is sixty percent of GDP – except that there is absolutely no evidence that this remarkable statistic is true. It is not an official government statistic. Where does it come from? If it was sixty percent of GDP, most of the population would be working in construction, which obviously they are not.

People *want* to believe that China will crash.

Who wants to believe that China will crash?

The people who believe that China will crash also believe that China is a command economy, which obviously it no longer is, except in the sense that Europe is a command economy, and America has recently become a command economy. They *also* believe in Soviet growth statistics – that the Soviet Union grew just great, at least at first.

---

[409]https://www.themoneyillusion.com/?p=4964

Further, those who believe that China will crash, also believe it has already crashed: that China's prosperity is based on forcing
peasants into grinding poverty in sweatshops on two dollars a day, that China has no middle class (hence the supposed absurdity of the present building boom in china creating vast amounts of middle class housing, offices, and shops), and that Cuba's quite astonishing health statistics are true.

Their beliefs about China are incoherent, internally inconsistent, and mutually contradictory, showing that they don't really believe what they believe. I suspect that what they really believe is that basing a society on self interest is morally wrong, and therefore must surely be punished by the heavens. Obviously the right way to run a society is to put people like themselves, who know what is good for society, in charge and then make everyone else do what is good for society, and any society that allows greed to run riot is obviously doomed. Therefore, they subconsciously think, China is obviously doomed, due all the rampant greed that is not properly restrained by good government.

I just don't hear any one who confidently and sincerely believes that self interest is the proper basis for a society, predicting doom for China.

No doubt China will have a recession, sooner or later. No doubt some speculators will lose their shirts, sooner or later, for in a free economy, speculators take risks, unlike America where the elite gets bailed out by taxpayers when they bungle, but China is growing mightily, and will continue to grow mightily, with the usual minor interruptions from time to time.

US government endorses Mexican violence

2010-05-09 08:42:26

At live oaks high school, government policy is that Red, White and Blue is verboten on Cinco de Mayo.

Compare and contrast with Saint Patrick's day:

Numerous blogs have objected: x^{410}, x^{411}, x^{412}, x^{413}, x^{414}, x^{415}, x^{416}, x^{417}, x^{418}, x^{419}, x^{420}, x^{421}.

By enforcing what the thugs want, the government endorses and supports that thuggery. The government will empower any group that supports bigger government, for

[410] https://michellemalkin.com/2010/05/06/whose-country-is-it-anyway/
[411] https://volokh.com/2010/05/06/discourteous-to-wear-american-flag-images-on-cinco-de-mayo/
[412] https://volokh.com/2010/05/06/disagreement-need-not-equal-discourtesy/
[413] https://justpiper.com/2010/05/did-live-oak-high-school-lower-the-us-flag-on-cinco-de-mayo/
[414] https://www.garylsnyder.com/my_weblog/2010/05/american-flag-shirts-ignite-firestorm.html
[415] https://biglizards.net/blog/archives/2010/05/the_soft_bigotr.html
[416] https://antzinpantz.com/kns/?p=25576
[417] https://www.thepoliticalclass.com/2010/05/students-wearing-american-flag-shirts-on-cinco-de-mayo-sent-home-by-school-principalaccused-of-being-racist.html
[418] https://www.libertyblog.com/2010/05/what-its-come-to.html
[419] https://rhymeswithright.mu.nu/archives/301314.php
[420] https://www.violenceworker.com/my_weblog/2010/05/does-this-flag-offend-you.html
[421] https://conservativerenaissance.wordpress.com/2010/05/06/where-is-the-tolerance/

example Mexicans as a voter block, and disempower any group that objects to bigger government. So, predictably, Mexican thugs were empowered by the school administration, the administration being part of the government.

China catching up
2010-05-09 15:19:06

Hourly Wages for China's Factory Workers

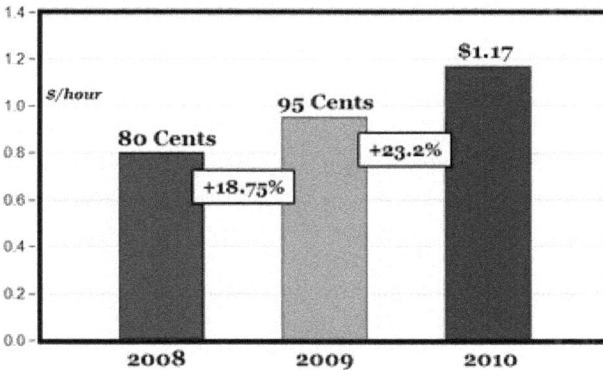

The NYT reports[422]

> Liang Huoqiao, a 22-year-old plastics worker, joined a small group of men and women studying a 40-foot-wide list of companies seeking workers.
>
> "You can walk into any factory and get a job," he said.
>
> ...
>
> He expected his pay to double in the next five years and added that he already had set his priorities.
>
> "For sure, I want to buy a car," he said. "Car first, then maybe marriage later."

Official statistics smell of official truth
2010-05-11 14:23:55

Mandel points out [423] that there is something mighty funny about official US economic statistics.

---

[422]https://www.nytimes.com/2010/02/27/business/global/27yuan.html?adxnnl=1&ref=business&adxnnlx=1267279899-BX+KaWAzVmdp/DFKk1s+nA
[423]https://innovationandgrowth.wordpress.com/2010/05/10/economics-statistics-in-an-alternative-universe/

The left as astroturf

2010-05-13 06:21:52

Whenever one sees supposedly insurrectionary leftism, one usually detects a government official sponsoring it, as for example in the recent suppression of US flags[424] on Cinco de Mayo.

Observe the recent firebombings in the Greek riots, where the "rioters" murdered three people.

Here are a couple of videos of the "rioters" firebombing police.

The "rioters" charge the police, and bang on their shields with light sticks, making no attempt to jab through the gaps at the actual bodies of the cops, nor using sticks heavy enough to even shake the shields. No axe handles or baseball bats.

Hey guys, if you want to bang on armored cops, I have a sledgehammer that would make a pretty good mace. It goes through concrete mighty fast.

They then fall back, and hurl firebombs[425] - but they do not hurl firebombs at the police, but at the ground in front of the police. One cop gets one of his boots splashed with burning petrol. He rolls around, and a couple of other cops put him out. In the second video[426], same scene shot from a different angle, we observe that the cops make not the slightest attempt to arrest the firebombers for attempted murder, and the rest of the mob for assault and as accessories to attempted murder. It is all theater. When they see that one of the firebombs has actually hit, the theater pauses.

When right wing militia listens politely to an FBI provocateur at a meeting proposing that they bomb someone, they all go to jail for plotting crimes. The "rioters" firebomb a cop, and everyone acts like it is an unfortunate accident – which of course is exactly what it is.

The "rioters" in the Greek riots are government employees put on the streets by government sponsored unions that are themselves as much part of the government as the police were – and predictably, in a supposed riot supposedly between police and government employees, the only people actually murdered were neither police nor government employees.

Yale Harvard and Basel style Free Enterprise

2010-05-16 07:55:12

After the collapse of socialism, the elite support free enterprise – they support it the way they support free speech.

If anyone is allowed to disagree with the orthodoxy taught at Yale and Harvard, or even doubt it, this endangers the free speech of people from Harvard and Yale, and similarly if any enterprise run by people from Harvard or Yale could go bust, this endangers the free enterprise of people from Harvard and Yale.

[424]https://blog.reaction.la/culture/us-government-endorses-mexican-violence.html
[425]https://www.youtube.com/watch?v=Y-ZNilpmH5E
[426]https://www.youtube.com/watch?v=KDU1-1_xUMc

Basel II is tens of thousands of pages of regulations, no one knows how vast it is, because not all the regulations can be found in any one place, but it could all be replaced by two simple rules: Politically correct victim groups shall always find it easy to borrow money, regardless of their ability or intention to pay it back, and politically well connected businesses shall always make money, regardless of whether they are competently run or not.

The seeds of the crisis were the CRA and the ratings agencies. I have discussed the CRA at length, but the CRA would have been resisted had it not been for other changes in the system that insulated the players against the consequences of making bad loans. These changes, guaranteeing that badly run businesses would succeed, started with the bailout of the ratings agencies in the seventies, forty years ago.

Back then, the ratings agencies were in trouble, because they had made a lot of bad calls. It seemed that whenever an institution was going under, the guys at the credit rating agencies were the last to know about it. Back then, they sold their assessments of credit risk to subscribers. So no one wanted to subscribe.

So in the seventies, the regulators stepped in to *make* people use the credit rating services. In 1975 the SEC created the Nationally Recognized Statistical Rating Organization (NRSRO) designation. Credit rating agencies so designated received what was in effect a grant of governmental power. The SEC then relied on the NRSRO's credit risk assessment in establishing capital requirements on SEC-regulated financial institutions – which meant that for SEC-regulated financial institutions to borrow and lend, they *had* to get rated. A cascade of regulatory decisions followed over the years, each decision forcing more and more reliance on the risk assessments issued by these demonstrably incompetent institutions – and less and less reliance on other people's risk assessment. For more and more organizations, it became *illegal* for them to make their own judgments about risk.

By the 1990s, as Levine and Partnoy tell us, the NRSROs were not selling assessments of credit risks, but licenses to issue securities. The rating agencies did not genuinely assess risk, nor did anyone really expect them to. Nor could repeatedly demonstrated incompetence reduce demand for their services, so the ratings agencies had no incentive to provide correct credit ratings. Since their income was entirely dependent on the state granting them power, they did, however, have an incentive to make *politically correct* credit ratings. If you lend to the poor, the oppressed, etc, and you are run by good old boys from Yale and Harvard, and you make donations to the right politicians, the NRSROs have a very powerful incentive to give you a good credit rating. And if you have a good credit rating, you can borrow as much as you like – and if you go bust, the government will bail you out.

Badly run companies that had been empowered to borrow as much as they pleased got in trouble – and were bailed out for the same reasons as they had been empowered to borrow as much as they pleased.

In addition to corruptly favorably rating the politically correct, the NRSROs corruptly favorably rated those who simply gave them money, which is perhaps what those who complain about "deregulation" have in mind. The banks creating structured financial products would first pay the rating agencies for "guidance" on how to package the securities to get high ratings and then pay the rating agencies to rate the resultant products – a glaring conflict of interest, though one less apt to lead to bailouts when the proverbial hits the fan.

Now since all this dirty dealing has cost the taxpayer trillions, you may well ask what measures have been taken to punish the NRSROs for bad conduct, or give them incentives for better conduct in future, or indeed restrain them from continuing to do this stuff?

All the strengthened regulation is regulation to make people continue to treat NRSRO ratings as true, even though it has become horrifyingly apparent that the ratings are generally false. All the strengthened regulation is more of what caused this mess in the first place. Any real reform would necessarily start by abolishing the legal privilege of NRSROs, would have to start by rolling back regulations to what they were in 1974. Instead, compulsion and bailouts are being applied to make NRSRO ratings true, or to enable people to continue pretend that they are true. Their power has been increased, their misconduct unpunished, and their incentives have become even worse.

How to fix the financial crisis

2010-05-21 17:33:34

Proposed reforms, both left and right, are unlikely to have any effect on the continuing massive misappropriation from the financial system. It is absurd that people are discussing obscure details of the credit swap market.

To fix the financial crisis, we have to revoke, or at least denounce and denigrate, Marie Curie's Nobel prize.

When they gave a Nobel prize to Marie Curie for being female, that did not hurt anyone except more deserving potential Nobel prize winners. But handing out phony Nobels on the basis of sex, race, and nationality necessitated handing out phony degrees on the basis of race and sex, and handing out phony degrees on the basis of race and sex necessarily led to a crisis where these phony degrees were being ignored by employers, so employers necessarily had to be forced to give out well paid phony jobs on the basis of race and sex.

But being given well paid phony jobs on the basis of race and sex failed to result in recipients living a middle class lifestyle, so lenders had to be forced to give out a middle class lifestyle on the basis of race and sex.

Which has led to our present financial crisis. It all began with Marie Curie. Each lie required a new and bigger lie. We need to start by acknowledging that genders and races tend to have different abilities - that if you are looking for people that are the best at something, whether the fastest runners or the greatest mathematicians, they will almost all be of one particular race and gender, and some races will be completely absent, and if you are merely looking for people that are acceptably good at something, for example accountants, basketball players, or donut makers, they will be mostly of one particular race and gender.

We cannot end the crisis unless we admit who is defaulting on their mortgages, we cannot admit who is defaulting without admitting that they cannot perform their jobs either, we cannot admit they cannot perform their jobs without admitting that their degrees are phony, and we cannot admit their degrees are phony without admitting that many Nobel prizes, starting with Marie Curie, were phony.

I predict an Obama win

2010-05-22 13:32:49

With these tactics, Obama should be able to win in 2012 And 2016, and ...
Of course, winning by such tactics may well result in a victory as useless as that which Patrice Lumumba won when the Congo became independent. Two or three weeks after independence, the government of the Congo had largely vanished from underneath Premier Patrice Lumumba, even though parliament continued to meet and vote him ever greater powers and additional titles for several months.

More google censorship

2010-05-24 10:22:00

Obama's social security number was issued in Connecticut in 1977[427] – which is mighty odd if he was born in America. Normally social security numbers are issued at birth. Getting a social security number from some random state at some random date is an indicator of immigration fraud. If you have a bit of political pull, *someone* will give you a social security number.

Mission accomplished

2010-05-26 13:10:22

[Paychecks from private business shrank to their smallest share of personal income in U.S. history during the first quarter of this year][428]
At the same time, government-provided benefits — from Social Security, unemployment insurance, food stamps and other programs — rose to a record high during the first three months of 2010.[429]

But has everything goes to hell in a handbasket, it will all be blamed on free markets, despite what Brutally Honest calls[430] "change some continue to believe in".

The fundamental political strategy is that the more moochers, the more votes there will be for mooching.

---

[427] https://www.wnd.com/index.php?fa=PAGE.view&pageId=152773
[428] https://www.usatoday.com/money/economy/income/2010-05-24-income-shifts-from-private-sector_N.htm
[429] https://www.usatoday.com/money/economy/income/2010-05-24-income-shifts-from-private-sector_N.htm
[430] https://www.brutallyhonest.org/brutally_honest/2010/05/obamas-mission-accomplished.html

The past is always changing
2010-05-28 06:12:24

Only the future is certain. The past is always changing.

The Congo was the poster child for the dreadful evils of colonialism. We were supposed to look at how cruelly the Belgians treat the poor natives, look at how many natives colonialism has murdered to maintain its savage rule. In 1961, it got independence. The whites fled rape and murder. Two or three weeks after independence, the Congo became a savage hell hole, and has remained that way ever since, Zimbabwe in fast forward. The whites fled the Congo faster than they have fled Zimbabwe, so the descent into savagery was faster. Yet now, the outcome of decolonization has been forgotten, and the Congo is back to being the poster child of the evils of colonialism, and we repeat the same disaster over and over again: Haiti foreshadowed the Congo, the Congo foreshadowed Zimbabwe and South Africa.

Until the Soviets collapsed, 99% of Academia enthusiastically agreed that the Soviet Union's command economy was growing much faster than the US's old fashioned semi market economy, and the remaining 1% agreed that it was growing at least as fast – or at least that is what they said when anyone was listening. Since the general consensus outside of Academia was that the Soviet Union was a festering economic basket case whose central plan existed only on paper, collapsing into disorderly pillage in actual practice, one wonders what happened to any academic inclined to say that the Soviet Union was a festering economic basket case, whose plans and statistics were utterly disconnected from the chaotic and destructive reality.

Before 1972, every historian of science agreed that Darwin's big idea was natural selection, and those of them that addressed the issue of Lamarck and common descent agreed that Lamarck proposed common descent.

Natural selection, however tends to lead to disturbing thoughts and disturbing words, for example "Once the superiority of races with a prevailing aversion to incest had been established by their survival ..." Superior races! Oh the horror, the horror. Natural selection suggests endangered species have it coming to them, that women are not naturally equal to men, that genocide is, if regrettable, nonetheless natural and in the long run frequently inevitable, and lots of similarly horrifying stuff like that, and I have left out the really shocking stuff to avoid offending the readers too much. So it was progressively de-emphasized to students in the textbooks. But if you de-emphasize natural selection, this leaves a mysterious gap. What was Darwin famous for?

So in 1972, history was corrected, Winston Smith style. Darwin got common descent to fill the gap left by the de-emphasis of natural selection, just as Winston Smith invented comrade Ogilvy to replace the vaporized unperson Comrade Withers, and common descent was taken away from Lamarck. The textbook "Biology today" page 638

> ... in the Origin of Species. The central claim of that book can be fairly simply stated. According to the Darwinian theory, any natural group of similar species-all the mammal species, for instance-owe their common mammalian characteristics to a common descent from a single ancestral mammalian species.

And as for Lamarck, he got the shaft. Page 641

> Lamarck's theory is not a hypothesis of common descent, which ascribes the common characteristics of a particular species to their common descent from a single species. ... He claims that ... although all mammals are descended from reptiles, they are not descended from the same reptiles

Somehow, after 1972, no one in Academia was able to mention that before 1972 everyone thought that Lamarckism is the doctrine "that all plants and animals are descended from a common primitive form of life." (Century Cyclopedia)

Before 1972[431]

After 1972[432]

Just as one wonders what happened to academics before 1980 who were inclined to doubt the great success of central planning, one wonders what happens to academics after 1972 who remember that before 1972, the history of science was different.

We have always been at war with Eastasia

Someone in Academia received an order like that given to Comrade Winston Smith, and all of Academia fell into line, and remains in line to this day, a thousand megaphones attached to one microphone.

> The reporting of Big Brother's Order for the Day in The Times of December 3rd 1983 is extremely unsatisfactory and makes references to non-existent persons. Rewrite it in full and submit your draft to higher authority before filing.
>
> ...
>
> ... Withers, however, was already an unperson. He did not exist: he had never existed. ...
>
> ... To-day he should commemorate Comrade Ogilvy. It was true that there was no such person as Comrade Ogilvy, but a few lines of print and a couple of faked photographs would soon bring him into existence.

Freedom flotilla vs Israeli Defence Forces.

2010-06-01 12:01:52

Don't take a knife to a gunfight.

Israel is blockading Gaza. Activists attempted to force the blockade with pathetically inadequate weapons. Perhaps the intent was to suffer some pathetic casualties, that they could then whine about, or perhaps they were just stupid.

If you are going to engage soldiers and marines, you should either take no weapons at all other than moral force, which may not be all that effective, but will not get you killed,

---

[431] https://books.google.com/books?as_q=Lamarck&as_epq=common+descent&as_sub=&as_drrb_is=b&as_minm_is=1&as_miny_is=1800&as_maxm_is=1&as_maxy_is=1971

[432] https://books.google.com/books?as_q=Lamarck&as_epq=common+descent&as_sub=&as_drrb_is=b&as_minm_is=1&as_miny_is=1972&as_maxm_is=1&as_maxy_is=2010

or else weapons capable of doing some good. Hamas tried weapons that should have been capable of doing some good, but the Israeli Defense Forces proved otherwise. This leaves moral force only. If you take a knife to a gunfight, as these activists did, the appropriate response is to laugh at them and piss on their graves.

Minority mortgage meldown and diversity recession

2010-06-07 12:14:04

People are starting to realize wonder where all the money was pissed away to. The answer, of course, is that most of it was pissed away on affirmative action loans to members of protected minorities. Whose fault is this?

Steve Sailer blames primarily Karl Rove and George Bush[433]

There is much truth in this, but I would primarily blame Basel.

Under Basel, what matters to a financial institution is not whether its assets are safely invested, but whether they are officially declared to be safely invested. The people in charge of deciding what is officially safe have no incentive to make their estimates accurate, but powerful incentives to make their estimates politically correct.

[an earlier version of this post incorrectly said Basel II, for which I was called out in the comments. Most of the problems started with Basel I]

The coming collapse

2010-06-08 06:54:51

Doc Zero explains the perverse incentives that make collapse inevitable.

Americans are already bailing out Greece, so will be bailing out California. Add the unfunded state liabilities to the unfunded federal liability, there is no way the Federal government can make good on its debts. We are not just up for the federal deficit. We are up for the Greek and Californian deficit.

If Jews bleed, it does not lead

2010-06-10 08:03:53

The biggest story of the last few days has been Israel's interception of peace activist ship to Gaza, in which they killed nine peace activists.

Here is a picture of some peace activists holding down a soldier at knifepoint, with what appears to be a pool of blood on the bulkheads.

---

[433]https://www.vdare.com/Sailer/080928_rove.htm

When the the picture gets carried at all in the mainstream media, the knife and the blood gets cropped. Even Fox news has not shown the picture at all.

The Muslim press, however, are showing these photos as they are - which is not the first time the Muslim press in totalitarian terror states has shown itself to be more free than in the west - I guess Muslims get more slack than Dhimmi.

Doomsday postponed for a short time

2010-06-15 08:06:11

As I write this, Spain just ran out of money. Presumably the European central bank is going to print up a whole lot of fresh money and bail them out, if it has not done so already. If they are not swiftly bailed out, there will be a run on the Spanish banks, and the Spanish deficit will be instafixed as the government loses the ability to pay most people.

The underlying crisis is, of course, that the welfare state is broke. Greece is more broke than Spain, Spain more broke than Germany, Germany more broke than the US, but all the major governments are in a very similar hole.

So can we print our way out the crisis? So far, printing more money has been highly successful, but printing fresh money in such huge amounts is giving everyone an uneasy feeling. Will it work forever? Can it work forever?

Printing more money will eventually lead to inflation, other things being equal, but of course, other things are not equal. We are seeing deflation, not inflation.

The value of fiat money is speculative. It is valuable because people think it is valuable. Properly managed, fiat money is bubble that never bursts. Improperly managed, it bursts, and people start using gold, whiskey, ammo, and dried beans. With more and more fiat money being issued, and the value remaining high, we are seeing bubble behavior.

Hyperinflations start off in series of abrupt bursts. People notice that not only are prices rising, but that goods are getting short. There is a mad rush to unload money and load up on goods. For a little while, money becomes unspendable. After a while, normality returns, but with goods at much higher prices. Prices remain fairly stable for while, the government continues to issue lots of money, and then there is another burst. After this happens several times, inflation starts to become continuous and extremely rapid, and people stop using the fiat money.

So the first hyperinflationary burst, if it happens, which I rather think it will, will rather sudden and shocking. The warning will not be high inflation, but high inflation with shelves emptying. If the governments then start balancing their budgets by laying off civil servants, and cutting civil servant pensions, then we will return to stability - at a substantially higher price level. If, on the other hand, deficits continue, another burst will come soon after the first.

China continues moving to the free market

2010-06-20 15:00:10

The greatest limitation on the economic liberty of Chinese was capital controls. Recently the party took a big step away from capital controls by allowing ordinary Chinese to buy and sell gold as an investment. As Europe and the US moves towards capital controls, the party continues to move away from capital controls.

The Central Bank of China has announced:[434]

> Starting from July 21, 2005, China has moved into a managed floating exchange rate regime based on market supply and demand with reference to a basket of currencies.

It still "managed" but in the west, everything financial is managed. We have not had anything remotely resembling a free financial market since Basel.

---

[434]https://www.pbc.gov.cn/english/detail.asp?col=6400&id=1488

It is the past that changes
2010-06-27 12:30:31

The future is certain, it is the past that changes.

Moveon had a web page demonizing General Petraeus as General Betray Us[435]

Obama appoints General Petraeus in charge of Afghanistan, whereupon the page not only instantly disappears from Moveon.org, but also instantly disappears from Google's cache[436]. When the past changes, Google's spiders are quicker of the mark than they are for normal updates, suggesting human intervention to correct the past lickety-spit.

General Petraeus is infinitesimally to the right of the fired General McChrystal.

The policy that should be followed in Afghanistan is not that of General Petraeus, General McChrystal, President Obama, or President Bush, all of which are following infinitesimally different variations of the same lunatic extreme left policy: COIN.

The correct policy would be that of Lord Cromer, who brought peace, prosperity, and freedom to Egypt with only five thousand men. Unfortunately that policy was already politically incorrect in 1907.

The weak horse
2010-07-03 20:16:42

Mark Steyn brilliantly skewers our Afghanistan policy[437]. He primarily blames Obama, though the rot set in under Bush.

> Why would Putin, Ahmadinejad or the ChiComs take Barack Obama seriously when even a footling client such as Hamid Karzai can flip him the finger?
>
> ...
>
> The toppling of the Taliban was an operation conducted with extraordinary improvised ingenuity and a very light U.S. footprint. Special forces on horseback rode with the Northern Alliance and used GPS to call in air strikes: they'll be teaching it in staff colleges for decades to come. But then the Taliban scuttled out of town, and a daring victory settled into a thankless semi-colonial policing operation, and then corroded further under the pressure of the usual transnational poseurs. After 2003, Afghanistan became the good war, the one everyone claimed to have supported all along, if mostly retrospectively and for the purposes of justifying their "principled moral opposition" to Bush's illegal adventuring against Saddam. Afghanistan was everything Iraq wasn't: UN-approved, NATO-backed, EU-compliant. It'd be tough for even the easiest nickel 'n' dime military incursion to survive that big an overdose of multilateral hogwash, and the Afghan campaign

[435] https://web.archive.org/web/20080731153144/https://pol.moveon.org/petraeus.html
[436] https://freerepublic.com/focus/f-news/2540791/posts?page=1
[437] https://www2.macleans.ca/2010/07/01/where-nice-obama-has-got-us/

didn't. Instead of being an operation to kill one of the planet's most concentrated populations of jihadist terrorists, it decayed into half-hearted nation-building in which a handful of real allies took the casualties while the rest showed up for the group photo. The 2004 NATO summit was hailed as a landmark success after the alliance's 26 members agreed to put up an extra 600 troops and three helicopters for Afghanistan. That averages out at 23.08 troops per country, plus almost a ninth of a helicopter apiece. As it transpired, the three Black Hawks all came from one country—Turkey—and within a year they'd all gone back. Those 600 troops and three helicopters made no practical difference, but the effort expended on that transnational fig leaf certainly contributed to America's disastrous reframing of its interests in Afghanistan.

...

And so here we are, nine years, billions of dollars and many dead soldiers later, watching the guy we've propped up with Western blood and treasure make peace overtures to the Taliban's most virulently anti-American and pro-al-Qaeda faction

...

Green Jobs

2010-07-05 10:45:00

Abengoa SA was offered a $1.45 billion loan guarantee[438] by the U.S. Department of Energy to build a 250-megawatt solar plant in Arizona, and Abound Solar Manufacturing was offered a $400 million loan guarantee toward two plants where thin-solar panels will be manufactured.

The guarantees through the Recovery Act and other measures are expected by the awardees to create more than 5,000 jobs, according to a statement from the White House.

Government guaranteed loans usually wind up being repaid by the government. It is just a way of keeping expenditures off today's books. So this works out as $370 000 per job.

But in fact the impact on jobs, and green energy, will probably be negative, as the firms that actually create jobs are less well connected, and will know better than to attempt to compete with a business that has such government favor.

---

[438] https://www.marketwatch.com/story/obama-outlines-2-billion-in-clean-energy-funds-2010-07-03?reflink=MW_news_stmp

Palin still in charge

2010-07-07 16:47:51

So far, when the Republican establishment has endorsed a republican in a primary, and Palin has endorsed a different candidate, Palin's candidate wins. Looks like Republican party activists listen to Palin, and rank and file republicans listen to party activists. The next test of Palin's power is Lisa Murkowski against Joe Miller.[439] The party establishment are not only way to the left of the party base, they are also incompetent, corrupt, politically clumsy, and astonishingly stupid, the kind of stupid that only years of teaching in an elite university can induce.

Financial Reform

2010-07-08 20:09:47

TheMoneyIllusion nicely summarizes the financial reform legislation[440]

> I can't see how it addressed ANY of the major causes of the 2008 fiasco. But easily the most inexcusable aspect of the bill was that it didn't even address Fannie and Freddie. People excuse that on the basis that there is a lot of political support for F&F. But if you can't reform them right after a $165 billion taxpayer bailout, when will they be unpopular enough that we can address their flaws? ...

> And no ban on sub-prime mortgages? I thought that was the cause of the crisis.

He misses, however, the biggest failure of the financial reform legislation - that the NRSROs are still in business, rather than in jail[441].

The government has decided to not reform the NRSROs - because any reform, we are quite truthfully told, would put them out of business.

In other words, their business is completely dependent on corruption and gross improprieties that have cost the taxpayer a trillion, possibly trillions.

Indeed, the regulations that Lawrence White complains about look very much as if they were passed to keep the NRSROs in business.

As Lawrence White tells us[442] (from behind a paywall):

> By means of the high ratings that they awarded to subprime mortgage-backed bonds, the three major rating agencies—Moody's, Standard & Poor's, and Fitch—played a central role in the current financial crisis. Without these ratings, it is doubtful that subprime mortgages would have been issued in such

---

[439]https://theothermccain.com/2010/07/06/lisa-murkowskis-palin-problem/
[440]https://www.themoneyillusion.com/?p=5949
[441]https://blog.reaction.la/economics/yale-harvard-and-basel-style-free-enterprise.html
[442]https://www.informaworld.com/smpp/content_content=a913109445db=all~jumptype=rss

huge amounts, since a major reason for the subprime lending boom was investor demand for high-rated bonds—much of it generated by regulations that made such bonds mandatory for large institutional investors. And it is even less likely that such bonds would have become concentrated on the balance sheets of the banks, for which they were rewarded by capital regulations that tilted toward high-rated securities. Why, then, were the agencies excessively optimistic in their ratings of subprime mortgage-backed securities? A combination of their fee structure, the complexity of the bonds that they were rating, insufficient historical data, some carelessness, and market pressures proved to be a potent brew. This combination was enabled, however, by seven decades of financial regulation that, beginning in the 1930s, had conferred the force of law upon these agencies' judgments about the creditworthiness of bonds and that, since 1975, had protected the three agencies from competition.

"ethics"

2010-07-10 12:52:33

The Washington post complains about unethical science in China[443].

> Zhao is turning his attention to a topic Western researchers have shied away from because of ethical worries: Zhao plans to study the genes of 1,000 of his best-performing classmates at a top high school in Beijing and compare them, he said, "with 1,000 normal kids."

Politically incorrect science is "unethical"

Today western science is stagnant for the same reasons as it was stagnant from 1293 to 1648 – because it has been subordinated to religion.

Real GDP growth

2010-07-12 09:46:59

GDP is an ill defined quantity, for it counts cars produced, official credit ratings produced, and regulators producing regulation. With the best will in the world, it is hard to say how it is changing, and lately we have been seeing some pretty bad will. Attempting to calculate GDP is worse than adding apples to oranges, it is adding apples to moonbeams.

Supposedly GDP is growing, and growing fast – despite the fact that everyone is feeling poorer, and private sector jobs are declining. An amazing productivity increase, largely reflecting amazing productivity improvements by government and quasi governmental employees.

So let us look for a different measure: Taxable retail sales. Which are stagnant or down[444]. Population keeps growing, but they are buying less stuff, in part because they are being taxed more.

---

[443]https://www.washingtonpost.com/wp-dyn/content/article/2010/06/27/AR2010062703639_3.html
[444]https://www.businessinsider.com/retail-sales-deflation-2010-7

The politics of Hit-Girl

2010-07-13 17:11:41

For a long time the left has controlled the gates for movies, books, and comics, in part because of the government control of television. Lately, however, I have been seeing more and more politically incorrect stuff.

As you probably figured out if you watched the movie Kick Ass, Hit-Girl is a conservative, what with being home schooled and all

It is a great movie.

In the comic book, her politics is more overtly conservative than in the movie, not that she is pacifist hippie in the movie. Here are some political scenes from the comics:
Click on the images to see them in their full glory
Here she is on crime, punishment, and the effect of environment on sociopathy:

Here she is being home schooled:

Sam Colt

Wherein she passes the test on "what is a Democrat" with flying colors.

The death of science

2010-07-14 09:55:31

"Scientists" complain that the government is interfering in "science" by denying them regulatory authority over other people's economic activity[445].

Nasa's primary goal is to make Muslims feel good about Muslim science[446]. In 1903 December 17, the Wright brothers flew.

[445] https://www.baltimoresun.com/health/la-na-science-obama-20100711,0,5023153.story
[446] https://www.floppingaces.net/2010/07/13/barack-obamas-nasa-saves-america-reader-post/

In 1905 October 05, they demonstrated powered flight "of practical utility"

In 1908, they started making a profit.

In 1969 July 20, Commander Neil Armstrong landed on the moon, but the flight was not of practical utility.

So from the Wright brothers to the moon landing was 66 years, and from the moon landing to now has been forty three years - and in those forty three years, have been slowly giving up on manned presence in space, rather than developing rockets "of practical utility".

The "dispersal of power" that Mencius Moldbug talks about is that any profitable activity requires more and more permissions.

For each permission, I need to make a payoff - I personally have paid a great deal of money for permissions, and what is worse, had to be nice to the people shaking me down.

Obviously, each person from which a permission is needed is likely to try to capture the lion's share of the benefit of the permitted activity. If you need ten permissions to do something, and each of the people granting permissions attempts to capture one third of the benefit, the activity will not happen, and everyone will be worse off.

To the extent that this happens, the more powerful concentrate power in their own hands, so that you need fewer permissions, and have to make fewer, but possibly larger, payoffs. Then the activity proceeds, and the payoffs get made. I would expect, but do not know by direct personal experience, that those who find themselves cut out, those who suffer their power to stop economic activities taken away from them, complain that the administration is interfering with "science".

In a theocracy, priests are bureaucrats, so science is regulation and politics.

Old fashioned science involves replication and stuff like that, which is likely to cast doubt on the holy faith, therefore old fashioned science is anti scientific.

Thus a regime that favored old fashioned science would be deemed extremely anti scientific. If they called Bush and Reagan chimps, you can imagine what the reaction would be to a regime that funded old fashioned science and defunded postmodern science.

The ruling class

2010-07-18 19:15:11

Roissy links to an insightful article on the growing divide between rulers and ruled

> Never has there been so little diversity within America's upper crust. Always, in America as elsewhere, some people have been wealthier and more powerful than others. But until our own time America's upper crust was a mixture of people who had gained prominence in a variety of ways, who drew their money and status from different sources and were not predictably of one mind on any given matter. The Boston Brahmins, the New York financiers, the land barons of California, Texas, and Florida, the industrialists of Pittsburgh, the Southern aristocracy, and the hardscrabble politicians who made it big in Chicago or Memphis had little contact with one another. Few had much contact with government, and "bureaucrat" was

a dirty word for all. So was "social engineering." Nor had the schools and universities that formed yesterday's upper crust imposed a single orthodoxy about the origins of man, about American history, and about how America should be governed. All that has changed.

Today's ruling class, from Boston to San Diego, was formed by an educational system that exposed them to the same ideas and gave them remarkably uniform guidance, as well as tastes and habits. These amount to a social canon of judgments about good and evil, complete with secular sacred history, sins (against minorities and the environment), and saints. Using the right words and avoiding the wrong ones when referring to such matters – speaking the "in" language – serves as a badge of identity. Regardless of what business or profession they are in, their road up included government channels and government money because, as government has grown, its boundary with the rest of American life has become indistinct. Many began their careers in government and leveraged their way into the private sector. Some, e.g., Secretary of the Treasury Timothy Geithner, never held a non-government job. Hence whether formally in government, out of it, or halfway, America's ruling class speaks the language and has the tastes, habits, and tools of bureaucrats.

It is in the nature of government to grow, and so it swallows up everything. The parasite eventually destroys the host. Government has seized upon a multitude of justifications, the most recent justification being the welfare state, the coming justification being saving the earth. Insolvency approaches. Trees do not grow to the sky. That which cannot continue, will stop.

The left is astroturf, it is the voice of the state. But we have already reached the point where persuading people to vote for more government, or interpreting their vote as a vote for more government no matter how they vote has become ineffectual, depriving the left of any reason for existence, depriving democracy itself of the reason for its existence.

If you are not at the government's table, you are on the government's menu

2010-07-20 06:03:48

Vox Populi:
> While the economic value of anything depends on sellers and buyers agreeing on that value as civil equals in the absence of force, modern government is about nothing if not tampering with civil equality. By endowing some in society with power to force others to sell cheaper than they would, and forcing others yet to buy at higher prices even to buy in the first place modern government makes valuable some things that are not, and devalues others that are. Thus if you are not among the favored guests at the table where officials make detailed lists of who is to receive what at whose expense, you are on the menu.

The revolving door[447]:

---

[447] https://www.salon.com/news/opinion/glenn_greenwald/2010/07/15/fowler/index.html

> This is an administration that almost employs more Goldman Sachs officials[448] in financial and regulatory positions[449] than Goldman Sachs itself does.One of the first acts of Interior Secretary Ken Salazar was to hire[450] a BP executive to serve as a deputy administrator for land and minerals management. And now they've just hired to implement the new healthcare law someone who was just recently in charge of the lobbying and government activities of the nation's largest private insurer.

If someone genuinely opposed big business, he would opposed all government regulation and all taxes.

"Diversity"

2010-07-20 12:43:31

What academia means by "diversity" is people of all colors and all sexual preferences chanting their master's words in unison.

Steve Sailer[451] found an interesting paper[452] on admissions policy.

> At the private institutions in their study whites from lower-class backgrounds incurred a huge admissions disadvantage not only in comparison to lower-class minority students, but compared to whites from middle-class and upper-middle-class backgrounds as well. The lower-class whites proved to be all-around losers. When equally matched for background factors (including SAT scores and high school GPAs), the better-off whites were more than three times as likely to be accepted as the poorest whites.
>
> ...
>
> Having money in the family greatly improved a white applicant's admissions chances, lack of money greatly reduced it.
>
> ...
>
> Participation in such Red State activities as high school ROTC, 4-H clubs, or the Future Farmers of America was found to reduce very substantially a student's chances of gaining admission to the competitive private colleges in the NSCE database on an all-other-things-considered basis. The admissions disadvantage was greatest for those in leadership positions in these activities or those winning honors and awards. "Being an officer or winning awards" for such career-oriented activities as junior ROTC, 4-H, or Future Farmers of America", say Espenshade and Radford, "has a significantly negative association with admission outcomes at highly selective institutions." Excelling in these activities is associated with 60 or 65 percent lower odds of admission."

---

[448] https://www.salon.com/news/opinion/glenn_greenwald/2009/10/16/goldman
[449] https://www.salon.com/news/opinion/glenn_greenwald/2009/07/13/goldman
[450] https://motherjones.com/blue-marble/2010/05/bp-mms-revolving-door
[451] https://isteve.blogspot.com/2010/07/how-to-get-into-college.html
[452] https://www.mindingthecampus.com/originals/2010/07/how_diversity_punishes_asians.html

How to tell your political enemies from your friends

2010-07-20 16:47:01

Your enemies are fond of giving you bad advice. Some of your enemies call themselves your friends - and give the same dubious advice.

When the dubious advice comes primarily from your enemies, anyone who is actually your friend will at minimum treat the advice with appropriate cynism and suspicioun.

The NAACP calls the Tea Party racist.

No democratic solution

2010-07-24 09:11:26

Doctor Zero has a carefully thought out proposal on how to save America[453] through mass democracy, through getting 50% of the voters plus one behind the measures necessary to save America, behind measures that are carefully pruned to be the minimum possible measures that could save the country, measures that are as "moderate" as possible, which is not very moderate at all.

No way Jose. Democracy is doomed, or the country is doomed, or, quite likely, both.Both in Europe[454] and America[455] we are seeing the collapse of private employment – the much prophesied death of the host under the impact of the parasite is finally unfolding: People just are not getting into private jobs, and an ever diminishing proportion of private jobs are genuinely private, genuinely producing stuff that has a price and a market. Instead, it is stuff like "green jobs".

Of course, this means an ever diminishing number of voters that will vote for the survival of the host, ever diminishing prestige and influence for the elite members of the host, and ever increasing prestige and influence for elite members of the parasite.

The parasite cannot restrain itself to match the diminished capability of the host to support it. As things fall apart, the parasite will launch austerity measures to shrink its demands, but the austerity measures will shrink the parasite far more slowly than the host shrinks. Russian agriculture still has not recovered from the liquidation of the kulaks. Consider, for example, schooling. New York spends $17 713 per student per year, which fails to pass the smell test. It is past time for government to simply get out of the schooling business and let parents educate their children or not. *That* would be a cut. "Austerity" is never cuts, but merely reckless, extravagant, and self indulgent waste growing less quickly than the political elite would prefer. What we need is cuts, not "austerity". Can you imagine how few votes a candidate who proposed actual cuts would receive?

The BLS tells[456] us that the normal July youth labor force participation rate before 1989 was 81 to 86% (always looking at July figures, since young people tend to be at school least in July)

---

[453]https://www.doczero.org/2010/07/the-independent-question/

[454]https://www.theglobeandmail.com/news/opinions/nini-and-the-european-dream/article1642865/

[455]https://www.nypost.com/p/news/business/the_dead_end_kids_AnwaWNOGqsXMuIlGONNX1K

[456]https://www.bls.gov/news.release/youth.nr0.htm

Supposedly youth unemployment is a mere 18%, but since young people tend to be ineligible for unemployment relief, they do not necessarily register with the BLS, so a more realistic measure is the proportion presently employed, 51.4%, to the proportion looking for work or employed in good times, 84% in a typical july.

As everything goes to hell in a handbasket, the regime becomes more and more unpopular, but sound policies that would put everything right also become more unpopular – a vicious cycle we have regularly seen in Latin America which cannot be cured. Only the employed and productive vote for measures that would permit productive employment.

To actually cut government spending down to what the nation can afford, you examine each government activity, and compare it with private sector businesses that do the same thing or a plausible substitute. If the government activity is costing enormously more, as for example education, the government then abandons that activity. As a general rule, the more unthinkable it is for the government to abandon some field of activity, the more outrageously extravagant and wasteful the government's activities in that field are. So if you want to cut the government back, the first place to look is at those things that are unthinkable to cut back.

Science is the belief in the ignorance of experts.

2010-07-30 11:30:06

Pajamas media has found an excellent quote from Richard Feynman, which skewers every global warmer:

"The Pleasure of Finding things out" by Richard Feynman, page 187

> We have many studies in teaching, for example, in which people make observations and they make lists and they do statistics, but they do not thereby become established science, established knowledge. They are merely an imitative form of science-like the South Sea Islanders making airfields, radio towers out of wood, expecting a great airplane to arrive. They even build wooden airplanes of the same shape as they see in the foreigners' airfields around them, but strangely, they don't fly. The result of this pseudoscientific imitation is to produce experts, which many of you are-experts. You teachers who are really teaching children at the bottom of the heap, maybe you can doubt the experts once in a while. Learn from science that you must doubt the experts. As a matter of fact, I can also define science another way: *Science is the belief in the ignorance of experts.*

> When someone says science teaches such and such, he is using the word incorrectly. Science doesn't teach it; experience teaches it. If they say to you science has shown such and such, you might ask, "How does science show it-how did the scientists find out-how, what, where?" Not science has shown, but this experiment, this effect, has shown. And you have as much right as anyone else, upon hearing about the experiments (but we must listen to all the evidence), to judge whether a reusable conclusion has been arrived at. . I

think we live in an unscientific age in which almost all the buffeting of communications and television words, books, and so on are unscientific. That doesn't mean they are bad, but they are unscientific. As a result, there is a considerable amount of intellectual tyranny in the name of science.

Genuine science is replicable. And "replicable" does not mean two priests recite the same doctrine, it means they explain what they did in such a fashion that anyone else could do it also.

If they refuse to explain, they are not scientists, but priests of Gaea.

Unsupported and unexplained politically correct pseudo science appears all the time in "Science" and "Nature"

For example[457]:

> Despite the fact that these papers appeared in top journals like Nature and Science, none of the journal reviewers or editors ever required Briffa to release his Yamal data. Steve McIntyre's repeated requests for them to uphold their own data disclosure rules were ignored.

This sort of thing (that PC science is in practice exempted from data disclosure, and proudly proclaims results on the basis of secret evidence) has been an ongoing scientific scandal from the very beginning of the global warming movement, and everyone aware of this unscientific practice should have realized that global warming science is not science, but politics and religion, and that global warming scientists are not scientists, but priests of Gaea.

Environmentalism, and several other isms, are state sponsored religions, which because of state backing have the privilege of publishing their holy texts in scientific journals despite conspicuous and infamous failure to comply with the standards and rules of those journals.

Nine years later, Briffa's Yamal data for twentieth century temperatures turned out to be that one tree of ten selected trees grew unusually rapidly during the twentieth century as compared to fossil trees of the same type from the same area. These ten trees were selected by Bricca after a great many other trees in the same area were measured, but the rest of the measurements were not included.

The larger population of trees, taken as a whole, shows much the same growth pattern as the fossil trees.

Take out one tree from those ten, Yamal06, and most of the evidence for climate change vanishes. Restore the much larger set of tree measurements from which the ten trees were selected, and all of the evidence for climate change vanishes - the population as a whole is has the same growth rates as the fossil trees.

Take out one tree from half a dozen graphs of global warming in near a dozen papers, and suddenly they do not show global warming any more.

Bricca has, at this time, not yet explained why those ten trees, and not other trees in the same area measured in the same survey. And whatever his explanation, ten trees is not enough.

---

[457] https://network.nationalpost.com/np/blogs/fullcomment/archive/2009/10/01/ross-mckitrick-defects-in-key-climate-data-are-uncovered.aspx

The government likes data that supports more government power, rewards those that tell it what it wants to hear, and punishes those that tell it what it does not want to hear.

Environmentalism is a state sponsored religion, for it is perfectly visible to anyone that wants to look that it is not subject to the same standards as normal science, the story of Briffa and the Yamal data being one example of a great many.

People have lost their jobs for reporting that glaciers are advancing in a particular area, even though they fully agreed that most glaciers are retreating. This makes it hard to tell whether most glaciers are indeed retreating.

Environmentalism generally, and the Global Warming movement in particular, acts like a holy and sectarian religious movement, a religious movement backed by state power, not like science.

Recent events prove that on certain topics, they do not carry science, but are mere megaphones for the holy ranting of the priesthood.

Science is not that which the state decrees to be science. It is that which follows the rules of science, which unwritten rules correspond, more or less, to the written rules of the older and more prestigious journals.

If these journals are reluctant to apply these written rules on certain sensitive topics, then what appears on those sensitive topics will not be science, and hence what appears or fails to appear in such journals is not an indication of truth, but of religion.

In particular if the replacement hockey stick had been genuinely peer reviewed, then, in accordance with the unwritten rules of science, and the written rules of the older and more prestigious science journals, the data and calculations supporting the graph would have been made available. Had the data and graphs been made available, people would have objected nine years ago that ten trees are not enough.

Since not genuinely peer reviewed, since not in conformity with journal rules, therefore not genuine science, therefore mere theology.

Palin Power

2010-08-05 07:09:00

According to polls, Palin's Support for a Candidate Doesn't Matter or Is Mostly Negative[458], yet we observe that in practice that when Palin endorses a candidate that is way behind, that candidate shoots up in the polls, and quite often wins.

There are several possible explanations of this

1. People tend to give politically correct replies to polls, rather than what they genuinely believe.

2. Republican party activists do what Palin tells them to do, and republican party voters do what republican party activists tell them to do.

3. A nobody cannot beat a somebody. Get Palin's endorsement, you are no longer a nobody, you are a serious candidate, the one to beat.

I suspect all of these explanations are true.

---

[458]https://www.politicsdaily.com/2010/08/03/palins-support-for-a-candidate-doesnt-matter-or-is-mostly-neg/

A solution to the gay marriage and the covenant marriage problem

2010-08-07 17:31:57

The Other McCain agrees. Get the government out of the marriage business.

Let each church decide for itself what marriage is, which views the government should ignore, and let people draw up what contracts they choose for living together.

You have the right to contract. Let us have gay nuptial contracts, not gay marriages.

And the same for heterosexual relationships: If a seventeen year old girl can contract for gigantic college debts that cannot be expunged by bankruptcy, in return for some academic training that will not necessarily give her a career, then she can agree to a nuptial contract that government does not necessarily think is fair to women.

Rush Limbaugh - smarter than ten thousand ecology PhDs

2010-08-08 07:43:16

Back when BP's oil was spouting into the gulf of Mexico, Rush told us:

"The beach will fix itself"

"More oil spilled every year in Africa, in Nigeria, than so far in the Gulf, so it's not unique. It's not exceptional. It's not the largest. Mexico had a spill that larger than this, nobody talks about except apparently me"

And behold: The beach has fixed itself.

The reason that BP was drilling there in the first place is that giant oil plumes occur naturally from time to time in that location– not as big as this one, but comparable. There is an entire ancient oil eating ecology naturally present in the gulf

This supposed crisis is akin to the supposedly horrifying crisis of the radioactive boy scout - any man made radiation is deemed ten gazillion times worse than naturally occurring sources of radiation, and any man released oil is deemed ten gazillion times worse than naturally occurring sources of oil.

Just as the soil is full of living creatures things that turn dead leaves into compost, the Gulf of Mexico is full of living creatures that turn oil into asphalt. The asphalt sinks to the bottom, and eventually gets buried in mud. It appears that sea creatures ate most of the released oil, and cleanup crews collected only a tiny portion. No doubt it was rough on those sea creatures that cannot eat oil, which all the cute charismatic creatures from seagulls to crabs cannot, but nature is rough whether humans meddle or not.

And while the cute charismatic creatures had a hard time for a while, now the oil is gone.

The cost of government

2010-08-12 05:51:55

Fleischer explains why he is not hiring.[459] He must spend $74,000 to provide Sally with an $59,000 salary, of which after tax she gets $44,000 plus $12,000 in benefits. Plus he faces large uncertainty that these costs may be arbitrarily and unpredictably increased.

The recent substantial increases in the cost of employing people have not been reflected in substantial reductions in people's wages, thus wages are substantially above market clearing levels. The Fed could, I suppose, inflate their way out of this problem, using inflation to sneak the real value of wages down, thus causing employment to recover. Government could then point out that the bloated capitalists are increasing their oppression of the victimized proletarians, and use that as justification to make employing people even more expensive. Never let a good crisis go to waste.

Seventy percent taxes coming eventually.

2010-08-15 06:36:18

In Greece, payroll tax, value added tax, and income tax adds up to around seventy percent. It is perfectly clear that this is far above the Laffer limit - the private sector in Greece is largely underground and not quite cash, like a third world country. If someone is employed by the state he pays taxes on his income because employed by the state, but does not actually do any work, because employed by the state. If someone is not employed by the state, he usually finds a way to make a living that does not exactly involve taxable income as such, so he seldom actually does any *taxable* work.

But the Cathedral is not much affected by contact with reality. Dylan Matthews took a survey of the elite[460], to ask them where the Laffer curve maxed, and all of them that were among our masters answered 69% or 70%, or refused to answer. Such a high value is improbable, but what is really improbable is such perfect agreement on such an uncertain number. You cannot get perfect agreement on anything unless it is official Cathedral doctrine. And if a high Laffer maximum is Cathedral doctrine, then actions that would be insane unless you believe in a high Laffer maximum are the Cathedral program

Treasury committed to supporting too big to fail

2010-08-23 17:11:54

Government lacks the will to allow to big to fail firms to fail, and the will and competence to regulate them. If a firm is too big to fail, it will take advantage of that fact, leading to crisis and massive tax payer losses.

Intefluidity reports that Treasury is not willing to deal with this problem. Interfluidity tells us[461]:

---

[459]https://emilgh.tumblr.com/post/928756212/why-im-not-hiring
[460]https://voices.washingtonpost.com/ezra-klein/2010/08/where_does_the_laffer_curve_be.html
[461]https://www.interfluidity.com/v2/933.html

I believe these policymakers conflate, in full sincerity, incumbent financial institutions with "the system", "the economy", and "ordinary Americans".

...

Ultimately, this "minimalist" approach to managing the GSEs amounts to nothing more or less than keeping the existing system and proposing that it be better regulated, including specific regulatory suggestions that are foreseeably unlikely to withstand industry pressure. No offense to its very smart proponent, but this was a non-idea dressed up as reform.

...

Large, complex, leveraged and interconnected financial firms simply cannot be regulated, by the private or public sector. Without regulation they quite rationally maximize stakeholder wealth in a manner that happens to be socially and economically destructive. The only way around this is to change the incentives of all stakeholders, and that could only happen by placing them in a different kind of firm. We have to limit the size and composition of firms' creditor base, so we can be sure losses to creditors would be socially and politically tolerable. (We do this already, or try to, with hedge funds.)

Atlas did not shrug

2010-08-24 07:49:44

The cathedral has pursued a policy of compromising with and absorbing competing elites - thus it both allowed the big banks to capture the regulators (resulting in financial crisis, but consolidating the elite's power over ordinary Americans) and allowed the Soviet Union to infiltrate the US government (thus causing wars and communist victories, but consolidating the elite's power over ordinary Americans).

As Dusk tells us[462]:

> look at how much regulation the banking industry came under during the 1990s and 2000s to serve the interests of social justice by giving out more mortgages to poor and Non-Asian Minority home-buyers. Rather than bankers individually growing weary and ultimately withdrawing from their calling, they as collective corporations dove into coerced self-sacrifice head-first and for years swam around in big bucks. And if somehow the pool's drain opened up, someone else would keep them afloat – I mean, people aren't just going to let saints go under for serving the cause of social justice, right?

> Researchers, inventors, and artists too resent having to comply with state regulations such as meeting affirmative action targets – e.g., when appealing to the government for grant money, having to detail how some expensive piece of equipment will be used in equal measure by men and women,

---

[462] https://akinokure.blogspot.com/2010/06/should-atlas-shrugged-have-been-about.html

as well as by whites / Asians and NAMs. Or having to detail how some community arts outreach project will target all demographic groups equally, if a financially strapped arts group wants state funding for it. Nevertheless, as annoyed as they may be, on the whole the members of these professions are not in revolt, do not even give off the smell of stewing in resentment, and don't suffer from the high burn-out rates that Rand would've predicted.

...

What Rand fundamentally miscalculated was the ability of inventors, businessmen, etc. to not just slip out of their regulatory fetters but to then form them into lashes with which to whip their competitors, a phenomenon known as "regulatory capture."

Anti anti communism, the repudiation of McCarthyism, is the same phenomenon: We now know that McCarthy was correct, but politically inconvenient.

McCarthy named Fred Fisher on television as a hostile communist infiltrator within the American government – as indeed he was.

Let us not assassinate this lad further, Senator. You've done enough. Have you no sense of decency, sir? At long last, have you left no sense of decency?

Fred Fisher never denied being a communist. No one has ever said he was not a communist He was a member of the National Lawyers Guild, which we knew then to be a communist front organization, and subsequent intercepts has confirmed to be a communist front organization – therefore, a hostile infiltrator, sabotaging the US government from within.

The reason communist infiltration was tolerated and encouraged was that the Cathedral perceived itself to be using the Soviet Union, rather than being used by the Soviet Union.

Similarly, the Cathedral likes to import Muslims precisely *because* of their anti western attitudes.

To say that it was outrageous to criticize Fisher,was to say it was outrageous to worry about hostile people
exercising power in sensitive positions within the US government.

On the evidence revealed in the Venona intercepts, there is compelling evidence that the Lawyers Guild was a communist front organization.

The evidence presented by the House Unamerican activities committee also seem to me to be quite convincing, but someone might reasonably disagree – the evidence could plausibly be interpreted as evidence of anti anti communism, rather than evidence of communism, plus evidence that the benevolent and helpful soviet union
was benevolently assisting the benevolent and helpful Lawyer's guild to engage in helpful benevolence.

And that is precisely why anti communism came to be demonized – because the Lawyer's guild, with the direct and substantial support and assistance of the Soviet Union, was in fact assisting the Cathedral in its war against ordinary Americans, and was not directly assisting the Soviet Union in its efforts to conquer the world – so the Cathedral quite reasonably and realistically perceived themselves as using Stalin, rather than being used by Stalin.

The Lawyer's guild were doing what the Cathedral perceived as good – at the instigation and with the assistance of Stalin and the Soviet Union, and were not obviously doing anything the Cathedral might perceive as bad, like arranging for the Soviet army to shoot Cathedral members and bury them.

Thus the Cathedral could plausibly view the Lawyer's guild as the Cathedral infiltrating and manipulating the communists, rather than the communists infiltrating and manipulating the Cathedral.

The activities of the Lawyer's guild are evidence that the Cathedral was soft on communism and allowed themselves to be infiltrated. It is also evidence that the Cathedral strategy of being nice and doing favors was working, that infiltration was a two way street.

Remember when Khrushchev said "we will bury you" they immediately proceeded to reinterpret him as proposing a

relatively peaceful takeover that leaves the existing cathedral in place as Soviet apparatchicks, rather than shipping them off the gulag – revealing what they really wanted and hoped for.

They hoped for and expected the kind of Soviet takeover that was the implied backstory of those "Startrek the Next Generation" episodes created before the fall of the Soviet Union – though I am pretty sure the Soviet Union had a very different kind of takeover in mind, intended to deal with the Cathedral with hot lead and shovels, rather than giving Cathedral members cushy jobs as Soviet Apparatchiks.

The Cathedral realistically believed that communists could and would promote their ideal of a greater, more powerful, and more benevolent state, just as they realistically believe that Muslim voters will vote for more government. They were unrealistic in believing that the Russians shared progressivism or could be persuaded to share it.

They realistically hope to use the enemies of America against their American enemies, and unrealistically hope to convert the enemies of America to progressivism.

It is even less realistic to suppose that Muslims will be converted to progressivism, but observe the strident response of progressives when we ridicule this delusion: "*Raaaaacist!*"

The Cathedral sets a very high value on being reasonable and nice and civilized. I recall that when a warmist scientist addressed skeptical scientists, he urged them that if they took a more conciliatory position they would have "more influence" I don't remember his exact words, and they matter little because the message was primarily in the way his body language commented upon his words, the unspoken but gestured message being "accept a lot of warmist beliefs, and warmists will accept a little of skeptic beliefs, and we will see to it that you get grants."

And thus, contrary to what was predicted in "Atlas Shrugs", scientists have come on board with the Cathedral and abandoned science, rather than retreating to Galt's Gulch.

A similar tendency towards shear niceness was evident in the financial collapse. It was quite unthinkable that financiers who has pissed away billions of their clients money in nice behavior, should thereby become unemployed, or even have their wealth and power seriously diminished, or even have their control over other people's money diminished, or be asked to make any substantial changes in the way they managed other people's money.

And so the bankers are not heading off to Galt's Gulch either.

The Cathedral, though quick to accuse its American enemies of being extreme, uncompromising, and violent, is paralytically incapable of dealing with enemies that actually are extreme, uncompromising, and violent. It likes to ally with them against its American enemies, but even absent that inclination and strategy, is just generally incompetent and incapable at dealing with them, so in desperation ascribes its own niceness and willingness to compromise, to them.

Its tendency to compromise, to distribute power in tiny little bite sized chunks, means that stuff just does not get done - as for example, the fact that the buildings damaged and destroyed in 9/11 are still damaged and destroyed nine years later.

To repair or replace any of these buildings, needs a hundred approvals from a hundred Brahmins, which no normal American businessman is ever going receive for anything (hence our European levels of unemployment). Islamists, however, can achieve it, because of their ability and willingness to apply negative incentives to roadblock bureaucrats. Being nice to each of one hundred Brahmins, good members of the establishment, unfortunately precludes being nice to one businessmen. When, however, the businessman is a dangerously non nice Muslim, such obstacles can be readily overcome.

The Cathedral approach to coalition building means it has no ready answer to those that spit upon its coalition and murder its members, other to welcome them inside, as it welcomed Ward Churchill inside.

Anti anti communism was not necessarily crazy, since they perceived themselves to be using Stalin to make war on evil Americans, even though Stalin thought he was using them, but the mortgage disaster, which is still under way, was definitely crazy, dismantling technological civilization to avoid possible slight warming is seriously crazy, and the Muslim takeover of Europe is really seriously crazy.

The end is in sight

2010-09-01 10:26:46

For the last hundred years or so, people have been predicting that the welfare and affirmative action state would collapse eventually.

Well, it seems that "eventually" is getting close. Arnold Kling has a list of links[463] showing that all the welfare state social democracies are going to hell in a handbasket, with everyone else in even worse trouble than the US.

Arnold Kling predicts[464] a US debt crisis between 2015 and 2035. Public sector pensions are unpayable[465].

The welfare state has made a pile of promises it cannot fulfill, and like a debtor in trouble, has been rapidly escalating the promises.

When the president and the most prestigious academies are out of contact with reality, then the path to advancement is to deny reality. As the housing debacle illustrates, the elite is incurably insane. The process is self reinforcing - any contact with reality, or

---

[463] https://econlog.econlib.org/archives/2010/08/bond_bubble_wat_1.html
[464] https://mercatus.org/publication/guessing-trigger-point-us-debt-crisis
[465] https://mercatus.org/pensions

tendency to engage in reality testing, disqualifies you for membership of the elite. Only lowly contemptible insignificant people engage in reality testing, and as everyone knows, they are boobs and disgusting racists.

In beauty contests, the contestants are asked to demonstrate allegiance to progressivism, by asking them questions on which America is divided[466]. They must side with the Cathedral, or else they lose. Similarly in a job interview for any important position. If an executive doubts the Cathedral, the company is likely to be sued for a "hostile work environment", so a precondition for employment in any substantial corporation in any important position is sincere zeal for the holy faith of the Cathedral.

The tea party is not actually all that rightwing. They are right wing in that they support the extreme left status quo ante and oppose the even more extreme left status quo. They want to turn the clock back to Clinton, not 1950, but to save the day, would have to turn the clock back to 1900.

People planned on social security and medicare being there for them. They see the government blowing all the money on pork barrel spending and dud mortgages for non asian minorities, and they suspect that the welfare state on which they intended to rely is going broke fast. They want to preserve the quite left wing status quo of the Clinton years.

Hence the progressive parody of the tea party: "get the government out of my medicare".

Only the most extreme elements of the Tea Party movement leadership (Sharon Angle) actually propose to put social security on a sound footing, propose to make it a forced saving program, where you individually and personally own your social security trust fund, rather than a welfare program.

The welfare problem is a necessary result of the universal franchise. Singapore, and only Singapore, has a non catastrophic solution to the welfare problem. They were able to get away with a non catastrophic solution only because of the Singaporean/Confucian attitude that the rulers have the right to rule, provided things are going OK, which rewards long term orientation by politicians.

The stupidity of the voters, and the short term orientation of politicians means that a universal franchise guarantees social, economic, and political collapse once government becomes large enough to drag everything down with it.

The least radical solution that could actually work, could make the welfare state viable, is to implement Singaporean style welfare, social security and healthcare, and to restrict the franchise enough that such a solution wins majority support from those few entitled to vote – which solution is a lot more radical than anyone in the tea party will advocate.

We can divide the major political programs into three:
1. The ignorant and unthinking, who are the great majority, since there is no point in knowing this stuff or thinking about it.
2. Those who doubt the expansion of the state can go on forever, and fear the end is nigh: these are the tea partiers, who want to stop the boat right by the edge of the waterfall.
3. Those who believe the state can expand forever, because state expenditures are so much

---

[466]https://www.powerlineblog.com/archives/2010/05/026319.php

more productive than mere private expenditures: these are the elite, to whom thinking like the state thinks is a badge of status, and who therefore confidently believe that going over the waterfall will be fine because the boat will fly like a bird without any need for external support.

The practical solution, of course, is to back the boat away from the waterfall – a long way back from the waterfall, but it is too fiscally late to do that without blowing off most of the state's financial obligations, and politically impossible to do that without radically restricting the franchise. A program of recognizing bankruptcy, and throwing most of the population off the voting rolls is unlikely to be very popular.

After mass democracy

2010-09-07 13:57:30

A couple of hundred years ago, the conventional wisdom was that democracy with broad voter participation was unstable, violent, ruinous, and short lived.

A hundred years or so ago the world moved to mass democracy, universal franchise. Many people predicted that this would result in the masses trying to vote themselves rich, resulting in social and economic collapse

Well guess what. The masses have been trying to vote themselves rich, social collapse is under way, and economic collapse looms.

The success stories of governance are Singapore, Hong Kong, China, and Botswana, which would suggest the future is not democratic.

Mass democracy is visibly self destructing. In 2005 nearly half of births in California were on medi-cal, and the disappearance of statistics after 2005 suggests the situation is rapidly deteriorating, hence the present Californian meltdown. The world of "the Marching Morons" is now.

Clearly this is unsustainable - Liverpool and Detroit represent the future of democracy - majority underclass. Detroit is the future of California, Liverpool the future of England if the Caliphate does not take England first.

I am hoping for anarcho capitalism, but a more likely outcome is military dictatorship evolving into monarchy, or gangs evolving into feudalism.

Mencius suggests an interesting form of futuristic government: The sovereign corporation with cryptographic control over its weapons. The vote of the board creates a cryptographic secret that gives the CEO control over the weapons of corporation's security forces. If there is a coup by the armed forces against the CEO or the CEO against the board, the coupists weapons stop working.

Mencius' proposal reflects the typical nerdly assumption that guns are all powerful. In practice, the way that power works is that the elite males settle things between themselves by means that are not overtly violent, and then the outsiders find they face a united, and violent front from the elite males. Once the elite males have agreed amongst themselves, the weapons are merely an afterthought, making the cryptographic locks irrelevant - which would suggest that if Kingship revives, it will have more resemblance to traditional kingship than to Mencius's CEO.

Switzerland's plebiscitary democracy is also an outstanding success, though it could be argued that this mainly because it is sufficiently unwieldy to prevent the government from actually doing much, and therefore prevents the government from vote buying in the fashion that led to the meltdowns in California and Detroit. Switzerland is a blast from the past. The future is more likely to be China, though I think that anarcho capitalism, or the revival of feudalism are also possibilities.

The minimum necessary reforms are to stop the financial system leaking money, and put welfare on a sound basis - but only the most extreme elements of the tea party are proposing anything approaching this, and they are clearly far too extreme for the voters. If reforms that would actually enable the system to survive were on the table, Christine O'Donnel would be unelectable left, not the unelectable right.

To put welfare and affirmative action a sound basis means imitating Singapore's welfare, social security healthcare, and so forth. Pigs will fly first.

Let us consider the seemingly more achievable problem of stopping the finance system from leaking money. All bankers are criminals, for they were all party to the grossly improper loans that led to our present crisis. Any honest banker was fired, because any honest banker got in the way of affirmative action and got run over.

To stop the system leaking money, have to fire crooked bankers, and replace them with honest bankers. To replace them with honest bankers, have to end affirmative action lending. That does not seem too hard. After all 99% of the voters oppose affirmative action lending, and a clear and substantial majority oppose all affirmative action. But it is hard. We have affirmative action lending for a reason: As I said before:

When they gave a Nobel prize to Marie Curie for being female, that did not hurt anyone except more deserving potential Nobel prize winners. But handing out phony Nobels on the basis of sex, race, and nationality necessitated handing out phony degrees on the basis of race and sex, and handing out phony degrees on the basis of race and sex necessarily led to a crisis where these phony degrees were being ignored by employers, so employers necessarily had to be forced to give out well paid phony jobs on the basis of race and sex. But being given well paid phony jobs on the basis of race and sex failed to result in recipients living a middle class lifestyle, so lenders had to be forced to give out a middle class lifestyle on the basis of race and sex. Which has led to our present financial crisis. It all began with Marie Curie.

So if you roll back the most unpopular, extreme, and disastrous form of affirmative action, you then immediately face a problem with less extreme and more popular forms. And if you roll them back ... All solutions are either radical or unworkable. Roll back affirmative action loans, and pretty soon you are going to have to restrict the franchise, or bring affirmative action loans back.

The number of the beast

2010-09-08 07:36:08

And he causeth all, both small and great, rich and poor, free and bond, to receive a mark in their right hand, or in their foreheads:

And that no man might buy or sell, save he that had the mark, or the name of the beast, or the number of his name.

Greece Bans Cash Transactions Over 1,500 Euros[467]
The Italian government will ban the use of cash in transactions over 5,000 euros, lowering the ceiling from 12,500 euros[468]
In the UK a tax evasion crackdown on middle class professionals.[469]

Rigging the vote
2010-09-09 02:41:06

Rigging the vote seems to me to be redundant, since even the tea party supports unsustainable welfare, affirmative action, social security, and healthcare programs, yet oddly, vote rigging is under way. Pajamas reports vote rigging in Texas[470] and around the US[471]

When the only people with a chance of winning are lunatic left, crazy left, and demented left, why bother? I conjecture this is because the major function of government has become handing out the gravy to true believers. This leads to everyone believing more truly than the next guy, everyone trying to be twice as holy as everyone else, but it also leads to vicious battles between the insider true believers, and those they doubt believe truly enough. As more and more government is handouts to political factions, the stakes are higher, so electoral contests are starting to use any means necessary, for although the election makes only a minute difference in what policy the US will follow (observe, for example, that Obama has been pretty much indistinguishable from Bush) the election will make a huge difference in who gets the gravy.

The explosive expansion of the state
2010-09-10 11:24:12

Government employment is increasing relative to private employment, but only moderately, not explosively, yet the deficit is exploding. Part of this comes from what Doc Zero calls[472] the remora economy[473]. Private businesses attach themselves to the state, and the state attaches nominally private businesses to itself and commands them to serve its political objectives.

The private businesses make corrupt profits from their state connection, and the state creates costs that are nominally off budget, as for example, the health crisis and the recent financial crisis which was primarily a crisis of affirmative action loans. Government regulatory intervention in the economy is exploding, creating a multitude of invisible taxes,

---

[467] https://www.economicpolicyjournal.com/2010/02/greece-bans-cash-transactions-over-1500.html
[468] https://uk.reuters.com/article/idUKTRE64N36720100524
[469] https://www.telegraph.co.uk/finance/personalfinance/consumertips/tax/6967760/Middle-class-professionals-such-as-doctors-dentists-lawyers-in-tax-evasion-crackdown.html
[470] https://pajamasmedia.com/blog/it%E2%80%99s-time-to-worry-about-houston/
[471] https://pajamasmedia.com/blog/doing-the-dojs-job-for-them-demanding-valid-voter-rolls-before-november/
[472] https://www.doczero.org/2010/09/the-remora-economy
[473] https://hotair.com/greenroom/archives/2010/09/08/the-remora-economy/

off budget expenditures, and opportunities for corrupt profits by semi private businesses, such Al Gore becoming a billionaire from carbon credits.

The cause of the crisis

2010-09-13 12:36:45

One of a series of posts titled "the cause of the crisis", each discussing a different cause, but each of these causes caused or was caused by each of the other causes:

When the universal franchise was introduced a hundred years ago, people said the system would go to hell. Now it is going to hell.

Obviously a government cannot go on forever spending much more than it collects. For a while printing money and borrowing money will work, but eventually, it is bound to lead to trouble, and big trouble is approaching fast.

Government inexorably and rapidly gets more expensive and more intrusive. No doubt more taxes could be collected if they went after the politically well connected, but overall taxes are close to the Laffer maximum - if they raise taxes on those whom it is easy to raise taxes on, for example a tax on luxury yachts, they will get less money, not more money.

A tax on gas, beer, and cigarettes would work, but be unpopular with the electorate. A tax on bankers, educationists, and lawyers would work, but would be unpopular with the well connected - and even such taxes would merely postpone the day of reckoning. Government's existing commitments are unsustainable with any politically realistic, or even politically unrealistic, tax rise.

The welfare state is simply running out of money.

There are two related problems: Theocracy and democracy. The masses are stupid, the elite is theocratic.

Because the elite is theocratic, they compete for power by each being holier than the other, that is to say, more politically correct than the other - but because their religion is this-worldly, they are required to have religious beliefs about this word rather than the next, thus each member of the elite competes to be further out of contact with reality than the other.

Because the masses are stupid, they succumb to politicians promising that the voters can vote themselves rich.

A hundred years ago, progressivism was a sect of Christianity with ambitions for theocracy and world conquest. To better pursue these goals, it discarded theism, becoming theologically indistinguishable from universalist Unitarianism, thus evading the restraints imposed by the first amendment.

Consider, for example, the doctrine that men and women are equal - therefore the same and interchangeable: Women, supposedly, can be firemen and soldiers. Men, supposedly, can marry other men.

The modern progressive theory of equality is in fact a variant of Christianity.

Equality of men and women, and of the races, makes no common sense or biological sense. Men and women, for example, are biologically so different, that pretty much however you decide to measure them, chances are slim that they will prove to be equal.

When I discuss the matter with leftists, the main argument is some kind of skepticism with regard to efforts to measure people (which always end up demonstrating sexual and racial differences). For example, Gould is skeptical about IQ and race.

Roissy wonders why the elites are so stuck on the obviously false idea of literal equality[474]. Understood as a species of Christian belief, it makes sense, because the Christians believe that the most important part of the self is immaterial. If it's immaterial, then material differences have nothing to do with it. So Christians are free to believe pretty much anything they want about this most important part of the self, unconstrained by material evidence of any sort. They are free to believe that deep inside everyone, there is a core, an essence, that is not the slightest diminished by bodily infirmity etc. etc. I.e., the soul.

The progressives jettison God, replacing God with, presumably, Nature. So "equality before God" becomes "equality before Nature". That is, natural equality (of some unspecified sort). And this could be how the progressives manage to believe in some unspecified "natural" (biological or whatever) equality even though no evidence backs them up. Their belief is derived, not from evidence, but from the Christian heritage of progressivism. Their belief looks superficially like a scientific hypothesis because all the terms in it could be interpreted as referring to natural things, but it doesn't really have any empirical content, because "equality", while it could refer to something measurable, does not actually refer to anything measurable. Any attempt to measure something to test the claim of "equality" is attacked by progressives.

Progressives are using naturalistic-sounding words to talk about equality, but they are behaving as though it didn't make any sense to try to measure it, which is how Christians would behave with respect to attempts to rigorously test equality before God. Their reaction would range from skepticism that it could be done, to the sense that it doesn't even make sense to try, and finally to the certainty that it is heresy to even suggest such a thing and the person suggesting it is evil and possibly a sorcerer and should be burnt at the stake.

The progressive reaction to naturalistic attempts to assess equality is exactly the same as the Christian reaction would be.

The Christian view of equality is entirely impervious to empirical evidence, and so is the progressive view. It makes sense, then, to interpret progressives, when they talk about male and female equality, and about black and white equality, as really talking about the Christian soul, even though they themselves do not realize this is what they are doing because they have forgotten why they are going through these mental motions.

Mao's murders

2010-09-20 03:19:20

Rummel estimated that Mao killed wrongfully killed seventy seven million, and the Black Book of Communism estimates sixty five million - but, of course, it is notoriously difficult to say what a totalitarian terror state based on slavery and mass murder is up to. They called it an iron curtain because you could not see what was behind it. So how should we judge the accuracy of estimates?

---

[474]https://roissy.wordpress.com/2010/09/11/why-the-elites-prop-up-the-blank-slate

One good way is to see what happens to those estimates when new data arrives. If the estimates tend to go up when we get new information, the original estimates were on the low side. If they tend to go down, perhaps the original estimates were exaggerated.

Because the great leap forward was violently controversial even within the communist party, it is the crime of communism that the present party leadership finds least hurtful to investigate. The present leadership descends from those who resisted the great leap forward, and are therefore less implicated by these crimes. So they have recently allowed investigation[475].

Rummel estimated the great leap forward democide to be twenty seven million, largely a result of forced exactions of grain from starving peasants, akin to the Ukraine famine. More recent data indicates forty five million.

The communist party of China now believes in "Socialism with Chinese Character-istics" - which looks remarkably like Capitalism with Hong Kong Characteristics, and Hong Kong is itself the society that among present day societies most closely resembles Manchesterism, the capitalism that made the Industrial Revolution, which system was exported to parts of the third world by early nineteenth century colonists.

Losing to Islam

2010-09-24 03:06:09

Islam is theocratic. It intends to conquer. Shariah law, as interpreted by most Muslims, treats women fine. Trouble is, as interpreted by all Muslims, even Sufis, it requires that infidels submit to law that makes them second class to believers and that Muslims fight to impose such law - and we are in fact submitting to such law. The rather small Sufi minority merely propose less drastic measures to impose inferiority.

East Lansing, Michigan Police Department offers $10,000 reward in Qur'an-burning case[476]

> The department is offering **$10,000** for any information that would lead to the identification and prosecution of those responsible for this act.

In November 2009, a high school senior was suspended in order to protect him from violence when he wrote an essay criticizing perceived special treatment for Somali Mus-lims in his school. In Dearborn, Mich., Christian missionaries were arrested for prosely-tizing at an Arab festival. In Minnesota, the state accommodates Shariah's prohibition on interest payments by buying homes from realtors and reselling them to Muslims at an up-front price[477]. Thereby providing Muslims with preferential access to homes at the expense of infidels. Apparently the Constitution requires separation of Church and state, but no separation of mosque and state.

---

[475] https://www.independent.co.uk/arts-entertainment/books/news/maos-great-leap-forward-killed-45-million-in-four-years-2081630.html

[476] https://www.jihadwatch.org/2010/09/east-lansing-michigan-police-department-offers-10000-reward-in-quran-burning-case.html

[477] https://sheikyermami.com/2010/09/19/the-shariah-threat/

While Christianity is forbidden in government schools, Islam is preached and sponsored by the state.[478]

Molly Norris, the Seattle cartoonist whose artwork sparked the controversial "Everybody Draw Muhammad Day!" has gone into hiding, changed her name, and so forth. The state is not protecting her.

Similarly for the Sweden Democrats.[479]

In much of Europe, including England, people who criticize Islam are capriciously prosecuted[480]

One supreme court justice has proposed that burning the Koran be banned[481] - though none would suggest similar courtesy for the flag or the bible, or the 9/11 dead. When an obscure church proposed to burn the Koran its website was shut down, its insurance policy has been canceled, and its mortgage has been called in by its bankers.[482]

In England two men were arrested for watching a video[483] of a Koran burning[484]

Muslims are abducting infidel women, raping them, getting them pregnant, and forcibly marrying them as additional wives, and everyone is closing their eyes to it[485].

Our official moderate Muslim, Imam Rauf, is curiously evasive about 9/11.

How many Christians reacted violently to Piss Christ? Not a one, zero. How many Muslims reacted violently to cartoon Mohammed? Hundreds of thousands committed criminal acts, millions cheered them on.

All the great leaders of Islam were war makers, military leaders, conquerors, slavers. This just is not a pattern you see in Christianity. Not only did the original prophet of Islam massacre defeated populations, every subsequent great Islamic religious leader acted similarly - some better, some worse, but all directly commanded wars, personally led them, and took extreme measures to subjugate the defeated population. In contrast, absolutely zero great Christian religious leaders has done this - you do not see popes and bishops leading armies, burning towns, and personally ordering the rape of the women of the conquered.

Christian fanatics generally lock themselves in dungeons and meditate. Islamic fanatics blow themselves up.

Christian leaders that combined the role of military and religious leader have always been a marginal phenomenon, and phenomenon that occurred only among those directly at war with Islam: the Knights of Malta and the Knights Templar. Further, those combining Christian religious and secular power have frequently led their followers to disaster by recollecting Christ's command to forgive one's enemies and turn the other cheek at some highly inopportune moment, as Grand Master Bolheim of the Knights of Malta did.

Just as there is in all the world not one Christian who called for violence against the creators of Piss Christ and Andres Serrano, there is in all the world not one Muslim very

[478] https://www.nationalreview.com/blogs/print/246899
[479] https://gatesofvienna.blogspot.com/2010/09/all-meetings-of-sweden-democrats-banned.html
[480] https://gatesofvienna.blogspot.com/2010/09/charges-dropped-against-gregorius.html
[481] https://mansizedtarget.wordpress.com/2010/09/19/legal-realism-and-the-koran/
[482] https://www.steynonline.com/content/view/3505/26/
[483] https://www.moonbattery.com/archives/2010/09/still-more-kora.html
[484] https://www.civilliberty.org.uk/newsdetail.php?newsid=1079
[485] https://www.israelnationalnews.com/News/News.aspx/139738

few Muslims who condemned the fatwa against Molly Norris. In that sense, every single Christian in the entire world is opposed to holy war and seeks peace, and every single Muslim in the entire world supports holy war and seeks conquest.

Let us imagine the situation was reversed, and some notable Christian preacher was to call for the murder of Andres Serrano. Obviously, if this happened, which it never would, every other notable Christian leader would condemn that call. Compare and contrast with the call for the murder of Molly Norris. Not every Muslim has called for the murder of Molly Norris, but not one Muslim has condemned the call either.

Financial collapse still under way

2010-09-27 05:15:33

The Market Ticker ® complains that the banks and the regulators are flagrantly and massively violating laws that are necessary for borrowing and lending to work – violating every step that is necessary for the trust to work along the chain, with the result that our entire financial system is massively disfunctional, and continues to leak huge amounts of money. He gives lots of interesting details of a multitude of flagrantly criminal acts.

But he fails to ask how the widespread criminality began.

It began because the law both commanded and forbade affirmative action lending, and to comply, what was illegal had to be done, therefore, had to be made de-facto legal.

Repeating my much repeated rant yet again:

When they gave a Nobel prize to Marie Curie for being female, that did not hurt anyone except more deserving potential Nobel prize winners. But handing out phony Nobels on the basis of sex, race, and nationality necessitated handing out phony degrees on the basis of race and sex, and handing out phony degrees on the basis of race and sex necessarily led to a crisis where these phony degrees were being ignored by employers, so employers necessarily had to be forced to give out well paid phony jobs on the basis of race and sex. But being given well paid phony jobs on the basis of race and sex failed to result in recipients living a middle class lifestyle, so lenders had to be forced to give out a middle class lifestyle on the basis of race and sex. Which required every single banker to become dishonest or get a new job. Which has led to our present financial crisis. It all began with Marie Curie.

So if you roll back the most unpopular, extreme, and disastrous form of affirmative action, you then immediately face a problem with less extreme and more popular forms. And if you roll them back ... All solutions are either radical or unworkable. Roll back affirmative action loans, and pretty soon you are going to have to ridicule Marie Curie, and say her husband should have kept her in the bedroom and the kitchen, and not put her in the lab. And since no one wants to start walking down a path that ends in them saying it was inappropriate for Pierre Curie to try to make Marie Curie into a scientist, no one wants to stop bankers doing criminal things.

And so the financial system continues to leak money

No Pressure 10:10

2010-10-02 10:34:30

Murder children for a greener tomorrow.

Most honest political ad of all time.[486]

By now, you have probably seen the No Pressure video, depicting the warmist wish fulfillment fantasy where they get to blow up the heretics. It starts with a warmist teacher blowing up skeptical children, then depicts every people of every part of society being blown up, then finally the revolution devours its children, with a warmist blowing up another warmist for inadequate faith.

A lot of blogs are asking: "what were they thinking!";

Cull the skeptics[487], Infocult[488], The Catastrophist[489], Fascistic New Video[490], Greens want to blow you up[491], Chicks on the right[492], Boom![493], most self-defeating ad campaign *ever*[494], utter stupidity[495], decimation[496], massive Freudian slip[497].

Seems pretty obvious to me. They were thinking about power, which is what the global warming campaign has been about from the beginning.

The fascinating thing is that before the shitstorm hit all the good and great signed on saying what a great video it is. Blowing up children. Ha ha! So funny. Serves them right for doubting their betters[498]!

The video reveals the true character of our rulers. They think that murdering people who disagree with them is funny.

One commenter gets it right in revolting[499]

> Politics, which fundamentally is a struggle to control the most violent organization in society, attracts people that are amoral or whom otherwise lack consideration for their fellow men. The more expansive the state, the more attractive it is to these people. The more they dominate the state, the more expansive and activist it becomes.It's a vicious feedback loop ending only when the state kills the civilization that is its host, or so shocks the host's sensibilities that the people rebel.

---

[486]https://pajamasmedia.com/zombie/2010/10/01/most-honest-political-ad-of-all-time/
[487]https://noconsensus.wordpress.com/2010/09/30/publicly-crazy-1010/
[488]https://infocult.typepad.com/infocult/2010/10/no-pressure.html
[489]https://catastrophist.wordpress.com/2010/10/02/1010-no-pressure-video/
[490]https://pajamasmedia.com/eddriscoll/2010/10/01/red-lining-the-eco-insanity-meter/
[491]https://www.crashbangwallace.com/2010/10/01/bin-laden-goes-green-and-greens-want-to-blow-you-up/
[492]https://chicksontheright.com/2010/10/01/no-pressure/
[493]https://quotulatiousness.ca/blog/2010/10/01/no-pressure-boom/
[494]https://hotair.com/archives/2010/10/01/video-the-dumbest-most-self-defeating-ad-campaign-ever/
[495]https://sppiblog.org/news/the-environmental-activist-mind-set-the-age-of-utter-stupidity
[496]https://faustasblog.com/?p=23303
[497]https://clancop.wordpress.com/2010/10/01/a-disturbing-commerical-a-glimpse-into-the-mind-of-a-radical-environmentalist-group/
[498]https://hot-topic.co.nz/no-pressure-1010-on-the-button/
[499]https://www.thelibertypapers.org/2010/10/01/the-most-revolting-political-video-ive-ever-seen/

Falkenblog locates the guilty
2010-10-03 10:37:23

Falkenblog has an interesting quote from Harvard[500], wherein in 2003, back before the financial crisis, Angello Mozilla gives politically correct bullshit justifying every bad thing the banks did to cause the financial crisis on the basis of race and affirmative action.

> That means there is currently a homeownership gap of over 25 points when comparing white households with African Americans and Hispanics. My friends, that gap is obviously far too wide.
>
> ...
>
> One of the more obvious resolutions to the Money Gap is the elimination of down payment requirements for low-income and minority borrowers
>
> ....
>
> the credit score bar dividing creditworthy from high-risk borrowers, must be substantially lowered by the GSEs, the secondary market in general, and with bank regulators.

These are all quotes from a publication[501] of "The Joint Center for Housing Studies of Harvard University", which endorsed all the actions the regulators took to destroy our financial system, and urged more of the same.

Please keep in mind that everything this wrecking crew did is still in place, still in force. It became illegal to be an honest banker, that being *raaaacist*, and it still is illegal. Every single banker is a crook, is because no honest banker can make crooked loans, and the regulators require all bankers to make crooked loans. Undoing the damage would require an unthinkably radical transformation of our political system, something more akin to regime change and the collapse of democracy, than any mere election. As I have said so many times before, to fix the financial system will require and result in a society where it is possible to laugh at the Nobel committee for giving Marie Curie two Nobel prizes that for work that was unexceptional when men did it, and laugh at Pierre Curie for pushing his wife into the lab, when he should have kept her in the bedroom and kitchen.

Duelling Rallies
2010-10-04 16:46:18

Verum Serum compares the rallies:[502]

Notice the mass of buses at the left of the "one nation" rally – those were unionists who were bused, government employees, rather than people who chose to turn up by their own individual decision. To judge by the number of buses, the "one nation" rally was 90% astroturf. Had they relied on voluntary unpaid attendance, the rally would have been invisibly tiny.

---

[500]https://falkenblog.blogspot.com/2010/09/conventional-wisdom-in-2003.html
[501]https://www.jchs.harvard.edu/publications/homeownership/M03-1_mozilo.pdf
[502]https://www.verumserum.com/?p=17666

War with Islam

2010-10-12 00:50:03

The Muslim brotherhood has majority support in Egypt, and supposedly moderate Muslim organizations that are linked to western governments, and supported by them, are in large part Muslim brotherhood organizations.

Memri translates a sermon by the Brotherhood's "Supreme Guide[503]" posted on the Brotherhood's website.

> ... they are disregarding Allah's commandment to wage jihad for His sake with [their] money and [their] lives, so that Allah's word will reign supreme and the infidels' word will be inferior...
>
> ...
>
> ... the improvement and change that the nation seeks can only be attained through jihad and sacrifice and by raising a jihadi generation that pursues death just as the enemies pursue life.
>
> ...
>
> The Soviet Union fell dramatically, but the factors that will lead to the collapse of the U.S. are much more powerful than those that led to the collapse of the Soviet empire – for a nation that does not champion moral and human values cannot lead humanity, and its wealth will not avail it once Allah has had His say, as happened with [powerful] nations in the past. The U.S. is now experiencing the beginning of its end, and is heading towards its demise...

After 9/11, I started reading old books, and found our past had been rewritten. It turns out that Islam has always been at war with us, at war with all infidels. A substantial and important part of our history has been erased, perhaps because it is "racist"

Thomas Jefferson and John Adams asked the Barbary Ambassador what right they attacked us.

> The Ambassador answered us that it founded on the Laws of the Prophet, that it was written in their Koran, that all nations who should not have answered their authority were sinners, that it was their right and duty to make war upon them wherever they could be found, and to make slaves of all they could take as prisoners, and that every Mussulman who should be slain in battle was sure to go to Paradise.

America was out of this war from 1830 to 1960, because the French foreign legion, and French sponsored settlers, were taking the brunt of it. When the French pulled the settlers out, we started to get hit with increasing effectiveness, much as Israel got rockets when they pulled the settlers out of Gaza.

---

[503] https://www.memri.org/report/en/0/0/0/0/0/0/0/4650.htm

Over the past thirteen hundred years we never had peace with Islam, just higher and lower levels of war, and when we had very low levels of war, we accomplished it by meeting state level war with state level war, but substate level war with substate level war - we met met substate level war with settlers, settler militias, and state sponsored pirates and brigands. For over a thousand years, settlers, brigands, and pirates, have been the keys to defeating Islam. Observe what happened when we pulled the settlers out of Algeria, and the settlers out of Gaza.

The only time when we enjoyed peace from them was during the colonial period when any trouble from them resulted in colonialist settlers taking their land and their women.

To survive, we need far more modest goals, and need to apply far more drastic measures, and far cheaper measures.

Because war with Islam is permanent and irreversible, we must fight it by methods that are sufficiently economical that we can sustain them permanently. This requires that all measures be carefully evaluated for the minimum cost to us, and the maximum cost to them. Building schools for them to blow up fails to meet that criterion. Seizure or destruction of assets meets that criterion wonderfully, and it is an operation that can be privatized, and over the past thousand years of warfare, usually was.

The foreclosure scandal

2010-10-12 15:28:17

Did you make payments on your mortgage? Can you prove it? Can you prove you made the payments to the right entity? Who is the right entity? Does anyone know? Mortgage servicers don't have great incentives to get distressed homeowner's records correct[504]

The foreclosure scandal, at first sight, does not seem like much of a scandal. A bunch of people borrowed large amounts of money against houses, usually with false or nonexistent documentation of their income and assets and grossly inflated valuations of the houses. Then they did not make their payments. Then some random person attempts to foreclose on them, and they complain that the guy trying to foreclose lacks standing to foreclose. What is so bad?

Somehow, one does not feel any great sensation of outrage and pity, but yes, there is a scandal here and it is really bad. Also[505] very,[506] very[507] complicate[508]d.

The dud loans were made into dud mortgage backed securities, which were divided into tranches, some of the tranches being more senior, that is to say less dud, than the others. So when it all has to be unwound, it is a total mess and complete chaos. To make

---

[504]https://rortybomb.wordpress.com/2010/10/11/foreclosure-fraud-for-dummies-2-what-is-a-note-and-why-is-it-so-important/

[505]https://rortybomb.wordpress.com/2010/10/08/foreclosure-fraud-for-dummies-1-the-chains-and-the-stakes/

[506]https://rortybomb.wordpress.com/2010/10/11/foreclosure-fraud-for-dummies-2-what-is-a-note-and-why-is-it-so-important/

[507]https://rortybomb.wordpress.com/2010/10/11/foreclosure-fraud-for-dummies-3-why-are-servicers-so-bad-at-their-job/

[508]https://rortybomb.wordpress.com/2010/10/11/foreclosure-fraud-for-dummies-4-how-could-this-explode-into-a-systemic-crisis/

things worse, the various entities that arranged the loans were fly by night scamsters who cannot be found. Even worse, the senior tranches all wound up being sold to the government: Freddy Mac, Fannie May, the Federal Reserve, and the FHA.

Why does the feds holding senior tranches make things worse? Because the holder of the senior tranche should be defending his own interests, should be making sure that foreclosures benefit himself, should be organizing the foreclosures to be most lucrative to himself, but the federal government could not run a pie stand. The labyrinthine and rigid federal bureaucracy is at the top composed largely of people who graduated in political correctness from the most eminent universities. Which means that these assets (the rights to foreclose on various houses) are ill defended, therefore apt to be stolen at worst, and incompetently exercised at best.

So it looks as if houses are often being foreclosed to the benefit of those who merely hold the junior tranches and thus have no right to benefit by the foreclosure, or perhaps do not hold anything at all – it is difficult to tell, perhaps impossible to tell.

It is also unclear how much money the people being foreclosed upon actually owe – again, it is difficult to tell, perhaps impossible to tell. When the scammers sold mortgages on to the next guy in line, they tended to pad up the mortgage, tended to exaggerate the amount of money owing.[509]

But the big scandal is a fraud upon the taxpayer: Goldman and Sach, and other well connected and too big to fail securitizing entities guaranteed that 9999 out of 10000 mortgage notes would be valid[510]. It looks like few or none of them are valid. Thus the people that securitized these the mortgages are liable for the full value. Unfortunately, since the senior tranches were all purchased by the taxpayer, this claim against Goldman and Sach is unlikely to be exercised. It may well be exercised by the holders of junior tranches, which will produce further chaos.

More astroturf

2010-10-13 15:05:15

The one nation rally was largely AstroTurf, students bussed by their teachers, unionists bussed by their unions. If it was not hundred percent AstroTurf, it was close enough to one hundred percent that it was hard to see the difference.

Jon Stewart's "March to keep fear alive" rally is looking like it will be more of the same[511].

> On the morning of October 30th, **we're loading up a fleet of buses** here at 1515 Broadway and sending as many of you as we can down to DC for a free one-day, round-trip journey to join in the Rally to Restore Sanity and March to Keep Fear Alive. It's about a 5 ½ hour trip down 95 to our nation's capital

---

[509]https://papers.ssrn.com/sol3/papers.cfm?abstract_id=1027961
[510]https://rortybomb.wordpress.com/2010/10/11/foreclosure-fraud-for-dummies-2-what-is-a-note-and-why-is-it-so-important/
[511]https://bighollywood.breitbart.com/jjmnolte/2010/10/12/exclusive-mtv-astro-turfs-their-employees-to-attend-jon-stewarts-counter-beck-rally/

By and large, if a rally is partly AstroTurf, it is usually all AstroTurf, because you don't resort to AstroTurf if you can get real supporters to show up. If one lie, all lies, if one AstroTurf, all AstroTurf.

Conspiracy

2010-10-14 07:50:34

If you watch the reality show "survivor", you will have noticed that in any power struggle, the winners usually have invisible connections - there is a group that conceals from outsiders that it is a group. Conspiracy tends to be a substantial part of any winning strategy. Conspiracies are therefore as common as cockroaches and crabgrass. Conspiracy theory has a deserved bad name because it tends to be invoked to explain away unwanted evidence, as for example Chomsky explaining that the Khmer Rouge were good guys under attack by the CIA[512], shortly before he explained that they were bad guys installed in power by the CIA.

But while we should not believe in conspiracies with the ability to program millions of refugees to say unkind things about noble mild mannered agrarian reformers, nor conspiracies that can bring out large mobs on the streets to lynch beloved leaders of the proletariat, we should believe in conspiracies that link together a handful of powerful people in a handful of powerful, but supposedly separate and independent, organizations. The state department really was full of commies.

By definition, a conspiracy is small. Astroturf, therefore is a signature of conspiracy. If there is a real mob in the streets, a conspiracy is unlikely to have much control over it.

Another good signature of conspiracy is people mysteriously rising to power from nowhere, as the current leader of the British Labor party. Ed Miliband has a mysteriously invisible powerbase. Before 2005, no one had heard of him. Then he is nominated to a safe seat - which usually only happens to people who have been working for years to inherit the seat, promptly becomes minister, and then, leader of the labor party.

Tracing connections, we find a lot of odd links between the London School of Economics, the people who made the 10:10 no pressure video, and Ed Miliband - revealing the presence of a greenie conspiracy that is
1. Powerful
2. Composed of morons
3. Unable to get its agenda through

Foreclosure fraud chaos

2010-10-14 14:09:40

Pines and Associates reports that[513]:

---

[512]https://reaction.la/chomsdis.htm
[513]https://marinfamilyaction.org/minutes/Minutes050510.pdf

Most [mortgage] loans are securitized and most investors have filed class action suits. He finds those suits and joins them on behalf of clients as a "special interest" in the suit.

This is Armageddon for the financial system. The underlying problem is that finance runs on trust, and these days they are all crooks, so the entire financial system has seized up.

Any solution to the problem that could possibly work is far more drastic than anything proposed by anyone on either side of politics. For starters, you would have to send everyone involved in the CRA scam to prison, roll affirmative action back all the way to Marie Curie, and that is only the beginning of what is needed.

The enormous mortgage-bond scandal

2010-10-15 13:53:28

Felix Salmon has found an interesting document[514] in the financial crisis inquiry hearings.

It seems the banks not only knew that the loans they were selling to investors generally failed to meet underwriting standards, they were so careless as to have documents lying around saying so in plain English.

Seems like they were a bank of morons. When I was involved in criminal conspiracies, none of us would write in plain English, and we would very rarely speak in plain English.

But if you are a regular visitor to his blog, that we are ruled by dim witted criminals is unlikely to surprise you. What has, however, surprised me, is that the political branch of the conspiracy failed to swiftly throw the bankster branch to the wolves and blame them for everything. If I was in Obama's shoes, in 2009 I would have been preparing federal prosecutions to generate interesting headlines just before the 2010 mid term elections, but instead both political parties continue in cover up mode.

The ruling elite is too soft on each other to hold on to power for very much longer. As soon as we get a really big crisis, are likely to fall.

The whitewash proceeds

2010-10-16 16:08:17

One of the bigger criminals in the mortgage scam was Former Countrywide CEO Mozilo. The SEC has made a symbolic settlement with him and a couple of his accomplices for seventy two million dollars, not a dime of which he has to pay personally, and which would be peanuts even if he had to pay it personally. As a part of the agreement, all potentially embarrassing details associated with his crimes are sealed from nosy outsiders.

What little money will be paid, will be paid from an escrow fund the company set up to cover shareholder litigation – and since Countrywide was taken over by the FDIC, this means that the government is paying the money to itself.

---

[514]https://blogs.reuters.com/felix-salmon/2010/10/13/the-enormous-mortgage-bond-scandal/

Elections do not matter.

2010-10-18 08:51:37

The most extreme of the "right wing" candidates are proposing measures far too feeble to make a difference. Consider for example, the mortgage scandal. Where is the candidate that suggests that to fix our financial system, the bums (the entire financial sector of wall street and the regulators to which they are connected by a revolving door) need to be fired for incompetence and imprisoned for fraud?

A lot of people are proposing "solutions" for the mortgage crisis – but all these "solutions" propose that the people in charge of the too-big-to-fail banks and their regulators will remain powerful, important, and out of jail, despite demonstrated criminality and gross incompetence.

The ruling elite has lost the capacity to discipline itself. Power is slipping out of their feeble hands, falling into the street.

Our society has reached that awkward state, too late for reform, too soon to shoot the bums, but that stage is usually irreversible. It will eventually reach the time to shoot the bums stage.

Illegality[515] by our elite is provoking illegality by ordinary middle class people[516]. As Market Ticker tells us:

> This is where lawlessness leads us - to more lawlessness. Once you commit a lawless act against someone **and are not punished for it** you have invited them to retaliate **with complete disregard for the law in their response.** You are only required to deal ethically and morally with an ethical and moral entity across the table - one who ignores the law **loses their right to demand that respect in return.**
>
> This mess**begins** with the securitization and sale of these mortgages in the first instance. It begins with whether or not the original banks actually transferred the notes **at all** (there's plenty of evidence they did not) and whether the representations and warranties were complied with when these securities were sold to investors (we **know** in many cases - if not all - they were not, from FCIC sworn testimony.)
>
> **We have turned a blind eye to these lawless acts for the better part of a decade - not one indictment has issued for securities fraud over these matters. And it's not just mortgages - we know banks were involved in ripping off communities such as Jefferson County, we know they are alleged to have been involved in rigging municipal debt offerings (which raised the cost of living for everyone through higher taxes) and yet not one bank officer or bank itself has been placed under indictment for any of it. Further, the FBI warned in 2004 of an "epidemic" (their words) of mortgage fraud, and instead of it being prosecuted the agents were pulled and reassigned.**

---

[515] https://blogs.reuters.com/felix-salmon/2010/10/13/the-enormous-mortgage-bond-scandal/
[516] https://market-ticker.org/akcs-www?post=169420

We have had two **sequential** administrations - Bush and now Obama - that have **intentionally** refused to prosecute any of this lawless behavior. This refusal continues to this very day with admissions in depositions **under oath** of the commission of **literal** tens of thousands of felonies **per month** (each instance of falsely swearing before a court is a separate count of fraud upon the court and, in the case of "robosigning", forgery - affixing a notary's signature by other than the actual notary.) **Yet despite this having been confirmed in multiple depositions going back several monthsnot one indictment has issued thus far and Attorneys General talk about not wanting to "upset" the banks or the "economy."**

Foreclosure Scandal

2010-10-19 09:01:38

Here is what is presently known and understood about the foreclosure scandal.
Violations of PSAs[517]
Worse than you think[518]
The long and the short of it is that securitization was organized by the too-big-to-fail banks, and was done incompetently, corruptly, and criminally.

Winning will be another Republican disaster

2010-10-20 07:35:04

Everyone on the Republican side is sucking up to the anti capitalist left - including Sarah Palin and Christine O'Donnel. None have the will to reverse the policies that are ruining the economy, making the middle class poor and insecure.

So, when elected, will get the blame for the consequences of these policies. Since the supposedly hard core capitalism of the Republicans will not work, obviously the solution must be more socialism.

Sarbanes–Oxley, the regulatory door revolving, and Basel, have installed in power a permanent business elite that cannot lose power no matter how incompetently they screw up, and cannot be prosecuted no matter what criminal deeds they commit – foreclosure-gate, the ratings agencies, and the leadership of the too-big-to-fail banks being examples of this problem.

The regulatory apparatus that locks this elite in place and protects them against market forces has to be removed – a program that is unthinkably and unimaginably radical, far more extreme than the most extreme of the supposedly extreme tea party candidates.

The problem is not the dramatic expansion of government spending. The problem is the vastly more dramatic explosion of the regulatory state such as, for example Sarbanes–Oxley, which has largely criminalized the great engine of jobs creation, ended the forma-

---

[517] https://www.nakedcapitalism.com/2010/10/josh-rosner-could-violations-of-psa%E2%80%99s-dwarf-lehman-weekend.html
[518] https://www.cnbc.com/id/39634568/Foreclosure_Fraud_It_s_Worse_Than_You_Think

tion of new small businesses, and Basel, which gives the state, and such private enterprises as the state chooses to privilege, the task of assessing financial risk.

Sarah Palin proposes an insignificantly tiny reform

2010-10-22 06:59:34

Sarah Palin observes that National Public Radio has purged one of its commentators for mentioning the unmentionable,[519] and suggests that National Public Radio be defunded for silencing debate and attempting to promote ignorance. Several other prominent Republicans have said the same thing, or endorsed Sarah Palin saying it, Sarah Palin being merely the most famous and influential of more republicans than I can shake a stick at.

This is a tiny, tiny, step towards defunding the left. To actually defund the left, need to abolish the illegal and unconstitutional departments of Education and energy, the National Endowment for the arts, and the environmental Protection Agency.

Of course if we cannot roll back Basel, despite the fact that under Basel's regime of politicized lending the entire banking system of the west has been leaking vast amounts of money and continues to do so, we cannot roll back funding for the left.

Numerous blogs are thrilled because a noted political leader has proposed we actually move slightly right, rather than merely proposing we move left slightly slower, and promptly been supported by lot more: x^{520}, x^{521}, x^{522}, x^{523}, x^{524}, x^{525}, x^{526}, x^{527}, x^{528}, x^{529}, x^{530}, x^{531}, x^{532}, and more blogs than I can shake a stick at.

The thrilled response to Sarah Palin's suggestion shows how rare such suggestions are.

---

[519] https://www.facebook.com/note.php?note_id=444532058434#!/notes/sarah-palin/juan-williams-going-rogue/444532058434

[520] https://www.riehlworldview.com/carnivorous_conservative/2010/10/juan-williams-was-fired-because-hes-black.html

[521] https://althouse.blogspot.com/2010/10/sarah-palin-juan-williams-going-rogue.html

[522] https://www.nationalpolicyinstitute.org/2010/10/21/sarah-palin-calls-for-congress-to-defund-npr-over-juan-williams%E2%80%99-firing/

[523] https://www.redstate.com/aarongardner/2010/10/21/on-npr-and-juan-williams/

[524] https://www.frugal-cafe.com/public_html/frugal-blog/frugal-cafe-blogzone/2010/10/21/sarah-palin-on-nprs-firing-of-juan-williams-despite-his-criticism-of-her-she-says-i-will-always-support-his-right-the-right-of-all-americans-to-speak-honestly-about-the-threats-this-country-f/

[525] https://www.thedailybeast.com/blogs-and-stories/2010-10-21/juan-williams-behind-his-firing-by-npr/

[526] https://blogs.courant.com/susan_campbell/2010/10/sarah-palin-just-tweeted-this.html

[527] https://www.washingtonexaminer.com/politics/ap/npr-fires-news-analyst-after-remarks-about-muslims-105430498.html

[528] https://chopitupmag.com/2010/10/21/juan-williams-fired-over-muslim-comments/

[529] https://thehill.com/blogs/blog-briefing-room/news/125225-in-wake-of-williams-firing-republicans-want-npr-funding-examined

[530] https://politicalderby.com/2010/10/21/honesty-will-get-you-fired/

[531] https://www.hollywoodreporter.com/news/fired-npr-analyst-stands-muslim-31840

[532] https://politicalticker.blogs.cnn.com/2010/10/21/huckabee-calls-on-congress-to-cut-npr-funding/

The supposedly unelectable Sarah Palin
2010-10-26 16:57:55

The Democrats assure Republicans that Sarah Palin is unelectable, and that for her to be nominated for president in 2012 is their wet dream, because it would assure Obama of a second term, that if Republican nominate Sarah Palin, Democrats will be celebrating.

At the same time, the Democrats are quietly pushing the supposedly much more electable Michael Rubens Bloomberg as Republican presidential candidate in 2012, creating opportunities for him to receive favorable publicity, giving him lots of respect in Democrat controlled publications. If he is so much more electable, why are the Democrats pushing him and mobilizing to prevent Sarah Palin from getting the nomination?

Never accept advice from your enemies.

The White House misses no opportunity to get the supposedly highly electable Michael Rubens Bloomberg some favorable publicity - Obama golfs with him, floats his name as treasury secretary, conspicuously sends prominent members of his government to conspicuously seek Bloomberg's supposedly wise advice. If I ask someone's advice, I do not announce it with a fanfare.

This is mighty odd behavior for a White house that supposedly would celebrating if the supposedly hopelessly unelectable Sarah Barracuda gets the nomination, rather than the supposedly terrifyingly electable Michael Rubens Bloomberg. As they miss no opportunity to tell us they hope for Sarah Palin's nomination, they also miss no opportunity to tell us they are terrified of Bloomberg's nomination – and miss no opportunity to make Bloomberg's nomination happen.

War on masculinity
2010-10-28 07:35:02

Roissy has a couple of great posts about the war on masculinity "Belittle League[533]" and "The medicalization of maleness[534]"

hyperinflation of the US$
2010-10-29 11:46:21

A great storm first manifest as clouds on the horizon. The Republicans are going to wish they had not won the 2010 November elections.

Supposedly US inflation is near zero, yet food, fuel, and heating oil has risen substantially.

Gonzalo points out[535]

> Grains as a class have risen over 33% year-over-year. Refined oil products have risen just shy of 13%, with home heating oil rising 18% year-over-year.

---

[533]https://roissy.wordpress.com/2010/10/27/belittle-league/
[534]https://roissy.wordpress.com/2010/01/21/the-medicalization-of-maleness/
[535]https://gonzalolira.blogspot.com/2010/10/signs-hyperinflation-is-arriving.html

In other words: Food, gasoline and heating oil have risen by double digits since 2009. And the 2010-'11 winter in the northern hemisphere is approaching.

Supposedly, food in the supermarket is not rising, or not rising yet, yet bulk prices of the commodities you need to live on have risen by thirty to fifty percent.

If this has not shown up in the supermarkets yet, it is going to show up mighty soon.

The storm, inflation rates that are quite obviously disruptive and unacceptable, will likely be raging vigorously some time in 2012. There may well be continued reluctance to admit what is happening. I will not be much surprised if official statistics and the New York Times announce that everything is coming up roses even in 2012

Officially, all is roses today, yet Case Research reports[536]

Fixing the financial system

2010-10-30 15:33:27

We are in trouble, the entire west is in trouble, in substantial part because the financial system has been leaking a lot of money. So has every other part of the governing apparatus, but the financial system is the biggest hole in the bucket.

Now a lot of people are saying that this is a revolutionary election, it is about fundamental change. Thomas Sowell, a man I enormously respect, tells us this is a crossroads election[537]. But is not. The Democrats are driving the bus towards the precipice in top gear with the pedal flat to the metal, the Republicans propose to proceed with the pedal not quite flat to the metal. Some of the unelectably extreme elements of the Tea Party are suggesting a lower gear. In Britain, they applied supposedly radical cuts - which "cuts" some how result in a substantial increase in government spending. Before the "cuts", an ordinary Briton had to be crazy if he planned to work, marry, have kids, and support his own kids. After the "cuts", he still had to be crazy if he planned to work, marry, have kids, and support his own kids.

But let us focus on the biggest single money leak: The financial system, for all the other problems resemble that. If we had the will to fix the financial system, we would have the will to fix all the other problems.

The Market Ticker proposes a general audit of the banks[538]: Shut down the insolvent banks, and remove their management permanently from the banking industry. This seemingly addresses the problem of crooked financiers. If we cannot jail them, we can at least fire them. Unfortunately, it does not ask *why* we are overrun with crooked bankers.

In America, the problem was the CRA and affirmative action lending. The regulators required a banker to make loans to certain voting blocks that there was no way could legitimately be made - so only crooked bankers survived. If a banker is still in business, he

[536] https://www.caseyresearch.com/editorial/3791?ppref=CRX175ED1010A
[537] https://townhall.com/columnists/ThomasSowell/2010/10/29/a_crossroads_election
[538] https://market-ticker.org/akcs-www?post=170706

is a criminal. But world wide, we saw a similar outbreak of crooked lending, often with very different beneficiaries.

The common factor in all this crooked lending was Basel: Basel means that regulators are the ultimate decision makers as to what is a risky loan and what is a safe loan - which means that politically correct loans are necessarily supposedly safe, and politically incorrect loans are necessarily supposedly unsafe - which means that a banker has to be corrupt.

So to fix the banking system, have to undo Basel. This sounds easy. The left claims that Basel is deregulation, therefore extremely bad and the big cause of our financial troubles; The right claims that Basel is regulation, an explosive expansion of regulation, therefore extremely bad and the big cause of our financial troubles – except however that only one minor candidate, widely viewed as ludicrously extreme, proposes to undo Basel.

Every candidate claims to hate the banksters twice as much as every other other candidate - but again only one candidate proposes to purge the banking system of zombie banks and crooked bankers.

You will notice the the fix for the financial system is the wholesale rollback of thirty years of financial regulation (or, as the left call it, deregulation), the mass firing of the good and the great, the powerful, the important and the influential, a large portion of the most eminent graduates of our most eminent universities, and the imprisonment of a significant fraction of them. Simply apply a similar fix to every part of our society, and the problem is solved.

We have a society that believes that children should not be spanked, that thieves should not be flogged, that women should not suffer adverse consequences for bearing children by men other than their husbands – and that graduates for the most eminent universities should not lose their jobs for corruption or incompetence.

Vote Cthulhu

2010-11-01 06:00:29

Why vote for the lesser evil?

Bush, of course, launched numerous expensive new programs and entitlements, and failed to restrain the inherent growth of Clinton's affirmative action easy mortgage program. He encouraged the growth of that program, though to judge by the screaming of the Democrats at the time, probably slightly less than the Democrats would have done.

But even if Bush had launched no new entitlements, restraining the inherent growth of Clinton's mortgage program would have been unthinkably drastic and "racist", would have been "cuts", "cuts" directed at particular racial groups supposedly for racist reasons, "cuts" immeasurably more extreme and controversial than anything any tea party candidate dares speak out loud about, "cuts" far more dramatic than the quite controversial cuts happening now in Britain. To maintain the Clinton status quo against the inherent growth of Clinton's programs would have required unthinkably drastic "right wing racist cuts".

Every institution tends to grow. Institutions are made of people. They exist because they give those people what they want, so people in them always want more of that institution. Market institutions, such as firms, are inherently limited, because if the customer says "no", the institution fails to grow, or vanishes altogether. Government institutions have no such inherent limits, so always grow barring frequent, extreme, and drastic "cuts".

The growth of government in America was restrained by federalism, by market competition between the states. When the constitution was gutted, that restraint was removed. Almost everything the feds do except the post office, the patent office, and warfare, is unconstitutional. If all that stuff was passed back to the states and states such as California were allowed to go bankrupt, state to state competition and state bankruptcies might slow growth to levels that could be accommodates without social collapse.

There is a natural selection process going on– government programs that *can* be stopped half way, generally are, or at least are slowed, so government tends to be dominated by programs that inherently have limitless growth that can end only in social collapse or total domination of every aspect of society.

If any politician stops affirmative action mortgages, he launches himself on a path where he is going to stop all affirmative action and wind up in front of the television cameras ridiculing Marie Curie's Nobel prizes and women scientists in general. You cannot stop affirmative action half way. The inherent logic and needs of affirmative action, like most successfully expansionist government programs, require total domination of every aspect of society, or complete repudiation.

The dominant part of government is programs that cannot be cut half way, can only be cut off at the roots, because the ones that can be cut half way, frequently are.

In the private sector, natural selection selects well run firms, so firms are mostly well run, and where most firms are badly run, for example retailing, well run firms such as Walmart tend to dominate.

In the government sector, natural selection selects programs whose growth is impossible to restrain For example: If you give "under represented groups" their fair share of Nobel prizes, you soon have to give them their fair share of degrees. If you give them their fair share of degrees, you soon have to give them their fair share of well paid high status jobs. If you give them their fair share of well paid high status jobs, you soon have to give them their fair share of mortgages. If you give them their fair share of mortgages, the economy collapses. So there is no help for it but to resist and ridicule giving them their fair share of Nobel prizes.

You cannot have half affirmative action, and half not, because if you do, either the half that is not affirmative action be racism and sexism, or the half that is affirmative action must be fraud, lies, pretense, and special privilege, must itself be racism and sexism. This is the formula for a successful government program – that any attempt to restrain its growth must be politically outrageous and extraordinary.

It follows that the biggest and most uncontrollable programs will be those that to cut is unthinkable, and that the only cuts of those programs that can succeed is total abolition. Compare and contrast with the most "radical" of the Tea Partiers.

If you can cut a program by five percent or ten percent, then it is unlikely to be a big problem. Most government is programs that cannot be cut by five or ten percent, cannot even have their growth much slowed, except by abolition.

If George Osborne slows the growth of Britain's National Health scheme to levels that Britain can afford, in a few years the National Health Scheme will consist entirely of committees of expert authorities sending memos to other committees of expert authorities, while Britons die in the streets of readily treated ailments. Indeed, we are already seeing the horror stories in the British press. George Osborne tells some government entity that is blowing ludicrous amounts of money that it will have a few hundred million pounds less money that it asked for, a mere drop in an overflowing bucket. The entity finds some pathetic and deserving client, whose very life has come to depend on them spending a minuscule amount money on him, and announces that they will save a few pounds by letting him die. And then they do it.

Yet another vote for European style Social Democracy

2010-11-04 05:35:09

As Europe collapses,[539] Americans vote to be like Europe.

The republicans now have control of the purse strings, and, among other things, have promised to reduce next years deficit from \$1470 000 000 000 to \$1370 000 000 000. We are in a bus heading towards a precipice at seventy miles and hour, and the republicans promise to slow down to sixty five miles an hour[540].

Any tea party candidate that made vague noises in the general direction of doing something to preserve America and avoid total collapse, lost. That position just is not popular.

The only solution is that after the collapse comes, we have to install a system other than democracy with broad or universal franchise.

When the franchise was extended to all males, people predicted that eventually the voters would fall for politicians promising that they could vote themselves rich, and everything would collapse. Observe. The voters have fallen, and now collapse is in sight.

Yes, Obama is a Muslim.

2010-11-05 12:33:53

I doubt Obama believes in anything, not in God, not even the evidence of the senses - but to be officially a Muslim, you have to publicly pronounce the Shahada: "There is no God but Allah, and Mohammed is his prophet". Obama did as a child, and recently repeated in public as an adult[541]. To cease to be a Muslim, you have to publicly reject that proposition, which he has not done, or publicly accept a contrary proposition, such as "Jesus is Lord", which he has not done.

To be officially Christian, you have to be baptized in the name of Jesus, and call Jesus "Lord", which Obama has not done, nor has his "Christian" pastor, the Reverend Wright, done.

As for what I am: I think that Mohammed was a mass murdering pedophile rapist who made up all that stuff about angels telling him the word of God. I think Jesus was

[539]https://www.hudson-ny.org/1636/riots-looting-chaos-france
[540]https://voxday.blogspot.com/2010/11/republican-irrelevance.html
[541]https://wtpotus.wordpress.com/2010/08/19/barack-hussein-obama-took-shahada/

making an honest and sincere effort to reform Judaism into a more peaceable faith, both for the general good and to protect Jews from getting squished by Romans, but the evasiveness of his prophecies reveal him to be a mortal.

"Nation shall rise against Nation, and Kingdom against Kingdom". And verily I tell unto you bears shall shit in the woods.

Jesus' prophecies for the fall of Jerusalem and temple were only marginally more impressive. He did not give an approximate date, nor tell us that the Romans would be the ones to do it – thereby keeping his ass covered against the possibility that Rome would fall before Jerusalem did – which ass covering reveals him to be a mortal, though it also suggests the books of the New Testament were written up before seventy AD. If they had been written up after the fall of Jerusalem, his prophecies probably would have been sharpened up a bit by the chroniclers. The argument that the New Testament must have been written after seventy AD is people irrationally hostile to Christianity going overboard in their desire to piss on Christianity. To cast doubt on Christianity, you merely have to cast doubt on the proposition that Jesus lives, not on the proposition that Jesus lived. The argument that the books of the bible were written long after the ministry of Jesus is an effort to disprove the existence of Jesus the man, which effort is silly – there is plenty of historical evidence that Jesus lived, preached, was crucified by Pontius Pilate, and stayed dead.

What I do believe in is that our senses give us straightforward access to reality as it really is, to things in themselves, that we are not trapped in Plato's cave because we can reach through the windows and break things apart to see what they are really made of, that with due care and competence, categories and concepts can be and should be constructed to correspond to the likeness and origins of particular things, reflecting commonalities between particular examples of real things. I believe that all words are defined by pointing at examples, or defined by other words that were defined by pointing at examples, that children rightly learn the meaning of words from the examples pointed at by their mothers, and that the ultimate authority of what words mean is the type examples provided by mothers and fairy tales to children – thus words mean what children think they mean, and not what ideologues and philosophers say they mean, that language, reality and the connection between language and reality are what children think they are.

While Obama is a Muslim, I not only doubt that he believes in Allah, but doubt that he believes that reality exists external to himself, or that words have any definite meaning.

Jihad watch reports Obama is Muslim

2010-11-08 08:33:57

Jihad watch reports on the anointed one's visit to India[542]:

> Obama is visiting ... a Muslim shrine. He has no plans to visit any holy places of the Sikhs (such as the Golden Temple, Amritsar), or any Hindu holy places, Buddhist holy places, or Jain holy places. Nor does he plan to

---

[542]https://www.jihadwatch.org/2010/11/obama-visiting-muslim-shrine-in-indiano-plans-to-visit-hindu-buddhist-or-other-shrines.html

visit Nariman house, the Chabad house in Mumbai that was the chief target of the jihad mass-murderers who killed 173 people in November 2008.

India is majority Hindu. All the faiths of India are in a state of war or near war with Islam, which conflict has within living memory been conducted at the level of full scale pogrom, mass murder, and full scale conventional military operations with tanks and columns of uniformed troops, as well as the more usual level of angry mobs and unconventional small scale operations deploying people out of uniform. Obama is being conspicuously rude to his Hindu hosts in visiting a Muslim shrine without visiting a Hindu Shrine.

Hyperinflation

2010-11-08 13:13:35

Officially, America has near zero inflation and a mere ten percent official unemployment. Odd that it has a mere ten percent unemployment when the proportion of young adult males with jobs has dropped a lot more than ten percent.

As with third world and Marxist countries, the government's reaction to bad news is to declare a new era of prosperity. The recession is officially over. With an unprecedented proportion of the workforce on the government payroll, productivity has officially risen to amazing heights and somehow, despite the big increase in the proportion of people on the government payroll, public spending has officially not risen much.

Unofficial inflation, however, is starting to look quite frightening:

Market Ticker tells us[543]:

> I just got back from the grocery store. Eggs, which were $1.60 two weeks ago, are now $1.99/dz. Butter? Two boxes for $6 - on sale. The same two boxes were $4.50 a couple months ago. Land-O-Lakes Brand? $4.89 - each. Cheese? 8oz bricks were commonly 3/$5 as recently as September. Now? $3.50 - for one.
>
> *But there's no inflation, you see.*
>
> Oh, and on the way home I passed the gas station. It was $2.59 for regular a couple of weeks ago. Now? $2.89. 30 cents in about 2 weeks, a 12% increase.

This is consistent with inflation rates of thirty to fifty percent per year, early hyperinflation rates.

Sarah Palin is, as usual, on the ball[544], while ruling class is floating away in La La Land, sincerely puzzled that the peasants are failing to eat cake.

This is the decisive test of Keynesianism. Of course, we already had a decisive test of Keynesianism: The Japanese crisis. Keynesianism failed dismally, to which the Keynesians replied that Japan's troubles were the result of not applying Keynesianism vigorously enough. This time, however, it has been applied vigorously enough. The results should

---

[543]https://market-ticker.org/akcs-www?post=171526
[544]https://www.nationalreview.com/corner/252715/palin-bernanke-cease-and-desist-robert-costa

be apparent by around 2012-2016. The fat lady has not yet sung, but so far, things are not looking good for Keynesianism.

Money is a matter of functions four,
a medium, a measure, a standard, a store.

There is a conflict between the use of money as a store and the use of money as a standard, since if everyone wants to store value at the same time, the value of money is apt to rise, and if everyone wants to use their store at the same time, the value is apt to fall. Keynesianism therefore addresses a real problem, but its proposed solution tells the ruling class what they want to hear – that they can buy votes with money they do not have, that they can eat their cake and have it to, which is of course not true, and not a solution to the problem. Keynesianism addresses a real problem, but is not a real solution.

It seems to me that a sounder solution would be to target the long run value of money. If people had confidence that in the long run, the value of money would be constant, that inflation would run for a few years to be followed by deflation, and deflation would run for a few years to followed by inflation, that what goes up must come down, then I doubt that natural fluctuations would be large or damaging. Fluctuations are large and damaging because there is no telling what the future value of money is likely to be, because Keynesianism makes money dangerously ineffectual as either a standard or as a store. This large uncertainty destabilizes the economy. The objective of monetary policy should be to give people confidence that the value of money will be the same in twenty or thirty years, even if it fluctuates a bit from year to year.

Of course, I am prescribing what an honest issuer of fiat money should do, if he cares about the long term, and wants everyone to continue using the fiat money he issues. Since issuers of fiat money sooner or later find themselves in a situation where the major question is whether the political leadership will survive another week, such advice is unlikely to be heeded. Keynesianism will continue to be believed, not because it is true, but because issuers of fiat money are compelled to act as if it was true.

The party of the state

2010-11-12 12:32:51

The number of federal workers earning $150,000 or more a year has doubled in the two years since President Obama took office

Update: Bill however argues this is less alarming that it seems:

> The big jump in % over $150K is all from the fact that the GS scale maxed out less than $150K in 2005 and over $150K in 2010. It's totally mechanical, an incident of drawing the line at $150K.

Britain goes totalitarian

2010-11-13 11:01:30

Sean Gabb, speaking very carefully to avoid saying things he could be arrested for, tell us[545]:

> Without thinking very hard, I can remember how Nick Griffin of the British National Party stood trial for having called Islam "a wicked vicious faith[546]". I can remember how a drunken student was arrested and fined for telling a policeman that his horse looked "gay[547]". I can remember how a man was arrested and charged and fined for standing beside the Cenotaph and reading out the names of the British war dead in Iraq[548]. I remember a case from this year where a pacifist unfurled a banner outside an army cadet training base. "Stop training murderers[549]", it said. His home was promptly raided by police with dogs, while a helicopter hovered overhead. He was arrested and cautioned. If I started mentioning the cases where Christian street preachers have been arrested for quoting the Bible, or where Moslems have set the police on people for alleged words or displays, or if I even alluded to the Public Order Act or the various racial and sexual hate speech laws, this article would swell immensely. It is enough to say that anything said in public is now illegal if someone complains to the police, or if the police themselves take against it. And, when something is not illegal, we are all getting used to the idea – second nature in most other countries – that we should "watch ourselves". Even I find that, if I discuss politics in a coffee bar, I sometimes drop my voice. A few weeks ago, I found myself looking round to see who might be within earshot.

How dumb is Obama?

2010-11-18 16:02:43

Obama is an affirmative action president. Affirmative action people are always stupid, incompetent, and corrupt. Is Obama stupid, incompetent and corrupt?

For corruption, observe that the infamous regulatory revolving door between Goldman and the Treasury continues to spin, even after the wall street financial system imploded, and similarly between Soros and the DoE. Perhaps Bush II was as corrupt as Obama, but Obama's corruption is more conspicuous.

As for stupidity – well clearly, he is a lot smarter than the most affirmative action blacks, such as his ivy league wife, and a lot smarter than the average white. But how does he compare with the elite?

---

[545] https://www.seangabb.co.uk/?q=node/358

[546] https://www.dailymail.co.uk/news/article-414343/BNP-leader-said-Islam-wicked.html

[547] https://mangans.blogspot.com/2005/06/man-arrested-for-calling-police-horse.html

[548] https://www.telegraph.co.uk/news/uknews/1515599/Protester-fined-for-naming-Gulf-war-dead-at-Cenotaph.html

[549] https://www.thisislondon.co.uk/standard/article-23796444-police-use-dogs-and-helicopter-to-swoop-on-pacifist-student.do

Recently an *anonymous* person who we are *told* is a Washington insider told us[550]
if you want to see President Obama get excited about a conversation, turn it to sports. That gets him interested. You start talking about Congress, or some policy, and he just kinda turns off. It's really very strange. I mean, we were all led to believe that this guy was some kind of intellectual giant, right? Ivy League and all that. Well, that is not what I saw. Barack Obama doesn't have a whole lot of intellectual curiosity. When he is off script, he is what I call a real "slow talker". Lots of ummms, and lots of time in between answers where you can almost see the little wheel in his head turning very slowly. I am not going to say the president is a dumb man, because he is not, but yeah, there was a definite letdown when you actually hear him talking without the script.

No – I am not going to call him stupid. He just doesn't strike me as particularly smart.

Well, so says an **anonymous** informant that we are **told** is a Washington insider.

So let us look at evidence whose veracity is easier to check:

We all know of his stumbles such as telling us that America has 57 states, and pronouncing corpsman "corpse man", but I am a very smart guy, and have done worse, and if I chide him on such things, will probably do something equally dimwitted in the same article as I chide him.

But I can fluently give a speech on complex topics from brief notes. Sarah Palin can fluently give a speech on complex topics from brief notes. Obama falls apart without a teleprompter. Without a teleprompter, he keeps it simple, and if lured onto complexity, starts to sound – black.

So, not stupid, but stupid by elite standards.

Intelligence is not the only requirement for a president. Blacks generally have more charisma than whites, more style, and are better able to think on their feet. Obama has more charisma and style than any major white politician, but now that the hype has faded away, it is apparent that he has not got much charisma and style by black standards. By black standards he is a bit of a nerd. Compare and contrast with most of the black republican candidates in recent mid terms. Most of them have lots of charisma. Blacks are also good at thinking on their feet, street smarts. Obama's ability to think on his feet is impressive. When the presidential seal fell off the podium, he ad libbed "It does not matter, you all know who I am" – but on more complex topics, considerably less impressive. Again, the Black Tea partiers gave a dazzling demonstration of ad libbing and thinking on their feet, considerably more impressive than that given by Obama. By black standards, Obama's ability to think on his feet is not all that impressive.

It looks to me that Obama was selected as the whitest possible black, rather than the black best qualified as a political candidate, that he was selected to prove there is no difference between whites and blacks, to prove that affirmative action does not give the results it so obviously does give. If you were selecting the black best qualified to win, you would come up with someone with a lot more charisma and street smarts than Obama, even at the cost of being a little bit dumber, you would come up with some one like the Tea Party candidates. Instead, they came up with someone as much as possible like a member of our very white elite, our very very white elite, the whitest possible dark skinned black.

---

[550]https://newsflavor.com/opinions/white-house-insider-on-obama-the-president-is-losing-it/

Hyperinflation coming, but not soon

2010-11-21 13:20:06

There is a lot of ruin in a nation.

Glen Bleck predicts catastrophic instant inflation completely collapsing the currency and government in a single two week crisis. That is not the way hyperinflation happens.

Hyperinflation consists of a series of hyperinflationary crises. In a hyperinflationary crisis, the value of money falls abruptly, typically to two thirds, half or a third of its previous value. The collapse occurs so suddenly that by the time most people realize that the hyperinflationary crisis has begun it, is already over.

And, after the crisis is over, people think normality is returning. After all, most of the government's debts have been inflated away. And sometimes normality does return. But usually the irresponsibility, criminality, and incompetence that led the government to run up unpayable debts is still present, so suddenly, when people least expect it, there is another hyperinflationary crisis. And then another. And another, until the government gets its act together or people just stop using its currency.

So when will the first hyperinflationary crisis hit? Europe is in worse shape than the US, and Europe still stands. So probably not for a few years.

Government probably will not collapse in the first hyperinflationary crisis, but there is a good chance it will collapse or undergo some fundamental change not long after. In 1994 I predicted governmental collapse around 2016, 2020, or 2025, or so. The American government has lasted a lot longer than most other governments, but there are numerous indications that its run is ending. That the buildings damaged or destroyed in the 9/11 attacks are still down is an omen, a manifestation of loss of cohesion and internal discipline withing the ruling elite. Park 51 cannot be repaired because to repair it needs permissions from lots and lots of authorities, and each authority wants the largest share of the vigorish.

Reflect on the proposed victory mosque at at Park 51. The factory at Park 51 suffered extensive damage in the 9/11 attack, due to parts the plane and parts of people landing on it, and could never be repaired or replaced, because any repair would require too many permissions from too many different authorities, each wanting the lion's share of the vigorish, so stands damaged and empty to this day, with bits of the 9/11 passengers still in it to this day.

But Imam Rauf, unlike the owner, has no trouble getting all the permissions he needs for a victory mosque, because if anyone creates difficulty for him, instead of paying off the bureaucrat making trouble, Imam Rauf drops a gentle hint that if Rauf does not get what he wants, some other Muslims, immoderate Muslims quite unlike the wonderfully moderate Rauf, might blow up the offender. Rauf, of course, understands that Islam is the religion of peace, but if he does not get what he wants, might inspire some of those dreadful misunderstanders of Islam to blow you up.

In the final stages of state decline, presaging final collapse, broader and broader state power, the power to destroy, is delegated to more and more people subject to less and less state discipline. Patent trolls are merely one more consequence of irresponsible judges with too much power and not enough restraint, and irresponsible overpowered judges are merely one more consequence of the expanding bureaucracy and regulatory apparatus that has prevented the towers from rising again.

The left rules, but like the Soviet Party, has lost faith in itself: Mencius remarks:[551]

Over a century ago, Lecky[552] found the core of liberalism in his portrait of Gladstone[553]:

Passion and casuistry seem naturally incompatible, but in Gladstone they were most curiously combined.

The perfect leftist is the fanatical hypocrite. While his beliefs correspond precisely to his own advantage, he believes in them furiously just the same. His opportunism does not even slightly detract from his sincerity, which is palpable and enormous. Indeed, if the situation changes and so do his interests, his mind will change as well. And change sincerely.

Alas, this character is easier to describe than find. In the day of Gladstone, liberalism was young and crazy and full of juice. Today? The movement exudes the overwhelming odor of fatigue. It remains both fanatical and hypocritical - but not in one person. Its fanatics, who could be broadly described as the amateur left, are devoid of any tactical cunning. And its hypocrites, who despite Robert Gibbs[554] constitute the professional left, are as passionless as an eggplant.

They try to care. They moan, they gasp, they writhe. But their eyes are dead, whore eyes. Now that we've seen it in the White House, we'd know it anywhere. You have to be an awfully blind fanatic not to see what you're looking at. Can the amateur left, the audience, the chumps who buy the magazines, find a professional leftist who actually cares about his ideals? They'll need a much brighter lantern than it took to find B.H. Obama.

In 2010, there is nothing fresh about the revolution industry. The idealistic professional leftist is the exact counterpart of the romantic porn star - a human impossibility. A porn star is a prostitute. It's simply impossible for a prostitute to feel, or even simulate, normal sexual passion. If any ordinary, amateur leftist were somehow transported into the White House, "enhanced patdowns" and Afghan wars would end tomorrow. But once a pro, always a pro. And who gets elected, but a pro?

And why has the ruling elite lost faith? The gate keepers to the elite demand proof of sincere radical leftism before anyone can be allowed in, require a demonstration of sincere leftism so extreme that no genuine leftist is likely to manifest it:

Gonzalo explains in Selecting for Cynicism in the Ivy League[555]

[551] https://unqualified-reservations.blogspot.com/2010/11/lightworker-wants-to-touch-your-junk.html
[552] https://en.wikipedia.org/wiki/William_Edward_Hartpole_Lecky
[553] https://books.google.com/books?id=L9hwqF0uEw0C&pg=PR30#v=onepage&q&f=false
[554] https://thehill.com/homenews/administration/113431-white-house-unloads-on-professional-left
[555] https://gonzalolira.blogspot.com/2010/11/selecting-for-cynicism-in-ivy-league.html

Chatting with my new classmates on my first day in Hanover, I quickly learned that none of this do-goodism was genuine. That wasn't my verdict— it was the verdict of my peers: The very ones who had done all this do-goodism admitted to me that it was not genuine—had never been genuine.

...

But community service or volunteer work was key: Any student serious about getting into an Ivy simply had to do community service or volunteer work.

Four years of high school meant eight "community service" extra-curriculars— one per semester. Anything more would seem like you were a "dabbler", and therefore "weren't serious". But anything less would show a "lack of commitment", which was equally bad. And the extra-curriculars had to be more or less aligned: You couldn't read to blind people one semester and then go save the whales in the next. Rather, you had to work on saving the whales in one semester, and then volunteer to work on an organic farm in the next: That showed you were "environmentally aware". Or else you had to tend a soup kitchen for the homeless, then read to the elderly in the next semester: That showed you were "socially engaged".

My fellow Dartmouth students, as well as students at all the other Ivies that I would get to know over the years, did all this do-goodism as a requirement, in order to get into a good school—an Ivy League school.

They did it in order to get ahead—and they were openly encouraged to do it: Not just by their parents, but by their high-school guidance counselors, their college prep advisors, even the visiting admissions deans of the very universities they were applying to—

—it was simply part of the admissions process: "It's like taking calculus," I still remember a girl named Debra, from Nebraska, telling me on the bus ride back to Hanover from Moosilauke Lodge. "You have to grind it out, and get it over with."

In 1985 I predicted the Soviet Union would fall, because the party had lost the faith.

A ruling elite sticks together, and presents a united face to all their inferiors. A ruling ideology, a theocratic state, like the Soviet Union, like the leftist ruled west, is a state where the elite derives its cohesion from shared belief. And when the theocrats no longer believe, the state will collapse at the first serious challenge.

Like Hell There's No Inflation

2010-11-22 09:04:15

Business Insider tells us:

Post Raisin Bran goes from 2.50 to 3.00 per box at Walmart.
My favorite yogurt goes from .50 to .58 each at Walmart.
Cherry tomatoes go from 4.98 to 5.98 per package.
Walnuts go from 9.98 to 13.98 per bag at Sam's.
Bottom round goes from 2.48 to 2.68 per pound at Sam's.

Al Dente tells us[556]

> What was once purchased for weekly meals at the supermarket for under $100, now exceeds $120. We have cut back on many items and we still pay more for our weekly food bill.

Econbrowser, however, tells us everything is coming up roses[557]:

> If the expectations hypothesis of the term structure (EHTS) holds, then these movements imply that as of 11/8, the average inflation rate over the next five years will be a breathtaking 1.6%!

Here is a free clue for Econbrowser: The tips market does not predict what the inflation rate will be. It predicts what the government will *report* the inflation rate to be - and indeed, the government is going to *report* near zero inflation during the next five years – because the government thinks you are stupid.

Losing to Islam

2010-11-25 08:57:14

Parapundit discovers that 130 000 US soldiers have suffered brain damage[558] in Iraq and Afghanistan.

This is far too high a price. We have to defeat Islam, but cannot do it this way. We have use methods that inflict much higher costs on Islam, at much lower cost to ourselves.

Decline of the west

2010-11-26 05:49:18

The last man on the moon left in 1972

The tallest building in the united states was finished in 1974.

Cars are becoming humbler.

US electricity production was growing exponentially until 1972. After 1972 it grew more slowly. Per capita electricity consumption seems likely to have peaked around 2007 or so[559].

Supposedly GDP is still growing rapidly, just as supposedly inflation is zero, but it seems improbable that GDP is growing when per capita electricity consumption is not.

---

[556]https://www.aldenteblog.com/2010/11/bacon-math.html

[557]https://www.econbrowser.com/archives/2010/11/inflation_fears_1.html

[558]https://www.eurekalert.org/pub_releases/2010-11/miot-msa111810.php

[559]https://www.eia.doe.gov/emeu/aer/pdf/pages/sec8_5.pdf

One could present all sorts of rationalizations for the decline in manned space exploration - for example that manned space exploration was a polite way of demonstrating superior capability to nuke the other side, and supposedly we are so much more civilized and mature now that the need for such chest beating has diminished.

However, by 2000, we have more compelling evidence of decline. The buildings damaged or destroyed in 9/11 have not been repaired or replaced.

The west is the past. America sinks into Eurosocialism, while Europe becomes the western satrapies of the new Persian empire. Every rising civilization was a lender, innovator, and investor, every declining civilization a borrower. California used to be the place where the future was invented, but no longer.

The west's lead was California's lead. And California is no more.

Where, for example, was the netbook commercialized? Who invented and built the "Amazon" Kindle? Who is today creating the blue light lasers that are the core of every DVD reader and writer?

The Kindle was developed in Taiwan, by Eink. It is some standard computing parts wrapped around a new display technology invented, developed and manufactured by Eink.

Indians looking to study abroad rate Melior in Singapore higher than Stanford in the USA.

Today, our universities turn out people trained in political correctness and "diversity". Every male CS graduate can parse a boolean expression, but most female CS graduates cannot, indicating that a male needs to be able to parse a boolean expression to get a CS degree, and a female does not. The end stage of this process is that no one needs to be able to parse a boolean expression, but everyone needs to be able to hate dead white males.

China leads the world in coal to liquids technology.

China leads the world in internet based transactions.

The simplest explanation for the fact that western research seems to have fallen off a cliff is that we are now reaching the point where hating dead white males is a more important academic qualification than anything else. Doubtless it is in reality more complicated than that, but the simplest explanation works quite well: Consider, for example, the recent demonization of Chagnon. The most striking factor was the ignorance and stupidity of the academic associations condemning him. They just did not know stuff. It was as if they don't read books by dead white males, as if they feared that reading such stuff might contaminate their minds with dangerous thoughts.

What we have had for some time in academia is theocracy, not meritocracy, and theocracy tends to promote those whose faith is most zealous and reliable. It is easier to have zealous and reliable faith if you are dumb as two planks glued together.

Who is at the top of Academia: I suppose the tip top crust are the people who condemned Chagnon, and people like the leading scientists of global warming, Mann and Phil Jones, who are demonstrably not nearly as smart as I am. Mann, for example, keeps making ludicrous and amateurish mistakes in his statistics, and any time Phil Jones wants something scientific done, he summons a post grad, and tells the postgrad to produce a chart that proves such and such, suggesting that Phil Jones cannot produce such charts, nor tell if the chart actually does prove such and such.

Mann's work demonstrates he is simply stupid. Mann's power over other scientists demonstrates that simply stupid people are on top. Stupid people on top provide a simple explanation of why science does not get done.

How did Mann get to the top? By telling the state what it wants to hear, by political correctness.

Demonstrably, the people in charge of science and research are **not** the tip top crust. They got where they are by hating dead white males more than anyone.

The fact that undergraduates are marked on the basis of race, gender, and political correctness is fairly harmless. That academics get power over other academics on the basis of political correctness has not been so harmless, and we are today paying the price, in that western research is failing.

Singapore has sustained its rate of growth. Taiwan has sustained its rate of growth. Therefore China is likely to sustain its rate of growth.

Assuming China grows like Singapore from now on, and the US grows like Europe (counting European growth as real, even though such growth as occurs is government employees, whose product is valued at cost, which cost grows at astonishing rate) then China should surpass the US in total GDP by 2019 or so.

China should surpass the US in GDP per head, as Singapore already has, by around 2045 or so. Taiwan should surpass the US in GDP per head in 2018 or so.

The financial system of the west is collapsing because the fed and its bureaucrats have the mission to replace financial panics with wise regulatory authority - which might work if wise regulatory authority had the will to punish elite wrongdoing the way financial panics did, and resist the desire of politicians to use the financial system as a piggy bank for vote buying the way bankers threatened by financial panics did. Since brave regulators are not to be found, the replacement is not working.

The last time the west stalled, it stalled for four hundred years under intellectual stagnation induced by theocracy, from 1277 to 1648.

We are seeing multiple simultaneous crises. Academia is a thousand loudspeakers controlled by one microphone, and that microphone in the hands of an idiot.

All the massive financial crime that the financial crisis exposed[560] continues unpunished and unabated, foreshadowing another, even bigger financial crisis coming up fast.

The graffiti on the buildings that are now owned by the Federal Reserve foretells our future.

We are also seeing an explosive gold rush in government as rent seeking monopolies multiply. Thus it used to be, for example, that the local council gave itself a monopoly of water and sewage, though there is in practice no rationale for the sewage monopoly - septic tanks and highly localized sewage farms are more economical. Large centralized sewage facilities beloved of councils and council unions suffer severe diseconomies of scale due to the high cost of piping sludge any reasonable distance. Seeing the lucrative flow of money, every other level of government gets into the act. Just as to get anything done, a private individual needs multiple permits from the council, each requiring him to hire numerous "consultants" at $400 per hour, the council needs multiple permits from state and federal governments, requiring the council to hire numerous "consultants" at $100

---

[560]https://blog.reaction.la/economics/mortgage-fraud-predatory-borrowing.html

000 per hour. The tip is emitting methane! Oh the horror. Someone official comes to officially look at the methane, charges $100,000 for looking, and issues an enforceable "recommendation" for an open ended and indefinite series of remediation measures, each of which will require another look.

Oh what did we do before there were people to officially and highly scientifically investigate the fact that tips are apt to pong? What would we do without government to supervise government? And surely any problems that might occur can be easily remedied by providing yet another layer of regulatory authority to regulate the regulators that are regulating the regulators that are regulating the local council.

This, like the housing boom is unsustainable. A single monopoly will charge inefficiently high prices and produce inefficiently low product, which is indefinitely sustainable. Multiple layered monopolies suffer a coordination problem that results in them charging infinite prices and producing zero product, as each attempts to get the majority of the squeeze.

This problem is remediable only through collapse or foreign conquest. As I have remarked several times, the reason that Dubai can build high towers and we no longer can, is that in Dubai, you only need the approval of one theocrat and one holy religion.

I hope for collapse, since foreign conquest is likely to be unpleasant. Last time around, however we had stagnation for four hundred years. Collapse would be preferable.

Democracy is self destructing, as it inexorably moves further and further to the left - the fate of the past democracies of Athens and Rome.

The war with Islam was lost on the playing fields of Sidwell Friends

2010-11-28 08:53:05

Roissy reports how when the Washington school to which the elite send their children made a poor sporting performance, their response to losing was childish, unsporting, and unmanly.

Pajamas Media reports[561] how unsportsmanlike attitudes are inculcated, and masculinity treated as a mental defect caused by testosterone poisoning.

If the Battle of Waterloo was won on the playing fields of Eton, America was lost on the playing fields of Sidwell Friends.

The childish and unmanly response of the kids from Sidwell Friends very much reminds me of the unmanly British response to military defeat in Basra.

Hurray for wikileaks

2010-12-02 03:33:34

We need to spy on the state. The state is our enemy. The government reads our emails. We should read theirs.

---

[561]https://pajamasmedia.com/blog/it%E2%80%99s-how-you-play-the-game-the-fate-of-western-civilization-and-grade-school-soccer/

I notice a lot of conservatives weeping big salt tears and calling for the assassination of Julian Assange because Wikileaks stole a pile of letters from the US government and made them public, Yet most of the letters in the latest leak reveal that the US government is run by leftists at every level from top to bottom, and thus most of the interesting, newsworthy, and embarrassing letters make leftists look bad and Obama look crazy. What is not to like?

This wikileak good for the US

2010-12-04 03:27:58

Pajamasmedia argues the leak is bad[562] for the US

> The fact is, the WikiLeaks drop gravely hurts the U.S., not so much in what's in the documents but in the disclosure itself. Imagine the U.S., China, Iran, Russia, North Korea etc etc all around a high-stakes poker table. WikiLeaks just took America's cards out of her hands and plopped one of them on the table, while keeping the rest of them for its own use. WikiLeaks has not done the same to the other players. This asymmetrical disclosure helps the other powers and hurts us, just by the fact that we don't control our cards anymore, and they still control theirs. We should be afraid of the unforeseeable and unintended consequences that this disclosure is bound to have. To not fear this is to not be prudent in the job of statecraft.

Well that would be true if the government was pursuing the interests of the US, but on the face of it, what is in Wikileaks suggests that the US government is pursuing the interests of the regnant left as an interest group, the interest of the Cathedral, that the government of the US does not much like America or Americans, that it thinks we are a bunch of stupid selfish white trash rednecks who pollute the earth and oppress and exploit the rest of the world, that it is just gut level hostile to ordinary Americans in flyover country, that the government is left wing elitist, regnant left, at the top and at every level.

Your government just does not like you. And electing politicians who do like you would not change much, because the real government is the permanent bureaucracy, whose conduct and policies is largely unaffected by the outcome of elections.

Anthropology stops pretending

2010-12-04 13:45:57

Anthropology stops pretending to have contact with reality, and positions itself as pure brainwashing[563].

---

[562]https://pajamasmedia.com/blog/gibbs-to-wikileaks-we-aint-scared-of-you/
[563]https://www.mindingthecampus.com/originals/2010/12/rigobertas_revenge_the_implosi.html

If Keynesians believed what they say they believe ...

2010-12-05 16:14:19

Nobel prize winning economist Krugman tells us we need stimulus, that is to say, more deficit spending. Government needs to spend more to stimulate the economy, he tells us.

Government spending puts money in peoples pockets. Then they spend stuff, so people get hired to produce stuff, so the newly employed get money too. Being employed rather than unemployed, they will produce and spend. So when the economy is in recession, government spending on pretty much anything is the best investment there can be – or so Keynesians tell us, so Nobel Prize winning economist Krugman tells us.

Despite the government vigorously applying the remedy that Krugman so enthusiastically recommended, the US economy is still in obviously in recession, not withstanding official government statistics that assure us that everything is coming up roses. Krugman tells us this is because the government did not spend enough. It needed to spend more. Spending cuts are destructive, they are economic illiteracy. That some republicans suggest spending cuts when unemployment is so high shows us that they are ignorant cavemen, unlike the highly sophisticated and knowledgeable Nobel Prize winning economist Krugman

But if a Keynesian believes in Keynesianism, should not he believe that tax cuts are better than spending increases? There is after all no such thing as a shovel ready project. Government spending programs take many years to get moving, and once moving tend to grow unstoppably. If the government has to manage the total level of demand, stimulating it in recession, cutting in booms (though somehow Keynesians never seem to think that a cut is necessary in booms) then taxes, which can be swiftly and easily raised and lowered, are the instrument to do it, rather than spending which cannot be quickly increased, and once increased, can never be cut.

If spending cuts in times of high unemployment are economic illiteracy, should not tax rises in times of high unemployment also be economic illiteracy?

Apparently not. According to Nobel Prize winning economist Krugman Republicans are economic illiterates for proposing cuts *and* they are economic illiterates for opposing tax rises[564].

If Keynesians actually believed Keynesianism was true, they would advocate tax cuts whenever unemployment was too high – and since a Keynesian never thinks unemployment is too low, they would advocate tax cuts day in and day out.

about one third banksters, two thirds ...

2010-12-06 14:06:01

The crisis is about one third theft by banksters, one third theft by rude, arrogant, and uncivil civil servants, and one third theft by the bastard spawn of welfare moms.

The split is not between rich and poor, but between tax consumers and tax payers.

I have emphasized the role of affirmative action loans in this crisis, and on the evidence, the great majority of the American dud loans were made to Hispanics – though it

---

[564]https://www.nytimes.com/2010/09/17/opinion/17krugman.html

was highly profitable for the wealthy banksters to arrange these dud loans, take the fees, and pass the loans onto someone else, and it was highly profitable for middle class loan offices to fill out the loan documents with whatever story would get the loan made, and then have the applicant sign a pack of lies that he was quite incapable of reading.

To which people reply by pointing at the crisis in Europe, where affirmative action lending is not a big problem. So in Europe, the problem is supposedly all banksters.

No it is not all banksters: The breakdown on the latest Irish bailout is[565] thirty five billion to bail out the banks, and fifty billion "to shore up the public finances and allow the government to keep making welfare payments and cover other expenses such as health and education."

So the stupid violent bastard spawn of Irish welfare mums are getting a major chunk of the loot, even though by a different mechanism to the way the stupid violent bastard spawn of American welfare mums got a major share of the loot.

The underlying mechanism of the crisis is that the regnant left (the Cathedral) buys as many votes as it needs to stay in power. As its internal discipline breaks down, it becomes more and more corrupt, hence more and more expensive, requiring ever greater expenditures on vote buying. To buy votes as cheaply as possible, it prefers low intelligence semi criminal immigrants and bastard welfare spawn, since their votes cost less, so sets about flooding society with low intelligence immigrants and bastard welfare spawn.

This does not mean there is any possibility that elections could fix the problem - there was no daylight visible between Bush and Obama, and very little daylight visible between Obama and Palin. Rather, what it means is that the measures that are taken to ensure that elections cannot fix the problem are becoming increasingly drastic.

Julian Assange is a hero

2010-12-07 12:48:09

Yes, he is a leftist, but he is an enemy of the regnant left, an enemy of the state, an enemy of my enemy. Why are all these rightists complaining when Assange makes Obama look like a dangerous lunatic and the state department look like deluded religious fanatics? Are these rightists loyal to a government that is at every level composed of men who hate them and regard them as enemies? Apparently so.

What took down the Roman Catholic theocracy was not the light of reason, not the enlightenment, but bigoted religious zealot theocrats like Martin Luther, who were rebelling because the Church was not theocratic enough. Julian Assange is one of those rebel theocrats.

Julian Assange's most important accomplishment was not leaking a pile of private emails that show our masters speaking unspeakable truths that no one speaks in public. What I found more disturbing was how often the cables were bland, how often they sincerely believed their deluded lies. What I found disturbing was not that these diplomats sometimes spoke the truth, but that they usually did not, that while hereditary aristocrats and monarchs can usually see the truth and are apt to speak it, and foreign politicians can sometimes see it and sometimes speak it, American diplomats can seldom see the truth

---

[565] https://www.guardian.co.uk/business/2010/nov/28/ireland-bailout-contribution-pensions

even when it is right in front of them. The cables are shocking not because they reveal what was unknown, but because they sometimes reveal what everyone know but no one says – but far too often, the cables are not shocking, far too often they reveal a theocracy that piously and sincerely believes in its official religion, far too often the cables reveal a frightening *lack* of hypocrisy.

Julian Assange's most important accomplishment was rubberhose[566], the predecessor to truecrypt[567]. In the long run, it is more effective to change society by changing the tools through which people interact, than by direct confrontation with the state. The state exists only because people think it exists, and is therefore far more fragile than it seems.

Julian Assange's "rape"

2010-12-09 06:10:45

Roissy has the details: The Assange "Rape": A Case Of SpurnedGroupies[568]

These girls, excited by his internet fame, pursued him, stalked him, and jumped his boner. He pumped them and dumped them both. Upon discovering they had been dumped and that he had banged them both, they then claimed rape – not on the basis that he had coerced them, but on the basis that he had refused to wear a condom, had been banging them both, and had refused to keep on banging them – on the basis that he treated them the way famous people usually treat the numerous women that eagerly pursue them.

Political correctness kills

2010-12-10 17:34:19

Pajamas Media has a long list of notable and obvious terrorists, who, as moderate Muslims, were invited into the highest reaches of the US government[569].

They only tell stories of high terrorists in the bosom of authority, simultaneously in authority in the US government, and in authority in Al Quaeda, neglecting to mention lowlier foot terrorists who actually carry out the killing, for example Hasan: the first terrorist to give an academic lecture with Power Point – to an Army audience – explaining his intention to commit a terrorist attack against his audience for the glory of God and the destruction of the infidel.

Pajamas media piously tells us that it does not want to see Muslims profiled – oh no, heaven forbid, the horror, the horror – merely held to the same standards as normal people.

But, of course, that is exactly the problem. Because profiling is such a horrible sin, because making generalizations on the basis of available evidence is such a horrible horrible horrible sin, people are bending over backwards to avoid drawing the conclusion that

---

[566]https://iq.org/~proff/rubberhose.org/

[567]https://www.truecrypt.org/

[568]https://roissy.wordpress.com/2010/12/08/the-assange-rape-a-case-of-spurned-groupies/   "Permanent Link to The Assange """Rape""": A Case Of Spurned Groupies"

[569]https://pajamasmedia.com/blog/political-correctness-kills-study-shows-how-terrorists-infiltrate-u-s-government/

a particular Muslim is a terrorist when it is glaringly obvious that the particular Muslim is a terrorist.

Fear of profiling not only means we strip search and grope three year old girls from Pasadena. It means that we wave through people covered in a Burkha. There is no middle ground. If you allow people to use all available evidence, they are profiling. If you don't allow them to use all available evidence, there is no limit to what evidence they are required to ignore.

Leftist fratricide

2010-12-16 16:57:12

The unity of the left in part derives from room at the top, that the ruling elite promised endless expansion – government jobs, and quasi governmental jobs like "diversity training", "human resources", and "sensitivity training", jobs for which one must demonstrate adequate leftism as a entry requirement. As the west moves into financial crisis, there is a marked shortage of additional room at the top. In Britain, the expansion of the state has halted, or considerably slowed, a change misleadingly described as "drastic cuts". For those Britons expecting natural progression into government jobs and government created jobs, it certainly feels like they have been cut, that they have been abandoned to drop into the underclass. The end of endless expansion is, to them, indeed a "cut".

So anti establishment leftist Julian Assange exposes the establishment leftists in the state department. Rotund establishment leftist Michael Moore supports Julian Assange, pays his bail, and smirks and rolls his eyes when discussing the ludicrous sex charges against him[570]. Immediately ugly diesel dyke feminists are thrown into a frothing rage[571] by that smirk and eye roll and call Michael Moore a rape enabler.

The unity of the left is expensive, and starting to exceed the capability of states to pay. The left is therefore moving into a crisis analogous to the reformation. The reformation was a loss of unity in the theocracy which made the age of reason possible. Today's theocracy is suffering from a similar weakening.

On the other hand, Roissy, like Unwin, argues that rationalism can only dominate in a patriarchal society, for which proposition Oprah is plausible evidence.

High returns on IQ between countries, but low returns within country

2010-12-21 10:04:30

If we control for academic qualification, there is zero or negative return on IQ within a country. That is to say, of two people of different IQ but same country and the same academic qualification, the smarter one will have similar or lower socioeconomic success.

---

[570]https://theothermccain.com/2010/12/16/merry-christmas-america-feminists-attack-michael-moore-as-rape-apologist-over-swedish-case-against-julian-assange/

[571]https://tigerbeatdown.com/2010/12/15/mooreandme-on-dude-progressives-rape-apologism-and-the-little-guy/

If we do not control for academic qualification, IQ still does not make a very large difference. Of two people of very different IQ, but the same country, and academic qualifications typical for their IQ, the much smarter one will not be much richer

I think it likely that this is a manifestation of the observed fact that high IQ people tend to be nerds, socially low status, tend to get in trouble socially.

However, if we compare between countries, countries where people have slightly higher average IQ tend to be much more prosperous than similar countries with slightly lower average IQ.

A two standard deviation difference in an individual person's IQ predicts only about a 30% difference in his wage. But half a standard deviation difference in a country's average IQ score predicts a 200% difference in the average wage in that country.

Why do high IQ people do so badly?

Suppose you have a bunch of people together. And the crowd makes a mistake about X, or, which comes to much the same thing, a high status person in the crowd makes a mistake about X. The high IQ kid is going to say "X is wrong". But no one else in the crowd can tell whether X is right or wrong. They will think it is a matter of opinion, like what flavor of icecream is better, or a matter of authority, an arbitrary rule decreed by someone, and this kid is wrongfully claiming authority to decree that rule.

And will conclude that the smart kid is inappropriately throwing his weight around, is acting inappropriately for his status, they will be insulted, offended, and angered at what they incorrectly perceive as a claim of status and authority. And so will attempt to correct his swelled head, will tell him his status is low, and his status claim inappropriately high.

So the smart kid in the group, like the stupid kid in the group, is going to wind up at the bottom - and very likely with an income to match. The high IQ kid is going to be a social failure in a group where the majority is stupid.

In the kingdom of the blind, the one eyed man is at the bottom.

So if you want society to be run by smart people, that society has to stream the kids, group smart kids with smart kids, and dumb kids with dumb kids, and get its leadership from the leadership that emerges from leading the smart group.

If, on the other hand, society thinks that everyone should go to university, and the elite universities select their students primarily on political correctness and cultural similarity to the existing elite rather than smarts, then your society is going to wind up being run by people who are not much brighter than average, and most of the wealth and power is going to be in the hands of people who are not much brighter than average for that country.

The smart group will do well, but the smart individual will do badly. Thus a smarter country is much richer, but a smarter individual is little richer, and may well be be poorer.

It follows that the way for the smart kid to succeed is to get in with a smart group of about his own intelligence that is in charge of its own destiny, get in on the right track early, and the way for a country to succeed is to make the formation of such groups easy and natural.

The future is Muslim, Mormon, and Catholic

2010-12-25 07:42:05

Anglican Christmas church service, ten attend, eight with one foot in the grave. Sermon is about the other foot dropping.

Catholic Christmas church service, approximately one hundred attend, most of them young. Sermon is about Christmas being a time for children.

Some months ago I checked the graveyards. To judge by the absence of angels, graveyards one hundred percent protestant.

The end of the road to serfdom

2010-12-26 06:46:01

Hayek, in "The Road to Serfdom" predicted the welfare regulatory state must inevitably become the totalitarian terror state.

Observe: We have arrived. America is now a totalitarian terror state.

In 1992 I visited Cuba. Thereafter, I argued it was a totalitarian state, because when I asked certain questions some people fled, fearing that merely hearing the question would result in them being punished for the thoughts it might elicit, and others answered furtively.

Yesterday, I asked someone very close to me a question apt to have a politically incorrect answer (I cannot identify him further, for he swore me to secrecy)

He looked around furtively. We were on top of a hill overlooking the Coral Sea in a semi rural area, the other side of the world from his workplace. He lowered his voice. He then proceeded to utter a series of politically correct platitudes, with gestures and grimaces reversing their meaning, his grimaces implying the opposite of the ostensible meaning, the same sort of communication coded against possible eavesdroppers and hidden microphones that I encountered in Cuba, where they would swear loyalty to communism, while making a gesture of their throats being cut.

Like Havel's green grocer, the truth would destroy his career.

This is the behavior that in 1992 I saw in Cuba and thereafter used as evidence that Cuba was a totalitarian state, a state of omnipresent fear.

So if Cuba was totalitarian in 1992, America is totalitarian in 2010. We have arrived at the end of Hayek's "Road to Serfdom".

In America, unlike Soviet Russia, we don't send dissidents to Alaska, and although lots of American psychiatrists are eager to diagnose political deviation as mental illness and treat it with electroshock and lobotomy as they do in Cuba, government has as yet declined to employ them in this capacity. But what government does do is ensure that political deviation blights your career. If a company knowingly employs political deviants, it is apt to be sued by quasi governmental organization for a "hostile work environment", in which lawsuit, no evidence will be presented of anyone saying unkind things to those for which the work environment was supposedly hostile, but evidence *will* be presented that employees had subversive thoughts – often evidence that they expressed subversive thoughts far from their workplace, as perhaps on a hill overlooking the Coral sea the other side of the world from his workplace – so the company will be punished, for failure to punish subversive thoughts.

Hayek, in "The Road to Serfdom", argued that regulatory welfare state must inevitably become totalitarian. Lo and behold, totalitarianism has arrived. Most people, everyone with some position in society, everyone with something that could be taken away from them, are very, very frightened.

And what is totalitarianism? Hayek's totalitarianism seems to be pretty much Havel's totalitarianism, and here is Havel on totalitarianism:

> The manager of a fruit-and-vegetable shop places in his window, among the onions and carrots, the slogan: "Workers of the world, unite!"

> Why does he do it? What is he trying to communicate to the world? Is he genuinely enthusiastic about the idea of unity among the workers of the world? Is his enthusiasm so great that he feels an irrepressible impulse to acquaint the public with his ideals? Has he really given more than a moment's thought to how such a unification might occur and what it would mean?

> I think I can safely assume that the overwhelming majority of shopkeepers never think about the slogans they put in their windows, nor do they use them to express their real opinions. That poster was delivered to our greengrocer from the enterprise headquarters along with the onions and the carrots. He put them all into the window simply because it has been done that way for years, because everyone does it, and because that is the way it has to be.

> If he were to refuse, there could be trouble. He could be reproached for not having the proper decoration in his window; someone might even accuse him of disloyalty. He does it because these things must be done if one is to get along in life. It is one of the thousands of details that guarantee him a relatively tranquil life "in harmony with society," as they say.

> Obviously the greengrocer is indifferent to the semantic content of the slogan on exhibit; he does not put the slogan in his window from any personal desire to acquaint the public with the ideal it expresses. This, of course, does not mean that his action has no motive or significance at all, or that the slogan communicates nothing to anyone.

> The slogan is really a sign, and as such it contains a subliminal but very definite message. Verbally, it might be expressed this way: "I, the greengrocer XY, live here and I know what I must do. I behave in the manner expected of me. I can be depended upon and am beyond reproach. I am obedient and therefore I have the right to be left in peace."

> This message, of course, has an addressee: it is directed above, to the greengrocer's superior, and at the same time is a shield that protects the greengrocer from potential informers. The slogan's real meaning, therefore, is rooted firmly in the greengrocer's existence. It reflects his vital interests. But what are those vital interests?

Let us take note: if the greengrocer had been instructed to display the slogan 'I am afraid and therefore unquestioningly obedient,' he would not be nearly as indifferent to its semantics, even though the statement would reflect the truth.

The greengrocer would be embarrassed and ashamed to put such an unequivocal statement of his own degradation in the shop window, and quite naturally so, for he is a human being and thus has a sense of his own dignity. To overcome this complication, his expression of loyalty must take the form of a sign which, at least on its textual surface, indicates a level of disinterested conviction. It must allow the greengrocer to say, "What's wrong with the workers of the world uniting?"

Thus the sign helps the greengrocer to conceal from himself the low foundations of his obedience, at the same time concealing the low foundations of power. It hides them behind the façade of something high. And that something is ideology.

As Bruce Charlton points out[572]:

If you go into an institutional environment - a government office, a school or college, a hospital or doctor's surgery, a museum, public transportation - and you observe posters adorning the walls on politically-correct topics such as diversity, fair trade, global warming, approved victim groups, third world aid - remember Havel's essay, and that the correct translation of such posters is as follows:

"I am afraid and therefore unquestioningly obedient"

Such posters are a coded admission of submission to ideology - except in the rare instance where they advertise genuine corruption by ideology.

The frequency of such posters nowadays, compared with a generation ago, is a quantitative measure of the progress of totalitarian government.

astroturf "anarchism"

2011-01-02 04:17:59

The Belmont club reports on left "anarchism", taking the movement at face value, as if it was what it appears to be.

the purest and most uncompromising of which are the anarchists.

In fact, left anarchists are astroturf.[573] They are the government threatening those that would restrain its growth.

Repeating my previous post on the Greek riots:

---

[572]https://charltonteaching.blogspot.com/2010/08/vaclav-havels-poster-test.html
[573]https://blog.reaction.la/culture/the-left-as-astroturf.html

Observe the recent firebombings in the Greek riots, where the "rioters" murdered three people.

Here are a couple of videos of the "rioters" firebombing police.

The "rioters" charge the police, and bang on their shields with light sticks, making no attempt to jab through the gaps at the actual bodies of the cops, nor using sticks heavy enough to even shake the shields. No axe handles or baseball bats.

Hey guys, if you want to bang on armored cops, I have a sledgehammer that would make a pretty good mace. It goes through concrete mighty fast.

They then fall back, and hurl firebombs[574] – but they do not not hurl firebombs at the police, but at the ground in front of the police. One cop gets one of his boots splashed with burning petrol. He rolls around, and a couple of other cops put him out. In the second video[575], same scene shot from a different angle, we observe that the cops make not the slightest attempt to arrest the firebombers for attempted murder, and the rest of the mob for assault and as accessories to attempted murder. It is all theater. When they see that one of the firebombs has actually hit, the theater pauses.

When right wing militia listens politely to an FBI provocateur provocateur at a meeting proposing that they bomb someone, they all go to jail for plotting crimes. The "rioters" firebomb a cop, and everyone acts like it is an unfortunate accident – which of course is exactly what it is.

The "rioters" in the Greek riots are government employees put on the streets by government sponsored unions that are themselves as much part of the government as the police were.

The evil empire

2011-01-03 09:13:14

Wikileaks Cable 10Paris58[576] reveals the extent of US rule over Europe. If Europe is further left than the US, broker than the US, and more @%# than the US, this primarily that the American ruling elite has a freer hand in ruling Europe than in ruling the US, due to the US constitution, and the American tradition of liberty.

In Cable 10Paris58, the writer announces that France is insufficiently left wing, therefore an American program of intervention in French internal affairs is required to move France further left.

"Gay Pride" is another illustration of the same process. When the US implemented "Gay Pride" in the US, it implemented "Gay Pride" world wide. And what is a gay pride parade called in Spanish? el día del Orgullo Gay

The use of the American neologism "Gay" reveals who is calling the shots, who planned and organized this event.

Let us reflect on Aristide's rule in Haiti:

The US intervened in Haiti to install Aristide at gunpoint *and it also intervened in Haitian society and culture to* convince Haitians that this was a good thing, was benevolent

---

[574]https://www.youtube.com/watch?v=Y-ZNilpmH5E
[575]https://www.youtube.com/watch?v=KDU1-1_xUMc
[576]https://190.224.163.182/wikileaks/cable/2010/01/10PARIS58.html

and progressive[577].

The US demanded an election. It then demanded an election rigged in Aristide's favor. He won, was overthrown. US demanded with threat of violence that he be reinstated. He was reinstated again, overthrown again. US invaded, installed him on the presidential throne with the guns of US marines, and, just to make sure Aristide did not get up to any mischief, surrounded him with an ***all white praetorian guard***.

You will probably read all over the internet and the mainstream media that the numerous occasions in which Aristide was removed from power were evil American plots by evil America to deprive Aristide of his immensely popular and well deserved power. Each of the supposedly anti American sources saying that stuff is a US state department muppet – someone from the state department has his arm up the speaker's @$$ and his fingers are moving the speaker's lips – pretty much in the way the praetorian guard were moving Aristide's lips.

They are indeed anti American - because the US state department and the US ruling elite is anti American.

Just look at the races of the actors. The people who installed Aristide were white Americans. The people who guarded him were white people of undisclosed nationality. (Not all that undisclosed - when everything fell apart, Aristide's praetorians were rescued from black Haitians by the US marines) The people Aristide fled were black Haitians.

It is not the Joos, it is Harvard and the State Department, not a sinister Jooish plot, it is a sinister Harvard plot. It is a government conspiracy to impose more government on those who can least resist it - the French being less able to resist than Americans, and the Haitians being less able to resist than the French.

The 1994 intervention in Haiti is not in itself all that important, Haiti being just a small pimple, but it is important in what it reveals - like Cable 10Paris58[578] it reveals the true face of US imperialism.

Anti semitism

2011-01-07 08:27:09

As Moldbug tells us:

> Anti semitism is the faulty, paranoid, and obsessive belief that Jewish elites
> are significantly different from gentile elites.

Jews, as Jews, simply were not an are not influential in the development of the theocracy that ruled us. Jews really do not matter so much, so any belief system that causes one to focus on Jews sends one crazy, detaches one from reality. If we look at the elite and bad conduct by the elite, and start asking:
"Who is a JOO? Look I see a JOO! See the JOO!" then we are apt to attribute to the elite an ethnic solidarity that it conspicuously lacks. The elite is disproportionately Jewish, and hates Jews, entirely white, and hates whites, mostly anglophone, and hates anglophones, mostly American, and hates Americans and America.

---

[577] https://www.google.com/search?q=%22Operation+uphold+democracy%22+psyop
[578] https://190.224.163.182/wikileaks/cable/2010/01/10PARIS58.html

Before any Jew was allowed to get anywhere near the reins of power, he had to convert to progressivism, or plausibly pretend to. Lots of them did so, as the progressive theocrats intended, which was highly beneficial for those Jews that converted and ascended, but a disaster for Judaism, and none too good for the Jewish people as a people.

Progressivism is an American branch of left protestantism, which sought theocratic power, in particular wanted all educational institutions to inculcate all children, especially Jewish and Catholic children, in their religion. Since the American constitution forbade this, they over time, ditched Christ, ditched redemption, and in large part ditched God. This started in 1900 or so and was largely completed by the time they were running reeducation, denazification and anti-colonialism.. They retained, however, a great pile of Christian and specifically protestant beliefs that are incompatible with Judaism as a religion, a culture, and a society. If Jews were influential as Jews, progressivism would be post Jewish, rather than post Christian. But progressivism is, in practice, a post Christian heresy from Christianity.

For an example of the post christian character of progressivism, consider the ludicrous progressive belief that all people are equal in ability and virtue and so forth, which is what remains of the Christian belief that all people are equal in the sight of God, after God and Christ have been removed from the belief system.

The proposition that men and women are literally equal, that races are equal, leading to the conclusion that they are interchangeable, that women can be soldiers and firemen, men can marry other men, can only be understood as proposition about souls, rather than bodies, and when this doctrine is doubted, the reaction is religious rather than empirical. Understood as a species of Christian belief, it makes sense, because the Christians believe that the most important part of the self is immaterial. If it's immaterial, then material differences have nothing to do with it. So Christians are free to believe pretty much anything they want about this most important part of the self, unconstrained by material evidence of any sort. They are free to believe that deep inside everyone, there is a core, an essence, that is not the slightest diminished by bodily infirmity etc. etc. I.e., the soul. The progressives jettison God, replacing God with, presumably, Nature. So "equality before God" becomes "equality before Nature". That is, natural equality (of some unspecified sort). And this could be how the progressives manage to believe in some unspecified "natural" (biological or whatever) equality even though no evidence backs them up. Their belief is derived, not from evidence, but from the Christian heritage of progressivism. Their belief looks superficially like a scientific hypothesis because all the terms in it could be interpreted as referring to natural things, but it doesn't really have any empirical content, because "equality", while it could refer to something measurable, does not actually refer to anything measurable. Any attempt to measure something to test the claim of "equality" is attacked by progressives.

Progressives are using naturalistic-sounding words to talk about equality, but they are behaving as though it didn't make any sense to try to measure it, which is how Christians would behave with respect to attempts to rigorously test equality before God. The Christian reaction would range from skepticism that it could be done, to the sense that it doesn't even make sense to try, and finally to the certainty that it is heresy to even suggest such a thing and the person suggesting it is evil and possibly a sorcerer and should be burnt at the stake - and if you express doubt about natural equality, the progressive reaction you will get is not an appeal to empirical evidence, but condemnation and threats.

Progressivism is today influential world wide, and everywhere it is primarily American. For example "Gay pride" was applied throughout Europe often before it was applied in America, but with made in America propaganda, directly translated and retain American idioms, and often American neologisms, such as "Gay" as the new euphemism for homosexual; the hand of the master was visible; the muppet's lips were moving, but the voice was not that of a local. Similarly American schoolchildren are taught about America, and are primarily taught that America is the most evil nation in the world, and German schoolchildren are also taught about America, and are primarily taught that America is the most evil nation in the world.

But, I hear you ask, if the Cathedral, the progressive ruling elite, is primarily American, rather than Jewish, why is it so maniacally anti American? Why you, ask, do they hate people like you and me. Surely that they hate Americans shows they are not Americans, do not think of themselves as Americans, therefore must be Jews?

Alas, self hatred is depressingly common, and progressives hate themselves, and therefore hate everyone like themselves, and therefore they hate you, and hate me, for reasons I will now explain:

Central to Christianity is sin and redemption. Christians are held to a standard so high that they cannot possibly attain it, and even if they attained it, they are condemned by original sin; we are all sinners and should be ashamed and guilty. But the preacher offers us a way out. Accept Christ as Lord, Christ will forgive you, Christ loves you, Christ will shoulder the load. Yes, you are a sinner, but Jesus loves you. And thus, central to progressivism is sin. Progressives are held to a standard so high that we cannot possibly attain it, and even if we attained it, we are condemned by original sin in that we are beneficiaries of colonialism slavery racism and blah blah blah. But the sensitivity trainer cannot offer us a way out, since God is dead and Jesus never existed. And so progressives are required to hate themselves. And they do.

The Progressives, the Left, the Cathedral, does not hate non Jewish whites because it is disproportionately Jewish; it hates all whites because it is white and hates Jews disproportionately because it is disproportionately Jewish. It hates America and Americans because it is primarily American.

The most honest political ad of all time[579] illustrates the perils of the politically correct only listening to each other. When they speak, their purpose is not truth, but power – and since they understand power as meaning the capacity to harm, everything they say is a lie intended to harm the hearer – and since they listen respectfully, indeed worshipfully, to each other ...

The ruling elite is theocratic, hence the nickname "the Cathedral". Their religion is simultaneously altruistically self hating, as illustrated by environmentalism and the fact that the disproportionately Jewish elite hates Israel and Jews, yet contradictorily, at the same time nihilistic and cynical, with the Alinksyite approach that anything goes in the pursuit of power, a contradiction resolved in their own minds since they are pursuing total, limitless, and absolute power, not on their own behalf, but on behalf of the oppressed

---

[579]https://blog.reaction.la/global-warming/no-pressure-1010/

and downtrodden – they are doing it for the proletariat, for the colonized. And if the proletariat and
the colonized are so rude as to talk back to their betters, well then, they are doing it for the trees.

The Cathedral will destroy everything, starting with itself, just as the most honest political ad of all time[580] ended with the murder of the narrator. Its self hatred renders it powerless against more self confident theocracies, such as Islam, and its self destructiveness renders it incapable of holding power for very long even absent external enemies.

If the Jews were running things, we would have decent airport security like they have in Israel, instead of naked body scan and genital gropedown. If the Jews were running things, the CIA would operate more like Mossad and less like the Keystone Cops.

The antiprofiling fetish is a left superstition and ritual, derived from progressivism's Christian roots, not a Jewish superstition and ritual – so it is obvious who is in charge.

Similarly, Israel had no banking crisis, despite the fact that their banks are full of Jews, who are doubtless as crooked as bankers elsewhere: The reason there is no banking crisis in Israel is because banks in Israel did not make political loans to voter blocks and special interest groups notorious for not paying their debts; such loans being a progressive, rather than Jewish, superstition. And when the US government put the heat on banks around the world to buy mortgage backed securities, Israel "refused to support the world banking system". Since when did we have a *world* banking system? One worldism is a progressive superstition centered on the UN, and the UN hates Jews.

The left is lily white (as we saw at the "rally to restore sanity") and hates whites. The left is dominated and largely controlled by America and anglophones (as we saw with the export of the "gay pride" program to the non English speaking world) and hates anglophones and hates Americans most among anglophones. The left is disproportionately Jewish, and hates Jews.

We are not ruled by Jews. We are ruled by people who hate themselves and hate us and hate Jews most of all.

Here is the Bank of Israel's take on the Global financial crisis[581]: You will notice that while everyone else is lying about it, they are telling the truth:

> What are the factors that led to the global crisis?
>
> > The main factor that initiated the crisis was the accumulation of mortgages in default in the US as a result of the reversal of the trend of US housing prices. This occurred against the background of easy mortgages over a period of several years during which mortgages were provided to homebuyers who did not have sufficient ability to repay them. The losses spread to large financial institutions in a number of countries through the globalized financial markets, which facilitated the creation and marketing of complex financial instruments world wide. These instruments had a variety of terms to deal with default that had

---
[580] ../global-warming/no-pressure-1010.html
[581] https://www.bankisrael.gov.il/deptdata/pikuah/crisis_faq/crisise.htm

not been in use in the past and some of the instruments were sold and guaranteed by large financial institutions. Large investment houses worldwide held the view that advances in the study of finance had enabled a better understanding of these products and the correct valuation of the products and their guarantees. In retrospect, the risk assessment of these products was extremely deficient. Thus, significant losses were incurred by these large financial institutions and their customers. As a result, uncertainty regarding the financial stability of these institutions spread at a surprisingly quick rate and activity in the markets for more basic financial products-in which these same investment houses are active-was also affected.

How has the crisis so far affected the Israeli financial system relative to its effect on the financial markets and institutions in other advanced economies?

One of the main causes of the global financial crisis was the provision of mortgages, primarily though not exclusively in the US, to borrowers with insufficient ability to repay them. As a result, housing prices rose sharply in these countries, as did the prices of financial assets. When the financial institutions began to realize that they had provided mortgages to homebuyers with insufficient ability to repay them and these individuals were forced to sell their homes, a downward trend began in the prices of houses that served as the collateral for not only sub-prime mortgages, but higher quality mortgages as well. The drop in the value of other assets also eroded the collateral for loans that were made by the financial institutions in these countries. These developments, together with the collapse of the markets for mortgage-backed securities, had a multiplier effect that among other things led to the collapse of several financial institutions in the US, the UK and Europe. The large-scale provision of such mortgages in these countries to individuals with insufficient means to repay them was not, however, characteristic of the Israeli financial system

You will observe that members of the Israeli elite can and do speak close to the the truth about the crisis, (the problem was mortgages to deadbeats) while members of the American elite, including their European muppets, cannot and do not. (Supposedly the problem was "excessive leverage".) Thus the financial crisis was brought to you by progressivism, not by the Jews, despite the disproportionate presence of Jews in finance and financial regulation.

Gabrielle Giffords needed killing

2011-01-09 11:47:15

And so do most of congress, most of the regulators, and most of the businessmen in the revolving door between business and regulation.

All the conservative criticism of her seems to be disappearing off the web, but what the hell, she stank, critics pointed out she stank, so someone killed her. It might have been a leftist who did not think she was left enough, but chances are, was a conservative. Yes, chances are that unkind remarks by conservatives got her killed. Pity it was not someone who mattered more. Her platform was to create lots of high paying jobs in government and quasi governmental activities - in other words, to transfer wealth from productive people who mostly voted against her, to unproductive people who mostly voted for her, thus moving the nation generally leftwards.

As the nation plunges into bankruptcy, as the Cloward–Piven crisis approaches, we might kill enough similar wrongdoers to eventually get out of the crisis. I don't really see any other path to resolving the crisis other than watering the tree of liberty in the usual fashion.

Gabrielle Gifford's shooter was a lefty

2011-01-11 06:27:24

Two down for the price of one!

I should have seen that he was a lefty from the fact he made no effort to escape. A rightist assassin would have attempted to cover his own ass.

He seems to have been an antisemite of Jewish descent – classic left wing crazy.

Right wing rhetoric probably contributed. The left's self hating identity crisis certainly contributed. But the root cause of rising tensions is the approaching Cloward–Piven crisis.

The root cause of the approaching Cloward–Piven crisis is that the government has purchased itself a left wing electorate, which electorate daily gets more expensive, and purchased left wing unity, which daily gets more expensive. A shakeout approaches. During that shakeout, some part of the left will be thrown overboard. The Cloward Piven strategy is that there will be a violent self coup in which that part of the left which is deemed insufficiently left wing will be thrown overboard – thus as little of the left as possible will be thrown overboard.

I would, of course, prefer a solution in which the established left was purged from government and quasi governmental institutions in the way that Germany was denazified. Check the resumes sent to every institution that is governmental or government backed. If some substantial proportion of the resumes give left wing credentials, then the institution should be suspected of being government sponsored leftism. If hiring practices favor those with left wing credentials, as for example the Department of Education, the Department of Energy, the NEA, the State Department, and so on and so forth, then the institution is a government sponsored leftist wing organization. The organization should be abolished, and membership of that organization should be treated the way membership of a Nazi organization was treated in postwar Germany.

The British government is trying something moderate, something in the middle between these revolutionary extremes, muddling through. It does not appear to be working, though early days yet, to soon to tell what the outcome will be.

To avoid or resolve the Cloward Piven crisis by normal constitutional and democratic means is going to look at least a little bit like the revolutionary de-leftification strategy I outlined above, modeled on de-nazification, for the basic problem is that a left wing electorate, and left wing unity, costs too much. Even the ultra leftist Cloward–Piven strategy, of resolving the crisis with a left wing self coup, has a little bit of de-leftification in it. After the Cloward–Piven self coup, some leftists who are at present the recipients of large amounts of government largess, are going to find themselves re-defined as rightists and cease being recipients of government largess.

Curious cuddles between the Cathedral and Islam

2011-01-11 15:26:00

If someone is a called a "moderate Muslim", he is probably part of the establishment, part of our ruling elite, or spends much of his day in their circles.

If someone is a Muslim, and part of our ruling elite or close to it, he is probably a terrorist, or spends much of the rest of his day in their circles.

There is at most one degree of separation between the elite, and Islam. In contrast, there are several degrees of separation between the elite, and conventional Christianity.

Exhibit A in this story is Abdul Rahman al-Amoudi, who spent a great deal of time walking and talking with US presidents Clinton and Bush and the usual parade of the good and the great – and who also addressed terror rallies demonizing the US. In 2004 was an unindicted co-conspirator in a plot to assassinate the man who is now King of Saudi Arabia. So Abdul Rahman al-Amoudi is zero degrees of separation between the Cathedral and the terrorists.

Well, perhaps the Cathedral just happened to have one bad apple? But it's other Muslim apples have smelly connections also.

Suhail Khan: Wikipedia tells us "Khan serves on the Board of Directors for the American Conservative Union, the Indian American Republican Council, the Islamic Free Market Institute, and on the interfaith Buxton Initiative Advisory Council. He speaks regularly at conferences and venues such as the Conservative Political Action Conference (CPAC), the Council for National Policy (CNP), the Harbour League, and the National Press Club and has contributed to publications such as the Washington Post/Newsweek Forum On Faith, the Washington Post, Foreign Policy, and Human Events."

Suhail Khan is Senior Fellow at the Institute for Global Engagement, a Christian organization dedicated to religious freedom worldwide.

And yet this same Suhail Khan, moderate, pillar of the establishment, advocate of tolerance, also seems to spend a lot of time with people dedicated to blowing up infidels[582].

So Suhail Khan is one degree of separation between the Cathedral and terrorism.

---

[582]https://www.vimeo.com/user5584908/videos

Similarly for *Imam* Feisal Adbul Rauf, of the ground zero victory mosque. So of three Muslims that I noticed as being Cathedral insiders, three had ties to terror.

It does not appear the Cathedral is consciously and cynically cozying up to terrorists – Suhail Khan put quite a bit of effort into appearing to be moderate. Rather, they turn a blind eye to terrorist connections, because to do otherwise would be racism and discrimination – while quite slight and vague connections to conventional Christianity cause them to reel back in shock and horror, like a vampire at the sight of the cross, as they do from Sarah Palin.

They want to include Muslims, but terrorism is as central to Islam as the Eucharist is to Christianity, and so if someone is an important Muslim, he is apt to have important connections to terror, and if a Muslim is in with the Cathedral, he is an important Muslim. In contrast, if a nominal Christian knew what the Eucharist was, the Cathedral would treat him with extreme suspicion.

This is not a pro terror bias, but an anti discrimination bias – which bias in practice means we are not allowed to discriminate against people trying to kill us.

Exterminationist rhetoric
2011-01-12 16:37:49

McCain has some good examples[583] of the left calling for the murder of its enemies[584].

The reason rhetoric is heating up is that we are drifting into the Cloward–Piven crisis, and the Cloward–Piven strategy only makes sense if we suppose that in the crisis, the left *will* attempt to exterminate its enemies.

The blood libel against Sarah Palin
2011-01-13 08:51:11

What is a "blood libel"? It is an irresponsible and frivolous accusation of murder, like the one made against Sarah Palin, made with the intent of justifying real murders.

The left have long been issuing exterminationist rhetoric, and this blood libel has led to an explosion of calls for the murder of alleged rightists[585]. x[586]

This blood libel looks to me like preparation for the real murders that the left hopes to commit during the coming Cloward–Piven crisis.

The left is, of course, outraged at the term "blood libel". It perceives only the right as using violent rhetoric. It sees nothing violent and menacing about its own rhetoric, because, after all, supposedly everyone knows rightists need killing, hence supposedly nothing controversial about saying so. And so, the use of the term by Sarah Palin and numerous bloggers and commentators[587] seems to them ludicrously inappropriate.

---

[583] https://theothermccain.com/2011/01/11/when-did-sarah-palin-say-put-him-against-the-wall-and-shoot-him/

[584] https://theothermccain.com/2011/01/11/vitriolic-rhetoric-anyone/

[585] https://neoneocon.com/2011/01/12/sarah-palin-and-the-blood-libel/

[586] https://legalinsurrection.blogspot.com/2011/01/blood-libel.html

[587] https://www.niemanlab.org/2011/01/blood-libel-how-language-evolves-and-spreads-within-online-worlds/

Since Sarah Palin supposedly knows how peaceful and benevolent the left is, the fact that she used such a term supposedly proves she cannot possibly know what it means. That she implies that the wonderfully peaceful left is violent and murderous is surely an accident, and proves how stupid she must be.

To progressives, who can see no violence or threats coming from anyone progressive, the term seems obviously inappropriate. Sometimes they say it is inappropriate in mild, civilized, and reasonable language, sometimes in language[588] so incendiary as to prove the term is entirely appropriate[589].

In considering the entire screaming match, one must keep in mind that we are approaching a crisis in the next decade or two in which political violence is possible, likely, and may well be necessary. *Someone* is going to get defunded, and they will likely resist it.

So, as Sarah Palin said, keep your powder dry.

No enemies to the left, no friends to the right

2011-01-16 14:50:46

A leftist has no enemies to the left, and no friends to the right. Thus everyone that he is a friend to, is an enemy to him, and everyone who is a friend to him, he is an enemy to.

Back in the day of the Soviet Union, we regularly saw this dynamic with the "popular front". The popular front, a coalition between moderates and radicals, would seemingly be dominated and led by moderate bourgeois, which moderates would be swiftly dumped once the front took over. But not only would the radicals think they had it coming for not being left enough, the moderates themselves seemed to feel they had it coming for not being left enough.

We also saw this dynamic in the Soviet Union during the purges. An influential Soviet officer and/or party member, a long way from Moscow, surrounded by armed people personally loyal to him, would be summoned to Moscow to face torture and death. Instead of looting the armory and fleeing for the hills, off he would dutifully go to Moscow.

And today, we once again see this dynamic in the Tucson murders. Jared Lee Loughner murdered a bunch of leftists. Naturally, many people, myself among them, figured Loughner for a Tea Partier, but it soon became apparent that Loughner was a leftist killing them for insufficient leftism.

And so, naturally and predictably, Loughner was forgiven, but the Tea Party was not. J Eric Fuller, who was shot in the knee by Loughner, announced his forgiveness of Loughner[590], but threatened to kill Tea Partier Trent Humpries[591].

Here is a word of advice for any leftists planning to die in blaze of glory killing those who commit themselves insufficiently to the one true faith: Practice on a shooting range first. Get them in the head or torso, not the knee. Remember: torso.

---

[588] https://www.themidnightreview.com/2011/01/sarah-palins-blood-libel-comment.html

[589] https://silencedmajority.blogs.com/silenced_majority_portal/2011/01/palin-uses-anti-semitic-slur-in-newest-rhetorical-outburst.html

[590] https://www.azcentral.com/news/articles/2011/01/14/20110114giffords-shooting-victim-loughner-parents.html

[591] https://www.kgun9.com/Global/story.asp?S=13849741

Creeping progressivism

2011-01-17 12:44:48

Mc Cain is horrified when a bunch of progressive lawyers demand that banks have their paperwork in order before foreclosing[592]. He does not realize that he has implicitly conceded everything that matters to those progressive lawyers.

He complains that this will have a detrimental effect on the availability of credit:

> this action could have a catastrophic impact on home values and mortgage lending ...
>
> ... lenders are discouraged fromoffering mortgages except to the most affluent and credit-worthy buyers.

Surely, after recent events, lenders should *not* be offering mortgages except to the most affluent and credit-worthy buyers.

The problem is not that a bunch of lefty liberal lawyers demand that banks have their paperwork in order. The problem is that the government intervened to make mortgages easily available any deadbeat, and that this necessitated taking a few short cuts with the paperwork, indeed necessitated taking a lot of quite drastic shortcuts with the paperwork.

And now the government is demanding *both* that mortgages continue to be easily available to any drunken unemployed deadbeat wetback, *and* that the banks keep their paperwork in order.

The remedy is not that the government should refrain from demanding clear, simple, straightforward and accurate paperwork before foreclosure. The remedy is that the government refrain from demanding that mortgages continue to be easily available to any drunken unemployed broke deadbeat wetback,

The New Civility

2011-01-18 07:24:37

"View from the right[593]" spots the fine print in a buried news story:

> James Eric Fuller, 63, who was shot in the knee, had told The Post on Friday, the day before his arrest, that top Republican figures should be tortured and their ears severed.
>
> "There would be torture and then an ear necklace, with [Minnesota US Rep.] Michelle Bachmann and Sarah Palin's ears toward the end, because they're small, female ears, and then Limbaugh, Hannity and the biggest ears of all, Cheney's, in the center," Fuller said.
>
> Also on Friday, Fuller stopped by the home of gunman Jared Lee Loughner and told a neighbor he was going to forgive the shooter, The Associated Press said.

---

[592]https://theothermccain.com/2011/01/16/liberals-cheer-as-lawyers-attempt-to-destroy-the-housing-market-in-maryland/
[593]https://www.amnation.com/vfr/archives/018447.html

A leftist has no enemies to the left, and no friends to the right, so if shot by someone lefter than thou, the shooter cannot be an enemy.

Europe crosses the Rubicon

2011-01-20 08:56:18

Ireland has started to issue its own Euros[594], or rather counterfeit its own Euros, since it has no legal authority to issue Euros – not that anyone worries about legal authority these days.

If any one country of Europe can get away with issuing Euros, then the political benefit is captured by the one country issuing Euros, while the inflationary effect is experience by all of Europe. This guarantees over issue of Euros.

The proposed cure for this problem is more central authority, a United States of Europe – but there was already central authority to stop people from issuing their own Euros. Irish issue of Euros is illegal, but the European Central Bank lacks the balls to say so, and forming a United States Of Europe would not give the European central bank a testosterone infusion.

The two most powerful democratically elected people in Europe, Ms.Merkel and Mr.Sarkozy, have, under pressure from their voters, prescribed a solution: The Deauville pact.

The Deauville pact if implemented would mean that Greece and Ireland would go broke. Irishmen would go the ATM, attempt to withdraw cash from their bank accounts, and no cash would come out. Pensions and doles issued by the Irish and Greek governments would bounce – that is to say, solvent banks would turn them down, and while insolvent banks would cheerfully accept them, the insolvent banks would be unable to give cash for them.

The European Central Bank is, however, reluctant to go along with this plan. But if they are reluctant to stop people spending Euros they do not have, or unable to stop people spending Euros they do not have, Euros will, in the end, be worthless.

The more solvent countries of Europe could save themselves from this shipwreck by issuing their own currencies – franks and marks. Of course, that would be easier if they actually were solvent. That Europe is drifting into a system that makes financial collapse unavoidable is more of a symptom than a cause. Genuinely solvent nations would unhesitatingly cut the wastrels off without a penny, to teach them thrift, which is what the the Deauville pact proposed. The problem is that every bureaucrat fears that if one government goes broke, people will doubt the next. Big spending governments fear to let bigger spending governments go broke, lest their own solvency be doubted.

The Deauville pact was more the politicians of France and Germany assuring each other and the voters that they were indeed solvent and could act in the macho manner that solvent enterprises can act, than it was any real intent to act.

---

[594]https://online.wsj.com/article/SB10001424052748703814804576035682984688312.html

Brad De Long explains he was wrong

2011-01-20 14:01:02

Wrong, that is in that he failed to appreciate his own his immense genius, and wrong in that he failed to appreciate that the progressive left wing account of economics was ever more staggeringly true than he thought it was:

According to him[595], he was wrong to think that:

> highly leveraged banks had control over their risks. With people like Stanley Fischer and Robert Rubin in the office of the president of Citigroup, with all of the industry's experience at quantitative analysis, with all the knowledge of economic history that the large investment and commercial banks of the United States had, that their bosses understood the importance of walking the trading floor, of understanding what their underlings were doing, of managing risk institution by institution. I thought that they were pretty good at doing that.

Funny about that. What those not under the thumb of Cathedral, such as the Israeli Central Bank and the Chinese seem to think is that he was wrong about was to imagine that the state could direct great barrels of mortgage money deadbeat borrowers with any prospect of the money being paid back.

According to him[596], he was wrong to think that:

> that the Federal Reserve had the power and the will to stabilize the growth path of nominal GDP.

> that no advanced country government with as frayed a safety net as America would tolerate 10% unemployment. In Germany and France with their lavish safety nets it was possible to run an economy for 10 years with 10% unemployment without political crisis. But I did not think that was possible in the United States.

Which is a roundabout way of saying he was not wrong to think that the government could cure unemployment by printing lots of money and spending it, and the fact that it has printed vast amounts of money and spent it, causing only inflation and not restoring employment, is proof that the government is not spending enough money. The treatment, he tells us, is just fine, just needs to applied more vigorously.

And he was also wrong to think that other economists were as smart as he was:

> I did not think that there were any economists who would look at a 10% shortfall of nominal GDP relative to its trend growth path and say that the government is being too stimulative.

---

[595]https://delong.typepad.com/sdj/2011/01/what-have-we-unlearned-from-our-great-recession.html
[596]https://delong.typepad.com/sdj/2011/01/what-have-we-unlearned-from-our-great-recession.html

It seems that all these other silly economists were so silly that they accurately predicted what the results of the governments policy would be – stagflation.

Official government inflation is still near zero, but the inflation people see when they do their shopping is quite shocking.

Brad De Long explains he was wrong

2011-01-20 14:13:53

Wrong, that is in that he failed to appreciate his own his immense genius, and wrong it that he failed to appreciate that the progressive left wing acount of economics was ever more staggeringly true than he thought it was:

According to him[597], he was wrong to think that:

> highly leveraged banks had control over their risks. With people like Stanley Fischer and Robert Rubin in the office of the president of Citigroup, with all of the industry's experience at quantitative analysis, with all the knowledge of economic history that the large investment and commercial banks of the United States had, that their bosses understood the importance of walking the trading floor, of understanding what their underlings were doing, of managing risk institution by institution. I thought that they were pretty good at doing that.

Funny about that. What those not under the thumb of Cathedral, such as the Israeli Central Bank and the Chinese seem to think is he was wrong to imagine that the government could direct great barrels of mortgage money deadbeat borrowers with any prospect of the money being paid back.

Who called the financial crisis before it happened?

2011-01-25 07:18:51

Among others, Ron Paul, in his speech to the house, proposing amendments to the laws that caused the crisis[598]

> ... the government's policy of diverting capital into housing creates a short-term boom in housing. Like all artificially created bubbles, the boom in housing prices cannot last forever. When housing prices fall, homeowners will experience difficulty as their equity is wiped out. Furthermore, the holders of the mortgage debt will also have a loss. These losses will be greater than they would have been had government policy not actively encouraged over-investment in housing.
>
> ...
>
> The connection between the GSEs and the government helps isolate the GSEs' managements from market discipline. This isolation from market discipline is the root cause of the mismanagement occurring at Fannie and Freddie ...

---

[597] https://delong.typepad.com/sdj/2011/01/what-have-we-unlearned-from-our-great-recession.html
[598] https://www.lewrockwell.com/paul/paul282.html

I hope my colleagues join me in protecting taxpayers from having to bail out Fannie Mae and Freddie Mac when the housing bubble bursts.

... The flip side of regulatory capture is that mangers and owners of highly subsidized and regulated industries are more concerned with pleasing the regulators than with pleasing consumers or investors, since the industries know that investors will believe all is well if the regulator is happy. Thus, the regulator and the regulated industry may form a symbiosis where each looks out for the other's interests while ignoring the concerns of investors. ...

... the government increases the likelihood of a painful crash in the housing market. ...

Needless to say, there was only one vote for addressing the looming financial crisis. Looking at the tea party candidates, I think if the Tea party did a clean sweep, if every single congressman had belonged to the tea party, I think there would have been two or three votes for addressing the looming financial crisis.

Ambac argues fraud committed for profit caused the crisis
2011-01-27 07:56:41

I of course, argue that government pressure to make mortgage loans caused the crisis. After all, the specific examples bad loans that Ambac lists in its lawsuit against Bear Stearns[599], are all loans that were made to poor people, though Ambac provides no information that would identify the race of these poor people. Ambac, however, argues that Bear Stearn made bad loans, lied that the loans were fine, and sold them on to the next sucker in order to collect fees. Ambac in its lawsuit against Bear Stearns explains the global financial crisis as caused by fraud conducted for profit, rather than caused by government policy.

It is, however, apparent that Bear Stearns kept a lot of bad loans, and took losses on them, even though it unloaded most of the bad loans onto various suckers by means of fraudulent warranties and representations. I argue therefore that Bear Stearns was under pressure to please regulators by lending to the supposedly poor and oppressed, which poor and oppressed are notoriously unable and unwilling to repay loans, and finding itself with a pile of bad loans, proceeded to unload as many of them as it could, by fair means and foul, many of them onto Ambac.

If, in the end, the government winds up compensating Ambac, and the Bear Stearns boys who made these fraudulent warranties and representations to Ambac go unpunished as individuals, we should conclude that Bear Stearns was carrying out government policy, that this fraud, like so many others, was committed out of political correctness. If, on the other hand, those who committed these massive frauds are themselves individually punished, for committing lucrative frauds that sank the world economy, then this will be evidence for the fraud was committed for profit.

Against the theory that the fraud was conducted for profit, is the fact that this is a civil lawsuit, even though fraud, and fraud that cost the taxpayer trillions, is a criminal

---

[599]https://www.scribd.com/full/47547012?access_key=key-3t5vxurwy5lu71lxf5y

offense. That there is not the slightest suggestion that any of these many acts of fraud will be punished criminally, suggests that these frauds were committed not for gain, but for political correctness.

The financial crisis inquiry report

2011-01-29 10:11:33

The government has investigated the "2008" financial crisis and released a detailed report[600]. (Actually it was the 2005 crisis, in that the panic set in towards the end of 2005 , but the government successfully covered things up and managed to get all the major players to pretend that everything was normal until 2008.)

The summary and conclusions are of course, piles of lies, intended to divert attention from those actually guilty.

Overall, it sticks to the cover story that hardly anyone noticed anything out of the ordinary until 2007. It correctly observes that regulators failed to use the authority that they had, and to the extent that they used their authority, used it corruptly in ways that worsened the crisis – from which it concludes that the regulators need more power and to exercise that power more forcefully.

It correctly observes that

> The kings of leverage were Fannie Mae and Freddie Mac, the two behemoth government-sponsored enterprises (GSEs). For example, by the end of 2007, Fannie's and Freddie's combined leverage ratio, including loans they owned and guaranteed, stood at 75 to 1.

So the next time you hear someone say that leverage caused the crisis, that is actually a euphemism for saying that government-sponsored enterprises were the major players causing the crisis, not an explanation of the crisis. After all, as the Republicans on the committee point out, leverage only produces bad results if you lose money, and the question therefore is how such large amounts of money were lost. So what, then, did Fannie and Freddie do to piss away large amounts of money?

It also tells us that

> As early as September 2004, Countrywide executives recognized that many
> of the loans they were originating
> could result in "catastrophic consequences."

Yet fails to quote that testimony or document in full. Surely those who saw the crisis coming, knew what was causing the crisis, yet we don't hear what they said back then.

The report is overcooked, presenting conclusions without the data from which those conclusions were drawn.

Crabtree testifies to large numbers of abandoned houses in 2006, of entire neighborhoods collapsing, of the lawns unmowed, the houses empty except for homeless people squatting. If the mortgages were busted in 2006, surely the crisis was in full swing in

---

[600]https://c0182732.cdn1.cloudfiles.rackspacecloud.com/fcic_final_report_full.pdf

2006? Why then is every commissioner telling a story that has the crisis suddenly manifesting in 2007/2008?

In November 2005 I said "Now is the time to panic", and it appeared to me that everyone did panic, within a few days of me saying it. People gave the commission the same testimony.

> Warren Peterson, a home builder in Bakersfield, felt that he could pinpoint when the world changed to the day. Peterson built homes in an upscale neighborhood, and each Monday morning, he would arrive at the office to find a bevy of real estate agents, sales contracts in hand, vying to be the ones chosen to purchase the new homes he was building. The stream of traffic was constant. On one Saturday in November 2005, he was at the sales office and noticed that not a single purchaser had entered the building. He called a friend, also in the home-building business, who said he had noticed the same thing, and asked him what he thought about it. "It's over," his friend told Peterson.

Why then does the commission stick to the story that this crisis happened in 2008?

Bad loans were made. The money was lost in bad loans. Why were those bad loans made?

The Democrats on the commission conclude that bad loans were made for profit:

> We find that the risky practices of Fannie Mae—the Commission's case study in this area—particularly from 2005 on, led to its fall: practices undertaken to meet Wall Street's expectations for growth, to regain market share, and to ensure generous compensation for its employees. Affordable housing goals imposed by the Department of Housing and Urban Development (HUD) did contribute marginally to these practices.

Peter J. Wallison argues that affirmative action and affordable housing contributed massively to these practices, in particular the HUD "Best practices initiative"

If a financial entity was failed to follow HUD "best practices" it was likely to be sued for racism, redlining, and any number of vague crimes that can never be disproven, so everyone had to follow "best practices" and if a company followed HUD "best practices" it was bound to make huge numbers of bad loans.

"Best practices" required that the lender accept "non traditional" evidence of ability to pay – and the reason such evidence was non traditional is that it is not evidence. If a mortgage business followed HUD "best practices", as in practice it had to do, best practices meant in practice that they were allowing borrowers or their loan officers to make $#!% up.

Muslim democracy is dangerous

2011-01-30 06:58:24

The reason there are so few Islamic democracies is that the majority of Muslims vote for war, rape, murder, and terror, with the result that democracies with substantial Muslim populations tend to be short lived. Muslim democracy is dangerous because Muslim voters are dangerous, and should not be permitted.

Egypt looks like it will produce more of the same – the winners will likely be the Muslim Brotherhood, which will unleash terrorism and rape against the Christian minority, and resume war against Israel as a first step towards war against all infidels everywhere. The Stratasphere calls US policy "Jimmy Carter Diplomacy[601]". The vast majority of Egyptians will vote for the Muslim Brotherhood[602], which organization assures our gullible ruling elite that they are moderates, while everywhere pursuing a policy of terrorism.

At best, Islamic democracies produce governments that look the other way on terrorism, and go easy on terrorists, for example Indonesia. At worst they elect regimes that propose to murder everyone everywhere who is not as passionately Muslim as those elected, as for example Algeria, where the Algerians freely and fairly elected a party, the Islamic Salvation Front, that thought that very few Algerians were sufficiently Muslim to be allowed to live.

Usually, however, they elect merely terrorist regimes, like Hamas. The Hamas regime has merely executed a few hundred Gazans for witchcraft, and few thousand for apostasy, but has applied most of its energies to terrorism against its neighbors, so it is pretty much in the middle as Islamic elected regimes go, though more extreme than is typical for long lived Islamic elected regimes.

Egypt a test case for war with Islam

2011-02-07 05:25:17

Is there a difference between "Islamic extremism", and Islam?

The British prime minster proposes Egypt as a test case[603]:

> This highlights, I think, a significant problem when discussing the terrorist threat that we face. There is so much muddled thinking about this whole issue. On the one hand, those on the hard right ignore this distinction between Islam and Islamist extremism, and just say that Islam and the West are irreconcilable– that there is a clash of civilizations. So, it follows: we should cut ourselves off from this religion, whether that is through forced repatriation, favoured by some fascists, or the banning of new mosques, as is suggested in some parts of Europe . These people fuel Islamophobia, and I completely reject their argument. If they want an example of how Western values and Islam can be entirely compatible, they should look at what's happened in the past few weeks on the streets of Tunis and Cairo : hundreds of thousands of people demanding the universal right to free elections and democracy.

[601] https://strata-sphere.com/blog/index.php/archives/15889
[602] https://pajamasmedia.com/rogerkimball/2011/01/29/what-sauce-will-barack-obama-use-when-he-eats-his-words/
[603] https://www.number10.gov.uk/news/speeches-and-transcripts/2011/02/pms-speech-at-munich-security-conference-60293

The point is this: the ideology of extremism is the problem; Islam emphatically is not. Picking a fight with the latter will do nothing to help us to confront the former.

It looks to me that those hundreds of thousands of people are demanding free elections, democracy, guaranteed government jobs, government subsidized food, war with Israel, and the right to rape infidel women.

Those who want to believe there is a difference between Islam and Islamic extremism, and that we are at war with one but not the other, are going to wind up telling themselves that Jews need killing, infidels need raping, and the masses need government jobs and government food.

Losing in Afghanistan

2011-02-09 06:21:45

When the US accepted the Karzai government it snatched defeat from jaws of victory.

There is not point in continuing the war in Afghanistan unless we start by killing Karzai and everyone near him.

A government that executes people for converting to Christianity[604] is always going to be a safe place for people to organize terror against infidels.

Mainstream media backs Romneycare for GOP presidential candidate

2011-02-12 17:44:52

Supposedly Romney, the creator of Romneycare, the medical system that inspired Obamacare, is the GOP's best hope for defeating Obama. So the mainstream media unanimously tells us.

Probably true, but there seems little point to such a "victory".

At CPAC, Presidential Candidate Romneycare upbraids Obama for high unemployment, and all the press, the same press that worships Obama, the same press that goes weak at the knees at the sight of the great Obamessiah, cheers Presidential Candidate Romneycare to an echo. Suddenly the press, who whom any truth about the great Obamessiah used to be the most vicious and depraved racism, thinks it is wonderfully inspiring for Presidential Candidate Romneycare to blame the great Obamessiah for unemployment.

So what would Presidential Candidate Romneycare have done about unemployment that differs from what Obama did? Somehow he neglects to tell us.

You can tell who has the real power by whose job is permanent, and who can lose his job. The public servants cannot lose their jobs. Politicians are competing to be the Public Relations department of the permanent government. This was most evident in

---

[604]https://www.dailymail.co.uk/news/article-1354246/One-legged-Afghan-Red-Cross-worker-hanged-converting-Christianity.html

the pitch made to CPAC by would-be Presidential Candidate Grinch: Gingrich calls for eliminating EPA, expanding domestic energy production[605]

But, of course, he does not propose to eliminate the Environmental Protection Agency. He proposes to convert it into an agency that focuses on "science, technology, markets and incentives."

Not that there is any danger of a presidential candidate Grinch. The Republican Party hates him for endorsing Scozzafava, from which act of treachery he can never recover, and the permanent government fears he is not sufficiently enthusiastic in his support for the permanent government. Of the available enemies of the Republican Party, the permanent government has clearly and unambiguously decided it wants Presidential Candidate Romneycare, the Republican President that could best defend the most recent big expansion of government, Obamacare.

But suppose the universally despised Grinch, hated by both left and right, somehow got to implement his plan: Trouble is that the Environmental Protection Agency is composed entirely of anti capitalism environmentalist activists who think factories are simply sinful in themselves, that destroying jobs, any jobs, is an act of Godliness. The Environmental Protection Agency is jobs for the lefty boys. Leftist activists got rewarded with permanent government jobs. You cannot remake it into a pro market organization. You have to shut down lefty government organizations, and if righty government organizations are to be created, they have to be created from scratch with jobs for the rightists. The fact that Grinch proposes conversion, rather than abolition, tells us that a President Grinch would be handing out even more jobs for the left wing boys, not jobs for the right wing boys, more rewards for left wing activists in the revolving door between government and activism.

If the president was the boss, or the president and congress was the boss, he could lay off agencies that were not performing, or were not going along with his agenda, the way Chief Executive Officer, or Chief Executive Officer and the Board of a company can, and frequently does, lay off divisions that are not performing, or are merely not part of the Chief Executive Officer's vision of what the company should be doing.

That this never happens, cannot happen, is just unthinkable, no matter how dreadfully an agency screws up, tells us who has the real power.

What would happen if the public elected officials that actually tried to exercise power?

President Reagan is often praised for overthrowing the Soviet Union, or contributing substantially to the overthrow of the Soviet Union, but most of what he did to overthrow the Soviet Union was moral pressure, threats, and inspiration, and much of what he actually did militarily to bleed the Soviet Union, to tie it down in more wars than it could afford, thereby depriving it of the power to intimidate its subjects, was illegal, and very nearly got him impeached, even though foreign policy is generally regarded as the one area where a president is actually allowed to do stuff. His efforts to change things internally, to put an end to unpopular and expensive federal bureaucracies, simply had no effect, and if there was any danger of them having effect, then, since he was damn near impeached for attempting to implement the policy he was elected on against the Soviet Union, he surely

---

[605] https://thehill.com/blogs/e2-wire/677-e2-wire/143279-gingrich-calls-for-elimnating-epa-expanding-domestic-energy-production

would have been impeached had he implemented the internal policy he was elected on, of cutting unpopular government expenditures.

The origins of multicultural rule

2011-02-13 03:30:35

Hbd Chick has been discussing the origins of multicultural rule.

I have been reading old books. The ideology that races, ethnicities, and genders, are the same in mean and distribution, and if they are not it is because of oppression and someone must be punished, is several hundred years old. It first exercised sufficient power to intimidate its enemies and reward its friends in Britain in 1890, as illustrated by the pressure applied to James Anthony Froude, and by the elevation to the heights of the none too bright John Jacob Thomas.

Affirmative action for women had the whip hand in Europe in 1910 – consider for example Marie Curie getting not one but *two* Nobel prizes for work that was entirely routine when men did it. Can you remember anyone who discovered any of the other hundred odd elements? You cannot, because all the other elements were discovered by men. She got Nobel prizes not for doing exceptional science, but for doing science that was exceptional *for a woman*, just as when people praise Obama's speaking skills, which are far inferior to Sarah Palin's, they mean he speaks well *for a black man*.

As early as 1904, academics are tiptoeing around the fact that the great Zimbabwe in Africa was built by Hebrews, and that as these Hebrew settlers interbred with local blacks, their workmanship deteriorated. (The tribe that claim to have built it recall that they are Hebrew descended, recall their journey from the middle east, have a religion that much resembles Judaism, look significantly less black than their neighbors, and were, in the twenty first century, gene tested revealing substantial Hebrew blood) The fact that the builders were of a visibly different race to their neighbors and claimed to have immigrated from the middle east is only mentioned by the indelicate, even in 1906. It was not something a proper academic would mention, since it might suggest that black people just cannot build or maintain cities.

From about 1880 to 1940, the ideology is clearly and overwhelmingly Christian, in particular Protestant Christian socialist, though these Christians were somewhat embarrassed by the bible, due to its reactionary views on family, marriage, women, divorce, adultery, homosexuality, and so forth, and were in the process of discarding it.

From 1920 to 1940, we see the center of power in this ideology, the holy church of multiculturalism and environment, shifting from Europe to the US. After World War II, the US was wholly dominant, and Harvard the high Cathedral of the religion. Since the holy doctrine must be taught in government schools, what little Christianity remained in the doctrine was ruthlessly suppressed, in order to superficially appear to comply with the first amendment, though arguably the doctrine was being taught in government schools with a more explicitly Christian tinge before the war. Jews only show up in the multicultural ruling elite after the remnants of Christianity are purged from the doctrine – fifty or sixty years after it first exercised theocratic power.

The new Egypt

2011-02-15 15:19:00

Earlier I argued that no Muslims should be allowed to vote anywhere in the world[606], least of all in Muslim majority countries.

Brutally honest has some interesting survey results[607] on what the Egyptian majority will vote for:

> • *84% favor the death penalty for people who leave the Muslim faith.*

Now 84% is an interesting number, considering that something like ten or fifteen percent of Egyptians are Christians (the number is rapidly diminishing due to rape, murder, and flight). So, supposing that no Christians support the death penalty for those that leave the Muslim faith, looks mighty close to 100% of Egyptian Muslims support the death penalty for those that leave the Muslim faith.

The survey neglected to ask how many supported Egypt going to war with the nearest infidels, but since 54% favor suicide bombings of civilian targets, chances are a considerable majority favor war.

The Wallison dissent

2011-02-16 09:33:41

Steve Sailor, is as always great reading, and he issues some comments that on the Wallison dissent that everyone who wants to understand the financial crisis should pay attention to.

Peter Wallison tells us[608]

> Profit had nothing to do with the motivations of these firms; they were responding to government direction.

Rather than direction, they were responding to government pressure and persuasion. Basel gave government not so much the power and authority to dispense off budget funds to friends and voter blocks, but rather to heavily influence and pressure banks to dispense off budget funds to friends and voter blocks. Since government, or those authorized by government, decide what is risky and what is not, rather than those actually making the loans, any loan that is politically correct is unlikely to be deemed risky.

Steve Sailer tells us:[609]

> Among profit-seeking lenders there will always be optimists and pessimists about the ability of marginal borrowers to pay back their home loans. Government policy from 1991 onward was heavily biased toward being nice

---

[606]https://blog.reaction.la/war/muslim-democracy-is-dangerous.html
[607]https://www.brutallyhonest.org/brutally_honest/2011/02/about-that-egyptian-freedom-movement.html
[608]https://www.aei.org/docLib/Wallisondissent.pdf
[609]https://econlog.econlib.org/archives/2011/02/the_wallison_di.html

to optimist lenders and not nice to pessimists lenders This nurtured a climate in which the businesses of the optimists grew and people in the middle shifted toward optimism, while pessimists moved toward other lines of work.

Consider Angelo Mozilo of Countrywide, who on January 13, 2005 catastrophically pledged $1,000,000,000,000.00 in mortgages by 2010 to minority and lower income borrowers. The government can't force anybody to lend a trillion bucks to bad risks. A billion dollars, sure. But a trillion? The lender has to want to do it.

That doesn't mean that politicians weren't intimately involved in cultivating Mozilo's delusional state of mind where he thought he was doing well by doing good and vice-versa.

There's no question that Mozilo was first prodded down this path by the hoopla over the stupid early 1990s Boston Fed "study" of discrimination in mortgage lending. Crucially, the Clinton Administration's threat in 1994 to extend the Community Reinvestment Act paperwork requirements to nonbanks like Countrywide led Mozilo to sign a treaty with Clinton's HUD secretary Henry Cisneros promising to lend like Countrywide was covered by the CRA.

But, Mozilo became infatuated with Cisneros's "vision" and put Cisneros on Countrywide's board. They both became convinced that lending vastly more to Hispanics was a great business idea.

If you didn't believe that, well, you'd better keep your mouth shut because you could be sued for discrimination, and regulators could make your life hell. So, the government helped change the culture of mortgage lending in part by selecting more credulous people like Mozilo for favorable attention and giving more skeptical people a hard time.

Another example is Kerry Killinger of Washington Mutual. He survived 29 Community Reinvestment Act reviews as he bought up other lenders by making huge pledges of minority and lower income lending, up to $375,000,000,000 for the acquisition of Dime Bank. So, there is a selection effect. The government gave the thumbs up to optimists expanding and the thumbs down to pessimists. So, the culture of lending shifted toward credulity.

On Steve Sailer's blog you can find much useful research you cannot find anywhere else, because it is just too horribly politically incorrect, but he does suffer from the fallacy of seeing jooz everywhere, and therefore believing the market is rigged by jooz against people like Steve Sailer. I hope some day to debate him on this topic – I argue that Jews are converts to progressivism, rather than progressivism being a sect of Judaism, (the Mencius Moldbug theory that progressivism is crypto calvinism[610]) and that progressives were

---

[610]https://unqualified-reservations.blogspot.com/2007/06/cryptocalvinism-slightly-tweaked.html

ruling the system and stealing all the money back when progressives were still nominally Christians[611], and did not allow any Jews to get in on the vig.

Democracy in Tunisia

2011-02-16 11:58:48

The promised democracy in Egypt is an infection from an outbreak of democracy in Tunisia.

Yet strangely, Tunisia has fallen off the headlines. How is democracy working out in Tunisia, you might ask?

Wonder no longer![612]

> Thousands of Tunisians have also arrived by boat to the Italian island of Lampedusa prompted Italy to declare a humanitarian state of emergency and ask the European Union for 100 million euros in aid to bring the situation under control.

Democracy in action

2011-02-17 11:59:35

Lara Logan, CBS chief foreign correspondent

was beaten and gang raped by a mob of 200 enthusiastic pro democracy protestors chanting "Jew, Jew"

---

[611] https://blog.reaction.la/culture/the-origins-of-multicultural-rule.html
[612] https://www.adnkronos.com/IGN/Aki/English/Security/Algeria-10000-Tunisians-have-crossed-over-border-since-Ben-Alis-fall_311684904464.html

There is an effort to blame Mubarak for this, but if the goons of a US ally had done this, if the goons of a man who accepted peace with the west had done this, the mainstream media would be covering this with headlines the size of tombstones, instead of piously sweeping it under the carpet.

No one is going to be punished for this, and the good progressives really do not want anyone to be punished, since whites and Americans are always in the wrong, and the enemies of civilization always in the right. I doubt that even Lara Logan wants anyone punished for this, for she is surely a true believing progressive. Only a true believing progressive would have wandered into a mob of savages without adequate backup, preferably backup from such evil white capitalist imperialists as the men of Blackwater or Executive Outcomes.

This incident reminds me of that Yellowstone park incident where a woman who had seen too many Disney movies poured honey on the hands of her little girl, and asked the girl to feed the bear. The bear, of course, ate the girl, starting with her hands.

Like the commenters at Atlas shrugged[613], I can't wait to hear her report after her recovery calling for understanding of her rapists and how it's all Bush's fault.

No friends to the right

2011-02-17 13:43:37

No enemies to the left, no friends to the right

Left wing journalist Nir Rosen ridicules Lara Logan's rape[614]. Seems that because Nir Rosen is even further left than she is, the stupid slut deserved to get raped.

"Lara Logan had to outdo Anderson. Where was her buddy McCrystal."

That she is supposedly a buddy of the insufficiently left wing McCrystal is a suggestion that she is insufficiently left wing.

Kosovo Democracy

2011-02-18 13:15:32

Muslim democracies vary in how Muslim they are. For example Turkey is mildy insane and somewhat homicidal. The majority disfavor murdering apostates, but murdering apostates is nonetheless a respectable political program, and government is reluctant to seriously punish it. Indonesia is insane and homicidal, and Egypt is frothing at the mouth insane and homicidal. As close to a hundred percent of Muslims favor murdering apostates, because any Muslim that doubted it would be suspected of apostacy.

But, among the varying degrees of madness and evil, there has to be one state among the Muslim democracies that everyone recognizes as the least insane and least evil, and that state is Kosovo, a place where Americans are popular, and can drink whiskey without

---

[613]https://atlasshrugs2000.typepad.com/atlas_shrugs/2011/02/egypt-army-saves-cbs-news-lara-logan-after-rape-and-beating-by-egypts-freedom-loving-protesters.html

[614]https://dailycaller.com/2011/02/15/nir-rosen-trashes-lara-logan-dismisses-her-sexual-assault/

getting their heads cut off. (Of course, Dubai is saner, because it is ruled by the best, but if ruled by the people of Dubai, would probably as bad as the others)

Lara Logan and the media rules
2011-02-20 06:18:07

Caroline Glick analyzes the coverage[615]:

> Identity politics revolve around the narrative of victimization. For adherents to identity politics, the victim is not a person, but a member of a privileged victim group. That is, the status of victimhood is not determined by facts, but by membership in an identity group. Stories about victims are not dictated by facts. Victim stories are tailored to fit the victim. Facts, values and individual responsibility are all irrelevant.
>
> In light of this, a person's membership in specific victim groups is far more important than his behavior. And there is a clear pecking order of victimhood in identity politics.
>
> Anti-American Third World national, religious and ethnic groups are at the top of the victim food chain. They out-victim everyone else.
>
> After them come the Western victims: Racial minorities, women, homosexuals, children and animals.
>
> Israelis, Jews, Americans, white males and rich people are the predetermined perpetrators. No matter how badly they are victimized, brave reporters will go to heroic lengths to ignore, underplay or explain away their suffering.
>
> In cases when victim groups are attacked by victim groups - for instance when Iraqis were attacked by Saddam, or Palestinians are attacked by the PA, the media tend to ignore the story.
>
> When members of Western victim groups are attacked by Third World victims, the story can be reported, but with as little mention of the identity of the victim-perpetrators as possible. So it was with coverage of Logan and the rest of the foreign reporters assaulted in Egypt. They were attacked by invisible attackers with no identities, no barbaric values, no moral responsibility, and no criminal culpability.

$1,200 billion increase cut by $60 billion
2011-02-22 16:39:36

The "right" triumphantly announces that it has cut spending by 60 billion

Before these mighty cuts, the projected 2011 deficit was $1,645 billio[616]n, an increase in spending, and an increase in the deficit, of 1,200 billion as compared to our last comparatively normal year, 2005.

[615]https://www.carolineglick.com/e/2011/02/lara-logan-and-the-media-rules.php
[616]https://gonzalolira.blogspot.com/2011/02/we-owe-how-much-waiting-for-big.html

After these mighty cuts, the projected deficit is, I suppose, reduced to a mere 1,585 billion, though of course chances are that somehow, by the end of the year, it will turn out to have actually been something south of $1,700 billion.

And, of course, this does not count a trillion or so of off budget expenditures, among them being that the federal reserve has purchased a large number of worthless mortgage backed securities and suchlike, and will not tell anyone how much.

So both parties, democrats and republicans alike, have moved far, far to the left, the extreme right of this year being far to the left of the extreme left of a few years back. Indeed, the same is true of the entire society. The government, all schools, all universities, all churches, and all institutions, are moving to the left with explosive speed. Big businesses are appointing CEOs by ideology and affirmative action - which strategy is in fact successful since success is by government favor, not competence, and ideology and affirmative action wins government favor. To appoint a CEO on the basis of competence, ability to make business turn a profit, you would have to be crazy.

Today's Christian right believes that marriage and family law should treat husbands and spouses as if men and women were the same in mean and distribution, and played the same roles in sex and reproduction, and had the same desires and intentions with regard to sex and reproduction, and find the horribly sexist words of Jesus on divorce and suchlike far too embarrassing to mention. If family law should treat men and woman as interchangeable, why object to gay marriage? To make a principled opposition to gay marriage, the Christian right would have to make a principled opposition to the family law that treats husbands and wives as alike and interchangeable, that assumes there are no significant differences between the nature of men and women, which position would be horribly sexist, hence the Christian right would never dream of taking such a stand, a stand that in 1950, no one would have ever dreamed of doubting, nor would today's Christian right ever dream of mentioning certain parts of the Bible that until recent decades were familiar to everyone. Just as not one nominated political candidate would today dream of suggesting measures that might significantly reduce the deficit, not one Christian preacher would today mention bits of the Bible that support patriarchy.

In the recent elections, the only candidate who was proposing significant cuts was Christine O'Donnel, widely derided as a lunatic extremist, and a witch. And she only proposed significant cuts during the primaries. As soon as she got the republican nomination, as soon as she faced the main election, and had to get votes from the mainstream, she immediately threw that policy overboard, and headed back to the "center" – headed back to what is now the center, but a few years back would have been the crazed lunatic left.

And indeed, Christine O'Donnel was crazy (though probably not a witch) because if you want to be taken seriously as a political candidate, you have to go along with policies that will destroy our society in the very near future. We are all in a bus, the bus is heading for a cliff at seventy miles an hour and the pedal is flat to the floorboards. If you are serious candidate, you discuss whether the pedal should be flat to the floorboards, or almost flat to the floorboards. Releasing the pedal, let alone applying the brakes, is not something any serious, responsible, sane, normal candidate would mention. You would have to be crazy – a lot crazier than Christine O'Donnel – to propose such a thing. You would have to be almost as crazy as a corporate board who appointed a CEO on the basis of his ability to turn a profit, rather than for his ideology, race, and gender.

I am reminded of the last days of the Roman empire in the west. In AD406, it was completely crazy, ludicrous, and absurd, to suggest that the barbarians could possibly threaten Rome. In AD410, the goths looted Rome, and raped every Roman woman. In AD412, it was *still* completely crazy, ludicrous, and absurd, to suggest that the barbarians could possibly threaten Rome, which bizarre response strikingly resembles the British failure to notice their humiliating defeats in Basra and the Persian Gulf. Rome failed to pull itself together in the way it had after past defeats, because it denied that it had been defeated, denied that the Roman empire in the west had ceased to be.

Total government debt was nine trillion, though this depends on how you count it - the nine trillion does not count the governments rapidly soaring pension commitments, nor the alarming multitude of promises it has made to backstop gambles made by bankers.

In the US there are about ninety million people who file tax returns and pay income tax (another forty million file tax returns, but pay no income tax[617]). So if you are one of those ninety million tax paying households, your household's share of the debt is about one hundred thousand dollars, and this year it will grow by about eighteen thousand dollars. It is not impossible that such a debt will be paid - it is physically possible to pay it. Whether it is politically possible to get people to pay it is another question. If you are a hundred thousand dollars in debt, and you ran up the debt in a big one off expenditure, like buying a house, you can probably pay it back. If you are a hundred thousand dollars in debt and you ran it up going to fancy restaraunts, going on trips, and buying friends, and you are still going to fancy restaurants and buying expensive friends, and next year you are going to be one hundred and twenty thousand dollars in debt, no way are you ever going to pay the money back.

So what happened: Why is everyone moving left, even the Christian right, even libertarians, even white nationalists and suchlike?

One factor is that western governments around the world have decided to elect a new people, through mass migration from the third world, on a scale that significantly, substantially, and rapidly alters the political balance.

Another factor is that in a program akin to the Soviet program to create New Soviet Man, the government is attempting to transform the people, through a highly politicized education system, an education system whose political intensity is rapidly increasing[618].

But why, you may ask? "Communist plot, Jooish plot, Islamist plot, Harvard plot?"

No, its a government plot, though to call it a Harvard plot is not far wrong. There are more conspiracies, committees, and special interest groups than you can shake a stick at, and all of them want to suck at the tit of the state. It is the nature of government to grow, and liberty to shrink. Government is a metastatic cancer. Each cancerous node spawns a dozen more. There are half dozen communist conspiracies each trying to smash each of the others, despite the expiration of their foreign sponsors, at least two Gaean conspiracies, one big tranzi conspiracy with extensive links to the two main Muslim conspiracies, ivy league academia is a seething mass of conspiracies that no one can possibly keep track

---

[617]https://finance.yahoo.com/news/Nearly-half-of-US-households-apf-1105567323.html
[618]https://althouse.blogspot.com/2011/02/medical-school-ethics-courses.html

of, and there are many more, not that one can draw any sharp distinction between a conspiracy and a special interest group.

Growth of government is not driven by ideology, or even political institutions, rather ideology is driven by the government's need to justify the growth of government.

Government originates in a stationary bandit, a bandit king, a bandit so successful he deters or exterminates all competition. The government at first consists of little more than the bandit himself. Taxation consists of him suggesting that the eminent give him and his boys land and money, thus taxes, though capricious and erratic, are quite low. Laws are few, verging on nonexistent, but enforced with brutal efficiency, the main law being that no one else does any banditry.

All organizations tend to fall apart. It is simply difficult to have a large bunch of people efficiently coordinated. Organizations that are actually effective originate in intense competition, and sooner or later are apt to decay - the Peter Principle, Parkinson's Law, etc.

Absent intense competition, they decay very badly indeed.

Over time bureaucrats, laws, taxes, quasi governmental organizations, and regulations multiply like vermin. Eventually, laws, taxes and meddling bureaucrats become a serious burden, and the bureaucrats face the need to persuade everyone that a horde of bureaucrats is a good thing.

The left (both Democrats and Republicans near equally) is the bureaucracy's PR apparatus - a collection of government sock puppets, astroturf. Its mission is to persuade us that six hundred pounds of fat is a healthy and handsome physique, and that government has never been better, that more laws are good for you, the government is here to help you, and more government will help you more. Thus from time to time the story about what government is good for changes, yet the central theme, that government is good for you, never changes.

Ever since the original bandit chieftain, government has moved ever further leftwards, and will always move ever further leftwards until checked by crisis and collapse, or reformed by internal totalitarian terror, "left" being whatever rationalization justifies more government today, which rationalization is apt to change from time to time.

You cannot fix the problem by excluding the Joos, or getting rid of the commies in the state department, or even by excluding Harvard old boys (though excluding Harvard old boys would help quite a bit). The whole damn thing, including the patent office and the post office, has got to go.

Thus we see numerous supposedly anti government people telling us that the fact that government does X and proposes to do Y is itself proof that X is necessary and good, and Y would be even better.

The deficit is out of control because the government is trying to buy support, and buy internal cohesion. If it cuts some elements of itself off from the the trough, there will be internal warfare between different elements of the government. The government unions will physically attack legislators as they have in Wisconsin, the Pentagon will bomb the state department, as it has already bombed state department proxies, and the police will raid the DEA for drugs and the NEA for loose cash. If, on the other hand, it cannot get a coalition that supposedly represents fifty one percent of the voters to bless its budget, the budget will not be reduced. Instead there will be external warfare between the government and the people. The militias will shoot IRS reveneurs. Hence the import of cheap voters from overseas.

When the Soviet Union was about to fall, one of the symptoms that I noticed, yet was not widely reported, was warfare between the army and GOSPLAN. The army would randomly stop trucks, and if the trucks contained food, seize the food to feed the troops. The Soviet army would seize what it, or its suppliers needed, as if it was living off the land in a hostile occupied country, as, of course, it was.

Transnationalism is just an effort to obtain legitimacy from "world opinion", when legitimacy can no longer be obtained from local voters – to obtain legitimacy from all those poor third worlders without the inconvenience and potential for civil war of allowing them to enter the advanced countries. The European Union is undemocratic because each European government wants to be able to have Brussels "force" it to do what it knows perfectly well it is going to wind up doing anyway.

From the fact that the deficit is $1,600 billion, and that the "right" triumphantly announces that it has cut spending by 60 billion, which "cut" will somehow fail to prevent the deficit from growing rapidly, I predict collapse in a decade or two – armed conflict between elements of the government, or between the government and the people, or, very likely, both. I have been making a similar prediction, for the same decade, since 1994, and events seem to be proceeding on schedule. The near civil war in France, and the violence by state unions in Wisconsin, are the beginning.

The decline of civilization reflected in fantasy novels
2011-02-25 04:20:13

Black gate observes the replacement of heroes by anti heroes, and the replacement of morality by anti morality[619]:

> Thus we can be confident that the murderous, blaspheming anti-hero who rapes and tortures children will never utter a racist thought, be disgusted by homosexuality, or express skepticism about any religious stand-in for Judaism or Islam.
>
> ...
>
> Abercrombie and others cannot rightly be accused of amorality nor can they correctly be portrayed as bold skewerers of sacred cows. They're simply skewering someone else's cows while respecting their own.

The commenters reactions reveal just how sacred these cows are. One of the commenters replies: "at that point you stood exposed". Exposed! Exposed! Oh the horror, the horror!

Another of the commenters pretends to sophistication, rather than advocacy of a different morality:

---

[619]https://www.blackgate.com/2011/02/20/the-decline-and-fall-of-the-fantasy-novel/

I don't see this as any kind of moral statement. Modern audiences are just more interested in complex characters, and that's reflected in their book choices.

It seems that torturing children makes a hero complex, but prejudging people according to their race or species, as Tolkien's characters were apt to do, does not.

Bryan Caplan's challenge

2011-03-03 06:42:20

Bryan Caplan wants people to go on record predicting the future of Egypt[620] before the future becomes apparent, as compared to our usual procedure of claiming one knew all along afterward.

As I said before, democracy with universal franchise does not work. It works worse with Muslims. No Muslim should be allowed to vote anywhere, especially in countries with substantial numbers of Muslims.

Egypt might get another dictator like Mubarak, but if it gets democracy, will suffer war and economic disaster, both of which will be blamed on Jews. Egyptian democracy will at best resemble Indonesian democracy: economic decay, quiet tolerance of terrorism against the west, with some arrests of those who terrorize westerners, but reluctant foot dragging in arresting them and slap on the wrist sentences in the unlikely event they get arrested, semi open tolerance of terrorism and mass violence against local infidels. At worst they will elect a government that thinks that everyone who voted against them are apostates who need their heads cut off, and that most of those who voted for them are also apostates who need their heads cut off, but most likely will elect something in between, somewhat resembling Hamas. Egypt will not officially abandon the peace agreement with Israel, but will abandon it in reality.

2011-03-06

2011-03-06 11:38:19

I see it regularly claimed that financial crisis reflected de-regulation. I was mighty puzzled. Deregulation? Has not Basel been a spectacular landslide of regulation, with massive apocalyptic government takeover of the financial system, with government deciding who shall be winners and who shall be losers, with government allocating lending to favored groups and away from disfavored groups? Eventually I discovered that this "deregulation" was the[621] Gramm-Leach-Bliley Bill[622], also known as the Financial Services Modernization Act of 1999, a bill *three hundred and eighty five pages* long, which repealed *one* page of the seventeen page Glass–Steagall Act of 1933

Among the many catastrophic things things Gramm-Leach-Bliley did was to make takeovers dependent on loaning to poor and non asian minorities, which had the effect

---

[620]https://econlog.econlib.org/archives/2011/03/the_future_of_t.html
[621]https://banking.senate.gov/conf/confrpt.htm
[622]https://banking.senate.gov/conf/confrpt.htm

that people who believed that lending to poor and non asian minorities was safe wound up in charge, and people who believed it was unsafe wound up unemployed.

This in turn led to lots of disastrous lending by bank managers infamous for their extreme political correctness.

It is often pointed out that most of the dud lending was not covered by the CRA - but just as breathing is covered by the commerce clause, all lending is in effect covered by the CRA.

Angelo Mozilo of Countrywide on January 13, 2005 catastrophically pledged $1 trillion in mortgages by 2010 to minority and lower income borrowers, very little of which has been paid back. The Clinton Administration's threat in 1994 to extend the Community Reinvestment Act paperwork requirements to nonbanks like Countrywide led Mozilo to sign a treaty with Clinton's HUD secretary Henry Cisneros promising to lend like Countrywide was covered by the CRA[623]. But what really went wrong is that Countrywide sincerely believed that lending vastly more to Hispanics was a great business idea - because a banker that did not genuinely and sincerely believe that would not have been able to take over lots of other people's banks with other people's money the way that Mozilo was able to.

Fossil life found in meteor fragment

2011-03-06 19:36:45

You have probably seen the photos of alleged fossil microorganisms in meteorites, but these are unconvincing. Look hard enough, and you will find faces in rocks. Lots of people have found supposed fossil microorganisms that turned out to be random shapes in rocks.

More impressive are asymmetric amino acids. The meteorite Ivuna Cl1 contained 372 parts per billion of l glutamic acid, but only 8 parts per billion of d glutamic acid[624], indicating that that glutamic acid came from living things. That there was glutamic acid but no leucine indicates that those living things died millions or billions of years ago, hence unlikely to be the product of earthly contamination of the meteorite. Seeming fossils by themselves would not be impressive. Finding traces of biological amino acids with what look like fossilized earthly microorganisms is a pretty good indication that these are indeed real fossils – in which case the most primitive forms of life on earth probably arrived from elsewhere.

Losing the peace to Islam

2011-03-10 08:02:40

The liberal theory is that they are going to deal with Islam by getting them to convert from Islam to liberalism.

---

[623]https://econlog.econlib.org/archives/2011/02/the_wallison_di.html
[624]https://journalofcosmology.com/Life100.html

This has worked against Christianity. Even the Christian right has converted wholesale away from Christianity to progressivism - they continue to oppose divorce, gay marriage, and abortion, but haveconceded on patriarchy and endorsed a system of family law that legally treats men and women as identical and interchangeable, which means that in practice it treats fathers as expendable, dangerous, and harmful. Having accepted the legal interchangeability of men and women they have no principled grounds to oppose gay marriage and so forth. If there are no differences between men and women, if equal in the sense of interchangeable, how can one oppose interchanging them? If men cannot be made carry children, how can you make women carry them? And so on and so forth. Having conceded on patriarchy and unequal marriage, having abandoned biological reality, all else follows, the entire liberal program follows.

So, if it has worked against Christianity, why not Islam?

Liberalism wins against Christianity not by appeal, for it is demonstrably unappealing. Observe that the more liberal the church, the emptier the pews. Nor does it succeed by reason, for Christianity has religious beliefs about the next world, which can never be disproven by reason, while liberalism has religious beliefs about this world, which beliefs are quite demonstrably false. Liberalism wins against Christianity because liberalism is a theocratic religion, and uses the power of the state to inculcate Christian children in liberalism, and to pressure churches to preach liberalism instead of Christianity. If a Christian church preaches illiberal Christianity, the state will disfavor its leading adherents in a variety of unpleasant ways, up to and including spurious sex abuse charges, state abduction of wives and children, Waco massacre, and so on and so forth, while if the preacher preaches liberal Christianity, he quietly gets all manner of favors, faith based state initiatives and so on and so forth, so if a preacher wants to get ahead, he gets with the liberal program.

This does not work against Islam, for Islam is also a theocratic religion, and forcibly resists this. Teach Muslim children liberalism, and someone might cut your throat. Pressure the mosque, and they will pressure right back. Howard, the Australian prime minister, attempted a program of state sponsored "moderate Islam", and as long as his hand was on it, any Muslim preacher that wanted the benefits of state sponsorship sounded at least a little bit "moderate" – but as soon as Howard was removed from power the strings that Howard had attached were swiftly snipped, leaving only state sponsorship of violently illiberal Islam.

So in the US Christians kids are forbidden to participate in collective prayer in school while Muslim kids are compelled to participate in collective prayer in school. As a result of this and many similar measures throughout the west, Muslim mosque attendance is high and rising, Christian Church attendance is low and falling.

In the West we see many converts to Islam, few converts to Christianity. We particularly see unmarried women in their most fertile years converting to Islam.

One article[625] claimed total Christian converts to Islam in Britain 100,000, (mostly women), with 5,200 converted in the most recent year

Another article[626] claimed total Muslim converts to Christianity in Britain was 3000

---

[625]https://www.dailymail.co.uk/news/article-1343954/100-000-Islam-converts-living-UK-White-women-keen-embrace-Muslim-faith.html

[626]https://jmm.aaa.net.au/articles/14689.htm

– a ratio of thirty to one total converts in favor of Islam.

Sample lists of Muslims in the west converting to Christianity are overwhelmingly male[627] – typically about one woman for every three males, while western converts to Islam are mainly women[628], mainly women[629].

Since the converts in one direction are mainly men, and converts in the other direction mainly women, this indicates the ratio in Britain is near a hundred female converts to Islam, for every female convert from Islam to Christianity.

The liberal program of gender abolition does not seem to appeal to its supposed beneficiaries. It is often said that in all of history there has never been gay marriage, but the reason that in all of history there has never been gay marriage, is that in all of history, there has never been a society in which marriage and family law treated husbands and wives alike as "spouses". The one is as unnatural as the other. Perhaps gender abolition will work in the future when biotechnology has progressed to the point that children are decanted, rather than born, but it is not working today.

More astroturf

2011-03-15 17:26:44

Your taxes at work – the government stages protests demanding more government.

The "One Nation Working Together Rally" got lots of ridicule because all the protesters had professionally made mass produced signs. So these protesters as they stream out of their taxpayer paid for buses are handed professionally made mass produced signs that are made to *look* like home made signs.

thanks to Sharp Elbows[630], via Lonely Conservative[631] and Moonbattery[632]

Observe all the school buses shipping protesters in. A better use, no doubt, for your education dollars than teaching children hateful lies demonizing American history.

Observe the guy with the crutch, who is presumably about to pretend to be a cripple

Observe the protesters signing off. Why do protesters need to sign off unless they are getting paid to show up? Could be worse. They could be paid to poison children's minds.

Reactor disaster

2011-03-20 04:31:26

The television is full of panic stricken horror about the supposedly horrible horrible horrible horrible nuclear disaster in Japan.

This disaster looks like being worse than three mile island, but not nearly as bad as Chernobyl.

How many died as a result of Chernobyl?

[627] https://www.muslimjourneytohope.com/watch.asp
[628] https://www.islamfortoday.com/converts.htm#COTW
[629] https://www.defendtheprophet.com/study-white-women-in-uk-converting-to-islam-more-than-men
[630] https://sharpelbowsstl.blogspot.com/2011/03/union-rally-turns-st-louis-into.html
[631] https://lonelyconservative.com/2011/03/video-union-demonstrators-bused-in-on-school-buses/
[632] https://www.moonbattery.com/archives/2011/03/school-buses-br.html

Sixty people died. Pretty similar compared to coal mining disasters, of which there are many each year, killing in total world wide thousands of people every year, usually without making much news.

People have been trying to get alarming cancer statistics from the vicinity of Chernobyl, and have come up empty.

If Chernobyl has elevated cancer rates in its vicinity, as is frequently alleged, somehow no one has been able to produce persuasive epidemiological evidence for it, the only epidemiological evidence being a high risk of thyroid cancers among children that were under four at the time of the incident or conceived but not yet born – **leading to the deaths of nine children from thyroid cancer! Nine! Nine! Nine!** That is the worst anyone has been able to come up with for a great horrible horribly disastrous Chernobyl cancer epidemic disaster.

Nine!

How the middle eastern revolutions are working out.

2011-03-21 11:41:48

As the US goes to war to secure victory for the revolutionaries in Libya, let us take a look at how the revolution is going in Egypt[633]:

1. Muslim terrorists who were lurking in the dark are now in control of the streets of Egypt, not the army.

2. Schools have been closed since January 25 out of fear that terrorists will come into the school to rape and kill students, and the school administrators do not want responsibility for that.

3. There are no police to speak of since they are the enemies of the Muslim Brotherhood. The police are hiding from the terrorists, and there is no 911 to call.

4. There is a complete breakdown of law and order — not just in Cairo, but in all of Egypt.

5. Women are being attacked, mugged and assaulted in broad daylight.

6. The once-banned militant Islamic preachers are now back from exile and are openly preaching hate toward Christians, the West and Israel.

7. Priests are being beheaded in their own apartments.

8. Churches are being burned to the ground.

9. On March 8, thirteen Christians were killed and 150 were injured — 48 of them seriously.

10. The army is acting impotently, if not sympathetically, with the Muslim Brotherhood. In fact, the army is infested with Muslim Brotherhood members.

[633]https://michaelyoussef.squarespace.com/michaels-blogs/the-folly-of-the-leftist-media.html

11. The new government recently appointed by the military council is made up of cabinet members who are on the record as against the peace treaty with Israel. They also are sympathetic to the Muslim Brotherhood.

We are arming and aiding our enemies.

Bryan Caplan wanted people to go on record predicting the future of Egypt[634] before the future becomes apparent. My prediction[635] has come true

Radiation levels normal and falling at Fukushima nuke reactor

2011-03-22 06:27:41

NPR, usually the first to panic about evil nuclear energy, is reporting some very undramatic numbers from the Fukushima reactor[636]

Radiation inside the plant is arguably dangerous, but radiation at the plants main gate is 0.647 milliserverts per hour. By comparison, when you take a flight, you get about 0.04 milliserverts per hour from cosmic rays, so standing at the main gate is fifteen times worse than flying. So someone who flies to Japan from New York, and then wanders up to the main gate to take a look, and hangs out at the main gate for half an hour or so, is likely to get more radiation from his flight than from the nuclear power plant.

Of course if your house is in front of the main gate, 0.647 milliserverts an hour is still a problem if it remains that high year after year - but if your house was in front of the gate, it is no longer in front of the main gate, because the tsunami washed it away, in which case radiation levels are a long way down on your list of troubles, and in any case, radiation levels will not remain that high for long.

Losing the war with Islam

2011-03-24 07:38:20

FilmLadd gives a pre mortem[637] on our defeat:

> On September 20th, 2001, President Bush gave a speech to a Joint Session of Congress after the attacks on 9/11[638] to rally the nation and steel its citizens for the days of strife to come.

> A few hours after the speech I received a call from a friend in military intelligence. The first words out of his mouth?

> "We lost."

---

[634]https://econlog.econlib.org/archives/2011/03/the_future_of_t.html

[635]https://blog.reaction.la/economics/bryan-caplans-challenge.html

[636]https://www.npr.org/blogs/health/2011/03/20/134658088/radiation-data-near-nuclear-plant-offers-little-cause-for-concern

[637]https://filmladd.com/?ArtOfWar

[638]https://www.americanrhetoric.com/speeches/gwbush911jointsessionspeech.htm

The coming collapse

2011-03-27 15:10:08

Under the old US constitution, around 2000 or so, in order for the bureaucrats to spend money on something the house of representatives, the senate, and the president, had to agreed to spend money. Thus in order to do stuff, politicians had to pass a budget, and bureaucrats had to spend within that budget. Passing the budget was power, and politicians were eager to work on the budget, each one wanted a budget, so he could get his own fingerprints on it, for the budget dispensed money, and money is power. Back in the day, you would have found it hard to stop politicians from budgeting even if you held bayonets against their throats.

The new rules that have gradually taken effect are that bureaucrats may spend money unless the house of representatives, the senate, and the president agree to refuse to spend money – kind of like a family where the kid can appeal to daddy, then mommy, then grandma, and the least restrictive parent wins. And if daddy stuck to "No!" not withstanding being overruled by Grandma, a most horrible screaming would ensue.

This renders budgets irrelevant, so no one has much interest in passing them. Budgets have been an empty ritual for a decade or so, and now you just cannot get politicians to bother to show up for the meaningless ritual commemorating a political system that has passed away

The new rules necessarily lead to crisis and financial collapse, so unless republicans grow a pair, pass a budget, and insist that no spending be done except as authorized in the budget, the US is pretty much doomed.

Of course, such insistence would probably require calling out the militia and involve extensive fighting in the streets. All the mass media, probably including Fox news, would protest that a return to the constitution as it was around 2000 or so is a return to the dark ages, and equivalent to the rise of Hitler, so the Republicans understandably lack enthusiasm.

If you look at the federal register, you will observe that it used to consist of rules, prefabricated quarrels. Everything went in there assuming that someone was going to be told what to do, and would try to find some way around it, so it was necessary to pin down precisely what they were to be told to do, so they could not weasel out between the commas. Now there are no rules. The federal register continues to grow at about one hundred thousand pages a year, but no one cares what is in it. Bureaucrats exercise discretion, case by case, and the federal register records meaningless makework performed by low level bureaucrats. So now, there are no rules, and no budgets, no constraints. It is somewhat surprising that they continue to pretend to have a federal register, when they have stopped pretending to have a budget. Regulators continue to ritualistically make rules, not because anyone cares about what the rules say, or because the rules say much of anything, but because rule making signals they are paying attention to certain activities.

As a result the federal government is a string made of sand. Lacking all discipline, it necessarily lacks all cohesion. Today, there are neither rules nor budgets.

The way a government works, the way that a government can exist, is that you have a bunch of elite males (women tend to be largely irrelevant to the process) who settle their internal disputes by means short of violence, and then present a united front to outsiders. The insiders are then stronger than any one outsider, or any natural group of outsiders, and can use violence unopposed, hence the saying that government is a monopoly of legitimate violence. Any one outsider, or small group of outsiders, any small group of subjects of the state, faces the entire elite united, the entire apparatus of the state. So he loses, and losing, his resistance is seen a illegitimate.

Political correctness undermines the cohesion of the politically correct, and the lack of a budget or rules are a manifestation of this lack of cohesion. Lack of a real budget eventually leads to hyperinflationary currency collapse. Hyperinflationary currency collapse is usually followed by regime change, not because the collapse undermines legitimacy and provokes revolution, though it tends to do so, but because it is a manifestation of lack of cohesion and discipline. If the elite cannot hold themselves to a budget, neither can they resist revolution. Regime change and hyperinflation are not caused by each other, but by lack of cohesion and discipline.

Financial collapse is probably a decade or two off, though it could happen as early as 2012. As long as every bureaucrat has a no limits credit card, can probably buy off trouble and buy up unity. Thus revolutionary change is likely to follow, rather than provoke, financial collapse and hyperinflation.

Of course, regime change does not mean the regime will get better. It could easily get worse. However, in the coming armed struggle, people who believe in revolutionary change will have an advantage, so it is going to be patriots versus communists, and the patriots are better shots.

Suppose the patriots win? What then? One solution would be to revert the electoral system so that only heads of taxpaying households vote. A better solution would be to revert the constitution, so that the only permitted activities of the federal government are war, interstate transport, and the post office - and the federal government has no authority to collect income tax. States could do all the stuff the federal government does today, but because of interstate competition, probably will not.

But governments will slither out of any constraints – a more realistic good outcome is a chain of wars and crises that destroys the capacity of the government to do very much.

The Bush-Obama regime in the US resembles the Freis-Allende regime. Freis was a supposed right winger, but his solution for dealing with the left was, like Bush the younger, to move far, far left, in an effort to hog the center - but of course the center simply moved far, far left, resulting in the election of far leftist Allende by a rather thin plurality, just as Bush the Younger's swerve left led to the election of Obama.

Obama, like Allende, plays at being good cop, with the supposed revolutionary far left being the bad cop - but the good cop and bad cop are quite visibly in cahoots.

Allende, like Obama, ran gigantic deficits in an effort to buy up legitimacy, which gained him quite a lot of support, but not quite enough. Pretty soon the money ran out, whereupon Allende ceased to woo support by playing father Christmas, and instead revealed the iron fist – proceeded to apply old fashioned Marxist methods.

The US government however, has more financial credit than Allende had. How much more, no one knows, though we shall soon run into the limits, at which point Obama, or his designated bad cops, will reveal the iron fist.

Perhaps the Cloward Piven strategy will succeed, leading to transnational socialist dictatorship. The Cloward Piven strategy is that once the money runs out, transnational socialists should blame deregulation and capitalism and apply the iron fist.

I think it unlikely that this strategy will succeed. The socialists are most likely going to get shot. That does not, however, necessarily mean that things will get better. We might find ourselves with national socialism, rather than transnational socialism, for once the shooting starts the multiculturalists will be revealed to be weak, and to be revealed as weak while in power is apt to be fatal. Once the $#!% hits the fan, subsequent events are likely to be surprising and unpredictable. One good thing is that if the army splits into factions after the pay runs out and logistics collapse, all the guys training troops in acceptance of homosexuality and so on and so forth will be in the tranzi faction, but all the troops that have seen battle will be in other factions.

There will be hyperinflation in the next couple of decades, possibly within the next few years, possibly as early as 2012. The signal for the start of hyperinflation will be empty shelves in the shops, as it was in Allende's Chile. Following hyperinflation, probably violence, and probably regime change. After that, my crystal ball grows cloudy.

"Deep Cuts"

2011-03-29 18:13:31

Harry Reid, leader of the RepublicanDemocratic party in the Senate, attacks the Republican party because some far right extremists want to make "deep cuts" in government spending

Senate Majority Leader Harry Reid [639] accused Tea Party lawmakers of destroying budget negotiations

> "We've tried to wait patiently for them ... but our patience and the American people's patience is wearing very thin,"

> "Tea Party Republicans are scrapping all the progress we have made and threatening to shut down the government if they do not get *all of their extreme demands.*[640]"

How extreme, I hear you ask, are these dreadfully extreme extremists? How extreme are these "*extreme demands*"

You may have heard that these horribly extreme extremists want to cut sixty one billion dollars off this years one thousand six hundred billion dollar deficit, so that spending will only increase by 1151 billion instead of 1200 billion. That is what I had heard.

But the Office of Management and Budget has analyzed these dreadful cuts, these terribly deep cuts, these drastic cuts, and found that they are only nine billion dollars in this year[641], reducing our 1645 billion dollar deficit to a mere 1636 billion dollar deficit. Most of the cuts consist of supposedly slightly slower growth in future years.

---

[639] D-NV

[640] https://www.lvrj.com/news/reid-vows-to-reject-overhaul-of-social-security-118814724.html

[641] https://www.chicagotribune.com/news/politics/sns-rt-politics-us-usa-contre72r4t6-20110328,0,5491136.story

In short, it is a shadow battle. The parties are only pretending to quarrel. The difference between an elected Democrat, an elected Republican, and an elected Tea Party Republican, is imperceptibly slight.

In truth, expenditures are set by the permanent government, and the political parties have little power, and not much desire for actual power either. Not only is Harry Reid a sell outtool of the Cathedral, but the major reason he is denouncing the Tea Party Republicans as extremists is to distract attention from the fact that they are just as much sell outs.

In theory, Obamacare cannot be implemented unless the House of Representatives votes to fund it. It is a theory no one in the House of Representatives is much interested in testing. In this sense, Obamacare is bipartisan - indeed tripartisan, since the Tea Party Republicans are not willing to stand up and pass a budget that refuses to fund all the things they supposedly oppose.

Laffer curve

2011-03-31 06:50:24

If the government taxes 0% of GDP, it will not get any money. If it attempts to tax 100% of GDP it will not get any money either, since there will be no above ground wealth. So somewhere between 0% and 100% is the tax that maximizes revenue.

Genghis Kahn and Raffles believed that the tax that maximizes revenue is quite low, close to 0%. Today's politician's believe it is quite high, somewhere close to 100%. I suppose that in a society with elaborate bookkeeping and large organizations, the maximum would be higher, so they could both be right about the respective societies that they ruled.

When the mandarins told Kublai Khan that he could not rule China from horseback, they were telling him that a bureaucracy, an elaborate apparatus of rule, can efficiently extract higher taxes than a gang of horsemen – that the revenue maximizing tax collected by a large and expensive bureaucracy is markedly higher than the revenue maximizing tax collected by horsemen, that bureaucrats and regulations are, for the ruler, a good investment.

But, on the other hand, naturally bureaucrats *would* say that. Maybe Kublai Khan would have had more net revenue, and thus been able to support a larger army, if he had gone right on ruling the empire from horseback. When the Mongols adopted bureaucracy, they ran out of puff. Perhaps bureaucracy, regulation, and high taxes is *not* a good investment for the ruler. This is the Mencius Moldbug argument: that economically efficient, rational, revenue maximizing absolute despots would be better than what we have got. It might well be true, though actual, rather than theoretical, absolute despots have a tendency to irrationality.

So we need empirical data. The Bush tax cuts were advocated on the basis that they would increase revenue. Some people say they reduced revenue, others say they increased revenue[642]. This depends on how you measure things. If you want to prove that the Bush tax cuts increased revenues, you look at revenue raised from people who had been highly taxed before the tax cuts, in which case it looks very much that the tax cuts increased

---

[642] https://www.washingtontimes.com/news/2010/feb/3/bush-tax-cuts-boosted-federal-revenue/

revenue. If you look at total revenue, looks like they reduced revenue, perhaps because a lot of people who had formerly paid some income tax, now paid no income tax. Overall, the experience of the Bush tax cuts suggests that taxes on the rich in the US are well above the Laffer maximum, taxes on the poor are well below the Laffer maximum. So if the government has to have more money, it has to do what European governments do: Tax the working poor[643].

Consistent with this theory, more expensive governments, high welfare governments, tend to tax the poor. Their redistribution is more progressive than the US, but their taxation is a lot less progressive than the US, suggesting that attempting to tax the rich more than they are taxed already just does not pay, suggests that as taxes hit the Laffer limit, and the state needs more money, it has no alternative but to tax everyone, including the working poor, at the Laffer limit – thus tax everyone who works in the above ground economy at much the same rate.

One such expensive government is the Greek government. Facing financial crisis, it raised taxes, across the board, taxing everyone more, rich and poor alike, with the result that[644]:

> Compared with the first two months of 2010, revenues declined this year by 9.2 percent

This suggests that Greece is well and truly on the wrong side of the Laffer maximum. Now obviously a rational self interested despot would only wish to tax at the Laffer maximum. Since taxes are universally unpopular, one might suppose a democracy would tax at well below the Laffer maximum – but clearly, at least some democracies are taxing above the Laffer maximum, and all democracies are taxing rather close to the Laffer maximum.

While a rational self interested despot would only wish to tax at the Laffer maximum, a rational self interested bureaucrat might well wish to tax far, far above the Laffer maximum, since that maximizes the power of the mandarins relative to the power of the men on horseback. If Kublai Khan had taxed at lower rate, his power would have depended more on horsemen and less on mandarins, regardless of whether higher taxes or lower taxes are revenue maximizing.

A mandarin is more concerned with relative power than absolute revenue, and would be quite happy if the private sector and non government middle class was completely annihilated, even if meant some substantial reduction in his own standard of living. Indeed, during the Allende regime Vuskovic made this argument explicitly, arguing that the regime should continue to socialize enterprises despite the fact that socialization immediately resulted in the enterprise losing money and producing fewer goods at higher prices, that to defeat the enemies of the regime it was necessary to destroy their power base, which was the private sector regardless of the economic consequences – that whether enterprises were socialized or destroyed, either result consolidated the power of the regime. Allende's socialism was exceptionally destructive because it was concerned with transferring goodies from enemies of the regime (the private sector) to supporters of the regime

---

[643]https://proteinwisdom.com/?p=25980
[644]https://www.ekathimerini.com/4dcgi/_w_articles_wsite2_1_08/03/2011_381979

(government sector unions) without paying much attention to the fact that once upon a time these goodies had been used to create wealth. Vuskovic and Allende employed Marxist rhetoric, class struggle rhetoric, but were in fact representing government as an interest group. Their "land to the peasants program" did not transfer land to the peasants, but to administrators from the cities who had good university degrees but no experience in producing anything, and the boys who deployed the violence that implemented the land program were city boys from the universities, not local peasants. If you are a politician dependent upon support from big government, the elite universities, and big government unions, your policies are going to resemble those of Allende and Vuskovic, whether or not you accept Marxist ideology and Marxist rhetoric.

As I have said before, the Bush/Obama regime strongly resembles the Freis/Allende regime, and history seems to be repeating itself, on a considerably larger scale.

Although the Allende regime had much rhetoric about peasants and workers, it was a regime of the new class, just like today's Washington. The peasants and workers never showed up except as astroturf. The people who showed up for Allende at riots were pretty much the same people as today show up for the Democrats in the Wisconsin troubles – unionists rolled out by big government unions, many of them paid for showing up, and students studying to become members of the new class on class assignment. The violence that preceded the overthrow of the Allende regime was a bourgeois revolt against the new class, the violence was private middle class versus new class, which revolt was appeased by a military regime which imposed major concessions on the new class, in favor of the private sector middle class.

So, in the light of that analogy, what is the solution? Britain and Europe are, I think, too far gone, and for them, like Chile, the only solution is military despotism, which will, perhaps, in time re-evolve into monarchy, but the American middle class remembers its revolutionary origins, and this time might well carry revolt all the way through, violently reimposing a constitution that forbids the Federal government to do anything much except defense and interstate transport.

Mencius has argued that the only way you can root out the New Class is something like denazification, which he argues that only something like a military despotism or foreign occupation could implement. Getting rid of the New Class is more like getting termites out of your house, than getting a burglar out of your house. It will require a great deal of dispersed and detailed violence, which violence Mencius envisages being applied by something like the military police, or the Waffen SS.

But, contrary to Mencius, we have seen in the war with Islam that the private sector is a lot more efficient at producing dispersed and detailed violence, so the best solution would somewhat resemble anarcho capitalism. Even a military despotism is going to have to delegate the application of violence more broadly than it can fully control, and in Latin America, the path to victory usually did involve delegating a lot of violence to militias and vigilantes. Military despots are just bureaucrats with guns. The bureaucracy gets in the way of the efficient and detailed application of violence.

Observe that as California collapses, the ever growing taxes and regulation only afflict the law abiding, only afflict the demographic categories that vote republican[645]. But if

---

[645] https://www.nationalreview.com/articles/255320/two-californias-victor-davis-hanson

Spanish speakers are free from taxes and regulation, why not everyone? If the laws are enforced in such a partisan fashion, *everyone* should resist.

Theocracy

2011-04-08 05:47:08

All Most theocratic religions are officially anti theocratic, in the sense that supposedly people believe in the official religion because it is simply the truth, not because of state sponsorship, and if anyone doubts the truth, they are supposedly seeking the power that rightly belongs to those who preach what is simply the truth, so it is those horrid heretics that are the theocrats. Thus the well paid wise progressive from Harvard sees a church in a wooden shack in the countryside, and cries in horror and outrage "Theocracy!". Islam, the most theocratic of them all, is openly theocratic in the sense that they claim that God literally rules them, which however means that they have to pretend their doctrine is unchanging.The Roman Catholic Church on the other hand, was after 1277 almost as furtive about theocracy as Harvard. Official lists of forbidden thoughts, such as the condemnations of 1277, were officially unofficial. The Spanish inquisition was operated by kings, and the Church, like Harvard, merely advised kings on the truth.

And if the truth requires frequent rewrites of history and the forceful suppression of dangerously inconvenient facts, such is a perfectly legitimate and reasonable response to the irrationally foolish heretics. We have to help people perceive the truth by lying to them, as for example "hide the decline". That is the way you do science. You delete the data you know to be misleading, and replace it with data that shows what you know to be the truth because it is the official consensus. All properly scientific scientists do that, and if they don't they deserve to lose their jobs. We know all scientists are reliable, because they are continually peer reviewed to make sure they stick to the consensus of their peers – and if their data fails to correspond to observation, who cares. It is more important that it correspond to the real truth than mere observation.

So how do you tell a theocratic religion if it fails to post a big label saying "Theocracy"?

Theocratic religions are always stronger the closer people are to the center of power, because they originate and are upheld by the center. That is how you tell a theocratic religion. That is what a theocratic religion is.

Thus:

Washington is more progressive than flyover country, and Cairo more Islamic than the Egyptian delta

The American rich are more progressive than the American poor, and the Egyptian rich more Islamic than the Egyptian poor.

Ivy League educated Americans are more progressive than Cow University educated Americans, and similarly in Egypt, those with higher status Egyptian educations are more Islamic.

And that is how you can spot a theocracy.

A theocracy that requires improbable beliefs about the next world can nonetheless recruit people who are sane, in that they can recruit people who have the required beliefs about the next world, but base their beliefs about this world on reality testing. The Jesuits were good at that. But progressivism is a religion, or substitute for religion, which requires beliefs about *this* world – thus tends to recruit people who are crazy and/or stupid. And as the required purity of belief becomes ever more and more extreme, the required real or feigned insanity becomes crazier and crazier, as magnificently illustrated by the events surrounding Major Hasan.

The Major Hasan incident illustrates the required craziness, Nobel Prize winning economist Paul Krugman illustrates the required stupidity.

The craziness is illustrated by the fact that when Major Hasan gave a power point presentation on why he was going to murder his audience, they all listened politely and respectfully, is illustrated by the fact that the State Department is installing the guys who raped and sexually mutilated Lara Logan into power in Egypt, is illustrated by the fact that Imam Rauf who is erecting a victory mosque at ground zero on the body parts of his enemies is hailed as a moderate and gets government funding.

If anyone had said of Major Hasan "Hey, this guy is saying he is going to kill us! Let us lock him up right now and throw away the key", that would have been *raaaciist*. They would have been *discriminating*.

Our policy of exporting democracy to Muslims is as transparently demented as our policy of affirmative actioning Hasan to Major. It is as crazy to allow Muslims to vote anywhere in the world as it was to affirmative action Hasan to Major instead of locking him up.

US policy is to export democracy at gunpoint in the expectation that it will turn Muslims into progressives – but quite obviously democracy is having the opposite effect. Democracy turns them into Islamists – and anyone who could not have foreseen it was going to turn them into Islamists was batshit crazy, willfully blind to the glaringly obvious.

An individual Muslim ruler who decides for war, or, more commonly, actions likely to provoke war, gets a warm glow of religious piety by so doing, but faces the consequences of his actions, because his decision makes a large difference to the likelihood of bombs falling through his roof. Since most Muslims are not in fact very pious, he, instead of piously deciding for war, swigs down a shot of whiskey, snacks on some pork, then impiously decides for peace and adopts measures to encourage tourism and western investment - for example as the United Arab Emirates does.

A Muslim voter who votes for trouble gets as much of a warm glow of piety as a ruler who decides for war, but since one vote makes no difference, does not increase the chances of bombs landing on his head. So just as western voters piously vote for redistribution of wealth and preservation of the environment regardless of the consequences to themselves, Muslims piously vote for hatred, murder and war regardless of the consequences of for themselves.

The most peaceable and prosperous Muslim states are long established monarchies with secure hereditary rulers, such as Kuwait, Qatar, and the United Arab Emirates. Muslim party states are considerably less peaceful. The more power is distributed, the more a Muslim state will act Islamic – the more it will make war upon us infidels.

The shape of things to come

2011-04-10 07:10:16

We are seeing a political singularity - the leftwards slide that has been under way since 1710 or so is going faster and faster.

Many people have already commented on the ludicrous absurdity of calling 1% cuts in a budget that rose 27% in three years, "drastic". Supposedly this makes the Tea Party not merely conservative, but "ultra conservative".

If the tea party is ultra conservative, what then would we call someone who attempted to restore the status quo of 2004? Super fanatical ultra nazi right wing extremist?

In the blogs people are presenting the usual Keynesian rationalizations for spending money that we do not have – but the Keynesian rationalization assumes that goods are going unsold and that we have deflation, whereas in reality there has been no deflation and we are starting to see empty shelves that can only be filled at substantially higher prices, foreshadowing rapid inflation soon. We have already seen substantial inflation that the US government is lying about, and the dire state of the supply chain foreshadows a lot more inflation. The Keynesian excuse for big spending, if it ever had any validity, has no validity today. It looks to me very much as if an inflationary shock is coming down the overly tight supply chain on top of the already disturbing rate of inflation – not a hyperinflationary shock – that is probably a decade or so down the road, but shocking enough.

We are not seeing a technological singularity. Technological change slowed down in 1970, at about the same time as political correctness started to be enforced on science and scientists by increasingly drastic means. The last man on the moon left in 1972. The tallest building in the united states was finished in 1974. Cars are becoming humbler. The history of science was abruptly rewritten in 1972, with natural selection being deprecated. Instead of Darwin being famous for natural selection, after 1972 he was supposedly famous for common descent, which necessitated common descent being removed from Lamarck. Lamarck was abruptly rewritten so that after 1972, he supposedly had proposed separate and parallel evolution instead of branching evolution with family resemblances between species resulting from common descent, though you can still get his original books from the internet archive.

That which cannot continue, will stop. Trees do not grow to the sky. This does not, however, necessarily mean that freedom will be restored and everything will be lovely. The last time we had theocracy, we had stagnation for four hundred years.

The explosive expansion of spending and regulation represents a collapse of discipline within the ruling elite. The way the system is supposed to work, and the way it mostly did work several decades ago, is that the American Federal Government can only spend money on something if the House of Representatives, the Senate, and the President agree to spend money on that thing, so no government employee can be employed, except all three agree he should be employed, so the government cannot do anything unless all three agree that it be done. A public servant, and indeed his entire department, was apt to be fired if he pissed off anyone. Conversely, the individual was free to do anything, unless all three agree that he be stopped from doing that thing. We are now approaching the reverse situation, where for an individual to do anything requires a pile of permissions from diverse governmental authorities, but any governmental authority can spend money on anything unless there is near unanimous opposition to them spending money.

Obviously this cannot continue. Eventually the money runs out, in that we shall have a hyperinflationary crisis, and revert to some other form of money, such as the gold standard. As that happens, the increasingly lawless behavior of the rulers against the ruled will become increasingly lawless behavior of the rulers against each other. Civil war, or something close to civil war, or the dire and immediate threat of civil war will ensue.

At that point, we will have the political singularity, probably around 2025 or so. Beyond the singularity, no predictions can be made, other than that the results will be surprising. It is possible that tax producers will win over tax consumers. I hope for that outcome. The alternative is centuries of poverty and stagnation. Whether it is probable, I cannot say. Such an outcome, however, necessitates the ending of democracy with universal franchise, since tax consumers substantially outnumber and outvote tax producers.

Conservative bloggers declare victory
2011-04-10 09:21:38

According to Strata and others, the outcome of the budget negotiations (to reduce by one percent spending that was recently increased by by thirty percent) was a mighty victory[646].

By a vote of approximately ten to one, the US House of Representatives voted to continue at slightly lower speed on a course that leads to bankruptcy, hyperinflation, social collapse, and, if we are lucky, civil war in the next decade or two.

Hide the decline, part umpteen
2011-04-12 15:01:18

Stephan and Rachit cored lots of trees, to estimate weather in past years. In a cold climate, near the tree line, a tree will generally grow more if the weather is warm than if it is cold, though lots of other things affect it too. Still, if you check lots of trees over a wide area of very cold land, other factors will probably average out, and the rate of growth, the width of the tree rings, will largely indicate temperature. And Stephan and Rachit cored a *lot* of trees, over a lot of very cold land, while being attacked by hordes of ravenous mosquitoes.

Yet somehow, strange to report, only about a tenth of the trees they cored were used to construct a hockey stick graph. Most of their data was quietly buried as unwanted, but leaked in the climategate files documents/briffa-treering-external/stepan. Recently Climate Audit took a look at this neglected data.

Why, you may ask, were some trees included and other trees, the vast majority of the trees, not included?

Climate Audit constructs a graph of growth[647]. The red line is the growth rate of the small set of trees the Anthropogenic Global Warmists chose to use for their hockey stick of doom. The black line is growth rate for all of the trees that Stephan and Rachit cored

---

[646]https://strata-sphere.com/blog/index.php/archives/16268
[647]https://climateaudit.org/2011/04/09/yamal-and-hide-the-decline/

while fighting off mosquitoes, including the vast majority of trees which the the Warmists somehow chose to not use.

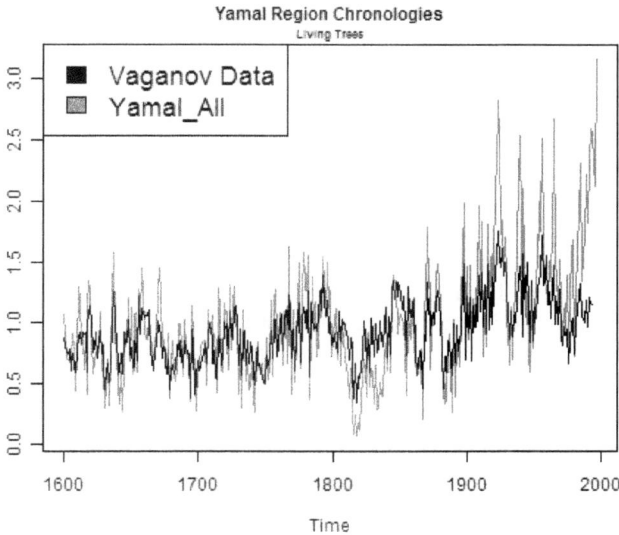

Observe that the red line, the cherry picked trees, show something dramatic and unusual happening in the twentieth century, especially the late twentieth century, show something like a hockey stick. The unselected trees, the vast majority of the trees, show a slight warming trend over centuries, but no more so in the twentieth century than in any other century.

Who rules the world?

2011-04-17 08:48:42

Tracing rulers academic connections yields an interesting picture. Thus Mugabe, like so many third world rulers, comes from the London School of Economics, but Harry Lee Kuan Yew was educated in Singapore. And lo and behold, Mugabe was installed in power by the "international community" aka the tranzis, while Harry Lee Kuan Yew was installed in power by Singaporeans.

A similar trace is visible in the Ivory Coast, where shortly before I wrote this, the "international community" held a blatantly rigged election, wherein Muslim cannibals were elected, under the leadership of a Muslim cannibal educated in an American Ivy League university. Since it was likely that the new elite would eat the old elite and their cats, the old elite was reluctant to acquiesce, so, as usual, the "international community" sent in peacekeeping troops. The "international community" says it is quite horrified that the new elite is killing the old elite and their cats, and sometimes eating them as I write this, and I suppose it truly is horrified, but not so horrified that they hold back from imposing the new elite. If massacres and sometimes cannibalism is taking place, it is supposedly all the old elite's fault for resisting the benign prodemocracy forces of transnationalism.

This much resembles the Tranzi reaction to the crimes of Mugabe, and the Tranzi reaction to the Hutu genocide of the Tutsi, which genocide was supposedly not happening, was happening but was supposedly the fault of the old colonial elite, not the new Tranzi elite, and which the Tutsi supposedly brought upon themselves by their evil collaboration with the old colonial elite.

The man being imposed by Tranzi troops in the Ivory coast is Alassane Ouattara, educated in a US Ivy Leage university, and then sent directly from the Ivy League to the World Bank (a classic tranzi institution to rule those benighted third worlders) and then sent directly from the world bank in a rigged election to directly rule the ivory coast. He is not an ivory coast politician, but a World Bank bureaucrat. Seems, however, that because of the great respect for cultural diversity in the Ivy League, they overlooked to teach him that eating people is wrong. He may not personally eat people, but in the glorious Ivy League tradition of tolerance, is alarmingly tolerant of those that do.

The man being overthrown by tranzi troops in the Ivory coast is Laurent Gbagbo, who was also educated in a western university, though a somewhat less classy and prestigious one than Ouattara, but unlike Ouattara arrived in back in the ivory coast as a mere ordinary teacher, and worked his way up to ruler in local politics, unlike Quattara who worked is way up in the World Bank bureaucracy, and arrived in the Ivory coast from overseas to rule.

The power transfer in the Ivory Coast looks like it may have much the same effect as it did in Rhodesia, where politically unreliable farmers were removed from their farms, to be replaced by politically reliable non farmers, resulting in a total collapse of production. If the tranzis create a desert in the Ivory coast, as they did in Rhodesia, this will confirm that they would rather destroy wealth, than let anyone politically unreliable control it.

The same transnational elite runs the US, most of Europe, and most of the third world. Observe that when "gay pride day" was exported to most of the world, they used the made in US Ivy League word "gay" which shows who is calling the shots.

India was initially ruled by the LSE, but in India local elites have taken charge, and Singapore was independent of the LSE from the day it became independent of Malaysia. Stalin thought he was running the western progressive ruling elite, but the reason they were so on board with Stalinist infiltration is that they thought they were running Stalin. Maybe they were, but they were not running Khrushchev. China, they thought, was run by Stalin, and they ran Stalin, so they thought, but China was not run by Khrushchev, and they did not run Khrushchev.

So we have, already, furtively and conspiratorially, a united ruling elite that runs the US, Europe, and most third world shitholes - observe, for example, what is happening in the Ivory Coast - made-in-France massacres of the Christian and animist minority. The French ruling elite get the money, the power, and the chocolate, and the local Muslims get to kill and eat infidels, and their cats.

However, the tranzi elite does not run that part of the formerly third world that is doing OK, indeed getting out from under that transnational ruling elite seems to be a precondition for doing OK. You cannot get rich unless you let competent people run production, and if you let competent people run production that is a threat to tranzi power. The tranzi elite colonized in the name of uprooting colonialism, a strategy that, as in Rhodesia, is apt to create deserts. In Singapore and Hong Kong the local eurasian elite, colonialist descended, held power. In Botswana, the partially black, colonial descended elite held on power for a while, but may have lost it now. Zimbabwe, a tool of the tranzis, invaded, Botswana had to turn the tranzis for help, and the tranzi assistance came, naturally, with strings attached, with the result that Botswana, like South Africa, may now be descending into the usual African chaos. Hard to tell, since the each elite hides behind the other.

So at present, if the world ruling elite simply dropped their cover, the transnational elite would rule a large part of the world, but not enough of the world to call themselves "United World Government" in place of "United States Government"

The end is not nigh

2011-04-21 11:03:56

But it is in sight.

There is a lot of ruin in a nation, but we have had a lot of ruin.

The US government lacks cohesion, and is insolvent. Lack of cohesion means that in a crisis it is apt to disappear, dissolve into its parts, with each part seeking its own interest. Insolvency means a crisis is looming.

I would expect the Euro to collapse before the US dollar, and the Euro is not going to collapse all that soon, and I would expect Europe to collapse politically before the US government collapses politically, and European political collapse is still far off. I predict interesting times in the 2020s.

A lot of people have made the metaphor that the Democrats have been driving the bus towards the cliff at one hundred miles per hour, and the Republicans propose to slow down to ninety eight miles per hour, but are willing to compromise for ninety nine miles per hour. What are they thinking?

Noble prize winning economist Krugman explains what he is thinking, which is pretty much what the Office of Management and Budget explains it is thinking, so I suppose this is what they are all thinking: The government is going to save pots of and pots of money by economizing on various things, especially health care.

How, you may ask, is it going to economize on health care?

Among the many measures the government is deploying to save pots and pots of money on health care, is that the government is forming two large new bureaucracies with the job of telling hospitals, doctors, and patients, how to save money on health care.

Whom the gods would destroy, they first make mad. Like a poker player in the grip of tilt, our ruling elite plan to solve their problems by doubling down on what got them into trouble.

Consensus

2011-04-22 16:30:20

When Galileo explained the scientific method, he condemned consensus:

The testimony of many has little more value than that of few, since the number of people who reason well in complicated matters is much smaller than that of those who reason badly. If reasoning were like hauling I should agree that several reasoners would be worth more than one, just as several horses can haul more sacks of grain than one can. But reasoning is like racing and not like hauling, and a single Barbary steed can outrun a hundred dray horses

Peer review is consensus. Consensus is religion, not science. Peer review works as depicted in this excellent cartoon[648]: Click on the snippet of the cartoon to see the full cartoon.

Observe the priestly robes worn by the scientists

The survival prospects of democracy

2011-04-26 03:00:40

Until the American Republic demonstrated impressive longevity, the conventional wisdom was that democracy was inherently short lived. As soon as the masses discovered they could vote themselves rich, it would implode.

Today, we observe that if it does not fall apart immediately, the elite import cheaper votes, and then it falls apart.

The latest casualty of democracy is the Ivory Coast. According the the mainstream media, everything is just lovely on the ivory coast, now that the Ivy League graduate and World Bank Bureaucrat has been installed by international forces over the evil dictator.

Yet somehow there are lots of anecdotes of ethnic cleansing[649] and cannibalism, and those who are owed money by the Ivory Coast government are worried because the ports are closed, the banks are closed, and the crops are rotting in the fields[650].

In the Ivory Coast, we see the worst possible outcome of democracy. First the top elements of the local elite imported cheap votes, then the transnational ruling elite used those imported voters as political cover to take power away from the top elements of the local elite, which process went out of control resulting in the ejection of the entire local elite - including the people who operated the farms, the banks, and the ports. In the process, the cheap imported voters physically displaced the people who built and operated those farms and ports, and in some cases, ate them.

You think that could only happen in the third world? Observe Detroit, though in Detroit they did not drop all the way to cannibalism.

What we are seeing in the Ivory Coast is an alliance of the top people (Ivy League and transnational bureaucrats) and the bottom people (Islamic illegal immigrants who have never had much contact with western civilization) displacing the middle people (farmers, bankers, and the like). Unfortunately neither the top people, nor the bottom people actually produce anything. The transnational elite, unlike the local elite that has just been replaced in the ivory coast, is parasitic and unproductive.

---

[648]https://dresdencodak.com/2011/04/19/dark-science-09/
[649]https://www.timeslive.co.za/africa/article1030651.ece/I.-Coast-villages-in-ruin-after-raids
[650]https://blogs.ft.com/beyond-brics/2011/04/18/ivory-coast-eurobond-triumph-of-hope/

The Ivory Coast, where the banks are closed, the ports are closed, and the cocoa crop is rotting in untended fields, is the future of democracy. The city of Detroit is the future of democracy. Democracy collapses faster when you have blacks and/or Muslims voting, but Liverpool is starting to look a lot like Detroit. In Detroit, the two legged feral animals are entirely black, in the ivory coast, entirely Muslim, but in Liverpool, mostly white, Democracy, rather than race is the critical factor. The Ivory Coast would still be one of the most prosperous nations in Africa were it not for democracy. In the Ivory Coast, democracy means that they really do eat the rich. They have always been black, but were not eating people until the recent elections. In the US, towards the end, we will very likely see members of one voting block eating members of another voting block, just as we are now seeing on the Ivory Coast.

And in America we cannot vote our way out of this problem, due to a combination of ballot box stuffing, as in the ivory coast, and the government electing a new people, as in the Ivory Coast.

Democracy has got to go, and is going to go, and the only question is how much damage it will do when it falls, and what will replace it.

The end state of democracy is members of the winning voter blocks eating members of the defeated voter blocks as the lights go out. Democracy is not the American Republic, but the Ivory Coast.

Democracy in America started off as a republic of white property owning males, in a land where every hard working man could expect to eventually acquire property, so that most males eventually became eligible to vote. The franchise inexorably expanded, because politicians always want voters whose votes are cheaper to buy. And when there were no more cheap votes to be had by expanding the franchise, they set about importing cheap low IQ voters, the end state of this process being the Ivory Coast.

The ruling coalition of top and bottom, of ivy league and primitive savages, tends to get ever smaller at the top, and ever more inferior at the bottom, as at the top the self perpetuating elite becomes ever smaller and more detached from reality, and at the bottom, the votes it relies on get ever cheaper. Vote buying is democracy's weakness, because the ruling elite winds up relying on the cheapest and most easily manipulated source of votes, which tend to be the worst people – people incapable of operating a civilization, a ruling underclass[651], as in Detroit.

The ruling coalition of Ivy league and human garbage becomes ever smaller at the top, looking down on ordinary members of the elite, such as farmers from a vast height, till for lack of numbers the top element of the coalition loses control of the bottom element of its coalition – thus in Detroit, the community organizers took over, in the Ivory Coast, the cannibals. The pretended democracy became all too horrifyingly real.

The transnational elite now have possession of the Ivory Coast banks and ports, but lack the ability to operate them. Even less can the horde of savages that they have unleashed operate them.

---

[651]https://unqualified-reservations.blogspot.com/2008/02/theory-of-ruling-underclass.html

Democracy in the Ivory Coast

2011-04-27 08:04:11

The UN refugee agency estimates that over a million people have fled[652]. Many of them are hiding in the jungle, and many of them have no food.

However, it piously avoids saying who is fleeing whom, and why.

The great majority of refugees are westernized Christians and animists fleeing Muslims with a markedly lower level of civilization. The great majority of refugees are not immigrants or the children of immigrants, but people who have lived on the coast for generations, who have now become exiles.

The refugees are people that made the Ivory Coast function. Those that drove them out are immigrants, many of them illegal immigrants, or the children of illegal immigrants, that come from inland areas with a marked lower level of civilization, lower living standard, and less westernization – and less ability to operate a society that is, by African standards, advanced.

These immigrants were allowed in, in part to provide cheap labor, but in large part to provide cheap votes. In due course, the tranzis bid for these cheap votes, and got them. One of the things they offered in return for these cheap votes, was a takeover of the Ivory Coast by the new voting block, offered them the land and housing and equipment of the old voting block.

What has happened in that inlanders led by tranzis have taken the coast away from its previous inhabitants, and driven the coastal people inland into the jungle.

These refugees are not fleeing a storm, or an earthquake. They are fleeing democracy in action.

The Ivory Coast illustrates the two great problems of democracy: The fact that bids for votes have no limit, since the politicians are bidding with the promise of stolen goods, and the propensity of governments, pursuing a cheaper vote, to elect a new people. A government composed of people native to the ivory coast elected a new people, a people not native to the ivory coast, and that new people, in turn, elected a new government, a government of tranzis in place of a government of people native to the Ivory Coast.

Tranzis tend to have a socialist outlook, that stuff such as banks, ports, farms, belong to the people collectively, rather than individually, so it is natural for them to bid for votes with *all* of other people's property. And then those other people make problems, and have to be chased away from their property. And so they were.

Google is evil

2011-05-08 06:19:02

Firefox reports your IP and all nearby wifi systems to Google. Thunderbird reports your IP to Google. From the nearby wifi systems, Google can locate you relative to nearby wifi points.. From a multitude of browsers reporting in, it can locate wifi systems relative to each other. When it does ground level photo drives for Google Earth, it locates wifi systems relative to streets and houses. Knowing the location of some wifi systems relative to

---

[652]https://www.voanews.com/english/news/africa/decapua-ivory-coast-displaced-26apr11-120707649.html

streets and houses, it can locate all wifi systems relative to streets and houses. So when you launch a search for a sexual preference, or a politically incorrect fact, Google can tell where you are sitting, what house you are in, when you search for unapproved knowledge[653]. It keeps this information forever.

The intent is that when you search for a restaurant or some such, Google will know to provide information about local restaurants. But Google notoriously plays ball with governments. More sinister uses are also possible. And why does Google need to know the geographic location where your email is coming from?

To turn this off:

Mozilla Firefox
+ Type 'about:config' in the address bar
+ Click through the warning
+ Type 'geo.' in the search box. A list of items appears
+ Doubleclick on the geo.enabled item till it reads 'False'
+ Rightclick on the 'geo.wifi.uri' item and select 'Modify'
+ Modify the item from evil google to 'https://localhost'
Mozilla Thunderbird
+ Select Tools/Options/Avanced/General/Config Editor
+ click through the warning
+ type 'geo.' in the search box. A list of items appears
+ Doubleclick on the geo.enabled item till it reads 'False'

Google piously proclaims:

> Your privacy is extremely important to us, and Firefox never shares your location without your permission.[654]

This is of course a lie. Firefox never shares your location to advertisers without your permission – but it does continually send your location to Google without your permission.

If your privacy was actually important to Google, the browser would only send this information to Google when advertisers requested it and you gave them permission.

"Democracy never lasts long"

2011-05-09 14:02:39

In 1814, John Adams, second president of the United States, and one of the revolutionaries that founded it, said

> Remember, democracy never lasts long. It soon wastes, exhausts, and murders itself. There never was a democracy yet that did not commit suicide. It is in vain to say that democracy is less vain, less proud, less selfish, less ambitious, or less avaricious than aristocracy or monarchy.

---

[653]https://www.mozilla.com/en-US/firefox/geolocation/
[654]https://www.mozilla.com/en-US/firefox/geolocation/

And that was the common wisdom at the time. Democracy in the United States, the work of the revolutionaries, has lasted a lot longer than anyone expected, but the end is now in sight.

I hope that after democracy, we will get, in at least some small parts of what once was the United States, anarcho capitalism, or failing that, monarchy, but the usual successor to democracy is a brief period of oligarchy swiftly followed by the worst form of dictatorship: popular dictatorship. Mencius Moldbug hopes that popular dictatorship will transition to monarchy, but consider that in the case of Rome, that took a very long time.

One small ground for optimism is that we are seeing a fair bit of crypto anarchy, as business goes underground, and non state armed forces, both legal and illegal, are growing stronger. The rise of crypto anarchy could lead to anarcho capitalism, at least for the wealthy, and the rise of private armed forces could lead to feudalism, but I fear that the way to bet is popular dictatorship.

The difference between popular dictatorship and monarchy is illustrated by the difference between Botswana and Zimbawe. Mugabe, endorsed by the London School of Economics to rule Zimbabwe, had to allow and encourage one group to loot another, in order to maintain a base of support. Similarly, Ivy League Graduate Ouattara, sent to rule the Ivory Coast by the world bank, now presiding over the place as the Muslims that gave gave him his legitimacy run amuck.

When the colonialists left, most of Black Africa turned into hellholes, with the notable exception of Botswana, now 53 in world GDP, far above any other black African country. When Botswana became independent they elected the man born to be King, and the place remained in good shape so long as he lived. Till the day he died, it was the fastest growing economy in Africa. So long as he lived, the place had low and stable taxes, and the best economic and personal freedom in Africa – because he was elected on the basis of his royal birth, not elected on the basis of paying off one group with the lives and property of another group.

Unfortunately, popular dictators, such as Mugabe, have the same need to pay off their supporters as democratically elected presidents, such as Quattara, so I am less optimistic than Mencius Moldbug about the prospects for America transitioning to a relatively benign monarchy via one man one vote once. When the deluge commences, let us aim for anarchy and/or feudalism, rather than monarchy. It takes generations for the sons of dictators to become monarchs, and in the meantime you get most of the disadvantages of democracy with none of the benefits.

Democratic Peace

2011-05-13 10:47:44

For a while, the theory of Democratic Peace was popular, widely believed, and widely argued. Supposedly democracies do not go to war with each other.

On the basis of this theory, Osama Obama and Bush have been promoting democracy in the middle east. Supposedly, if Muslims get to vote, they will vote against making war on us.

Of course, one could look at much the same evidence and conclude that countries that are capitalist and predominantly free market do not go to war with each other, and that countries with McDonald's franchises do not go to war with each other.

The last theory, in addition to being better supported by the evidence, also has more plausible theory behind it: If two countries both have McDonald's franchises, they have business connections to the world, and thus to each other, so you have vested interests in both countries in favor of peace.

The democratic peace theory was always based on wishful thinking and torturing the evidence till it confesses. The three most dreadful recent wars were the American civil war, between democracies, the first world war, mostly between democracies, in the sense that the Kaiser's war budget had to voted by democratically elected legislators, and World War II, which was primarily caused by a democracy, the Weimar Republic, suicidally voting for totalitarians. Proponents of the Democratic Peace theory argue that does not count, because Nazi Germany certainly was not democratic, but the notorious propensity of democracies to commit suicide in a messy fashion certainly ought to count. The Nazi party came to power in accordance with the Weimar Republic rules, because they got more votes than any other party in the Weimar Republic ever did in any election. The only reason that they did not get an outright majority is that lots of people were voting for the communists, so though there was no clear majority for any one party, there was clear majority in favor war, terror, and bringing democracy to an end.

Now, the US has successfully exported democracy to Egypt. And how shall we be rewarded?

The most likely winner of the election proposes to end the peace treaty with Israel, confront Israel, and allow terrorists to operate from Egypt[655]. None of the candidates are saying "war", but they are proposing to act in a way that makes war likely, and perhaps unavoidable.

Lifestyles of the benefactors of the poor

2011-05-16 06:58:05

The other McCain has an interesting tale to tell:

Recently the World Bank, led by the leading socialist candidate for the french presidency, in its endless efforts to help the poor, helped the poor backward illegal immigrant Muslim majority of the Ivory Coast take over from the slightly less poor and slightly more advanced native Christian minority of the Ivory Coast.

But how do these people live when not tirelessly serving the poor?

The managing director of the International Monetary Fund, former French Foreign Minister, and until now leading socialist candidate for the French presidency, Dominique Strauss-Kahn, was recently busted for raping a hotel maid in his three thousand dollars a night hotel suite[656]

---

[655] https://www.rightsidenews.com/2011051113485/editorial/world-opinion-and-editorial/israels-new-neighbor-egypt-radical-nationalist-president-islamist-dominated-parliament.html

[656] https://theothermccain.com/2011/05/15/frenchman-shocked-to-discover-its-illegal-to-sodomize-your-hotel-maid-in-u-s/

I find the psychology of it interesting. He was in a foreign country, she was in her own country, still the most powerful country in the world despite our recent decline, she was an employee in her place of employment, he was a guest, which puts her in the strongest possible position get retribution for rape, and him in the weakest possible position to weasel out of it, in the position where one is most likely to get busted. These people think they own the whole world - and usually they are right.

Why did the USG kill Bin Laden out of hand? And why did almost all Americans approve of killing him out of hand, rather than charging him and trying him, or questioning him under torture and then charging him and trying him?

Because no one, not even the US president, trusts US courts to convict against foreign pressure, or acquit against foreign pressure.

It will be interesting to see what happens with these charges. It will also be interesting to see what happens to the career of whoever is in charge of the Midtown South New York police precinct.

I suspect that after he is released on bail, these charges will go nowhere fast, much like the careers of the police who busted him. His behavior suggests that that is what he believes, and the reaction to the killing of Bin Laden suggests that this belief is widely shared.

Anne Mansouret confirms rape of Tristane Banon by DSK
2011-05-17 10:01:42

It seems that the chief of the IMF has been in the habit of raping women for quite some time - and no one called him on it until today.

Ann Mansouret confirms that her daughter, Tristane Banon was raped by Dominique Strauss-Kahn[657]

So far, the hotel management has had balls the size of apples, the south central cops have had balls the size of apples, and, to my considerable surprise, the judge has had balls the size of apples. But, of course, the higher this goes up the judicial system, the smaller the testicles.

Herman Cain
2011-05-17 11:26:10

The rest of the republican field is now acting as if Herman Cain is the man to beat, acting as if he is now the front runner for Republican candidate and president, which makes him the front runner for the moment, though it is a long way to go to the 2012 presidential elections.

I suspect this may be charisma envy. Obama has a lot of charisma, so Republicans are looking for someone with charisma. Herman Cain has more charisma than Obama, and more charisma than the rest of the republican field put together, though he is not as smart as the rest of the republican field, nor even as smart as the Obamessiah. Still, if you,

---

[657] https://www.agoravox.tv/actualites/politique/article/affaire-dsk-tristane-banon-michele-30239

unlike Obama, are not proposing to micromanage America, how much smarts do you need?

Does he have character, something that the Obamessiah conspicuously lacks? The democrats and the rest of the republican field are now putting his life under examination, so I suppose we shall soon learn about his character, or lack thereof.

It is a long, long way to the 2012 presidential elections, but they are Herman Cain's to lose. A short while ago, the republicans had no candidate. Now they have a potential candidate and a plausible winner.

It will be an odd sight if in the 2012 presidential elections, we have two black candidates, one of them noticeably less bright than past presidents, and the other noticeably less bright than that. But if Herman Cain sticks to the program he is running on in the primaries, running on the American dream and American exceptionalism, he will be less bad than any recent president.

However, if he gets the nomination, he will probably swerve left, as the rest of the Tea Party has.

Obama's Birth Certificate Forged

2011-05-18 16:46:16

What Obama released is a composite photoshopped together from multiple documents.

Archive Index Systems spots undeniable photoshop artifacts in the released birth certificate.[658]

The background text, from one certificate, is slightly curved, which is what you get if you scan some paper that is not perfectly flat - the document was scanned from a book, so near the book binding did not lie perfectly flat. The name of the hospital is not curved– so was not scanned from the same document. The name "Barack" has white around it, being lifted from a document without the birth certificate background, lifted from a document that is not a birth certificate. They should have hired me. I do much better forgeries than that. This is a crude and amateurish job – typical government work.

Democratic apocalypse

2011-05-21 02:39:50

The latest events in the middle east are not looking too favorable for the theory of democratic peac[659]e.

I said this in an earlier post, and this is just an "I told you so" repeat. Things were bad then, and they are getting worse now, as the middle eastern parties converge to the center and the mainstream – revealing that the center and the mainstream favors suicidal war on infidels.

If nearby Jews and Christians are on the firing line, Jews and Christians further away, for example in US airliners, will be next in line. If they kill the Copts, the Israelis are next, if they kill the Israelis, we are next.

---

[658]https://www.scribd.com/doc/55594183/Obamas-Cert-of-Birth-May-10-2011-News-Realease
[659]https://www.nationalreview.com/corner/267321/arab-spring-turns-fall-winter-follow-stanley-kurtz

The difference between Islamists, and what passes for "secular democrats" in the middle east, is insignificant., much like the difference between Republicans and Democrats in the US. No matter which party wins the elections, the outcome for the US will be much the same. The Islamists favor war on infidels, and the secular democrats favor slightly more selective war on infidels, just as in the US, the Democrats favor national *socialism*, and the Republicans favor *national* socialism.

The Middle Eastern kings generally favor peaceful coexistence with infidels. The popular dictators, for example Bashar al-Assad in Syria and Qaddaffi in Libya, could be intimidated into reducing their level of violence against infidels with moderate amounts of violence. Democrats, however, will have to be killed. If we are to live, they will have to die.

It should be US policy that no Muslim anywhere gets to vote. Not in America, not in the West, and especially not in Muslim majority countries. Voters are dangerous, and Muslim voters are exceptionally dangerous.

A voter votes to demonstrate his allegiance to virtue, and or the group to which he belongs, thus is apt to vote unselfishly, because his vote affirms his support for virtue, without making any difference to the prospects that he will actually be forced to be virtuous, since his vote is merely one of millions. And if the official religion deems suicidal war to be virtuous, the voter will vote for suicidal war, whereas a King hopes to bequeath his country to his sons, so selfishly chooses policies that lead to peace and prosperity.

In the US, non white votes are encouraged to vote to demonstrate allegiance to their race or ethnicity, thereby demonstrating virtue, while white voters are encouraged to demonstrate lack of allegiance to their race or ethnicity, thereby demonstrating virtue. If you are a Muslim, however, virtue is demonstrated by support for death. They say "We love death more than you love life". It is fairly obvious that Muslim Kings do not love death, because if they decided for death, they would quite likely be killed. A voter, however, can vote for death, without altering his chances that the policy will actually be put into effect. As a result, it will be put into effect. They will vote for measures that force us to kill them all. A Muslim voter demonstrates virtue by demonstrating that he loves death, which he does by voting for whatever policy will force us to kill him.

No compromise is possible, since the median Muslim voter does not demonstrate his virtue by voting for policies that will lead to Israel withdrawing to pre-1967 borders, or policies that will lead to the US withdrawing from the middle east, or policies that will support and uphold the family by excluding sexual corruption and controlling female sexuality, but by voting for policies that will likely get him killed. It will probably be easier to stop them from voting than to kill them all, but in the end, will have to do one or the other.

Censorship

2011-05-26 11:13:05

Like a frog boiled, we have now reached Stalinist levels of censorship. They won't send you to the gulag, but in the later days of Stalinism they seldom did that. Rather, your career depended on compliance

I was listening to Chris Rock's hilarious rant "We hate black people too!" and my son became alarmed, lest some one sneak up on my house and listen near the windows.

Everyone in America tells the official story of the banking crisis: "de-regulation". The Israeli central bank correctly blames government intervention aimed at making loans available to poor people with bad credit - though even the Israeli central bank somehow neglects to mention that in America, those poor people were not poor white males.

Observe that every fiction book must have properly counterstereotypical characters to rebut the characteristics of race and sex. Thus, for example, John Ringo, having committed the unpardonable sin of a few lines about stereotypical blondes in "live Free or Die" has to make the main character of the sequel ("Citadel") a counter stereotypical blonde. In the sequel, the rhetoric about freedom mysteriously mutates into anticolonialist, or de-colonist, rhetoric, perhaps because merely having a counter stereotypical blonde as main character is insufficient penance for making a joke about blondes. Everything published must serve the higher purpose of inculcating correct political attitudes.

If you are an executive, and you use the word "blonde" as a noun your company can get whacked with a multimillion dollar lawsuit, and if you are an untenured academic and use the word "blonde" as a noun you will never get tenure. (Tenured academics, however, can and regularly do say "blonde" without losing tenure.)

Everyone is terrified of tripping over some incredibly obscure rule of political correctness that they have never heard of. My favorite in this regard comes from the history of science. Among the many recent rewrites of the history of science is that before 1972, Darwin's big idea was natural selection, and the idea that families of species were related by blood, were actual families, with a common ancestor, was attributed to Lamarck and other predecessors of Darwin. After 1972, history was abruptly rewritten - though the original books by Lamark are still around and continue to say what they so plainly said. Yet whenever I raise this story as an example of PC, no one dares notice that old books say what they said, and that Lamarck says what he said.

> O'Brien held up his left hand, its back towards Winston, with the thumb hidden and four fingers extended. "How many fingers am I holding up, Winston"
>
> "Four"
>
> "And if the party says it is not four but five—then how many?"

I point people to what Lamarck said:H Elliot's translation of Lamarck's book[660] , pages 19 to 38, Lamarck discusses of species, the fact that forms naturally occur in group. Pages 38 to 39, he explains them by common descent, by shared blood or sap from an individual common ancestor, Page 179, he gives a family tree of the animals, And I point them to what old books say he said, and yet, upon being notified that since 1972 the politically correct position is that Lamarck did not say what he said

Page 641 "Biology Today", 1972:

> Lamarck's theory is not a hypothesis of common descent, which ascribes the common characteristics of a particular species to their common descent

---

[660] https://www.archive.org/details/zoologicalphilos00lama

from a single species. He claims that mammals are produced by the gradual complexification of reptiles and that this elevation is going on constantly. Although all mammals are descended from reptiles, they are not descended from the same reptiles.

They will dutifully say that O'Brien is holding up five fingers, dutifully say that the position stated in Page 641 "Biology Today", 1972, is true, even though they never heard of it until I raised as an example of political correctness gone crazy. What appears in a 1972 textbook supposedly must be true, even if it flatly contradicts what appears in a 1965 textbook, and flatly contradicts the source materials it describes. Oceania was at war with Eurasia: therefore Oceania had always been at war with Eurasia.

Check the origins of the theory of common descent, that similar species are similar because related by blood or sap, and try it on someone. Anyone who is in the slightest bit politically correct will chicken out. All the books that address the topic before 1972 say that Lamarck proposed common descent[661] in the sense that families of species are families by blood, all the respectable books after 1972 that address the topic say he did not[662]. And therefore, every respectable person will say he did not, no matter that what the textbooks said before 1972, no matter what Lamarck himself said.

A lot of ruin in a nation

2011-05-27 10:54:29

Many bloggers, myself among them, have been predicting hyperinflation, socio economic collapse, and violent political change. But a lot of countries are in worse shape than the US, and they have not collapsed yet. Spain has all the US problems, less credit, more of a command economy, and the two Spanish political parties are agreed on reforms too miniscule to make significant difference, which reforms are nonetheless denounced as war upon the poor and the working class. These barely perceptible reforms provoke threats of armed revolution from the unions, which threats are hot air, but might well becomes real if actual reforms likely to actually fix the situation were applied.

The first country to go is Belarus, which has "market socialism" (Spain's economic system with knobs on) and a government deficit that is sixteen percent of GDP. In Belarus, hyperinflation is starting, and violent political change is in sight.

So if Belarus is only now going, the fall of the US from much the same causes is in sight but not yet close. I would guess Greece is two or three years behind Belarus. Once Greece goes, we will see what used to be called the domino effect, and is now called contagion. Several other European countries will swiftly follow.

After that, my crystal ball goes cloudy.

---

[661] https://books.google.com/books?as_q=Lamarck&as_epq=common+descent&as_sub=&as_drrb_is=b&as_minm_is=1&as_miny_is=1800&as_maxm_is=1&as_maxy_is=1971

[662] https://books.google.com/books?as_q=Lamarck&as_epq=common+descent&as_sub=&as_drrb_is=b&as_minm_is=1&as_miny_is=1972&as_maxm_is=1&as_maxy_is=2010

Governor Romneycare promises to be a better Obama

2011-05-30 06:38:51

Governor Romneycare is campaigning to be the Republican presidential candidate. He tells us that:

> Every turnaround has three rules. Focus, focus, focus. Focus on what's most important, devote all your energy to that which is broken. ... Instead of focusing his energy on the economy he delegated the stimulus to Nancy Pelosi and Harry Reid, and they built a stimulus which grew government jobs but didn't grow private-sector jobs. And then he went to work on his real agenda. And that was cap and trade, to raise energy costs; card check to unionise at places of employment where the employees didn't want unions; Obamacare, where the federal government takes over health-care; and regulatory reform relating to the financial services sector, which of course scared the heck out of anybody in the financial sector. He went to work on this agenda. And virtually every aspect of his agenda increased the degree of uncertainty that existed in the employment sector.

Employment is a means to an end: We don't need employment, we need productive employment. The only thing the government can do to enable productive employment is to stop enabling unproductive employment.

What you subsidize, you get more of. What you tax, you get less of. The taxpayer has massively subsidized the finance sector, and we *now have far too many people employed in finance*. Most of them need to lose their jobs. The vast majority of them need to lose their jobs.Clearly we do need regulatory reform in the financial sector, since people in the financial sector have been misbehaving. And since they have been misbehaving, we do need to scare the heck out of them. The problem with the Obama financial reform is that it has not fixed anything that was wrong, and has *not* scared the heck out of them.There now are a bunch of civil lawsuits alleging massive fraud. The fraud was committed to unload dud loans. Why no criminal lawsuits?

The government under Bush vigorously encouraged the banks to lower their credit standards, which resulted in dud loans. The government issued a series of white papers arguing that low credit standards were wise and profitable, that high credit standards were racist, and grounds for racial discrimination lawsuits. None of this has been reformed under Obama. The government cajoled the banks, threatened them with racism lawsuits, and enabled politically correct bankers to take over politically incorrect banks, which politically correct bankers (in particular Kerry Killinger of Washington Mutual) proceeded to make gigantic quantities of dud loans. The government, under Bush and Obama, has altered accounting rules to make it easier for the financial sector to lie about money, in particular "Mark to Myth".

The financial sector is still unreasonably large, unreasonably opaque, implausibly profitable, and receives gigantic government handouts. We need a dramatically smaller and more transparent financial sector. The overwhelming majority of people working in the existing financial sector need to be unemployed and seeking alternative forms of employment. The finance sector is too politicized: too left wing in that the government uses it to dispense money to favored voting blocks, generally voting blocks of poor people, too right wing, in that it makes a small number of people inordinately rich though crony capitalism and selective government favor, and too left wing, in that those inordinately rich people, such as Kerry Killinger, seem to have become inordinately rich through their commitment to left wing politics and their cozy relationship with left activist organizations such as Acorn. The Obama regime has been an improvement in that today such cuddly relationships between the left and the finance sector now come under hostile scrutiny from the Republican party, while under the supposedly right wing Bush, everyone ignored them, Democrats and Republicans alike. Despite all the outrage about Obama's selective government favor to left connected businessmen, we getting arguably getting less of that under Obama than we got under Bush, precisely because of all the outrage.

During the supposedly right wing Bush government, the conspicuously left wing Kerry Killinger was made remarkably rich, in that through regulatory favor his bank was given charge of lots of well and responsibly run bank, which he proceeded to run irresponsibly and incompetently, losing through incompetence the paperwork that kept track of where the assets were, and lending for political reasons piles of money to people with neither ability nor the inclination to repay it. To sustain these activities, he committed massive fraud, in that through a mixture of incompetence, lost paperwork, and deliberate deception, he misrepresented dud loans to resell them. The government continues to support and protect similar fraud.

Some of the blame for Kerry Killinger rests with Clinton, and some of it with Obama, and quite a bit of it lies with the congress that was dominated by Democrats during the latter years of Kerry Killinger's rise, but the most conspicuous, objectionable, and incompetent far left wing crony capitalist of recent times got most of his loot under the Bush presidency,

Further, these subsides are granted to some organizations but not others, in that one organization gets implicit or explicit government guarantees, and another organization does not, one organizations gets one set of rules, and another organization gets another set of rules. This is crony capitalism, which results in stupid and incompetent people running things, as illustrated by the banks massively mucking up their paperwork and losing a vast variety of paperwork in a vast variety of ways. Goldman and Sach is full of PhD's from Harvard, yet they did not know the crash was happening until over a year after everyone that I knew saw that a well founded panic was happening. This is so stupid that it seems likely to be politically induced stupidity. Since no one in the government or the finance sector wanted to believe these policies were leading to disaster, they were unable to see the disaster even when it was actually happening. On the other hand, the unending paperwork screw ups revealed in the foreclosure scandals are just plain ordinary everyday stupidity and incompetence, suggesting that that Harvard awards PhDs more on the basis of political orientation and connections than on ability.

What we need is a total purge of the finance sector, through widespread massive bankruptcy induced by truthful accounting, and the withdrawal of special government favor and privileges granted to some organizations but not others, so that the only bankers remaining are those old fashioned types that believe that anyone who needs credit does not deserve credit, the kind who lend you an umbrella when the sun shines, and snatch it back when it rains. *That* would scare the heck out of them.

Monetary growth

2011-05-31 08:26:56

So, the monetary base has tripled.[663]

According to Milton Friedman, the price level will therefore triple "after large and variable delay"

One interpretation of this event is that the Keynesians are doubling down. Since large doses of Keynesianism did not work, they conclude a bigger dose is required.

I am inclined, however, to regard the economics departments of Ivy League universities as primarily megaphones of the government, one microphone, many megaphones, bellowing ignorant and stupid propaganda justifying whatever the government is doing today, regardless of whether the propaganda is consistent with their justification of what the government was doing yesterday.

On this interpretation, the monetary base initially doubled late in 2008 through the government handing out eight hundred billion to their pals in finance to keep them from going bust, then rose more slowly in 2009 by an additional five hundred billion, through massive vote buying and payoffs to cronies, and now as the election comes in sight, rising again, five hundred billion so far, for more vote buying, and today's Keynesianism is merely a rationalization as to why this is a good thing.

On this theory it is going to go right on accelerating all the way to the election, by which time the monetary base will probably have quadrupled from its 2008 levels, possibly quintupled.

Death panels

2011-06-02 16:41:21

No, Obama is not setting up death panels. He is just creating rules that hospitals can only comply with if they quietly and unofficially have death panels for medicare patients[664].

If a hospital discharges a patient who lingers on for years sucking up lots of expensive services outside the hospital, the hospital is penalized. If, however, the potentially expensive patient should conveniently croak while in hospital ...

In a number of European countries, quite a lot of patients die "under deep sedation" – in other words, medically administered barbiturate overdose, murdered.

If the patient is dead of IV drug overdose with a drug clicker in his hand that controls the amount of fentanyl in the IV, then that is suicide or death by misadventure.

If the patient is dead of IV drug overdose with *no* clicker in his hand, murder. And that is the way patients in Europe die when they die "under deep sedation".

Pain control is morphine or fentanyl. "Deep sedation" is lots of barbiturates. Barbiturates are deadly in large doses.

---

[663] https://research.stlouisfed.org/fred2/series/BASE
[664] https://strata-sphere.com/blog/index.php/archives/16565

Barbiturates are not to prevent pain, but to prevent the patient from making a fuss about his medical treatment, or making a fuss about dying – or from making a fuss about lack of medical treatment, lack of food, and lack of water, hence given with IV, but without clicker.

There are legitimate medical uses of barbiturates, typically to keep patients from making trouble when the doctor is giving them an examination that is painful and embarrassing, for example a colonoscopy. But there are seldom legitimate reasons to give barbiturates to a patient lying in a hospital bed, and there are never legitimate reasons for a patient to die "under deep sedation" while lying in bed. Yet somehow quite a lot European patients do die "under deep sedation".

The usual procedure for extreme pain control is to give the patient a clicker, whereby the patient directly controls the level of morphine or fentanyl, up to a limit. If no limit, this also gives the patient the option of voluntary euthanasia, by clicking hard enough.

"Sedation" means barbiturates, which means not controlling the patients pain, but rather controlling the patient.

These barbiturates are applied through the IV, without the patients knowledge, consent, or control, thus death during deep sedation is involuntary euthanasia: murder of the inconvenient and unwanted.

If the patient is dead with a lethal quantity of fentanyl inside him, and fentanyl clicker in his dead hand, obviously voluntary euthanasia or death by misadventure.

If the patient is dead with a lethal quantity of barbiturates inside him, the barbiturates administered by IV with no barbiturate clicker, obviously involuntary euthanasia: murder.

"Deep sedation" is never given with a clicker, therefore always involuntary euthanasia, murder. There is a lot of medical murder in Denmark and many other European countries, and now hospitals in the US have a compelling financial incentive to do the same with potentially expensive medicare patients, including medicare patients that have something expensive but not swiftly lethal wrong with them that will create endless expenses after they are discharged from hospital.

Again the brilliance of Sarah Palin

2011-06-04 15:21:15

In her supposedly non campaign tour during which she is theoretically not seeking the republican presidential nomination Sarah Palin told us:

> Come on, everyone knows who Paul Revere, the silversmith and patriot is.
> "He warned the British that they weren't gonna be takin' away our arms, uh, by ringing those bells, and um, makin' sure as he's riding his horse through town to send those warning shots and bells that we were going to be sure and we were going to be free, and we were going to be armed.

Of course all the good progressives, including the supposedly respectable right wing, have been brought up on the hate America first history which erases from our past the fact that Paul Revere was fighting gun control, and which erases from history anything related to his fight against gun control, such as ringing the bells to sound the alarm, such as warning the British that any attempt to disarm the people would be resisted with deadly force.

So they promptly sneered at her supposed ignorance

"Not the history channel version" they said. "Not the version we were taught in school", revealing their own ignorance.

Indeed was not, for the version you were taught in school, the version on the history channel, was the hate America first version.

Whether she gets the nomination or not, she reveals how ignorant and out of contact with reality our elite is. She is the one and only major politician running against our ruling elite.

Paul Revere's ride was to fight gun control. The Pilgrim father's were not thanking the Indians for giving them corn, but thanking God for his wisdom in commanding capitalism, or guiding them back to capitalism. And Darwin's big idea was natural selection, not the idea that similarities between different species are due to blood relationships, common descent. Common descent, in the sense that families of species, such as the mammals, are actual families by blood if you go back far enough, was Lamarck's big idea. Darwin's big idea was that natural selection was a plausible explanation for different races arising, and developing into different species.

A golden oldie on the minority mortgage meltdown

2011-06-08 06:07:06

Ann Coulter rarely gives links, and frequently employs hyperbole and humorous exaggeration, so when she reports entirely ridiculous real events, it is difficult to be sure whether she is engaging in humorous hyperbole, or things really are that outrageous. Vdare has helpfully annotated one of her posts with links[665], and I have added a little more annotation. And yes, Ann Coulter was not making this up. The government really is as ludicrous as she depicts it[666]:

> If Obama plans to hold Wall Street accountable for its own bad decisions, it will be a first for the Democrats.For the past two decades, Democrats have specialized in insulating financial giants from the consequences of their own high-risk bets. Citigroup and Goldman Sachs alone have been rescued from their risky bets by unwitting taxpayers four times in the last 15 years.

> Bankers get all the profits, glory and bonuses when their flimflam bets pay off, but the taxpayers foot the bill when Wall Street firms' bets go bad on – to name just three examples – Mexican bonds (1995), Thai, Indonesian and South Korean bonds (1997), and Russian bonds (1998).

> As Peter Schweizer writes in his magnificent book Architects of Ruin[667] "Wall Street is a very far cry from the arena of freewheeling capitalism most

---

[665]https://blog.vdare.com/archives/2010/01/29/ann-coulter-on-the-minority-mortgage-meltdown/
[666]https://www.anncoulter.com/cgi-local/article.cgi?article=352
[667]https://amzn.to/lmgLgL

people recall from their history books." With their reverse-Midas touch, the execrable baby boom generation turned Wall Street into what Schweizer dubs "risk-free Clintonian state capitalism."

Apropos of the Clintonian No-Responsibility Era, Goldman Sachs and Citibank became heavily invested in Mexican bonds after a two-day bender in Tijuana in the early '90s. Any half-wit could see that "investing" in the dog track would be safer than investing in a corrupt Third World government controlled by drug lords.

But precisely because the bonds were so risky, bankers made money hand-over-fist on the scheme – at least until Mexico defaulted.

With Mexico unable to pay the $25 billion it owed the big financial houses, Clinton's White House decided the banks shouldn't be on the hook for their own bad bets.

Clinton's Treasury Secretary, Robert Rubin, former chairman of Goldman, demanded that the U.S. bail out Mexico to save his friends at Goldman. He said a failure to bail out Mexico would affect "everyone," by which I take it he meant "everyone in my building."

Larry Summers, currently Obama's National Economic Council director, warned that a failure to rescue Mexico would lead to another Great Depression. (Ironically, Summers' current position in the Obama administration is "Great Depression czar.") [Hyperbole, he was finance Czar, which was arguably even more ludicrous]

[Most] Republicans in Congress said "no" to Clinton's Welfare-for-Wall-Street plan.

It's not as if this hadn't happened before: In 1981, Reagan allowed Mexico to default on tens of billions of dollars in debt – Mexico claimed the money was "in my other pair of pants" [hyperbole – the actual excuses were more complicated but even less plausible] – leaving Wall Street to deal with its own bad bets.

As Larry Summers expected, this led like night into day to the Great Depression we experienced during the Reagan years ... Wait, that never happened.

At congressional hearings on Clinton's proposed Mexico bailout a decade later, Republicans Larry Kudlow, Bill Seidman and Steve Forbes all denounced the plan to save Goldman Sachs via a Mexican bailout.

So the Clinton administration did an end run around the Republicans in Congress and rescued improvident Wall Street bankers by giving Mexico a $20 billion line of credit directly from the Treasury's Exchange Stabilization Fund.

Relieved of any responsibility for their losing bets, Wall Street firms lept into buying other shaky foreign bonds. Soon the U.S. taxpayer, through the International Monetary Fund, was propping up bonds out of South Korea, Thailand, Indonesia, then Russia – all to save Goldman Sachs.

The IMF could have saved itself a lot of paperwork by just sending taxpayer money directly to Goldman, but I think they're saving that for Obama's second term.

Throughout every bailout, [some] congressional Republicans were screaming from the rooftops that this wasn't capitalism. It was "Government Sachs." As Rep. Spencer Bachus (R-Ala.) put it, the same rules that apply to welfare mothers "ought to apply to rich Greenwich, Conn., investors who are multimillionaires."

But Wall Street raised a lot of money for the Democrats, so Clinton bailed them out, over and over again.

Before you knew it, once-respectable Wall Street institutions were buying investment products[668] even more ludicrous than Mexican bonds: They were buying the mortgages of Mexican strawberry-pickers. Why shouldn't Wall Street trust in suicidal loans no sane person would ever imagine could be paid back? Time after time, when their bets paid off, they pocketed huge fees; when their bets failed,[669] they sent the bill[670] to the taxpayers.

With nothing to fear, the big financial houses bought, repackaged and resold investment products that included loans like the one issued by Washington Mutual[671] to non-English-speaking strawberry pickers earning a combined $14,000 a year to purchase a $720,000 house[672].

But the financial wizards on Wall Street were trading these preposterous loans as if they were bars of gold. They may as well have bet the entire U.S. economy on a dice game in an alley off 44th Street.

Every mortgage-backed security bundle was infected with suicidal, politically correct loans[673] that had been demanded by community organizers[674] such as Barack Obama — as is thoroughly documented in Schweizer's book[675].

On the off chance that mammoth mortgages to people who could barely afford food somehow went bad, Wall Street firms could be confident that their Democrat friends would bail them out.

Even the Republicans would have to bail them out this time They had strapped the dynamite of toxic loans[676] onto the entire economy and were threatening to pull the clip. Wall Street[677] had infected every financial institution in the country, including completely innocent banks. [rationalization - in the

[668] https://www.vdare.com/seiyo/080922_borrower.htm
[669] https://vdare.com/jb/ltcm.htm
[670] https://vdare.com/jb/WallStChangingCulture.htm
[671] https://blog.vdare.com/archives/2008/09/26/washington-mutuals-last-press-release-ever/
[672] https://blog.vdare.com/archives/2008/11/11/
[673] https://vdare.com/malkin/mortgages.htm
[674] https://vdare.com/sailer/080907_organizer.htm
[675] https://amzn.to/lmgLgL
[676] https://vdare.com/sailer/090222_gramm.htm
[677] https://www.vdare.com/pb/080930_pujo.htm

savings and loans crisis, the government protected Main Street from Wall Street without bailing out Wall Street. In the S&L crisis if a bank went down they rescued the depositors, not the bankers. In this crisis, the government bailed out Wall Street at the expense of Main Street, Bush as much as Obama.]

But now Obama says he's going to "fight" Wall Street, which is as plausible as claiming he'll "fight" the trial lawyers.

As Schweizer demonstrates, whenever the Democrats "regulate" Wall Street, the innocent pay through the nose, while Wall Street swine lower than drug dealers and pornographers end up with multimillion-dollar bonuses so they can run for governor of New Jersey and fund lavish Democratic fundraisers in the Hamptons.

Crisis and collapse is capitalism's way of moving assets, employees and resources from those who unproductively misuse them, to those who productively exploit them. If the government prevents crisis and collapse, you wind up with stupid cronies in charge instead of competent capitalists. This leads, as with Japan's crisis, to permanent stagnation. America's growth since the crisis has been phony. Creative statistics have substantially understated inflation[678], thus counted inflation as economic growth, and have counted government expenditure as creating value, even when the government, as with "cash for clunkers", spent money on destroying value. The economy is in fact declining at about the same rate as the number of white males employed is declining. The racial balance of employed people suggests that those employed are lower IQ than they used to be, and thus less productive than they used to be, and the balance of jobs also suggests that that those employed are lower IQ than they used to be, and thus less productive than they used to be, the biggest growth in this month being employment by McDonalds - the US economy is increasingly doing stuff characteristic of third world economies, and is doing less stuff characteristic of America. Just as you could tell that the Communists had undeveloped the areas they conquered from the character of the exports and their imports, which resembled those of other third world countries, you can see the same thing happening in America. Supposedly the US is growing, yet it is exporting less high tech, and importing more high tech.

Let us consider the latest cool hi tech toy - Apple's smartphone. Designed in America by smart white males, then the design and the brand name is licensed to Chinese firms to actually build it. Now, however, those chinese smartphone manufacturers are rapidly switching to building android smart phones, which means that the software is still written by smart white males, but the hardware is designed by smart Chinese males.

It used to be that the smartest Chinese males migrated to America, so that they could do great stuff. Now, I see the smartest white American males migrating to Asia so that they can do great stuff.

Bailouts are always bailouts for the incompetent. If governments keep the incompetent in power, they exclude the competent from power. So the best emigrate. And I see them emigrating.

---

[678]https://www.shadowstats.com/

What would have happened if no bailout in 2008?

2011-06-09 18:33:43

Steven Horwitz has the experiment.[679]

Yes, inferior races have smaller cranial capacities on average

2011-06-12 09:54:50

So what is a politically correct intellectual allowed to say?

Lately, people who are quite politically correct and academically respectable[680], are acknowledging that Gould and Lewontin were wrong and making $#!% up, and no heresy charges ensue. Indeed, they have been pissing on Lewontin since 2003. Now if Lewontin is wrong, then the races are genetically different in important ways, if Gould is wrong, then Darwin is right that races are the origin of species, and Morton was right[681] that negroes and native Americans have smaller cranial capacities than whites.

So what is the version that a politically correct person with career that could be subject to reprisals now permitted say about races? Lewis et-al piously assure us that though cranial capacities differ significantly, this is wholly a function of environment, offering no explanation or evidence for this.

In 1972, holy writ became that genetic differences between races are insignificant, and that races are entirely social constructions. Supposedly we only imagine that humans come in different races. Supposedly there is no phenotypic or genotypic difference between so called races. Supposedly, not only is it impossible to tell what race someone is by looking at his DNA, it is also impossible to tell by looking at his face!

Of course that was obviously ridiculous, so people were reluctant to actually say it. But it was quite dangerous to contradict it. So official doctrine tended to be sort of endorsed, and quietly contradicted. People continued to study races, racial differences, and genetics, but used the word "populations" as code for races, and got away with saying things that would have got them into very big trouble if they had used plainer words.

And then in 1996 Nei et al[682] said "human populations are known to vary considerably over evolutionary time and thus the evolutionary rate would vary from population to population", and produced a bunch of diagrams implying that certain "populations", for example the "Nigerian population", had not evolved much from the common ancestor of man and chimp.

Suddenly the hammer came down hard, though plenty of academics before Nei had said worse. Nei et-al recanted and repented, and piously proclaimed that there is no significant genetic, evolutionary, or phenotypic difference between "populations".

This strictness put people in something of a bind, since strict conformity prohibited what any fool could see, and an entire field of academic study.

---

[679]https://www.coordinationproblem.org/2011/06/recalculation-in-the-commerical-real-estate-market.html
[680]https://johnhawks.net/weblog/
[681]https://www.plosbiology.org/article/info:doi/10.1371/journal.pbio.1001071
[682]https://reaction.la/1996-nei-takezaki.pdf

In the twenty first century, the strictness seems to have eased up somewhat, so what now is permitted to be said? What is the official line?

Since it was supposedly impossible to tell people's race merely by looking at them, terminology that acknowledged such distinctions became politically incorrect. Thus race, supposedly, refers to continent of origin. Thus Turks and Iranians were supposedly Asians, and Chinese also supposedly Asians, thus supposedly the same race.

This was particularly confusing in Britain. Since they had to call all sorts of people Asians who were obviously not Asians, they had difficulty calling actual Asians, for example Chinese and Vietnamese, "Asians". They tended to call actual Asians "orientals" or some such instead, though with much fear that such language was politically incorrect. And since they so many of the people that they were required to call "Asian" look very like people from Somalia or Morocco, they tended to call Somalis and Moroccans Asians, since they were unclear on the rationale for assigning people to the correct racial group. Supposedly Moroccans are Africans, even though they are obviously not Africans, any more than Iranians are Asians. So in England, Somalis tend to be "Asians", and Chinese not "Asians", contrary to the use of language that the politically correct intended. Instead of racial terminology referring to continent or origin, without regard to the supposedly invisible appearance, it merely became confused.

The intent was to force people to categorize races on the basis of continent of origin without regard to actual race, since supposedly they are all alike, but the actual effect was that people used racial terminology inconsistently and incoherently.

This confusion, however, gave the politically correct a way out of the bind in which they had put themselves:

The politically correct are now allowed to acknowledge that natural differences exist, but supposedly races as conventionally defined do not correspond to these natural populations. Only the politically correct are allowed to notice these naturally distinct populations, thus the politically correct are now allowed to be as racist as they like. The politically correct can now even acknowledge what Nei was reprimanded for acknowledging, that certain populations evolved at a slower rate than others, that some populations evolved more rapidly towards the use of complex artifacts, and other populations also evolved quite rapidly, but in directions other than towards intelligence and use of artifacts.

But no one else is allowed.

For the rest of us, it is still the case that it is supposedly impossible to tell someone's race by his genes or physical appearance, and as I write this, the columnist Andrew Bolt is undergoing a heresy show trial over this very question[683], even though he has repeatedly recanted, repented, apologized, and denounced his previous views.

Andrew Bolt got in trouble for noticing that the chief beneficiaries of grants to aboriginal Australians and affirmative action were not natives living in poverty on reservations, but people who were more than 98% white by ancestry and members of the white ruling upper class culture, often descended from people who had also been members of the white ruling upper class culture and also been beneficiaries of government grants.

He is now undergoing an extremely lengthy show trial.

From his recantation and apology, we now know it is terribly racist to think that race has anything to do with race. Rather, race is socially ascribed or self chosen. It is horribly racist to deny that certain people are aboriginals just because they look 100% white and have never had more exposure to aboriginal culture than that which is obtained by reading National Geographic.

Thus when the politically correct tell us that races as socially defined have nothing to do with natural differences really existing between different human kinds, what they actually mean is that races as socially defined *better not* have anything to do with natural difference really existing different human kinds, and if they do have something to do with such difference, you are going to be in big trouble. It is not a statement about popular usage of racial terms, but a threat. Use racial terms that way or else what was done to Andrew Bolt shall be done to you!

Probability of fiat collapse

2011-06-13 20:09:07

I observe that people are still buying and selling long term corporate bonds at prices that indicate low inflationary expectations.

On the other hand, total value of world gold is about fifteen trillion dollars, which indicates a lot of people expecting partial or total collapse of fiat money

That people are buying and selling government bonds at prices that indicate low inflationary expectations is not necessarily indicative of anything, since there are a lot of funny goings on the government bond market, but the corporate bond market is probably not all that manipulated, hence a genuine indicator.

So there are a lot of rich, and therefore presumably competent, people who expect collapse of fiat money, and a lot of rich , and therefore presumably competent, people who think this extremely unlikely.

There is a black swan bias: People tend to discount the probability of events that happen less than once in a lifetime, so under estimate the likelihood of fiat moneys vanishing.

There is a bubble bias. People think that this time it is different, that trees grow to the sky, so over estimate the likelihood that gold will grow to the sky.

So much for the wisdom of crowds. There is a crowd with great confidence in fiat money, and there is a plausible rationale to call that crowd crazy, and a crowd with great confidence in gold, and there is a plausible rationale to call that crowd crazy.

So, time to consider the underlying forces, the basic mechanisms at work.

Suppose that there was in the world one central bank, issuing one fiat currency, the base money for all other moneys, all other central banks, which are not so central. Suppose this bank is ruled by a wise hereditary ruler, King Hamurrabi, immune to external pressures. He has a sweet gig, so he does not want to spoil it by issuing too much money, by abusing his power. Everything will work. There is no way he will issue so much money that people stop using his money altogether. The world will operate on fiat money for ever and ever, with no prospect of change, nor any problems ensuing that would make people much desire change.

Unfortunately, after a while King Hamurrabi's royal guard tell him "Hey, Ham, you got a sweet gig running, we want some of it."

So now there are a hundred people who can issue fiat money in the name of the Bank of King Hamurrabi, instead of one. Soon they are issuing too much, way too much, and after a while, people lose faith in King Hamurrabi's fiat money altogether. As long as King Hamurrabi bank was one man who could, and would, make decisions for his long term benefit, there as no way fiat money could possibly end. When his bank was a hundred men, each one pursuing his own good without all that much concern for the good of the other ninety nine, there was no way fiat money could possibly continue.

In Europe, theoretically only the central bank can issue Euros. In practice however, every European government, and every major European bank, can issue Euros.

And in America, every too big to fail institution can in effect issue dollars.

What happens is that on a Thursday, a European government sees it is not going to be able to make payroll on Friday. So it robs the banks. And when the national government proceeds to rob the national banks to make payroll on Friday, rules or no rules, the European Central bank proceeds to bail the national banks out on Saturday with completely illegal money issue, rules or no rules, because it well knows that if it did not, the banks would be surrounded by screaming mobs on Monday.

Under Basel, banks, governments, and regulators have become so intimately connected that there is no market discipline on banks. Banks seek political favor, not profit. If they lose money it is not a problem, except for the taxpayer. Irresponsible political lending abounds, leaking money. So every European government can effectively issue fiat money, and every major bank can effectively issue money. Institutions guaranteed formally or informally by the taxpayer are allowed to take complicated risks, risks too complicated for the regulators to understand, even if the regulators were not bank employee shortly before they became government employees, and due to become bank employees again in the near future. From time to time these risks blow up, but the bankers concerned will usually be fine if they lent lots of money to pals of politicians, and to voting blocks that the politicians were wooing.

To save fiat money would require a restoration of discipline. A restoration of discipline needs a central bank that allows irresponsible behavior to be punished by important people actually running out of money. To restore discipline, the money issuers need to say no. Pigs will fly first.

Entryism goes public

2011-06-15 05:53:52

The SEIU is a far left organization, far far further to the left than any elected Democrat will admit to being. It is the voice of the state organized as political interest group. It has always been a major force backing "moderate" Republicans.

Entryism consists of a small, secretive, and disciplined organization infiltrating a larger and less disciplined organization, an organization whose goals, motivations, and members the entryists despise, and then taking over that organization and using its funds, assets, and membership list for the entryists own purposes, rather than for the original purposes of the organization.

Entryism is the reason that all organizations tend to turn left, unless they are controlled by rightist ideologues who actively try to keep them right.

Entryism has always been a very secretive profession, immoral though not illegal. But, under campaign finance law, engaging in electoral politics without registering *is* illegal. So the left is routinely and massively committing prohibited acts, which prohibited acts have routinely and massively been ignored by the campaign finance authorities.

Although SEIU never seemed to worry about those laws in the past, they have now formed a Republican Action Committee[684], so what they are doing is now legal *and now visible*.

The declared aim of the Action Committee is, truthfully enough, to give us more government. They neglect to add "And the destruction of the icky reactionary white racist Republican party", but attitude of the SEIU to republicans is well known. As with the entryist Dede Scozzafava, they will always give defeating the Republican party higher priority than getting their "Republican" elected.

Actual Greek riots

2011-06-17 06:00:32

Last year the riots were entirely fake, astroturf government rioters theatrically engaging in pretend conflict with government police. This time, there was some fake violence, and some quite real violence.

In the previous riots, government protestors threw Molotov cocktails from short range, not at police, but in front of policemen's feet. And then they stood around, with the police making no effort to arrest them. In this riot, Molotov cocktails were thrown from long range and landed amidst the police from above. They were actually trying to harm policemen, and were acting as if they believed that police would try to arrest them.

We also saw plenty of government astroturf theater, for example a mob banging on a wall or crowd barrier - but they were not putting their shoulders into it. Whenever it looked like the barrier would fall, they eased up their already rather gentle banging.

Once again, the Greek government has cut expenditures, and increased tax rates.

The increase in rates is perverse, since it is obvious that rates are well above the Laffer limit, on rich and poor alike, and every time they raise rates, revenues fall substantially, due to massive tax evasion and people dropping out. The futile tax rate rises fit with the astroturf element of the protests. The government is protesting itself as part of austerity theater: "See, we are being as austere as we can be." and the government is raising taxes, regardless of the fact that they well and truly on the falling side of the Laffer curve to show that they are being as austere as they can be.

But, perhaps to their surprise, high unemployment and high taxes may have caused some real protestors to show up.

---

[684]https://newmediajournal.us/indx.php/item/1853

McConnell tells Obama he can stick it in a little bit
2011-06-20 08:19:54

House Republican leader McConnell tells Obama he can stick it into the Republicans just a little bit, but not all the way, and must stop if it starts to hurt. Short debt limit hike possible[685]

> Congress and the White House could raise the debt limit for a few months while they seek a comprehensive, long-term budget deal, Senate Republican leader Mitch McConnell said on Sunday.

Looks like we are headed for a budget deal wherein the debt limit is raised now, and in return, Democrats and Republicans agree that after the next election, whoever is elected then will "cut" government spending – meaning slow the rate of growth of government spending.

Thus this year they will agree, that after the next election they will agree, to slow the rate of growth of expenditure for the year after that. Thus Republicans will raise the debt limit in 2011, and will get in return a promise of good intentions to have a budget in 2013 that plans to spend less money in 2014 than some wished to spend.

I always have difficulty keeping straight which politicians are republicans, and which democrats.

Philips curve, stimulus
2011-06-21 16:55:43

If stimulus works, if Keynesianism is a good enough approximation to the modern American economy, there should be a relationship between unemployment and inflation, the Philips curve. Higher unemployment should lead to lower inflation, and vice versa.

There is no relationship.

---

[685] https://ca.news.yahoo.com/short-debt-limit-hike-possible-mcconnell-195539802.html

Keynesianism says that unemployment is caused by lack of aggregate demand, which should also manifest as falling prices, deflation.

Supposedly, when there is insufficient aggregate demand, stimulus is needed, there is unemployment, but no inflation. Stimulus will not cause inflation, it will cause people to be employed. Only when just about everyone is employed, when there is sufficient aggregate demand, will increased aggregate demand cause inflation.

Of course prices never seem to fall in practice, so Keynesians then say that lack of inflation is deflation. And if it looks like prices are rising at an alarming rate, Keynesians then say that lack of *core* inflation is deflation.

Now you might think that core inflation is stuff like food and fuel, stuff where the price is easy to define and measure, stuff you cannot do without. But no, core inflation is stuff like ipods, washing machines, and laundry detergent. And since you cannot really say how the value of yesterday's ipod compares with today's ipod, the wise folk at the Bureau of Labor Statistics will make a hedonic adustment.

Now ipods are certainly getting better, but you might find it hard to say how much better. The wise folk at the Bureau of Labor statistics, are, however, wise, being civil servants, and have no difficulty saying how much better ipods are getting

Now you might think that washing machines and laundry detergent are getting more expensive and markedly worse, since they are no longer very effective in getting clothes clean, possibly thanks to regulations restricting power usage, water usage, and the use of phosphates in laundry detergent, but the wise folk at the Bureau of Labor statistics know that they are getting better and better, because, after all the purpose of those regulations was to make them better (not better for getting clothes clean, but better nonetheless). So even though your clothes are not as clean, modern washing machines get a big hedonic adjustment. Today's washing machine is supposedly more washing machine than yesterday's washing machine.

In short, core inflation is inflation in those items were no one can possibly make an accurate estimate of inflation. And, unsurprisingly, core inflation tends to be a lot more politically correct, which is to say lower, than non core inflation.

If there is massive unemployment, there must be insufficient demand, which can be remedied by stimulus. And if stimulus fails to remedy it, obviously there was not enough stimulus. And if stimulus leads to inflation – well, it cannot lead to inflation while there is massive unemployment, so there is none.

The flaw in Keynesianism is that "aggregate demand" involves adding apples to oranges. It ignores, as trivial, the questions of what will be produced, what jobs will people do. It simplifies the economy enough that government can manage it. That Keynesianism is a simplification does not make it wrong. All theories are necessarily simplifications. What makes it wrong is that the world does not behave as described.

billion prices inflation estimate

2011-06-23 12:04:31

The billion prices project spiders prices off the internet, and gets results broadly similar to the BLS[686], about thee percent per year, which surprises me, since over the last three years the BLS has been applying "hedonic adjustments" to all manner of goods where hedonic adjustment is impossible or implausible[687]. Today's supposedly three percent inflation as measured by the BLS is a lot higher rate of inflation than what the BLS was measuring as three percent inflation three years ago.

Three percent a year is high enough to cast doubt on the Keynesian account of the economic crisis, but it is low enough to not worry much about inflation. The billion prices project shows prices rising two percent in the last five months, which is five percent annualized, high enough to thoroughly discredit the Keynsian account of the crisis, and high enough to make one a bit worried about inflation, but not a symptom of imminent hyperinflation.

On the other hand, online goods tend to be small lightweight consumer durables, such as cameras, cell phones, scissors and so forth, where in some countries (but not the US) progress continues, tending to reduce their price relative to goods that are less easily traded internationally, such as medical services and education, and relative to prices with a higher material content and lower skill content, such as food and fuel. So the billion prices project probably honestly under estimates inflation, due to innate bias in what it follows, while the BLS, which attempts to follow everything, is apt to look too hard for rationalizations to interpret prices as falling, and not hard enough for prices rising. The continuous commodities index indicates sixty percent inflation per year, which is apt to make one worry about hyperinflation. Recollect that the early stages of hyperinflation do not hit everything at the same time. Real estate is the last to rise, urgent necessities the first.

An example of dubious hedonic adjustment by the BLS is that the BLS tells us that washing machines have become much better[688], even though it is obvious that they are not washing clothes as well as they used to, nor lasting as long as they used to, an anecdotal recollection confirmed by consumer reports testing.

The US is getting dirtier and shabbier, the cars are smaller and less powerful, and the tallest building in the US was built in 1972, even though computers are getting more powerful, and internet connections faster, thus uniformly positive hedonic adjustment looks distinctly suspicious. While positive hedonic adjustment for computers is fair enough, there should be broad categories where hedonic adjustment is stable or going downwards, and there are not. Or better still, they just should not attempt to do hedonic adjustment, because it is impossible to do honestly.

There are parts of the world that look the way we thought 2010 would look back in 1972. The US, on the other hand, really does not look as if hedonic adjustments should always be positive over the past forty years. As in Cuba and North Korea, the buildings

---

[686]https://bpp.mit.edu/usa/
[687]https://www.bls.gov/cpi/cpihqaitem.htm
[688]https://www.bls.gov/cpi/cpihqaappliance.pdf

in the US are getting older and shabbier.

Here is what 2010 was supposed to look like, when were looking forward to 2010 from 1970:

You will notice a couple of other futuristic looking buildings in the same photo, and in different views of the same hotel, I see a third futuristic looking structure, though Marina Bay Sands hotel is the biggest and most science fictional of them all. Singapore, by and large, looks the way 2010 was supposed to look like: Clean, shiny, and science fictional.

That thing on top of the hotel, the Skypark, is not merely a decoration to look sci-fi. It is a gigantic swimming pool, indeed an imitation island, with a view. So that guests can swim, and still see the view, the swimming pool has no visible wall holding the water in:

Due to the curve in the wall, you can see in the distant part of the photo the hidden gear that holds the water in The invisible wall ensures that the guests get the best possible view, and supports the illusion of being on a tropical island in a limitless ocean.

If the US look liked Singapore, *then* I would believe it when the BLS gave everything a positive hedonic adjustment. But the fact is the US is just getting dirtier and shabbier. The US is still cleaner and shinier than Europe, but the US today just does not look like a society where everything deserves a positive hedonic adjustment over time.

real inflation

2011-06-27 12:12:52

There is precision, and there is accuracy. It is unwise to attain more precision than accuracy, for one is apt to fool oneself, and worse still to attain precision at the cost of accuracy.

You cannot measure inflation on goods that are changing, without making questionable subjective judgements. Goods that are not changing are stuff like food and fuel. An accurate measure of inflation would not include goods that apt to change, which measure would understate the difficult to define or measure improvement of standard living, but accurately state the cost of living.

So how is inflation going on stuff that we can measure accurately?

It is starting to look a lot like hyperinflation:

CNBC tells us[689]

> Just in April—the most recent month for which data is available—grapes went up nearly 30 percent, cabbage jumped about 17 percent and orange juice surged more than 5 percent.
>
> ...
>
> The government's main gauge of inflation, the Consumer Price Index, is increasing at a 3.6 percent annualized rate, a higher reading but not enough to provoke any policy action to control prices.
>
> But a look at prices compiled by the Bureau of Labor Statistics tells a different story.
>
> The BLS numbers show a climate of continually rising prices across a wide swath of food categories—a tally of 76 items ranging from ground beef to soda to dairy products.
>
> ...
>
> Measuring the past month's performance, the BLS found prices gained on 45 of the items it monitors. But over the past year the trend is much stronger, with 66 of the 76 items higher in price, some by staggering numbers.
>
> Coffee, for instance, is up 40 percent. Celery is 28 percent higher while butter prices rose 26.4 percent. Rounding out the top five are bacon, at 23.5 percent, and cabbage, at 23.3 percent.
>
> April 2011, meanwhile, was a bad month for fruit prices as well. Joining grapes as big gainers in the fruit aisle was grapefruit, which rose 15 percent. While cabbage led the vegetables, broccoli rose 2.5 percent in the month and about 12 percent for the past year. Smoked ham was 7 percent higher and potatoes jumped 6.1 percent.
>
> Federal Reserve Chairman Ben Bernanke has used the term "transitory" to address the surge in food and energy costs, reasoning that temporary factors such as weather and $4 a gallon gas were pressuring prices.

---

[689]https://www.cnbc.com/id/43498072

He might be right, but it looks to me the other way around - that food and fuel are showing the real rate of inflation, while "core inflation" shows how easy it is to fool yourself with sufficiently overcomplicated statistics. We shall know in a year or so.

His faith that food and fuel prices are temporary appears to me to based on faith in Keynesianism, which is in turn based on faith in progressivism. He would be better off having faith in the great Cthulhu, which unlike Keynesianism can never be disproved.

I shall revisit this post in 2012 October.

You can't trust bankers

2011-06-29 05:33:28

"You can't trust bankers" says Nassim Nicholas Taleb, author of "The Black Swan: The Impact of the Highly Improbable[690]"
Taleb is an econometrician and trader - meaning he makes his money betting on financial instruments, like a professional poker player.

Bankers specialize in asymmetric risk. They borrow a lot of other people's money, and every day they make a small, reasonable, predictable profit with it, and take their fee, except that once in a while they have a gigantic loss, and decline to refund their fees.

When banks get sufficiently large, and sufficiently interconnected, the loss becomes really rare, but really gigantic, and taxpayers find themselves on the hook.

Bankers have a variety of mechanisms for generating asymmetric risk, but one of the biggest is maturity transformation. Singapore survived the financial crisis in fine shape, possibly because the Singaporean central bank monitors its financial institutions for maturity transformation, and is apt to remind investors from time to time that certain debts and loans are *not* implicitly backed by the Singaporean government nor the Singaporean central bank.

Maturity transformation is borrowing short and lending long. This works most of the time, because when one short term lender calls in his loan, another short term lender makes a loan. People lend short, however, because they are worried about a rainy day, and want their money available when it rains. And when it rains, it is apt to rain on everyone at once – the black swan – so everyone calls in their short term loans at the same time – which is apt to become the time when long term loans are selling at a horrible discount.

Asymmetric risk tends to become fraud, because the financier arranges matters that when he wins, he wins, and when he loses, someone else loses and he does not. So the financier is encouraged to increase fat tail risk, rather than reduce it.

To give financiers an incentive to control and reduce fat tail risks, to reduce the risk of black swan events, you have to make sure that bad things happen to them if they lose large amounts of other people's money in a black swan event. I suggest unlimited personal liability for financiers as Lloyds of London used to have, debtors prison, and indentured servitude, to the extent that a financier is in a position to negligently or intentionally expose other people to risks that they will find hard to judge, predict, or observe. This will give the financier an incentive to judge, predict, limit, and report such possibilities,

---
[690]https://amzn.to/k4W9x3

and make contractual provision for such events, rather than brush the possibility of such events under the carpet.

Taleb's proposed solution, however, is less drastic: That government should refrain from making a bad situation worse. That rather than preventing financial institutions from failing, which merely leads to less frequent but bigger collapses later, government should allow them to fail early and fail often.

More fake violence in Greece

2011-06-29 11:11:26

A little of the violence is real, indeed more and more of it is real, but the vast majority of it is still imitation violence by astroturf, which I conjecture is imitation riot theater instigated by the government against itself to dramatize its imitation austerity theater.

Observe the trash fires at 0:14. Real rioters burn stuff more valuable than trash, and light bigger fires.

Observe at 0:24 the group of protestors armed with white sticks, all the sticks identical, and all rather small and light, suitable perhaps for disciplining a woman or a small boy, but definitely not the sort of thing that one should strike a man with, particularly a man wearing armor. That the sticks are light, indicates pretend violence. That the sticks are identical, indicates astroturf. Someone has got in a big batch of mass produced sticks, and handed them out. The sticks are white, for maximum visibility, to make a good image, rather than to shatter the bones of one's enemies.

At 0:51 , observe some real violence - directed, of course, at a non state enemy.

At 1:06, observe the police detonate a noisy teargas canister a couple of feet downwind of their own feet, rather than at the protestors. Similarly at 1:16, where the police are almost teargassing themselves.

At 1:42 observe a little petrol unsurprisingly fail to set a stone building on fire – someone has thrown a tiny little molotov at a target that it cannot possibly harm. Indeed, places where it is so obviously safe to place a molotov are few and far between. Someone set this molotov for the least possible risk of damage.

At 2:10, another white stick, absolutely identical to every other white stick we saw in the video. The whole riot evidently has a single weapons supplier, a strong indication that this is an astroturf rent-a-mob riot. Observe the way he is carrying the stick, revealing how light it is.

Quantitative easing comes back again from the undead

2011-06-30 08:39:27

QE2 was supposed to end, and it has. However, as it ends, the federal reserve opens up open ended dollar lending to foreign central banks[691]. Supposedly there is no risk, since these are central banks, and we all know central banks always repay their debts.

---

[691] https://www.marketwatch.com/story/global-central-banks-keep-dollar-swap-lines-open-2011-06-29?link=MW_pulse

Poorer, dirtier and shabbier

2011-07-01 17:58:31

In the comments, some have disagreed with my proposition that BLS statistics are unbelievable because the US is becoming dirtier and shabbier. Dirtier and shabbier is rather subjective, so reasonable people can disagree.

Obviously California has become poorer, dirtier, and shabbier, but this is not necessarily indicative of the USA as a whole. Possibly California might be exceptional due the federally sponsored movement of very large numbers of Mexicans into formerly white areas by affirmative action lending, and the state government's self destructive tax and regulate policies, as for example just a couple of days ago, the Californian government shot itself in the foot by attempting to tax Amazon.com, with the result that Amazon abruptly fled, as thousands of smaller businesses have fled over the last couple of years[692].

So let us look for statistics less subject to manipulation and subjective judgment than the consumer price index.

According to the government's disputed measure of inflation, US GDP per head is increasing. If GDP per head was increasing, we would see electricity consumption per head increasing and life expectancy increasing. Both are decreasing.

Life expectancy[693]

The green line is gdp per head as a percentage of 2005 value - or what the BLS claims is GDP per head.

The red line is power used per head as a per head as a percentage of 2005 value.

caption id=" " align="aligncenter" width="390"

includegraphicslatex/images/power_and_gdp.gif

You will notice that the green line, alleged gdp per head, goes up about five percent a year more than the red line, power use per head. I find this hard to believe. Perhaps you find it easier to believe.

Total electricity production from EIA[694]

Population assumed to be growing linearly between the 1990, 2000, and 2010 censuses. GDP figures from the BEA[695]

Defund the left

2011-07-02 14:07:40

The reason the battle in Wisconsin is so bitter is that the Wisconsin Republicans are doing what Reagan attempted to do and failed to do: Defund the left.

Previously schools were required to buy health insurance through the teachers union. Being free to shop around for health insurance appears to save over half a million dollars

---

[692] https://thebusinessrelocationcoach.blogspot.com/2011/06/calif-business-departures-increasing.html
[693] https://articles.latimes.com/2010/dec/09/news/la-heb-stroke-20101209
[694] https://www.eia.gov/electricity/data.cfm#summary
[695] https://www.bea.gov/national/index.htm#gdp

per school The dissenting opinion[696], The Stratasphere[697], Public School Spending[698]

That is over a half a million dollars a year of taxpayer funded left wing activism in every school district, some of which appears to have been spent on rentamobs.

Taxing beyond the laffer maximum

2011-07-02 18:33:08

Why do governments tax beyond the Laffer maxium?

You have probably read about the California's Amazon tax. Amazon said it would flee the tax, promptly did so, and so, predictably. instead of gaining two hundred million, the state lost taxes on something like one hundred and fifty million of income[699].

Some people blame retailers such as Walmart, and there is much truth in that, but bloggers are not without influence, supplying, as they do, something politicians and judges crave more than money.

In Greece, the private economy is vanishing. The government applies ever more extreme measures to get people to submit their taxes, yet the very extremism of the government's measures is becoming counter productive. A poor working class Greek pays 27 cents income tax on the marginal dollar, plus 23 cents vat (sales tax) on everything he spends, leaving him about half, and of course the well off, the people who actually make the economy go, pay substantially more. If someone in Greece owns a business, and operates it in a legitimate above ground manner, the business profits get taxed as profits, then they get taxed as income when paid out to the owner, and then when the owner finally spends what little remains, he pays vat.

Clearly this is counterproductive, and yet the main form of "austerity" in Greece is to raise tax rates yet further, which of course every time results in an immediate and substantial decline in tax revenue.

The Californian state government certainly knew that the Amazon tax would result in substantial loss of revenue, and the Greek government appears to be aware that every increase in tax rates results in massive and immediate loss of revenue, because they denounce those they tax as wicked and immoral, which denunciation implicitly acknowledge that these people are going respond to increased tax rates by wickedly and immorally paying less taxes.

The attitude expressed by these words may well explain these counterproductive actions. Government thinks it wicked for private people to keep their own money, which wickedness deserves punishment, regardless of whether the punishment actually benefits the government. Government selects people with politically correct attitudes, in practice pro government attitudes, a loyalty and value expressed and displayed by irrational support for higher taxes. Thus taxes against people who don't have a lot of votes tend to

---

[696]https://www.thedissentingopinion.com/2011/05/another-district-drops-wea-trust.html

[697]https://strata-sphere.com/blog/index.php/archives/16707

[698]https://www.publicschoolspending.com/daily-updates/wisconsin-media-lacks-the-courage-to-confront-wea-trust-insurance-scam/

[699]https://www.cbs19.tv/story/15003531/california-nexus-tax-bill-crashes-website-owners-says-performance-marketing-association

exceed the Laffer limit, though taxes against people with lots of votes are in the US substantially less than the Laffer limit, and in Europe, with a few notable exceptions such as Greece, somewhat below the Laffer limit.

"The Barbarian Invasions"

2011-07-04 10:07:42

I watched an old 2003 movie, "The Barbarian Invasions" which the right love, because it depicts the ruling progressive left elite as decadent, corrupt, hypocritical, incompetent and destroying the civilization that they rule, and the ruling progressive elite love, perhaps because it is about their favorite topic, themselves.

When someone who is not part of the ruling elite watches this movie, the first message he sees is that socialist health care is a disaster, inflicting third world squalor and neglect upon the sick.

The next thing he sees is all the good progressives sneering at the USA as hateful and deserving destruction, while a hick town in the US provides smiling faces and scientifically and technologically advanced medical treatment, something notably lacking from the Canadian hospital, where even the priest just goes through the motions while waiting for patients to drop dead.

After that, the next thing he sees is that part of the problem is that the elite class of corrupt progressive government medical administrators cream off all the money for themselves, abandoning their patients and nurses to crime, squalor, disease, and death, abandoning even fellow members of the elite when they are so unfortunate as to become ill.

After that, the next thing the viewer sees is that union bosses and organizers are criminal thugs who shake down everyone, including the workers they supposedly represent, with the quiet threat of brutal violence.

And the next thing he sees is that progressives are personally immoral, disloyal, lazy, irresponsible, incompetent, and feckless, yet very comfortably off at the expense of the taxpayer.

Yet when I saw the ads for this movie, I see ruling elite progressives their target audience. The ads say that if you are one of the superior ruling progressive elite, you should watch this movie to get a warm fuzzy feeling about how superior you are. And I read the reviews, and find they did get a warm fuzzy feeling about how superior they are.

So what does a ruling elite progressive see when he watches this movie?

What I suspect he gets is what the priest was dispensing to the patients in the first scenes of the movie: Absolution. The forgiveness of sins.

Perhaps the good progressive hears that even though he and his kind screwed up totally, he is smarter and more cultured than the revolting masses, and if he is destroying our civilization, our civilization had it coming because of colonialism and imperialism and all that, and no matter how bad he may be, his good intentions make him such a superior person.

Whatever it is that he hears, the fact that the movie's absolutely devastating depiction of leftists and leftism does not trouble him, implies that it is not news to him.

Solving the immigration problem

2011-07-05 05:32:51

Roissy complains that Libertarians are in favor of open borders and that open borders are having disastrous consequences.

But what is having disastrous consequences is not open borders by themselves, but open borders combined with democracy and the welfare state.

Even if the government had the will to stop the flood of low IQ migrants, the effect would be limited. Does not stop drugs.But, more importantly, democratic welfare state government inherently lacks the will. The problem is not employers desire for cheap labor, but the desire of government and bureaucracy for cheap votes, republican politicians almost as much as democrats. Cheap votes are in the interest of government as an interest group and voting block. Government as an interest group wants people to vote for more government and more taxes, and poor low IQ voters can easily be paid and bamboozled to vote for more government and more taxes.

The only feasible solution to the immigration problem is open borders, restricting the franchise to property owners with sound credit rating, and ending welfare – or ending democracy altogether, which the way the wind is blowing is looking increasingly probable.

Retrodicting climate

2011-07-09 16:01:44

Warmist climate models do a fine job of retrodicting the climate, yet a woefully bad job at predicting the climate.

Their prediction tends to be doom in the next few years, while their modeling of the past is perfectly spot on. Thus their predictions grow old fast.You have probably heard that sulphate emissions from China temporarily saved the world from the dire and horrid effects of global warming, explaining away the politically inconvenient failure of the world to warm over the past thirteen years. "Sulfur stalls temperature rise[700]"

But that China's coal use was growing rapidly was known in 2007, when the IPCC models predicted horrid climate doom for 2011. China's coal use has been growing at about the same speed as now from about 2000 onwards.

So to *now* announce that sulphates explain away the lack of warming is a retcon.

Today's temperatures are well below the temperatures that the models predicted, well below the range that the models deemed possible, far below the uncertainty that the models admitted to[701].

---

[700]https://blog.sciencenews.org/view/generic/id/332152/title/Sulfur_stalls_surface_temperature_rise_
[701]https://clivebest.com/blog/?p=2277

"Don't call my bluff" says Obama

2011-07-15 15:33:37

"Don't call my bluff" says President Obama, thereby implicitly admitting he is bluffing. He then storms out of the meeting.

Any white trash redneck can negotiate better than that. If Obama played poker, he would lose his shirt.

This is one of those days when the affirmative action job holder needs a white male to do his job for him. You should never acknowledge the slightest possibility that you might be bluffing, or that any reasonable person might think you are bluffing. And you never storm out of negotiations. You wander out acting bored, and tell the other guys that you might contact them again sometime, maybe in a few days. Or maybe not. If you were to storm out, it would show you care, which would show the other side that they have hand over you.

Supposedly, the borrowing limit has to be raised before August the second, or the US stops paying its bills. This is baloney, a fake deadline. The president could cancel the stimulus, thereby freeing up the remaining unspent stimulus money, or could start selling off the gold in Fort Knox, or hold a land auction for some of the immense area of unused and under used land owned by the Federal government, but the closer the president gets to the real deadline, the worse his negotiating position. If Republicans hold tight till after the fake deadline, then shortly after the fake deadline but quite some time before the real deadline, the President will concede. He has already implicitly admitted it.

Although there is substantial overlap between the dumbest whites and the smartest blacks, affirmative action has the unintended effect of abolishing that overlap. The bell curve is flat in the middle, but falls of very rapidly at the edges. So if you take an extreme group, the very worst at something, such as crime, or the very best at something, such as maths or running, they will overwhelmingly be of one particular race and sex.

If people are admitted to some elite activity on merit, then those admitted will be rather similar in merit. If it is difficult to get in, most people admitted will have just barely made it in, so they will mostly be of very similar merit. Apply affirmative action for some people of a readily identifiable group, for example females to engineering, and then almost everyone of that group will be of strikingly inferior to those admitted on merit. In a group of a hundred or so, chances are that every single member of the non affirmative action group will be of visibly greater merit than the very best of the affirmative action group. Overlap will be insignificant, and in a highly elite group, there will be no overlap.

I suppose there must be some white trash rednecks who negotiate worse than Obama, but of course they would never negotiate, so if you ever see a white trash redneck negotiating, or playing poker, he is a better poker player and a better negotiator than President Obama, because there is no affirmative action for white trash rednecks.

Obama's connections

2011-07-16 16:54:40

If you read blogs like this, you probably already know that Obama's family and friends on both the black and white sides were communists and terrorists for three generations.

You are probably also familiar with Moldbug's theory that when Stalin was running the US state department, the US state department was also running Stalin, that the various wars that the US was involved in were not only proxy wars with the Soviet Union, but were in large part proxy wars between the Pentagon and the State Department, wars in which the Pentagon's contractors have frequently come very close to shooting State Department employees, and have with great regularity shot state department contractors, that the reason that the State Department was so comfortable with Stalin's agents was that they believed, in part correctly, that Stalin was their agent, that the reason that the CIA was so reluctant to believe the Soviet Union was falling is the same reason that NASA was so reluctant to believe the Challenger Space Shuttle was about to explode.

You may have known, but I did not know until today, that Obama's family had state department connections from a long way back[702]

> Another photo, published in a Honolulu newspaper in 1959, shows Stanley Dunham escorted by uniformed U.S. Navy officers, greeting Barack Obama, Sr., as he arrived in Hawaii from Kenya ...the Kenyan did not meet Dunham's daughter, Ann, in a classroom. This would fit the chronology: Classes started on September 26. Ann was pregnant by early November. Obama [Senior] was housed at the University of Hawaii's East-West Center facility funded by the Asia Foundation, itself funded by CIA.

> ...Ann ran a "micro-financing" project, financed by the Ford Foundation, in Indonesia's most vulnerable areas. Supervising the funding at Ford in the late '60s was Peter Geithner, whose son would eventually serve hers as U.S. secretary of the treasury. In addition to the Ford Foundation, the list of her employers is a directory of America's official, semi-official, and clandestine organs of influence: the United States Information Agency, the United States Agency for International Development, the World Bank, the Asian Development Bank. While running a project for five years in Pakistan, she lived in Lahore's Hilton International. Nothing small time, never mind hippyish.

> In sum, though the only evidence available is circumstantial, Barack Obama, Jr.'s mother, father, stepfather, grandmother, and grandfather seem to have been well connected, body and soul, with the U.S. government's then extensive and well-financed trans-public-private influence operations.

> ...

> The point here is that this network was formed precisely to help the careers of kindred folk, while ruining those of others, and to move the requisite

---

[702]https://www.claremont.org/publications/crb/id.1852/article_detail.asp

money and influence unaccountably, erasing evidence that it had done so. Exercising influence abroad on America's behalf—the network's founding purpose—never got in the way of playing a partisan role in American life and, of course, of taking care of its own.

...Meyer explained what he was about in his book *Facing Reality* (1980).

Meyer and his upscale CIA colleagues considered themselves family members of the domestic and international Left. They believed that America's competition with Soviet Communism was to be waged by, for, and among the Left.

Which implies that the real enemy, the big important enemy, was not the Soviet Union, but the American way of life.

The curious solvency of Japan

2011-07-18 16:58:08

By any objective measure, Japan is more broke than Italy. Indeed, nearly all the advanced countries are as broke as each other, but some of them are in trouble, and some of them are not. Japan can borrow money at low interest. Italy cannot.

Looking at past financial crises, there is no objective level of solvency at which a country goes down the tubes. They get along fine until they do not. Even when it is obvious that a country is trouble, people continue to lend it money on the assumption that an even bigger idiot will lend it more money with which to repay the first idiot. And they are always right, until they are wrong.

National bankruptcies are like bubbles, are in fact bubbles. And there is no way to say when a bubble will pop, because if there was a way to say when a bubble would pop, it would pop before then.

So people believe that there more and bigger idiots for Japan, so it is safer to lend to Japan, than to lend to Italy.

Smart people believe that there will be more idiots to come though for Japan, than there will be for Italy.

It is easier to understand Italy's insolvency than Japan's. Italy cannot print its own money. If it runs out, it has to stiff its borrowers, including its banks. If it stiffs its banks, they have to stiff their depositors.

The European Union, like Japan, can print its own money, but it is easier to understand the European Union's insolvency than Japan's. One day there might suddenly be no more European Union. If Germany decides to go back to Deutschmarks, euros probably will not be worth anything any more. The European Union might become unreal tomorrow morning - it is looking rather insubstantial this afternoon. Japan on the other hand has been around for thousands of years. Its national anthem is over a thousand years old, and its imperial dynasty has been seated on the Chrysanthemum Throne[703] since 660BC. Japan looks mighty stable, compared to the governments of Europe, which notoriously have been prone to come and go.

---

[703]https://en.wikipedia.org/wiki/Chrysanthemum_Throne "Chrysanthemum Throne"

The idea that a country and its government might still exist, but that its money might suffer a sudden and massive loss of value, that a broke government is apt to find its money worthless, the idea that fiat money is merely fiat, is one that many people find very hard to grasp. A lot of Germans still do not understand the German hyperinflation.

So it is more plausible that if the Japanese government starts to go broke, you will be able to unload your Japanese bonds on an idiot of last resort. that you will be able to find a bigger idiot to take Japanese bonds off your hands, than that if the Italian government starts to go broke, you will be able to unload your Italian bonds on an idiot of last resort, that you will be able to find a bigger idiot to take your Italian bonds off your hands.

Anthropogenic CO2

2011-07-22 12:55:55

A replication of part of Clive Best's analysis.

The theory of catastrophic anthropogenic global warming assumes a number of points without evidence, assumptions that might well be true, but which they have made no attempt to test.

One is that warming would be a bad thing, another is that the world is very sensitive to quite small CO_2 greenhouse effect, supposedly because the CO_2 greenhouse effect will be enormously amplified by the H_2O green house effect.

And another is that human burning of coal and oil can have a significant effect on atmospheric CO_2. The latter point seems reasonable, since the amount of coal and oil that has been burnt is comparable to the amount of CO_2 in the air. It is, however, insignificant compared to the amount of CO_2 in the ocean, and the ground. The threat of acidifying the oceans with CO_2 is incompatible with the threat that human are capable of significantly affecting the amount of CO_2 in the air. If CO_2 in the air rapidly equilibriates with CO_2 in the oceans, then for humans to make a significant difference by burning coal would be like humans raising the level of lake Michigan by spitting in it. There is a *lot* of CO_2 in the oceans. It is physically impossible for humans to change the acidity of any substantial part of the oceans.

CO_2 in the air has been rising, at about half the rate that would be expected if all the CO_2 in the coal we are burning stayed in the air, but, over the last twenty thousand years, CO_2 has been a lot higher than it is now, and a lot lower than it is now, so the recent rise may well reflect forces far mightier than puny humankind. Usually rise in CO_2 follows rise in global temperatures by a couple of hundred years, so we would expect CO_2 levels to be naturally rising today, because we are recovering from the little ice age that ended during the nineteenth century.

Clive Best[704] therefore proceeded to do what the "consensus" failed to do, and assess carbon flows from isotopes. He concluded that over a decade or so, the atmosphere equilibrates with some much larger carbon reservoir.

One of his lines of evidence was that in the fifties, nuclear testing added a lot of carbon fourteen to the atmosphere, which, according to wikipedia, disappeared from the atmosphere over a decade or so.

---

[704]https://clivebest.com/blog/?p=2391

Wikipedia being notoriously unreliable, I am replicating his data analysis, though we all rely on Cromer et al's data.

Cromer et-al reported C14 measurements to 1983[705], and their data is on the web[706].

The value they report, d14C, is not the absolute level of carbon 14 in parts per million, but the change, the difference between the observed level, and the historic level before nuclear tests raised it.

I loaded their data into an open office spreadsheet[707], and plotted it.

The grey line is an exponential decay, that is to say, a straight line on a logarithmic graph, of the form exp(-date/ 5330 days)

The fact that it fits the decline so well, once atmospheric nuclear testing stopped, indicates that carbon fourteen is equilibrating with a reservoir vastly larger than the atmosphere over a period of 5330 days.

And if carbon fourteen is equilibrating, so is carbon twelve and carbon thirteen, so is the carbon from coal.

So humans can no more have a significant affect on the carbon dioxide levels in the earths atmosphere, than they can raise the level of lake Michigan by spitting in it.

---

[705] https://cdiac.esd.ornl.gov/trends/co2/cent-verm.html
[706] https://cdiac.esd.ornl.gov/ftp/trends/co2/vermunt.c14
[707] latex/images/D14.ods

Shot the organ grinder

2011-07-24 13:25:51

Anders Behring Breivik shot the organ grinder instead of the monkey, the puppeteer, not the puppet.

The government of Norway is electing a new people. He did not like it.

Mencius Moldbug doubts that right wing terrorism can be effective, without a corresponding conspiracy within the government or within the armed forces. I disagree. I think this action will be highly effective in influencing the government, but the government is more a symptom than a disease, the real disease being that Norwegians have lost the will to continue to exist, which problem terrorism cannot remedy.

Norwegians, and westerners generally, are failing to reproduce, biologically or culturally, for lack of fathers. Men are not volunteering to get married, because of a society and legal system hostile to husbands and fathers. The courts treat husbands and fathers as evil by definition, while television treats them as nincompoops.

High levels of illegitimacy and low levels of boys growing up with their biological fathers indicate a father shortage, which indicates that the marriage terms are too unfavorable to men to equalize supply and demand. The last time supply and demand was reasonably equal was 1830 or so, at which time marriage was severely and radically unequal in favor of men, and to the disfavor of women, marriage being a contract in which a women irreversibly gave up extensive rights over herself, her property, and her own body to a husband, in return for his irreversible commitment to support her and his children by her.

The natural state, absent contract, is that a woman can abort, or give up children, and the father, similarly, has no obligation to support his children or their mothers. Couples can leave this natural state only by formally witnessed contract, that is to say marriage, which contract has to have terms that reflect supply and demand.

Such a contract, to equalize supply and demand for fathers, cannot treat men and women as interchangeable, it must give men terms that are nearly the opposite of the terms it gives women – the woman must commit to love, honor, and *obey*. Not that many men want to be pissed on the way a television dad gets pissed on.

The welfare state that Norwegians imagine will support them in their old age is collapsing. To prevent the collapse, the state brings in dark skinned Muslims to replace the grandchildren that Norwegians are not having. The outsiders, however, lack any inclination to support aging Norwegians, so the collapse is accelerated rather than prevented. Norway's overall fertility rate is replacement, which is very high by European standards - but that reflects the average over outsiders breeding far above replacement, and Norwegians breeding far below replacement. Norway, like the rest of Europe, is suffering a massive increase in the never married and the divorced.

Norway has a generous welfare system supporting children, which is pretty good for people who are happy to bring up children on welfare, but not really a major benefit for a white middle class couple married to each other. It winds up being another Jizya paid by Dhimmi to Muslims.

A preliminary review of the works of Anders Behring Breivik

2011-07-25 16:49:52

Shortly before killing a bunch of people, mainly the children of the elite, Breivik published two works:

A movie, the knights templar which has too much fine print for the medium, and proceeds too fast for the amount of fine print. I suppose the intent is to get you in the right frame of mind for his print works, or it might be he was just in too much of a hurry to get killing people to do a good job on the movie, and of course, his extremely lengthy, well read, scholarly and well researched manifesto thesis 2083 A European Declaration of Independence by Anders Behring Breivik.docx Did I mention it is rather lengthy, because it is rather lengthy.

His rationale for killing a bunch of people is that in order to defeat Islam, it is first necessary to defeat the Cultural Marxists (i.e. diversocracy, enforced political correctness), then restore patriarchy, then nationalism, and only then will it be practical to defeat Islam. His schedule has war with Islam for control of Europe starting around 2083. Before 2083, the job is to remake Europe to be capable of resisting Islam.

The analysis is sound as far as it goes, but the trouble is that while Charles the Hammer could remake Europe to make it capable of resisting Islam, a guy with some guns and a few tons of explosives cannot.

Rational terrorism

2011-07-26 10:15:15

A lot of people, myself included, have suggested that Breivik's terrorism was unlikely to be effective[708], but he has information we did not. If his account and perception of reality is accurate, if his thesis about the reality of Norwegian society today is correct, then his terrorism mostly killed bad people who were soldiers for the evil side, and may well have the intended effects, over the lengthy intended time frame.

Brievik is handsome, intelligent, scholarly, and well read, a natural member of the elite, but in a society dominated by gangs, grew up in a white gang of vandals and thugs, mainly because the chicks dig gang bangers, particularly if their gangs are connected to the right gangs. Chicks dig bad boys, chick do bad boys, and Breivik tells us that in Norway, as in much of the US, the baddest boys get government funding and police protection. And if you are a bad boy with government funding and police protection, you get the girls.

He smoothly made the transition from the gang elite to the nominally non gang academic elite.

According to Brievik, Norway is organized similarly to the way the Democratic party in the US in areas with a substantial non asian minority is organized. The government directly funds the Democratic Party machine, (as for example the health insurance scam[709]) the Democratic party machine funds and is in large part composed of community organizers, who get government money and police protection, the community organizers fund and are in large part composed of gangsters who rob, vandalize, mug, and shakedown prostitutes and good time girls for money, drugs, booze, and sex. The gangsters get out the vote, and adjust population composition along voting district boundaries, and get government money and police protection. If there are too many of group X in the congressman's district, they ethnically cleanse members of group X out.

In order to travel around without being beaten up, you have to have the correct gang affiliations, which you get primarily through politics. But suppose the price of the right gang affiliations is too high? Sometimes politics has to be backed by force. Well then you can do a drive by shooting thereby persuading this other gang that is causing your gang grief to adopt more favorable attitude.

With this social order, it is frequently rational to do a drive by shooting, to shoot up the street. A couple of guys from your gang shoot up example street. The gang that rules example street needs to make peace with you, so lets your gang hang out on example street, so you get to beat up the chicks in example street, take their money, and fuck them.

---

[708]https://blog.reaction.la/politics/a-preliminary-review-of-the-works-of-anders-behring-breivik.html "Permanent Link to A preliminary review of the works of Anders Behring Breivik"

[709]https://biggovernment.com/kolson/2011/02/23/wisconsin-unions-insurance-scam-at-stake-in-collective-bargaining-reform/

And the chicks dig it - hence the reproduction and childbirth statistics from those parts of America resemble the reproduction and childbirth statistics from Norway as a whole.

In Norway even females with high educational qualification, if they have children, generally have children without marriage or any long term relationship, and my personal observation (not of Norway, but of other parts of the world) is that upper class women who have children without marriage or a long term relationship, commonly have children by thugs whom they financially support.

This act of political terrorism was also yet another gang shooting, with the important difference that Breivik, having what he plausibly claims to be a clearer perception of how things work than the average gang banger, went after members of the top gang, instead of its dark skinned minions.

Since Brievik is likely to be doing a long time in jail, he may not necessarily be reproductively successful, but in the US, a gang banger who does a long time in jail for shooting up the street for his gang nonetheless usually manages to have a couple of dozen kids on welfare by a couple of dozen women, so Brievik's strategy may well be personally successful from a Darwinian perspective.

For Brievik's strategy to be long term successful, his new Knights Templar need to succeed in getting laid. The top gang in Norway has been favoring gangs of the new people, the imported underclass voters, and disfavoring gangs of the previous people, gangs formed from the previous inhabitants of Norway. If this terrorist act results in a change of that policy, then gangs of the previous people, the new Knights Templar, will get more pussy, money, drugs and booze.

Gangs dominate, so you join a gang. Your gang, however is politically disfavored, so the girls give you less pussy, and less of their wages, welfare money, child support money, drugs, and booze, than they give members of other gangs. What should you do? Maybe you should do a drive by on a gathering of the most powerful gang of thugs of them all. That is what Breivik thought, and he is clearly a lot smarter than the average gang banger.

How well run is Oslo?

2011-07-28 04:12:12

According to the bloggers who speak for our ruling elite (such as Matthew Yglesias) Norway is wonderfully well run. But according to the terrorist Breivik, it is run much like Chicago, where the ruling party's political mobilization of the disproportionately criminal underclass has produced a criminal party.According to the terrorist Brievik, the ruling elite, having imported a new people to keep voting them into power, having imported vast masses of underclass voters, has a party apparatus whose lower levels are heavily underclass, and rife with underclass behaviors, with lower levels of the party apparatus overlapping with the leadership of underclass gangs of thugs, with criminals on the party payroll.

According the terrorist Breivik, Norway's previous people are suffering total collapse of the family, with even the upper class substantially fatherless.

Who is right? Breivik is closer to the facts, is a personal eyewitness, but might be crazy. I go to you tube, and search "Oslo riots". What I see looks like what I would expect to see in a city where, according to Breivik, there are large areas where you cannot pass without the correct gang affiliations, consistent with his account of a party that has franchised part of its power to criminal gangs, Chicago style.

Breivik reports the collapse of the family: Norway's reproduction statistics look like total collapse of the family. People are having children without getting married or expecting a durable relationship. In America this is primarily an underclass phenomenon, but in Norway appears classless in the statistics, possibly because the new people (mostly underclass) have strong restraints on female sexual misbehavior, so in the statistics we are seeing an average over the underclass of the previous people and the mostly underclass new people, the underclass of the previous people behaving even worse than the elite reproductively, and the the new people behaving better than the elite reproductively.

So on the whole the, the evidence suggests to me that it is the terrorist Breivik that is sane, and it is the spokebloggers for our ruling elite that are crazy.

The debt limit charade

2011-07-31 09:00:19

US politicians are engaged in passionate debate and confrontation over the debt limit and spending. The question is whether to "cut" two trillion over the next ten years, which is to say, about two hundred billion dollars a year, which is to say, whether, after ten years, spending will be five or six trillion dollars a year more than it is now, or whether it will be five or six trillion dollars a year more than it is now, assuming that the US government still exists in ten years.

Politics, they say, is the art of the possible, though others say it is war by less lethal means. And if politics is the art of the possible, one must proceed with small incremental changes. So if every year we have another teensy weeny confrontation like this one over teensy weeny little issues, and every year we cut another two trillion over ten years, which is to say, two hundred billion per year, then, at the end of ten years, instead of federal spending having grown by five or six trillion per year, it will have grown by three or four trillion per year, assuming we win every such confrontation, which we will not.

Spending increases are irreversible. No one ever proposes actual cuts, merely increases less than planned. Government departments are immortal, all of which follows from the fact that bureaucrats are unsackable. Even if they completely piss of the president and congress, and demonstrate total incompetence combined with gross insubordination, as the SEC did over Ponzi schemes, they are still completely fireproof. And there is always a good reason for yet another government department, for if a government department screws up spectacularly, as they so regularly do, the remedy is always the creation yet another government department, rather than the disappearance of the old.

Wisconsin, one state in fifty states, is the extraordinary exception, the one state where the elected politicians rolled the permanent fireproof government, or at least made a serious attempt to do so. They may well fail, but the results so far are interesting.

Reagan attempted to defund the left, and failed.

In Wisconsin they actually are defunding the left, hence the extraordinary reaction. The savings accomplished were dramatic, revealing how much of government spending was in reality funding for the left - which in turn reveals that the left is 99% astroturf, that leftists are on the payroll.

To actually accomplish anything, it would be necessary to defund the left nation-wide, and to make government employees fireable nationwide, which would not be politics as normal, not be incremental change, but be difficult to accomplish by means short of regime change.

The left is currently defined by its policies on race and sex, rather than class. In the US, this is a natural consequence of the legacy of slavery and the mass importation of voters from Mexico. In Europe, it is rather an artificial consequence of the European left taking its marching orders from the US left, resulting in a policy of transforming Europe into an Islamic state, a condition even less pleasant than turning California into Mexico.

However, the American left position on race and sex today is as indefensible as its position on socialism was in 1949. The strategy of handing out a middle class lifestyle on the basis of race and sex led to economic crisis and collapse.

If the left, which is to say the state, stops giving people a middle class lifestyle on the basis of race and sex, then people who have middle class jobs on the basis of race and sex, as for example most of your human resources department, expose the scam by not living a middle class lifestyle, whereupon is becomes embarrassing to give them middle class jobs on the basis of race and sex.

If the left, which is to say the state, stops giving people middle class jobs on the basis of race and sex, then people who have degrees on the basis of race and sex expose the scam by their inability to get jobs, whereupon it becomes embarrassing to give them middle class degrees on the basis of race and sex.

If the left, which is to say the state, stops giving people middle class degrees on the basis of race and sex, then Marie Curie and company are left high and dry.

As the left runs into troubles with its position on class and race and sex, it increasingly becomes purely the party of the state. The trade unions are state trade unions, the race baiters are government and party employees.

At the same time as leftist ideology becomes more more fake and bankrupt, the rate of movement leftwards becomes faster and faster, foreshadowing a political singularity.

I attempted to fit the growth in regulation and the growth in expenditure with best fit to simple power law rules. The functions contained a term sqrt(T-t), or 1/sqrt(T-t), where t is the date, and T is around 2016-2027.

The fit was not nearly good enough to give a very definite date, but the basic scenario is a regulatory singularity: For example:

1933: 17 pages Glass–Steagall Act

1999: 385 pages Gramm–Leach–Bliley Bill, also known as the Financial Services Modernization Act

2010: 2305 pages Dodd–Frank Wall Street Reform and Consumer Protection Act

The fit was not all that good, but most hyperexponential curves have a singularity coming up soon once you get to the part of the curve that is obviously hyperexponential.

Although pensions are a disaster in the long term, what is driving the deficit in the short term is explosive growth of regulation: for example the financial services act replaced sound lending with politically correct lending, which in turn resulted in bailouts. The growth in regulation also prevents investment in the sense that any investment requires an ever growing pile of permits that are ever more difficult to obtain. This produces an imbalance between savings and investment, which needs to be remedied, and Keynesians believe should be remedied by government dis-saving.

Stagflation

2011-07-31 19:30:17

Once again, the economic news[710] is "unexpected" bad. Official inflation is supposedly 3.2% annualized while real GDP is supposedly 1.3% annualized. I suspect actual inflation is higher, which would mean that actual growth was correspondingly lower, but even if we take these figures at face value, they still do not support the Keynesian account of the crisis.

There are several explanations of recessions and depressions:

The one most approved by government, and most apt to get glittering prizes at ivy league universities, is Keynesianism. If there is unemployment, aggregate lack of demand for workers, there must be insufficient aggregate demand for goods, so government should print up some money and spend it. This analysis never fails to be a hit with politicians.

Then there is the recalculation theory: Lots of capitalists make big mistakes, thinking some activity is profitable (such as perhaps lending money to deadbeats to buy houses). The balloon bursts, they discover they have been investing in the wrong stuff. Lots of people who formerly had jobs in real estate, building houses, banking, and so forth now have to find new ways of making a living, which is hard.

Then there is the regime uncertainty theory. Today, the major objective of businessmen is not finding lucrative ways to apply capital to create wealth, but to get an Obamacare waiver. They are not hiring, because they fear unpredictable punishment.

Then there is the regulatory explosion. To create jobs, a businessman needs to invest. To invest, needs lots of permissions and permits, a rapidly increasing number of permissions and permits. Cannot get them. Savings therefore exceed investment.

In the immediate aftermath of the housing bust, the problem was probably recalculation and the regulatory explosion, but now it is regime uncertainy and the regulatory explosion.

Science stagnating in the west

2011-08-03 17:52:31

John Goodman reminds us:

> How many new drugs, Dr.Lajos Pusztai asks, were approved for breast cancer treatment in the past decade? His answer: seven. None was much different from drugs already on the market.
>
> Yet in the same decade, he said, there were 8,000 publications in medical and scientific journals on breast cancer and more than 3,000 clinical trials

---

[710]https://www.bea.gov/newsreleases/national/gdp/gdpnewsrelease.htm

at a cost of over $1 billion. "What came out of this is seven 'me too' drugs," Dr.Pusztai said.

Until about 1946 or so science in the west was advancing rapidly. However, shortly after the war ended peer review was widely adopted, and at about the same time science history was abruptly rewritten so that science had always practiced peer review, and at the same time also rewritten so that Roger Bacon, instead of being imprisoned in solitary confinement on bread and water[711] by the Church for advocating the scientific method as in the earlier histories, was instead supposedly placed under "a form of house arrest" for advocating astrology[712]. With the adoption of peer review, the scientific method was de-emphasized. It was not written out of history, but in the new version of official history, the scientific method lost its starring, heroic, and revolutionary role in western civilization. The scientific method was still routinely taught in schools, though after the seventies, less so.

It is hard to say exactly when science slowed down, but after we landed on the moon, obviously slower. I suspect that the decline is caused by peer review and the de-emphasis of the scientific method, but because it is hard to say when science slowed, hard to say what caused it. I say the problem is that if the scientific method is central to science, then it is science, but if peer review is central, then nothing distinguishes "science" from any other state sponsored theocratic priesthood. That is my explanation of the problem, but your interpretation of the evidence may differ.

Julia Szabo reminds us:[713]

> many Americans frustrated by declining health and understandably eager to improve their quality of life are booking flights to state-of-the-art facilities where they can expect to receive high-tech treatments (for orthopedic injury, arthritis, multiple sclerosis, spinal injury, COPD, cardiovascular disease, and many other conditions) that American hospitals simply cannot offer.

> Many are returning home significantly improved — like Bartolo Colon. Sidelined by a series of arm and shoudler injuries, the pitcher underwent adult stem cell therapy in May in the Dominican Republic. Samples of his fat and bone marrow were processed for his own stem cells, then injected into the afflicted areas of his arm to repair ligament damage and a torn rotator cuff. The procedure had previously been shown to work for sidelined race horses; that was good enough for Colon, who is now at work for the Yankees, in the pink of health, delighting his fans.

It seems that the reason this therapy is not available in the US is that the science underlying the therapy subtly discredits one of the arguments in favor of abortion – demonstrating that science in the US is subservient to progressive theology.

---

[711] https://books.google.com/books?id=wMUKAAAAYAAJ&pg=PR94#v=onepage&q&f=false
[712] https://books.google.com/books?id=Gy3Vp7TurVUC&pg=PA19&lpg=PA19
[713] https://pajamasmedia.com/blog/adult-stem-cells-work-better-msm-only-likes-embryonic-kind-hmm/?singlepage=true "Adult stem cells heretical"

US federal government burn rate is 8% of GDP

2011-08-05 15:38:51

The burn rate is a eight percent of GDP. Total debt is one hundred percent of GDP.[714] Federal government accounting is a riddle wrapped in a mystery inside an Enigma, which has lead some people attempting to make sense of its books to become somewhat paranoid, myself amongst them. If you have ever run a small business, you will know how hard it is to figure out how the business is really doing, even if you are a smart guy who knows a bit of accounting and understands the business. If it is a large business, and those doing the accounts do not really want to know how the business is actually doing ...

The recent debt limit shenanigans, however, revealed the burn rate, the rate at which the federal government has to borrow money or print money. Between April sixteenth and August the first, the national debt increased by 238.357 billion in 77 days, which is about 1.13 trillion dollars a year, surprisingly close to the reported deficit. The actual burn rate is likely a fair bit higher than that, because July is a good month for tax payments.

That is unsustainable, but it is not hyperinflation in 2012. More like hyperinflation in 2026

The prehistory of the left

2011-08-06 13:15:41

Vladimir, Moldbug, and Foseti discuss the prehistory of the left, also known as the United States Government[715]. Prehistory ends, and history starts, in the 1950s, because history before then got rewritten beyond recognition.

Communism or universalism

2011-08-07 11:46:36

Mencius Moldbug proposes to explain what is wrong with the current political order by pointing out what it has in common with communism, thus he proposes to call the current regime communist[716], in that genuine opposition is for the most part successfully repressed. According to Moldbug Communism is "Democracy without authentic political opposition".

Not so. Communism is primarily an economic system.

I would call the current regime the Cathedral, and its ideology universalism. There are important differences between communism and the present social order.

The biggest and most dramatic is the economy: Communists implement a government owned command economy. Universalism aims at a nominally private economy subject to government command, similar to that implemented by the German Nazi Party, and the Cathedral has not yet entirely achieved this goal, though it is well on the way.

[714]https://lonelyconservative.com/2011/08/more-great-news-us-borrowing-now-tops-gdp/
[715]https://foseti.wordpress.com/2011/08/03/eisenhower/?like=1&$_{w}pnonce = 07e4fabd85$
[716]https://unqualified-reservations.blogspot.com/2011/08/reuther-memorandum-1961.html

Communists imprison or shoot their opponents. The Cathedral quietly blights the careers of its opponents and destroys their good name. Communism is totalitarian, while the Cathedral applies repressive mock tolerance. Thus a lot more opposition persists under the Cathedral than persisted under communism.

Communists implement tyranny, where every commissar is even more terrorized than those he terrorizes. Universalism seeks to implement anarcho tyranny, where Cathedral members have vast power over non Cathedral members, but the president cannot fire a bureaucrat, let alone shut down a department, no matter how spectacularly that bureaucrat messes up. Universalist governments are incohesive. Communist governments are cohesive till they collapse.

Communists claimed to rule on behalf of the working class, claimed to *be* the working class, and if any worker doubted it, he was likely to be shot. Universalists claim to be such wonderful nice guys that they rule on behalf of everyone, except perhaps white males, and deserve to rule because they are so very nice.

Communists strongly believed in economic development. Whenever the proles could not get jam today, that was because the communists were investing in a brighter tomorrow, though when I went to Cuba, it looked like no one had built anything since communists took power: all the facilities were old, and in dire need repairs, maintenance, and paint. When East Germany fell, and west Germany attempted to privatize the factories, the factories were still largely World War II era, despite all this supposed investment.

Universalists, on the other hand, are so very nice that increasingly they claim to rule on behalf of the trees, rather than human beings, which unfortunately necessitates the suppression of evil factories, evil mining, and so forth, measures that are causing the death of millions through famine, poverty, and disease, and may well cause the death of billions. Songbirds eat mosquitoes, so, since universalists care so much for songbirds, cannot permit people to use excessively deadly poisons against mosquitoes. In this they are direct opposite of communists, who casually spewed poisons over the land in their efforts to develop economically.

The size of the difference between universalism and communism

2011-08-08 16:04:46

Moldbug points out that universalist regimes such as the US government and its satellites, suppress dissent too, though by means less drastic and obvious than communist regimes, and that universalist regimes had disturbingly cozy relationships with communist regimes, were full of fellow travellers until there was no one left to travel with. He proposes, therefore, to call them all communist.

But, Vladimir points out[717]:

> If you read that Ruritania was communist until 1989 and then became Universalist, chances are you'll have a highly correct picture of its political system both before and after — even if you know absolutely nothing about Ru-

---

[717]https://foseti.wordpress.com/2011/08/03/eisenhower/#comment-5177

ritania other than this single fact. A contrast between two words that packs
so much accurate information is, in my opinion, certainly worth keeping.

And you will also have a highly correct picture of its economic system before, and the
ways in which that economic system is changing after.

The big difference between universalist and communist regimes is economic, with
universalist regimes seeking a Nazi type economy, with extensive ad hoc intervention,
command, and control, but nominally private ownership and no central plan, while communist regimes intended open state ownership and a central plan.

In the past, this (fascism) has been a more rational system than state ownership and
a central plan, but with too much state intervention, the lack of a central plan produces
chaos. It only works if enough capitalism remains. The financial system appears to be
reaching this point, and the American health care system has clearly reached this point.
The best medical system in the world is probably Singapore, which has a fully socialist
system for the poor and the unfortunate, and a fully capitalist system for the vast majority. For the poor in Singapore, there are death panels and a central plan. The Singaporean
middle class, however pays for their health care, and get what they pay for, with the result that genuine free market competition yields costs that are substantially lower than in
other countries.

London riots

2011-08-09 10:46:54

The police shot Mark Duggan in London, as they beat up Rodney King in Los Angeles.
Likely Mark Duggan needed killing, and it was instant justice, or possibly not. There is
disagreement over who fired first.

Real violence, not astroturf mock violence, ensued. There have been three days of
rioting, looting, and racist assaults by blacks on whites over much of England, and the
riots continue[718].

I think we have a better quality of looter and arsonist in the US, since in the US they
waited for the investigation to complete.

Another thing they do not have in England is Korean snipers on rooftops with AK47s
to clean the streets. For lack of those snipers, the shops are burning.

The police are trying very hard to "lower tensions" and be "non threatening" which
looked to me like cowardice and weakness, and that is the way it looked to the rioters. On
BBC video I saw a mass of cops wearing armor and carrying shields, and traffic jam of
cop cars driving slowly past them. A team of young black men carrying big rocks dashed
in front of them, hurled rocks at cars, and raced back with dazzling speed and athleti-
cism, almost as if they were dancing. The spin as each black hurled his rock, stopped and
turned, was graceful and spectacular. Obviously they expected a mighty horde of cops to
give chase, but nothing happened. So they did it again. And again. The cops acted like
potted palms. If the cops wanted to be non threatening, and non provocative, they were
succeeding.

---

[718]https://www.guardian.co.uk/uk/blog/2011/aug/08/london-riots-third-night-live

When I looked at the Guardian's riot blog a few minutes ago there were no incidents of police protecting a person or his property. There was however one report of a private citizen, armed only with a knife, protecting a journalist and his property.

The Guardian journalist Jason Rodrigues reports:

> I was forced to swerve away from them but crashed to the ground. Just as one of the thieves grabbed my bike from under me a red van raced screeched around the corner and smashed into a parked car. Two young men then got out and the man in passenger seat then put his hand in his pocket and threatened to pull a on knife on the thieves

Very British. The lack of AK47s and rooftop snipers is apparent.

Here is a video of police being highly non threatening, non confrontational, and non provocative.

Observe, four unarmed, unarmored rioters confront eight cops armed and in full armor. Some of the cops show fear. Emboldened by this, a large horde abruptly materializes to support the four unarmed rioters. Police rapidly become so non threatening, non confrontational, and non provocative that a cynic might think it looks remarkably as if they are running like rabbits. Compare and contrast with Jason Rodrigues' account of two young men facing down a large gang with the threat of deadly force.

Suppose the armed and armored cops had stood their ground. Firstly, if they had shown willingness to stand their ground the mob would not have attacked. And if the mob had attacked, whosoever in the mob was frontmost, would have suffered injury or death, and pretty soon no one in the mob would want to be frontmost, so that no matter what the mob's advantage in numbers, they would all be waiting for someone else to go first.

Obama says it is not his fault

2011-08-10 13:54:29

In a boring and unusually uncharismatic speech, Obama explains that America's credit rating downgrade is not his fault, and it is not his job to fix it.

I found this speech more entertaining and more informative when I watched it with the sound off. A basic requirement for a politician is real or well faked sincerity. Watching Obama with sound off, it is apparent that he is not a very good liar.

His "I am the moderate adult in the room" spiel collided incongruently with his "Tea party terrorists bombed America's credit rating" spiel. Logically, the words made sense I suppose. The speech would have been congruent if presented as text. As words they were congruent, but his face was all wrong for his words, trying too hard.

Another case of the affirmative action president. Clinton could lie very well, and Bush could persuade himself to believe whatever was convenient to believe. Obama can do neither.

Mark Duggan did not shoot

2011-08-12 11:39:30

Mark Duggan's gun was not fired, and before his death, he expected to be murdered. This suggests that his family's account of his killing is true – that he was not killed in an exchange of fire, but was murdered by police, in which case the attacks on police that started these riots were legitimate, no matter how illegitimate the ensuing arson, looting, and random racist assaults.

Though the British cops generally go easy on the underclass, they are the hounds of hell on people with guns. Since they are the hounds of hell on members of the bourgeoisie who use guns to defend their property, since British police casually break every law in order to punish these respectable legal gun owners, and expend huge amounts of time and effort to legally or illegally get middle class property owners who use guns to protect their property, it is plausible that they behave similarly to members of the underclass who use guns to protect their drugs.

Police devoted extraordinary resources to getting Mark Duggan, just as they devoted even more extraordinary resources to taking down Tony Martin, a 55-year-old Norfolk farmer who shot a burglar in self defense. Compare and contrast with their casual negligence when members of the middle class are robbed or have their property destroyed by arsonists.

Inspector Gadget tells us[719]:

> We want to carry out a baton charge at a line of angry youths who are setting fire to a huge wheelie bin in the doorway of a post office, but we are told to 'hold the line'.

No big effort to prevent people from starting fires, but a gigantic effort to prevent people like Tony Martin from using guns on underclass habitual criminals.

Since they were putting remarkable effort into pinning something on Mark Duggan, it is plausible that, as claimed by the protestors, they eventually decided to take a short cut.

Meanwhile, those who attacked property in the riots get off lightly[720]. Harriet Harman is seeking the looter and arsonist vote[721], as is Ken Livingstone[722]

The rioters are underclass, are living on welfare, or, which comes to much the same thing, are employed in low level government jobs (either way, they don't work and do not have to discipline themselves). Most of them are imported underclass, though some of them are native British underclass[723].

---

[719]https://inspectorgadget.wordpress.com/2011/08/09/we-dont-need-the-army-we-need-the-order-to-charge/

[720]https://www.telegraph.co.uk/news/uknews/crime/8696787/UK-riots-the-young-yobs-back-on-the-streets-despite-David-Camerons-pledge.html

[721]https://www.youtube.com/watch?v=UgXuX32ot8w

[722]https://blogs.telegraph.co.uk/news/andrewgilligan/100100126/ken-livingstone-the-rioters-need-someone-to-%E2%80%9Ccare-about-them-and-speak-for-them%E2%80%9D/

[723]https://www.anncoulter.com/columns/2011-08-10.html

These are people who, whether nominally employed or not, are paid for their votes, in most cases, brought to Britain for their votes. These are welfare state mobs[724].

When the government collects money from group A, and gives it to group B, one should not be very surprised if law enforcement, the judiciary, and regulatory authorities also favor group B over group A.

In America, we have the problem of racist flash mobs forming to attack whites, x[725], x[726], x[727] similar though not identical to Britain's rioter problem. And as with Britain's rioter problem, the authorities roll over and play dead.

Recall that Major Hasan, before he murdered a bunch of people at Fort Hood, was affirmative actioned into a job for which he was clearly unqualified. He is still drawing pay for that job, while those who heroically stopped him at great risk to their own lives, have, predictably, been laid off[728].

The government is on the side of the mob. Of course it is on the side of the mob. That is what democracy is. And a democratic government prefers a poor and ignorant mob whose votes come cheaply. And if the natives are not like that, will import a new people to get rid of the old people, which process is now under way.

Inspector Gadget thinks that if police were just allowed to whack people, they would make short work of the rioters, but if you want to get ahead in today's police force, it is not the rioters you should be making short work of, it is those who have the insolence to work, marry, raise their own children, save money, and invest.

People are saying that it is shocking the state is too weak to maintain order, we need a stronger state. Rather, the problem is that the state is *not on the side of property*, so property gets set on fire. The state was plenty strong enough to railroad Tony Martin for defending his property.

Ruling majority underclass

2011-08-13 10:36:06

Following the British riots (which have not exactly ended, but have diminished to merely routine levels of violence, robbery, and arson) the British Labor Party went trolling for looter and arsonist votes, while the conservative party tried to get the votes of those members of the underclass that were worried about being robbed or burned out of the homes – the parties acted as if taxpayer votes were irrelevant since they could be taken for granted, the objective was for the conservatives to split off enough underclass votes.

The ideology of entitlement is the orthodoxy in Britain. Those that work and operate businesses are supposedly bad people, so deserve to have their stuff taken and given to good people. The government is failing to adequately confiscate stuff, so supposedly it is understandable that the oppressed masses must rise up and do it themselves. The conservative party objects to this theory, but is not quite prepared to reject it altogether.

---

[724]https://jadedhaven.wordpress.com/2011/08/10/welfare-state-nihilism/
[725]https://www.todaystmj4.com/news/local/126825018.html
[726]https://blogs.the-american-interest.com/wrm/2011/08/07/american-tinderbox/
[727]https://www.alternativeright.com/main/blogs/zeitgeist/the-flash-mob-phenomenon/
[728]https://www.jihadwatch.org/2011/08/fort-hood-jihad-mass-murderer-still-getting-military-paycheck-heroes-who-took-him-down-fired.html

Perhaps they are arguing that rioting, looting, and arson is wrong because the conservatives are doing a good enough job in taking money from the sinfully employed and giving it to the virtuously unemployed, but it is hard to tell what they are saying because their mouths are full of cotton wool

How big is the underclass?

British illegitimacy is 41%, and you can add to that exceeding brief marriages with last long enough only for the wife to get pregnant with her welfare entitlement and her claim on the husbands income as well as assets, so that she can set to screwing random thugs without the encumbrance of a husband. Not all underclass members are illegitimate, and not all illegitimate children and their mothers are underclass, but the groups are likely to be of very roughly comparable size.

Income and power, or lack thereof, is not an indicator of underclass status, for some welfare recipients get a *lot* of welfare. Consider Professor Lionel McIntyre, "professor" at the American Ivy League University of Columbia. He sucker punched a female colleague in a discussion of "white privilege", giving her a black eye, and then punched out a male who politely remonstrated him. The bouncers did not throw him out. He did not lose his job. When he repeatedly failed to show up in court, the court hearing got repeatedly postponed. If you fail to show up, you will get a hefty sentence and warrant made out for your arrest – even if you failed to show up because they gave you the wrong hearing date. He was eventually sentenced to three days community service. His behavior demonstrates that though a well paid Ivy League professor, he was still underclass. Getting a "job" by affirmative action has the same detrimental effects on character as living on welfare, because affirmative action employees frequently do little or no work, seldom show up, and so on and so forth. Affirmative action is just a more generous welfare package. The same is true of much government employment. You don't necessarily need to show up. Observe that those looters in the British riots that had jobs, had government jobs.

Interestingly, *Professor* Lionel McIntyre does not appear to give any classes at Columbia University. How is that for white privilege! Similarly, the British National Health, the nations largest employer, mostly employs people whose supposed jobs do not involve any form of patient contact. I suppose some of them do something, but I suspect that for most of them, their primary job is voting for more national health service.

Affirmative action employment, and government employment is, in large part, thinly disguised welfare and crime, and as a result the recipients frequently show underclass behavior and underclass attitudes, even though they get better welfare and commit more lucrative crime than most of the underclass.

Consider that in the US a very large proportion of female university students take "women's studies" courses, and a very large proportion of black university students take "black studies" courses. In most cases they are taking on serious debt to go to university, so these courses are costing them serious debt without them learning anything useful. The implication is that they believe that they will get a job without being expected or required to produce value, that they will get an affirmative action pretend job – a better class of welfare, one that does not require them push their welfare tickets out of their bellies.

So what this adds up to is that if you are a British taxpayer, you are well and truly outvoted, and if you are an American taxpayer, you are outvoted and it is going to get worse. The state takes money from group A, and gives it to group B, and also favors group B in regulation and law enforcement. In the US, Professor McIntyre can punch a woman. You cannot. In Britain, the rioters can attack people, and you cannot defend yourself. The police and the courts and so forth are not on your side. They are on the side of the likes of Professor McIntyre, who, if he was in Britain, would probably be found helping himself to a free plasma television set while white professors teach classes.

The underclass has been legalized, and the middle class has been illegalized.

Affirmative action and lies

2011-08-15 06:56:25

Suppose group A and group B differ in mean and distribution in some desirable or undesirable quality. Chances are that there is a lot of overlap in the middle, but when you select the very best, perhaps for some prestigious and well paid job, and the very worst, perhaps to lock them up and get them off the streets, the bell curve, the normal distribution, implies not much overlap. Because not much overlap, if the state enforces affirmative action there will be very little overlap between those who earned the prestigious job, and those affirmative actioned into the prestigious job. Most of the affirmative action job holders, on casual inspection seemingly all of them, will be incapable of fulfilling the normal requirements of the job. (For a notorious recent example, female firefighters during the 9/11 fire.)

Often, to everyone's great relief, they will just stop showing up at work, while remaining on the payroll, turning affirmative action into welfare, yet another tax that businesses must pay, which welfare has the usual destructive effects on the recipients.

Hence the outrage at the bell curve: The mathematics of the normal distribution shows that affirmative action is always going to be a disaster.

The same thing applies for affirmative action enforcement of criminal and honor codes, for selection of the worst rather than the best. Authority is going to refrain from expelling, firing, or imprisoning people who quite obviously would have been imprisoned or fired had they been white, making the differences between the two groups glaringly obvious, even though if you look at people in the middle, there is a great deal of overlap.

Thus affirmative action results in very conspicuous group privilege and very conspicuous group differences – that people of the favored group rarely perform their jobs, and regularly get away with stuff a normal man would not be allowed to get away with, as if members of the favored group were wild animals in a zoo. If you select a black at random and a white at random, you cannot reliably predict which one will be better. If you select a black and white prestigious job holder at random, the white is almost certainly going to be substantially better than the black. Just about every white prestigious job holder will be better than just about every black prestigious job holder. (Unless of course, it is basketball, where affirmative action works the other way around, and every black on the team is better than any white on the team.) That is not racism, that is the mathematics of the normal distribution. Every fireman is better than every "firefighter".

Professor Lionel McIntyre of the highly prestigious Columbia university had a discussion about white privilege with a female employee at that university, in which he sucker punched her in the face. Another employee remonstrated, whereupon Professor Lionel McIntyre punched him in the face.

As soon as I said "sucker punched her in the face", you knew he was black. You cannot conclude from the fact that so and so punched a woman in the face that so and so is black. You can, however, thanks to affirmative action, conclude from the fact that so and so holds a prestigious job, and yet he punched a woman in the face, that so and so is black. Thanks to affirmative action, you *can* prejudge individual cases, as if blacks were a different species, whereas formerly you could not.

The bouncers did not throw Professor Lionel McIntyre into the street, which would have happened if he was white.

Professor Lionel McIntyre did not lose his job, which would have happened if he was white.

Professor Lionel McIntyre was charged, but failed to appear in court. The court, instead of convicting him in absentia and issuing an arrest warrant, set another date. And another. And another. Eventually he deigned to show up, and was given three days community service.

The intent of affirmative action was to make it easier for everyone to politely ignore group differences, but the actual consequence has been to make the differences dramatically obvious, and most obvious to members of the elite, though members of the elite can least afford to speak the truth.

The pious lie relies on there being lots of overlap, enough overlap to obfuscate the ugly and hurtful truth. Affirmative action drastically reduces the overlap, near enough eliminates it, leaving the ugly truth bare ass naked.

Long ago, the elite could piously believe whatever they wanted to believe about supposedly oppressed groups, and piously denounce those unfortunate enough to have actual contact with those groups as "racist"

Affirmative action has the unintended effect that the elite now know better than anyone that group differences are disturbingly large and ugly, the opposite of what it was intended to do, while enforcement of political correctness forces them to hypocritically lie more than anyone on this topic.

Stereotypes confirmed

2011-08-15 19:41:55

The ever insightful Steve Sailer spotted[729] a German newspaper telling the truth about the English rioters[730]:

Almost all suspects are foreigners, no job, and a sizeable criminal record. About half of the defendants are minors, yet their parents fail to show up in court.

Although England has a massive native underclass, the overwhelming majority of the looting and burning was done by the imported underclass, the new people.

---

[729]https://isteve.blogspot.com/2011/08/die-welt-most-defendants-confirm-all.html
[730]https://www.welt.de/politik/ausland/article13542760/Die-meisten-Angeklagten-bestaetigen-alle-Klischees.html

Rick Perry (Bush III) replaces governor Romneycare

2011-08-17 02:12:22

Governor Romneycare was the establishment's favored candidate for president, anointed as front runner, to make Obamanism bipartisan. It has, however, become obvious that his campaign is dead on arrival (strange for a supposed front runner) so the establishment has now anointed Rick Perry, a politician indistinguishable from Bush, as its preferred candidate, shortly to be proclaimed front runner.

Governor Rick Perry provided subsidized tuition, and indeed subsidized everything, to illegal aliens, importing not workers, but welfare voters, which is the Democrat program of replacing the old people, with their irritating habits of independence, with a new people, who can be trusted to be suitably dependent. It is illegal for an illegal alien in Texas to work, but he has a right to remain in Texas, and a right to welfare, creating incentives for the kind of immigrant who can be relied upon to vote for the destruction of America when he gets naturalized, as he has a right to be after remaining in the US collecting welfare for a sufficient length of time.

For America to remain America, it has to be legal for illegal immigrants to work, but illegal for them to receive welfare. That or build an iron curtain. Otherwise, the original Americans will become second class citizens to a dependent underclass that is affirmative actioned to supremacy over them, as the former British have become.

Governor Rick Perry also stands on both sides of government healthcare issue, just as Bush did.

> the Mexican and U.S. sides of the border compose one region, and we must address health care problems throughout that region

Rick Perry, like George Bush, stands for the replacement of America and Americans, welfarism, and government health care. His actual policies are far to the left of the policies and program that he presents to republican voters. He is a two faced candidate, presenting a left wing face to the establishment, to power, and a right wing face to the voters.

In the 2008 election, John McCain was the Republican presidential candidate. He won the Republican nomination thanks to abrupt and frequently retrospective rule changes in his favor, but subsequently lost the election because Republicans would not vote for him. The dead-in-the-water showing of Governor Romneycare suggests they won't vote for Rick Perry (Bush the third) either, even if the alternative is Obama.

Despite massive and obvious lack of enthusiasm for Rick Perry (the establishment loathes him because he is not quite as far left as Obama, and the Republicans loathe him because he is third coming of Bush) he may well "win" the nomination, which is to say, be given the nomination by the Republican establishment over the outraged screams of republican voters as John McCain was.

What if they gave an election, and nobody came? Republicans would not vote for John McCain. They are not going to vote for Rick Perry.

Chicks dig jerks, 1513AD edition

2011-08-17 10:30:33

In "the Prince", Machiavelli observed:

> fortune is a woman, and if you wish to keep her under it is necessary to beat and ill-use her; and it is seen that she allows herself to be mastered by the adventurous rather than by those who go to work more coldly. She is, therefore, always, woman-like, a lover of young men, because they are less cautious, more violent, and with more audacity command her.

Observe that Machiavelli is familiar with what we now call game, and takes for granted that his audience is familiar.

Roissy is rediscovering[731] what was well known up to around 1830 or so, though he is now placing it on the sounder basis of evolutionary psychology.

Some time between 1830 and 1860, I have not pinned the date down exactly, a thick fog of what we now call politically correctness set in, obscuring the ugly truths about the differences between men and women, among many other things, and radically rewriting history. Over the years, political correctness became ever more extreme, ever more severe, and the rewrites of history ever more drastic, blatant, and outrageous. We think that people in the 1950s were politically incorrect, but people in the 1950s thought that people before 1910 were what we would now call politically incorrect, and people in the 1890s thought that people in the 1830s were what we would now call politically incorrect.

Trees don't grow to the sky, and that which cannot continue, will stop. Since we have coined the pejorative phrase "political correctness", what we now call game is being rediscovered[732], and human biodiversity rediscovered[733], perhaps the end will soon be in sight. It is not in sight yet. Even those who revel in their supposed political incorrectness and indignantly ridicule the left will not tolerate some of the more disturbing truths[734].

They will perhaps tip their toe in the 1950s, but not go all the way. The 1890s, let alone the 1830s, are of course entirely unthinkable to them, yet from 1830 onwards, it is all lies, each lie leading to an even bigger lie.

Further, if one merely goes back half way, to the 1950s or the 1890s, one is in a logically inconsistent position. Political correctness logically requires ever greater political correctness. Being half politically correct is incoherent and internally inconsistent. One has to go all the way back to the cultural and historical facts that people before 1830 knew were true, for example that democracy does not work, that men were *not* created equal – which very few people are yet prepared to do.

---

[731] https://heartiste.wordpress.com/2011/08/16/chicks-dig-jerks-more-scientific-evidence/
[732] https://heartiste.wordpress.com/
[733] https://isteve.blogspot.com/
[734] https://esr.ibiblio.org/?p=3567

Past getting rewritten right now

2011-08-18 17:49:00

Commentary magazine spots a rewrite in progress[735]. I just checked his claim by comparing the current version of the state department 2002 list of consulates against the google cached version of that list. In google's cached version, the US in 2002 recognized Jerusalem as part of Israel. In the live version from the state departments servers, not only does no one in the world now recognize Jerusalem as part of Israel, the US back in 2002 did not recognize Jerusalem as part of Israel either.

Normally I would not bother mentioning such a relatively minor rewrite of history, but I report it because the change is happening right now and shows up on google's servers. Wikipedia's Jerusalem article has reported for some time that no one recognizes Jerusalem as the capital of Israel. You can usually see the latest version of the past appear first on Wikipedia, so this revision of history has been under way for some time.

Thus, for example, the 2007 version of Wikipedia's Jerusalem[736] article begins:
> Jerusalem is the capital and largest city of Israel in both population and area, with 732,100 residents in an area of 125.1 square kilometers (49 sq mi). Located in the Judean Mountains, between the Mediterranean Sea and the northern tip of the Dead Sea, the city has a history that goes back as far as the 4th millennium BCE, making it one of the oldest cities in the world. Jerusalem has been the holiest city in Judaism and the spiritual center of the Jewish people since the 10th century BCE

The latest and greatest version begins:
> Jerusalem is the capital of Israel, though not internationally recognized as such. If the area and population of East Jerusalem is included, it is Israel's largest city in both population and area, with a population of 763,800 residents over an area of 125.1 km2 (48.3 sq mi).[3][4][iv] Located in the Judean Mountains, between the Mediterranean Sea and the northern edge of the Dead Sea, modern Jerusalem has grown far beyond the boundaries of the Old City.

Similarly the section of the article that was formerly titled "Capital of Israel" has been retitled "Political Status".

Wikipedia changes, and in due course the documents it cites are corrected to agree. Only the future is certain. The past is always changing.

Rick Perry and the underclassing of America

2011-08-19 11:06:18

Rick Perry proposed to give every female child Gardasil vaccine at government expense.

Gardasil protects against a sexually transmitted disease that causes cancer in women and male homosexuals. It rarely affects male heterosexuals in advanced countries. The vaccine is expensive, and has dangerous side effects, so should only be given to those that need it: sluts sexually active females and gays. If a girl is planning to ride the cock carousel, then she should definitely take it shortly before she starts.

---

[735]https://www.commentarymagazine.com/2011/08/16/obama-bush-jerusalem/
[736]https://en.wikipedia.org/w/index.php?title=Jerusalem&oldid=178417106

But the vaccine is only effective for four years. Rick Perry was giving the vaccine to eleven year old girls. Even if an eleven year old is planning to ride the cock carousel, by the time she started doing so, chances are the vaccine would have worn off.

The concern is that everyone should take it, so that those who actually need it do not feel like weirdos. Some children are going start having sex at twelve or thirteen, so let us vaccinate them all so that those having sex do not feel socially excluded.

But they should feel like weirdos, rather than normal children risking their health, and taxpayers paying up, for the sake of wierdo's feelings.

Vaccinating children against a sexually transmitted disease normalizes the underclass lifestyle. Wasting money on a dangerous and expensive vaccine sends a message: "Everybody has sex starting at age eleven. It is all perfectly normal and government approved. All you twelve year old girls should be screwing your pimp uncles."

That Perry's policy favored underclass sexual behavior, is consistent with Perry's policies favoring non working illegal immigrants. They are both directed at underclassing America.

I cannot object to anyone who comes to America to earn an honest living, but Perry's policies encourage people to come to America to vote themselves a living, and encourage them to behave the way that people vote themselves a living usually do behave. Taxpayers should not have to pay for, nor be forced to pretend to approve of, the underclass lifestyle.

The state should remain neutral between lifestyles, rather than trying to protect people from disapproval. Piously protecting sexually active twelve year old girls from people thinking unkind thoughts about them violates freedom of speech, freedom of religion, and reveals an hostility to America, a preference for the kind of society that Britain has become, where you will be arrested for calling an ugly horse "gay", but not for burning down shops in front of police, where everything is policed except crime.

Giving Gardasil to eleven year olds is not a public health measure, but rather state speech to make sexually active children feel better about themselves. State funded and state coerced speech is a violation of freedom of speech. Giving gardasil to sixteen year olds could arguably be a public health measure, but giving it to eleven year olds is primarily a symbolic act, not a practical act. Symbolic acts are speech – taxpayer funded and state supported speech.

People who need Gardasil vaccine should be encouraged to take it. And encouraged to pay for it. If it was cheaper, safer, and longer lasting, there might be an argument for giving it to everyone free for the sake of herd immunity, for the sake of the externalities, but a vaccine that only lasts four years is not going to create herd immunity, particular when you give it to those who are at the least risk.

If it is a public health measure, you want herd immunity, which means you want to vaccinate the at risk population every four years. Gardasil for eleven year olds is a state sponsored speech measure, not a health measure. The primary reservoir of the HP virus is older males having sex with each other. If you are genuinely worried about public health rather than inculcating the correct attitudes in twelve year olds, vaccinate the gays every four years.

Rick Perry, multiculturalist

2011-08-19 18:53:02

On the campaign trail, seeking the republican presidential nomination, he piously bows his head in prayer, he supposedly doubts evolution, but he imposed on Texas schools a course denigrating Christianity and whitewashing Islam.

"Atlas Shrugs" sarcastically describes the course:[737]

> While Islam "spreads" and "extends," presumably in the same way that dew forms on flower petals, Crusaders "wrest political control of the Holy Land form Muslim rulers, damaging the positive relations that had previously existed." Nowhere is it mentioned that the Crusades were prompted by two crises: (1) the ruthless treatment of Christian pilgrims attempting to see Jerusalem, which was under Muslim control, and (2) Byzantine Emperor Alexius's plea for European knights to help him take back territory that had just been overrun by an invasion of Muslim Turks.

The course teaches kids that:

> The religion that the Prophet Muhammad preached provided his followers an ethical and moral vision for leading a life of righteousness. By the time of his death in 632, loyalty to Muhammad and Islam also provided an important means for forging solidarity among various Arab tribes who had previously been engaged in petty rivalries and wars against each other.

neglecting to mention that Mecca surrendered to Mohammed because Mohammed cut their trade routes by terrorism against trade caravans, neglecting to mention the numerous massacres of Jews committed by Mohammed.

OK, fair enough to leave out all that hurtful stuff done by Mohammed and his followers you think? Then why is it fair enough to include some of the hurtful stuff done by crusaders and colonialists. And why is it fair enough to leave out all the stuff that crusaders and colonialists were reacting to, such as stubborn and persistent Islamic terrorism and slave raiding. Why report the bad stuff that Christians did if you are not going to report the bad stuff that Muslims did?

There needs to be some mention, however polite, of the fact that from the very beginning Islam expanded by war and terrorism, and that the crusaders and colonialists were reacting to this very serious problem.

When Rick Perry pretends to doubt evolution, he reveals that he believes Christians are morons, for a man of his background does not doubt evolution.

---

[737] https://atlasshrugs2000.typepad.com/atlas_shrugs/2011/08/perryaga-curriculum-shocking-example-of-islamic-propaganda-forced-upon-unsuspecting-students-attendi.html

Stagflation August

2011-08-20 02:29:50

> While inflation has been running at an annualised rate of 3.6% over the past
> three months, higher than the Fed's target 2%, said Brett Hammond, senior
> economist at TIAA-CREF, "in order to get the economy moving again, a
> little inflation isn't a bad thing".

If Keynesianism is true, you are not supposed to have rising inflation and unemployment at the same time. It is only moderate stagflation, but it is rising, and shows every sign that it will go on rising.

There will be war

2011-08-20 19:15:53

Brad deLong tells us:

> it took me only two monthstwo months!to conclude that America's best
> hope for sane technocratic governance required the elimination of the Republican Party from our political system as rapidly as possible.

Since Republicans are supposedly terrorists, elimination is apt to mean lining them up against a wall and shooting them.

Democracy is internal peace. It means both sides have decided to live together and tolerate each other. When one side decides it is not going live with the other side, not going to tolerate it, there is nothing the other side can do. Democracy can only continue so long as no substantial minority wishes it to end.

War is easy, peace is hard. Peace requires both sides to continually make an effort to keep the peace. It takes two to make peace, only one to make war. If the Democrats decide they do not want democracy, there can be no democracy. Republicans can win or lose, but if they win, their leader will be a Pinochet or a Sulla, not a Reagan. Or both sides might lose, and the country could wind up with rule by warlords and people's militias, probably a more attractive option than rule by Sulla.

The experience of Latin America shows you cannot hold an election when one side is trying to win by any means necessary. If one side is prepared to win by any means necessary, the other side has to stop them from winning by any means necessary, in which case the election is at best not be plausibly democratic, and at worst will be full scale civil war.

In each election, the Democrats have engaged in more ballot box stuffing than the last one. At some point this is going to get out of hand.

What is wrong with Haiti

2011-08-22 08:52:20

After the earthquake, Haiti suffered something even more devastating than an earthquake, something even more devastating than a genetically low IQ population, something far more brutal and destructive than rule by genetically low IQ overlords.

Worse than cholera, worse than the earthquake, Haiti suffered a devastating influx of aid agencies and high IQ Harvard graduates with billions of dollars of aid money.

Rolling Stone tells us[738]

>

> CHF, which works out of two spacious mansions in Port-au-Prince and maintains a fleet of brand-new vehicles, is generally considered one of the most ostentatious NGOs in Haiti. It is also one of the largest USAID contractors in Haiti and enjoys a cozy relationship with Washington: Its president and CEO, David Weiss, is a former State Department official and lobbyist. "There is a shocking lack of transparency and accountability in aid, and it's crystallized in this relief effort," says Schwartz, the anthropologist. "For an NGO in Haiti, the criteria for success is raising money, filling out paperwork and making sure the money is 'accounted for' — meaning they can show donors that they spent the money. But nobody goes out there and judges the project, or even verifies that the project exists. In the majority of the cases, nobody even talks to the community."

>

> Bertin Voise, a 30-year-old carpenter, lives with his wife and five other members of his family in the courtyard of what was once a spacious home in Ravine Pintade. It is now marked with a giant red "X," signifying that it is not only irreparable but a hazard. Standing outside his broken house, Voise tells us that he has every intention of rebuilding it, as soon as he has enough money. This clearly bothers Lee, who has just finished explaining how CHF wants to raze houses like his and replace them with two-story steel-framed plywood shelters. While the construction of new homes is taking place, Lee wants to move everyone into temporary shelters in the area — what she calls "T-shelter hotels." She seems excited by the idea. Voise, who would have to relinquish his four-bedroom home for one slightly larger than a doghouse, is unmoved.

...

> There was a great deal of frustration among international actors that the current Haitian administration couldn't just take land under eminent domain to dump rubble or build housing

Which problem was soon fixed by the election of a Haitian president sponsored by the usual suspects from Harvard.

> But despite all that has been promised, almost nothing has been built back in Haiti, better or otherwise. Within Port-au-Prince, some 3 million people languish in permanent misery, subject to myriad experiments at "fixing" a nation that, to those who are attempting it, stubbornly refuses to be fixed. Mountains of rubble remain in the streets, hundreds of thousands of people continue to live in weather-beaten tents, and cholera, a disease that hadn't been seen in Haiti for 60 years, has swept over the land, infecting more than a quarter million people.

...

---

[738]https://www.rollingstone.com/politics/news/how-the-world-failed-haiti-20110804

"At least with Duvalier, we had lights."

Let us think about that carpenter and that doghouse. If low IQ peasant owns some land, and can get some wood, even if only roundwood, and some mud and some stone and such, he will, in time, build a quite nice house for himself.

If, however, he is in temporary housing, built for him by his high IQ betters from Harvard, he won't do anything, he cannot do anything, and those high IQ people from Harvard are not really going to do anything much for anyone other than themselves. As is proven by the fact that the gigantic flood of money and PhDs have left Haiti covered in mud, refugees, and human excreta.

There is no effective way to help people, if they are not allowed to help themselves.

Expect leftist violence in 2012

2011-08-26 17:09:15

When the left, aka the government, wants an opponent or apostate harmed or killed, they don't do it the way totalitarian regimes do it. It is more like "Who will rid me of this turbulent priest". And that is what we are now hearing.

The way it is done is not that someone at the top signs a death warrant, and a KGB goon is directed "take care of this guy", communist style. Rather, news gets around with a wink and a nod that certain crimes will be overlooked, and anyone who pays too much attention to such crimes will be the one that gets in trouble. It is not as reliable and effective as death warrants, but it is often adequate to get the job done.

In 2008, the message to the leftist rank and file was that they should allow Republicans to meet and organize unmolested. We are now seeing, in preparation for the 2012 elections, a different message.

In 2008, leftists organized to protest the Republican National Convention, and some of them organized to prevent the Republican National Convention. The latter were, of course, squashed like bugs, for going further than the authorized policy of the official government left.

The two FBI informants are now, starting 2011 February, in deep shit, which sends a message not to trouble innocent peace loving protestors with their innocent peace loving Molotovs next time.

One informant is charged with domestic violence and such. Perhaps, by shear coincidence, he happens to be actually guilty. This therefore does not necessarily send a message. What, however, is happening to Brandon Darby does send a message, and that message is "Go for Republicans this time".

Brandon Darby, wearing a wire, asked a couple what they were going to do with their Molotov cocktails. They gave the answers you would expect, and then the FBI were all over them like a rash. One confessed, one alleged that Darby was a provocateur, but then retracted the allegation[739] when he discovered that the prosecution had a tape of a phone call he had made to a co-conspirator.

---

[739]https://www.startribune.com/templates/Print_This_Story?sid=45694662

And everything was fine for Brandon Darby until 2011. Then, starting 2011 February, we hear the voice of authority, the voice of the left, the voice of the state, the New York Times and PBS, denouncing Brandon Darby as an evil agent provocateur, who encouraged these poor innocent easily led lads to make Molotov cocktails and say disturbing things into his hidden mike.

Of the two informants, two are down. The message is, that if you should see some deeply caring young progressives with deeply caring Molotov cocktails to encourage progress, you had best not mention it.

Which also sends the message that if you are a deeply caring young man, doing something about Republicans is unlikely to get you into real trouble this time around. The Justice Department, the New York Times, and PBS, is going to be on your side, so how much trouble can you get into?

Just as the treatment of Senator Joe McCarthy implied that suppressing communist spies was suppressing freedom of speech, in the same way, the message is now going out that suppressing Molotov cocktails is suppressing freedom of speech.

Global warming causes mandatory evacuation

2011-08-28 05:29:22

Or rather the *ideology* of global warming causes mandatory evacuation. The actual weather was merely an unusually wet and windy weekend, slippery roads and slightly more falling trees than usual. In New York, the storm caused subways to shut down and loss of power – well actually the storm did not cause either one. Politicians panicked by fear of the wrath of Gaea shut down power and subways.

Seven felonies a day

2011-08-29 05:32:33

A few years back I remarked that the average respectable middle class male had committed hundreds of felonies, each worth many years jail time. Things have become worse since then:
The Silicon Greybeard reminds us:[740]

> Where were you when owning wood became a felony?

> ...

> Looking around my house, not one piece of wooden furniture - either the ones I built or the ones I bought - has a label telling the genus and species it came from along with the country of origin. Certainly the toothpicks and knife handles don't. I see perhaps 2 dozen felonies within eye shot.

> ...

---

[740]https://thesilicongraybeard.blogspot.com/2011/08/more-tales-from-over-regulated-state.html?show-Comment=1314325831434#c6991110756808100193 "More Tales From the Over Regulated State"

... we will phase in enforcement of the declaration requirements for additional chapters containing plants and plant products covered by the Lacey Act, including (but not limited to) Ch. 12 (oil seeds, misc. grain, seed, fruit, plant, etc.), Ch. 13 (gums, lacs, resins, vegetable saps, extracts, etc.), [vegetable saps and extracts? like olive oil, maple syrup? - gb] Ch. 14 (vegetable plaiting materials and products not elsewhere specified or included), [the wildcard so they can arrest you for anything - gb] Ch. 45 (cork and articles of), Ch. 46 (basket ware and wickerwork), Ch. 66 (umbrellas, walking sticks, riding crops), Ch. 82 (tools), Ch. 93 (guns), Ch. 95 (toys, games and sporting equipment), Ch. 96 (brooms, pencils, and buttons), and Ch. 97 (works of art). ...

...

... anyone who exports, transports, sells, receives, acquires or purchases such products in the United States, may be prosecuted.

Of course, this is primarily applied against businesses, because businesses have more money lying around to steal.

Are you wondering why the economy has not recovered?

Why Are Finland's Schools Successful?

2011-08-30 07:11:56

Progressives suggest it is because Finland is so wonderfully progressive[741].

However, a refugee from Finland took a look at that article, and reports that it is because progressives lie like rugs[742]:
> no different from the now infamous official state radio programs in 70's Finland that proclaimed how much better everything is in the Soviet Union, with our useful idiots reporting from their visits to some artificial Potemkian model kolkhoz that was superior to the Western world in every way. Really, this whole article is just beyond parody. But damn, now I know how those Russian defectors back in the day felt like every time the useful idiots "educated" them how their own lying eyes had deceived them.

Somewhat similarly, I notice that not only does Cuba have wonderful health care statistics despite the total absence of medicine or treatment, but also European countries have wonderful health care statistics even in those countries where they apply involuntary euthanasia (barbiturates) to everyone who shows up with some potentially expensive ailment. There is no legitimate hospital use for barbiturates other than keeping patients quiet while they undergo some painful or humiliating procedure. If you keep them quiet while they are just lying in a hospital bed, they are apt to die of it.

---

[741] https://edubirdie.com/blog/why-are-finlands-schools-successful "The country's achievements in education have other nations doing their homework"

[742] https://fourthcheckraise.blogspot.com/2011/08/waiting-for-pooperman.html

Why democracy will always elect a new people

2011-09-01 06:51:36

Lately Mencius Moldbug has been off his best, so, looking back to his greatest hits, here is a golden oldie[743]

The democratic state needs votes, to give it legitimacy, so is always looking for ignorant stupid cheap voters that it can buy to bulk up its astroturf. And so the franchise expands. And when it can expand no more, then fresh voters are purchased from outside.

The article is full of wonderful gems

> For the intellectuals, a tiny minority, to build a working majority with the tools of trans-democracy, they must discover and diligently exploit a vast pool of empty heads.

> And these people, who are human beings, but not in any sense philosophers, will be alien to the intellectual. Friendship will be asserted - but the relationship is not friendship, for friendship is a relation of peers based on human affinity and human sympathy. The aristocrat has no genuine human connection to the coal miner, the ghetto criminal, the illegal day-laborer. They are, at best, his clients - his peons, his pets. This reality, sordid on its face, cannot be revealed. The aristocrat cannot accept it; the client cannot accept it; the bourgeois cannot be allowed to see it.

> Thus the passion of the late 20th-century trans-democrat for, in Brecht's word, electing a new people.

> ...

> Are there any individuals who must be legally protected from disrespect? Is there any crime of lèse-majesté, per se? The answer is: no. America is not a dictatorship; the load-bearing pillar of political power is not a single human being; therefore, legally and in fact, Americans are free to laugh at anyone.

> But are we free to laugh at everyone? There are no protected individuals. A search for protected class[744], however, produces quite a number of hits. Consider the penalties for disrespecting, singly or en masse, a member of a protected class. Do they not bear a strange resemblance to those for offending Stalin, in Kiev in the '70s? Professor Volokh certainly thinks so.

> Thus, Maine's law. There is no crime of lèse-majesté in America; there never has been. Every day, however, Americans are prosecuted and/or persecuted for the crime of lèse-peuple.

> Naturally, it is not a crime to disrespect the entire People. Not that anyone bothers - because, quite frankly, in 2010 it is almost comical to consider America as a single political community. No; it is only a crime to disrespect

---

[743]https://unqualified-reservations.blogspot.com/2010/11/democracy-cis-and-trans-maines-law.html
[744]https://en.wikipedia.org/wiki/Protected_class

the sacred vessels of trans-democracy - the aliens among us. The workers and peasants, or such as we have these days; the human fuel of progressive government. By disrespecting the vessels, of course, we threaten the chemists, just as by disrespecting Stalin the young Professor Volokh threatened the entire Soviet state.

Is this a coincidence? How could it possibly be a coincidence? Hence, Maine's law. Try it yourself. You'll find it works all over the place.

For instance, we find that the worse the crimes of the dictator, the worse the penalty for disrespect. Stalin is a mass murderer of colossal scale, so constant adulation is required. Brezhnev is a mere corrupt bureaucrat, so no one is executed for muttering about him.

Through the prism of Maine's law, we extend this principle, and what do we derive? Where are the American gulags, the mass graves, of lèse-peuple? Well, for instance, one could look on Wikipedia[745]. Normally, when people flee, it means someone else chased them out. More broadly, we find that we have derived... Auster's First Law[746].

Every day in every university in America, all injustices committed by Americans of tribe A against tribe B are wrapped into a ball, monstrously exaggerated, and thrust as a burden of guilt onto all members of tribe A. Who shudder at the load, but sigh and carry it. As for injustices (ie, crimes) committed by Americans of tribe B against those of tribe A, it is almost taboo to mention them, and certainly taboo to connect them. Each is its own random and inexplicable event - the responsibility of the criminal alone, and no one else. After all, it's not like he was following orders - like some NKVD officer. And it's purely coincidental that he's so well-informed about the enormous crimes of tribe A.

And when we contemplate this strange and hideous spectacle, are we surprised that tribe A is the native, cis-democratic electorate, and tribe B the alien, trans-democratic votebank[747]? We are not. And hence, the fundamentally suicidal nature of democracy unfolds itself to us. Well, it never hurts to know your fate.

The price of silver
2011-09-02 06:44:07

A lot of people are wondering why silver is not going up.

It is quite simple. Gold is money, the one and only true money. Silver is not money, ceased to be money around 1870 or so. People are buying gold in expectation of an increase in monetary demand. The imminent collapse of fiat moneys will boost demand for gold, not silver.

---

[745]https://en.wikipedia.org/wiki/White_flight
[746]https://www.amnation.com/vfr/archives/000933.html
[747]https://en.wikipedia.org/wiki/Votebank

Why is gold money? Network effects. It is money because it is money, and silver is not money because it is not money. Gold is money because large numbers of people expect large numbers of other people to treat it as money.

How best to buy gold?

2011-09-04 07:36:00

I don't evaluate the situation as so serious yet that one needs to buy physical gold and sit on it, but one needs to buy claims on gold that can be turned into physical gold that one can sit on should the situation deteriorate further, as it most likely will. Can anyone tell me what gold investments most plausibly make such a promise?

A lot of gold funds are investments in promises to deliver gold, rather than investments in gold capable of being delivered. The time is fast approaching when they are *not* going to deliver. Today, the credibility of gold funds is not so important, but may well become important rather suddenly.

Did the banksters steal the five trillion?

2011-09-05 06:26:09

Taleb, a very smart guy for whom I have immense respect, says the five trillion in effect wound up being stolen by the banksters[748].

If we just look at events over the last few years, that is obviously untrue. In the USA the money was for the most part pissed away in politically correct loans to irresponsible people, most of them Hispanic, many of them with no jobs, who purchased million dollar houses no money down and never made a payment. If the house went up they flipped it, if it went down they lived in it rent free, and many of them are still in those houses even today. In other countries the scam varied, but the general pattern was that money was pissed away on major voting blocks and/or the politically well connected, not directly on the banksters.

But since Taleb is a smart guy, that cannot be what he means. What he is talking about is asymmetric risk: Heads the the bankers win, tails the tax payer loses. The bankers make big bets, and if the bets pay off, pocket the profits. If the bets go bad, the taxpayer pays up. In this sense, the bankers stole the money, not in the sense that the money went directly to them. They were willing to make politically correct bets because if the bets paid off, they would make money, and if the bets went bad, the taxpayer would lose money.

Taleb moans plaintively that the banks are allowed to get away with this because they are so politically powerful. While he is smart about risk and economics, this is just political stupidity – that or, more likely, political correctness. If you trace the political debate on the risk before things blew up, it was the left that wanted the financial institutions to take bigger risks. Politicians of all parties, but especially the left, like being able to use financial institutions as a political slush fund to pay off voting blocks, interest groups, and special friends. If financial institutions were apt to lose their own money, they would be

---

[748]https://globalpublicsquare.blogs.cnn.com/2011/09/02/the-great-bank-robbery/

substantially less cooperative. Government guaranteed financial institutions mean that politicians and bureaucrats can covertly spend money and the bill does not show up until several elections later.

Gay Marriage: A modest proposal

2011-09-05 19:00:10

It is apparent that the modern institution of marriage is profoundly ill suited for producing and raising one's biological children. I suggest, therefore, that just as we no longer use the word "gay" to mean merry and light hearted, we introduce a new word and new kind of contract, reproductive contracts, for people who intend to have children together and raise them. And for "marriage", allow anyone to marry anyone, or any group of people or animals, for any length of time five minutes or longer. Thus three men, a horse, and a dog, could marry for seven minutes to have sex in the alley between Van Ness and Polk Gulch, but let us have a different word, and a different contract, for the case where the intent is to bear and raise children.

Among such contracts we need it to be possible to make a contract where a woman commits to always be sexually available to a man and to never have sex with someone else, and the man commits to always support her and father his children by her, and to never provide significant support to any other sexual partner – which is not the commitment men and women are making in today's "marriage"

Such a contract, to be a contract, would if broken, have bad consequences for the party that broke it.

We need to provide a range of possible contracts some of which are optimized for reproduction. If an eighteen year old girl can commit to gigantic college debts for an education of unpredictable value, debts that cannot be expunged by bankruptcy, she can commit to be always sexually available to one man, and only that man.

Many, though not all, Islamic societies are markedly more successful than western societies at reproducing culturally and physically and at providing children with fathers, and they do this by providing a wide variety of marital contracts, rather than one size fits all.

I have been reading "Sex and Culture" by JD Unwin, which makes an impressive survey of a wide range of societies over time, and provides compelling evidence that women's emancipation leads to the collapse of civilization.

He has a politically correct explanation of this phenomenon. His theory is Freudian, and thus we know it to be false. Supposedly sexual repression diverts sexual energy to building civilization. Supposedly, sexual repression creates civilizational energy.

One problem with this politically correct explanation is that though the Classic Greeks controlled female sexuality with an iron hand, there were no similar constraints on male sexuality. Xenophon's ten thousand raped, whored, and fornicated their way from Asia to Greece, impregnating every concave surface along the way, while energetically building civilization.

Still, it is clear that changes in the Greeks reproductive practices immediately precede changes in their culture and civilization, and similarly with a huge variety of other cultures and civilizations he examines

> Thus, when first they attract our attention by the abundance of their energy, the Hellenes are of the opinion that diseases are due to the action of certain malignant powers which can be coerced by incantations or swayed by prayers. Only certain men, the priests of Asclepius, know the proper words, so they must be consulted. After the earth has completed a few more revolutions, the Hellenes defeat the Persians at Marathon. After a few more revolutions each city appoints a state-physician, who is paid out of public funds; private practitioners also set up; surgery becomes a favourite method of treatment. Men begin to specialize in diseases of the eyes, ears, or teeth. Moreover, one of the leading physicians, Hippocrates, has nothing but contempt for charms and incantations. In his opinion they are both vulgar and superstitious; he lays stress on a quiet reserved manner at the bedside.

> The earth continues to revolve, then we notice that once more the Hellenes are changing their opinions. Clinical histories are replaced by cures which can be classed only as magical; amulets return to favour.

> Physicians no longer regard incantations and purifications as vulgar; they even adopt them in the course of their own treatment. In a word Hellenic therapeutics return to what they, had been a few orbits ago.

He found strong commonalities between cultures that correlate sexual practices strongly with world view and strongly with the success or failure of the culture. One might expect the world view to change first, with success or failure following, but instead, sexual practice was the leading indicator, and world view changed later, following, rather than preceding, the rise of the culture.

His theory predicts that the future of Western civilization is the collapsing ruins of Detroit and Liverpool, in that the symptoms he finds reliably foreshadowing the decline of past civilizations have well and truly recurred in our civilization.

Now, however, the state of the ruins of Detroit is more visible to us, a sociobiological account of the same data seems more plausible:

Under conditions of high paternal certainty, men invest in their children. They raise their sons, thus transmitting their culture. They do stuff for posterity - and thus are visible to the historians. When paternal certainty diminishes, the culture vanishes from the history books, for historians, like sons, are posterity, and without paternal certainty, men don't care about posterity.

Under conditions of high paternal certainty, resources are transferred by men to women and children. Under conditions of low paternal certainty, men stop investing in wives and children, and resources are transferred from women and children to some high status adult men: This is the culture celebrated in rap songs as pimps and bitches, the sexual and reproductive system advocated by blogs on game. The game blogs explain that that is a necessary response to female immorality and a legal system that fails to support marriage, and so it is.

There is of course a great deal of ruin in a nation. Rome was not burnt in a day. The collapse he predicted has been happening as predicted since he wrote in 1934, and yet we are still in a predominantly rationalistic culture. It is a long way to the bottom.

The lowest, most primitive level of culture in Unwin's analysis is "zoistic".

Above zoistic culture there is manistic culture, above manistic, deistic, and above deistic, rationalistic.

1. Zoism - subhuman, animal level culture.A zoistic society has no religious beliefs - it is not that they do no believe in the supernatural, but rather that they do not believe in the natural. Everyone at a zoistic level of culture engages in magical thinking, attributing to themselves and other people capabilities we would consider supernatural. They think that dead bodies walk, and the ghosts of the dead hang around, but they swiftly forget the recently dead, because they live in an eternal present. They have difficulty distinguishing between their dreams and the past. Stuff that happened long ago and stuff that happened in their dreams last night are one and the same. They dispose of the dead like garbage, and do not tend the graves of the dead. Zoists have no ghosts, because they forget, and no gods, because they attribute magical powers to everyone, including themselves. In their dreams, they meet supernatural beings as equals, and so, they suppose, in the past they also met supernatural beings as equals. A typical example of zoistic thinking is the jury in a medical malpractice lawsuit, where the lawyer seldom bothers to give the jury a concrete explanation of how the doctor caused or could have avoided a bad result.

2. Manism. Some special men are attributed supernatural powers, much more than regular men. These men engage in mystical chants, and rattle magical stones and necklaces, as for example, the expert witness in a silicone or asbestos lawsuit. These special men can smell out other men who use their magical powers to do harm, thus witchfinders and radioactive pollution. Manists have special graves for real or imagined dead sorcerers, and engage in rituals commemorating these powerful ghosts. New ageism tends to be manist. Deism with lots of saints is close to being manist, and conversely, Manism with a small number of immensely powerful and important ghosts is close to being deism.

3. Deism: We all know what deism is.Deism with god far away, a god who dumped problems on us and commands us to solve them as best we can, is pretty close to being rationalism.

4. Rationalism: There is no supernatural, or if there is it is far, far away, and long, long ago.

A typical example of zoistic culture is the indictment of Napoleon Chagnon, "Darkness in El Dorado", which ignored not only evidence and reason, but cause and effect. Chagnon supposedly caused death, disease, and violence to the people he studied not through any causal mechanism, not through any physical material process, but through thinking Darwinist thoughts, Darwinist thoughts being cruel, violent, and bloody. There was no need to provide any causal connection through alleged deeds by Chagnon, no proposed concrete mechanism linking his allegedly evil ideas to the alleged evil consequences.

Similarly you have doubtless seen it frequently explained that communists were killed in country X because the CIA wished them to be killed, without any need to provide a material physical explanation of how CIA wishes became militia nooses. We joke that the CIA killed the communists by broadcasting mind control rays that turned the masses into enraged space bats, but when we make this joke, no one gets it, because they see no need to propose some physical material method, some alleged concrete deeds, whereby the CIA turned its wishes into dead commies.

A typical system of justice in a zoistic or manistic culture, is that when something bad happens, the shaman takes a large dose of hallucinogenic drugs, and on the basis of his dreams, declares that so and so caused the bad thing - again, observe medical lawsuits, asbestos lawsuits, and political correctness lawsuits. These are all examples of zoistic culture, which makes no distinction between natural and supernatural, or manistic, which makes little distinction, and supposes the supernatural to be exceedingly common. It is zoistic if the lawyer does not bother with an explanation of how the accused caused harm, manistic if the lawyer produces an expert witness, who chants magical formulae in place of an explanation.

The highest level of culture is rationalistic. In a rationalistic culture, there is natural and supernatural. But supernatural stuff is the business of the Gods, as in a Deistic culture, and unlike a Deistic culture the Gods are far far away, and for the most part, long long ago. In a rationalistic culture anyone claiming supernatural stuff in ordinary everyday life gets odd looks. In a rationalistic culture, if the jury cannot understand the mechanism whereby the accused supposedly caused harm, they will not convict.

In a rationalistic culture, no one would invoke our mistreatment of Gaia and her resulting righteous wrath to explain a flood or hurricane. They might theoretically believe in the wrath of Gaia if raised in that church but would think someone who proposed it as a direct causal mechanism in actual life disturbingly crazy, would think someone who said "the earth has a fever" a bit peculiar.

Intermediate levels have ghosts, spirits, demons, gods, etc taking an active role in daily life. There is a distinction between natural and supernatural, stronger at the higher levels of culture, weaker at the lower levels of culture, but at the intermediate levels of culture there is lots of supernatural stuff going on in everyday daily life. At the Zoistic level, there is no natural, at the rationalistic level, no supernatural.

JD Unwin attributes cultural level to sexual practices, with a Freudian, therefore false, explanation.

An alternative possiblity is that both the sexual practices and the cultural level are caused by something else: Adult males inculcate rationality in their children and transmit civilization, while women tend focus on physically nurturing children, rather than teaching their sons how to be men.

I would go with a Roissian explanation. Roissy[749], like Dr JD Unwin, attributes the collapse of civilization to the collapse of patriarchy, but the proposed mechanism is different.

The general spirit of the Roissy explanation is that Patriarchs built and maintained civilization, one of the key mechanisms being that producer protector males got pussy, got assigned the patriarch's daughters, thus got a wife and family as reward for building civilization.

If women get to choose, they choose player sperm. Players, such as Roissy tries to be, undermine civilization.

---

[749]https://heartiste.wordpress.com/

Another mechanism is that Patriarchs transmit civilization to their children, and players do not, for players are rarely present in the lives of their children.

To the extent that men are uncertain of paternity, they reduce investment in raising children. The major male contributions to childraising are physical protection, and socialization in extended relationships, socializing children to relate to the larger, more distant, society - thus men transmit civilization. In our society, the majority of children are fatherless.

We are in a civilization that is approaching majority fatherless. The evidence in "sex and culture" can reasonably be interpreted as implying that in monogamous civilizations with severe constraints on wives and mother, paternal investment is markedly higher, resulting in marked differences in children, than in civilizations with less severe constraints, though that is not the interpretation the author suggests.

The evidence Unwin assembles shows that the civilization that puts women on a pedestal and chains them to it, will beat the hell out of both the culture that just chains them up, and the culture that lets them lek freely.

Today, however, we have technological means for providing paternal certainty that are more reliable than chaining women to a pedestal.

The "lack of energy" Unwin depicts could equally be interpreted as lack of economic and cultural capital.

It is not clear that women even like equal rights in matters pertaining to sex and reproduction. On anecdote and casual observation, there seem to be lot more women than men converting to Islam

The conversation about Polanski indicates widespread belief that alpha males of one's own in group should be entitled to rape lesser females,

Polanski's rape was actual rape, plea bargained down to nominal statutory rape, not actual statutory rape, and it seems to me that most of those supporting Polanski are female members of his in group – males are less supportive of other males raping – males don't like the competition, lower status males don't like the possibility that high status males of their own group might bang their women. Women don't really mind that possibility. They mind being raped by low status men, which is of course in actual practice quite vigorously suppressed in Muslim societies. They are disturbingly relaxed about the risk of being raped by high status males like Polanski.

This is also visible in the crime victimization survey data – the wife of a male head of household has an unmeasurably low rape/sexual assault rate, while all other categories make only moderate difference, indicating that males do a far more vigorous job of policing their wives against sexual assault than women do to protect themselves or even fathers do to police their daughters, as we would expect from sociobiology, evolutionary psychology.

Googling up interviews with western converts to Islam from Christianity, most of them are young single fertile age women. Googling up interviews with western converts from Islam to Christianity, few of them are young single fertile age women.

In Britain, I found data indicating three thousand converts from Islam to Christianity[750], one hundred thousand converts from Christianity to Islam[751].

It looks to me as if women are voting with their feet to say that Sharia is a pretty good system for women, and the reaction of those in Polanski's in group suggests that this attitude is widespread, in the sense that the Polanski case also suggests that women do not much like equality, as we would expect if evolutionary psychology is true, and political correctness is false.

FHFA sues Goldman Sachs

2011-09-06 13:01:55

Until recently, it has been near impossible to see daylight between the Obama regime and the Banksters, but now, banksters are being thrown overboard.

The FHFA sues Goldman Sachs for common law fraud.[752]

I conjecture this is in preparation for the 2012 elections

One complication is that they are suing Goldman Sachs for bad behavior committed by Goldman Sachs Mortgage Securities, a firm that has absolutely no assets.

Allegedly a manager of Goldman Sachs Mortgage Securities would put on his mortgage securities hat, and make up a bunch of outrageous lies about the mortgages, and then take off that hat and put on his hat as a manager of Goldman Sachs, and totally believe those outrageous lies that he had just told himself. "Hey", he says, "I am the victim here."

Wearing his Goldman Sachs hat, this poor innocent victim would buy the securities on behalf of Goldman Sachs, from the evil fraudster, Goldman Sachs Mortgage securities (from himself wearing his other hat), and then innocently and sincerely resell them to Goldman Sachs' customers, such as the predecessors of the Federal Housing Finance Agency .

That Goldman Sachs Mortgage Securities has no money leads me to conjecture that though all the lies were told while wearing the Goldman Sachs Mortgage Securities hat, all the profits that accrued from these lies accrued while wearing the Goldman Sachs hat.

The Federal Housing Finance Agency was created to take up all the bad mortgages of Fannie, Freddy and the rest.

That a government sponsored enterprise purchased this %@& - that Goldman Sachs was telling the lies its customers asked it to tell them.

Sarah Palin's speech

2011-09-07 08:59:28

Sarah Palin has issued a typically brilliant and insightful speech[753], while still teasing on the issue of whether she is going to run. I think at this stage, getting a bit late to run,

---

[750]https://jmm.aaa.net.au/articles/14689.htm

[751]https://www.dailymail.co.uk/news/article-1343954/100-000-Islam-converts-living-UK-White-women-keen-embrace-Muslim-faith.htm

[752]https://www.businessinsider.com/goldman-fhfa-lawsuit-2011

[753]https://www.sarahpac.com/posts/governor-palins-speech-at-the-restoring-america-tea-party-of-america-rally-in-indianola-iowa-video-and-transcript

better carry on in her lucrative career as a public intellectual, saying the things officially accredited public intellectuals cannot say.

She starts off with the usual baby kissing flattery of the audience, and then, eventually, after quite a lot of flattery, gets down to business.

> It's called corporate crony capitalism. This is not the capitalism of free men and free markets, of innovation and hard work and ethics, of sacrifice and of risk. No, this is the capitalism of connections and government bailouts and handouts, of waste and influence peddling and corporate welfare. This is the crony capitalism that destroyed Europe's economies. It's the collusion of big government and big business and big finance to the detriment of all the rest

Every so often, she slips from her folksy working class small town mother of three language, to the language of who she really is - a member of the political elite

"so many demographics represented"

Uh Sarah, folksy small town women do not check out the demographics of their audience to make sure it adequately covers a majority of the voters. "Demographics" is a not at all a folksy lower middle class word.

While Howard could speak from the hip and remain pitch perfect in his persona, Howard the little aussie battler, supposedly exactly the same class as the median voter, when Sarah Palin speaks from the hip, who she really is tends to show through - a wealthy and highly trained professional politician.

Skipping over all the stuff on how great Americans are, and how she is a folksy lower middle class woman just like the voters:

She lays out a program of what needs to be done to restore the American dream and end Euroschlerosis. And if all the voters were white middle class voters like most of her audience, I expect she could pass it - barely. All the cheers are in the parts where she flatters the audience. Whenever she starts getting more intellectual, the audience stands quietly, puzzled and confused.

The intellectual substance of her speech, analyzing how the US actually works, and how it could and should work, starts at 9:50 into the video, after nearly ten minutes of giving the audience a hand job.

If anyone could sell this to the average, aka dumb, American, it is Sarah Palin, but I fear it is just going over their heads. And of course the elite congratulates them. Hey, if you don't understand what Sarah Palin is saying, it is supposedly proof that she is stupid, not you.

> We sent a new class of leaders to D.C., but immediately the permanent political class tried to co-opt them – because the reality is we are governed by a permanent political class, until we change that. They talk endlessly about cutting government spending, and yet they keep spending more. They talk about massive unsustainable debt, and yet they keep incurring more. They spend, they print, they borrow, they spend more, and then they stick us with

the bill. Then they pat their own backs, and they claim that they faced and "solved" the debt crisis that they got us in, but when we were humiliated in front of the world with our country's first credit downgrade, they promptly went on vacation.

No, they don't feel the same urgency that we do. But why should they? For them business is good; business is very good. Seven of the ten wealthiest counties are suburbs of Washington, D.C. Polls there actually – and usually I say polls, eh, they're for strippers and cross country skiers – but polls in those parts show that some people there believe that the economy has actually improved. See, there may not be a recession in Georgetown, but there is in the rest of America.

Yeah, the permanent political class – they're doing just fine. Ever notice how so many of them arrive in Washington, D.C. of modest means and then miraculously throughout the years they end up becoming very, very wealthy? Well, it's because they derive power and their wealth from their access to our money – to taxpayer dollars. They use it to bail out their friends on Wall Street and their corporate cronies, and to reward campaign contributors, and to buy votes via earmarks. There is so much waste. And there is a name for this: It's called corporate crony capitalism. This is not the capitalism of free men and free markets, of innovation and hard work and ethics, of sacrifice and of risk. No, this is the capitalism of connections and government bailouts and handouts, of waste and influence peddling and corporate welfare. This is the crony capitalism that destroyed Europe's economies. It's the collusion of big government and big business and big finance to the detriment of all the rest – to the little guys. It's a slap in the face to our small business owners – the true entrepreneurs, the job creators accounting for 70% of the jobs in America, it's you who own these small businesses, you're the economic engine, but you don't grease the wheels of government power.

So, do you want to know why the permanent political class doesn't really want to cut any spending? Do you want to know why nothing ever really gets done? It's because there's nothing in it for them. They've got a lot of mouths to feed – a lot of corporate lobbyists and a lot of special interests that are counting on them to keep the good times and the money rolling along.

It doesn't surprise me. I've seen this kind of crony capitalism before. It's is the same good old boy politics-as-usual that I fought and we defeated in my home state. I took on a corrupt and compromised political class and their backroom dealings with Big Oil. And I can tell you from experience that sudden and relentless reform never sits well with entrenched interests and power-brokers. So, please you must vet a candidate's record. You must know their ability to successfully reform and actually fix problems that they're going to claim that they inherited.

Real reform never sits well with the entrenched special interests, and that's why the true voices of reform are so quickly demonized. Look what they say about you. You are concerned civilized citizens and look what they say about you. And just look what happened during the debt-ceiling debate. We'd been given warning after warning that our credit rating would be downgraded if politicians didn't get serious about tackling the debt and deficit problem. But instead of making the real cuts that are necessary, they used Enron-like accounting gimmicks, and they promised that if they were just allowed to spend trillions more today, they'd cut billions ten years from now. By some magical thinking, they figured they could run up trillion dollar deficits year after year, yet still somehow avoid the unforgiving mathematics that led to the downgrade. Well, they got a rude awakening from the rest of the world, and that's that even America isn't "too big to fail."

When we finally did get slapped with that inevitable downgraded, the politicians and the pundits turned around and blamed us – independent commonsense conservatives. We got blamed! They called us un-American and terrorists and suicide bombers and...hobbits...couldn't understand that one.

And what is the President's answer to this enormous debt problem? It's just spend more money. Only you can't call it "spending" now. Now you got to call it "investing." Don't call it "spending." Call it "investing." It's kind of like what happens with FEMA and some of these other bureaucratic agencies that don't really want to refer to our centralized federal government as "government." Now it's called the "federal family." Am I too old to ask to be emancipated? Never thought I'd say it, but I want a divorce.

No, the President's answer to our debt problem is: Incur more debt. Spend more money (only call it "investing"). Make more folks even more reliant on government to supply their every need. This is the antithesis of the pioneering American spirit that empowered the individual to work, to produce, to be able to thrive and succeed with fulfillment and with pride; and that in turn built our free and hope-filled and proud country.

He wants to "Win The Future" by "investing" more of your hard-earned money in some harebrained ideas like more solar panels and really fast trains. These are things that venture capitalists will tell you are non-starters, yet he wants to do more of them. We're flat broke, but he thinks these solar panels and really fast trains are going to magically save us. He's shouting "all aboard Obama's bullet train to bankruptcy."

The only future that Barack Obama is trying to win is his own re-election, and he has shown that he's perfectly willing to mortgage our children's future to pay for it. And there is proof of this. Just look closely at where all that "green energy" stimulus money is "invested." See a pattern. The President's big campaign donors got nice returns for their "investments" in him to the tune of billions of your tax dollars in the form of "green energy" stimulus funds. The technical term for this is "pay-to-play." Between bailouts for Wall Street cronies and stimulus projects for union bosses' security and "green energy" giveaways, he took care of his friends. And now they're on course to raise a billion dollars for his re-election bid so that they can do it all over again. Are you going to let them do it all over again? Are you willing to unite to do all we can to not let them do it again so we can save our country?

Now to be fair, some GOP candidates also raised mammoth amounts of cash, and we need to ask them, too: What, if anything, do their donors expect in return for their "investments"? We need to know this because our country can't afford more trillion-dollar "thank you" notes to campaign backers. It is an important question, and it cuts to the heart of our problem. And I speak from experience in confronting the corruption and the crony capitalism since starting out in public office 20 years ago. I've been out-spent in my campaigns two to one, three to one, five to one. (And, by the way, I don't play that game either of hiring expert political advisors just so they'll say something nice about me on TV – if you ever wonder. You know how that game's played too I'm sure.) But the reason is simple: It's because like you, I'm not for sale. It's because we believe in the free market. I believe in the free market, and that is why I detest crony capitalism. And Barack Obama has shown us cronyism on steroids. It will lead to our downfall if we don't stop it now. It's a root that grows our economic problems. Our unsustainable debt and our high unemployment numbers and a housing market that's in the tank and a stagnant economy – these are all symptoms. Politicians are so focused on the symptoms and not the disease. We will not solve our economic problems until we confront the cronyism of our President and our permanent political class.

So, this is why we must remember that the challenge is not simply to replace Obama in 2012. The real challenge is who and what we will replace him with. It's not enough to just change up the uniform. If we don't change the team and the game plan, we won't save our country.

Yes, we need sudden and relentless reform, and that will return power to "We the People." This, of course, requires deeds, not just words. It's not good enough for politicians to just be throwing our way some vague generalities, talking about some promises here and there. It's time that we hold them accountable. It is amazing to me that even some good conservatives run away from being honest and straight up with us about what needs to be done. They don't want to rock the boat. They can't hurt future election prospects evidently. They just talk vaguely about cuts and then they move on. They're too busy saying what they think we want to hear, but instead they should be telling us what needs to be said and what needs to be done. So, let us today in this field have that adult conversation about what needs to be done to restore America. Let's do that now.

In five days time, our President will gift us with yet another speech. In his next speech he'll reveal his latest new super-duper "jobs plan." It will have more lofty goals and flowery rhetoric, more illogical economic fantasies and more continued blame and finger-pointing. But listen closely to what he says. All of his "solutions" will revolve around more of the same – more pay-offs for his friends and supporters. His "plan" is the same as it's always been, and that's grow more government, increase more debt, take and give more of your hard-earned money to special interests. And this is such a problem. But you know what the problems are. We could go on all day about the problems caused by the status quo in Washington. Status quo I think is Latin for "more of the same mess that we're in." That status quo won't work any more. We could go on all day about the problems, but you know them because you live them everyday. So, let's talk about real solutions. I want to tell you what my plan is. My plan is a bona-fide pro-working man's plan, and it deals in reality. It deals in the way that the world really works because we must talk about what really works in order to get America back to work.

My plan is about empowerment: empowerment of our states, empowerment of our entrepreneurs, most importantly empowerment of you – our hardworking individuals – because I have faith, I have trust, I have respect for you.

The way forward is no more politics as usual. We must stop expanding an out-of-control and out-of-touch federal government. This is first: All power not specifically delegated to the federal government by our Constitution is reserved for the states and for we the people. So, let's enforce the 10th Amendment and devolve powers back locally where the Founders intended them to be.

Second, what happened to all those promises about staying committed to repealing the mother of all big government unfunded mandates? We must repeal Obamacare! And rein in burdensome regulations that are a boot on our neck. Get government out of the way. Let the private sector breathe and grow. This will allow the confidence that businesses need in order to expand and hire more people.

Third, no more run away debt. We must prioritize and cut. Cancel un-used stimulus funds, and have that come to Jesus moment where we own up to the debt challenge that is entitlement reform. See, the reality is we will have entitlement reform; it's just a matter of how we're going to get there. We either do it ourselves or the world's capital markets are going to shove it down our throats, and we'll have no choice but to reform our entitlement programs. The status quo is no longer an option. Entitlement reform is our duty now, and it must be done in a way that honors our commitment to our esteemed elders today, while keeping faith with future generations. I don't think anything has irked me more than this nonsense coming from the White House about maybe not sending our seniors their checks. It's their money! They have paid into Social Security all of their working lives; and for the President to say, "ah, we may not be able to cut their checks," ah, well, where did all their money go, politicians? It's like the Commander-in-Chief being willing to throw our military under the bus by threatening that their paychecks may not arrive. But the politicians will still get their checks and their secure retirements, and he'll still get his posh vacations. Aren't you just sick to death of those skewed priorities? It's all backwards. Our seniors and our brave men and women in uniform being used as pawns – I say it's shameful, and enough is enough. No more.

Fourth, it is time for America to become the energy superpower. The real stimulus that we've been waiting for is robust and responsible domestic energy production. We have the resources. Affordable and secure energy is the key to any thriving economy, and it must be our foundation. So, I would do the opposite of Obama's manipulation of U.S. supplies of energy. Drill here, drill now. Let the refineries and the pipelines be built. Stop kowtowing to foreign countries and dictators asking them to ramp up production and industry for us, promising them that we'll be their greatest customer. No, not when we have the resources here. We need to move on tapping our own God-given natural resources. I promise you that this will bring real job growth, not the politicians' phony "green jobs" fairy dust sprinkled with wishes and glitter... No, a hardcore all-of-the-above energy policy that builds this indestructible link between made-in-America energy and our prosperity and our security. You know, there are enough large conventional natural resource development projects waiting for government approval that could potentially create more than a million high-paying jobs all across the country. And this is true stimulus. It wouldn't cost government a dime to allow the private sector to do these. In fact, these projects will generate billions of dollars in revenue. Can you imagine that: a stimulus project that actually helps dig us out of debt instead of digging us further into it! And these are good-paying jobs, and I know that from experience. For years my own family was supported (as Todd worked up on the North Slope) by a good energy sector job. America's economic revival starts with America's energy revival.

Fifth, we can and we will make America the most attractive country on earth to do business in. Here's how we're going to do this. Right now, we have the highest federal corporate income tax rate in the industrialized world. Did you know our rates are higher than China and communist Cuba? This doesn't generate as much revenue as you would think, though, because many big corporations skirt federal taxes because they have the friends in D.C. who right the rules for the rest of us. This makes us less competitive and restrains our engine of prosperity. Heck, some businesses spend more time trying to figure out how to hide their profits than they do in generating more profits so that they can expand and hire more of us. So, to make America the most attractive and competitive place to do business, to set up shop here and hire people here, to attract capital from all over the globe that will lead to an explosion of growth, instead of chasing industry offshore, I propose to eliminate all federal corporate income tax. And hear me out on this. This is how we create millions of high-paying jobs. This is how we increase opportunity and prosperity for all.

But here's the best part: To balance out any loss of federal revenue from this tax cut, we eliminate corporate welfare and all the loopholes and we eliminate bailouts. This is how we break the back of crony capitalism because it feeds off corporate welfare, which is just socialism for the very rich. We can change all of that. The message then to job-creating corporations is: We'll unshackle you from the world's highest federal corporate income tax rate, but you will stand or fall on your own, just like all the rest of us out on main street.

See, when we empower the job-creators, our economy will soar; Americans will get back to work.

This plan is a first step in a long march towards fundamental restoration of a strong and free market economy. And it represents the kind of real reform that we need. And, folks, it must come from you. It must come from the American people. Real hope is in you. It's not that hopey-changey "stuff" that we heard about back in 2008. We've all learned that. And real hope isn't in an individual. It's not in a politician certainly. And that hopey-changey stuff that was put in an individual back when Barack Obama was a candidate – that hopey-changey stuff didn't create one job in August, did it? That's the first time that's happened in the United States since World War II. Real hope comes from you. Real hope comes from realizing that we the people can make the difference. And you don't need a title to make a difference. We can get this country back on the right track. We can do it by empowering the people and realizing that God has richly blessed this most exceptional nation, and then we do something about that realization.

Don't wait for the permanent political class to reform anything for you. They won't. They can't. They can't even take responsibility for their own actions. Our credit is downgraded, but it's not their fault. Our economy's in turmoil, but it's not his fault. It's the tsunami in Japan or the Middle East uprising. It's Irene. It's those doggone ATM machines.

Folks, the truth is Barack Obama is adrift with no plan because his "fundamental transformation" is at odds with everything that made this country great. It doesn't make sense. He doesn't make sense. Unbelievably our President declares that he "believes in American Exceptionalism... just as the Greeks believe in Greek Exceptionalism." Well, the path he has us on will make us just as "exceptional" as Greece, alright – with the debt crisis and the stagnation and the unemployment and uprisings and all.

Perry not the establishment candidate

2011-09-08 07:59:45

In a previous post, I remarked that with Governor Romneycare dead on arrival, Perry was now the establishment candidate. Seems I was wrong[754]. Looks like the establishment still has a hard on for Governor Romneycare.

If Governor Perry (welfare for Mexicans, underclass is the new normal[755]) is the anti establishment candidate we are doomed, though perhaps doom will come a little slower than with governor Romneycare.

NGO astroturf

2011-09-09 10:37:09

NGO stands for "Non Government Organization". The butcher and the baker do not call themselves non government organizations, because they actually are non government organizations. Any organization that calls itself a non government organization turns out in practice to be largely a government organization. It follows therefore, that an NGO is a government doing something evil.

One such operation is funding astroturf protests in Israel[756]

> She noted that when she headed ACRI's Tel Aviv office, ACRI had 5,000 members, while today it has less than 800, and it was only able to muster about 5,000 people to its December human rights march by relying on the active staff of the 120 NGOs that participated.

If the ostensible purposes of the NGO, such as feeding the hungry, were actually being accomplished, would not the sponsoring government or governments want their name all over the place? That NGOs are governments acting furtively implies that they are governments acting badly.

One of the many evil things that western governments do through NGOs is pursue the destruction of Israel, by funding political activity both inside and outside Israel.

That there is such an entity as "the Palestinians" reflects the fact that Palestinians get paid for being Palestinian, paid rather a lot. There was no such entity, no such people, until the money started flowing.

And who pays them? It is remarkably difficult to find out, almost as if paying them was some sort of criminal plot. But, contrary to the common complaint, it is not the Arab governments. The money flows, furtively, from the West.

The Paris conference (who?) provided 7.7 billion in Palestinian aid over three years 2008-2010. Note that no one seems to want to have their names on these payments.

Actual direct aid for Israel from the US in 2008 was 2.38 billion, which seems remarkably similar to western aid to Palestinians – except that aid to Israel is done with trumpets blowing, and aid to "Palestinians" is done furtively.

---

[754]https://www.latimes.com/news/politics/la-pn-rick-perry-rove-20110907,0,7339010.story
[755]https://blog.reaction.la/culture/rick-perry-and-the-underclassing-of-america.html
[756]https://wikileaks.org/cable/2010/02/10TELAVIV439.html

This is consistent with Mencius Moldbug's analysis that the US is not the ally of Israel but its major enemy[757], or rather that the State Department and Harvard are the major enemies of Israel, even though the rest of the US, including most of the not insignificant Pentagon, is allied to Israel.

Why all organizations move left

2011-09-10 09:05:48

All organizations move ever leftwards.

Wikipedia was founded by a conservative libertarian, or conservative Randian, and has been moving progressively leftwards,so that it is now one of the voices of the state, which is to say, one of the voices of the left, one of a thousand megaphones controlled by a single microphone.

People tend to say "all organizations move left except for explicitly right wing organizations", but that is not so. Libertarian organizations move leftwards on statism, Neo Nazi organizations move leftwards on race and affirmative action, and Christian Right organizations move leftwards on marriage, the family, and homosexuality.

Christianity should be right wing on social issues because the New Testament has a conservative position on marriage, the family, and homosexuality. According to the New Testament: * Wives must obey their husbands.

- Homosexuals will suffer eternal damnation.

- Men may only divorce their wives for fornication (infidelity or lack of virginity).

- Wives may not divorce their husbands for any reason whatsoever.

- A divorced woman may never remarry, but a divorced man may remarry.

Yet strange to report, today's Christian right takes a position on marriage and the family that in the fifties would have been perceived as hippy dippy left wing, and 1830 or so would have been considered pretty much demented and far out insane.

So why have Christian organizations been moving left? Well I can tell you why libertarian organizations have been moving left, and presumably the same applies with Neo Nazis, Christians, and whatnot.

The state directly funds and sponsors left wing entryism into anti state organizations, for example "Critical Review", which is a state funded entryist organization that attempts to move libertarians, and libertarian organizations, leftwards. If you are a libertarian activist, and you cooperate with "Critical Review", you can get paid. Don't cooperate? Then you don't get paid.

---

[757]https://unqualified-reservations.blogspot.com/2009/05/democraphobia-goes-slightly-viral.html

Similarly, the blogger "The Agitator" campaigned as a libertarian, but was only libertarian on those issues agreeable to the left. He was opposed to the police and army, but supported all the rest of the state, and opposed the rights of private property, for example he opposed the right to eject a journalist from private property. And in due course, he received a financial reward from the Huffington Post, an organization that runs at a loss dispensing money to left wing activists - basically it launders money from the state, rendering it nominally private, and then dispenses that money to left wing journalists and bloggers. The state does favors to nominally private businesses, which "donate" to the Huffington Post, and the Huffington Post then financially rewards people, such as the blogger, who follow the line.

In addition to the carrot, there is the stick. If your employer is sued for racial or sexual discrimination, the political opinions of his employees constitute evidence of racism, sexism, and whatnot. So, best not to hire people with unsuitable political opinions.

Why unemployment is high and rising

2011-09-10 11:56:06

If anyone wonders why unemployment is high and rising, and is inclined to discuss aggregate demand and suchlike, just read Coyote Blog: Dispatches from a Small Business[758]

Lets roll

2011-09-11 07:38:55

On 2001, September the 11th, on United Airlines Flight 93:

At 9:27am, Tom Burnett called his wife, reporting the hijacking. She informed him of the attack on the two towers, from which he concluded the hijackers intended to fly them into a building.

At 9:30am Sandy Bradshaw, flight attendant, called her husband:

"Have you seen what's happening? Have you heard? We've been hijacked."

They talked about their children, and told each other they loved each other.

At about 9:37am Jeremy Glick called from the plane to his wife to report the hijacking. He learns about the attack on the two towers, and realizes what the hijackers are planning.

Todd Beamer tried to call his wife, but could not get through. At 9:45 he found himself talking to Verizon Customer service. He tells them that one passenger is dead. He doesn't know about the pilots. One hijacker is in the rear of the plane, claiming to have a bomb strapped to his body, blocking access to the hijackers in the cockpit. He tells the operator that they plan to jump the hijacker with the bomb.

"I know I'm not going to get out of this."

---

[758]https://www.coyoteblog.com/coyote_blog/2011/08/this-is-an-awesome-idea-i-want-to-propose-california-do-much-more-of-this.html

At 9:47, Jeremy Glick called his wife again, and tells her that all the male passengers are going to rush the hijackers.

At 6:54am Thomas Burnett called his wife Deena Burnett again

"A group of us is going to do something," he told Deena.

Deena told him, "No, Tom, just sit down and don't draw attention to yourself."

"Deena, if they're going to crash the plane into the ground, we have to do something. We can't wait for the authorities. We have to do something now. Pray, just pray, Deena. We're going to do something,"

Sandy Bradshaw told her husband that she was boiling water to toss over the Islamic hijackers.

Todd Beamer tells the Verizon operator to sing the twenty third psalm, "The Lord is my Shepherd" with him.

In the background of Sandy Bradshaw's call to her husband, some men preparing to die fighting were singing the twenty third Psalm.

> The Lord is my Shepherd; I shall not want.
> He maketh me to lie down in green pastures:
> He leadeth me beside the still waters.
> He restoreth my soul:
> He leadeth me in the paths of righteousness for His name' sake.
>
> Yea, though I walk through the valley of the shadow of death,
> I will fear no evil: For thou art with me;
> Thy rod and thy staff, they comfort me.
> Thou preparest a table before me in the presence of mine enemies;
> Thou annointest my head with oil; My cup runneth over.
>
> Surely goodness and mercy shall follow me all the days of my life,
> and I will dwell in the House of the Lord forever.

Another passenger, Elizabeth Wainio was speaking to her stepmother.

At 9:59-10:00am Tod Beamer drops his phone. In the background, the Verizon operator hears him say to other people on board the plane "Are you ready guys? Let's roll."

Elizabeth Wainio tells her stepmother.

> "I have to go. They're about to storm the cockpit"

She hangs up without giving her stepmother a chance to reply.

Sarah Sandy Bradshaw's tells her husband

> We're all running to first class
>
> I've got to go. Bye.

She drops the phone, without hanging up.

Jeremy Glick, more optimistically, interrupts his 26-minute call to his wife, by saying:

> Hold the line. I'll be back.

These warriors took out the terrorist with a bomb without him having a chance to explode. Perhaps the boiling water disoriented him for long enough.

They then broke into the locked cockpit. During the struggle, the hijackers flew the plane towards the ground, indicating that the passengers were gaining control of the cockpit. At the very end, just before the crash, the black box records people speaking in English about guiding the plane.

Obama's Day of Rage

2011-09-13 10:22:40

A Day of Rage has been declared for this coming Saturday by an obscure leftist group, one sufficiently obscure that anything bad that happens can be blamed on it.

They will be raging at Wall Street. In 2008, it became obvious that Wall Street had blown trillions of other people's money, and yet no Day of Rage back then. What has happened lately?

What has happened lately is that the Obama regime has been trying to separate itself from accusations of crony capitalism by Sarah Palin and others, for example by suing their Wall Street buddies for crimes committed by Wall Street at the instigation of the regulators, crimes committed with a wink and a nod from Fannie and Freddy.

To show that the left is not so palsy-walsy with Wall Street, we shall see some "anarchists" smashing windows and lighting fires on Wall Street, while the police are strangely inactive and ineffectual, and those arrested, if any, go largely unpunished.

They have not yet figured out what their demands are going to be, but it is safe to predict that they are *not* going to demand that businesses that lose lots of money should be allowed to go bust.

Crony Capitalism

2011-09-17 15:39:57

Palin's brilliant speech on Crony Capitalism[759] seemed to go right over the heads of most of the voters, but the party faithful understood it, and now this talking point is being used to hammer Obama at every opportunity[760].

After it has been repeated one thousand times, the voters might well get it.

Potentially, democracy can stop the government from buying up businessmen. Pity it cannot stop the government from buying and importing low IQ voters. The Mexican underclass is moving en masse to California, because the welfare is better. Even if Mexico was not lower IQ on average, the kind of people California attracts with welfare being legal, and employment being illegal, are substantially lower IQ on average, which is the way politicians like them, but I digress:

Back to Crony Capitalism: Zombie has had a wonderful cartoon created explaining Crony Capitalism in the Solyndra case[761]. Palin's September 3rd speech may have gone

---

[759]https://blog.reaction.la/politics/sarah-palins-speech.html
[760]https://www.newsmax.com/Headline/obama-solyndra-shelton-cronyism/2011/09/16/id/411300
[761]https://pajamasmedia.com/zombie/2011/09/09/solyndra-for-dummies/

over the voter's heads, but Zombie's September 9th cartoon makes it all perfectly clear even to the median voter.

No one shows up for Day of rage.

2011-09-18 11:52:45

Less than a dozen protestors showed up for the promised day of rage at wall street. Either people are not enraged, or, more likely, they decline to swallow the story that Fanny, Freddie, the FHA, and the rest of the government alphabet soup now merged into FHFA were poor innocent victims led astray by the manipulations of their evil wall street partners.

Four years ago, it became apparent that vast sums of money had mysteriously disappeared. Yet no protests against wall street, apart from the usual SEIU astroturf[762]. On 2011 September 2nd, the Obama regime announced a massive lawsuit blaming wall street for all of this[763]. Lo and behold, a day of rage against Wall Street is promptly scheduled for 2011 September 17.

I predicted we would see the usual astroturf rentamob and some fires and broken windows, but, contrary to my prediction, no rentamob, and without a rentamob, no one shows up– which tells us how much traction the blame-wall-street story is getting.

Recall Obama's boast and threat against Wall Street: "My administration is the only thing between you and the pitchforks.!" Who is standing between Obama and the pitchforks?

According to a sympathetic news source, thousands showed up - which they illustrate with a photo of nine.

"hundreds of protestors"

2011-09-19 04:31:57

ABC news tell us that "hundreds of protestors"[764] showed up to occupy Wall Street, yet their photo shows only nineteen, count them, nineteen protestors, twenty one if we suppose the two well dressed men mingling with police are also protestors, twenty two if we suppose the guy in the distance is also a protestor.

One might suppose that this is just part of a much bigger crowd, but every protestor except one is looking inwards to the center of the shot, indicative of everyone being rounded up for a photo opportunity.

---

[762]https://michellemalkin.com/2009/10/25/seiu-leads-new-banking-shakedown-campaign/ "the usual astroturf"

[763]https://www.businessinsider.com/youre-guide-to-the-fhfa-bank-lawsuits-2011-9 "Obama shifts the blame"

[764]https://abcnews.go.com/blogs/headlines/2011/09/protesters-begin-effort-to-occupy-wall-street/

So much for Obama's pitchforks! The average voter probably does not know what happened to the money, but it is apparent that the kind of person who is politically aware has a pretty good idea.

Vice Provost for Diversity & Climate
2011-09-19 12:58:26

And what, you may ask, connects these two fields?

The Center for Equal Opportunity had criticized the University of Wisconsin for its grossly race based admissions, and cast doubt on the impartiality of its grading and graduations.

And so the University of Wisconsin's Vice Provost for Diversity & Climate organized a mob to beat the crap out the heretics, who were giving a talk at a hotel. The mob invaded the hotel. The people giving the talk escaped, but hotel employees were assaulted.

Statement from Tom Ziarnik, General Manager of DoubleTree:

> First and foremost, it is our job to protect the guests of our hotel.
>
> When threats were made by the protesters to rush the hotel, we secured all entrances to the property. Many protesters were telling us to "call the police" and "we want to be arrested." Unfortunately when escorting meeting attendees out of the hotel through a private entrance, staff were then rushed by a mob of protesters, throwing employees to the ground.
>
> The mob became increasingly physically violent when forcing themselves into the meeting room where the press conference had already ended, filling it over fire code capacity. Madison police arrived on the scene after the protesters had stormed the hotel.
>
> These protesters were not guests of the hotel and were repeatedly informed that they were trespassing on private property and needed to leave, per Madison General Ordinance Sec 23.07.
>
> We are extremely grateful that no one was seriously injured and no property was damaged.

Let us reflect on the large turnout that the Vice Provost for Diversity and Climate obtained, and the rather small turnout that showed for the "Day of Rage"

The title "Diversity & Climate" implies very great power to punish and reward, to permanently destroy people's lives and careers. How many, I wonder, would have shown up to riot without threat of punishment, or hope of reward? For this riot, hard to tell how much is government astroturf – other than the fact that it has been a very long time since anyone saw left riot in the US without government astroturf.

Hat tip Protein Wisdom[765], What If?[766], Althouse[767]

---

[765] https://proteinwisdom.com/?p=30557
[766] https://moot.typepad.com/what_if/2011/09/the-marketplace-of-ideas.html
[767] https://althouse.blogspot.com/2011/09/its-alinsky-vs-alinsky-now-rational.html

Zombie reports the day of rage

2011-09-19 16:58:48

Zombie reports the day of rage. All the pictures showing them marching down the street, symbolically confronting capitalist institutions, and so forth, show a group of less than twenty, but there is also a photograph of hundreds of people gathered in a park listening to a speech, which gathering looked genuine enough, not much indication of astroturfing.

I conjecture that there were a few hundred people that wanted to see some raging, but not themselves actually be exposed to risk by it. Zombie remarks that in San Francisco, they had trouble attracting an audience.

It looks as though in New York, they were able to put together an audience of a few hundred in Zucotti Park, but the masses declined to confront the symbols of capitalism and finance in Wall Street. Upon marching them out of Zucotti park, the crowd shrank.

According to Zombie in San Francisco, when they confronted various symbols of capitalism and finance in San Francisco, a few stern looks from the rentacops shepherded them out of trouble.

No enemies to the left, no friends to the right

2011-09-20 08:28:35

Everyone, including most on the right, wants to kiss up and brown nose leftwards, while condemning and denigrating rightwards, for the left has the power, delivers the gravy, and punishes its enemies.

Recall that video during the 9/11 ceremony. Reacting to the ceremonial folding of Old Glory, Mrs.Obama turns to her husband and says, "All this just for a flag." She then shakes her head and rolls her eyes while the president nods in agreement[768].

That her words were "all this for just a flag" is based on lip reading. For short sentences, lip reading is notoriously unreliable, but Obama's flacks have not proposed any alternative words that fit her lip movements, and even if she had not said a word, her expression and body language conveyed her meaning.

And, just as when Obama issued a crudely photoshopped birth certificate, we see the right piling on to rationalize

Klavan piously tells us[769]:

> I'm not even sure I can read her expression — which might be one of appreciation, as if she were saying, "Wow, isn't it wonderful, all this for our flag."

You can't read expressions, Klavan? Raised by wolves, were you?

> Obama is not a Muslim. He wasn't born in Timbuktu. He doesn't rub his hands together when he's alone and mutter, "The economy is almost destroyed. One more stimulus package should do the trick! Bwahahahaha."

[768]https://www.youtube.com/watch?v=g2SQUXjxUS8
[769]https://pajamasmedia.com/andrewklavan/2011/09/19/obama-is-wrong-not-evil/

Figure 2: Obama smirks at the dead

Obama is[770] a Muslim, his place of birth is suspiciously concealed[771], and while he does not rub his hands together when he's alone and mutter, "The economy is almost destroyed. Bwahahahaha.", he does rub his hands together with glee at every successful blow he makes against the old economy of free men and free markets, of innovation and hard work and ethics, of sacrifice and of risk, and every step towards replacing it with the new economy of connections and government bailouts and handouts, of waste and influence peddling and corporate welfare.

Palin surges

2011-09-22 12:07:08

Palin's poll numbers are shooting up[772].

Although her speech on crony capitalism seemed to go right over the audience's heads, since then the party faithful have been banging away on message, and it looks like it is penetrating. Zombie's cartoon should explain crony capitalism to anyone[773].

Maybe democracy can work against crony capitalism. Democracy tends to self destruct in massive vote buying, as tax consumers outnumber taxpayers, but should not self destruct in influence peddling, which is more a problem with Royal Courts. After the message has been repeated one thousand more times, probably will get through.

No enemies to the left, no friends to the right

2011-09-22 16:22:51

"What if" is a right wing/libertarian blog. Yet strangely, is incapable of seeing evil[774] – when evil is on the left.

---

[770] https://blog.reaction.la/science/yes-obama-is-a-muslim.html

[771] https://blog.reaction.la/politics/obamas-birth-certificate-forged.html

[772] https://hotair.com/archives/2011/09/20/oh-my-palin-within-five-of-obama-in-new-marist-poll/

[773] https://pajamasmedia.com/zombie/2011/09/09/solyndra-for-dummies/

[774] https://moot.typepad.com/what_if/2011/09/wrong-not-evil.html

When however alleged evil is on the right[775], has not the slightest difficulty in seeing evil.

Those who kiss upwards, can usually be relied on to spit downwards.

Similarly consider his reaction to the comedian Imus:

> IMUS: That's some rough girls from Rutgers. Man, they got tattoos and—
>
> McGUIRK: Some hard-core hos.
>
> IMUS: That's some nappy-headed hos. I'm gonna tell you that now, man, that's some—whew. And the girls from Tennessee[776], they all look cute, you know, so, like—kinda like—I don't know.
>
> McGUIRK: A Spike Lee[777] thing.
>
> IMUS: Yeah.
>
> McGUIRK: The Jigaboos vs.the Wannabes[778]—that movie that he had.

"What if" tells us[779]:

> When I first heard the tape play, I felt a little sick. One can hear ugly speech easily with the communications available to us today. But, to hear these kinds of comments about college students is particularly gross.

The problem being that Imus's are low status, while Obama's words are high status - and so will never make "What if" feel a little sick.

The astroturf arrives to "Occupy Wall Street"
2011-09-26 05:52:03

Until yesterday, the movement to occupy Wall Street was genuine, with a handful of lunatics and a few homeless hippies who had lost their way to the 1969 San Francisco love in. The hilariously tiny turnout, and the general level of idiocy, was an embarrassment to the left, revealing that the left is not a mass movement, but an elite movement, that the left is merely the voice of the state, that there is no mob with pitchforks[780] that the state is protecting the rich from. And so, predictably, the astroturf showed up.

To provide some decent numbers, and some protest signs that showed a connection to this universe, the Professional Staff Congress Union, and a bunch of students turned out by the professors of the City University of New York, came out to "Occupy Wall Street"

When the "left", also known as the United States Government, calls a protest, if they astroturf it, it looks astroturfed. If they don't astroturf it, hardly anyone shows up, and those that do show up are an embarrassment.

---

[775] https://moot.typepad.com/what_if/2005/01/bad_gets_worse.html

[776] https://en.wikipedia.org/wiki/Tennessee_Lady_Volunteers_basketball "Tennessee Lady Volunteers basketball"

[777] https://en.wikipedia.org/wiki/Spike_Lee "Spike Lee"

[778] https://en.wikipedia.org/wiki/School_Daze "School Daze"

[779] https://moot.typepad.com/what_if/2007/04/a_day.html

[780] https://abcnews.go.com/blogs/politics/2009/04/obama-to-banker/

Herman Cain is front runner for Republican Presidential nomination

2011-09-27 17:49:43

Governor Romneycare is, or was, the establishment Republican nominee. When his campaign turned out to be dead on arrival, Rick Perry was the emergency backup establishment republican nominee. But Herman Cain now leads 28% to 17%[781]

Herman Cain has from the beginning been the main Republican Republican nominee. Back in May I said "It is a long, long way to the 2012 presidential elections, but they are Herman Cain's to lose." They still are.

It has often been said that social security is the third rail of US politics. Touch it, and you die. But this has more to do with establishment protectiveness of social security, that public attitudes. Observe that the number two candidate for republican presidential nominee has touched it, and the leading candidate appears to be sitting on it.

Herman Cain keeps saying that we should go to the Chilean retirement system. He could have said the Singaporean system, or the Australian system, both of which are variants on the Chilean model, but no, he chose Chile as the exemplar.

The core benefit of the Chilean model is that old folks do not become tax consumers, so tend to vote for secure private property rights.

"Arctic ice hits near record low"

2011-09-28 08:03:20

"Arctic ice hits near record low, Threatening Wildlife"

Since we have been observing the total ice area for thirty years, on average, assuming that there is no long term warming trend, arctic ice will hit a *near* record low one year out of ten.

But, of course, there are two poles, so in one year out of five either arctic or antarctic ice will hit a near record low. And of course, there is also the rest of the world to have near record events in.

So over the last thirty years, maybe a trend towards warming, and maybe not.

To judge, we need a longer view. Debunk house gives us a two hundred and forty year view, and then a thousand year view[782].

Its more of the same. Sometimes things get colder, sometimes they get warmer. If these were graphs of the stock market, they would not be much help in deciding whether to invest or not.

---

[781] https://theothermccain.com/2011/09/26/shocker-herman-cain-leads-perry-28-18-in-new-zogby-poll/
[782] https://debunkhouse.wordpress.com/2011/09/19/warming-island-climate-reconstruction/

Andrew Bolt convicted of heresy and impiety

2011-09-28 16:44:01

Andrew Bolt was convicted for impugning various people by accusing them of being white, merely because they and their parents on both sides were physically and culturally white. This [783] has been declared to be a racist insult.

Having created special privileges for black people, many of our ruling elite naturally declared themselves to be of the privileged caste, though few of them have ever been close enough to an actual black to spit on them, nor would they send their children to a school where there was any danger of any substantial number of actual blacks attending . To doubt their entitlement is clearly a racist insult, which must be punished.

Anita Heiss is as white as I am, has never lived anywhere that any significant number of blacks lived, and would never lower herself to live anywhere that any significant number of blacks lived.

Herman Cain: Not the affirmative action candidate

2011-09-29 16:56:54

Because Herman Cain has black accent, and tends to use simple sentences to express himself, while Barack Hussein Obama has a ruling class accent, I initially got the impression that Obama was smarter. I should have known better.

Herman Cain will answer tricky questions extempore. No teleprompter for him. Who then is smarter? He has lots of facts at his fingertips. If someone expresses himself simply, it is apt to indicate he cannot express, nor understand, complex ideas, but if someone expresses complex ideas simply, it means he is smart, has charisma, and the common touch.

Herman Cain is smart, has charisma, and the common touch.

Repression

2011-10-02 13:04:00

A conservative blog[784] by an anonymous right wing academic announced that it had been suppressed, shortly after he was outed. And then, predictably, the announcement of censorship was itself censored. The original announcement of the end read[785]:

> I hesitated in writing this, but I have two choices at this point: 1) open political activism including this blog, 2) my career. I don't want to get into too many details here, but I was given this choice.... I want to thank everyone from the bottom of my heart for reading, commenting and encouraging me to continue. Thank you all for your messages of support of my efforts, which will now be at the grass roots level only. I want to make it clear that in

---

[783] calling people white
[784] https://theblogprof.blogspot.com/
[785] https://legalinsurrection.com/2011/09/farewell-to-the-blogprof/

no way am I burned out (almost 3 years now I have kept a consistent pace). In fact, I am more energized than ever. I also do not blame my employer. They are doing what they see is in the best interest of the institution.

Which was promptly revised[786] to:

Due to yet anther media inquiry by a lefty 'journalist' pretending to be middle-of-the-road, let me just be clear that I work for the best employer there is, and this will help me do my job better. I made this decision *on my own*. And that's all there is to it.

"I was given a choice" disappeared from the blog.

This is theocracy: In theocracy, the state enforces the rule of the priests, that no one can disagree with the priests, and the priests endorse the state, the high priesthood being Harvard and the federal bureaucracy, such as the secret science manufactured by the EPA.

If the theocracy is diffuse, rather than having all power concentrated in a single high priest, pope, or holy King, an unintended side effect of theocracy is that in the course of coercing the rest of society the theocracy coerces *itself* to become ever more extreme.

Over time, a theocracy tends to become ever more extreme, and the more extreme it becomes, the faster it becomes extreme, forming a political singularity until anti theocratic reaction ends it, as with Pinochet or the Thermidorian reaction, or until a single leader takes total power in the theocracy, as with Stalin, who can unilaterally set the orthodoxy of the theocracy without himself being coerced.

Stalin is often interpreted as the originator of the great terror, but that is not how Russian history looks to me. Rather, my interpretation of events is that the state under the Czars started leaning moderate left, which led to the state leaning immoderate left, which led to the overthrow of the Czars by social democracy, which continued to lean ever further left leading to communist coup against social democracy, and the state continuing to lean ever further left, until it started to look like the state would wind up murdering every single Soviet subject for failure to be sufficiently left, and at this point Stalin seized despotic power in order to halt the terror. We don't see Stalin urging the party to commit terror. Instead, we see him publishing papers such as "giddy with success" intended to persuade the party to calm down and ease up. It looks to me that the Soviet terror was the spontaneous outcome of the natural dynamics of theocracy, and despotism was needed to break the cycle of extremism leading to ever greater extremism. Stalin saved the party from murdering everyone in the Soviet Union including party members, or rather saved the party from murdering everyone in the Soviet Union especially party members

The French revolution shows all these tendencies. Under the monarchy, rightism was repressed, for example the doctrine that the races of man were separate species became dangerous to one's career. The suppression of rightism and the encouragement of leftism lead to the collapse of the monarchy, and eventually to the terror, which led to the red terror, which was ended by the Thermidorian reaction.

The first amendment was intended to prevent this kind of problem, but the first amendment is now being worked around in various ways: For example speech gets de-

---

[786]https://theblogprof.blogspot.com/2011/09/end.html

fined as money, making campaign finance laws applicable as happened to Kirk Shelmerdine. Admission to better universities requires the plausible appearance of left wing views, and students are from time catechized, and need to give politically correct answers in those catechisms. Businesses are subject to discrimination lawsuits if they employ people who disapprove of affirmative action – it is not sufficient that a business practice affirmative action, it must do so sincerely believing in the rightness off affirmative action.

And, as with the commerce cause, the more grounds that have been discovered to set aside the first amendment, the more grounds that will be discovered – a problem that cannot be remedied until both sides have had their turn being suppressed. There will never again be support for the first amendment until the left has experienced a Sulla or a Pinochet.

US dollar rises, because Euro smells even worse

2011-10-03 05:29:53

The value of the US dollar has risen, as valued by gold and by the fiat currencies of countries that are relatively solvent.

The apparent cause of this is not that there has been any improvement in the prospects for the US dollar, but that a chaotic dissolution of the Euro zone looks likely, so traders are switching to the most liquid asset that there is.

Fiat currencies whose sponsoring government have in substantial part a Chilean style retirement system (Singapore, Switzerland, and Australia) tend to behave like gold.

This suggests that were America to adopt such a system, the expectation that gold is likely to become money would cease, and gold would become more like a normal commodity, with the result that it would have a price, instead of being what everything else is priced in, and that price would fall.

Thus if you think that there is a decent chance that the US can get out of this crisis without passing through disaster, investing in assets located in more solvent countries may well be safer than gold.

Progressives are not commies.

2011-10-08 13:30:30

1. Commies propose the government run everything by a central plan. Progressives propose the government run everything with no plan at all.

2. Commies believe that underdevelopment is a sin committed by wealthy capitalists against poor people, and propose to fix this by commanding stuff to be developed. Progressives believe that development is a sin committed by wealthy capitalists against Gaea and the trees, and propose to fix this by prohibiting stuff from being developed.

3. Commies believe in democracy, and indeed believe in it so much that they will shoot anyone who votes incorrectly. Progressives believe in democracy, and if large

numbers of people keep voting incorrectly, will import a foreign underclass to out-vote them.

Herman Cain wrote his own book

2011-10-09 08:34:23

Often when a politician campaigns for an important post, he promotes a book about his life. And almost always that book is ghost written.

I compared the partial transcripts of his interview with O'Donnell, with an extract from the book discussed by O'Donnell[787]. They are similar in style. Likely the book was edited by a white editor, because most English language books are edited by a white editor, but if so that editor did not do enough editing to change the style or vocabulary much. If it is ghost written, the ghost limited himself to transcribing large chunks of Cain's own words.

Under attack Cain's diction became more complex and less black - which means the apparent simplicity of his diction is the result of effort to keep it simple and to sound authentically black. Compare and contrast with Obama, the affirmative action president, who tends to fall apart when he hits a complex sentence on his teleprompter, putting stress in the wrong places thus mangling the meaning. Obama is trying to not sound black, but is not quite smart enough to handle elite diction. Cain is trying to sound authentically black, but is smart enough to handle elite diction. When Obama extemporizes under pressure, he sounds markedly blacker. When Cain extemporizes under pressure, he sounds whiter.

Normally when I see a black man in a high status job I assume he is stupid and has been affirmative actioned into his position, because that is the way to bet, nine times out of ten. I made that assumption about Herman Cain, but obviously I was wrong. Obama speaks in complex sentences to obfuscate the fact that he was affirmative actioned into his job. Herman Cain can afford to speak in simple sentences because he does not have to prove that he was not affirmative actioned into his job.

Obama's thing is that he is half black man who is culturally part of the elite. Cain's thing is that he is a black man who is smart enough to handle authentic American civilization – that Cain is black and yet also real American, while Obama is a real member of the elite, but not a real American. So Cain is playing up his blackness, while Obama is playing up his elite culture – a culture Obama is not quite smart enough to handle.

Obama is only half black and half American. Cain's story is that Cain is all black and all American.

Don't pressure Cain to denounce affirmative action – to do so would undermine his blackness, which is already under attack from white liberals like O'Donnell. The fact that he is smart enough that he could make it without affirmative action is what you need to conclude he is no friend of affirmative action.

---

[787] https://www.theatlantic.com/politics/archive/2011/10/lawrence-odonnells-offensive-interview-with-herman-cain/246328/

Pinker on violence

2011-10-11 07:18:05

Pinker argues that there has over time, been a great decline in violence,[788] mistaking progressivism for progress. "The better angels of our nature"

This is the doctrine that progressivism is niceness, is the better angels of our nature, and conservatism is nastiness. The rise of the better angels of our nature is the rise of progressivism.

Pinker tells us that murders have declined. Googling around for such statistics, the first thing that I stumble upon[789], page 14, shows a substantial increase in the UK murder rate per thousand from 1900 to the present, and an extraordinary, gigantic, and astonishing rise in indictable offenses per thousand.

There are more real crimes committed, more people in jail, and vastly more actions that the state deems crimes – and if what the state deems a crime is not truly a crime, then that is state violence.

The staggering rise in indictable offenses represents an increase in private violence, or an increase in state violence, or both. I would guess it to be a moderate rise in private violence, and a gigantic, colossal, terrifying and horrifying rise in state violence against the subject. It is often said of modern Britain that everything has been criminalized, except crime, which has been decriminalized. The statistics on indictable offenses show that either that is true, or else there has been a gigantic explosion in criminal behavior.

In modern times, no one is drawn and quartered, but a lot more people are in jail than there used to be. But Pinker rather likes jail. Jail resembles the progressive utopia, with free housing, free food, free medical care, and a good deal less of all those nasty freedoms that progressives rather dislike. As legislation multiplies the number of crimes, and welfare increases, the difference between being in prison and out of it evaporates. If the whole world resembles prison, Pinker will be ecstatic.

If less murderers are executed, that is, Pinker thinks, a diminution in violence. If more hard working middle class husbands are thrown out their homes for imaginary offenses and lose access to their children, that also, thinks Pinker, is a diminution in violence.

Pinker compares the genocides recorded in the bible, with modern times – but the bible covers thousands of years, while modern times are considerably shorter. Take any one century of biblical time, and typically there are no extraordinary crimes in that century, or at least none that directly affect the children of Israel, while there have been quite a few extraordinary crimes in our most recent century.

Pinker reminds us that war has diminished in recent times – meaning diminished since the development of nuclear weapons, and diminished further since the fall of communism, but that diminution is not necessarily because we are more peaceable, but because the risk of extraordinary violence has increased. Nuclear weapons promote peace by making war potentially more dreadful.

The fall of the Soviet Union promoted peace the same way the fall of Napoleon did. World Wars one and two were at least as dreadful as the Napoleonic wars, and arguably a

---

[788]https://www.edge.org/3rd_culture/pinker07/pinker07_index.html
[789]https://www.parliament.uk/documents/commons/lib/research/rp99/rp99-111.pdf

good deal worse. No long term trend is apparent on that timescale.

The widespread peace following the fall of the evil empire resembles the widespread peace following the defeat of Napoleon. If the cold war was mild by historical standards it is largely because World War Three is likely to be a humdinger.

Pinker tells us:

> In Western Europe and the Americas, the second half of the century saw a steep decline in the number of wars, military coups, and deadly ethnic riots.

And the first half of the century?

The reason the second half of the century was more peaceful than the first half, was because the first half was unprecedentedly horrifying. A better comparison would be Europe following the fall of Napoleon, with world following the fall of the Soviet Union, by which measure we are not doing well, or Europe following the rise of Napoleon and nationalism, with the west following the rise of Germany and communism , by which measure we truly suck.

And what is happening outside "Western Europe and the Americas"? The end of colonialism caused a horrifying rise in violence. While India seems to be finally recovering from its abandonment by the British, some parts of Africa are still collapsing with no bottom in sight.

Pinker glibly glosses over this, because that is mostly progressive violence, for example the genocide of the Tutsi and the ethnic cleansing of the Ivory Coast, of which violence progressives rather approve, much as they approve of state violence against middle class husbands and the imprisonment of a large part of the population, therefore, to Pinker, that violence does not count. Nothing happened in the Ivory Coast, as far as Pinker knows.

The Great Recession

2011-10-14 07:04:30

The gray bar represents the official recession, which is all over now, and supposedly everything is now lovely, because the economy is supposedly growing like gangbusters. (Actually government handouts to their pals is growing like gangbusters, which handouts are recorded as GDP growth, since everything the government spends money on is supposedly for value.)

The income is "real" income, which is to say income adjusted by the official inflation numbers, which, like the official GDP data and the official end of the recession, are becoming increasingly hard to believe. If the official inflation numbers are to be believed, the average real income in all income quintiles has fallen by ten or eleven percent, and if we doubt official inflation numbers, then by a fair bit more.

The state sponsored interpretation of this data by the official Harvard Economists, who know more economics that I do because Harvard tells us they do, is that it is proof the stimulus was not big enough. The problem with this account is that the official inflation for the last year was around four percent, which high and rising, though as yet well short of hyperinflation. The official account is Keynesian. If the Keynesian account is true you cannot have rising inflation, falling employment, and falling incomes, because it completely trivial for private enterprise to produce wealth no matter how besieged they are with blood sucking parasites. Stagflation is impossible, therefore inflation must be low, even if to the eyes of mere mortals who lack credentials from Harvard it looks alarmingly high.

The radical left interpretation of this data (and today's radical left is a trial balloon for tomorrows official left, with whom it is dangerous to disagree) is that this problem is because the richest one percent are getting all the the boundless wealth that Keynesianism tells us is completely trivial to produce.

("One percent" you may recall were the president's words, which the supposedly grassroots crowd occupying the front lawn of Wall Street immediately echoed in massive chorus, like children at school repeating a drill by rote.)

However the top twenty percent, and the top five percent, are taking much the same beating as the median household, so though I do not have figures for the top one percent, this explanation is unlikely. If the top one percent were scarfing it all up, their income would have doubled.

Here is my explanation. During the Bush/Obama regime, we rapidly moved to European levels of regulation and state intervention, and so our income levels are now rapidly falling to those of a European country. When what made America unique went away, what made America rich went away.

I think it unlikely that this problem can be fixed by democratic means. The public service controls the government, not the politicians, and the Ivy League Universities are the holy church of the public service. Rolling back regulation would involve something more like regime change, for it would require a political purge of the public service. Everyone who applies to university issues a list of the extra curricular activities demonstrating that they are sufficiently left wing. A necessary step to remedy the problem is to go through those lists, and purge the public service of everyone who has submitted proof of his left wing character, which all of them, since you don't get a higher position in the public service without credentials, and you don't get the required credentials without demonstrating your political position.

Short summary of "Fast and Furious"

2011-10-15 12:58:18

Many blogs have covered[790] all this for a long time, in great depth, among them Human Events[791]. I am not going to do so, but I need to mention such an important event, if only for my own records:

To create favorable publicity for gun control, and to make true the oft repeated lie that ninety percent of Mexican drug cartel weapons come from the US, the US government supplied two thousand guns to Mexican criminals who were legally prohibited from buying guns in the USA. Sixty of the guns were found at crime scenes in the US, and hundreds of deadly crimes were committed using the weapons in Mexico. Thirty four of the

---

[790]https://pajamasmedia.com/blog/fast-and-furious-demonstrates-ruling-class-country-divide/
[791]https://www.humanevents.com/article.php?id=45398

weapons were 0.50 sniper rifles. The government department that actively did this was the ATF, but every major government department and the entire mainstream media have been accessories after the fact. "Fast and Furious" has been vigorously investigated by some elements of the Republican party – and equally vigorously ignored by other elements of the Republican party.

"Fast and Furious" confirms what we all know: That the government wants criminals armed, and productive citizens disarmed, in order to make its subjects dependent on the state.

My position on guns is that the difference between honest people and criminals is pretty obvious, and that honest people should be armed with any weapons they deem appropriate, including full auto guns, rocket launchers, mortars, and the like, and criminals disarmed, of everything including sticks. Unfortunately, if government is allowed to define who is a criminal, it is apt to decriminalize burglary of an occupied residence, while criminalizing the use of "gay" as a curse word, even if one manages to elect politicians who disagree quite vigorously with this. Observe today's Britain.

Reflect that even if we elect Herman Cain president, with a Republican house and senate, the government criminals that implemented "Fast and Furious" will still be employed by the government, will still be in power, and will be immune from firing, or even from having their power diminished. Consider: A civil servant can easily do a great deal to get a politician to lose his seat, but a politician cannot fire a civil servant. Who then has the power? Consider that if a private citizen, or even a politician, ran guns to criminals, he would be in jail for a very long time, but no one imagines that any of the very large number of civil servants involved in "Fast and Furious" will suffer any adverse consequences thereby. To punish these men would constitute regime change, would require armed revolution and fighting in the streets.

And now back to my regular blog topics.

The cause of the decline

2011-10-16 13:59:06

Lately there as been a lot of concern about the increasingly visible decline of the west, notably Peter Thiel on "The End of the Future"[792]:

> ... we are undergoing cultural decay — ranging from the collapse of art and literature after 1945 to the soft totalitarianism of political correctness in media and academia to the sordid worlds of reality television and popular entertainment

> ... how do we even know whether the so-called scientists are not just lawmakers and politicians in disguise, as some conservatives suspect in fields as disparate as climate change, evolutionary biology, and embryonic-stem-cell research, and as I have come to suspect in almost all fields?

> When tracked against the admittedly lofty hopes of the 1950s and 1960s, technological progress has fallen short in many domains. Consider the most

---

[792]https://www.nationalreview.com/articles/print/278758

literal instance of non-acceleration: We are no longer moving faster. The centuries-long acceleration of travel speeds — from ever-faster sailing ships in the 16th through 18th centuries, to the advent of ever-faster railroads in the 19th century, and ever-faster cars and airplanes in the 20th century — reversed with the decommissioning of the Concorde in 2003, to say nothing of the nightmarish delays caused by strikingly low-tech post-9/11 airport-security systems. ...

... One cannot in good conscience encourage an undergraduate in 2011 to study nuclear engineering as a career....

... In the next three years, the large pharmaceutical companies will lose approximately one third of their current revenue stream as patents expire, so, in a perverse yet understandable response, they have begun the wholesale liquidation of the research departments that have borne so little fruit in the last decade and a half.

...

The single most important economic development in recent times has been the broad stagnation of real wages and incomes since 1973, ...

Incomes, stalled since 1973, are now falling[793], across the board, afflicting all income quintiles, with no end in sight. Japan has been in decline for over a decade. There is no reason to think that this decline will end until its causes are remedied– and if never remedied, we may well wind up like so many vanished civilizations before us.

Since the decline effects all of society, every aspect of society, we have the luxury of looking of looking for causes where the light is best.

Let us look at three well studied instances of decline: the Space Shuttle Challenger explosion, Wikipedia, and Washington Mutual. I did not select these cases because they all support my thesis, but because they are conspicuous and good information is available for what went wrong.

1.The space Shuttle Explosion

Low ranking engineers explained to their superiors in detail that the Challenger would explode if launched in cold weather and explained in detail how and why it would explode, but the high ranking "engineers" neither understood nor believed[794].

> **Chairman Rogers**: Well, let's read it. "Loss of mission"– this is actual loss.
>
> "Failure effects summary: Actual loss. Loss of mission, vehicle and crew due to metal erosion, burn-through, and probable case burst, resulting in fire and deflagration."
>
> ...
>
> **Mr.Mulloy:** But about halfway through, after we had looked at all of the

---

[793]https://blog.reaction.la/economics/the-great-recession.html
[794]https://history.nasa.gov/rogersrep/v5part1a.htm#2

data, the conclusion and recommendation charts that Mr.Lundhad prepared came in and the logic for his recommendation, which did not specifically address don't launch 51-L, what itsaid was that, within our experience base we should not operate any solid rocket motor at any temperature colder than we have previously operated one, which was 51-C.

Chairman Rogers: Didn't you take that to be a negative recommendation?

Mr.Mulloy: Yes, sir. That was an engineering conclusion, which I found this conclusion without basis and I challenged its logic.

Mulloy then repeats over and over again that he was not able to understand the explanation of why the shuttle was going to blow up, from which he concluded not that he was an idiot, but the engineers telling him it was going to blow up were idiots.

"And this was a rather surprising conclusion, based upon data that didn't seem to hang together, and so I challenged that."

Further, in describing how it did blow, he reveals he still does not understand the explanation of how it did blow up. In other words, he is an idiot, and, being too stupid to understand why the space shuttle was going to explode, and not wanting to believe it was going to explode, insisted on it being launched. Mulloy not only did not understand why the space shuttle was going to explode, but after it exploded, and the cause of the explosion had been found, studied, and explained again step by step, still did not understand how it exploded.

So how is it that Mr Mulloy, and people like him, who do not know $#!% shit from beans, are in charge of people who knew and understood stuff?

2. Wikipedia

Wikipedia has less information, and less useful information, than it used to. This reflects its policy of presenting the official view on everything. Where there is no official view, facts tend to get deleted as unsupported, or not encyclopedic, or some such. Truth and knowledge is supposedly what comes from universities and the mainstream media. If not in the universities or the mainstream media, is supposedly not truth. This leads to particularly bitter contention in political fields like climate science, evolutionary psychology, race, and Darwinism, but causes widespread damage in many non political fields, for example on computer science, since the vast majority of computer science knowledge is not academic.

Contributors are instructed: "Wikipedia is an encyclopedic reference, not an instruction manual, guidebook, or textbook. Wikipedia articles should not read like ... instruction manuals."

When I look something up related to computer science, it is normally because I am working on a project, and need to know how to do something, so I need something that reads like an instruction manual, guidebook, or textbook. Further, anyone who knows computer science stuff is usually an engineer, so is apt to write like a textbook or instruction manual. The effect and application of the not-a-manual rule is to prohibit contributions from people who actually do stuff, which contributions they intend to share with other people who actually do stuff, in favor of contributions by people who do not do stuff, and are incapable of doing stuff – which is to say, in favor of academic knowledge.

3. Washington Mutual

Washington Mutual was able to take over many other better run banks, not because shareholders had confidence in Washington Mutual, but because regulators had confidence in Washington Mutual willingness to enthusiastically hurl vast amounts of money in the general direction of desired voting blocks. Kerry Killinger, CEO of Washington Mutual, became rich and powerful in substantial part through his cozy relationship with left wing activist organizations such as Acorn, which enabled him to control regulators as much as it reflected the fact that regulators controlled him.

Washington Mutual took out ads condemning themselves for racism, and was given a bunch of other, more soberly run banks, to loot and destroy.

Banks were told by regulators[795]: "Lack of credit history should not be seen as a negative factor ... In reviewing past credit problems, lenders should be willing to consider extenuating circumstance"

If a bank prevented people with no credit history from borrowing, this was a practice with "disparate impact"– which is "Raaaacism". "Disparate impact" means you cannot apply standards at which non Asian minorities fail disproportionately– such as having documented income, a past history of paying their bills, and so on and so forth.

When your regulator tells you that you "should" make easy money loans, you will make easy money loans, or suffer dire punishment. And indeed, banks that did not make easy money loans did suffer dire punishment – they got taken over by Washington Mutual and its merry band of idiots.

It is clear that Kerry Killinger and Angelo Mozilo sincerely believed that lending unemployed no-hablo-english wetbacks money to buy million dollar houses no money down was a good idea. They conned everyone of gigantic amounts of money, but their biggest victims were themselves and their banks.

They did not pretend to believe in order to become rich and powerful, rather the regulatory apparatus efficiently selected stupid people who sincerely believed stupid things to become rich and powerful. If their beliefs had been feigned and cynical, a lot more of the disappeared money would have stuck to them.

That Kerry Killinger was quite genuinely stupid was also demonstrated by the inability of Countrywide and Washington Mutual to manage their paperwork. Many of the titles that passed through their hands now have no paper trail showing who is the rightful owner, which suggests that bank was for the most part staffed by people whose IQ was below 105.

---

[795] https://www.foxnews.com/story/0,2933,424945,00.html

Because political correctness requires stupid beliefs, selection for people who are sincerely politically correct, such as Kerry Killinger, selects stupid people, who in turn hire and promote other stupid people, so that no one in his bank could do a banker's paperwork.

This is consistent with Codevilla's analysis[796]: That that we are ruled by a ruling elite, credentialed but not educated by the very best universities, that is increasing narrow, ignorant, out of touch, and stupid!

> Today's ruling class, from Boston to San Diego, was formed by an educational system that exposed them to the same ideas and gave them remarkably uniform guidance, as well as tastes and habits. These amount to a social canon of judgments about good and evil, complete with secular sacred history, sins (against minorities and the environment), and saints. Using the right words and avoiding the wrong ones when referring to such matters– speaking the "in" language– serves as a badge of identity. Regardless of what business or profession they are in, their road up included government channels and government money because, as government has grown, its boundary with the rest of American life has become indistinct. Many began their careers in government and leveraged their way into the private sector. Some, e.g., Secretary of the Treasury Timothy Geithner, never held a non-government job. Hence whether formally in government, out of it, or halfway, America's ruling class speaks the language and has the tastes, habits, and tools of bureaucrats. ...

> ...regardless of where they live, their social-intellectual circle includes people in the lucrative "nonprofit" and "philanthropic" sectors and public policy. What really distinguishes these privileged people demographically is that, whether in government power directly or as officers in companies, their careers and fortunes depend on government....

> Professional prominence or position will not secure a place in the class any more than mere money. In fact, it is possible to be an official of a major corporation or a member of the U.S. Supreme Court (just ask Justice Clarence Thomas), or even president (Ronald Reagan), and not be taken seriously by the ruling class. Like a fraternity, this class requires above all comity – being in with the right people, giving the required signs that one is on the right side, and joining in despising the Outs....

> Much less does membership in the ruling class depend on high academic achievement. ... But didn't our [ruling elite] go to Harvard and Princeton and Stanford? Didn't most of them get good grades? ... getting into America's "top schools" is less a matter of passing exams than of showing up with acceptable grades and an attractive social profile. American secondary schools are generous with their As. Since the 1970s, it has been virtually impossible to flunk out of American colleges. And it is an open secret that "the

---

[796]https://spectator.org/archives/2010/07/16/americas-ruling-class-and-the/print

best" colleges require the least work and give out the highest grade point averages. No, our ruling class recruits and renews itself not through meritocracy but rather by taking into itself people whose most prominent feature is their commitment to fit in. The most successful neither write books and papers that stand up to criticism nor release their academic records. Thus does our ruling class stunt itself through negative selection. But the more it has dumbed itself down, the more it has defined itself by the presumption of intellectual superiority.

We have statistical evidence that our ruling elite selects people who fit in at the expense of ability[797] – that people who are excessively able in unappreciated ways do not fit in.

Participation in such Red State activities as high school ROTC, 4-H clubs, or the Future Farmers of America was found to reduce very substantially a student's chances of gaining admission to the competitive private colleges in the NSCE database on an all-other-things-considered basis. The admissions disadvantage was greatest for those in leadership positions in these activities or those winning honors and awards. "Being an officer or winning awards" for such career-oriented activities as junior ROTC, 4-H, or Future Farmers of America, say Espenshade and Radford, "has a significantly negative association with admission outcomes at highly selective institutions." Excelling in these activities "is associated with 60 or 65 percent lower odds of admission."

all other things being equal, being an officer in the ROTC is likely to get you excluded from a prestigious university– any fool can see that political correctness counts more than ability or experience – whether in college admissions, or Obama's picks for the federal reserve, or the post of CEO of HP, people are chosen primarily for their theology not their ability.
Codevilla continues:

Laws and regulations nowadays are longer than ever because length is needed to specify how people will be treated unequally. For example, the health care bill of 2010 takes more than 2,700 pages to make sure not just that some states will be treated differently from others because their senators offered key political support, but more importantly to codify bargains between the government and various parts of the health care industry, state governments, and large employers about who would receive what benefits (e.g., public employee unions and auto workers) and who would pass what amounts to indirect taxes onto the general public. The financial regulation bill of 2010, far from setting unequivocal rules for the entire financial industry in few words, spends some 3,000 pages (at this writing) tilting the field exquisitely toward some and away from others. Even more significantly, these and other products of Democratic and Republican administrations and Congresses

---

[797] https://www.mindingthecampus.com/originals/2010/07/how_diversity_punishes_asians.html

empower countless boards and commissions arbitrarily to protect some persons and companies, while ruining others. Thus in 2008 the Republican administration first bailed out Bear Stearns, then let Lehman Brothers sink in the ensuing panic, but then rescued Goldman Sachs by infusing cash into its principal debtor, AIG. Then, its Democratic successor used similarly naked discretionary power (and money appropriated for another purpose) to give major stakes in the auto industry to labor unions that support it. Nowadays, the members of our ruling class admit that they do not read the laws. They don't have to. Because modern laws are primarily grants of discretion, all anybody has to know about them is whom they empower.

This means that there really is no private enterprise any more. Everything is to a greater or lesser extent run by the ruling elite– and the ruling elite is not very bright, and is steadily getting dumber.

If someone is important and under pressure to perform (perhaps the board, being composed of major shareholders, wants the CEO to make a profit and will fire him if he does not) he will surround himself with the smartest people he can get– the Google policy. But if he is under no pressure to perform, he will prefer that those lower in status than him are not quite as bright as he is, other wise he is apt to find himself in the uncomfortable position of Mr Mulloy, wherein a low status person explains why he is wrong about something, and he fails to understand the explanation. Since our ruling elite exclusively works in fields where there is no pressure to perform it naturally finds itself more comfortable inducting new members of the ruling elite that are dumber than the existing members, so that with each generation, our ruling elite gets stupider and stupider. Once upon a time, the ruling elite was kept smart by the continual infusion of smart people from business, and was prevented from declining by an hereditary elite, but now, completely self enclosed, and under no pressure to perform, a purported meritocracy by slow degrees becomes an idiocracy.

I predict that wherever membership of the government bureaucracy is controlled by some meritocratic test, the test will be subverted to that it no longer has much to do with intelligence, because bureaucrats do not much like smart people.

Observe that even at Google, though they get the smartest engineers that they can, they have a very different policy for other parts of the company. Those that might have to deal with the state, are selected to fit in, and if you are dangerously smart, you are unlikely to fit in.

We are in decay because the our ruling elite, including our top scientists (who are not really scientists, but rather a priesthood who preach pseudo scientific rationales for whatever our rulers desire to do), are steadily getting dumber and dumber.

Government hires protestors to demand more government
2011-10-17 18:12:10

Powerline found an interesting job advertisement[798] in Craigslist:

---

[798]https://www.powerlineblog.com/archives/2011/10/help-wanted.php

Under the job category "new york craigslist > brooklyn > jobs > government jobs", people looking for a government job are invited to:" FIGHT TO HOLD WALL STREET ACCOUNTABLE NOW! MAKE A DIFFERENCE! GET PAID![799]"

I knew they were getting paid to protest, but until now there was some deniability - students were being turned out to protest by their professors, employees of government unions were being turned out to protest by their union bosses, ngo employees were being turned out by ngo bosses, rather than a flat out overt offer to get paid to show up and protest.

Fun hate fact about the bell curve

2011-10-21 11:38:29

Today's hate fact is hyperexponential decay.

The normal survival function (the number of cases in a normal distribution that are more than x, one minus the cumulative distribution) approaches zero as x increases hyperexponentially, which is to say, very fast. This often makes it possible, under many common circumstances, to draw conclusions about individual cases, to infer a particular person's character and or ability from his race or sex, and to infer a particular individual's race or sex from his ability or character, to draw conclusions about particular identifiable people from average racial characteristics.

Normal distribution, probability density of cases having value x:

$$\frac{1}{\sqrt{2\pi\sigma^2}} e^{-\frac{(x-\mu)^2}{2\sigma^2}}$$

Normal Survival function, proportion of cases x or more:

$$\int_x^\infty \frac{1}{\sqrt{2\pi\sigma^2}} e^{-\frac{(y-\mu)^2}{2\sigma^2}} \, dy$$

This is the probability that a particular case will exceed x, for example the proportion of people in the population that exceed x, where x is some characteristic that is normally distributed, such as height or intelligence or criminality.

I have used the less common definition, integral from x to infinity, (normal survival function) rather than the more common definition, integral from minus infinity to x (cumulative normal distribution), since minus infinity is counter intuitive, and the fact

---

[799]https://newyork.craigslist.org/brk/gov/2618821815.html

that there are very few really smart people, and very few really violent people, is intuitive, so we want the function to approach zero, the number of people smarter than x, rather than unity, the proportion of people dumber than x.

Survival function at the extremes:

$$\left[\frac{\sigma}{(x - \mu)\sqrt{2\pi}} + O\left(\frac{1}{(x-\mu)^3} \right) \right] e^{-\frac{(x-\mu)^2}{2\sigma^2}}$$

For x more than one or two standard deviations above the mean, the following approximation to the normal survival function is good enough:

caption id=" " align="aligncenter" width="171"

$$\frac{\sigma}{(x - \mu)\sqrt{2\pi}} e^{-\frac{(x-\mu)^2}{2\sigma^2}}$$

Obviously any category that is likely to be of interest (such as the category of people competent enough to do such and such, or the category of people wicked enough to do so and so) is going to deviate from the mean by one or two standard deviations, so we can almost always use this approximation.

And now for today's hate fact:

Notice that the normal survival function falls off hyperexponentially, in other words, very abruptly, falls off faster than exponentially.

This is what makes it possible to deduce facts about people's characteristics from their race in particular individual cases, and their race from their characteristics in particular individual cases.

It follows from hyperexponential decay that if you select a subgroup from the population that meets some high standard, for example the entry requirements of a university course, or fails some low standard, for example performs an act that is both stupid and criminal, then the vast majority of those selected will only just meet the standard.

Hyperexponential decay means that if you have finite population of cases, you are going to hit zero mighty fast.

So if you have one standard for white students, and another standard for black students, there is a good chance that every single black student in a class will be inferior to any white student in that class, since the vast majority of blacks will be close to the their minimum, which is lower than the white minimum. Similarly for women in computer science classes.

Even though there is a lot of overlap in the population as a whole, in the selected category, very little overlap, so chances are that in any small group of the category, such as students at a class, every person who got in on his merits will be better than any single person who got in on affirmative action.

Thus for example: a class of fifty students, six of them are black. None of the white essays are plagiarized, all of the black essays are plagiarized[800].

If there are a thousand blacks in the university, there is going to be some overlap. If there are six blacks in the class, probably not. Particularly as the likes of Michelle Obama are not in the class, because they probably got a luxury all expenses paid scholarship to grace Princeton with their presence.

Conversely, if you look at the work of a person who is a member of a group where they were selected for being good enough, and yet that work is is not good enough, you can be pretty sure he belongs to the category benefited by affirmative action. You can tell the skin color of first lady Michelle Obama from the fact that her Princeton University senior thesis is incoherent and full of has spelling and grammar errors[801]. Obviously, you cannot conclude that someone is black from the fact that their essay is no good, but from the fact that it is senior thesis at an ivy league university, and nonetheless no good, you can tell that she is black. Thanks to hyperexponential decay, even Princeton cannot find enough black women who can write decent essays.

The Ivy League are hard up for enough black men, hard up for enough females, and to make their quota of black female graduates, they have to really scrape the bottom of the barrel, first lady Michelle Obama being what they find at the bottom of the barrel.

If a crime is violent, you cannot necessarily know the perpetrator is black. If a crime is stupid, you cannot necessarily know the perpetrator is black. But if a crime is violent and stupid, you can be pretty sure the perpetrator was black, thanks to hyperexponential decay:

Two women attempt to pass a counterfeit $50 bill at McDonald's. The cashier refuses it. One of them punches the cashier, a large male. He retreats. They jump the counter. He flees all the way to the corner. Then they attack him in the corner[802]. He loses control, beats the crap out of both of them, damn near kills one of them. Guess the race.

Left political singularity
2011-10-22 12:32:35

The French Red Terror, the Soviet Great Terror, the Cambodian autogenocide, and many others were all examples of what I call left political singularities.

Left wing repression tends to make things lefter, which tends to worsen left wing repression, which makes things even lefter, which ...The process only stops when the latest despot starts to realize he is not left enough, he is being outflanked on the left, is going to be overthrown by those even lefter than himself, and promptly gets rid of everyone important who is even lefter than he is.

Right wing repression does not have this effect, because right wing repression, for example Pinochet, pressures people to forget about politics, whereas left wing repression reaches into every person's life and forcefully pressures them to piously say the politically correct things. Left wing repression forcibly politicizes everything, even your personal private sexual activities. Right wing repression depoliticizes everything.

---

[800]https://www.isegoria.net/2011/10/six-out-of-50/
[801]https://www.atimes.com/atimes/Front_Page/JC04Aa01.html
[802]https://www.youtube.com/watch?v=dQafDUUCkpY&feature=related

In Stalin's pamphlet "Dizzy with success" it looks to me he was trying to thwart the terror, but terrified that if he tried to thwart it too vigorously, would be its next victim.

Under Tsar Nicholas II, the way to power came to be to be lefter than thou. The safest way to ally was no enemies to the left, no friends to the right. And so everything from there on moved ever lefter. And the lefter things got, the more the way to power was to be lefter than thou, the more dangerous it became to have friends to the right, so the lefter things became, the faster they moved left, consuming each leader in turn for insufficient leftism.

Left wing repression tends to make things lefter, which tends to worsen left wing repression.

We see a similar wind up in the French Revolution. The King moves left, leftists, in particular Rousseau and Voltaire, do very well, so everyone moves left. Voltaire and Rousseau were repressed by the supposedly right wing authorities only enough to generate favorable publicity for their works. The old order was condemned by highly successful intellectuals who somehow wound up with lots of money and young women. Where were the defenders of the old order? Not even the King defended it.

There is an obvious and plausible defense of hereditary monarchy and the hereditary principle: If power is up for the grabbing, there will be a lot of grabbing, and this will at best dissipate lots of wealth, and at worst kill lots of people. The replacement for King Log is apt to be King Stork. Past democracies and republics were apt to degenerate into advance auctions of stolen goods, and often those in power were reluctant to yield power when they were supposed to, so that election became civil war. In the lead up to the French Revolution, we see those attacking the monarchy prospering and succeeding, and we did not hear anyone defending the monarchy, not even the Monarch. Charles the First of England defended hereditary monarchy, first with the pen, then with the sword, and though he lost temporarily, and lost his head, in the end he won, but Louis the Sixteenth of France did as much to undermine monarchy as any man.

Voltaire tells the French that the monarchy needs overthrowing. Well, if the monarchy needs overthrowing, and and an intellectual can do very nicely under the monarchy while calling for its overthrow, likely an intellectual could do even better if it was overthrown, and those intellectuals had to step into the vacuum and replace it. And having stepped into that gap, they declined to imitate the monarchy's tolerance for its enemies and disdain for its supporters.

King Charles the First told us that the King should protect the subject's life, liberty, and property, but the subject should not concern himself with politics, that being the King's business. King Louis the sixteenth however, told us that the King "must always consult public opinion; it is never wrong". Well if the King himself says that, who is going to deny it? When the King himself will not defend the Royal prerogative, who would? And thus under Louis the sixteenth, an ever leftwards process was set in motion, culminating with the red terror in 1795.

Another way of stating this theory is that when a political belief system intent on gaining power, what I have been calling a theocracy, even if there is no God involved as such, finds it has been pushing on an open door, the push continues, till it blows up in their face and faith.

Leftism is such a belief system, rightism is not, rightism merely being a coalition of random odds and sods being rolled by leftism, and random odds and sods who disagree with leftism on any of a thousand different points of doctrine. Leftists, unlike orthodox Christians, can always be outflanked by purer and more extreme leftists, leftism being a this worldly doctrine, and so the push proceeds. Feminists get outflanked by gays, gays by transgendered.

More astroturf riots in Greece.

2011-10-23 15:01:54

At one minute fifty seconds in this you tube video[803], a man carrying a burning molotov cocktail rushes up to police. They don't react. He hurls it onto the ground, not at them, but right in front of himself. There is a huge spectacular whoosh as burning petrol sprays everywhere. They react only slightly. He runs away. They don't chase him.

They act as if they knew in advance that a man was going to come rushing at them and hurl a molotov cocktail, not at them, but right in front of himself.

At forty seven seconds in this video[804] a molotov hits right behind a cop. He does not turn around. He acts as if he knew in advance the molotov is coming and will land a short but safe distance from him.

You are supposed to believe that unless the Greek government gets more money to allieviate the condition of the oppressed masses, there will be communist revolution, but it is all fake and staged.

At two minutes and five seconds in this video[805] you see a fuse burning, then an explosion goes off. It is right on the gutter, in the safest possible place for an explosion, where there is no risk it might hurl stuff onto anyone on the pavement.

Alrenous, however, links to some real Greek rioting[806], which I would interpret as copycats getting carried away.

The lesson of Gaddafi

2011-10-25 03:41:41

The brutal death of Gaddafi teachers all rulers a lesson: Emulate Syria, Iran, and Turkey. Obstinately continue to do bad things to Americans, do not give in. Do not imitate Gaddafi, who stopped doing terrorism, backed off and went on his best behavior after Ronald Reagan killed various members of Gaddafi's family. Still less should you emulate Egypt, and be an American ally.

---

[803]https://www.youtube.com/watch?v=LSi0iNIaRLU

[804]https://www.youtube.com/watch?v=0j5m6wOh5JU

[805]https://www.youtube.com/watch?v=S6iBhdy-njA

[806]https://107.20.137.49/?h=345&w=600&src=https://www.newsit.gr/files/Image/00-ARTEMIS/20-10-2011/37.jpg

Herman Cain sticks it to political correctness

2011-10-26 11:31:48

At 41 seconds into the ad, the speaker says: "We can do this, we can take this country back", and *takes a drag on a cigarette.*

So who are we taking it back from?

We are taking it back from the scolds and self righteous naggers.

Obama could take a public dump on the American flag and no one would blink, indeed, in a sense he has done so, but this ad is shocking them.

Of course blacks have long been taking advantage of being black to say shocking things that whites are not permitted to say, for example Chris Rock telling us that when he is about to withdraw money from the ATM, and fearfully looks behind him, "Ah'm looking for niggas", plus all the wonderfully truthful things that they have been saying about women, and white women in particular, but such permissiveness does not extend to black conservatives, still less to their white campaign managers.

And now to manufacture a Kent State Moment

2011-10-27 04:49:37

But alas, no protestor is volunteering to die, and no cop is volunteering to be the designated bad guy.

The Occupy X encampments are drawing ridicule, because the incentives provided to draw campers (free food, free camping gear, free sleeping bags and a free urban campsite) tend to attract failed would-be members of the crust. The occupiers discredit the left by being over educated and under intelligent, and remind us that though a training in leftism is prerequisite for membership of the crust, there are not enough upper crust jobs for every idiot with a training in leftism and little else.

And so, time to end the occupations with a grand confrontation.

Randomly selecting the first news story on the Oakland confrontation, the first identified protestor in the story[807] is: "Max Alper, 31, a union organizer from Berkeley" – a paid employee of a union. The unions at these protests are somehow always government unions.

I suspect what is happening here is not an attempt to generate dramatic riot footage, Greek style, which would probably just piss off most Americans, who are rapidly coming to the conclusion that the occupiers are spoiled brats whose fathers neglected them by failing to provide some vitally needed spankings, but rather to get some copy cat protestor to actually throw rocks at police accurately, instead of throw rocks and somehow always miss, thereby provoking some genuinely enraged cops to genuinely beat the crap out of the offender, who would then alas die in hospital, thus supplying a martyr. But every cop knows if he gets caught on video performing the Kent State Moment, he is going to be a human sacrifice. The plan is for some *other* cop to be the human sacrifice. Oakland cops are notorious for beating the stuffing out of people, which is probably why they were

---

[807] https://www.washingtonpost.com/national/tense-scene-in-oakland-after-police-protesters-clash-at-site-of-dismantled-occupy-camp/2011/10/26/gIQAyFwLIM_story.html

selected for this riot - but I doubt that any cop is going to beat the stuffing out of anyone when the entire world mass media is eagerly awaiting the event.

At the moment the designated victim is Olsen, who was hit in the face by a police projectile, causing him to bleed a few drops of blood[808]. Kent state it is not.

Lew Rockwell drinks the left's Koolaid

2011-10-30 08:05:26

According to LewRockwell.com

> the protesters were peaceful, the only ones acting out with petty violence being loudly chastised by the crowd. The most belligerent participants by far were law enforcers, who responded to thrown bottles and civil disobedience with tear gas and rubber bullets.

Reflect that the original plan of the Occupy Wall Street movement was not to camp out in public parks, but to camp inside major buildings symbolic of capitalism in general and Wall Street in particular, planning to relive the sixties occupations of University Campus admin buildings that gave the extreme left total control of the campus. Recall that they repeatedly attempted to do so, and in every case swiftly got the heave ho from rentacops, security, and custodians, sometimes with a bit of pepper spray, but usually they swiftly retreated in the face of the firm and calm determination of the greatly outnumbered handful of rentacops, with very little fuss and drama.

And yet police somehow, strange to report, find it terribly difficult to remove these guys from a public park without great drama and spectacle.

Similarly, London is somehow strangely unable to clear out the tents of a Potemkin village occupation whose tents are empty at night[809]. "Occupy Wall Street" are the state and police are the state.

LewRockwell.com and Bruce Majors are attempting to ally leftwards. It is pointless. There is no left. The left is the state and the state is the left. "Occupy Wall Street" are just astroturf puppets of the people who gave you the bailout.

The organization "Libertarian Republicans" are not libertarian. They think Governor Romneycare is Libertarian, and Herman Cain is not. Whosoever purports to ally with some supposedly small faction of the left, allies with the state. Although there are one hundred and one factions within the state, each struggling with each other, they are all within the state, none are outside the state. To ally with one, is to ally with the state, which is to ally with them all against the people.

According to "Libertarian Republicans"[810]

> For 2012, the choice for all Republicans, including Libertarian Republicans is now Mitt Romney

---

[808]https://www.indybay.org/newsitems/2011/10/25/18695124.php

[809]https://www.telegraph.co.uk/news/picturegalleries/picturesoftheday/8847958/Pictures-of-the-day-25-October-2011.html?image=18

[810]https://www.libertarianrepublican.net/2009/07/for-2012-choice-for-all-republicans.html

So if you are a libertarian, you supposedly must support Romneycare, the system on which Obamacare was based.

Whosoever allies with one leftist, allies with every single one, for all leftists, whoever much they quarrel with each other, are united to rule everyone else. Whosoever sees some good in "Occupy Wall Street", somehow winds up seeing some good in bailouts and Obamacare. All leftists are one leftist, and whosoever allies with one of them, allies with all of them.

Whosoever discovers that there is some good in "Occupy Wall Street" because supposedly they oppose bailouts, will soon be found arguing that the sinfulness of bankers makes some bailouts regrettably necessary, and we must support Governor Romneycare for president because he is electable and Herman Cain is not.

This in part illustrates the conspiratorial nature of the left, with its innumerable front organizations, but it also illustrates the evil nature of consensus. Since the evil and the insane do not shift, consensus always winds up being fully dominated by the evil and the insane, so if you look for allies on a side dominated by consensus, you wind up as part of the echo chamber for the evil and the insane.

When we are in a society larger than the society of evolutionary adaptation, larger than the society of the ancestral environment, we automatically and irrationally overweight consensus, all of us, myself included, though I do so less than some.

People who overweight consensus less than others are disagreeable people by definition: They disagree. But nonetheless everyone errs in the direction of overweighting consensus and status, no one, not a one, errs by underweighting it, just as we always eat too much sugar and do not get enough exercise. Consensus in a large society always necessarily winds up dominated by the evil and the insane, since the insane will not shift, and the evil will conspiratorially manipulate the appearance of consensus, thus one should never believe anything because of consensus. If the main evidence for X is consensus, rather than primary evidence, X is probably a lie.

In the ancestral environment, topics of conversation were immediately empirical: ("Good fishing at those rocks when the tide is coming over them"), thus consensus was reliable. The less immediately empirical the facts in question, the more dangerous consensus. Thus in the modern environment, where facts tend to be third hand and elaborately processed, we tend to be excessively credulous towards consensus, just as we tend to eat too much sugar. When the consensus concerns status questions ("so and so is a racist"), it automatically is going to go into a positive feedback loop, automatically becoming ever more extreme, and ever less sane, creating an environment where madness is conformity to the good and the great, and sanity is deemed evil, and, worse than evil, low status.

Riot choreography

2011-11-04 05:09:54

Supposedly, according to Associated Press "Port of Oakland reopens after Wall Street protesters remove blockade that had shut down operations overnight"

They very much wish that Wall Street protestors had been able to shut down operations

Supposedly there was a general strike in Oakland yesterday, a strike, which, however, strangely only affected city operations.

But what in fact happened was revealed by the Police Association: according to to Police Officer's Association, objecting to being police being choreographed as riot bad guys.[811]:

> the Administration issued a memo on Friday, October 28th to all City workers in support of the "Stop Work" strike scheduled for Wednesday, giving all employees, except for police officers, permission to take the day off.

So the Port of Oakland was only shut down because the city government shut it down, and as much of the city as they could. With all port workers given a day off, not much to blockade.

The protestors tweeted about buses transporting protestors, which leads me to suspect that the city unions then bused the city employees to the protest in city buses, though I don't have direct proof of that:

The police officers also shed light on the protestors triumphant reoccupation of city property after being thrown out which much spectacular and photogenic violence, during which a protestor supposedly suffered brain damage after a blow to his head that caused only very minor bleeding.

> On Tuesday, October 25th, we were ordered by Mayor Quan to clear out the encampments at Frank Ogawa Plaza and to keep protesters out of the Plaza. We performed the job that the Mayor's Administration asked us to do, being fully aware that past protests in Oakland have resulted in rioting, violence and destruction of property.

> Then, on Wednesday, October 26th, the Mayor allowed protesters back in – to camp out at the very place they were evacuated from the day before.

Evidently the purpose of Mayor's order was not to remove the encampment, but to stage a Kent State Moment.

The officers also complain that the City Government is supplying astroturf:

> The Mayor and her Administration are beefing up police presence for Wednesday's work strike they are encouraging and even "staffing,"

The police officers complain that the city government's behavior is "confusing". To make sense of the confusion simply recall that the state is the left, and the left is the state. Leftism is the state at prayer, the ideology of the state, and the Ivy League its churches.

---

[811] https://www.opoa.org/uncategorized/an-open-letter-to-the-citizens-of-oakland-from-the-oakland-police-officers%e2%80%99-association/

No friends to the right

2011-11-04 08:59:13

Men's Warehouse sends their staff to join the protest, with pay.

Which means, of course, *they send warehouse security away.*

Suckers!

Whosoever attempts to ally leftwards, engages in a one way alliance. It is like making concessions to Palestinians.

épater la bourgeoisie

2011-11-06 12:38:22

Occupy Wall Street is the rage of a privileged elite. Here are some images of the digs of some of those arrested[812].

Most of Occupy Wall Street have no demands at all - they are just astroturf, like the grotesquely well paid "striking" employees of the City of Oakland, sent by the the Mayor

---

[812]https://dailycaller.com/2011/11/02/opulent-homes-of-the-99-percent-slideshow/5_1/

to join the protest on full pay. The protestors did not block the Port, rather the Mayor told her port employees not to show up for work. They were "blockading" an operation that had been shut down by the Mayor. It was confrontation theater, the appearance, but not the substance, of confrontation.

Yet there is real rage: Of course, at the protests, hard to tell the real rage from the choreographed rage, though when they smash up a Whole Foods shop or a Men's warehouse, obviously there is some real rage. Rage is perhaps more evident in the art world, where official artists blessed by the government as real artists (unlike mere kitsch peddlers who have to humbly rely on people voluntarily choosing to buy their stuff) tend to produce utter garbage[813], to show their contempt for the bourgeoisie that are forced to pay them, the San Jose dog turd being an infamous example. The message of the San Jose dog turd is "I can shit on you, proving I am more powerful and important than you are." The dog turd statue is spittle directed at la bourgeoisie.

The TSA conveys a similar message: "We can capriciously humiliate you and degrade you, and you dare not resist, or even complain, so we are powerful and you are powerless." Obviously security should be given back to the control and discretion of the airlines, and in particular, the captain should carry a gun, and have final decision making authority over security. No one dares propose abolishing the TSA, even though it is obvious that such abolition would be hugely popular.

Most real Americans think that money is status, think a wealthy guy is high status, though unless he is rich enough to fly by private jet, he gets the TSA treatment like everyone else, and probably with knobs on, since the TSA does not like wealthy Americans. A lot of George Washington's resentment of the British may have been that though he had land, money, education, and military experience demonstrating courage, leadership, and competence, the British did not consider him a gentleman, and since he was not a gentleman, felt his money and land to be rather illegitimate and improper. The "Occupy Wall Street" mob view the wealth of the productive with disdain similar to that with which the British viewed Sam Adams.

One striking difference between the "Occupy Wall Street" mob and real Americans is that the the "Occupy Wall Street" mob thinks that only the virtue industry is high status: They think that only their inferiors should degrade themselves by producing goods or services that la bourgeoisie actually want and are willing to pay for. They think a low paid job in the virtue industry is higher status than a rich man who produces what la bourgeoisie actually want. Their vision of their personal bailout is not that the government bails them out by giving them a well paid job, but that the government bails them out by giving them a virtue industry job, a job where they get to morally or culturally improve their inferiors whether their inferiors like it or not.

The politicians do not rule, merely compete for the job of public relations officer for the permanent and fireproof government employees. Government employees were made fireproof to supposedly depoliticize the public service, yet somehow recruitment has become more political than ever it was, as illustrated by the infamous Department of Justice, the EPA, and the SEC. The "Occupy Wall Street" mob reveals these people who rule us are inferior to us, dislike us, and like to harm us.

---

[813]https://althouse.blogspot.com/2011/11/cleaning-lady-cleans-artwork-making-it.html

A real change of government would require a mass political purge of government employees.

Herman Cain charged with making a woman feel bad about herself

2011-11-08 05:02:17

And if a woman says whatever it is that she is saying (not that anyone is telling us what she is saying) the man must be guilty, right?

His offense was that a woman claims to feel offended - which is pretty standard female reaction to a strong man who fails to make a pickup when she was expecting one, or who makes a pickup, and then makes a pickup of someone else, or who makes a pickup and then does not follow through, perhaps he was only joking, or who is already married and faithful to his wife.

This issue is much debated between PUAs and MRAs, between Pick Up Artists and Men's Rights Activists.

PUAs say that men lead and women follow, that as bird must fly, and a fish must swim, men and women must follow their innate natures, that men must be strong.

MRAs point out that that is illegal. That by law men must submit and women command. Since women who command are unhappy, angry, and disagreeable, because they are acting against their natures, and are prone to issuing commands that are mutually contradictory and impossible to obey, the MRA solution is to run away.

Show me a household where the housework is equally and fairly shared, including such traditionally female tasks as picking up stuff, and I will show you a marriage where the husband sleeps on the couch, and once in a week or so the wife's lover drops in to bang her on the main bed, rough her up a bit, take her money, and leave a mess for the husband to clean up.

When in doubt, do what Sean Connery would have done.

Watch Barbra Walters get wet when Sean Connery refuses to be bullied.

Sean Connery regrets nothing!

If Herman Cain refuses to be bullied, as Sean Connery refused to be bullied, the female voters will respond to Cain much as Barbra Walters did to Sean Connery.

There is a large and rapidly growing discrepancy between what is theoretically illegal, and what is in fact acceptable and commonly done. We are all felons now. The average honest respectable middle class entrepreneur has offenses worth several hundred years of jail time. It is near impossible to anything important in a way that is wholly legal, unless you are government employee, or an employee of a quasi governmental organization.

Such laws are enforced selectively, against such people as Herman Cain. Any political candidate that fails to please the ruling elite will get this treatment. No candidate that could possibly get us out of this mess will please the ruling elite, so any candidate that could possibly get us out of this mess will be charged with hate crimes and suchlike.

The average busy professional commits three felonies a day[814]. Make sure you commit

---

[814]https://www.amazon.com/gp/product/1594035229/ref=as_li_qf_sp_asin_il_tl?ie=UTF8&tag=jims-blo0e-20&linkCode=as2&camp=1789&creative=9325&creativeASIN=1594035229

a few felony hate crimes among them.

True story: Governor Arnold Schwartzenegger was bicycling icognito, a press man with him, but no secret service. A woman recognized him and said "Oh my God, it is President Clinton"

To which he replied, "No, I am the other sex offender."

Our sex offenders are better than their sex offenders!

The sins of "Occupy Wall Street"

2011-11-11 04:37:50

This should not be necessary, but I observe right wing blogs blissfully unaware of what has been going on, so, a list:

1. Astroturf: Large protests consist mostly of students sent in by their professors, and employees sent in by their employers. The routine day to day organizing is by people employed by government unions and ngos, who theoretically are not paid to protest, but are somehow at the protest day after day while their employer continues to pay them. Both the government unions, and the ngos, receive their money from the government. Ngo employment, despite the name *Non* Governmental Organization, is listed as government employment in the job ads. The people at the camps however, are only about half or a third astroturf – if you don't count free food, free laundry service, free camping gear and a free campsite as payment. If you count that as payment, they are all astroturf.

2. Confrontation Theater: Fake conflicts are staged with the collaboration of authorities, so that they can appear to be a formidable force. Thus, for example, when they "blockaded" Oakland port, what shut down the port was not that it was blockaded, but that the people who normally work in the port had been sent away by the city government to blockade it[815]. In another infamous Oakland example, the protestors were removed from the park with great drama and thousands of police, only to be immediately re-admitted. Similarly with the fake occupation of London. The tents are just there for show.[816] Only a handful of protestors remain at night. The cleaning staff could just clean up the mess and throw the tents in the trash, if they chose to do so. Note that when these guys attempted to occupy important symbols of capitalism, businesses had no difficulty removing occupiers with a handful of security guys and very little drama. They also had no difficulty making sure that if any protestors got hurt in the process, they got hurt off camera. Similarly, observe that it takes only a handful of rentacops to remove these guys, but it somehow takes thousands of police

3. Vandalism and Assault:In the Oakland protest as they marched down the street they did not only attack Whole Foods, but numerous businesses. If it was not occupied by defenders, they attacked

4. Cowardice: They attempted to blockade Americans for Prosperity, while the police displayed curious lack of interest. Americans for Prosperity sallied forth to lift the blockade. In the ensuing dust up, OWS seriously injured only an old lady, while Americans for

---

[815]blog.reaction.la/politics/riot-choreography.html

[816]https://www.telegraph.co.uk/news/religion/8846402/Only-one-in-10-St-Pauls-protesters-stay-overnight.html

Prosperity injured only healthy young males. If any young males on the Americans for Prosperity side got hurt, they were manly enough not to make a fuss about the matter. See also target selection above in the Oakland march.

5. Social dysfunction. Their camps stink of filth, and are unsafe. When the boy scouts camp, it works. When the Tea Party holds a protest, they leave behind no mess. You can tell the occupiers are subhuman by the odor.

6. Snobbery: A major issue with occupiers is unemployment and under employment, as one might expect of those attracted by free food and free place to crash. Those of them that are not employed in the virtue industry are only interested in virtue employment, which is to say, high status employment. Joe the Puppeteer does not want to paid by people who want to watch puppets. He wants to be paid by the state. Joe the Plumber makes good money, but is low status. Joe the Puppeteer is, alas, temporarily between grants, but holds the qualification "Master of Fine Arts", which not only makes him high status, and not only makes him too high status to do plumbing, but also makes him too high status to attempt entertain paying customers with his puppets.

Real eviction for fake Occupy Denver
2011-11-14 05:05:48

You can tell that when Occupy Denver was finally evicted, it was a real eviction (not a pretend eviction to be immediately followed by them being allowed back in as happened with Occupy Oakland) because this time, no Kent State Moment, no highly dramatic confrontation footage, no gigantic hordes of police dressed in maximum menace gear.

Seems that when you actually evict the Occupiers, you don't need nearly as many police as when you pretend to evict them. Two hundred police evicted Occupy Denver, a few of them dressed in riot gear. Thousands of police were strangely unsuccessful in evicting Occupy Oakland. But as in Oakland, it is apparent that the same people are running both the eviction and the occupation. Those arrested in the eviction are not getting legal representation from the Occupy Movement. They are going to be getting court appointed lawyers, which in practice means prosecution appointed lawyers. When I last saw a court appointed lawyer at work, he got about thirty of his clients convicted in twenty minutes, some of them for crimes they could not possibly have committed.

If you get busted in a pretend eviction as at Oakland, you get a real lawyer, for free, for maximum courtroom drama. If you get busted in real eviction, you are on your own. Since court appointed lawyers make up for low fees by high volume and high speed processing, there is unlikely to be any drama. No matter how low the pay for a job, it is mighty good pay if you don't actually have to do the job.

The Occupations had become an embarrassment. The occupiers are filthy, they stink, disease is starting to spread. They are stupid, incompetent, criminal and dysfunctional. The ruling elite, people with highly advanced degrees in basketweaving from elite universities, want to run Wall Street, but are revealed to be incapable of running a camp.

They are going to make a final attempt to shut down Wall Street briefly[817], and then, looks like that will be the end of "Occupy". Since they have been consistently unsuccessful

---

[817]https://www.crainsnewyork.com/article/20111111/FINANCE/111119966

in their attempts to enter defended privately owned offices, this will probably take the form of a street blockade, with police protecting their blockade from being broken, in the way their blockade of Americans for Prosperity was so swiftly broken.

While the Occupiers chant "pigs", and "police brutality", I expect we shall see the police, not the Occupiers, enforcing the Occupiers coming brief blockade of Wall Street. If instead the police turn a blind eye to the occupiers obstructing people, as they did at the Americans for Prosperity Confrontation, I expect that theoccupiers will again be dealt with as they were at that confrontation.

I hope that when the occupiers attempt to blockade Wall Street, the police will be mysteriously busy elsewhere, as they were for the Americans for Prosperity blockade, but expect to see firm enforcement of the official story line, wherein fearful Wall Streeters supposedly quail before the might of an enraged populace, protected by the thin blue line of the police.

But, though I fear we are likely to see covert police backing of the blockade, I hope to hear again the wonderful chant by the occupiers of "Arrest that man! Arrest that man! ..." as followed their unsuccessful blockade of Americans for Prosperity, when the police only showed up after the occupiers had gotten the worst of it.

On the one hand, if our rulers were rational, what they would do is have the police shut down Wall Street supposedly for the safety of Wall Streeters, but the other hand, our masters are apt to drink their own Kool-Aid, and believe themselves to be not the state, but the mighty masses revolting against the state, in which case they will once again have the police mysteriously absent from the confrontation.

Stultum facit fortuna

2011-11-16 09:43:20

Whom fortune wishes to destroy, she first makes mad.

Consensus leads to the madness of crowds, not the wisdom of crowds. As we move to a government ruled by consensus, and intrusively pervading every aspect of society with its power, madness and evil prevails.

The wisdom of crowds happens when you collect people's guesses or estimates for some fact, without them consulting each other, without them forming consensus first.

The opening anecdote of the book "The wisdom of crowds[818]" relates Francis Galton's surprise that the crowd at a county fair accurately guessed the weight of an ox when their individual guesses were averaged (the average was closer to the ox's true butchered weight than the estimates of most crowd members, and also closer than any of the separate estimates made by cattle experts)

But the book also has many examples of the madness of crowds. The book tells us, when members of the crowd consult each other first, when they influence each other's opinions, when they update their Bayesian priors from the priors of those around them, the crowd becomes markedly less wise, often becomes insane.

---

[818]https://www.amazon.com/gp/product/B002VM0L3Q/ref=as_li_tf_tl?ie=UTF8&tag=jimsblo0e-20&linkCode=as2&camp=217145&creative=399373&creativeASIN=B002VM0L3Q

The crowd, he tells us, goes mad when the members of the crowd are too conscious of the opinions of others and began to emulate each other and conform rather than think differently.

In other words, consensus is apt to be madness.

And now I depart from the book, and tell you my own observations on my own authority, not that of James Surowiecki[819].

Our communications skills were evolved for the hunt and for war, where groups were small and feedback from the environment was strong, immediate, and impossible to ignore. Ignore it, you would soon get hurt.

Humans are not well adapted to the mental life of large groups, to "the life of the mind", meaning life without forceful feedback from the senses, feedback that is frequently accompanied by physical pain to force us to pay attention.

With larger groups, more feedback from people and less feedback from the environment, consensus building is apt to go into positive feedback loops, even without deliberate manipulation by the insane and the evil.

A bubble is a manifestation of a spontaneous positive feedback loop by the sane.

Add the evil and insane to the mix, and consensus will reliably go wrong. The sane update their views from the consensus, the insane do not update so the consensus moves towards the insane, the evil lie and manipulate the Overton window, so the consensus moves towards what the evil purport to believe.

Linguistics theory, Chomsky's universal grammar, is best understood as grantsmanship (the evil), an effort by academics who did not know or care much about foreign languages to take control of a juicy chunk of academia from polylingual language geeks. The lies about language continually and radically changed, reflecting not the pressure from the sane, nor updates on the basis of information, but, like the abruptly changing Soviet line, moves in a struggle over grants and power. Global Warming is similarly a combination of grantsmanship (the evil) with the death-to-humankind greenies (evil and insane).

Anti dietary fat science is primarily the insane dominating the consensus (greenies and animal rights activists who are entirely unmoved by either evidence or the opinions of the sane).

The financial crisis is a combination of bubble (the sane are apt to spontaneously go off the rails by paying too much attention to each other and not enough to external reality) with evil (political loan allocation) and with the evil and insane (affirmative action going ever lefter than thou.)

The destruction of fatherhood, the financial crisis, and lots of others, including global warming, are all manifestations of the left singularity. Lefter than thou is the way to power, so whatever direction the consensus tends to move, whether spontaneously as in a bubble or through madness, becomes a path for the evil to gain power, ("Hey, we are all agreed on X, so we need to enforce X") so whatever the direction that the consensus happens to be moving defines leftism, whereupon the evil push it ever further in that direction. ("We need to enforce X even more than it is already being enforced. Grant all power to us, and we will take care of X")

---

[819]https://www.amazon.com/gp/product/B002VM0L3Q/ref=as_li_tf_tl?ie=UTF8&tag=jimsblo0e-20&linkCode=as2&camp=217145&creative=399373&creativeASIN=B002VM0L3Q

Thus in the left singularity evil and madness invariably ally, to pursue ever escalating heights of madness.

The scientific method, (short form: "take no ones word for it") was a conscious effort to be mindful of this flaw in our natures, and socially enforce behavior that protects the group from it. The scientific method is replication. He who invokes "consensus" preaches not science, but authority and faith.

The twinkle up, twinkle down consensus building behavior of OWS, on the contrary, is an effort to socially and coercively enforce this flaw in our nature, from which the evil and the insane benefit.

The corporate form is also an effort to protect us from this flaw in our nature. The board appoints the CEO, and monitors him, but is not supposed to second guess him and direct him. Consensus is socially prohibited. The board chooses one guy, and goes with what he thinks. If they don't like it, they choose another, but they are not supposed to switch too often, and not supposed to meddle. When the board meddles, people in the investor class tend to view this as improper and corrupt. They are supposed to look over his shoulder and keep an eye on what he is doing, but are not supposed to second guess him, short of firing him.

The reason that rentacops were so effective in dealing with OWS is the corporate form:

The shareholders theoretically appoint the board (though more commonly it appoints itself, and subsequently perpetuates itself). The board appoints the CEO, and delegates to him full power over the assets of the firm. He is not supposed to suffer any interference from the board, short of being suddenly fired, and mostly he does not.

He in turn delegates the full power of the property owner down the line (or at least he is supposed to), and in the case of security, delegates to the guys in each building. Thus, when OWS attempted to occupy, the security guards did not need to consult with a bunch of suits, who would in turn consult with a bunch of lawyers, who would consult with ... instead the security guards had all necessary authority to act ex tempore without consulting anyone, to exercise the sort of power over trespassers that a private owner would. When dealing with outside intrusion, some poorly paid guy was able to speak with the full authority of the owners, the shareholders, since the shareholders had granted full authority to the board, the board to the CEO, and the CEO ... all the way down to some poorly paid guy who has a stungun and pepper spray in his desk. When the security guys decide to throw out some unwanted visitors, that is usually morally and legally the same as if they personally owned the building, for those who actually do own the building fully delegated that moral and legal authority to them.

Of course, just as it all too frequently happens that board does meddle, it also all too frequently happens that corporate decisions are made by committees, but it is not supposed to happen. Committee management and matrix management is a manifestation of the mid level management hugging power to themselves. One is likely to see a meeting of twenty high status people, and one lower status person who does not speak much, the lower status person being the one who actually knows the matter being discussed, the one who is actually responsible for giving effect to the supposed consensus of the meeting. But corporations are not supposed to make decisions by meetings and consensus, and mostly they do not. To the extent that they do, they deservedly suffer ridicule.

The OWS model would have the shareholders gather in a crowd, and twinkle up and twinkle down at each other. In the corporate model, the poorly paid guy with a stungun in his desk is the avatar for the shareholders. He is the property owner, in their place, exercising their full authority to deal with unwanted visitors. He does not file a report to the shareholders proposing courses of action and wait for them to twinkle the various courses of action up or down.

Regulation, however, interferes with the corporate model. To do something that is regulated, the corporation finds it has to get buy in from dozens, perhaps hundreds, sometimes thousands, of meddlesome people.

In regulation, the evil and insane, which is to say the consensus, prohibit the sane (the corporate form) from acting, and even from sanity. In the banking crisis, they demanded conformity not only in action, but in thought.

Markets are also a way of avoiding consensus, since each participant in the market is expected to outsmart all the others, thus as in science, replicate the research of each of the others. The laws against "insider trading" attempt to prohibit this, but do not have the effect of enforcing consensus. Price control and rationing does have the effect, but we are not getting that problem.

The corporate form is mostly sane because consensus is socially discouraged, replaced by delegating concentrated power freely, and concentrating power as much as practical. The scientific method is sane, if actually followed, though markedly slower and less efficient than the corporate form, because consensus is discouraged for replication ("take no one's word for it"). The market is mostly sane, because market participants are supposed to strive to each be smarter than the rest, rather than to conform. Corporations exist because markets require more decision making by more smart people, because markets replicate decision making. Corporations economize on decision making, by telling people what to do.

Since committee decision making is expensive, as well as tending to madness, a corporation that finds itself holding meetings to make decisions should consider outsourcing the activities that are causing this problem to the market.

Peer review enforces consensus in science, as regulation enforces it against corporations. And so the the insane take over the asylum.

Why has science stopped progressing?

Peer review came into broad application around 1942 or so, and that is pretty much when science stopped progressing. Technology continued to progress until 1972, and some areas of technology continue to progress today, but large areas stopped progressing in 1972, and many additional areas of have very recently stopped progressing, at least in the West.

Because of peer review, Einstein's special relativity paper would not be publishable today. Any paper that is publishable today has lots and lots of citations to prove it is in line with the consensus. Einstein's paper conspicuously lacked citations, because it was not in line with the consensus. Einstein was not an academic, and not a PhD, his paper had few or no citations, and radically up ended existing physics.

When I was taught special relativity, they did not tell us Einstein was right because the holy consensus tells us so, they had us replicate the calculations and review the evidence that Einstein presented in "On the Electrodynamics of Moving Bodies" just as if Einstein was some patent clerk with neither PhD nor academic position.

Einstein attempted to present special relativity as his dissertation, and it was rejected. If rejected as his dissertation, would surely have been rejected had it ever been submitted to peer review. So instead he submitted for his dissertation a don't-rock-the-boat paper that contained nothing very new or interesting.

Each person replicating the research of each of the others can be costly. A corporation reduces the cost of this, enabling the employment of people who are not bright, by telling them what to do. Externally a corporation is market oriented, each corporation replicating the research of all the other corporations in the market, but though externally a corporation is market oriented, internally, a corporation is socialism, but what people fail to notice is that internally it is socialism on the pattern of the Nazis, the socialism of the Führerprinzip, not the socialism of the modern left whose massive dysfunction we see on display at Occupy Wall Street.

This sounds like corporations are oppressive, and they are, but in practice it means that a low pay low IQ security guy does not need to hold a meeting, nor wire the board for instructions, when a bunch of bad guys attempt to occupy the office. Full concentration of power to the CEO is supposed to be accompanied by full delegation of power from the CEO, and usually it is.

The Führerprinzip is that you don't have committees and you don't have votes and you don't have consensus. Each leader (Führer in German) is delegated full authority in his own area by his leader.

According to allied propaganda, the Führerprinzip is that the Führer is above the law and incarnates the German people, but rather, the Führerprinzip is more the common sense observation that committees are dreadfully bad at making decisions, and you should appoint a smart guy with full authority to deal with X, and hold him fully responsible for any foul ups in X.

This maximizes the capability of hierarchical organizations to get lots of stupid people to perform functions that would require smart people, were they a multitude of independent operators in the market, and lowers the high cost of figuring out what to do.

In contrast, organizations that have lots of committees tend to be horribly Dilbertesque. In practice, the socialism intended by the modern left is markedly worse than the socialism practiced by Hitler, in roughly the same proportion as the socialism practiced by the communists murdered more people than the socialism practiced by Hitler. Rather than people being empowered by participation, they are oppressed by meetings that they do not want to go to, and strangled by red tape.

Leftists want to slice power into lots and lots of tiny little slices, and share that power out between lots and lots of people, but this in practice is horribly disfunctional. What it does is not empower people but instead ensure that decisions are evil and insane, in other words, ensure that decisions are left wing. It also increases the cost of decision making. If a decision is sufficiently important that it is worth spending the time of a lot of important people on it, then it should be made by the market, or by the scientific method, not by consensus.

Because the socialism of the Nazis was inherently saner than the socialism of the modern left, it was inherently less left wing, hence its markedly lower murder rate. And thus the modern left, which is to say the modern state, reaches into science, markets, and corporations to remake them all into its own image, which is to say, make them all inherently evil and insane.

Cops protecting the occupation

Police protect astroturf to obstruct Seattle traffic
2011-11-19 12:27:27

The Seattle Times tells us that[820]:

> Hundreds of demonstrators marched onto Seattle's University Bridge Thursday halting traffic during the evening rush hour in one of several rallies nationwide for "Jobs Not Cuts."

You may ask: How did they manage to get "hundreds" to show up, and how could "hundreds" halt traffic?
They were able to halt traffic because

> Seattle police escorted the group from the University of Washington to the University Bridge, and later reported there had been no conflicts in what they termed "the peaceful demonstrations."

Peaceful because the police by protecting the astroturf prevented motorists from getting where they wanted to go, which the motorists probably felt was not at all peaceful. And "hundreds" showed up at the protest assembly site where the march to obstruct traffic was prepared because[821]:

> ... a couple hundred people were milling about. ... representatives from various unions. However, despite the fact that the protest was being held on the University of Washington's campus, precious few students.

> ...I overheard a young woman saying something about how attending the protest was part of her gender/women's studies class.

Paper precious metals start to evaporate
2011-11-19 12:59:05

Gerald Celente purchased six figures worth of gold futures, with the intent of taking physical delivery
He won't be.
Jim Willie tells us[822]:

---

[820]https://seattletimes.nwsource.com/html/localnews/2016793710_protest18m.html
[821]https://www.the-spearhead.com/2011/11/18/report-from-occupy-protest/
[822]https://news.goldseek.com/GoldenJackass/1321563600.php

The CME has advised that 1.42 million ounces of registered COMEX silver inventory is unavailable for delivery due to MF Global bankruptcy, as well as 16,645 registered ounces of gold also unavailable for delivery.

He tells us that there will be naked shorting of gold, but it seems to me that MF Global was already doing naked shorting.

The corruption that led to this disappearance of paper gold was Obama and EU related, so rather than drawing the general conclusion to avoid paper gold, I would draw the conclusion to avoid financial instruments regulated by the US or EU.

In general, it may not be a good idea to utilize financial instruments regulated by an insolvent state, therefore one should try to arrange one's financial instruments to be regulated by a state that whose retirement system is primarily Chilean style or no retirement system at all – one should avoid financial instruments regulated by states with pay-as-you-go retirement systems, since pay-as-you-go retirement scheme is a synonym for fraudulent book keeping. If one lie, all lies.

Nightfall

2011-11-19 18:23:16

Is this the end?

Civilization is an artifice, progressivism is what you get when you apply the social instincts that were adequate in a small band of half a dozen males wandering through the jungle eating ants and leaves. Civilization requires several inventions and virtues that are counter intuitive, and have to be continually re-learned, reinforced and enforced.

1. Cleanliness. You cannot have cities unless people and places are clean. Without cleanliness, people cannot live close to other people, because they get diseases. Thus, dirty people are bad, need to be treated as bad, repugnant, undesirable people, and similarly dirty places. Civilized people stay out of dirty places, or they get rid of the dirty people and clean those places up. Progressives tend to be dirty. Recall the astonishing piles of filth and trash left behind after the One Nation rally, the Occupy Wall Street encampments drowning in their own slowly accumulating garbage, and the stench and disease characteristic of Britain's public hospitals.

2. Respect for private property, freedom of contract, and freedom of trade. Adam Smith explained how this solves the coordination problem. Violating these rights complicates the coordination problem, making it unmanageable and impractical to coordinate large numbers of people. Nuclear families are naturally socialist, and this works well enough provided that Dad is benevolent dictator for life. It tends to fail even within families if Dad is not benevolent, or not dictator. The larger the group, the larger the necessary role for private property, freedom of contract, and freedom of trade. For big groups, every intrusion on property is a disaster.

3. The scientific method. Progressivism rejects the scientific method for the "scientific" consensus, such as peer review. We continually need to ask "how do you

know that", rather than relying on a suitably prestigious authority - we need to use what Wikipedia deprecatingly calls "original research" - which is to say, replicated research, not original research. Without this, society becomes riddled with superstition, and lives in the demon haunted dark - for example recycling rules, and the dietary rules against animal fat. Science ended around 1942 or thereabouts, as peer review replaced replication. The demon haunted dark closes in upon us, shutting down nuclear power, forbidding fracking for natural gas, superstitiously terrified of dangerous compounds at one thousandth their harmful levels. Science needs to be restored.

The need for the scientific method is a phenomenon of large groups. In small isolated groups, everyone is close to the original evidence, the testimony of the senses. In large groups we become overly reliant on what other people tell us, which can circulate entirely disconnected from the testimony of the senses https://xkcd.com/978/. The scientific method is a continual demand that such disconnects be watched for, detected, and rejected.

4. Fatherhood. Males need to raise their children, which requires rules for families that make it attractive for males to stick around, in other words: patriarchy and female chastity. As the rules have been changed to be less and less favorable for males, more and more children have been deprived of their natural fathers, and even when fathers stick around, they are less and less involved in their children's lives.

5. Crime needs to be suppressed. It should seem odd and shocking that we need to lock our doors and take the keys out of our cars. It should be bizarre and horrifying that there are large parts of the city where it is simply hopelessly unsafe for an outsider to go. There are plenty of societies where the victimization rate is a hundred or a thousandfold lower than it is in the modern west, for example Singapore, and they accomplish this using methods that horrify modern progressives. Gangs that attack random people in the street should be as bizarre and improbable as man eating crocodiles eating people in the municipal pond.

If you have a plan for victory over progressivism, don't think of making entitlements expand at a one percent slower rate, think of restoration of the basic requirements for civilization, think of civilization protecting itself by enforcing them against the savages and subhumans.

The right is also left of reality
2011-11-21 17:09:09

Alternative right correctly points out that Darwinism, which is to say reality, is far to the right of what either the mainstream left, or the mainstream right, dares think.

but the science of human nature demolishes more than just bitchy feminism[823].

---

[823]https://www.alternativeright.com/main/blogs/hbd-human-biodiversity/hbd-left-and-right/

A number of people in the manosphere have pointed out that today's Christian right churches take a position on marriage, divorce, and female chastity that in the fifties would have been seen as radical hippy dippy leftism, but back to the topic addressed by "Alternative Right" - evolution and racial inequality. (On another day, I will address evolution and gender inequality)

The origin of species, full title: "On the Origin of Species by Means of Natural Selection, or the Preservation of Favoured Races in the Struggle for Life"

Darwin tells us:

Descent of Man, Chapter 01

> Do the races or species of men, whichever term may be applied, encroach on and replace one another, so that some finally become extinct? We shall see that all these questions, as indeed is obvious in respect to most of them, must be answered in the affirmative, in the same manner as with the lower animals.

Descent of Man, Chapter 05

> Man accumulates property and bequeaths it to his children, so that the children of the rich have an advantage over the poor in the race for success, independently of bodily or mental superiority. On the other hand, the children of parents who are short-lived, and are therefore on an average deficient in health and vigour, come into their property sooner than other children, and will be likely to marry earlier, and leave a larger number of offspring to inherit their inferior constitutions. But the inheritance of property by itself is very far from an evil; for without the accumulation of capital the arts could not progress; and it is chiefly through their power that the civilised races have extended, and are now everywhere extending their range, so as to take the place of the lower races.

Descent of Man, Chapter 07

> At some future period, not very distant as measured by centuries, the civilised races of man will almost certainly exterminate, and replace, the savage races throughout the world. At the same time the anthropomorphous apes, as Professor Schaaffhausen has remarked,* will no doubt be exterminated. The break between man and his nearest allies will then be wider, for it will intervene between man in a more civilised state, as we may hope, even than the Caucasian, and some ape as low as a baboon, instead of as now between the negro or Australian and the gorilla.

Pepper spray theater

2011-11-23 03:17:37

Observe that when the video begins, all the students obviously know that the designated group of pepper sprayees is going to be pepper sprayed, and everyone has taken their positions to spray, to be sprayed, or, for the great majority, to watch the spraying in the confident knowledge that only the designated evil bad guys will be spraying, and only the designated innocent victims at the designated spray point will be sprayed.

In the first five seconds of the video, top right, a cop pats a protestor on the shoulder, murmurs something in a friendly manner and the protester replies in a friendly manner "you are shooting us, that is fine, that is fine", which sounds like the actor playing the good guy discussing the upcoming scene with the actor playing the bad guy, a few moments before they get into character.

The police in this video are not Davis City cops. They are university cops[824] Their bosses are far left, far, far left.

If the students are obstructing the cops, they are all obstructing the cops, yet most are acting like the audience for the prospective spraying, and the prospective victims are acting like the prospective victims. The script, evidently, has been leaked.

If a Southern Sheriff was the bad guy in the video, it might be believable. If they were Davis City police, might almost be believable. But these are University cops answerable to management that is to the left of Mao, answerable to the same management that astroturfed the students to the protest. Chances are the kids are being sprayed with tomato sauce.

You will notice that when the protestors attempt to occupy an office building, the rentacops handle it without creating a spectacle for the cameras, while here, everyone knows well in advance that a spectacle is going to unfold, and what the spectacle will be - it is the cops whose bosses are enthusiastic supporters of Occupy, and who are sending in student astroturf for course credit, that act out the spectacle. The spectacle, as at Oakland, is played by the cops with the leftmost bosses, not the cops with the rightmost bosses.

Next climategate installment.

2011-11-23 10:32:41

From Watts up[825]

I have not read through these, and it took me a long time to understand and read through the first batch[826].

The biggest and most important fact about the first batch is not that some of the documents were anti scientific, but that none of them reflected a scientific inquiry. All of them, every single one, were the internal documents of a political and religious campaign. None of them, not a single one were the internal documents of a scientific inquiry. It was not that some of those documents stank badly, but that every single one smelled at least a little bit funny.

---

[824]https://cityofdavis.org/police/press-releases/repository/2011-11-19.cfm

[825]https://wattsupwiththat.com/2011/11/22/climategate-2-0/

[826]magnet:?xt=urn:btih:e106283c92224d89fa6e9178b87147ee11c4392f&dn=Hadley+CRU+Files+%28FOI2009.zip bittorrent.com%3A80&tr=udp%3A%2F%2Ftracker.publicbt.com%3A80&tr=udp%3A%2F%2Ftracker.ccc.de%3A80

Women drivers

2011-11-27 06:08:37

Women drivers have more serious crashes than male drivers. Obviously sexism it to blame, and car manufacturers must be punished[827]. Poor fragile women driving a car need more protection from evil men.

Strangely, the summary neglects to inform us about what happens to the passengers and cars of women drivers.

Supposedly the crashes are "comparable" – but if female crashes are comparable to male crashes, should not women passengers also have a higher injury rate than male passengers? To ascertain whether the crashes are comparable, what we really need is data on *passengers* of women drivers, as compared to passengers of male drivers.

If the cause of the problem is that women are fragile, that should be easy to detect. In an accident, males in the car would be at lower risk than females in the same car – the sex of the driver should be irrelevant. That the problem is driver related suggests that the cause of the problem is that women tend to be terrible drivers.

MF Global Obama

2011-11-29 05:51:05

John Corzine was the US Government, in the same sense, and to the same extent, as the Occupy Wall Street protestors are the US government. He stole his depositors money, and pissed it away, not on wine, women and song, nor on gambling on stocks nor horses, nor at the casino, nor on purchasing little boys for sexual purposes, but gambling on Greece.

You know how the occupiers demand virtue jobs at government expense? Jon Corzine was betting on the great productivity of Greeks who have virtue jobs at government expense.

Jon Corzine is a politician, an important power in the Democratic Party, he was the Senator from New Jersey, and then became Governor of New Jersey, a rapidly rising star in the Democratic Party. When the Democrats, to everyone's shock and amazement lost New Jersey, he was appointed chairman and CEO of MF Global Inc, by much the same people who caused him to be nominated Senator and Governor. As a politician, he sponsored Obama, Obama held a fund raiser in Jon Corzine's home on Fifth Avenue, and as Chairman and CEO of MF Global he funded Obama – and Greece. He was expected to return to politics as soon as a post sufficiently important for a man of his stature could be found for him.

When you see photographs of Jon Corzine, they are the sort of photos a politician arranges to have taken of himself, not the sort of photos a businessman arranges to have taken of himself.

"Occupy Wall Street"[828] are just astroturf puppets of the people who gave you the bailout, and Jon Corzine is one of the people who gave you the bailout.

---

[827] https://www.nlm.nih.gov/medlineplus/news/fullstory_117782.html
[828] https://blog.reaction.la/politics/lew-rockwell-drinks-the-lefts-koolaid.html

MF Global recently made a bond sale with an unusual clause, saying the interest rate on the bonds would rise 1 percent if Jon Corzine ended up being appointed to a post in the Obama administration, indicating that MF Global was perceived as primarily governmental, rather than private, as what in England is called a quango, quasi governmental organization, and in most of the world, an ngo, non governmental organization - the "non" being euphemistic or ironic.

The finance system is in collapse because our ruling elite is buying up an underclass with finance system money, and it is running out.

Was Jon Corzine ordered to help out the Greeks at the expense of himself and his depositors?

Unlikely: But the elite of which he is part has a consensus, a quite delusive consensus, and he would not have been placed in charge of other people's money had he not shared or plausibly appeared to share those delusions in full. He was placed in charge of other people's money because, like Angelo Mozilo appointed to Countrywide and Kerry Killinger appointed to WaMU, he was mad as a hatter.

That he gambled with his depositors money, intending to keep the profits if he won, but they would take the losses if he lost was evil. That he gambled on Greece is insane. No one sane bets on Greece with his own money unless someone is twisting his arm. Thus John Corzine personally exemplifies the fact that consensus always winds up dominated by evil and madness[829] because the sane shift, but the insane don't shift, and the evil lie about what they believe.

The lek mating system

2011-11-30 12:51:31

In a lek based mating system, males and females regularly gather at some location and the males put on a display. The females inspect the displays, then, after much wandering about, have sex with one of the males, never to meet that male again.

Absent patriarchy, humans predominantly mate on the lek system[830].

In monogamy and polygyny children have natural fathers. In lekking, they don't. Today, most children do not live with their father. Therefore, lekking is the today predominant system, not monogamy, not serial monogamy, not polygyny.

Lekking.

In general, a species that leks will obviously produce fewer offpring than a monogamous species, about half as many. Hence the fall in fertility.

In the general span of history surveyed by Udwin in "Sex and Culture", societies that reproduce by lekking disappear, while monogamous societies expand and overwhelm their neighbors.

---

[829]https://blog.reaction.la/economics/stultum-facit-fortuna.html
[830]https://whiskeys-place.blogspot.com/2011/11/sadness-american-and-british-versions.html

Timing the coming hyperinflation

2011-12-02 06:47:01

We have a bubble in government paper. Assessing the end of the bubble is, like assessing the end of any bubble, hard.

Bubbles climb a wall of worry. At the beginning, everyone worries that the asset is overpriced. As more and more people hold more and more value in the bubble asset, that signifies that fewer and fewer people are worried. Supposedly, government paper is the only safe asset left, so most people prefer to hold it, even though interest rates are far below inflation.

Eventually almost everyone is convinced that the bursting of the bubble will not happen for a long, long time, and just about everyone has as much of their assets in the bubble as they are ever going to have. At which point, at the point of maximum confidence in the bubble asset, it starts to fall in value. The bubble bursts when confidence in the bubble asset stops rising.

So when the hardcore gold bugs have given in, when the prophets of hyperinflation having repeatedly been proven wrong, stop issuing new redated prophecies, that is when we shall suddenly discover that the world cannot indefinitely have a far larger amount of assets in the form of taxpayer futures than it has ever had before.

Of course, if you have read this far, you want me to stick my neck out, and give a date.

Bubbles are unstable, and can suddenly collapse for no reason at all, or because the child calls out that the emperor has no clothes. Often confidence just stops growing for no particular reason, and the asset starts to fall, and confidence collapses.

The sooner the collapse, the less damage is caused. But the trouble is that this bubble is being centrally managed by powerful people, who will do anything to keep confidence up, short of actually balancing their budgets, so though the collapse could start at any moment, I think there is a good chance this bubble will go all the way to its absolute limit, which looks to me to be around 2026.

I used to say 2025, so I am adjusting my prophecies, which is itself an indicator of the collapse being imminent. Food prices and fuel prices are soaring, and though the government is telling the truth about fuel prices, it continues to deny, or at least substantially delay the truth, about food prices.

If the collapse comes sooner than 2026, then in trying to predict the time of the collapse, we are trying to predict crowd psychology, meaning we are trying to predict madness, which is notoriously unpredictable. The best tool for predicting crowd psychology is charting.

I therefore attempted to fit the commodities index on to the run up towards German hyperinflation. Unfortunately, it does not fit well. Commodity prices are growing linearly or exponentially with time, rather than hyperexponentially. Looking at the chart to 2008, the fit predicts hyperinflation in 2012; looking at the chart to 2009, the fit predicts hyperinflation early in 2011, which obviously did not happen; looking at the chart to the middle of 2010, the fit predicts hyperinflation in 2013 June; looking at the chart to today, the fit predicts hyperinflation in 2014 June. A method that yields ever later prophecies is probably predicting crisis too soon.

So, I will say that hyperinflation is unlikely before late 2014, but will happen 2026 or earlier.

Climategate 1 and 2

2011-12-03 13:34:42

Climategate 1 is self summarized by the famous line:

> Mike's Nature trick[831] ... to hide the decline.

Climategate 2 is self summarized by the theme: '

> help the cause

Climategate 1

> I've just completed Mike's Nature trick[832] of adding in the real temps to each series for the last 20 years (ie from 1981 onwards) and from 1961 for Keith's to hide the decline.

Meaning hide the fact that alleged proxy measured temperatures for the past several hundred years failed to replicatealleged instrumentally measured temperatures for recent decades by replacing the proxy with "the real temps".

The theme running through through the over a thousand emails and three thousand other documents was that these "scientists" were hiding unfavorable information, and were, as Harry Readme complained, making up favorable information. Every document, one way or another, supports the story that global warming is indeed Mann made, in that the evidence for it is Michael Mann made.

Climategate 2

> <3115> By the way, when is Tom C going to formally publish his roughly 1500 year reconstruction??? It would **help the cause** to be able to refer to that reconstruction as confirming Mann and Jones, etc.

> <3940> They will (see below) allow us to provide some discussion of the synthetic example, referring to the J. Cimate paper (which should be finally accepted upon submission of the revised final draft), so that should **help the cause** a bit.

> <0810> I gave up on Judith Curry a while ago. I don't know what she think's she's doing, but its **not helping the cause**

---

[831] https://climateaudit.org/2011/03/29/keiths-science-trick-mikes-nature-trick-and-phils-combo/
[832] https://climateaudit.org/2011/03/29/keiths-science-trick-mikes-nature-trick-and-phils-combo/

I have not read a lot of the Climategate 2 documents, whereas I have read most of the Climategate 1 documents.

It looks to me that the Climategate 1 documents were hand selected by human judgment to tell a coherent and complete story, whereas the Climategate 2 documents appear to be more of a grab bag of random stuff. Climategate 1 is a story, Climategate 2 is a pile of emails.

But since grabbed from a team of human beings, a uniting theme appears anyway:

While the uniting theme of the Climategate 1 documents was that the warmists were not practicing science, the uniting theme of Climategate 2 is that the warmists are engaged in a holy crusade.

Climategate 2, unlike Climategate 1, contains a lot of emails where scientists expressed doubt in anthropogenic global warming, but often these demonstrate the response to doubt. Doubt is treated as sinful, evil, doubt needs punishment, as for example, the effort to cancel Pat Michaels's PhD[833].

Whereas Climategate 1 showed us that these were salesmen and political campaigners, rather than scientists, Climategate 2 showed us that these were priests, rather than scientists.

All Republican nominees extreme left by 1996 standards.

2011-12-04 13:35:34

There is Governor Romneycare, who created the original of which Obamacare is a copy.

There is Governor Perry, a man who fully supports the underclassing[834] and the suppression of Christianity by state power combined with state sponsorship of alternatives to Christianity such as Islam[835].

There Newt Gingrinch, who talks like a right winger, but is an entryist.

He supported the key element of Obamacare, the individual mandate. He supported Scozzafava, an extreme left candidate inserted into the Republican party by an openly entryist far left organization.

He points out that we end up taking care of the uninsured anyway, and proposed to fix this by providing more socialism for everyone, rich and poor alike.

The correct solution for the uninsured is not to make health care more socialist for everyone, but to provide ~~death camps~~ free government doctors and hospitals with ~~death panels~~.

If you don't want to face the ~~death camps~~ free government doctors and hospitals with ~~death panels~~, you pay for your own health care.

The long term trend is for any semi socialist industry that everyone depends on is to become ever more socialist, more left wing, more oppressive, ever more tyrannical, and ever more murderous (example, British National Health System treats elderly people who are having trouble breathing with barbiturates - which depress breathing)

---

[833]https://www.australianclimatemadness.com/2011/12/climategate-2-0-ipcc-bias-and-defending-the-cause/

[834]https://blog.reaction.la/culture/rick-perry-and-the-underclassing-of-america.html

[835]https://blog.reaction.la/culture/rick-perry-multiculturalist.html

If, however, you have a government hospital system that only treats the poor and the desperate, the natural trend is that no one cares how shitty the government health cares is provided the private system is fine, so a free public system with for pay private tends over time to approximate the libertarian solution: That those that cannot pay, shall have little or no medical care.

If you have socialist health care for the poor, and private health care for the rest, then the natural tendency of government to cruelty, tyranny, murder, and corruption, tends over time to approximate private health care plus some pious rituals to make people feel better about dumping those that are poor and sick and who no one cares about.

If, however, you have socialist health care for everyone, you wind up with the state exercising power of life and death over everyone.

Gingrich in 2005 wanted to fix problems with a bit of socialism for everyone, rather than a bit of socialism for the poor.

Today, you need to simulate politically correctness, which is to say left wing views, to get into university. Tomorrow, you may well have to simulate left wing views to avoid getting your organs harvested for the greater good.

Sarbanes-Oxley:

2011-12-11 12:14:17

Sarbannes-Oxley does to double entry accounting, what the Occupy Movement did to poop control.

Sarbannes-Oxley was correctly predicted to be a gigantic job killer and an obstacle to innovation. It has also turned out to be a license to steal, as has been demonstrated dramatically in the collapse of MF Global.

You know how the Occupy crowd is calling for personal bailouts and high status government funded virtue jobs. In Europe, by and large, their equivalents *have* government funded virtue jobs. President Obama and company tell each other that this is an investment in our future, and after they say it enough times, they start to believe it. And so, when MF Global's clients thought they were investing in gold futures or such, Jon Corzine (former Democratic party Governor of New Jersey) being wiser than his social inferiors who do not know that investing in gold is politically incorrect and investing in Greek bonds is politically correct, and thus bound to be highly profitable, took their money and invested in loan guarantees to governments without telling them, which were ultimately investments in virtue jobs for the kind of people who at Occupy encampments are apt to poop in grossly inappropriate places, thus ultimately "investments" in people inadequately toilet trained and disinclined to do any real work.

And Jon Corzine's accountants and auditors, PricewaterhouseCoopers, in accordance with Sarbanes-Oxley, somehow neglected to tell anyone the money had gone.

Civilization is the art of living together in large numbers without killing each other too often, and economics the art of coordinating human activity in large numbers without slave labor and killing fields.

Civilization began with burying your poop. God told the Children of Israel he did not like to see stools lying around, and that if you hung out with diseased or dirty people, or ate animals that had died rather than being killed, you would get unholy cooties from them. God commanded them to bury their poop. God was pleased with their obedience, and performed miracles for them – the most common important miracle reported in the bible being that during war and conflict, their enemies would be shattered by plague, and the Children of Israel would not. Until the modern era, armies were struck down by plague a lot more than they were struck down by fire and steel, so the winner was often the last army to get sick– which, the bible tells us, was apt to miraculously be the Children of Israel.

Modern technological civilization, the widespread application of science and technology to improve people's living standards, is based on the joint stock company. In North Korea, we see what happens when you attempt to do it by the old fashioned means, by slave labor and killing fields[836]. Slave labor and killing fields are not totally incapable of effectively coordinating the labor and capital of large numbers of people, but they are clearly less effective than the joint stock corporation. The joint stock corporation is built on double entry accounting, which treats the corporation as a being that owns property and does business separate from the particular people that actually carry out the actions of defending that property and using it to do business. The left, starting with Rousseau, have always been fundamentally hostile to civilization, all of it, lock stock and barrel. Thus with Sarbannes-Oxley the modern left did to double entry accounting, what the Occupy movement did to poop control. Sarbannes-Oxley, no less than modern university courses, is part of the left's war on western civilization and modern technology.

PricewaterhouseCoopers accounts and audit for MF Global showed MF Globals "investments" in guarantees of for government bonds as off balance sheet liabilities, as if MF Global still had the money. But the big "liability" was that the money was already gone. It had been spent– and ultimately spent on Greek rioters and suchlike. It was not a liability, still less a liability that could be appropriately listed off the balance sheet. The money was gone, and the "liability" was that it was not very likely to return. A liability is money that you are at risk of having to pay out in the future. This was money that had already been paid out in the past. By treating this as a potential liability, PricewaterhouseCoopers misled MF Global's clients that MF Global still had their money, when in fact MF Global no longer had their money.

If it had merely been a liability, then if that liability had come due, MF Global would then have gone bust and its creditors would have been out of luck, but the clients would have been able to withdraw their money, while the creditors would not have been paid their liability. But it was not a future liability, but a past actual loss. The money to pay the clients was no longer there. The money had already been spent, in part on Greek rent-a-rioters. Or, as President Obama would say, "invested in the struggle for justice".

PricewaterhouseCoopers was the same accounting firm that also somehow failed to notice[837] that Freddy and Fanny had pissed away most of their money and lots of other people's money on no money down million dollar mortgages to unemployed no-hablo-english wetbacks – another triumph of Sarbannes-Oxley accounting. Back in 2002, Democratic Party Senator Jon Corzine was shocked, shocked to find that Fannie's accounts were

---

[836]https://reaction.lakillingfields.html
[837]https://www.wallstreetbear.com/board/view.php?topic=7297&post=26253

a teensy weensy bit vague as to where the money was and who had it.

Sarbannes-Oxley killed IPOs[838]. It used to be that venture capitalists would fund an entrepreneur and, if the venture succeeded, sell it to shareholders. Today, however, the compliance costs are too great, which makes it a lot harder to cash out.

Supposedly, Sarbannes-Oxley prevents fraud:

> Most senior company officers and auditors can attest that Sarbanes-Oxley is difficult and expensive to comply with. While the legislation prevents accounting fraud and material misstatements, designing, implementing and following lots of internal controls procedures at all levels of the organization prevents employees and managers from focusing on running the company.

Yet let us compare the bad stuff that happened before Sarbannes-Oxley, with the bad stuff that happened after Sarbannes-Oxley. It does not look as if the legislation prevents fraud and material misstatements.

Before Sarbannes-Oxley Enron did funny stuff with its books. A bunch of accountancy students went over its books, smelled something funny, word got out, investors and creditors panicked, suddenly Enron found itself unable to buy stuff except for cash on the barrelhead, and unable to sell stuff except for stuff it could actually deliver on the spot, unable to sell stuff except for what was in the barrel– which meant that Enron could no longer buy nor sell. Suddenly Enron's paychecks started bouncing, and shortly thereafter, no one was showing up for work, the landlords were chucking their stuff in the street, and so on and so forth.

So, the federal government announced that something must be done, and created Sarbannes-Oxley, which theoretically forbade doing funny stuff with the books.

In the present crisis, a lot of strange accounting has come to light, strange accounting often curiously similar to that conducted by Enron - but due in part to Sarbannes-Oxley, only came to light *after* numerous financial institutions bit the dust, whereas before Sarbannes Oxley, it came to light before Enron bit the dust, and caused Enron to bite the dust.

The way real accounting works is that accountants ask people who actually operate the company where money and valuables are, and what was done with past money and valuables, what happened to the previous years money and valuables, and do some spot checks to make sure that the money and valuables reported to be there actually are there.

Theoretically this also happens in Sarbannes-Oxley but in practice it is is apt to be the other way around. Instead of listening, the godlike accountants tell people, and rather than the accounts reflecting reality, reality is supposed to be adjusted to reflect the accounts, much as peer review results in the scientific community telling the experimenter what he observed, instead of the experimenter telling the scientific community what he observed.

By examining Enron's accounts carefully and cynically, people could, and did, discover that Enron was deeply in debt and losing money hand over fist, and was therefore unlikely to be able to pay for goods it had purchased, nor supply goods it had been paid

---

[838] https://online.wsj.com/article/SB10001424052748704662604576203002012714150.html?mod=google-news_wsj

for. There was no way that someone examining MF Global's accounts could tell that MF Global had already pissed away its client's money on European welfare bums. That is the difference thatSarbannes-Oxley made.

Woman charged with making a false rape accusation!
2011-12-12 04:50:11

A woman is being charged with making a false rape accusation!
   Gasp!
   Are pigs flying? Has the revolution come? Is marriage going to be legally restored?
   No.She is charged with making a false rape accusation against a minority[839]. She should have done what everyone else does, make false rape accusations against lower income and/or rural members of the majority ethnic group of males.

Worse than a crime, a legalism
2011-12-16 16:53:28

MF Global did worse than embezzle client funds. They embezzled client funds *legally*[840]
   Very large numbers of investors may be in the same position as MF Global's investors, who thought they were investing in gold, businesses, and suchlike, but were in fact investing in Greek rioters, Italians on welfare, and public servants taking early retirement.

Why the left always wins.
2011-12-17 20:13:34

And the non left always loses.
   "Coordination Problem" is treating this as a deep and puzzling mystery[841]. Obviously they have not been reading Moldbug.
   Leftism is a form of theocracy. The state endorses the belief system, and the belief system endorses the state. The priests (the Ivy league professoriat) get power and the state gets power. Indeed, since there is no fixed doctrine or direction of leftism, it is merely theocracy. Any theocracy is in a sense leftism, which is why leftists are so fond of Islamists – but since Islamists, unlike leftists, *do* have a fixed and definite doctrine, an unchanging holy book, they do not return the affection.
   Leftism is the state, and the state is the left. Leftism is the state at prayer.
   Naturally, those who intend to remake society in their interests, adhere to the faction that has been successful in remaking society in their interests. The left is simply the gang

[839]https://www.telegraph.co.uk/news/worldnews/europe/italy/8949325/Italian-gipsy-camp-burned-down-by-vigilantes-after-false-rape-claim.html
   [840]https://newsandinsight.thomsonreuters.com/Securities/Insight/2011/12_-_December/MF_Global_and_the_great_Wall_St_re-hypothecation_scandal/
   [841]https://www.coordinationproblem.org/2011/12/could-it-be-that-the-mistake-theory-of-government-policy-is-mistaken.html?cid=6a00d83451eb0069e20154386c041a970c#comments

that has been winning, and so keeps on winning, while the right is whoever is getting run over by the bandwagon. The process is inexorably self accelerating.

Leftists are confident that Islamism has no fixed essence, that Islam can be whatever leftists would like it to be, because leftists have no fixed essence.

Most theocracies do have a fixed essence - because those without a fixed essence destroy themselves quite rapidly. In a theocracy the way to power is always to be holier than the next guy, to be lefter than thou, and if the religion does not have a book and immutable doctrine to anchor it, this results in doctrine becoming ever more extreme and ever more crazy.

Leftists project onto Christianity their own theocracy, and onto Islam their own fluidity. When they see Muslims taking "moderate" positions, for example the Muslim brotherhood's gradualism, they conclude that Muslim brotherhood is well on the way to being progressive, but in reality the Muslim brotherhood's gradualism is Mohammed's gradualism. Mohammed favored the salami slicer procedure for eradicating opponents, so favoring more abrupt repression of heretics does not make a Muslim more Muslim than a gradualist, whereas favoring more abrupt repression of heretics does make a leftist lefter than a gradualist.

Leftists tend to be staggeringly ignorant of cultures and societies different from their own, since any actual knowledge of such societies is likely to be politically incorrect, or have politically incorrect implications. Since the way to power is to sincerely and loyally believe every single one of ten thousand points of ever shifting leftist doctrine, and reality is apt to contradict leftist doctrine, the way to power is to avoid knowing the difference between shit and beans. Even if reality fails to contradict today's leftist doctrine, it might contradict tomorrow's, so knowing reality can get you into trouble. Perhaps tomorrow it will be necessary to believe that beans remain unchanged after passage through a mule, in which case should you have ever believed otherwise, you will be a global warming denier or something equally heinous.

It is always safe, and apt to be profitable, to be lefter than thou, whereas right wing deviation is apt to be punished. This has been the case for a couple of hundred years. Even when slavery was in effect, it was apt to be hazardous to argue in favor of slavery, while very safe, and wonderfully respectable, to argue against it, and to argue for the dignity of the negro race, the inherent equality of women, that labor and the poor are oppressed. Dickens was wonderfully respectable, taking the safe, respectable, and popular position. Carlyle was not. In a conspicuous display of affirmative action the reasonably literate black schoolteacher John Jacob Thomas was in 1869 paraded around London as a brilliant intellectual, like a monkey dressed in a business suit - not primarily because he was a reasonably intelligent counter stereotypical black man, but because he was a reasonably intelligent counter stereotypical black *leftist*. And if anyone doubted the supposed brilliance of John Jacob Thomas, it cannot be because Thomas really was not all that bright, it must be because the doubter hates blacks and favors slavery. The doctrine first enunciated by Thomas is still around as Ebonics, and to doubt what we now call Ebonics was as hazardous back then as it is now.

And indeed, by and large the doubters did favor slavery, in the sense that they believed that blacks needed white rule for their own good or they would revert to savagery. And by and large, the doubters were right. For example, when the whites fled the Congo, cannibalism and genocide returned. Since the progressive finds it perfectly obvious that blacks are on average precisely equal to whites, and woman on average precisely equal to men in every respect, there can be no reason for doubting this other than hatred of blacks and desire to harm them. And thus, if one makes unkind remarks about women's driving and parking skills, one will on most blogs be promptly banned, lest your horrid hatred of womankind causes trouble for the blog owner.

The good leftist will not only perfectly confident that women are just as good at driving as men, he will also be agnostic as to the difference between beans and shit, just it case that too becomes a point of leftist doctrine.

Does this mean we are doomed to always and forever move ever leftwards? Of course not. Trees do not grow to the sky. They grow to a certain height, then fall over. But we will move ever leftwards until we run into crisis and collapse. Chances are that democracy and the United States will end before the ever leftwards movement ends. Predicting when a tree will fall is chancy, but predicting that a tree will fall is certain. If you are in bus moving at high speed, and the driver is blind and insane, the bus will stop eventually.

Paul leading in Iowa

2011-12-20 08:42:04

As the last non leftist still standing, Paul is now leading in Iowa[842], the first actual vote of the Republican nomination.

Paul twenty three percent, Mitt Romney twenty percent, Gingrich fourteen percent, ten percent or less for all the rest.

It is not "Anybody but Governor Romneycare", but rather "Anybody but yet another leftist like Obama/McCain/Romneycare"

In the 2008 election the radical leftist McCain got the nomination, because the non left vote was split. So now Republicans don't want to split. They all pile on to whatever non leftist is currently hot.

Expect therefore banner headlines quoting some of the more entertaining bits from the newsletter "Ron Paul and Associates", for example that in the LA Riots order was only restored when it came time for blacks to pick up their welfare checks.

Paul's snark was not literally true, because blacks don't literally have to pick up their welfare checks - they get a cashcard to which welfare payments are automatically credited. But what is true is that every month crime is substantially lower from first of the month to the fifth of the month, when criminals are busy blowing their welfare checks, and the LA riots followed that pattern.

Indeed I think the switch from welfare checks to welfare cashcards was in large part to reduce jokes about the monthly crime drop and the monthly crime rise.

---

[842]https://www.publicpolicypolling.com/main/2011/12/paul-takes-lead-as-gingrich-collapses-in-iowa.html

The word "theocracy"

2011-12-21 08:15:52

A lot of people complain about my use, and Mencius's use, of the word theocracy, to refer both to past systems were God endorsed Caesar, and Caesar endorsed God, and the present system where Political Correctness endorses the state, and the State endorses Political Correctness.

So I am trying to crowdsource some less confusing terminology.

Without the word "theocracy", how does one concisely explain why society moves ever leftwards?

One way around this problem is to use the concept of a ruling clerisy, since the word "clerisy" has in the past been used to refer to what is in common in the exercise of political power by priests and bishops, and the exercise of political power by journalists, academics, and intellectuals.

Trouble is that "clerisy", when used unironically, merely means the class of learned persons, when what we want to refer to is the class of persons learned in the state supported and state supporting belief system. Obviously we want the ironic meaning of clerisy – the class of ignorant brainwashed but officially credentialed holders of officially true opinions, the class of people learned only in political reliability.

So "clerisy" like "theocracy" brings in unwanted meanings.

So could anyone who does not like my use of the word "theocracy" try to come up with an explanation of why the left always wins and the right always loses is, using different words?

We have a winner

2011-12-22 05:32:23

I crowdsourced the task of finding a word[843] to describe the political and social order that is leading us to doom, in a way that explains the fundamental driving forces, explains why the left always wins.

Hwan Lewi:

> How about 'atheocracy'? It should be instantly recognizable as derivative of 'theocracy' and thus retain most of the descriptive and shock value, and it gets around the deism/non-deism issue.

From now on, atheocracy it is. In addition to being clear, it avoids pissing off those reactionaries who favor a genuinely Christian theocracy.

Digressing, I fully agree that that a genuinely Christian theocracy would be a good system. I also think that a theocracy genuinely based on the pagan religion of the early Roman monarchical period would be a good system.

The Roman monarchy worked fine when the King was elected for life by the Senate and the people of Rome, and endorsed by the Gods. When the Gods started to bend to

---

[843]https://blog.reaction.la/economics/the-word-theocracy.html

whatever the prevailing wind was, the monarchy started to become corrupt and decadent. So Kings were removed. Thus began the Roman Republic. Elections were now more much more frequent. This worked fine for a while, but almost immediately the Republic started an ever leftwards drift, which soon became intolerable - so intolerable that the army stopped tolerating it.

The leftward drift was abruptly reversed by Sulla, who implemented a hard reset similar to that advocated by Mencius Moldbug and restored the old Republic. The restored old republic worked fine for a generation, but this failed to fix things permanently, since the reset led to a drift to military dictatorship. One generation later, civil war resumed and dictatorship followed.

Blacks chimp out for Christmas

2011-12-30 07:33:20

La Griffe du Lion finds that though the average criminality of blacks is substantially higher than that of whites, the variance is substantially lower[844]. This predicts that under a firm and effective law enforcement environment, in which only the most criminally inclined misbehaved, a black majority area would be safer than a white majority area. However in a lax environment, in modern anarcho tyranny where everything has been criminalized, except crime, which has been decriminalized, the difference between blacks and the more evolved types of human[845] is exceptionally visible, and the fact that no one can speak of it exceptionally ludicrous.

Just as affirmative action makes the differences between blacks and whites starkly visible to everyone[846] at the same time as it makes it a criminal offense to notice, or even think about, those differences, law enforcement that primarily targets the honest and productive similarly makes the differences between the honest and productive, and those born to welfare to live on their votes, starkly visible to everyone.

The propensity to commit crime is extremely sensitive to the level of enforcement. A modest tightening of enforcement, such as Singapore with its floggings and swift justice, reduces crime by a factor of a hundred or a thousand. The punishments in Singapore are not hundred times more severe, nor is justice a hundred times swifter, but crime is reduced by more than a hundred fold.

The fact that some societies have no difficult in reducing crime to zero for all practical purposes, reducing it to levels so insignificant as to have eliminated it for all practical purposes, shows that the supply of crime is extremely elastic to the price of crime.

In such an environment, only the most exceptionally criminally inclined are likely to misbehave. La Griffe Du Lion's analysis shows that though the typical black is criminally inclined, and the typical white is not, the exceptionally and extraordinarily criminally inclined individual is typically white, not black. Just as very smart people are overwhelmingly male, due to the greater male variance in IQ, very criminal people are overwhelmingly white. When we see niggers chimping out en masse, they are doing stupid stuff -

---

[844]https://www.lagriffedulion.f2s.com/prison.htm
[845]https://mbe.oxfordjournals.org/content/13/1/170.full.pdf
[846]https://blog.reaction.la/politics/fun-hate-fact-about-the-bell-curve.html

minor assaults. Black flash mobs are seldom deadly. Nothing anyone did in this video would be surprising or disturbing if a single white individual did it. What is surprising and disturbing is a mob doing it. What is disturbing is not the edge of the black bell curve, but the center.

Singapore does not allow us to test this theoretical prediction, because by and large, they just don't let black people in, however the America of the past does allow us to test this prediction, since back then, most crimes would get you immediately hung from a tree. Consistent with this prediction, we read Nehemiah Adams in "A Southside View of Slavery" telling us how peaceable and well behaved negroes are. Similarly, Froude in "The Bow of Ulysses" never pays the slightest attention to whether or not he is in an all black area. Carlyle in "Occasional Discourse on the Nigger Question" remarks on how negroes thrive under white rule and are made into good people, and argues that God and/or Nature makes it the duty of whites to so rule backs for the good of their souls, and if not so ruled, blacks will prey upon each other.

But obviously rule by today's whites does not benefit today's blacks – indeed state policy is to turn everyone, regardless of race, into underclass[847], in order to move the electorate left. If everyone, regardless of race, are pimps, whores, and thieves, they will reliably vote for the sort of politics that the good and the great know they should vote for.

The solution, therefore, is not separation of whites and blacks, but just, efficient, and swift law enforcement, preferably with offenders hanging by their necks from trees, something that democracy is unlikely to provide us because we have wound up with rule by those who steal the money of the productive to buy themselves the electorate they want. And the electorate that they want is on display in the above video.

Economic effect of leftism

2012-01-04 08:56:44

I found the 2005 and 2010 values for nominal gross state product of US states. I looked up Wikipedia for which states were right to work states. Over the five years, right to work states grew ten percent relative to non right to work states[848] –

That is to say, after five years, the average growth in nominal GDP for a right to work state was 1.231, that is to say, twenty three percent, five percent a year, while the average growth in non right to work states was 1.135, that is to say, thirteen percent, or two and half percent per year – probably negative real growth when inflation is taken into account.

Most left wing policies are federally enforced, rather than state enforced, thus this must massively understate the economic effect of leftism. Chances are that the effect of state plus federal leftism over five years is far higher than ten percent of GDP - which explains our current economic decline: Society has massively moved left, therefore must become correspondingly poorer.

If a state is not "Right to work", this means that a "bargaining unit" can be unionized by vote – so if fifty percent of the people in your "bargaining unit" sign up, and vote in a secret ballot, you find some of your pay is being deducted to support full time political

---

[847]https://blog.reaction.la/culture/rick-perry-and-the-underclassing-of-america.html
[848]https://blog.reaction.la/misc_upl/right to work.ods "Open office spreadsheet"

activists, and you are now on a union health care scheme that provides markedly fewer benefits and markedly higher cost than your old health care scheme.

This sounds bad, but in practice is worse. For the individual, signing or not signing makes no difference to the likelihood that a deduction will be made from his pay, since he is unlikely to be the one that makes a difference between 50% and 49%, but it makes a very large difference to the likelihood that he will have his legs broken. So the rational individual choice is to sign regardless of what the individual thinks of the union. This is not too bad, provided a secret ballot is required, but a secret ballot is not always required. Sometimes you get a union imposed on the basis of card check alone, that is to say, on the basis of broken legs, depending primarily on how cozy the union is with the government, as compared to how cozy the employer is. Federal legislation requires a secret ballot, but of course, the federal government is not required to obey its own laws, and frequently does not.

In a right to work state, however, you only get dues deducted from yourself individually if you yourself individually sign up, with the result that the dues tend to be lower, and the union health scheme does not suck so much, and, of course, the rational individual choice is *not* to sign up regardless of what the individual thinks of the union, making leg breaking correspondingly more hazardous.

In practice, right to work states do not have markedly fewer strikes and labor disputes. They do, however, have markedly fewer full time left political activists.

Ron Paul, only non leftist left standing

2012-01-04 10:24:11

The three major candidates are Governor Romneycare, the man who provided the model for Obamacare, Ron Paul, and Rick Santorum.

Rick Santorum's nephew tells us[849]:

> When Republicans were spending so much money under President Bush, my uncle was right there along with them

Rick Santorum's claim to fiscal conservatism is that he supported Clinton on welfare reform. Unfortunately he also supported Bush on pissing away mortgage money on deadbeat borrowers. Paul is the only one in the race who opposed the financial crisis before it happened.

Paul is the only Not Romney that survived under fire. We shall see how Rick Santorum does when he comes under fire. He is already being monstered as Bush the third. If Rick Santorum goes down under fire, then Ron Paul will be the only Not Romney remaining.

---

[849]https://dailycaller.com/2012/01/03/the-trouble-with-my-uncle-rick-santorum/

Economic Decline

2012-01-11 20:05:00

The BLS is arguably understating inflation and unemployment. According to Shadow-stats[850], the real rate of inflation is more than two percent higher than reported, and the real rate of GDP decline more than than two percent a year worse than reported.

There really is no such thing as the real rate of inflation. To estimate inflation, you need to compare apples with oranges, which requires a judgment call. Increasingly, the BLS has been making judgment calls in the direction that will flatter its masters – which does not, however, prove those judgment calls are false.

The amount of computing power that an hour's work will buy has gone up an astonishing amount, and continues to rise rapidly. Televisions are cheaper by this metric and considerably better. Unfortunately the amount of food, housing, healthcare, energy and education that an hour's work will buy has fallen, and continues to fall.

It has been falling for a long time, at first slowly, and now, faster and faster.

Once again, I repeat, the last man left the moon in 1972, the tallest buildings in the US were completed in 1972, and the coolest cars built in 1972.

If you cannot afford to feed, house, and educate your children, if driving to work gets a bigger problem every day and you cannot casually go and see your relatives, the falling cost and improved quality of smartphones is small consolation.

If we go by Shadowstats value judgments, then we see that GDP has been falling, the US has been in economic decline ever since Bush the elder replaced Ronald Reagan.

Shadowstats figures, like the government's figures, show a boom from 2001 to 2005 November, but everyone now knows this boom was fake. Manifestly, whether the Austrian theory of booms and busts is true in general, it has been true of recent events. People invested in housing, bankers supposedly created value through borrowing and lending, real estate agents supposedly created value by getting people in houses, and builders created value by building and improving houses. but obviously the builders were creating considerably less value than was believed, and the bankers and real estate agents were subtracting rather than creating value.

The boom was what the Austrian economic school calls malinvestment. People invest in the wrong things, so prices are wrong, so people do the wrong things, subtracting value, but getting paid as if they are creating value. Then, subsequently there is correction, which correction unavoidably makes people feel bad. Printing money to make people feel good just makes things worse.

People thought that housing would have more value than it did, because they thought that genetically low IQ Mexican immigrants were going to be magically affirmative actioned into successfully performing the middle class lifestyle, that in the near future they would have nice houses in suburbia, and in the near future they would be able to pay for nice houses in suburbia, so there would be the need for a lot more nice houses in suburbia, and a payment stream making those houses valuable.

This fantasy fell apart, though no one can speak about it, and mentioning it, even on supposedly right wing and libertarian blogs, is apt to result in being called a white

---

[850]https://www.shadowstats.com/alternate_data

nationalist, a hateful racist, and getting banned from that blog.

If we adjust for the fake boom and subsequent correction, we see not an abrupt decline starting in 2009, but rather a long arch, with growth slowing in the 1970s, the economy peaking soon after Reagan, and decline slowly and steadily accelerating since then.

So what is causing the decline?

If we look at the areas where we are declining, and where we are not, the answer is pretty obvious: Computers are pretty much unregulated. Every piece of software and hardware comes with a de riguer disclaimer that it is not promised to do anything useful, and may well do you great harm, and if so, not the manufacturers fault. Strangely, government, courts, and regulators have let them get away with it, probably because they are not quite sure what computers are or what they do.

Housing, health, energy, food, finance, and education, on the other hand, are massively regulated, and are largely managed by government or quasi government institutions.

Government is simply failing economically, and is taking with it major and vital parts of the economy.

The cure is going to be illegal health care[851], illegal finance, illegal food, and illegal housing, all of which is apt to create a demand for the illegal provision of defense and contract enforcement services, assuming we don't get conquered by hostile outsiders in the process, or, like the Roman Republic, switch to military despotism, a despotism that might, with painful slowness, eventually become monarchy.

In its death throes, government is taking over and destroying every part of the economy, and will probably reach computing soon enough. I have often mentioned Sarbannes Oxley as the height of far left madness, for it makes the foundation of the modern corporation, accounting, pretty much illegal, leaving investors in the dark. Sarbanes-Oxley accounts don't mean much[852].

Lately the government has been directly intervening into the management of companies, with cataclysmic results.

All these interventions have the effect that investment, instead of being directed at making money, is instead directed to political goals – spent on the underclass, and on professional left wing activists.

Sarbanes–Oxley theoretically dictated how accounting should be done, so that people could not cook their books. But no one knows how to comply with Sarbanes–Oxley, or what compliance with Sarbanes–Oxley would constitute, so they just hire someone sufficiently influential that whatever he does is likely to be deemed compliance with Sarbanes–Oxley.

Which means that no one knows what, if anything, the accounts mean. Observe that in the recent financial failures, everyone was working in the dark. The accounts failed to provide any sign that the money was running out until the checks started bouncing and people discovered that everything was gone.

Now on top of Sarbanes–Oxley, we have the Dodd–Frank Wall Street Reform and

---

[851] https://www.smartplanet.com/blog/rethinking-healthcare/yankees-pitchers-stem-cell-therapy-didnt-endow-superhuman-powers/5074

[852] https://blog.reaction.la/economics/sarbanes-oxley/

Consumer Protection Act, which turns all major financial institutions into quasi government enterprises, like Fannie and Freddy.

Such enterprises have no incentive to perform, and are above the law, making it likely they will act criminally.

This is already happening: A major part of Dodd–Frank was regulating derivatives. The big derivatives that scare people are bets on credit events, where a financier promises to pay if someone does not pay his debts. So if you lend to Greece, and are worried that Greece will not pay its debts, you buy a bet from a bank that Greece will pay its debts. If Greece stiffs you, the bank will pay you.

Before Dodd-Frank, when such bets were unregulated, those who lost the bet always paid up, or themselves went broke. Recent Greece failed to make payments on its government debt, and lo and behold, those who were stiffed by Greece, were stiffed a second time by Goldman Sachs which had made big bets that Greece would pay its debts, but now that finance is regulated by the wise and the benevolent, they wisely and benevolently deemed that the bet would not be paid.

Thus the practical effect of Sarbanes–Oxley is cargo cult accounting, and to criminalize real accounting, and the way the wind is blowing, the practical effect of Dodd–Frank will be cargo cult finance, and to criminalize real finance. The true nature of Sarbanes–Oxley is shown by MF Global, and the true nature of Dodd–Frank is shown by derivatives of Greek debt.

Anyone who offers investments through United States brokers has to comply with Sarbanes–Oxley, which means that US citizens are forbidden world wide to invest in anything with real accounting. You can bypass this, but it is not trivial. If you go with the flow, you wind up investing on the basis of Sarbanes–Oxley numbers.

Supposedly Sarbanes–Oxley has produced "better earnings quality" – but one would not expect Sarbanes–Oxley to produce better earnings, that not being the purpose of Sarbanes–Oxley. It is more likely that Sarbanes–Oxley has produced reported better earnings. The purpose of Sarbanes–Oxley was to produce truth, and it has not produced truth. On the contrary, whereas Enron's accounts, read carefully, revealed that Enron had been losing money for some time, and was broke, nothing in MF Global's accounts revealed that.

Enron went under because people stopped selling it stuff on credit, and stopped paying for stuff in advance. People were depositing money and gold in MF Global right up the last minute.

Enron went under because the truth in its accounts meant it could no longer suck in other people's money. MF Global went under because it was losing more money than it could suck in. Accounting did not fail for Enron. It failed for MF Global. Enron failed because people got wind it was in trouble. No one got wind that MF Global was in trouble.

Mitt Romneycare, enemy of capitalism

2012-01-12 13:26:51

Mitt Romneycare tells us:

In the general election I'll be pointing out that the president took the reins at General Motors and Chrysler – closed factories, closed dealerships laid off thousands and thousands of workers – he did it to try to save the business.

Now that is an unusual strategy for winning elections.

This shows us why a Republican Party socialist can never beat a Democratic Party socialist in an election. If you are going to oppose a Democratic Party socialist, have to oppose socialism.

This is politics 101. If you tell the voters that your opponent's policies are so wonderful that you will be just the same, only better, they are not going to be impressed.

Whatever it is that is most characteristic, distinctive, and controversial about your incumbent opponent, you have to say that that prominent and controversial characteristic stinks mightily. You have to say that your opponent is no damn good because his most prominent and distinctive controversial characteristic is no damn good, that Obama's socialism is destroying this country. Instead, Governor Romneycare sounds like the conspicuously fake opposition that communist parties would sometimes run against themselves, which fake opponents would not only lose by 0.1% to 99.9% but would quite genuinely lose by almost as much.

Paraphrasing: Oh, no I am not a greedy selfish capitalist, I am almost as kindly and benevolent as the great Obamessiah himself. I save jobs just like the benevolent Obamessiah does.

The right answer, of course, would have been that Bain Capital took care of the destruction side of capitalism's creative destruction, that for well run firms like Apple to exist, badly run firms have to be shut down and their assets sold to the highest bidder – which story would sound a whole lot better coming from someone responsible for the creative side of capitalism's creative destruction.

If a presidential candidate cannot say that Obama's socialism is ruining lives and destroying jobs, that candidate is not going to win against Obama.

Burning the past

2012-01-14 20:42:19

We are in the greatest era of book burning ever[853]. Libraries systematically destroy their older books, without allowing staff to go through the books and sort out the valuable ones, the ones that would bring enormous prices on Amazon.com.

This destruction allows a new past to be written, a demonized and hate filled past.

Now one might suppose that this destruction is unintentional, a mere result of perverse incentives, though what is the incentive that compels people to destroy books that would bring high prices on Amazon? But that Google gives limited access to our past, and that books are becoming lefter and lefter makes this destruction suspicious. For example the disturbingly politically incorrect Hakayit Abdullah by Munshi Abdullah is available on google only in snippet view. Why only snippet view? The translation was published

---

[853]https://www.cracked.com/article_19453_6-reasons-were-in-another-book-burning-period-in-history.html

in 1874, which makes it well and truly out of copyright everywhere in the world. Google only gives full access to a tiny handful of past texts. One can get around this by looking up texts on google book search, then downloading them from the internet archive[854]. Accessing our past is not criminalized, nor even particularly difficult, but it is systematically discouraged.

This restriction is not obviously politically selective. It is more of a wholesale restriction on the past. Both "Froudacity", the left wing, politically correct view on decolonization by a black man affirmative actioned to prominence, and "The Bow of Ulysses", a eulogy and funeral speech for colonialism that looked back to the good old days when colonialists were free to be pirates and brigands, are available only in preview, though of course, one can get them from the Internet Archive.

The author of "Froudacity" is also the originator of what we now call Ebonics - the idea that black speech is not inferior, not less capable of communicating ideas and instructions, but merely different– a proposal that merely has to be stated for its absurdity to be apparent, and merely has to be contradicted to create the most astonishing outrage, for to contradict it implies that blacks are, on average, not merely less literate but less verbal, less capable of human speech, and therefore, on average, significantly less human, speech being the defining human characteristic.

"The Bow of Ulysses", on the other hand, endorses the old colonialism, nostalgically recalling the days when Britain was not an empire, but rather British colonialists were pirates and brigands, who robbed, conquered and eventually ruled, gradually making the transition from mobile banditry to stationary banditry without the British government paying much attention. In "The Bow of Ulysses" Froude condemns nineteenth century imperialism as unworkably left wing, and inevitably leading to the destruction of the British empire, and thus the ruin of the subjects of the British empire, all of which ensued as he envisaged, while the author of "Froudacity" endorsed imperialism.

(Since I posted this, people have reported to me that they can access "The Bow of Ulysses" through Google, but I cannot, even when using Tor, or using a Singaporean proxy)

If we read "Froudacity" and "the Bow of Ulysses", we discover the remarkable and surprising fact that the imperialists, the ones that upgraded Queen Victoria from Queen to empress, were the same bunch as those then and now preaching ebonics. The imperialists, those advocating British Empire, were the left, and the colonialists were the right. And the colonialists correctly predicted that if this were to go on, we would get the left that we now have– one of the many strange facts one encounters if one reads old books. Reading the works of and about Garnet Wolsely we find that when the British subjugated the Boers, this was the left conquering the right, with a view to eventually producing today's black ruled South Africa, which the right predicted would be the way that it is in fact turning out to be.

The Google suppression of the past is not in itself directly politically biased, old left texts are not obviously privileged above old right texts, but it is politically biased in that the texts of the past are all non left by modern standards, and tend to discredit the politically correct version of history, so if you suppress old books on the basis of age without regard

---

[854]https://www.archive.org/details/translationsfrom00abdu

to their political content, you are suppressing the non left, since old books are mostly non left, and new books are mostly left.

Kim Standley Robinson, moves from far left in 1992 to frothing at the mouth insane left in 1997:

In his 1992 fiction book "Red Mars", regrettably over-idealistic environmentalists harm people who are trying to develop and settle Mars, harm people who are trying to make it habitable to humans.

In his 1997 fiction book, "Antarctica", evil developers seeking to develop and settle Antarctica harm idealistic environmentalists

In "Lucifer's Hammer", written in 1978 by Niven and Pournelle, civilization collapses, there is famine, and people start eating people The cannibals are not especially black, even though realistically, it is likely that the cannibals would be disproportionately black. The only guy who suggest that there might be a correlation between cannibalism and blackness is the horribly prejudiced ignorant hick.

In Lucifer's hammer the authors are careful to make the proportion of blacks among the cannibal army exactly and precisely the same proportion as blacks are a percentage of the US population, nonetheless today the book is deemed utterly outrageous and horribly reactionary for having any black cannibals whatsoever. Observe that in today's collapse of civilization books, all cannibals are white.

"Clone High" 2002-2003 is a cartoon series. It ridicules political correctness. In episode 11, "Snowflake Day; A very special holiday" Christmas has been banned, replaced by a silly made up festival "Snowflake day". Snowflake Day is celebrated in large part by telling everyone how hate filled and exclusionary Christmas was - which of course reveals that Snowflake day, not Christmas, is hate filled and exclusionary, reveals the intolerance of "tolerance". Again, I don't see any recent mainstream works making such criticism.

All the clones in Clone High have foster parents instead of real parents. Clone JFK has two daddies, which family, consisting of a teenage heterosexual boy, and two male homosexuals, is presented as vile, disgusting, ugly, perverse, unnatural, and disturbing, ridiculing the political correctness of "Heather has two mommies". His two daddies display stereotypical gay behavior, which stereotypes these days would be deemed hateful and hurtful.

Kage Baker's company series, for example "The Life of the World To Come", supposes that over the next three hundred years, political correctness will become ever more severe and oppressive - the background is "If this goes on". In 2004 it was possible for novelists to condemn political correctness as oppressive and still get published by mainstream publishers. No longer.

The science fiction writer John Ringo is pretty far right, as is obvious in his earlier books. In "The Last Centurion" published in 2008 by a mainstream publisher, a military coup saves the US from the excesses of democracy. Like Sulla, though with considerably less bloodshed, the military officers then restore the old republic and resign. The book optimistically promises that this restoration, unlike Sulla's, will last. Could he publish that today? Let us look at what he is publishing today:

In "Live Free or Die", published 2010, he tries very hard to contain his right wing slant, and play straight down the middle with obligatory bows to political correctness, piously endorsing the official line with amusingly transparent insincerity. Unfortunately, he committed the unpardonable sin of a few lines about stereotypical blondes.

So, alas, the sequel ("Citadel", published 2011) has to have as its main character a counter stereotypical blonde female. In the sequel, the rhetoric about freedom mysteriously mutates into anticolonialist, or decolonist, rhetoric, perhaps because merely having a counter stereotypical blonde as main character is insufficient penance for making a joke about blondes.

Writers are steadily moving left – each writer as time passes by produces works that are far the left of his previous works, reflecting what is politically acceptable at that time. The early Keith Laumer ridiculed democracy. The later Keith Laumer did not. In "The Governor of Glave", published 1963, he seems to take it for granted that everyone knows that democracy is a corrupt system run by people who are foolish, ignorant and evil. The planet Glave is what we would now call a terraformed planet. Earthlike conditions are maintained by some big high technology superscience machinery. The elite rules over their inferiors, but are getting tired of providing their inferiors with bread, circuses, and earthlike conditions. Most of the elite has left for a frontier world less infested with inferior welfare parasites. There is a democratic coup against the remaining elite. Finding democracy even less attractive, most of the remaining elite attempt to leave and/or go on Galt strike. The evil democrats refuse to let them leave, and force them to work under armed guard.

The heroic Retief arranges for their escape. As they escape, we see terraforming collapsing and the planet starting to revert to its natural inhospitable condition.

Similarly, in Keith Laumer's "The prince and pirate" 1964, the Prime minister and his party are vile treacherous cowardly scum. The prince is kingly and the pirate is bold and martial. Retief makes a deal between the prince and the pirate, which results in the prime minister being killed, something unpleasant happening to his party, and the prince becoming an absolute monarch.

The nearest thing to an anti democratic novel in recent times is "The Last Centurion", where the military restrain the excesses of democracy – but they then, like Sulla, leave politics so that democracy can continue, whereas the prince in "The prince and pirate" permanently ends democratic politics by killing quite a lot of politicians. We just don't see novels that unashamedly support technocracy, monarchy, or aristocracy any more.

"The Last Centurion" is far to the left of "The prince and the Pirate", "Live Free or Die" far to the left of "The Last Centurion", and "Citadel" far to the left of "Live Free or Die". I am pretty sure that anything written by John Ringo is as right wing as anything a major author dare publish, and what he publishes indicates that the rightmost thing that a major author can publish gets further left every year.

The latest evil from Google

2012-01-18 09:50:09

Google has recently been nailed in two more scandals: cold calling ignorant Kenyans with a scam offer and scary lies about Google's competitor[855], and vandalizing open source maps[856] which competes with Google Maps.

While Google is wonderfully politically correct, and would never dream of suggesting that black people are stupid, the scam service they are selling in Kenya is predicated on the assumption that black people are stupid.

Mocality is a Kenyan business whose main asset is a database of Kenyan businesses, and a web service for looking up those businesses. It creates, for every Kenyan business it can find, a short web page, directly competing with Google advertising. Kenyans look up Mocality when they want to find a business, rather than googling.

Google call centers would look up businesses listed by Mocality, cold call them, and try to telemarket them Google's hosting service.

Very few Kenyan businesses have the skills to create a web page, nor any compelling reason to acquire such skills when Mocality creates a web page free of charge for every Kenyan business, so they had no use for the hosting service that Google was selling.

So, part of the Google telemarketer script was that Mocality was supposedly going to charge businesses some extravagant fee for their listing, and that is why Kenyan businesses supposedly needed their own host and their own web page.

Inflationary crisis?

2012-01-19 07:16:14

According to the US census, estimated monthly sales have gone up ten percent in dollars between 2010 November and 2011 November[857]. Have living standards gone up? Clearly living standards are falling. Total physical volume of goods shipped by rail has been falling over the past year,[858] consistent with the general experience of falling living standards. Can anyone explain what is going on? This looks to me like slightly worse than ten percent year on year inflation, which is the inflation rate at which a significant risk of panicked flight from paper money sets in. Am I misreading these numbers in some silly way?

There is a lot of ruin in a nation. I have been predicting that we will probably not see hyperinflationary collapse for several years. I find this data surprising and confusing. Either we are booming, or we are inflating, and it does not feel like we are booming.

---

[855]https://blog.mocality.co.ke/2012/01/13/google-what-were-you-thinking/
[856]https://opengeodata.org/google-ip-vandalizing-openstreetmap
[857]https://www.census.gov/mtis/www/data/pdf/mtis_current.pdf "hyperinflation"
[858]https://www.businessinsider.com/wow-total-collapse-in-rail-traffic-to-start-the-year-2012-1

Not the cognitive elite

2012-01-25 06:56:26

According to Murray, in the bad old days of elitism, the university was full of good old boys, rather than the smartest, but now, our elite are a bunch of really smart guys.

Leading climate scientist Michael Mann and Nobel Prize winning economist Paul Krugman are really smart guys? The guys who write the New York Times are really smart?

A university selects for diligence, intelligence, ability to follow orders, and willingness to follow orders, thus a degree signals these things to employers, and a high degree from an elite university signals more of these things to employers. It also, however, selects for political correctness, or the well simulated appearance of political correctness, and as the left has become ever lefter, political correctness has increasingly become a signal of stupidity, real or pretended.

Who is the most influential scientist?

Michael Mann, a Yale PhD, who does not have enough brains to know when he is telling lies with statistics, and who has his students and employees perform any task that is intellectually demanding.

Once upon a time, the left position was arguably clever and sophisticated. By and by, it became more a collection of elaborate and extremely clever rationalizations for propositions that were quite stupid. Galbraith, Gould, and Chomsky were great rationalizers for obviously stupid propositions. Quote any of Chomsky's conclusions without the very clever lead up, he sounds like a monkey flinging $#!%. But there was a very clever lead up.

However, as leftism has become increasingly stupid, barefaced assertion has replaced clever rationalization. This transition is visible in the career of Paul Krugman, his Nobel prize winning work being clever rationalizations for politically desired stupid conclusions, his recent work being mere proclamations of holy dogma.

Observe the response by the KOS tribe to some guy making the point that Muslims have all the characteristics that the left attribute to Christians: It is a troop of monkeys flinging their $#!%[859] from the trees.

OK, that troop of monkeys is merely the rank and file leftists, not necessarily Harvard PhDs, (though chances are that quite a lot of them are Harvard PhDs, with advanced degrees in education and victim studies). Surely the leadership is, however, a lot smarter?

Well yes, the leadership is smarter, but that does not actually make them smart. Here is one of the top monkeys flinging his $#!%[860] from his tree.

This is the cognitive elite?

---

[859]https://www.dailykos.com/story/2012/01/21/1056966/-Do-You-Support-Human-Rights-This-this-Simple-Quiz#comments

[860]https://www.newyorker.com/humor/2011/11/28/111128sh_shouts_kenney

Ben Bernanke pledges to throw gasoline on the fire

2012-01-26 17:43:20

Bernanke pledges to keep interest rates low for at least the next two years[861] – meaning real interest are several percent negative. Large negative interest rates rapidly lead to economic crisis.

"The low level of inflation is a validation," Bernanke said. "There are some who were very concerned that our balance-sheet policies and the like would lead to high inflation. There's certainly no sign of that yet."

Really? Sales have gone up ten percent in nominal value, which only makes sense if the real rate of inflation is seven to ten percent[862]. The US economy is on fire, and Bernanke pledges to continue throwing gasoline on the flames.

Why the madness? Well, reading human souls is a chancy business, but here is my reading:

For political reasons the left, aka the United States Government, aka the guys who cannot be fired or lose their jobs no matter how badly they screw up, has been hurling great gobs of money at political insiders, such as favored bankers and financiers, and also great gobs of money at favored voting blocks, in particular Mexicans.

Therefore, everyone has to believe that these policies are not a matter of throwing America over the cliff for short term political and financial gain, even though the US economy appears to be falling off a cliff, but rather are sound and principled actions dictated by sound economic reasoning, and the reasoning is, um, ah, err, uh – Oh yes. Vitally needed Keynesian stimulus!

And if Keynesian stimulus is vitally needed, then we must be suffering serious deflation.

So everyone who knows how to get ahead convinces himself that we are suffering serious deflation, or at least that inflation is a very minor problem. And of course these guys don't do any shopping, and they don't know anyone who does their own shopping, so there is no inconvenient risk of reality butting its head in where it is not wanted. The Bureau of labor statistics notes that computers are greatly improving in value, televisions are significantly improving in value, and blithely closes its eyes to the fact that everything you need to live is getting more expensive.

And now, something even chancier than reading human souls: Reading the future: I think we are nine to eighteen months from an "Oh $#!%" moment when everyone except the ruling elite recognizes that the US economy is in total meltdown, and about three years to five years or so for the ruling elite to catch on.

There is a lot of ruin in a nation, and I still predict ruin around 2020-2025 or so, but this disturbing statement by Bernanke, and everyone's calm acceptance that it is perfectly reasonable, and that there is nothing even faintly suggestive of madness and evil about it, leads me to predict interesting times arriving sooner than that.

A lot of people think that the ruling elite is cynically aware of what it is doing, but

---

[861] https://www.washingtonpost.com/business/bernankes-own-words-on-interest-rates-asset-purchases/2012/01/25/gIQAD2lERQ_video.html

[862] https://blog.reaction.la/economics/inflationary-crisis.html "hyperinflation"

seems to me that everyone knew of the mortgage meltdown in 2005 November, whereas Goldman and Sach did not start unloading their mortgage exposure onto their customers until 2007. In the mortgage crisis, the elite from Harvard were the last to know. That is why they needed to be bailed out.

Similarly, when the Soviet Union was falling, after 1985 lots of people knew the fall was imminent, yet the left, aka the government, was still in denial well after it had fallen.

We are not ruled by an elite selected for intelligence, but rather for the ability to believe six impossible things before breakfast.

Why Bernanke is not panicking

2012-01-29 04:38:03

The stimulus is finally taking effect. As Zimbabwe and the Wiemar Republic demonstrate, one thing that governments armed with the ability to print fiat money really can do is stimulate.

From 2009 May[863] to 2011 November[864] total business sales in dollars rose twenty six percent, ten percent a year, which to me, though not to Bernanke, looks like good reason to scream panic and hit the brakes, to raise real interest rates to at least normal levels, and arguably higher.

The reason Bernanke is not panicking is that from 2008 July[865] to 2009 May[866], total sales fell by the same amount, so, Bernanke presumably figures, we are just getting back to normal, and indeed still have not gotten to back to anything like the old normal, because these are inflated dollars. Continue at this rate for a a year and a bit, then we will be back to the old normal, in terms of real value of goods sold,

So he proposes to continue at this rate for another year and a bit, to early 2014.

Which makes perfect sense if you think the US economy is still as capable of producing wealth as ever it was.

I don't think we can get back to the old normal without fundamental political change, and by fundamental change, I don't mean any of the current crowd of Obama look alikes that the Republican party is offering.

In a year and a bit, early 2014, it will become apparent whether I was right orBernanke was right.

Manufactured spectacle at Oakland

2012-01-31 02:35:27

The police toss smoke grenades, not tear gas grenades, a short distance upwind, between themselves and the protestors.

This is not riot control, it is a manufactured photo opportunity

[863]https://www.census.gov/mtis/www/data/text/mtis0905.txt
[864]https://www.census.gov/mtis/www/data/text/mtis1111.txt
[865]https://www.census.gov/mtis/www/data/text/mtis0807.txt
[866]https://www.census.gov/mtis/www/data/text/mtis0905.txt

Observe the hand motion. He is tossing a smoke grenade just in front, not at the protestors. If you are wondering how heavily outnumbered protestors accomplished their goal of occupying the city hall, despite announcing it at least a day in advance, the above photo explains the inexplicable.

And here are the protestors are in occupation, burning the vandalized and stolen city hall flag. Although the photo does not show it, police are watching a short distance away.

caption id=" " align="aligncenter" width="450"

*Another photo opportunity while police watch"[stolen flag burning][867][/caption]

There were amply sufficient police watching to have seriously cramped their style, and yet, they did not. First the photo opportunity, *then* the police intervene. When the police finally intervene, the protestors yield without any resistance or fuss, revealing police complicity in this photo opp.

This post placed in the economics category, as well as the politics, being an example of your tax dollars at work, the government funding agitation for more government funding.

Steyn nails it:

2012-02-03 03:41:18

Our Sick State:

> I don't quite know what you'd call these rituals, but the term "private health-care system" doesn't seem the most obvious fit. Indeed, as in so many other areas of American life — the Fannie-Freddied mortgage market, the six-figure college education — the main purpose of these dysfunctional labyrinths

---

[867] latex/images/flagburn.jpg "stolen flag burning*

ever more disconnected from any genuinely free market seems to be to discredit the very concept of a "private" system and thus soften up the electorate for statist fixes.

...

In free, functioning societies, it ought to be easy to buy a bottle of pills. The fact that it isn't is one reason why America has a real bad headache.

...

if you price your time, even if you price it at kind of minimum wage, the amount of time it takes, this is my problem, that everywhere you look now, you're seeing a remorseless transfer of time, and time is money, of time and money from the productive class to the kind of bureaucratic sclerosis class.

In a previous post of mine, I observe that the US health care system is socialism without a central plan, and capitalism without markets or prices[868]. Obama is not socializing it. He is making it more socialist than it was.

Inflation

2012-02-03 17:03:46

Total sales are rising ten percent a year in nominal terms[869]. Surprise surprise, shadowstats estimates ten percent inflation per year[870] if we use the measure of inflation that was used in the the 1980s. Hawaiian Libertarian[871] reports that that is pretty much what he is seeing when he puts his money down.

So what is the true rate of inflation?

There is no one true rate of inflation, since to estimate inflation, one has to compare apples and oranges, and there is no one valid way of doing this.

But if inflation is substantially less than ten percent a year, we are consuming substantially more goods this year than last year. Do you think we are consuming substantially more goods this year than last year?

But whatever the true rate of inflation might be, it is increasing. It is not increasing fast as I expected, not increasing very fast at all. It is increasing at about two percent a year, so if this year inflation was not ten percent, but eight percent, next year it will be ten percent a year, and the year after that, twelve percent a year. The rate at which prices increase, is itself increasing.

This does not sound all that terrifying, but recall that hyperinflation begins as the collapse of a paper bubble. Everyone wakes up one morning realizing that inflation is a lot higher than they thought and will only get worse, so they all try to unload their paper at the same time for tangibles: Land in productive use, gold, ammo, guns, non perishable

[868] https://blog.reaction.la/economics/how-to-do-health-care-right.html

[869] https://blog.reaction.la/economics/why-bernanke-is-not-panicking.html

[870] https://www.shadowstats.com/alternate_data/inflation-charts

[871] https://hawaiianlibertarian.blogspot.com.au/2012/02/inflation-escalation.html

food items, alcohol, and suchlike, also overseas non tangible assets, paper assets regulated by solvent governments.

Only to discover that they cannot all unload their paper money at the same time.

If the rate of inflation is high and increasing, sooner or later, it suddenly starts to increase a lot faster. Suppose inflation this year was seven percent, then next year it will nine percent, which is not imminent doom. If people are not panicking today, they are unlikely to panic tomorrow. The end is not nigh. But the end, nonetheless, is in sight.

The virtuous upper class?

2012-02-10 12:56:25

According to Charles Murray in the top 20 percent of citizens in income and education exemplify the core founding of industriousness, honesty, marriage, and religious observance. They raise their children in stable homes.

This is not my observation. My observation is that the the higher the socioeconomic status of the male, the better his behavior, but the higher the socioeconomic status of the female, the worse her behavior.

I could shoot down Pinker with readily available statistical data, which shows that moderns have become much more violent, that there is a broad trend to greatly increasing levels of violence. I have no data with which to shoot down Murray, just impressions and a gut feeling.

I cannot provide any statistics for sex and social status, the way I could for violence and modernity, just anecdotes and impressions. I hope that some of my readers can point me to some data that would differentiate between a woman with a degree in basket weaving and women's studies married to a high socioeconomic status male (and thus, I think, a stable marriage), and a woman with actual high socioeconomic status, as in the ability to actually hold a well paid job, for example a lawyer who actually shows up in court to argue law (and thus, I think, a violently unstable marriage, in the unlikely event she gets married at all)

We need to distinguish between a woman at university doing marriage 101, who is at university largely because that is where the guys with good prospects are to be found, who is likely once married to stay married, and woman at university who successfully prepares for a high status high income career (unlikely to marry or stay married)

My impression is that if the upper class on the whole are raising their own children, it is because upper class males are raising their children, and upper class females are aborting their bastard spawn.

What I see is that high socioeconomic status *males* have stable marriages and get to raise their own children, because they can compete with Uncle Sam the Pimp. Marriage leads to industriousness and religious observance, and industriousness leads to high socioeconomic status. Low socioeconomic status males have low marriage rates and high divorce rates and are not permitted to raise their own children, because they cannot compete with Uncle Sam the Pimp in money or status.

High socioeconomic status females do not have bastard children, because the child support provided by Uncle Sam the Pimp is less attractive for them than for low socioeconomic status females, and because high socioeconomic status females are smart enough to figure that males under child support orders are apt to simply give up trying and go broke, smart enough to figure that you are unlikely to have a high socioeconomic status lifestyle on child support. Instead high socioeconomic status females abort their numerous bastard spawn.

My observation of female lawyers (and by "lawyer" I do not mean a barista with a hundred thousand dollar debt to a law school, but a woman who actually practices law and gets serious money for doing so) is that their sex lives are pretty similar to stripper's sex lives. A stripper collects money five dollars at at time from drunk guys in bars, and gives most of it away to an ever changing parade of unsuccessful musicians, pimps, and small time thugs. A female lawyer collects money five hundred or five thousand dollars at a time from clients in business suits, and gives most of it away to an ever changing parade of guys practicing extreme sports, unsuccessful musicians, and thugs. The major difference is that the lawyer can afford to go to more expensive locations than the stripper to put out, locations where she gets screwed by ski bums and surfer dudes while the stripper gets screwed by whiskey bums, and that the lawyer will more reliably abort her bastard spawn than the stripper. When the stripper and the lawyer hit a certain age in their thirties when promiscuity becomes repulsive rather than intriguing, they both gradually transition to cat ladies in their forties, after a few sex tours during the transition to resorts notorious for the gigolos.

My impression is that if you want an easy lay, tropical beaches and the Mount Everest base camp work way better than a bar, though the lawyer chicks at Mount Everest base camp get no higher than the base camp. The girls having casual sex on the sand dunes with numerous wildly unsuitable males are all high socioeconomic status, even the backpackers, though as the women get older, they are more apt to be doing it with the barkeeper than a fellow tourist, and are less likely to be backpacking.

The barista with a hundred thousand dollars in law school debt will stay married should she manage to marry a high socioeconomic status male. The barrister will not marry him, and if she does marry him, will likely divorce him. Though I have no statistics to prove this.

Murray refuted

2012-02-13 11:14:50

I found Murray's major theses in Coming Apart: The State of White America, 1960-2010[872], hard to believe, in particular, that the elite is sexually well behaved.

Everyone knows that high socioeconomic status males have high rates of marriage, low rates of divorce, and look after their kids, but that high socioeconomic status career women are worse than truck bar strippers, at least at the very top, such as high priced female lawyers: they have low rates of marriage, if married have high rates of adultery and high rates of divorce, seldom have children, frequently fail to look after their children, if divorced with children invariably demand custody but are then apt to ditch the kids as

---

[872]https://www.amazon.com/gp/product/0307453421/ref=as_li_tf_tl?ie=UTF8&tag=jimsblo0e-20&linkCode=as2&camp=1789&creative=9325&creativeASIN=0307453421

inconvenient. When young they have a rapidly changing parade of males who tend to be thugs, unsuccessful musicians, ski bums, and similar shiftless lowlifes, to whom they are apt to give large amounts of money, a financial relationship that more resembles being a complete idiot than hiring gigolos (or at least I hope it does). When they reach the age when promiscuity ceases to be intriguing and becomes disgusting they are apt to become cat ladies. (However women who pursue careers in traditionally female areas do not tend to be bad, apart from high status women who work in Human Resources who tend to be bad despite it being a traditionally female area)

But, according to Murray, what everyone knows is not so. Supposedly, it is a myth.

However Murray then piously follows the pretense that there are no significant differences between men and women, and offers us, not statistics for high socioeconomic status career women, but for high socioeconomic status *people*.

According to Murray, the myth is not about high socioeconomic status career women, but about high socioeconomic status *people*. Heaven forbid that there might be anyone anywhere who might think that men and women are very different.

As usual, statistics that might potentially be politically incorrect, statistics that might reflect adversely on favored groups, are hard to find but Euro had some:

Euro quotes from chapter 14[873] of The Garbage Generation[874], available in full[875] on the internet

> Vassar economist Shirley Johnson calculated that every \$1,000 increase in a wife's earnings increases her chance for divorce by 2 percent....These working women, who earn \$20,000-plus, are the most likely of all women to be separated or divorced."
>
> ...
>
> According to this study, the odds that an executive woman will never marry are four times greater than for the average American woman. Only 5 percent of most women age thirty and up have never wed (the 1985 Census), whereas 21 percent of our executive women have never been brides."
>
> "Even if our women do marry, the probability of their divorcing is twice as great as the norm. Thirty percent are currently divorced, and another 10 percent are on second or third marriages. Forty percent of all our women have therefore been divorced–compared with just 20 percent of most women in their same age range."
>
> "The differences between our women and their male peers are even more striking. Less than half (48 percent) of our women are currently married– compared with a whopping 96 percent of executive men ... What's more, just 11 percent of the men have been divorced, compared with nearly four times as many of our women."

---

[873] https://fisheaters.com/gb9.html
[874] https://www.amazon.com/gp/product/0961086459/ref=as_li_tf_tl?ie=UTF8&tag=jimsblo0e-20&linkCode=as2&camp=1789&creative=9325&creativeASIN=0961086459
[875] https://fisheaters.com/garbagegeneration.html

While much of the bad behavior of high socioeconomic status career women may well be the result of hypergamy, not all of it can be explained in this fashion. Possibly some of it is the result of feminism. Feminism demands that men behave well, and demands that women behave "transgressively". High socioeconomic status people are more exposed to such doctrines, and more likely to conform to whatever they are exposed to, being selected for conformity.

Murray also claims that our universities are sorting out the cognitive elite.

Reading old books, it appears to me that sorting along cognitive lines was most selective and effectual quite some time back. Cognitive selection has been diminishing since at least 1950 and arguably since 1890.

The problem is that if you recruit on indicators that correlate strongly with intelligence, such as the SAT, you get politically incorrect results. So increasingly universities are recruiting on indicators of conformity, pliability, and political correctness, on which women and blacks score far better.

The increasing recruitment on conformity and consensus explains the bubble that Murray describes. It also explains obviously dim witted members of the elite, such as the world's most influential scientist, Michael Mann. (Though as one of my commentators points out, he is more a megaphone for the state, not a himself holding the microphone) Similarly Nobel Prize winning economist Paul Krugman, though not dim witted, is not all that bright. Mann and Krugman are *not* the cognitive elite.

There is a myth going around that Murray is a prophet of the libertarian right. Not so. Murray represents how far right, and how far libertarian you can be, and still be mostly acceptable in polite company: Which is not very right, nor very libertarian at all, as compared with reality.

Michelle Fields interviews the astroturf

2012-02-14 19:36:11

The supposedly 99% attempted to occupy the supposedly 1%, the CPAC conference.

But it seems the 99% were a bit hard up for warm bodies.

0 seconds:

Hot reporter chick Michelle Fields:

> So what are you guys protesting here for?

First poor black man:

> Don't start with me. I dunno.

Hot reporter chick:

> You don't know what you are protesting?

16 seconds:

third poor black man

I aint got anything nice to say about local one hunerd.

Hot reporter chick:

About what?

Third poor black man:

This whole situation

Hot reporter chick:

Are you getting paid right now?

Third poor black man:

Yeah, we all getting paid for this.

Hot reporter chick:

How much are you all getting paid?

Third poor black man:

It is like sixty dollars per head.

26 seconds:
In background we see an organizer with a shirt marked "Sheet Metal Workers Local 100", presumably the "Local One hunerd", the employer that the third black man is upset about.

The third poor black man explains that he is a member of the union, that union members who have been unemployed for a year or so are being paid to protest, a form of assistance that he seems less than enthused by.

50 seconds:
Hot reporter chick:

And do you know what you ... what this is?

Third poor black man looks around trying to figure it out.

Nuh.

He Looks around some more

I have no idea

Hot reporter chick

Do you know what this event is ... CPAC?

Third poor black man:

Nuh. They just tell me "You want to make sixty bucks, so come on." So I am here.

1 minute 3 seconds
Hot reporter chick:

All these people are paid?

Third poor black man:

Yeah.
You say *all* these people?

Hot reporter chick:

Yes, all these people

Third poor black man:

Yeah, they are getting paid. Sixty dollars a head, that is it.

Reproduction
2012-02-20 08:01:44

People that vote conservative tend to reproduce. People who reproduce tend to vote conservative. People who live in places where the environment is favorable to reproduction tend to vote conservative, because they are apt to worry about the future. Leftist in power make the environment less favorable to reproduction, thereby making the electorate lefter, by making the electorate less worried about the long term fate of the political system.

In the long run we are all dead – but our children are not.

The major factor stopping reproduction is inability to make a valid binding and enforceable reproductive contract, a contract wherein a man agrees to be a father to all his children by a woman and only by that woman, and that woman agrees to have children by that man and only that man, or else a binding and enforceable contract wherein a woman agrees to be always sexually available to one man and only that man and a man agrees to be a father to all his children by that woman and only by that woman

Observe that the Philippines, which has traditional marriage and has cute stewardesses, is the last Christian country on earth with a reasonable fertility rate.

This could not (ugly stewardesses and stewards) and would not (PC) happen on an American airline today.

Forbidding cute stewardesses is part of, either in intention or effect, a political policy of devaluing and denigrating the traditional role of women – which necessarily has the effect of reducing the number of women performing their traditional role.

If you have easy divorce, you have a policy of treating women as men. If you have a policy of treating women as men, you cannot cry vive la différence.

A state policy of not enforcing sex differences, becomes a state policy of forcibly suppressing sex differences – which necessarily tends to end reproduction, thereby moving society leftwards.

Notice I said reproductive contract. Gay marriage is in part a sincere attempt by gays to adopt a more monogamous lifestyle but it is in part a spiteful effort to épater le bourgeois, to render marriage ridiculous, disgusting and repugnant. The latter effort has succeeded, regardless of what good intentions some gays may have. As with any new euphemism, the euphemism swiftly becomes a swear word, and has to be replaced by a new word, for which I propose "reproductive contract".

The word "married", like the words "gay", "retard" and each previous euphemism, will necessarily become a curse word, is already becoming a curse word. I don't think most people in the gay marriage movement intend that "marriage" should become a curse word, rather, they genuinely hope to adopt less self destructive lifestyle that more resembles that of heterosexuals, but they did not intend that "gay" would become a curse word either. They intended that people would continue to use the word "gay" to mean cheerful and lighthearted, but of course what they intended did not happen. Instead "gay", like "retard", became an astonishingly potent curse word.

And some people in the gay marriage movement *do* intend that "marriage" should become a curse word, and are succeeding. When the state forces everyone to use the word "marriage" for relationships that are in many cases ostentatiously and spectacularly vile, disgusting, self destructive, and perverse, everyone will swiftly come to use the word "marriage" to mean a relationship that is vile, disgusting, self destructive and perverse. Such is the fate of every euphemism, and especially every state enforced euphemism. The left, aka the state, indignantly opposed "gay" becoming a curse word, and still piously pretend it is not a curse word, but by and large the left, aka the state, is enthusiastically pushing along the transition of the word "marriage" to curse word.

Pretty soon, just as heterosexuals who are having fun are no longer "gay", heterosexuals who have committed to be permanently together will no longer be "married", which outcome will disappoint some gays just as much as the transition of "gay" to curse word – but will greatly please a lot of politicians.

Laffer Maximum

2012-02-24 08:52:12

Britain decided to increase income tax on the top one percent of taxpayers to fifty percent. Predictably, revenues from the top one percent of tax payers collapsed[876].

This demonstrates the entirely unsurprising fact that a income tax of 50% plus VAT tax of 20% for an effective tax of 60%, is well above the Laffer limit.

I doubt that this came as any surprise to those imposing the tax. More likely the tax was imposed for political reasons, so that heavily taxed poor people would spitefully and self destructively vote for high taxes because rich people are taxed even more.

---

[876]https://michellemalkin.com/2012/02/22/uk-buffett-rule/

What the DenialGate fake reveals about warmists

2012-02-24 18:19:54

Peter Gleik phished some genuine files from the Heartland Institute. The files revealed what everyone knows, what no one has ever denied, and what the Heartland Institute has frequently announced: That the Heartland Institute is funding science that is skeptical of global warming, though its funding is ludicrously tiny, while Peter Gleik received half a million dollars to attack skeptics and help the warming cause.

He then created what he probably considered to be a truthful summary of these files and *fraudulently attributed his summary to the Heartland Institute*. Doubtless he thought of the summary as fake but accurate. The summary, however, is written from within the left worldview, not from the Heartland Institute worldview. It contained numerous tells, lines that gave away its true authorship[877], among them its description of Gleik as a climate scientist, rather than a political activist, and gave away much about the minds of leftists.

I hear a reader saying: "Surely it gives away much about Peter Gleik, not all leftists?"

But all important leftists are one leftist, since it is mandatory for all leftists to think alike about almost everything, whereas the right is a loose amalgamation of every interest group that is being stomped on by the left. Ordinary leftists at the bottom might have deviant thoughts on one issue or another, but a higher level leftist that gets half a million dollars to help the warming cause is going to be believe exactly and precisely what every leftist is supposed to believe on every single issue with absolute and genuine sincerity – or something that he is incapable of distinguishing from absolute and genuine sincerity. If you are remotely capable of having a deviant thought on any issue whatsoever, you do not get half a million dollars.

Now a lot of people say the fake memo cannot be Gleik's work, because you would have to be a gibbering idiot to write such nonsense, to imagine that anyone would believe the Heartland Institute would have written such nonsense - but being a leftist, or at least being a highly paid leftist, requires you to make yourself as dumb as a post. If it was not Gleik's work, it was work approved by Gleik, or credulously believed by Gleik, therefore, he really was that stupid – or rather it is mandatory for all leftists, no matter how clever to make themselves that stupid.

There are several lines in the memo that reveal it to be a fake, the most quoted being:

> His effort will focus on providing curriculum that shows that the topic of climate change is controversial and uncertain – two key points that are effective at dissuading teachers from teaching science.

Obviously climate skeptics do not believe that teachers who teach global warming are teaching science, but rather believe that teachers are teaching dogmatic worship of the goddess Gaia. The line presupposes that science is official truth, whereas skeptics believe that science is knowledge derived from the scientific method.

But what is more revealing is what was not there. The killer line from the climategate files was

---

[877] https://www.powerlineblog.com/archives/2012/02/global-warming-alarmists-resort-to-hoax.php

trick to hide the decline

Which self summarized what was revealed - that warmists cherry picked data that supported their position, and suppressed or "corrected" data that contradicted their position, with the result that all their alleged data was poisoned by "corrections" and cherry picking.

The Warmist response to this was to say that it was totally legitimate and completely ethical for scientists to make up data to show things that they knew to be true, and delete data that appeared to show things that they knew to be false.

Now since denialgate was intended as response to climategate, one might have expected the fake memo to contain the phrase "Trick to hide the X", where X is one of the many things that warmists believe is happening, such as melting glaciers, but skeptics have noticed is not happening.

That it does not contain that line reveals that warmists don't think "trick to hide the X" is incriminating - but the lines that it does contain reveal that they think that failure to believe in official truth *is* incriminating.

The skeptic analysis of the climategate files was that warmist scientists were cooking the data to conform to peer review. Gleik's analysis of the Heartland documents is that the Heartland Institute is heretically refusing to believe the official consensus.

Warren Buffet doubts gold

2012-02-27 11:02:24

Warren Buffet points out that land produces wealth, and gold does not[878]. His argument leads to the conclusion that had a Roman in the time of Caesar invested a talent in land, or deposited some money with the money lenders to earn interest, his descendents would now be worth 1067 talents, or about one trillion trillion trillion trillion trillion trillion dollars, whereas had that Roman buried a talent of gold in the ground, that Roman's descendents would now be worth about one talent, which is a few hundred dollars. Clearly there is a fallacy somewhere.

Warren Buffet tells us:

> The major asset in this category is gold, currently a huge favorite of investors who fear almost all other assets, especially paper money (of whose value, as noted, they are right to be fearful). Gold, however, has two significant shortcomings, being neither of much use nor procreative. True, gold has some industrial and decorative utility, but the demand for these purposes is both limited and incapable of soaking up new production. Meanwhile, if you own one ounce of gold for an eternity, you will still own one ounce at its end.
>
> What motivates most gold purchasers is their belief that the ranks of the fearful will grow.

---

[878]https://www.berkshirehathaway.com/letters/2011ltr.pdf

Not so. What motivates most gold purchasers is insurance against their fears becoming true.

> During the past decade that belief has proved correct. Beyond that, the rising price has on its own generated additional buying enthusiasm, attracting purchasers who see the rise as validating an investment thesis. As "bandwagon" investors join any party, they create their own truth – for a while.
>
> Over the past 15 years, both Internet stocks and houses have demonstrated the extraordinary excesses that can be created by combining an initially sensible thesis with well-publicized rising prices. In these bubbles, an army of originally skeptical investors succumbed to the "proof" delivered by the market, and the pool of buyers – for a time – expanded sufficiently to keep the bandwagon rolling. But bubbles
> blown large enough inevitably pop. And then the old proverb is confirmed once again: "What the wise man does in the beginning, the fool does in the end."
>
> Today the world's gold stock is about 170,000 metric tons. If all of this gold were melded together, it would form a cube of about 68 feet per side. (Picture it fitting comfortably within a baseball infield.) At $1,750 per ounce – gold's price as I write this – its value would be $9.6 trillion. Call this cube pile A. Let's now create a pile B costing an equal amount. For that, we could buy all U.S. cropland (400 million acres with output of about $200 billion annually), plus 16 Exxon Mobils (the world's most profitable company, one earning more than $40 billion annually). After these purchases, we would have about $1 trillion left over for walking-around money (no sense feeling strapped after this buying
> binge). Can you imagine an investor with $9.6 trillion selecting pile A over pile B?
>
> Beyond the staggering valuation given the existing stock of gold, current prices make today's annual production of gold command about $160 billion. Buyers – whether jewelry and industrial users, frightened individuals, or speculators – must continually absorb this additional supply to merely maintain an equilibrium at present prices.
>
> A century from now the 400 million acres of farmland will have produced staggering amounts of corn, wheat, cotton, and other crops – and will continue to produce that valuable bounty, whatever the currency may be. Exxon Mobil will probably have delivered trillions of dollars in dividends to its owners and will also hold assets worth many more trillions (and, remember, you get 16 Exxons).

Warren thinks that if you invest in cropland, rather than gold, then at the end of the day, you will have the cropland *and* the crops.

But alternatively you get a one way trip to the gulag as the great and the good, the wise and the virtuous, look for scapegoats to punish for the failure of utopia to arise at their command. They command utopia, notice that there is no food. Obviously those who own cropland must be at fault, and need to be punished.

What motivates most gold purchasers (and thus most bitcoin purchasers) is their belief that their fears might well prove correct, that without gold, they might find themselves penniless refugees, or, worse, without even the ability to become penniless refugees, because they lack the funding to leave a collapsing society.

Gold is an end of the world investment, insurance against total institutional collapse. We tend to underestimate fat tail risks such as total collapse, since the English speaking world has never had a total institutional collapse since the battle of Hastings in 1066.

This however, is survivorship bias. In the rest of the world, total institutional collapse has been rather common. What would have been the best investment for a Russian, an Austrian, a Hungarian, or a German in 1900? Survivorship bias causes us to overlook fat tail risks.

Warren Buffet correctly argues that gold will, on average, lose value. However there is a significant risk that everything except gold will lose value.

Warmist day of reckoning

2012-03-05 10:40:15

No global warming for the past fourteen years.
What is wrong with models that predict anthropogenic global warming[879]
The undead hockey stick[880]

Background to the hockey stick issue:

Warmists use a unique and non standard method for combining temperature proxies, such that if one combines a hundred supposed proxies, one of which, due to luck, cherry picking, or random error, shows a hockey stick, the entire graph of the supposedly combined proxies will be dominated by the one that shows a hockey stick, and not the ninety nine that do not. Thus the history of the hockey stick is the history of discovering smelly data among those supposed proxies, and demonstrating that the supposedly combined graph is fragile, in that when a small handful dubious cherry picked outlying items are removed, the entire graph radically changes shape.

The decline that had to be hidden in "hide the decline" was that the curve was pieced together out of random noise proxies, and thus they used one temperature indicator for one period, and a different temperature indicator for another period, patching together the story that they wanted the data tell from indicators that told different and contradictory stories, as if making a ransom note out of words and letters cut from a newspaper. What was hidden was that one supposed temperature indicator failed to agree with another.

---

[879]https://mises.org/daily/5892/The-Skeptics-Case#.T0eUhlmYO74.email
[880]https://bishophill.squarespace.com/blog/2009/9/29/the-yamal-implosion.html

Sarbanes Oxley

2012-03-07 06:39:55

I have mentioned the Sarbanes Oxley problem in passing in fairly regularly, but I should repeat all that in a specific post.

Capitalism cannot function without reliable accounting, and Sarbannes Oxley forbids reliable accounting.

Politicians had lots of good intentions when they passed Sarbanes Oxley, and lots of bad intentions, lots and lots of intentions, with the result that no one can possibly know what constitutes compliance with Sarbanes Oxley. In practice, the only possible way to comply is to hire someone who is sufficiently cozy with the regulators that whatever he winds up doing is deemed to constitute compliance.

Thus, no one knows what Sarbanes Oxley compliant accounts mean: In particular they do not know if a company that is reported as solvent and making money is making money, losing money, going broke, or already bust and only maintaining the appearance of operating by stealing from its customers. Sarbanes Oxley leaves businessmen and investors in the ark.

Koch brothers right to sue widow

2012-03-07 07:57:32

Cato was controlled by four men, all of them politically libertarian: The two Koch brothers, Edward Crane, long serving President, and William Niskan.

The anti libertarian right wing blog Bona Fides[881] favorably cites the far left pro Islam blog Counterpunch[882], in attacking the Koch brothers.

Crane and Niskan have taken an alarmingly large amount of money out of the Cato institute in the form of generous salaries and benefits, the Koch brothers have substantially funded it. They have not been happy with this arrangement. Niskan died, with the result that balance of power is now with his non political widow. Now the Koch brothers are suing his widow - they want to control what they paid for. How horribly greedy of them. ;-)

Counterpunch claims to be an anti state left blog. It continually attacks the Obama regime for capitalism, colonialism, imperialism, and making war on Islam, which might seem a refreshing contrast with most of the left that only objects when Republicans make war, but on every issue where they "attack" the state, they attack it for not exercising sufficient power, not hiring enough people for privileged government employment, and not confiscating sufficient wealth.

On the question of freedom of internet speech Counterpunch's position is "we must balance the constitution with child safety". "We" presumably being the state. They speak as if they are the state, as, of course, they are.

---

[881] https://www.counterpunch.org/2012/03/05/koch-brothers-worth-50-billion-sue-widow-over-16-00-of-nonprofits-stock/

[882] https://www.counterpunch.org/2012/03/05/koch-brothers-worth-50-billion-sue-widow-over-16-00-of-nonprofits-stock/

They are fanning the flames of hysteria on Fukushima, citing every absurd over reaction as evidence that even more extreme overreactions are needed. Supposedly the government is not evcuating a twenty kilometer zone contaminated with trivial and inconsequential levels of radioactivity in order to fan the flames of nuke hysteria. Supposedly it is evacuating because of end of the world radioactive levels.

Once again I remind you that Chernobyl spewed vastly more radioactivity than Fukushima, yet the cluster of cancers associated with Chernobyl killed six people, possibly as many as fifteen, (not counting the firefighters who were trying to put it out and workers in the plant itself when it blew up, just counting people in the towns around Chernobyl, just counting people who were not actually inside the fence or on the fence at any time). That is six. Not six hundred million, no sixty million, not six million, not six hundred thousand. Six, moral being that it is quite dangerous to be inside a nuclear facility when you can see flames coming out of the roof, but otherwise, not all that dangerous.

If radioactivity is horribly horribly horribly evil, then we need lots and lots of good government regulators regulating energy in general and nuclear power in particular - indeed the government needs to have its hands tight around the throat of technological civilization, since we cannot have abundant energy.

Nuclear hysteria justifies the government reining in technological civilization by limiting access to energy. Warmism serves the same agenda.

When a supposedly right wing blog favorably cites Counterpunch, it favorably cites the state.

When we look at the enemies of the Koch brothers, their enemies are our our enemies.

Yes, ten percent of Netherlands deaths are murder by government.

2012-03-07 12:30:56

Yes, ten percent of hospital deaths in the Netherlands *are* state sponsored murder, involuntary euthanasia.

Rick Santorum is attracting a great deal of outrage for his statement that to control medical costs in the Netherlands, ten percent of patients are involuntarily euthanized - murdered to save on medical costs. The mainstream media is producing a pile of articles claiming that he is lying.

"There is not a shred of evidence[883]"

Anyone who dies in hospital under deep prolonged barbiturate sedation is being murdered, for prolonged deep barbiturate sedation stops you from breathing, and ten percent of hospital deaths in the Netherlands occur under prolonged deep barbiturate sedation[884].

So Rick Santorum is telling the truth, and the mainstream media are lying, as are the dutch government and medical authorities.

---

[883]https://www.washingtonpost.com/blogs/fact-checker/post/euthanasia-in-the-netherlands-rick-santorums-bogus-statistics/2012/02/21/gIQAJaRbSR_blog.html

[884]https://www.ncbi.nlm.nih.gov/pmc/articles/PMC2292332/

A few hours under deep barbiturate sedation is risky enough that the manufacturers instructions require the patient to be constantly watched at all times until he is back to normal, because he is quite likely to stop breathing, requiring emergency measures to get him breathing again. After few days of deep sedation, the patient will surely stop breathing, and, absent appropriate emergency measures to get him breathing again, swiftly die.

The inevitability of murder under government health care

2012-03-07 17:22:39

At the age of eighty four, you have a heart attack. The ambulance comes around, it stabilizes you, it takes you, free of charge to the free government hospital, and the free doctors at the free government hospital conclude you need open heart surgery, a stent and a coronary bypass.

Now the government can provide the free ambulance, and the free stabilization to everyone. But there is no way it can provide the free stent and the free bypass to everyone, in part because free stuff always costs ten times as much as stuff that people pay for themselves (which is why free contraception is expected to cost $1000 per year).

The government could, and probably will, put you on the emergency waiting list to join the special emergency waiting list for open heart surgery, which waiting list will grow longer and longer until people dying on the waiting list balances supply and demand– but it cannot keep you occupying a hospital bed while you are on the waiting list, because if it does, it is rapidly going to run out of hospital beds.

So, one way or another, those hospital beds are going to be emptied.

One way around this is home care: The government sends you out to die in your own bed, but has people come to your house to make sure that the bed gets changed, that you have a bath from time to time, and that there is food available. This is expensive, but it is way cheaper than keeping you in a hospital bed to die, and a lot nicer for the patient to die in his own bed with his own family than to die in hospital so that the government can pretend it is treating him. But the trouble is that this is apt to make it embarrassingly obvious that the government is sending you to your own bed to die, that the government cannot and will not provide all the medical care that everyone needs. So to maintain the pretense that the government can provide all the medical care that everyone needs regardless of their ability to pay, it is going to clear those beds out by such measures as "deep sedation".

Some governments have gone the home care path, and have avoided murdering people – but those are governments that unashamedly run a two tier system, where the middle class pay for their own health care in order to avoid the waiting lists and the death panels. Governments that pretend to be running a one tier system, a system that supposedly guarantees unlimited health care for everyone, inevitably wind up committing murder. They also wind up furtively running a two tier system, except that instead of everyone with money getting into the upper tier, only those with the right connections get into the upper tier.

The hypocrisy and murder that results from government healthcare inevitably corrupts the entire society.

Why "free" is so expensive

2012-03-09 07:34:10

If you are spending your own money on yourself, you care very much how much it costs, and care very much how good what you get is. If you are spending someone else's money on someone else, aka "free", you don't care how much it costs, and you don't care if it does the recipient good or does him harm.

"What if"[885] has found an interesting example of "free"

Seems that the government budgeted eleven million dollars to provide free interview suits for four hundred job seekers, a cost of a mere thirty thousand dollars per job seeker, which expenditure was considered perfectly reasonable, proper, and legitimate. Ordinarily such a small, reasonable, and modest expenditure would not attract anyone's attention, even though very nice suits cost only a few hundred.

But as things turned out the eleven million dollars only managed to cover two free interview suits, for a cost of five million dollars per suit which was considered excessive, improper, and illegitimate, thereby attracting attention to this otherwise entirely ordinary and unremarkable expenditure.

Now if the government is providing "free" for some small and noisy interest group, this does not lead to disaster. But suppose the government wants to provide "free" for some very large group, for example "free" medical care, "free" contraception: Then the *$#!%* is going to hit the fan, because not even Uncle Sam the Pimp's magic no limit credit card can handle that sort of damage.

So what is a government to do? Answer, lie and murder to conceal the fact that it is not delivering on its promises. Hence the curiously large proportion of deaths under deep sedation in countries with "free" medical care.

Murray on the decline of marriage

2012-03-14 12:18:39

The right tends to have orgasms over Charles Murray, because he is a rightist that is tolerated by the regnant left, albeit barely tolerated, therefore wonderfully high status as compared to the rest of the right, since regular rightists are not tolerated by our masters, therefore regular rightists are low status. Is it not wonderful to be allowed to get close to Charles Murray, who is allowed to get close enough to our masters for them to spit on him?

But, if he is tolerated, he has to be far to the left of reality, indeed almost as far out in la la land as any Dean of Diversity Studies. From where I stand, having confidence in evolutionary psychology and the wisdom of our ancestors (but I repeat myself), I can barely see the difference between Charles Murray and the Dean of Diversity Studies.

I now critique his latest interview:[886]

Edward Luce interviews Murray on marriage, after chatting at length on whiter people dining.

---

[885]https://moot.typepad.com/what_if/2012/03/sarah-was-a-piker.html
[886]https://www.ft.com/intl/cms/s/2/628d8524-690b-11e1-956a-00144feabdc0.html#axzz1p1e4f200

Observe how the intro to this interview carefully delineates all the markers of high status:

> the waiter says the black-truffle pasta is still on the menu, and we both order
> it as a starter

By the way, I am writing this after snacking on pork belly, roast potatoes, and home made wine fortified with a touch of moonshine and a bit of fermented prickly pear juice for added flavor and vivid blood red color. Mmmmm, pork belly. And the prickly pear is guaranteed to obliterate all those delicate subtleties of flavor and color that might have gotten into the wine during the fermentation process. And some instant coffee to compensate for the alcohol.

There is something wonderfully proletarian about pork belly, even though it is almost the same meal as pork spare ribs with some supposedly authentic Chinese seasoning, a meal beloved of whiter people when their pretense of being vegetarian collapses. Similarly fermented prickly pear, which should be a whiter people drink due to being obscure, organic, supposedly healthful, and all that, is not in the least a whiter people drink because it is as vividly colored and potently flavored as the stuff that blacks drink. I did not deliberately compose this meal to ridicule Charles Murray and his whiter people interviewer. I ate first, then read the interview.

Are you not impressed by the fact that this interviewer eats with Charles Murray, a man whose status is so high that our masters let him get close enough to them for them to spit on him? Clearly the interviewer expects you to be impressed.

And, by the way, should you find yourself dining an expensive restaurant with an elite newspaper paying the bill, don't order black truffle pasta, because it contains only homeopathic amounts of black truffle. If you want to gain actual status from what you eat, try eating actual black truffles. If your expense account covers actual black truffles, then *that* will impress me. I am distinctly unimpressed by black truffle pasta. Back when we our ruling elite actually was elite, they ate truffles, so today's whiter people imitate them by eating overpriced spaghetti with truffles in the name. You can do a lot better than spaghetti on an expense account.

And only whiter people think they can tell the difference between varietal wines and regular plonk. With a varietal wine, you are supposed to demonstrate your knowledge about the variety, all of which knowledge you actually cribbed.

After numerous whiter people dining tips, in which we are once again reminded that this is an expensive restaurant and the Financial Times is picking up the tab, and the interviewer and interviewee frequently hang out at this expensive restaurant (did I mention it was expensive), we read some actual cultural critique.

> "Whatever the Victorians did right in England, we need to resuscitate over
> here," says Murray, between concluding mouthfuls of his pasta. "In the late
> 19th century, the entire English population were propagandized into buy-
> ing into a certain code of morals. I would be happy if we could emulate that
> in some way in America." Then he pauses: "But that gets into the whole
> question of whether the elite has the self-confidence in its own rightness."

The rot started with the Victorians. Victorianism was the political correctness of its day. The state intervened in the family to dismantle patriarchal marriage, which is to say, to dismantle traditional marriage, new testament marriage, a change as arrogant and destructive as gay marriage.

Previously everyone knew that society needed patriarchal marriage because women were lecherous animals, and unless firmly kept in hand, the family would collapse, followed shortly by society. The account of women that one today reads on Pick Up Artist blogs was the standard mainstream view in the Georgian period.

To rationalize this disruptive and coercive change, to persuade people it would not lead to the collapse of the family, the state proceeded with a propaganda offensive on how women were chaste and pure delicate flowers threatened by vile lecherous men, which today is taken to ever greater extremes in ever more one sided rape, date, and domestic violence laws - for all the horrible details read your favorite Men's Rights Activist blog. All the dreadful stuff that Men's Rights Activists are complaining about got started with the Victorian propaganda offensive that Charles Murray is so impressed by.

> Murray is now on to his barramundi, an Asian sea bass, while I have grilled sardines, both "drizzled with lemon"

Barramundi is deservedly high status because in places where you can get it reasonably fresh, it is very good. Washington is not one of those places. If you live in some place where people need to explain what barramundi is, the reason they need to explain is that it is not all that good. If you supposedly know about the variety of your varietal wine, you should know that barramundi needs to be fresh to be high status. Murray was eating *thawed* barramundi. Oh the horror.

Explaining about food status has made me feel like snacking on a bit more roast potato. And, by the way, we food cognoscenti call barramundi "barra" to show that we are so high status that the high status of barramundi does not impress us.

Maybe I will have some more instant coffee. Now if only someone would sell a coffee guaranteed to be slow roasted by oppressed workers forced to work in unbearable heat, perhaps I would get interested in varietal coffee.

> "If you are arguing that 22-year-old men are saying to their girlfriends, 'I just need a job and then I'll behave responsibly ...' Well, that's just bullshit. If you ask women in working class communities, they will say, 'Why should I marry these losers? It's like taking another child into the household.'"

The problem is that a working class job does not suffice to marry a working class woman, so working class men have no incentive to get working class jobs. Woman always marry up, and Uncle Sam the Big Pimp is higher status than a working class husband. Wives of upper class men are well behaved provided that they are slightly less upper class than their husbands, because Uncle Sam the Big Pimp is lower status than an upper class husband. Upper class career women, in particular lawyers are deadly, because they cannot marry men who are even higher status than themselves, so instead bang musicians, thugs, and sportsmen. As a result, they fail to marry or reproduce.

Any fertile age woman will tell you that only one man in thirty is barely acceptable. Since they seem to be getting laid we may conclude that Mister One In Thirty is a very busy man. As their fertile years start running out, they start looking for someone to marry, but how many men want to marry a woman whose fertile years are running out, and who will always compare him with two dozen of "Mister One in Thirty"?

I first had sex with my wife when she was a teenager, but the younger generation is finding that increasingly difficult to accomplish. So you get a job, keep your nose to the cubicle, and at the age of forty, get to marry a woman who has ridden a whole bunch of men she thinks are a lot better than you, and is getting close to forty herself. Oh what an incentive. Why even try?

The Gavi is going down fast

Naturally readers who are so high status that they read stuff by people sufficiently high status to eat with Charles Murray, who is so high status that our rulers allow him close enough to spit on him, would know that Gavi is an expensive varietal wine, and could doubtless give a lengthy discourse about cortese grapes and Italian vineyards. Perhaps the grapes were grown on the sunny side of the hill. Unfortunately I am out of moonshine and cannot easily get any more.

Technological decay

2012-03-19 09:35:40

Earlier I argued that technology in the west peaked in 1970, Tallest building 1972, coolest muscle cars, last man left the moon,though it continues to advance in some other parts of the world:

Unreasonable expectations[887] points at another indicator. The most advanced plane ever built, the SR71, was built in 1966, retired 1972. One would have expected stealthed mach three fighters and bombers to replace it, but instead, slower, lower performance stealthed fighters and bombers replaced it. Unreasonable expectations argues that all advances since then have been driven solely by advances in photolithography, and that when photolithography runs out, technological advance will end.

A number of posts have appeared by a number of people reporting slowing in technology, or actual decline in the level of technology: See Locklin for a summary and review[888].

I would instead predict that technological advance in the west will end. I see new technologies, such as the blue light semiconductor laser, which makes possible modern DVDs, e-ink, which made possible the kindle, and new construction methods for very large buildings, which make possible the remarkably cool asian airports[889], continuing to appear in Asia.

---

[887]https://veryunreasonableexpectations.blogspot.com.au/2012/02/reblag-technological-nadir.html
[888]https://scottlocklin.wordpress.com/2009/09/01/myths-of-technological-progress/
[889]https://www.graphichorizon.net/10-marvelous-photograph-of-famous-international-airports/

You can see where the future is being made. The Oslo cityscape looks as though it should be in sepia, for the nineteenth century look - similarly when you google up street scenes from Europe and the US and compare them with equivalent street scenes from China.

In the 1930s, they imagined the world of tomorrow would look shiny and futuristic. It does look that way, but not in the west.

What is causing it?

Contrary to Charles Murray, it looks to me that our elite is less and less elite, less and less selected for ability, creativity, and intelligence, that it is now primarily selected for conformity and political correctness, and secondarily selected for race and gender, and thus excludes the person who is smarter than those around him, who tends to have difficulty conforming, and is apt to show signs of noticing the more illogical aspects of the holy faith. You observe a lot more women in today's ruling elite, and women are noticeably less intelligent and logical, less capable of comprehending or advancing technology, and the smartest women are considerably less smart than the smartest men. There are no great female composers, despite the fact that women have been very strongly encouraged to go into music for several hundred years. There are no great female scientists, Marie Curie being a completely faked up poster girl and an affirmative action Nobel prize. So when you see lots of females in the elite, you are simply going to see less technology. You are going to see the really smart man (and he always is a man) simply have lower status and less time and resources to accomplish stuff.

If you read up on the challenger disaster, it is pretty obvious that the people making the decisions were just stupid, and engineers under them were markedly smarter. Mulloy simply did not understand Lund's presentation[890]. And because the bosses were just too dimwitted, the space shuttle fell out of the sky. Further, the reason Lund was low status and Mulloy was high status is because Mulloy was stupid enough to fit in with the elite, while Lund was just too smart to fit in.

Reading old books, it looks to me that in the US, selection on the basis of ability maxed in 1870 if we suppose breeding counts, and if we instead suppose that the college board test (which later became the SAT) is vastly more predictive than breeding, so that breeding should be completely and totally disregarded, then it looks to me that selection on the basis of ability maxed in 1910, when they started to worry more about the fact that high scorers tended to be affluent white males, than whether the exam accurately measured ability to benefit from the kind of material taught at college.

Ever since then, since 1870 or 1910, depending on how reactionary you are, our elite has just been getting dumber and dumber, hence, technological decline.

Why the elite is dumb and getting dumber

2012-03-20 05:44:34

When recruiting people for administration, administrators very reasonably look for past experience on the administration track. To him that has shall be given, to him that has not, even what little he has shall be taken away. However success at the lowest levels of the administration track is at best a poor indicator of intelligence, and in government, and in large schlerotic organizations choked on red tape, is a strong negative indicator of intelligence. Dumb people thrive in an environment where there are lots of committees, and lots of time is spent attending meetings.

This is a big problem with businesses that are immune from market pressures, businesses that like General Motors are too big to fail, with universities, and of course, with the biggest business of them all: Government. Professors of resentment studies are stupid. Government employees in management positions in the governing apparatus are really stupid, and are even more fireproof than professors of resentment studies.

Three cases that should be studied: The Challenger disaster, Washington Mutual, and Countrywide, where demonstrably stupid people were given power, catastrophically fouled up, and got into trouble for so doing. These are not the most stupid people of course, they are just the most stupid people doing stuff where stupidity can get you into

---

[890]https://history.nasa.gov/rogersrep/v5part1a.htm#2

trouble. In most areas of government, stupidity, such as letting the 9/11 hijackers do obviously suspicious stuff, will get you promoted. And no one can foul up resentment studies, even when resentment coursework leads to race hate gang rapes on campus. Recall that the Major Hasan case was supposedly not a tragedy because Hasan murdered a bunch of people. It was supposedly a tragedy because it might cause people to doubt that affirmative actioning Muslims into militarily sensitive positions of power was a good idea.So in looking at these cases, keep in mind that these cases are occurring where elite stupidity is likely to be the least severe, not where it is likely to be most severe. I am relying on unsympathetic investigations of disastrous stupidity, but stupidity is likely to be most severe in those areas where no amount of stupidity, no matter how disastrous the consequences, can get you into trouble and result in unsympathetic investigation.

Some people are going to say that because Mozillo and Killinger made hundreds of millions of dollars in the course of destroying their banks, they must be really smart people. But the smart people, the ones that knew that they were robbing the banking system blind, got the hell out in 2006, leaving people like Mozilo and Killinger to take the blame. There was a massive panic stricken exodus in late 2005, early 2006. Anyone that did not get out while the getting was good is stupid.

Consensus tends to be dominated by those who will not shift their purported beliefs in the face of evidence and rational argument, thus dominated by the evil and the insane[891], meaning by those who lie about what their beliefs are, and thus have purported beliefs that are unaffected by reality, and those who genuinely have beliefs unaffected by reality. To fit in with such a consensus, it helps if you are stupid. See the scientific debate on linguistic deep structure for a debate dominated by the evil, dominated by those for whom scientific theory was one more club with which to destroy their enemies in academic struggles over power and funding, and the scientific debate on red meat and animal fats in the human diet for a debate dominated by the insane, dominated by those for whom health means spiritual health, which is best obtained by not exploiting or oppressing animals. In both cases, stupidity, real or feigned, helps advance one's scientific career. Too much smarts will incur the wrath of a small but fanatical group, which no sensible person is going to provoke.

To compensate for the fact that success at low levels of management is a poor filter for people of ability, businesses look to universities to select management track people for them, so that only the very smart get started on that track. But increasingly universities accredit people in much the same way that large bureaucratic organization gives people experience on the management track. You are required to sincerely believe six impossible things before breakfast every morning, and it is a lot easier for stupid people to sincerely believe, to fit in.

Observe that one can get a computer science degree from a name university, despite total lack of ability to write a non trivial program. Course material is no longer filtering out the less clever, and political correctness and general requirements for conformity are filtering out the clever. This is a problem even with engineering courses, and it is a much bigger problem with management track postgraduate courses. If someone has a management track postgraduate degree in engineering from an elite university, he is pretty much

---

[891]https://blog.reaction.la/economics/stultum-facit-fortuna.html

guaranteed to be stupid, relative to an engineer from a no name university who has successfully done some actual engineering at work – which is what we saw happening in the Challenger disaster: Management track engineers not only did not want to believe the disturbing reports submitted by engineering track engineers, but were *unable* to understand those reports.

And that is what happened with the Challenger disaster: Murray signed off on a report by Lund that said that the Challenger was going to explode, but never understood what he was signing off on.

The lesson of the Challenger disaster is that a postgraduate engineering degree in management is like a postgraduate science degree in interdisciplinary studies: It is a degree in Stupid.

Since low level administrative experience does not select for intelligence, administrators rely on universities to filter for intelligence– but universities are not filtering for intelligence either. Increasingly, university degrees are degrees in Stupid, for example resentment studies degrees, interdisciplinary studies degrees, and even degrees in Smart, for example computer science degrees, let an alarming number of stupid people through the filter. An awful lot of Computer Science graduates just cannot write a non trivial program.

In the case of the Challenger disaster, the people who knew the Challenger was going to blow up, and wrote reports saying so, were engineers trained on the engineering track. At university they studied engineering problems. At work, they held their jobs on the ability to solve engineering problems. The people who did not know, and did not want to know, that the Challenger was going to blow up, were engineers who did postgraduate work on the business management track, trained to manage engineers, not to themselves engineer, and their careers were from the very beginning in management – they went directly from university to low level management. As managers, they were judged not on their ability to solve engineering problems, but on their ability to solve people problems – and if you are smarter than your boss, it is a problem.

If we look at Kerry Killinger, CEO of Washington Mutual, we find that Washington Mutual had reports saying that it was going to collapse, because its borrowers could only pay their mortgages by flipping their houses, so as soon as housing prices stopped rising, Washington Mutual's mortgages would collapse, just as NASA had reports saying that the Challenger was going to explode, which reports were, of course, ignored. Let us look at Kerry Killinger's resume, leading to his job as CEO. It is all that he served on the X committee, and was Chairman of the Y committee. Committees work by consensus, so tend to be dominated by the evil and the insane, so it helps to be stupid to fit in. His management background was a career in the track that tends to most strongly select for stupidity, conformity, and willingness to conform to what is stupid, evil and insane. Kerry Killinger came from a management track where ability to ignore reality is a major asset, and led his company to disaster by ignoring reality.

The Countrywide disaster was in large part caused by affirmative action, and by selection for true believers in affirmative action, which is to say, for stupid people. The CEO, Angelo R. Mozilo, was an affirmative action hire, and also a sincere believer in affirmative action lending. His bank became large and powerful in part by making special loans to politicians and regulators, in part by enthusiastically making loans to the supposedly oppressed, in other words, entirely by left wing politics. He made an enormous number of "VIP loans" to fellow leftists in positions of power. Since left wing politics requires sincere belief in no end of ridiculous stuff, leftists tend to be stupid, even when they do not affirmative action dimwits into power among themselves.

Angelo Mozilo is a particular case that affirmative action people in power tend to be stupid, and that leftists tend to be stupid. That leftists tend to be stupid is the most important case of the problem that those whose path to power went through committees tend to be stupid, evil, and insane.

To recap

Success in low level administration fails to filter out the stupid people, and is apt to filter out the smart people. So administrators rely on universities to filter smart people onto the administration track, and filter stupid people off that track. Unfortunately universities are no longer effectively filtering smart people in and stupid people out, as demonstrated by the fact that degrees in resentment studies, interdisciplinary studies, post graduate management studies courses for engineers, and so on and so forth are usually degrees in Stupid, are usually a reliable indicator of a stupid person, and that even among people with degrees in Smart, a substantial minority are stupid. Something like one third of Computer Science graduates just cannot write a non trivial program.

The ancestral environment of females

2012-03-27 08:17:19

The collagen in old bones of humans shows stable isotope levels similar to that of the old bones of wolves and hyenas, indicating that humans ate at the same trophic level as wolves and hyenas or higher, that is to say, the same position in the food chain or higher, which implies that almost all the food was meat, which implies hunting mattered and gathering did not matter, which in turn implies that women were kept like pets for their sexual, domestic, and reproductive services, that women were incapable of supporting themselves and were entirely dependent on fathers, brothers, and husbands, not only for protection, but also for food.

Women are psychologically adapted to this environment, an environment where they are property, perhaps much loved property, and if they are virtuous and lucky, more loved than a good hunting dog. Such psychological adaption leads to disturbingly counterproductive and self destructive behavior in the more favorable present environment.

Women are ill suited to make decisions about their own lives, because in the ancestral environment they did not get to make such decisions.

Thus, until women psychologically adapt to an environment where upper body physical strength and capacity for violence is less important, which will require centuries and perhaps millenia of evolution, emancipation and universal suffrage will remain entirely unworkable and impractical ideals.

Show me a marriage where the housework is equally and fairly shared, rather than being divided into man's work (taking out the garbage, unplugging the drains, mowing the lawn, and barbecuing meat) and woman's work (almost everything else)and I will show you a marriage where the husband sleeps on the couch, and once in a week or so the wife's lover drops in to bang her on the main bed, rough her up a bit, take her money, and leave a mess for the husband to clean up.

This is the Darwinist equivalent to the Judeo-Christian proposition that God created women to be a help meet for man

I first slept with my wife when she was very young, and we are still married much later, so I think I can speak impartially about other people's divorces: Divorce is almost always the woman's fault, always the woman's fault that I know of, and most of the time even though the wife grossly misbehaves, nagging, backseat driving, and speaking back to her husband, it is the wife who foolishly and self destructively initiates the divorce. If you give a woman equality, she will take supremacy, and if she takes supremacy, she will walk all over you and then completely lose interest in you and walk right out. In people's personal individual sexual lives, it is clear that equality between men and woman does not work out, that it reliably leads to complete disaster. If you treat your wife as equal, you will lose everything, and your life will be completely destroyed. Equality is not in a woman's nature, and this applies every bit as much to women educated in elite institutions and full of feminist ideology.

Contrary to what I claimed above about ancient bones, a feminist anthropologist has recently reported that among currently living South African Bushmen, gathered food accounted for about 80 percent of the calories and the culture was thus quite egalitarian

However, the old hunting and gathering lifestyle no longer exists, due in part to the fact that these days bush meat is obtained using rifles, which procedure for obtaining bush meat she excluded from consideration, thus I am inclined to doubt that it is possible for an anthropologist to observe the old hunter gatherer lifestyle, though doubtless easy to observe what she wishes the hunter gatherer lifestyle should have been. If she really did manage to find some genuine hunter gatherers, whose game really had not been eradicated by men with rifles, they were in a very marginal environment, thus likely to be atypical of our ancestors.

Tasmanian aboriginals would trade a good woman for a good hunting dog, at the ratio of one dog for one woman, and no one would think to consult either the dog or the woman. While modern reports on (no longer actually existent) hunter gatherers tend to support feminism, the old reports from the times when it was a major and important lifestyle, from the times when hunter gatherer lands were first being settled, depict women being treated like dogs.

The PUA doctrine on shit tests is the equivalent of the no longer fashionable eighteenth century Judeo Christian proposition that women are sinful, easily tempted, and thus apt to fail in their duty to be help meet for man and therefore need supervision and restraint.

Mental differences:

Women are better than males at reading people. The average women also has more verbal skills than the average man. She should: the average woman talks several times as much as the average man. They are also better at finding stuff than men.

Women, however are not smart in that they lack logic, and not smart in that they lack emotional wisdom, making extremely stupid choices, being unduly moved by immediate and momentary pressures. In these areas of life they vary from not too bright to dumb as a rock. Just as almost every man, as near all of them as makes no difference, is stronger than almost every women, as near all of them as makes no difference, there are quite important areas of life, such as logic, where most men smarter than almost every women. Even though women have more emotional intelligence than men in reading people, they have markedly less emotional intelligence than men in managing people, thus tend to be ill suited for management positions. There have been some very great female political leaders, such as Queen Elizabeth the first, Margaret Thatcher, and Golda Meir, but there have been no great female business leaders.

That IQ tests are gender normed should tell you that if they were not gender normed, women would test out less bright on average, as expected from the fact that their brains are smaller on average relative to body size. If it was men that would test out less bright, the tests would not be gender normed.

effect of status and intelligence

Today, among both men and woman, the longer the education, the fewer children that they wind up having, and the more elite and high status the education, the less the students are apt to behave sexually.

However, among men, the more successful the career, the higher the number of children. Optimal fertility tends to be associated with a shorter and less elite education, but a more successful career.

In women, but not in men, having a successful career depresses fertility, and results in pathological, perverse and self destructive sexual behavior. She has no more sex than a lower status woman, perhaps less, but what sex she does have is more immoral and self destructive, apt to hurt both herself and any relationships she might have. (Personal observation, I cannot provide any scientific studies to support this claim, and many people disagree with this claim) Studies do show that successful women have low reproduction rate, and successful men a high reproduction rate, indicating that successful women are not marrying successful men, consistent with personal observation.

However a women with an elite education who at a reasonably young age marries a male with a somewhat more elite education than she has, a man who earns more money that she does, even if only moderately more, is relatively well behaved compared to lower class women, in part because she is less sexually active, and, unlike the career woman, a lot less sexually active with criminals, musicians, sportsmen, bosses, and high status legal clients. (Personal observation, controversial and not universally accepted)

Where there is large variance in male reproduction rates, female preference for assholes (what used to be called cads) is adaptive for the individual female. She produces sons who will also be cads. (Darwinian theory)

society and civilizational collapse:

Reproduction is a prisoners dilemma problem. If the female is loyal, but the male defects, the male is better off. If the male is loyal, but the female defects, the female is better off. If both defect, both are worse off, if both loyal, both are better off.

If the female preference for cads is allowed free reign, we get a defect/defect equilibrium, resulting in more male energy being applied to male/male sexual competition, and less male energy being applied to offspring and posterity.

The solution, of course, is familial enforcement of a cooperate/cooperate equilibrium, with shotgun marriage being enforced on males, and chastity on daughters. Societies and social classes where the cooperate/cooperate equilibrium is enforced out reproduce and out invest societies that practice the defect/defect equilibrium, thus societies, and social classes in a defect/defect equilibrium disappear from history.

To illustrate the proposition that women are apt to make bad decisions, I will link to the reality show character Kate Gosselin, who evidently failed to notice that the father of eight children is irreplaceable. Kate Gosselin became a shrew and harridan who made life a living hell for the father of her children, and was videotaped doing so[892].

In a typical divorce (personal observation, not universally accepted) the wife spends an immense amount of effort and emotional energy into making life a living hell for the only man who will ever love her children, and should he fail to leave under his own power, perhaps fearing that his children will wind up in the hands of a stepfather who will at best treat his children as enemies, at worst treat them as vermin, murder his sons and hate fuck his daughters, then his wife proceeds to destroy her own life and her children's lives by divorcing him, despite the fact that raising children single handed does not work, and trying to have a love life with your children by another man hanging around works considerably worse. Stepfathers are the natural enemies of stepchildren. (Personal observation, universally accepted - and almost universally denied with pious hypocrisy).

It is glaringly obvious, yet somehow never mentioned, that most divorced women under forty with children fail to maintain a safe environment for their children.

The solution proposed by men's rights activists, equal custody, is a completely ludicrous solution to the problem that women are breaking up their families irresponsibly and self destructively: You can see the Katie Gosslin divorce on reality television. Most divorces are pretty much like that.

Men's rights activist sites piously whine that men are not equal to women, and should be - but we tried equality in 1850. It was a complete disaster and things have steadily gotten worse since then. As the pick up artist sites point out, women are not equal to men by nature, and treating them as equal leads to bad outcomes.

The reason men's rights activist sites are so whiny is that they accept the progressive ideology of equalism, and in their own lives they treated women as equals, and of course got treated like shit. Women are very nice and have all the virtues attributed to women provided you keep them in line, but not otherwise.

Once again, I cite the case of reality television person Kate Gossyln, who self destructively ditched her husband because that was the only way to hurt him more than she was

---

[892]https://www.the-spearhead.com/2012/02/28/men-not-rushing-to-kate-gosselin/

hurting him already, and was then astonished to find that no one else wanted to father her eight children.

The normal cause of divorce is that female psychology is maladapted to the modern environment.

In the ancestral environment, if a woman could get away with treating a man as an equal, let along an inferior, let alone bully him, then it was not a man, and so did not exist sexually or as a source of support.

In the ancestral environment, women were dangerously powerless, so natural selection made them always want to have more power, just as it made us always want to have more sugar, so that we are inclined to eat more sugar than is good for us, and women inclined to take more power than is good for them.

So women always push for more, and even if they have equality or supremacy, do not consciously realize it. Since they keep on pushing regardless, they rationalize that they cannot have equality or power. But if they succeed in getting equality or supremacy over their husbands, they will leave their husbands.

Pick up artists argue that to pick up women, you have to treat them badly. Well, I am no expert on picking up women, but I do know that to keep a woman, however you may acquire her, you have to treat her as a subordinate, a much loved pet, but however much you love that pet, you cannot afford to put up with too much shit from that pet.

Roissy argues that women want a master. This true and untrue. It is untrue in that they certainly do not believe they want a master. It is untrue in that they will struggle with alarming determination to get the upper hand over their husbands. It is true in that should they succeed in getting what they think they want, they will ditch their husband without the slightest thought of the disastrous effect on themselves and their children.

In the considerable majority of divorces, all of them that I know of, the cause of divorce was that the husband was too nice a guy to his wife, and therefore allowed her equality. Of course you should be nice to your wife, just as you should be nice to your dog, but if you allow her equality, she will walk right over you and walk right out, and will use the legal system to destroy you and destroy her own children. (Personal observation, controversial and not universally accepted)

The reason Men's Rights Activists are so angry and bitter is that they tried treating women as equals in their personal sexual lives, and, of course, suffered a total and complete disaster. Women just cannot be treated as equals. At best, you can get away with spoiling and indulging them like kittens. They are grossly maladapted to equality.

In the standard romantic story written for women, the love interest is a monstrous jerk or impossibly powerful male. However, he winds up twisted around the protagonists little finger, that being standard female wish fulfillment - but when the female's wish is completely fulfilled, the readers lose interest in the male, so the writer saves this fulfillment to the very end of the story.

In romances targeted at women, the asshole is invariably tamed, and frequently winds up twisted around the women's little finger, indicating that women want power over men. However, we observe that the romantic love interest never winds up mastered by the woman until the final curtain, consistent with the PUA contention that when the badboy is tamed, when the woman gets what she thinks she wants, the woman forgets about him and loses sexual interest

In "Buffy the Vampire Slayer", when Spike was the big bad of the series arc, it seemed that most of the audience were women hoping to see Spike with his shirt off. When Spike wound up wrapped around Buffy's little finger, the audience, the writers, and in due course Buffy herself, completely forgot that he existed. Various Spike related plot threads were left hanging in mid air, much like the father of Kate Gosselin's children.

Women want to wrap the man around their little finger, but they don't want a man that they can wrap around their little finger. They want what they do not want, and they don't want what they do want.

Nice guy love interests do exist in female romances, but is in a position of power over the protagonist: The protagonist's family gave her or sold her to the nice guy or some such improbable plot, as with the protagonist of "Red String" and her considerably older nice guy boyfriend.

What the protagonist and her twelve year old readers want, is not to have the power to get what they want, but rather that a man takes possession of them and gives them what they really want like it or not.

How marriage was destroyed:

We see heavy handed state intervention in marriage starting in the nineteenth century.

Before then, middle class families enforced marriage on terms violently unfavorable to women, which, according to contemporary accounts seems to have balanced supply and demand, or if there was an imbalance, it was that any respectable eligible bachelor was in extremely high demand by families with virginal daughters who were getting too old, "old" in this context meaning approaching twenty.

This resulted in the practice of unloading problem middle class females (for example suspected of lack of virginity, or getting horribly elderly, for example twenty three) on industrious upwardly mobile members of the working class, and compensating the husband by using influence to advance his career.

Aristocratic marriage, however, was in bad shape, with massive family breakdown. Theoretically the same norms applied to aristocratic marriage as to middle class marriage, but in practice these norms were massively violated and spectacularly disregarded, with frequent failure of aristocrats to reproduce.

In 1912, marriage was already violently asymmetric in favor of women, in that the duties of the husband were legally enforceable and enforced, but the duties of the wife were not.

Logically one would expect that this would lead to high demand for marriage by women and low demand by men, but since women are maladapted to a high status role, since they do not desire a relationship in which they have power, even though they contradictorily desire power within a relationship, it leads to low demand by both.

George Zimmerman, Trayvon Martin

2012-03-28 13:11:55

According to George Zimmerman, he turned his back on Trayvon Martin and was walking away, whereupon Trayvon Martin chimped out and attacked him from rear left. Circumstantial evidence supports this story, (for starters, there is no way a man like George Zimmerman is going to physically attack a man like Trayvon Martin with his fists) and there are no eyewitnesses contradicting it.

According to George Zimmerman *and eyewitnesses*, Zimmerman wound up on the ground, screaming for help, while Trayvon Martin pinned him down and continued to beat the *$%@!* out of him.

Imagine you are on the ground, with a big black male on top of you, not the photoshopped cherubic little boy the government media are depicting, but a big black male dressed in gang clothing[893], and that black is pounding away. What are *you* going to do?

The reason the media are pushing the story "white man attacks poor little black boy" is because the actual story "black man attacks mestizo" is an wedge cutting the Democratic part coalition apart.

There is no way Zimmerman is going to be convicted for shooting Trayvon Martin - not because he happens to be in right, which these days does not matter in the slightest, but because he is mestizo. There is no way in hell that mestizos are going to allow themselves to be classified as white when they come under attack by blacks. Mestizos have the privilege of defending themselves against black attack, a privilege that they vitally need, since they so frequently come under black attack.

You will notice that Republicans are hiding under the bed with the blankets over their heads hoping that this issue will go away. They should have jumped on a soapbox and set to work hammering the wedge into the Democratic party coalition, by loudly proclaiming the right of self defense, and pointing out that the Democrats are trying to take away the long established right of mestizos to defend themselves against blacks.

Republicans don't want Republicans to win. They want progressives to win, though they would mildly prefer them to be Republican progressives.

Photoshopping Trayvon

2012-03-28 18:00:01

The mainstream media have applied the magic of photoshop[894] to convert Trayvon Martin from a menacing thug who needed killing to a sweet innocent child.

Eyes enlarged to reduce apparent age. Nose reduced for cuteness. Chinline on viewer right of image altered to reduce apparent age. Hairline raised for larger forehead, to reduce

---

[893]https://www.riehlworldview.com/carnivorous_conservative/2012/03/why-was-trayvon-martin-photo-altered.html

[894]https://www.riehlworldview.com/carnivorous_conservative/2012/03/why-was-trayvon-martin-photo-altered.html

apparent age and give a more intelligent and gentle appearance. Facial hair reduction to reduce apparent age.

Mouth redrawn for gentle instead of menacing expression.

There are photoshop artifacts on the jawline and the mouth of the child image, revealing that the thug is the original image, and the child the photoshopped image.

Conservatives distrust official science

2012-04-01 05:37:17

Lately leftists have been moaning that conservatives have lost faith in the scientific community[895].

Conservatives distrust *official* science, because official scientist do not practice actual science, instead manufacturing official truth.

If you start arguing the scientific method, rather than "the scientific community", to a leftist, for example that warmists should make available the data that supposedly shows we are doomed if we don't obey them, they will react like a vampire exposed to sunlight. Leftists have not merely lost faith in the scientific method, they would like to burn anyone who advocates it at the stake. If you start arguing with a leftist that evolution is natural selection, and natural selection did not stop above the neck, they will call you a racist.

Now whenever I have argued with a leftist that official science is not applying the scientific method to X, they argue that applying the scientific method to X is impractical or immoral, therefore we should believe that whatever official government scientists do is science.

So, here is a test example, where applying the scientific method is easy, almost trivial: The Urban Hotspot effect.

The obvious way to measure the Urban Hotspot effect is to drive a thermometer from the countryside through the center of town then out into the countryside on the other side of town. Repeat at various times of day and various towns.

Now obviously no officially endorsed government funded scientist has ever done such a thing, presumably because if he did, his career would come to an abrupt end, for anyone who has ever gone looking for a picnic spot while driving through a rural highway on a hot day has noticed that the Urban Hotspot effect, if measured in such a fashion, would be quite high, and reporting a high Urban Hotspot Effect would have the same effect as saying "niggardly" in a room full of affirmative action English graduates.

So instead, he measures the urban hotspot effect in some highly indirect fashion involving obscure alleged Chinese historical records, that, strange to report, no one else is able to find.

What would happen if a scientist was to actually measure the Urban Hotspot Effect? Well the article I linked to above gives us a hint:

> scientific authority is too easily had or invented — from temporary statuses with slow-moving associations that take time to detect and reject rogue members, to fake statuses with make-believe organizations of their own inven-

---

[895]https://scholarlykitchen.sspnet.org/2012/03/30/why-is-science-both-more-important-and-less-trusted/

tion. Maddow recounts a situation in which a person masquerading as an authority was later kicked out of one association, relocated to another, was kicked out of that — but in the meantime, he was able to get cited litera- ture into the scientific record and into books that had large cultural conse- quences, including justifying at least one despot to terrorize a class of citi- zens based on this false science.

Notice that in the example given, there was no argument that the scientists results were incorrect, merely that they could legitimize the incorrect political position, So, doing actual science, will swiftly get you ejected from all professional associations, since politics is now so all embracing that any scientific result could have political consequences.

If you cannot do actual science on the Urban Hotpot Effect, you cannot do actual science on anything political, and these days, just about everything is political, so, to a good approximation, if anyone is an official scientist, chances are he is not doing science, and unlikely to be interested in doing science.

This may well explain our technological stagnation. Science relevant to engines be- came political, so engines stopped advancing. Similarly with one field after another, photo lithography being one of the last to fall.

What is the scientific method?

Well it cannot be entirely expressed in words, except cryptically and briefly. It can, however, be expressed by examples, as I have just done. Another good example illustrating the scientific method is the Sokal Hoax and Wood's exposureof the N Ray delusion[896]. WHO research into the effects of pesticides, and all research into the effects of low dose radiation, are conducted in much the same way that research into N Rays was conducted, but back then it was safe to doubt N Rays, whereas today it is seriously dangerous for one's career to doubt WHO.

Two famous and historically important summaries of the scientific method are:
1. the Royal Society's "nullius in verba", which means that when expert authority claims to know X, you are supposed to ask how they know X, and if they don't have a good answer, you are not supposed to believe them.
2. Richard Feynman "Science is the belief in the ignorance of experts"

Around the time that the Royal Society started weaseling on "nullius in verba" and the journals stopped insisting that those supplying politically correct science conclusions needed to provide their data and their methods of analyzing their data that supposedly led to their conclusions, official science and the scientific method parted company.

The rot set in earlier than that. The scientific method was in a bad way once they in- troduced peer review after World War II. If one reviewer of n can block unwanted truths, unwanted truths are never going to get through. For science to work, you need a system where you only have to impress one editor of n editors, not a system where you have to refrain from offending any one reviewer of n reviewers. Peer review is entirely deadly in its effects on science. Everything becomes political.

---

[896]https://www.scribd.cometwww.rexresearch.com/blondlot/nrays.htm

conservatives are not the only people losing faith in official science

2012-04-01 16:45:42

Amgen, the worlds largest independent biotech firm, ran a replication survey on fifty three widely cited landmark cancer research papers. Only six were replicable[897].

If conservatives are losing faith in official science[898], maybe that is an indicator that conservatives are in contact with reality.

Left wing tells

2012-04-06 11:03:46

Every time you twit a leftist with the Trayvon Martin incident, he will list how the evil racist George Zimmerman provoked Martin by the horrible racism of suspecting Martin of criminality – which implicitly admits what is explicitly denied, that the six foot one black Martin attacked the five foot seven mestizo Zimmerman, which in turn implicitly admits that leftists approve of the black racist attacks on whites that they so enthusiastically encourage[899].

Similarly, if you twit a leftist with "trick to... hide the decline", they will patronizingly explain to you that "decline" does not mean what it sounds like it means, but resist explaining "trick" or "hide" no matter how vigorously you twit them on it, implicitly admitting that they know full well that "trick" and "hide" mean exactly what they sound like they mean– which in turn implies that they don't care whether global warming is true or false, only that it is a way of getting the power to create a totalitarian world terror state and get rid of a few billions of excess population.

Over time, leftism has been getting more and more evil.

Leftists like to trace leftism to the left side of the french Estates General. Like every version of history that leftists like, this does not seem to be true. French leftism repeatedly dead ended disastrously, swiftly winding up in Bonapartism, and had to be repeatedly re-created by the English left, in much the same way the anti colonialist movement was manufactured by the imperial powers and forcibly imposed on the third world, much as Soros and the CIA are trying to restart leftism in the countries of the former Soviet empire after it dead ended in Stalinism.

The English left, not the Jews nor the French, is the source and origin of the world's left. What we now call progressive or reform Jews merely got in on a good thing during the twentieth century, but the greatest glories of the left predate the twentieth century, and thus predate significant Jewish participation in the left.

Before and shortly after World War II, English leftism was progressive protestantism, was nominally Christian, although for a century or so Jesus Christ had been demoted from the incarnation of God to chief community organizer, so that progressive protes-

---

[897]https://www.ahrp.org/cms/content/view/839/9/
[898]https://www.speak4sociology.org/?p=521
[899]https://ozconservative.blogspot.com.au/2012/04/video-test.html

tantism was well on the way to becoming Universalist Unitarianism, and Universalist Unitarianism was already scarcely distinguishable from militant atheism.

Reform Judaism was a conversion to leftism, and thus a conversion from Judaism to progressive protestantism, with the result that reform Jews, like progressive protestants, are not reproducing, while Orthodox Jews continue reproduce industriously as they always have.

The greatest glories of the left, and their most plausibly righteous accomplishments, were the emancipation of women, the emancipation of blacks, and the abolition of slavery. Every leftist project since then has been ever more dubious. Leftism requires ever more reforms, and thus, with the passage of time, pursues reforms that are ever less credible. I have already argued that the emancipation of women was an intolerable mistake, and a disaster that must and will be reversed, possibly through the collapse of our civilization, certainly through the collapse of our government. Haiti and South Africa[900] suggest that black emancipation also was a disaster, that blacks are better off ruled by whites than ruling themselves. What about slavery?

Of all the left wing projects, abolishing slavery was the most plausibly good, and the least plausibly evil. Debt based slavery is reasonably defensible, since the incompetent and improvident wind up with someone else making decisions for them, as they should. In practice, however, slavery tends to be war based, with members of incompetent and improvident groups being enslaved, regardless of individual competence and providence.

If some people are naturally slaves, and others naturally masters, which I rather think is the case, it seems unlikely that recently existent slavery was very precise in putting people in the right categories. So I would say that abolishing slavery was not too bad, but everything else was bad, and has been getting steadily worse.

All organizations move left

2012-04-17 05:39:02

With the purge of two of its best writers for "racism", the "American Spectator" completes the movement left. The current issue has an article "Neutral Objective Facts" whose subtext is that the mainstream media is not biased, it is just that reality has a liberal bias, and it is entirely hopeless to try to create a conservative media, because a a conservative media is overtly biased, hence disreputable, while the mainstream media is not.

Apparently photoshop jobs are just part of reality, and not a manifestation of overt left wing bias, whereas failure to echo Obama talking points is a manifestation of overt right wing bias.

Which if true, means that "American Spectator" has no reason to exist. Come on, show your true progressivism by cutting your own throats.

And what is "racism"? Why is the belief that the appearance and origin of a desk has a good correlation with the desk's value and usefulness not known as "deskism", and why is "deskism" unlikely to to destroy one's career?

---

[900]https://www.ourcivilisation.com/die.htm

Racism and Deskism

2012-04-17 11:12:11

What is "racism"? Why is the belief that the appearance and origin of a desk has a good correlation with the desk's value and usefulness not known as "deskism", and why is "deskism" unlikely to to destroy one's career, whereas the belief that the appearance and origin of a human has a good correlation with various desirable or undesirable characteristics is a horrid and unthinkable sin.

Racism, sexism, and so forth, is the act of using the same kind of reasoning to make inferences about people, as one would use to make inferences about anything else.

Thus in all of history there was never such a word, until the twentieth century, for in the twentieth century, various thoughts about this world have been prohibited, in much the same manner, and for much the same reasons, as various thoughts about the next were prohibited in earlier centuries.

Now some people will say that racism is *irrationally* making inferences from someone's appearance and origins, but in practice, no application of Bayes theorem to particular individual cases that includes this kind of information will ever be accepted as rational, thus no application of this information in any real life situation will ever be accepted as rational - though of course those crying "racist" will make an unprincipled exception for themselves. Knowing that visiting certain parts of the city will surely get them assaulted, they don't go there, and they spend stupendous amounts of money to ensure that their kids do not go to school with blacks.

Monsters among us

2012-04-20 13:44:08

One curious and difficult to explain aspect of the left, is the tendency to hate what is good and true and to love monstrous evil and barefaced lies. Thus, for example, compare the worshipful treatment of China from 1956 to 1972, with the high pitched moral outrage directed at China when the Chinese government ended mass murder and artificial famine in the late seventies, and set to replacing slave labor and command with wage labor and profitability in 1981. Similarly their affection for Islamists. While the left is evil, the company they love to keep is apt to be astoundingly evil, with the result that old fashioned Christians, those few of them that still remain, are apt to suspect demonic infiltration rather than communist infiltration. You will still today get denial that the old China used mass murder, artificial famine and slave labor, combined with hearty condemnation of the current use of wage labor in China. Similarly, no one notices when our "allies" ethnically cleanse Christians from their lands, having already rendered those lands judenrien.

Below the fold, you will find an outlandishly disgusting video, which reveals that leftists frequently lack the gag reflex, are disinclined to turn away in horror and revulsion from that which is horrible and revolting. A bunch of leftists, smiling, giggling, and joking, simulate cannibalism on a living person, and don't realize how it is going to look when normals view the video.

https://blog.reaction.la/videos/monsters_among_us.mp4

Roissy, now calling himself Heartiste, has an interesting explanation.[901]:

A lot of the leftist program, for example feminism and gay liberation, is just inherently revolting and disgusting, due to our adaption to the ancestral environment, so to get along in progressive circles, you had better not have a gag reflex – but the same gag reflex that makes us turn away from women pretending to be men, and men pretending to be women, also makes us turn away from evil.

Consider, for example, Germaine Greer. When young and pretty, she had lots and lots of sex with lots and lots of high status males, mainly musicians of mildly successful bands. However, though she had lots of sex, she never had a sexual relationship. She probably believed she had sexual relationships with lots and lots of high status men, but they did not believe they had a sexual relationship with her. She wanted to have children, and always expected that some suitably high status man would choose to have children with her, but who wants to hang out with a raging slut? Any guy that she considered good enough to have sex with was good enough that he had better options. It appears that she was uniformly treated as a filthy hole in which to relieve oneself, for we hear about her sexual acts from her and her feminist friends, not from the numerous men that banged her. I conjecture that men did not want to announce they were dropping their loads in Germain Greer, any more than they wanted to admit to wanking off in a filthy public toilet. Eventually, approaching menopause, she woke up to the horrifying reality that she was no longer sexually attractive except as a hole to drop a quick load in, and spent a fortune on IVF, attempting to have fatherless children - unsuccessfully.

If you notice this sort of thing, that Germaine Greer was disgusting, it will blight your career as much as saying "nigger" (or saying "niggardly" – leftists do not know etymology). And so, as an unintended side effect, the left is, as in the video above, disturbingly comfortable with evil and horror. A old fashioned Christian would say that women's liberation leads to demonic possession. I prefer the naturalistic explanation based on adaption to the ancestral environment[902], but Germaine Greer does look demonically possessed.

---

[901] https://heartiste.wordpress.com/2012/04/18/the-psychology-of-feminists-and-manboobs/
[902] https://heartiste.wordpress.com/2012/04/18/the-psychology-of-feminists-and-manboobs/

Rule by consensus has a similar effect. If you notice that the evil and the insane are having disproportionate influence over the consensus, you will not get far. If you want a career in progressive circles, you had best be incapable of noticing evil and madness.

Not the cognitive elite

2012-04-24 11:08:03

The immensely well paid staff of the World Bank issued a pile of nonsense about European financial problems in which they kept calling a positive feedback loop a negative feedback loop[903]. Obama's speechwriters issued an equally stupid speech to their black mascot in which they called the Falkland Islands the Maldives[904].

From time to time, people dig up tests that were given to high school kids in the eighteen seventies, and point out that today's Harvard postgraduates would be unable to pass them.

To which those defending our current elite reply that the curriculum is different. Supposedly it is not that our current elite does not know !#!%, and beans were not covered in

---

[903] https://www.google.com/search?q=%22negative+feedback+loops%22+OR+%22negative+feedback+loop%22+site%3Ahttp%3A%2F%2Fwww.imf.org%2F
[904] https://www.telegraph.co.uk/news/worldnews/southamerica/falklandislands/9207183/Barack-Obama-makes-Falklands-gaffe-by-calling-Malvinas-the-Maldives.html

their curriculum, beans being a menial old fashioned obsolete topic unworthy of their immense brains. While today's Harvard PhDs would flunk high school in the 1870s, 1870 schoolkids would, we are told, flunk Harvard. Well of course they would flunk Harvard. Back in the bad old days they did not know that whites are bad and blacks are good and that men are bad and women are good. Learn to chant "Four legs good, two legs bad", and you too can be a Harvard PhD in sociology or in interdisciplinary studies.

Perhaps I know the difference between a positive feedback loop and a negative feedback loop because of my background in computers, but why do I know the difference between the Falkland islands and the Maldives, while Obama's gigantic entourage of speechwriters and fact checkers does not?

What people know is not necessarily a good indicator of intelligence. There is a lot of stuff to know, and plausibly people know different things– but smart people know the stuff in their own field, like the difference between the Maldives and the Malvinas. And if you are going to use the concept of feedback loop to analyze the financial system, you should know the difference between a negative feedback loop and a positive feedback loop. And if you don't trust your audience to know, use the phrase "vicious cycle", or "run", which are usually more precise, accurate, and appropriate to any situation where one might be tempted to use "negative feedback loop" inappropriately.

You will notice I have not bothered to explain the difference between a positive feedback loop and a negative feedback loop, nor explain which are the Malvinas and which are the Maldives– because I figure that most people who read my blog are considerably smarter and more knowledgeable than Obama's staff or the IMF staff and would not appreciate being patronized.

Nazism descends from Lutheranism

2012-04-29 08:27:01

Just as progressivism, (by which I mean anglosphere mainstream leftism) descends from the Puritans, via the infamous and conspiratorial Exeter Hall, the Acorn of its day, and "super protestantism", looks like Nazism is descended from Lutheranism[905].

The apple does not fall far from the tree. Lutherans hated Jews, Puritans hated Christmas and men having sex with women.

Mencius argued that Nazism was genuinely right wing because it was not progressivism. This fits the definition of the "right", that whosoever disagrees with progressivism on any one point of ten thousand points of doctrine, is a rightist (and doubtless a racist also). If however, Nazism is, like progressivism, a child of the seventeenth century holy wars, this accurately describes its extensive commonalities with leftism.

Thus Nazis are rightists, in that they are not descended from puritanism, but leftists, in that they are descended from protestantism.

Thus World War II and denazification may be understood as an atheocratic continuation of the theocratic holy wars of the seventeenth century. Once the Roman Catholics were defeated and the Holy Roman Empire vanished, the protestants turned on each

---

[905]https://socialpathology.blogspot.com.au/2012/04/1932-german-election.html

other, since each sect of protestantism disagreed with a different aspect of Roman Catholi-cism, having little in common except that they deviated from Roman Catholicism on a few issues of a thousand issues.

Theocracy is inherently warlike. The warlike character of theocracy/atheocracy is ob-fuscated at present by the strategy of progressivism/puritanism to ally with the far en-emy, such as communists and Muslims, against the near enemy, ordinary white taxpaying Americans.

Hence the doctrine of democratic peace: Democracies never go to war with each other – provided we define all democracies where progressives lacked the upper hand as undemocratic. If, however, we ignorantly look at things like voting and elections, it looks very much as if democracies frequently do go to war with each other.

The Laffer Curve

2012-04-30 13:03:46

Let us suppose you are a smart ambitious guy, and have a big idea that you think can change the world, and make a great big pile of money. You run your idea before some angel investors, and they think it is worth a shot. So you, and they, form yourselves into a class C corporation. You are probably pretty well off, and they are probably really well off, so you are paying the maximum tax rate.

Miraculously, your idea turns out to be hot stuff, and the corporation makes a hun-dred million dollars - which sounds like a lot, but in order to get there, you had to cut the angel investors in for a share, the next round investors in for a share, various highly talented people who joined the company in for a share ... But before they get their share, the government wants its share.

Unfortunately the U.S. corporate tax rate is 39.2%. Now you have $60 800 000 in net income. If you are in the state of California, they want 8.84 percent corporate tax. So now you have 51 960 000. OK, this gets split between the various investors, the founding employees, and you, all whom are probably paying at the maximum marginal tax rate. So after it is paid out, the feds want 35%, and California wants 10%, so now that is down to 28 000 000 or so. And then you spend it, and there is sales tax, so now that is down to 26 000 000 or so.

Thus, three dollars for the taxman, one dollar for you.

Of course, should your plan fail, and everyone lose their money, that is your problem, not the government's.

It is often said that the Bush tax cuts disproved the Laffer curve, since they arguably reduced, rather than increased federal receipts, but that is because they were mostly tax cuts on the poor. They substantially reduced the number of people paying any income tax at all. To the extent that they cut taxes on the rich, they greatly increased receipts from the rich, almost enough to offset the reduced receipts from the poor.

Taxes on the rich in the US are far, far east of the Laffer Maximum.

There is plenty of room for the US government to raise more money by taxing the poor - taxing beer, cigarettes, and petrol. A Pigovian tax on single moms and broken homes would also, like the Pigovian tax on booze, improve behavior, while raising money without harming the economy too much - except of course that any money spent by the government, is, at the margin, spent on damaging and hurtful things, so that while a Pigovian tax on broken homes and fatherless children would improve private behavior, it would worsen government behavior. Giving money to the government is like giving money to a drunken mugger.

But if they want to raise revenue to get money to hand out to crony capitalists, taxing the rich is a dry well. They have to tax the poor. Taxing beer and cigs has reached their Laffer curve limits also.. The last untapped Pigovian sin tax is fatherless children and broken homes. If our rulers don't want to piss off the feminists by extending sin taxes to new sins, they have to do what Europe does: Tax fuel, food, clothes, and such.

In Europe, all the wells are dry. Europeans are far, far east of the Laffer curve maximum even for taxes on the poor, except that for reasons of feminism, they have not touched the last Pigovian sin tax.

Every time England, Spain, or Greece raise taxes, tax receipts immediately fall, and fall a lot. This rationalized away as Keynesian recession. Supposedly taxes are reducing demand. But for taxes to reduce demand, they would have to raise money, at least at first. Since the tax rises immediately lose money, they are not reducing demand, but reducing supply.

Nonetheless, if we look at the European "austerity" budgets, they are all tax rises today, spending "cuts" tomorrow, the "cuts" being that at some time in the future, expenditures will rise by less than planned, and people who expected to have government jobs and handouts someday in the future will, someday, not have them.

Predictably, the "austerity" tax rises raise tax rates today reducing revenue today, while the "austerity" spending cuts may reduce spending some time, some time, some day, so the European austerity budgets "unexpectedly" fail to reduce the deficits. Seems that most economic headlines these days have the word "unexpected" in them.

If you are going to cut the US deficit, the place to start is massive tax cuts on the rich, and end to handouts to crony capitalists and the poor. All government involvement in the finance sector, green energy, and the rest, is crony capitalist handouts. Social security supplemental is ninety nine percent handouts to the undeserving poor, for example people who say their sexual deviations and alcohol habit prevents them from working, or that they are victims of discrimination on the basis of mental handicap, race, criminal past, and gender, for example people suffering from a mental syndrome that forces them to scream obscenities at bosses, fellow employees, and customers, not to mention all those people with bad backs - but I digress. Back to the Laffer curve.

How far east of the Laffer Maximum is Greece? The proportion of Singaporean residents aged 25 to 64 in employment is 77.1% In Greece, about half that.

With that rate of labor participation, obviously the way for the Greek government to raise more money is to cut handouts and taxes, which is the opposite of what the Greek government is doing.

I notice that whenever these "unexpected" falls in revenue are discussed, people piously proclaim them as evidence for the truth of Keynesianism, which suggests that in Academia blaming revenue falls on the Laffer curve is as dangerous as blaming black dysfunction on a genetic propensity to stupidity and violence. When curiously few people are working, it is obviously the Laffer curve. (At least if we include regulatory burdens such as that employees are fireproof once hired as part of the Laffer curve burden.) But try getting an academic, or anyone whose job is government dependent, to say that.

Now with taxes like that, one might wonder how America functions at all. The answer is quite simple. If your business starts making any money, then you apply the same energy, effort, and ingenuity you spent creating the business to moving all income generating activities outside of the US. If it was not for tax dodging and the export of wealth generating activities, the US would be a third world hell hole.

Leftists intend:

2012-05-10 06:42:56

It is often said that leftists intend good, or that they intend the same things that all normal decent people intend.

Leftists intend, among other things, the deaths of several billion of supposedly excess population, in order to protect Gaia from the hand of man. For example the food to fuel mandates have created artificial famine in many parts of world.

Leftists intend, among other things, the destruction of technological civilization by cutting off its energy supply.

Leftists intend, among other things, to make most people slave laborers of the state dominated by leftists, thus maximizing the status and benefits of members of the state apparatus. This is considerably worse than private chattel slavery, since resources owned by a private owner are conserved, whereas resources owned by the state are wasted and destroyed.

Leftists intend and expect that they will use state superpowers for good, in pretty much the way that one expects one will follow a diet and exercise regime, but apart from the fact that it is difficult to use state power for good, it is also distasteful, like a very strict diet. Leftist want power itself, not the benefits that power brings, and one cannot really experience power except by making others suffer, so in practice, leftists delight in the use of power to make others suffer, and when their fellow leftists behaved in this manner, older leftists were unsurprised and undismayed – because any leftists that were surprised and dismayed changed sides.

Likely some leftists believe that with themselves as masters, all the slaves would be happy, but are not much interested in historical reality tests that suggest the contrary.

When the original anglosphere leftists, the puritans, punished people for holding hands, they could plausibly believe that they were doing good, protecting people from fornication, but when they burst into people's houses to find them celebrating Christmas, and destroyed the Christmas feast, they were enjoying the exercise of power to make people suffer, for the New Testament clearly endorses spraying a thin spray of Christian whitewash over old pagan festivals. If someone performs a 100% pagan festival, but he performs it to the Lord, and giveth God thanks, this makes it, the New Testament tells us, a 100% Christian festival. The Puritans believed that being holier than thou, they were righteously entitled to make thou suffer, and their anti Christmas measures suggest that their anti fornication and anti cruelty to animals measures ultimately rested on delight in making people suffer.

Anti fornication, and anti cruelty to animals had scriptural justification. Anti Christmas did not.

And through all the transformations their movement has undergone, ultimately transforming into modern anti Christian anglosphere leftism, this thread has remained constant, that they will snatch any justification that they are holier than thou, and thus entitled to have power over thou, and thus entitled to take righteous delight in making thou suffer.

They are not holier than me. They are evil power hungry hateful hypocrites, for those few of them that are young and naive leave the movement whenever it shows its true face, which it frequently does.

Effects of taxing and spending

2012-05-13 21:45:06

Back in 2009 Alesina and Ardagna[906] did a survey of the effects of large changes in fiscal policy.

Unsurprisingly they found that large revenue increases seldom increased revenue, indicating that most governments and most taxes are near their Laffer maximum, and that spending increases were not very stimulatory. Indeed often spending cuts stimulated the economy, which suggests that at the margin government spending is of negative absolute value, not just negative net value - that people would be better off if the money was spent blowing stuff up in distant lands.

This shows that supply side effects of large changes in fiscal policy substantially outweigh demand side effects.

This explains and predicts the failure of "austerity" in Britain and France, since the "austerity" consisted of increasing expenditure relative to GDP, but increasing taxes - measures to increase the power of the parasitic ruling class, and diminish the power of the productive class. For austerity to work, has to be austere for the rulers. Similarly, it predicts the failure of "stimulus" in the US, since the stimulus consists of the government doing even more damage than before.

Alesina[907] tells us that spending does not stimulate, and cutting spending does not depress. He provides a couple of politically correct explanations involving expectations for this observation, but fails to mention what seems to be to be the glaringly obvious explanation: That government transfer spending discourages people, especially women and protected minorities, from working, and that government direct spending consists, at the margin, not of roads, public safety, and garbage collection, but of evil people doing hurtful things[908].

---

[906]https://www.economics.harvard.edu/faculty/alesina/files/Large%2Bchanges%2Bin%2Bfiscal%2Bpolicy_October_2009.pdf

[907]https://mercatus.org/sites/default/files/publication/Fiscal%20Adjustments.%20What%20Do..Corrected%20Table.Alesina.pdf

[908]https://www.youtube.com/watch?v=ze3GB_b7Nuo

God is dead

2012-05-17 10:55:15

An excellent post by Jonathon Frost[909].

> If it's traditionalism you seek, you won't find it under any 21st-century basilica.

The actually existent Christian Church has capitulated to its heretical atheistic spawn, progressivism. And if a few fragments of resistance remain, they are going to go down soon enough.

Among the excellent links provided by Jonathon Frost is this one on Christian Marriage[910].

The original sin that led to modern Christianity/Progressivism was the Puritans lust for power. The Puritans believed, as their successors the modern progressives believe, that being holier than thou, they were entitled to exercise power over thou:

As I said earlier in the comments: in Cromwell's England, and in the puritan colonies in the Americas, most of the crimes and punishments concerned not crimes against property and the person, but crimes against the puritan interpretation of scripture, the most infamous such enforcement being the war on Christmas.

The puritans objected to Christmas supposedly because it was impure, being a pagan festival thinly spray painted with Christianity, with the underlying paganism quite visible under the spray coat of Christianity.

But here is what Paul has to say on this topic: Romans 14:

> [2] For one believeth that he may eat all things: another, who is weak, eateth herbs.
> [3] Let not him that eateth despise him that eateth not; and let not him which eateth not judge him that eateth: for God hath received him.
> [4] Who art thou that judgest another man's servant? to his own master he standeth or falleth. Yea, he shall be holden up: for God is able to make him stand.
> [5] One man esteemeth one day above another: another esteemeth every day alike. Let every man be fully persuaded in his own mind.
> [6] He that regardeth the day, regardeth it unto the Lord; and he that regardeth not the day, to the Lord he doth not regard it. He that eateth, eateth to the Lord, for he giveth God thanks; and he that eateth not, to the Lord he eateth not, and giveth God thanks.
> [7] For none of us liveth to himself, and no man dieth to himself.
> [8] For whether we live, we live unto the Lord; and whether we die, we die unto the Lord: whether we live therefore, or die, we are the Lord's.
> [9] For to this end Christ both died, and rose, and revived, that he might be Lord both of the dead and living.

---

[909]https://www.jonathan-frost.com/god-is-dead/
[910]https://dalrock.wordpress.com/2012/05/11/reframing-christian-marriage/

[10] But why dost thou judge thy brother? or why dost thou set at nought thy brother? for we shall all stand before the judgment seat of Christ.

The puritans believed that being holier than the next person, they were entitled to exercise power over the next person – which attitude is the essential core of leftism, and as gross a violation of scripture as anything their successors did. Had they truly stuck to scripture, they would have known that Christmas can be 99% pagan, and still be 100% Christian if the person celebrating what once were pagan rituals, what would still be pagan rituals if a pagan celebrated them, celebrates Christmas to the Lord, and giveth God thanks.

In the restoration, General Monck reinstalled a King and reinstalled an official Church, in order to put an end to a frightening power struggle, the frightening struggle for political and religious authority within the army.

You were not required to be a member of the official Church, and lots of people were not, but if you were not officially a member of the official Church, you were not allowed anywhere near the levers of power.

The job of a king is to reign, which means that by simply existing and being King, he prevents the negative sum struggle for power from destroying the wealth of the Kingdom and possibly getting lots of people killed. His job is to deny political power to anyone and everyone that wants it.

The job of a king as head of the official Church is to prevent a negative sum theocratic struggle for power, to prevent people from advancing their political ambitions by being holier than thou. By preventing a theocratic struggle for religious authority, he prevents religion from being perverted into an instrument of power, and thus prevents morals from being corrupted by those who most loudly proclaim their greater holiness.

The King is not required to be personally holy, and Charles the Second certainly was not. He is required to go through the motions of believing in the official religion pro forma, but no more than that, and Charles the second just barely went through the motions pro forma. What the King does do is merely by being head of the Church, he quells people from using their real or purported religious beliefs to advance their ambitions.

Which did not stop the Whigs from trying, but it limited how far they got. To the great disgust of the Whigs, King Charles the Second firmly denied and ridiculed claims by the holy whigs that they should get to tell other people what to do in order to be as holy as the Whigs were.

This theocratic order gave you complete religious freedom to believe any nonsense you wanted, unless, of course, you wanted a position near the levers of state power, in which case you had to be Anglican. And, as an Anglican you could still believe almost anything you wanted, including that there was no God, except that you would not get far believing that your superior holiness justified exercising authority over English gentlemen.

The restoration reimposed overt and official theocracy, which lasted from the restoration in 1660 to various acts allowing unofficial religions access to state power in and around 1828-1856. The restoration, and the accompanying purge of puritans from every governmental institution, in particular academia and the church, immediately eradicated the overtly covert and officially unofficial theocracy of the puritans, and immediately and greatly expanded freedom, to just about everyone's great relief.

People celebrated the introduction of official theocracy with anti theocratic pagan rituals such as the maypole dance, correctly perceiving the introduction of official theocracy as the end of theocracy.

As soon as overt and official theocracy abolished covert and officially unofficial theocracy, we got the greatest freedom seen in recent history - at least greatest for property owning males. If you owned your own home, even if it was a tarpaper shack with a dirt floor, you were more free than Englishmen had ever been before or since. For women, vagabonds, and for people who lived in their master's household, not so much

And two centuries later, as soon as overt and official theocracy was abolished, everything started to go to hell:

Two centuries later, the dissenting/nonconformist churches, aka puritans, went into politics, from which they had been excluded, and started doing left wing stuff - anti slavery, female emancipation, education for the poor, and so forth, all of which had the convenient side effect of getting their hands on the levers of power. And once their hands were on the levers of power, dissent on an ever growing multitude of this worldly questions became dangerous, as it had never been dangerous under the overt and official theocracy. By 1890, unofficial and covert theocracy was already noticeable, and lot more repressive, a lot more politically correct, than official and overt theocracy had ever been.

The first big move of the new theocrats was imperialism and anti slavery. Imperialism was anti colonialist - a shift of power and wealth from the colonies to London, from the colonists to the theocrats.

The colonialists were a bunch of pirates and brigands, most of whom had become stationary brigands, who mostly produced better and less oppressive government than the native stationary brigands, but they were still more or less openly in the business of robbing people at gunpoint, and those of them that were not slavers had slaver connections.

So it would seem obvious that the well intentioned government in London would do a much better job, that transferring power and wealth from those selfish greedy colonialists to the pious dogooders in London would make everything much nicer for the oppressed natives.

I suppose anti slavery did make things better for the slaves, such of them as were capable of looking after themselves, but imperialism/anti colonialism did not make things better for the colonies, despite, or perhaps because of, the cheerfully piratical character of the colonialists. Rather, imperialism prefigured Zimbabwe. Anti colonialism was the imperialists doubling down on everything that was wrong with imperialism.

The aristocratic values of the well off class were exemplified by the restoration and the Cavalier Parliament and it is clear that the restoration was perceived and experienced as freedom for everyone, even though it was more freedom for the well off. The masses celebrated their freedom by making rude gestures at theocracy, for example by the maypole dances.

The restoration purged all state and quasi state institutions, among them, academia. One might expect that this restricted academic freedom, and in one important sense it did. Academics were prevented from pursuing power by being holier than thou. This led to the rise of science. Before the restoration, people discussed the circulation of the blood primarily in the context of more important questions such as the relationship between God the father and God the son.

The Puritans are responsible for the Petition of Right, and thus for the doctrine that freedoms of wealthy males apply to all men (except for slaves, servants, vagabonds, women and so on and so forth). The puritans are responsible for the doctrine that an Englishman's home is his castle, yet strangely, somehow, when the Puritans were in power, puritan soldiers would kick down a man's door to discover if he was roasting a goose to celebrate Christmas, and then destroy his Christmas feast, whereas after the restoration and the puritans were purged, an Englishman's home actually *was* his castle.

Before the restoration, science was "the invisible college". After the restoration, science was "the Royal Society", whose slogan "Nullius in Verba" ("Don't take anyone's word for it") epitomized the scientific method, and indeed the way that science was practiced from the restoration to the 1940s or so, when peer review was introduced, we started taking the word of secret cabals of peer reviewers, and instead of experimenters telling the scientific community what they observed, the scientific community would tell the experimenter what he observed.

Science lasted three centuries after the restoration, died one century after members of dissenter churches were allowed to get their hands on power.

Theocracy seems like a horrid system, and I suppose we would be better off with true separation of information and state, prohibiting the state from running schools or funding education, art, and science, all of which are apt to turn into religion in disguise if the state purports to be secular.

The restoration system had theocracy kept on a short leash by the King, and the King kept on a long leash by the gentlemen. For this to work, required a strong class of gentlemen, where a gentleman was expected to uphold his honor, and do his own policing, where gentlemen were capable of physical violence and expected to employ it when necessary. There were no police during this period. The puritan army peformed police like functions before the restoration. Police were introduced in England 1850, not long thereafter in the US, California in the early twentieth century being the last to become what Britons before 1850 called "a police state" - one where the power of the state is exercised through the police, rather than by giving expression to the general consensus among important people.

At about the same time that non conformist churches were allowed access to the levers of power, the power connected to those levers started to dramatically increase. It looks to me that the nonconformist churches were kicking down an open door - that the class of gentlemen ceased to be capable of exercising power, that if you had a King and a theocratic church today, there would be no one capable of keeping them in line, nor anyone other than the theocrats and the police to support the King's power, so the King would become a puppet of police and political ideologues, which is pretty much the shape of modern dictatorships.

So though I agree with Mencius Moldbug that it has been downhill since the restoration, it does not follow that the restoration system can be restored. For it to be restored, we would need a live God, and we don't have one.

Trayvon autopsy

2012-05-20 13:41:04

Here is what you did *not* hear about Trayvon's autopsy, the dog that did not bark.

You did not hear about the mark of single blow, while Zimmerman looks like he had an argument with a cement mixer.

So Trayvon attacked Zimmerman. He was bashing Zimmerman, while Zimmerman refused to fight back, screaming for help, hoping it would stop, or that help would arrive. When it became apparent that Trayvon would not stop till Zimmerman was dead or gravely injured, and help would not arrive, *then* Zimmerman shot Trayvon.

Well of course he attacked Zimmerman unprovoked. He was black. And every single person that accuses Zimmerman of attacking Trayvon, adduces as evidence that Zimmerman provoked Trayvon by suspecting him of being a criminal merely because he was dressed like a criminal and acting like he was casing the joint.

But if Zimmerman provoked Trayvon, that is not reason to suspect that Zimmerman attacked Trayvon, that is reason to suspect that Trayvon attacked Zimmerman.

So what every single person that accuses Zimmerman really thinks is that Zimmerman deserved a beating for failing to show the respect that is due to blacks.

If you, a white guy, go into a gated community, or on a private road, or into a resort where you are not a guest, you expect someone to ask you what you are doing, and you answer politely. I know this because I have been the guy asking, and the guy asked. Everyone always answers politely. They expect to be asked. But though it is OK to ask a white guy, it is intolerably wicked to ask a black guy, and so Zimmerman supposedly deserved his beating.

Asking someone what he is doing in a restricted area is not provocation - unless, of course, the person being asked is black, because blacks are the masters of the universe.

Soros and the rest fund domestic terrorism

2012-05-25 18:29:15

Normally I would not mention this, because for me, and everyone outside the limits of acceptable discourse, that the big names of the left fund terrorism against their opponents is like reporting that bears shit in the woods and the Pope is Catholic, but lately people who foolishly thought they were within the limits of acceptable discourse have asked everyone to blog about Brett Kimberlin[911]. So here is the requested boring public service announcement:

Not only do bears shit in the woods, but the limits of acceptable discourse shift ever leftwards. Check your weapons.

---

[911] https://www.google.com/search?q=Brett+Kimberlin+terrorist

Clueless conservatives.

2012-05-27 07:22:49

In response to Brett Kimberlin's attacks, clueless conservatives want to conserve a system that is fundamentally broken, entirely hostile against them, and inherently structured to move ever leftwards at an ever increasing rate.

Michelle Malkin piously complains[912]:
> This is a convoluted, ongoing nightmare that combines abuse of the court system, workplace intimidation, serial invasions of privacy, perjury, and harassment of family members. McCain was forced to move with his family out of his house this week, and has just gotten a small taste of what Aaron and Patterico have been enduring over the past year. Aaron and his wife were fired from their jobs after their employer feared the office would be targeted next. Convicted bomber Kimberlin has filed bogus "peace orders" against Aaron, …

Hey, wonder how come a convicted criminal can use the legal system to attack conservatives, but conservatives, many of them lawyers, cannot use the legal system to protect themselves?

The left is the state, and the state is the left. The left is the state at prayer. The judiciary is the mailed fist of the left. Brett Kimberlin provides judges with a legal excuse to do what they want to do anyway, and a fall guy to blame if the action should turn out to be embarrassing. Every single judge, and every single public servant, is a leftist, because if he was not a leftist, they would not hire him. Lawfare works for the left, and against everyone who is not left, because the judges are in on it.

With enough light shone on this operation, the judges may well retreat and throw the entirely expendable Brett Kimberlin to the wolves, only to swiftly replace him with another convicted criminal similarly given early release to do some more crimes against the right and similarly funded by the pillars of the establishment. Blaming the convicted criminal Brett Kimberlin is foolish and pointless, because he is a nonentity, a tool, an entirely replaceable tool, who, having attracted attention, will soon be replaced. There are plenty more convicted criminals where he came from.

Anonymized funding for terrorists

2012-05-27 13:00:01

I was outraged to hear that Fidelity and Schwab had seemingly funded Kimberlin, but held off mentioning it because I suspected that they had merely been laundering other people's money in their role as financial institutions - which turned out to be the case[913]. It looks like some people funding Kimberlin unsurprisingly did not wish this to become known, thus Schwab's name was on the check, the way the bank's name is on a bank check

---

[912]https://michellemalkin.com/2012/05/23/free-speech-show-solidarity-for-targeted-conservative-bloggers/
[913]https://www.breitbart.com/Big-Government/2012/05/25/Kimberlin-Funders-Stunned-to-Discover-they-Fund-Kimberlin

- the equivalent of a brown paper bag full of small used notes, except that you cannot get a tax refund on a brown paper bag full of small used notes.

More clueless conservatives

2012-05-27 16:29:07

The Volokh Conspiracy naively, or pretending to be naive, piously asks about the Brett Kimberlin incidents[914]:

> One thing I do not comprehend about either story is the apparent reticence of local authorities. I would think local law enforcement would move heaven and earth to uncover who sicced SWAT on Patterico's home and it is unconscionable the local authorities in Montgomery County, Maryland would sit by and allow the continued abuse of legal process that has victimized Worthing.

I wonder if any commenter who attempts to explain this mystery to him gets instabanned.

Not the cognitive elite

2012-06-07 10:23:08

Theoretically elite colleges select people with very high scores on the college entrance exam, thus select very smart people, thus our ruling elite is composed of very smart people.

There are two problems with this story. One is that they do not in fact select people with very high scores[915] on the college entrance exam, and the other is that during the 1990s, high scores on the college entrance exam frequently ceased to correlate with being very smart[916].

LSAT is pretty much an IQ test, and if colleges aim for a high LSAT score, they are aiming for a high IQ student body, but during the 1990s SAT and PSAT ceased to correlate strongly with IQ, suggesting a loss of enthusiasm for dangerously smart students.

From the 1900s to the 1990s, college entrance exams in the US have been in large part test of IQ. Now, not so much.

At the same time as the change in testing, we see elite institutions taking in large numbers of students that seem to be pretty dumb: Thus, for example,Claremont McKenna College was admitting people that could not read[917], and faking up their test scores. The elite magnet school Thomas Jefferson High School for Science and Technology in Alexandria lowered the questions on its entrance exam so that they were two years below grade[918], which is to say, suitable for people of well below average IQ.

[914]https://volokh.com/2012/05/26/beyond-incivility/

[915]https://www.city-journal.org/2012/cjc0215jlcj.html "Lessons from Claremont"

[916]https://previous.us.mensa.org/join_mensa/testscores.php3 "Mensa derecognizes some college prep exams"

[917]https://www.city-journal.org/2012/cjc0524cj.html

[918]https://washingtonexaminer.com/opinion/columnists/2012/05/examiner-local-editorial-dumbing-it-down-even-thomas-jefferson/637631

The reaction of the various elite institutions to the Claremont scandal suggests that they are all guilty of faking up their intake test scores, and are more alarmed by the prospect that their own misconduct might come to light, than the prospect that the Claremont scandal might cast doubt on their own eliteness.

From 1928 to 1970, there was concern that affluent white males tended to do rather better on the tests than most, and there were innumerable efforts to fix this problem, but in the end, the only solution that proved satisfactory was taking race and sex explicitly into account, which solution was implemented. For some reason, in the US they lost interest in fixing the problem that affluent white males tended to do well, and were content to merely fix the problem that white males tended to do well.

Having fixed the problem that they cared about, they had no reason to move away from selecting for IQ, but manifestly they are. There must be a new problem that they care about.

The Thomas Jefferson scandal gives us a hint. They lowered their exam questions to make them suitable for applicants of below average IQ at the same time as they adjusted their recruitment procedures to recruit primarily for political correctness.

When academies first started recruiting on political correctness, they asked the candidate to submit an essay describing himself. Naturally, students took a look at what essays worked, and what essays did not, and swiftly discovered that what was required was an essay explaining how left wing one was. So pretty soon all the smart kids were submitting plausible and convincing essays that they were the second coming of Karl Marx. So the essay ceased to be a useful indicator of leftism, though it was reasonably well correlated with IQ.

So academies then started emphasizing extracurricular activities. Naturally, students took a look at what extracurricular activities worked, and what extracurricular activities did not, and swiftly discovered that what was required was extracurricular activities demonstrating how left wing one was. So pretty soon all the smart kids had manufactured organizations that generated the appearance of pursuit of various supposedly noble causes, without requiring much actual work for these supposedly noble causes. So the extracurricular activity ceased to be a useful indicator of leftism, though it was reasonably well correlated with IQ.

So the academies asked for "student information sheets" and these cannot be reverse engineered as the essays and extracurricular activities were, because the students do not get to see them, so cannot discover what constitutes a report that is useful for getting into an elite institution, nor how to manipulate teachers into generating such reports.

When an academy switches to heavily weighting "student information sheets", it tends to recruit stupid students, as in the Thomas Jefferson scandal, indicating that the desired characteristic in the reports does not merely fail to correlate with intelligence, but correlates negatively with intelligence. From this I conclude that the report that gets you into an elite institution says, in effect, that the student swallows the political propaganda he is taught mindlessly and unthinkingly.

Islamic theocracies have a similar problem with adverse selection, in that the holiest tend to be the most stupid.

Tea Party Express is far left entryist

2012-06-15 07:38:22

In its mailings, the Tea Party Express conceptualizes the political landscape of the US as "conservative republicans", "moderate republicans", "right wing democrats", and just plain "democrats". There is, it seems, only one liberal democrat, and no liberal or left wing republicans.

Thus betraying the writer's *real* viewpoint - that the far left is normal and mainstream, and all the rest are weirdoes, despite the fact that today's "conservative republicans" are for the most part far to the left of the Clinton Democrats.

If the left wing of the Republican party are "moderates" to you, then you are looking at the party from outside.

Every few years the supposed right adopts the positions that were unthinkably extreme a decade or so previously. For example today's "conservative republicans" generally support Obamacare light, which is far to the left of the Bush position on medical care, which was itself far to the left of Clinton position on medical care.

Actual republicans conceptualize the political landscape as just plain "republicans", "republicans in name only", "moderate democrats", and "liberal democrats".

Tea Party Express has twice called Sherrod Brown a liberal democrat, but it seems that no other Democrats are liberals, whereas lots of Republicans that are pretty far left are "moderates"

If Tea Party Express opposes "moderate republicans" in favor of "conservative republicans", why does it call them moderates? Does Ann Coulter call herself conservative?

Inflation

2012-06-16 20:34:35

If we believe the official inflation figures, supposedly living standards in the US are rising: Yet the proportion of people with cars is falling, the proportion of households with a car is falling faster, and the amount of meat people are eating is falling - consistent with a cpi rising at about the rate that shadowstats claims, about six to ten percent[919]

The official rate of inflation for 2012 April was 2.3% annualized.[920]

Inflation sounds like a well defined economic quantity, as does "quantity of money", but neither one is well defined. Inflation is poorly defined because we are comparing apples and oranges. I think that 2012 cars are inferior to 1972 cars, while those who compile the official cpi think they are enormously better, hence, as I have often argued, we are better off explaining the business cycle in terms of evil and madness, the wisdom of crowds and the madness of crowds, than in terms of such nebulous and undefinable quantities as inflation, quantity of money, and real GDP. People put scare quotes around "evil" and even around "madness" because these are not well defined, but at moderate levels of inflation, they are a lot better defined and more readily definable than "inflation" and "real GDP"

---

[919]https://www.shadowstats.com/alternate_data/inflation-charts
[920]https://www.tradingeconomics.com/united-states/inflation-cpi

Clearly, regardless of whether cars are getting better or worse, someone without a car has a substantially lower standard of living than someone with a car, and someone who is having meat for dinner has a substantially higher standard of living that someone who is having beans for dinner. So let us check these alleged figures against such common sense measures.

Nomnal GDP, unlike "real" GDP is reasonably well defined. Nominal GDP is growing at about 4.5%[921], so if official inflation is reasonable "real" GDP is growing at 2.2% per year. Population is growing at 0.91%.

But if real GDP was really growing, people would have more cars and more meat dinners. And they don't.

Mysteriously, the government stopped making the figures for total number of registered cars available in 2008, when the number started falling (or at least I cannot find the numbers, though some well connected people seem to be able to see them).

The last available data was for 2009, which showed a one percent fall relative to 2008[922] - and then the 2009 number disappeared, and no new numbers have appeared.

However, the number of cars is closely proportional to the the number of miles supposedly traveled - since the number of miles supposedly traveled is calculated from the no longer easily found number registered - and this has been falling at about 1% per year. Registrations are stable and falling from levels considered catastrophically low in 2008.

Since population is growing at about one percent a year, cars per person is falling at about two percent a year, indicating a fall in "real" GDP of something like one percent a year, instead of growth at 2.2 percent.

Indicating that inflation is understated by three or four percent a year, indicating inflation of five or six percent a year - not hyperinflation by any means but headed in that direction. This falsifies the Keynesian account of the current crisis. The problem is not demand side.

Since people are consuming less of stuff that matters a lot to them, "real" GDP is falling one or two percent a year. Since nominal GDP is rising at 4.5%, "inflation" must be 4.5% plus one or two percent.

Meat consumption in the US has also been falling about 1% a year, and there has been a shift towards cheaper cuts of meat (parts of the cow that used to be ground up are now steaks), and there has been a shift towards small portions of meat (parts that used to be roasts are now steaks). Total egg consumption was unchanged from 2010 to 2011, despite population increase. Eggs are a somewhat cheaper substitute for meat, thus stable egg consumption is consistent with the trend in meat products towards cheaper cuts and smaller portions. If people are getting poorer, we would expect them to substitute eggs for meat.

I expect a long term trend of people in the west getting substantially poorer as regulation continues to explode, accompanied by official statistics supposedly proving the opposite. I also expect the discrepancy between official inflation and actual inflation, and between official statistics generally and reality, to continue growing, as is typical in dysfunctional regimes.

---

[921] https://www.forecasts.org/gdpgrowth.htm
[922] https://misunderstoodfinance.blogspot.com.au/2010/01/4-million-fewer-registered-cars-in-us.html

This is a supply side crisis. It is perfectly obvious what is causing the collapse in supply - any small business blog will tell you how the government persecutes them, and everything causing the crisis is getting worse, with no way to reverse trends through politics as normal. The Tea Party movement did what democratic politics say you are supposed to do, won, and got only more of the same.

Democracy must end, and will end, the only question being how bad things get before we do what must be done. There is a lot or ruin in a nation. I hope and expect we get collapse around 2026, but things could easily end with a whimper, rather than a bang.

The PC trajectory

2012-06-19 08:05:28

VDare complains that PC is getting worse. Ya think[923]?

Vdare compares a truth telling 1994 article appearing in the mainstream press, which points out systematic legal, state sponsored, and private persecution of whites in majority "minority" regions, which today could never appear.

Of course, if you read old books, it is apparent that political correctness has been getting worse ever since the eighteen thirties or thereabouts.

"Conservatives" think that last year or last decade was lovely, but things have gone too far left since then, our current Republican Presidential candidate being more of the "back to last year" persuasion. He promises slightly less Obamacare, a deficit that escalates not quite as fast, but proposes to continue demographic replacement and continue affirmative actioning blacks and women into government employment even where they vastly overrepresented relative to their numbers in the general population, and continue affirmative actioning women into college, even though they are already overrepresented in college despite significantly lower typical LSAT scores.

Nazis, neo nazis, and white nationalists think the nineteen thirties or early nineteen forties was politically fine, that Franklin D. Roosevelt and social security was the greatest thing since sliced bread, and there is nothing wrong with social security that soaking the rich could not fix, but that things went too far left once Jews were encouraged to convert to progressivism and join the ruling elite and promptly launched the civil rights movement. They don't think there was any such thing as political correctness in the early twentieth century. In this sense, Nazis are leftists - and the Tea Party are also leftists.

But everything that is going wrong today was visible in the middle of the nineteenth century.

The first political correctness was the doctrine that women were naturally sexually pure and were oppressed by men's rapacious sexual lusts, a doctrine that would have met with hearty laughter and obscene jokes in any earlier period. This doctrine was enforced to justify the dismantling of patriarchy, and is, surprisingly, still going strong, with ever more unreasonable sexual harassment laws, and rape trials with rules ever more weighted against the accused and in favor of the accuser, with an ever expanding definition of rape.

---

[923]https://blog.reaction.la/culture/burning-the-past.html

Fertile age women lack maturity, future orientation, and ability to defer gratification[924], thus tend to make bad decisions, which is why they need supervision and control by their father, and subsequently their husband. Their voracious hypergamy is apt to undermine the family, hence the need for patriarchy, the need for social and legal enforcement of a marriage contract where a woman promises to always love, honor, and obey, in order to preserve the family against hypergamy. Like children, they should not be allowed to make binding contracts without the permission of their father or their husband. The first political correctness was, in early Victorian times, to prohibit anyone from mentioning any of this.

Around the eighteen seventies or eighteen nineties, blacks also got protection against people so unkind as to mention group differences, and things have been going downhill ever since. If you read old books about the Great Zimbabwe ruins, it is apparent that the writers are walking on eggshells.

While the civil rights movement was Jewish converts to progressivism being lefter than thou, everything before that was due to groups descended from Quakers and Puritans, who in the pursuit of power focused more and more on this world, and less and less on the next, becoming today's anglosphere left, which rules the world. A Jew who in the pursuit of power converts to progressivism is a converso, not a Jew, and if he should have any children, he is likely to have children with a non Jew, his Jewish identity swiftly dissolving into his Cathedral identity.

29% of British hospital deaths murder by the state

2012-06-22 06:49:58

The Liverpool Care Pathway. Which consists of heavily drugging them, and giving them no food or water. This will kill a healthy person in less than a week, and kill someone with breathing difficulties, for example an elderly person with pneumonia, in a few hours. The average life expectancy on the Liverpool Care Pathway is thirty three hours, indicating most patients were pretty healthy when it was decided to murder them.

The Liverpool Care Pathway was originally justified for treating terminal care patients, but is now routinely used for highly treatable ailments such as pneumonia, which ordinarily would only result in quite short hospital stay if actually treated.

Whenever a government makes the unfulfillable but extremely popular promise that it is going to provide everyone with all the medical care they really need, free or at affordable cost, it is planning to murder millions.

Conversely, whenever a government openly or semi openly repudiates that promise, as the Australian government did under Howard, it stops murdering people, instead sending excess patients to live or die at home. The Howard government replaced murder with extensive home care, which though expensive is less expensive than hospital care. This, of course, is always violently unpopular, because most of the electorate are women and idiots.

---

[924]https://dalrock.wordpress.com/2011/10/02/special-needs-employees/

Correction: Tea Party Express not wholly left entryist

2012-06-22 08:21:59

Earlier I accused the Tea Party Express as being left entryist, on the basis that its emailings tend to analyze the political spectrum as Democrats, right wing Democrats, moderate republicans, and conservative republicans, language that treats the left as normality and truth, and everyone else as deviations from normality and truth.

However, emailings have recently changed that terminology, and the Tea Party Express blog always analyzed the political spectrum as liberal Democrats, Democrats, Republicans in Name Only, and true conservatives, language that does not privilege the left point of view as normal and reality, and everything else as abnormal and untrue, language that instead implies that conservatism is normal and right for republicans.

Religiosity and fertility: Wrong metric

2012-06-23 06:48:52

Half Sigma finds that religiosity is correlated with fertility, and nothing else makes much difference. In particular, intelligence makes little difference, except that smart people tend to be less religious by the measure of religiosity used.

But

His measurement of religiosity is Biblical Literalism, which is more a measurement of which religion one subscribes to, rather than how much one subscribes to religion: Thus, a better conclusion is that some religions encourage fertility, and others discourage it.

A brief wander between religious gatherings reveal that some breed, and some do not, thus chances are that any measure one uses, will correlate or not depending on the extent that high fertility religion happens to correlate with whatever measure of religiosity one is using.

It seems likely that the correct measure is *attendance* to particular churches and religious organizations, rather than beliefs that do not in themselves directly affect sex and reproduction.

Secondly, fertility correlates negatively with educational attainment[925], but again, not with intelligence.

But if attainment, but not intelligence, then obviously attainment is the wrong measure: The right measure should be *attendance,* not attainment. We should treat educational institutions as yet another church or religious organization.

In which case we will find that the religion taught at some institutions discourages fertility, and the religion taught at other institutions encourages fertility. That reform Jews don't breed, while orthodox Jews and Mormons do breed suggests that the critical variables are hypergamy and patriarchy. To the extent a religion encourages hypergamy, it discourages fertility, and to the extent that it encourages patriarchy, it encourages fertility.

Attendance at educational institutions, viewed as religious attendance, encourages hypergamy. Girls are taught that they are entitled. They can have it all. A girl of average

---

[925]https://anepigone.blogspot.com.au/2012/06/education-religiosity-and-fecundity.html

looks can, she is told, have a career and a financially successful faithful lover who looks like Brad Pitt.

Half Sigma's measure of religiosity tends to favor churches that refrain from encouraging hypergamy. If the question had been "We are children of the universe, and there is a cosmic force that cares for us", I am pretty sure that religiosity so measured would be negatively correlated with fertility, massively so.

I saw the crisis coming: Why the fed did not.

2012-06-24 18:06:36

In 2010 April 3, Michael Burry asked "I saw the crisis coming. Why did not the Fed?"[926] His question was, in a sense, answered in the next two weeks.

In 2005 November, about four months after Michael Burry started betting his business by making big bets against mortgage backed securities, I said of the real estate market, and the easy money mortgages that were propping it up: "Now is the time to panic!"

At that time, among over mortgaged white people speculating in real estate in San Francisco, there was a mad rush to the exits, to get the hell out. In some cases this involved picking up some illegal immigrant from Home Depot, and inducing him with a pile of cash and a bottle of whiskey to sign a pile of papers he could not read , and then presenting him with the keys to a house mortgaged far beyond its worth, thus transferring a million dollar mortgage from a white guy, who it was politically and financially possible to persecute for not paying his mortgage, to a no-hablo-English mestizo with no job and no assets who was immune from getting into trouble for failure to pay, who did not even know that he now had a million dollar mortage, and would not have cared had he known.

The mortgages that Michael Burry was betting would fail rested on that mestizo making his payments, payments he could not possibly make and probably did not even know he was supposed to make. Back in 2005, I figured that this was bound to become noticeable quite soon, and was repeatedly astonished by how long the government managed to delay the day of reckoning with maneuvers ever more extreme and desperate. We all, we white speculators in the Bay area, figured that next week or next month, it would suddenly cease to be possible to unload over mortgaged real estate on no-hablo-English unemployed wetbacks, but it just went on, and on, and on. Similarly, Michael Burry was repeatedly astonished by how it continued to be possible to pretend that the mortgages he had bet against were still good. It just did not stop. Until it did stop.

That which cannot continue, will not.

Greenspan told us that he sat through innumerable meetings at the Fed with crack economists, and not one of them warned of the problems that were to come.

Immediately after making this op ed, Michael Bury was investigated by the FBI, and all his financial activities were audited by the usual alphabet soup.

From which we should conclude that if any of those crack economists had warned of the problems that were to come, and Greenspan had ratted him out for speaking too plainly, that crack economist would have been similarly investigated and audited, and unless squeaky clean, would have gone to jail.

---

[926]https://www.nytimes.com/2010/04/04/opinion/04burry.html

This illustrates the left singularity. Everyone is required to believe in lies and delusion, and the ruling elite required to be more deluded than anyone else. The closer one is to the center of power, the further from reality one must be.

In the beginning of the video[927],Michael Burry gives a one sentence summary of the cause of the continuing crisis:

> when the entitled elect themselves, the party accelerates, and the brutal hangover is inevitable

So, to end the crisis, either have to end democracy altogether, or drastically restrict the franchise.

At fourteen minutes into the video, he tells us what happened when he asked questions that should not be asked, and mentioned facts that should not be mentioned.

> In my letters to investors, I described a downturn that would be unprecedented, with no counterpart in the modern era. Wall Street's risk models would fall all at once, and every single CEO and every single politician would be disastrously wrong.
>
> I put my money where my mouth was. At its peak I was short 8.4 billion dollars worth of subrpime mortgages ... and at first we did lose. It was a negative carry trade. Investors, business partners, and even employees questioned strategy. Lawsuits were threatened, our distress was reported in the press, and Wall Street tried to squeeze our short.
>
> ...
>
> I had bet against America, and won.
>
> In 2010 I posted an op-ed in the New York times, posing what I thought was a valid question of the Federal Reserve, Congress and the President:
>
> > I saw the crisis coming, why did not the Fed?
>
> Never did any member of Congress, any member of Government for that matter, reach out to me for an open collegial discussion of what went wrong, or what could be done. Rather, within two weeks all six of my defunct funds were audited. The Congressional Financial Crisis Inquiry Commission demanded all my emails and a list of people with whom I had conversed going back to 2003
>
> And a little later the FBI showed up.
>
> A million in legal and accounting costs and thousands of hours wasted, all because I asked questions.

Clearly the chief mission of the Congressional Financial Crisis Inquiry Commission was to conceal, rather than reveal the cause of the crisis – the underlying cause of the crisis

---

[927] https://www.youtube.com/watch?v=1CLhqjOzoyE

being the government giving out easy money to voting blocks, in particular to non Asian minorities, something no one close to power can say, or even think.

Only one thing in this video will surprise anyone who reads this blog. It will all be old news to you except for the startling fact, appearing at 14 minutes into the video, that if someone is sufficiently a member of the establishment that he is entitled to give New York Times op eds, speaking plainly about the crisis will get him in very big trouble. I thought that the elite were pre-approved, that no one got into the elite who was inclined to rock the boat. Evidently, on the contrary, the closer you are to power, the more you have to watch your step, much as the outer party in Orwell's "1984" had even less political freedom than the proles, and inner party even less than the outer party. They don't rock the boat because they are scared spitless.

This has the effect of making piety, hypocrisy, and the bare faced endorsement of transparent lies high status, because it is what high status people do. High status people act scared spitless, so everyone else acts as if they were scared spitless, without the need for the direct repression and violence needed to make everyone else actually scared spitless.

It is an efficient use of repression, but means that the elite is further out of contact with reality than anyone else, thus that they are never going to realize that franchise has to be restricted, or else democracy ended. The change is going to have to come from outside the present elite, after the crisis becomes so severe that it becomes impossible to continue on the present course, and simultaneously impossible to change course.

Health care and stockholm syndrome

2012-06-29 05:48:52

Observing enthusiasm for government health care around the world, it seems fairly proportional to the amount of involuntary euthanasia, the amount of murder by the state.

Government healthcare has been demonstrably successful in moving the population and voters left, in large part in proportion to its propensity to murder people.

Thirty percent of hospital deaths in Britain are murder by the state. British hospitals literally stink of death, due to deplorable and obvious lack of basic hygiene. They don't apply enough hot water and bleach to cover up what they are doing, let alone prevent the spread of hospital acquired infectious diseases.

"Community acquired" diseases (a euphemism for hospital acquired diseases) are a big problem in Britain. These diseases are frequently anti biotic resistant. The proposed solution is to use less antibiotics, rather than the obvious solution: More hot water, soap, and bleach.

And predictably Britons are correspondingly enthusiastic about government health care.

However, when visiting Cuba, I noticed that there was lack of enthusiasm for its even more lethal government health care proportional to the availability of black market medicine. To the extent that people had to put their lives in the hands of the state, they loved the state. To the extent that they had an alternative, they did not.

We are already seeing medical tourism, regulatory arbitrage, and grey market medicine for advanced technologies. Dr Purita is a Florida doctor, but treats people in the Dominican Republic[928], where it costs less to bribe the regulators. The technology was developed in the USA, but due to regulatory obstacles, cannot be applied here.

Men's Rights Activists are whiny losers

2012-07-01 07:03:41

The reason men's rights activist sites are so whiny is that they accept the progressive ideology of equalism, and in their own lives they treated women as equals, and of course deservedly got treated like shit. They complain that men and women are not truly treated as alike, and therefore men get the short end of the stick.

Since men and woman are not alike, if they were truly treated alike, both would get the short end of the stick. In a previous post in the comments I observed that if the government enforced contracts on women in the same way they enforce contracts on men, it would be mighty rough on women.

Men's rights activist sites piously whine that men are not equal to women, and should be – but we tried equality in 1850. It was a complete disaster and things have steadily gotten worse since then.

A Voice for Men complained about Jenna_Myers_Karvunidis_-_Bigot,[929] which resulted in her issuing a grovelling apology: A big succes for men's rights :-) What was this woman's horrid crime? A false rape allegation? Demanding that accused rapists be treated as guilty until proven innocent?

Nope, she objected to males doing potty duty unsupervised on children they were not related to – in other words, she had a moment of sanity, making an unprincipled deviation from the equalist ideology she, and men's rights activists, theoretically subscribe to, for the safety of her own children.

In practice, almost everyone believes in equalist ideology when it is apt to have disastrous consequences for other people, but considerably fewer people believe in equalist ideology when it is likely have disastrous consequences for themselves or their own children. Instead, they make an unprincipled exception for themselves to what they theoretically believe in for everyone else.

As I have said many times before: Show me a marriage where the housework is equally and fairly shared, rather than being divided into man's work (taking out the garbage, unplugging the drains, mowing the lawn, and barbecuing meat) and woman's work (almost everything else) and I will show you a marriage where the husband sleeps on the couch, and once in a week or so the wife's lover drops in to bang her on the main bed, rough her up a bit, take her money, and leave a mess for the husband to clean up.

While he cleans up the mess the lover made, washing bodily fluids off the sheets, the husband explains that he is so enlightened and sensitive that he has an open marriage and is a polyamorist.

In my observation, in every successful marriage, if the husband theoretically believes in female emancipation, he quietly makes an unprincipled exception for himself and his

---

[928]https://www.nytimes.com/2011/05/12/sports/baseball/disputed-treatment-was-used-in-bartolo-colons-comeback.html

[929]https://register-her.com/index.php?title=Jenna_Myers_Karvunidis__Bigot

wife. Men's rights activist failed to make an unprincipled exception, and so encountered total disaster.

Women are not attracted to kitchen bitch husbands, equalist relationships, or men they are supporting due to earning more than them. Women loathe all of that, eventually, regardless of the feminist programming they have gotten that may tell them they should love being the marital dominatrix.

Further, it is not in a women's nature to just grin and bear it, to do their duty, so faced with a situation that is not to their liking, however much they are theoretically supposed to like it, they will cuckold, they will leave, they will find something else that suits them. And they will be happy doing so.

Where are the John Waynes, Steve McQueens, Clint Eastwoods, and Charles Bronsons of today? Men no longer have role models that would enable them to command and lead their wives the way that women want to be commanded and led, thus increasingly we see people failing to make the necessary unprincipled exception in their own lives.

Women are not naturally inclined to submit, notwithstanding John Norman's wishful thinking. But they are naturally inclined to find a man who can make them submit, overwhelming their willful and vigorous resistance. They want a husband who will lead and command, that they can honor and obey, even though they will struggle strenuously to dishonor and disobey. The John Norman novels depict women eager to obey submitting themselves to a man reluctant and diffident to command, thus he has PC males and non PC females, which is, alas, not at all the way it works in real life. Woman don't want to honor and obey, but they want a husband who makes them honor and obey, which is to say, a husband who is absolutely not a Men's Rights Activist.

Christianity yields to Zoism

2012-07-09 13:05:39

(That is Zoism, the politically incorrect term for primitive religion, not Zionism, the theory that Jews need a homeland and heavy weapons because people keep trying to kill them)

Theoretically, most western people still consider themselves Christian – including those that think that Jesus gay married Buddha and from time to time the loving couple visit earth in a flying saucer. But it is not the Christianity of 1950 or 1960. In the period 1900 to 1970, "Christianity" underwent changes that would have rendered it scarcely recognizable to anyone from the past two millenia, changes that render it psychologically inconsistent and no longer viable as religion. Christianity's time has ended, and the question is what system shall replace it, the main contenders now being Islam, itself afflicted by a related deadly ailment, and state sponsored Gaia worship. Mormonism and Orthodox Judaism are the healthiest remaining deistic religions, and will win in the long run if deism wins, but it is not obvious that deism will win.

An essential part of the definition of Zoism is that it is a magical belief system that resembles those of savages. The term is part of the now forbidden frame work for understanding cultures and civilizations that assumes that civilization is better, that some races and cultures are better than others due to race and or culture, and that savages are apt to be savage, simple minded, cruel, ignorant, and self destructive.

Unwin categorizes religious belief in four levels:

1. Zoism – subhuman, animal level culture.A zoistic society has no religious beliefs – it is not that they do not believe in the supernatural, but rather that they do not believe in the natural. At a zoistic level of culture all influential and high prestige people engage in magical thinking, attributing to themselves and other people capabilities rationalists would consider supernatural. They dispose of the dead like garbage, and do not tend the graves of the dead.

2. Manism. Some special men are attributed supernatural powers, much more than regular men. These men engage in mystical chants, and rattle magical stones and necklaces, as for example, the expert witness in a silicone or asbestos lawsuit. These special men can smell out other men who use their magical powers to do harm, thus witchfinders and radioactive pollution.

3. Deism: We all know what deism is. Deism with god far away, a god who dumped problems on us and commands us to solve them as best we can, is pretty close to being rationalism.

4. Rationalism: There is no supernatural, or if there is it is far, far away, and long, long ago, in the next world, not this one.

Notable exponents of Zoism are Oprah, and the best selling book "The Secret". "The Secret" is teaching the popular message that optimism will cause magic, that if you expect good things to happen they will.

If you expect good things to happen, you may well be more inclined to take the risk of trying to make them happen, but this is not what "The Secret" preaches. It preaches that you can do magic, that good things will be caused by your thoughts, not by an empirical chain of cause and effect wherein your thoughts cause you to act, and your actions cause good things to happen.

Unwin's studies of various societies suggests that where paternity is uncertain or unimportant, where fathers lack authority, societies tend drift down the scale of religions, from rationalism to Zoism, hence the death of Christianity. Patriarchal socities tend to move up the scale, matrilineal societies down the scale. Abrahamic religions are the religions of patriarchs.

Christianity used to be an unambiguously patriarchal religion. From the death of Jesus to before the second world war all Christians, all of them, one hundred percent believed, or at least made a pretense of believing, that at marriage the wife promised to love honor and obey till death do us part. All of them, one hundred percent believed, or at least made a pretense of believing, that a divorced women should not remarry, nor should a man marry a divorced woman. They notoriously tended to weasel around this in practice, but hypocrisy is the homage that vice pays to virtue. All Christians, all of them, one hundred percent believed, or at least made a pretense of believing, that in marriage a man and a woman consented to sex once and forever, that the wife had no right to withhold sexual gratification from the husband, nor the husband from the wife, that sex in marriage did not require continuing mutual consent, rather, to abstain from sex required mutual consent.

The Christian position on consent sounds in form as equalist as any modern leftist could desire, but in practice, because of unadmitted large differences between men and women, tended to favor the authority of the husband and undermine the power of the wife.

However the contrary position, that sex requires continuing mutual consent, as well as empowering the wife, necessarily leads to the result that marriage requires continuing mutual consent, necessarily leads to no fault divorce at will, abolishes marriage as Christians understood marriage for two thousand years.

These three positions:
1. That the wife honors and obeys,
2. that divorce is forbidden (especially for females),
3. and that withholding sex from one's husband or wife is forbidden,

are social conservatism. For two thousand years, Christianity was socially conservative.

One cannot today find a single Church that maintains these principles, and it is hard to find a Christian rightist so extreme as to endorse any of these principles. From everyone endorsing all three positions we have gone to no one endorsing any of these positions, with most of the change occurring in my lifetime.

There are some churches that equivocally tell us that the husband should "lead", but the marriage oath did not say "follow", it said "obey". In my marriage, I am the boss and always have been, and any marriage where the husband is not the boss, is apt to fall apart pretty quickly. You will not find any Church that says the husband should be the boss.

Today, there are no Christian social conservatives, none. If we are to revive social conservatism, must revive it on Darwinian grounds, or perhaps on the basis of a religious or quasi religious movement as yet unimagined.

If you abolish marriage (what social conservatives mean by marriage) empirically the consequence is apt to be the abolition of Abrahamic religions. Abrahamic religions caused socially conservative marriage, and correlation suggests that socially conservative marriage caused Abrahamic religions.

In a previous post I gave a more detailed account of these various kinds and levels of religion[930], and other examples of zoistic thinking by influential and powerful people in our society.

The distinguishing feature of Zoistic thinking is that mere desire or belief is sufficient to allegedly be the cause of the effect, without any need for the Zoist to provide a material explanation of cause and effect. Bad beliefs supposedly lead directly to bad outcomes and good beliefs supposedly lead directly to good outcomes without any real effort to provide a material account of belief causing actions and actions directly causing effects. Thus, for example, black criminality and female unreliability is supposedly caused by people expecting blacks to be criminal and females unreliable. Conversely, all government programs supposedly accomplish their intended effect, even if the intended effect is difficult, and perhaps impossible, to accomplish. For example Obamacare will supposedly accomplish numerous logically incompatible objectives, because it creates numerous bureaucracies to accomplish these objectives and tasks them to create regulations to accomplish all these logically contradictory objectives simultaneously. Costs are budgeted on the assumption

---

[930]https://blog.reaction.la/culture/gay-marriage-a-modest-proposal.html

that these bureaucracies will successfully square the circle.

Zoistic societies tend to high levels of conflict, eventually erupting in high levels of violence, because if anything bad happens, it is supposedly someone's fault, someone caused the bad thing by thinking bad thoughts, with no need to provide any causal mechanism, any concrete deeds, wherein this bad person's bad thoughts caused bad consequences through bad deeds. Consider, for example, the various pollution, medical malpractice, and discrimination lawsuits. One does not have to do anything concrete to discriminate or pollute.

The EPA (Environmental Protection Agency) regulations on micro particulates are a good example of this. The EPA finds it unnecessary to provide any evidence of concrete deeds that may have raised dust levels, nor concrete evidence that the dust has harmful consequences. Insufficient faith in the EPA is supposedly sufficient to cause harmful levels of dust, and proclamation by authority is sufficient to prove dust harmful. Supposedly the proclamation is based on empirical "studies", but ordinary mortals are not allowed to see the contents of these studies, providing the nominal form of empiricism and rationalism, but not the substance. The EPA is regulating not dust, which is in practice difficult or impossible to regulate, for reasons painfully familiar, but dangerous thoughts about dust. The EPA therefore, makes state sponsored Zoism mandatory.

Occupy LA performs riot theater

2012-07-15 06:45:29

Michael Blaze is a black artist and art entrepreneur who is sufficiently white, middle class, and upwardly mobile that if he shot a black criminal, would promptly be declared white by Mainstream Media. He is one of those blacks that whiter people like to associate with to prove they are not prejudiced without risking getting mugged, and, like those whiter people, is a good progressive.

He gives us an on the spot report of the occupy riot against LA Art Walk[931], in which he tells us that if it was black criminals rioting the police response would be very different, by which he presumably means a lot more effective. At 4:10 into the video he tells us
> "people are throwing cans, bottles ... agitators. There are maybe fifty or a hundred police, and they are taking no action."

A few cops get hurt by the Occupy LA mob, and a few of the Occupy LA mob get hurt by the cops, but in fact, it is cops and occupiers working together to disrupt LA Art Walk. The conflict between cops and occupiers is staged, because if it was real, the hundred cops would have arrested the thirty agitators one minute into the confrontation. Meanwhile the harassment and disruption of Art Walk and the thousands of people showing up at Art Walk to have a good time is real. Two hundred cops and thirty agitators gave everyone a bad time.

Michael Blaze shows his good progressive credentials by protesting at police arresting people for chalking, and tells us how bad the LA PD are for provoking this confrontation, but then at 7:30 in the video

---

[931] https://www.youtube.com/watch?v=aXMfxNfupc4

"this guy jumped up on the police and hit them ... *still* no arrests. Right now the police are not in control."

So people are arrested for chalking, for which they will probably get very small fines or, more likely, no punishment at all, but so far in the riot not arrested for assault, vandalism, and obstructing the roads.

At 8:50 in the video:

> "I cannot believe they are not being arrested. People are literally pushing on the police, and the police are restraining themselves. ... This is out of control. Something needs to happen"

Of course the police *are* in control, in that if their officers did not want a riot, they would just beat the stuffing out of the most riotous agitator, and then the second most riotous agitator, and then when they looked for the third most riotous agitator, he would be nowhere to be found. If they did not want a riot, they would arrest people for assault, rather than chalking.

So, why Art Walk, an event that is wall to wall with good progressives and whiter people? Why are they not attacking a gun show, or some conference sponsored by the Koch brothers?

(Whiter people is an epithet used by white people for other white people who ape the purported views and tastes of our rulers, the regnant left, with excessive enthusiasm and thoroughness. Recall me ridiculing Charles Murray for eating barra in Washington, and eating spaghetti with homeopathic quantities of truffle in it[932].)

Well the answer is, that they tried such targets, and such targets turned out to be tough. The original plan was to "Occupy Wall Street". They attempted to occupy various symbols of capitalism, and promptly got thumped. So they went looking for softer targets – which softer targets invariably turn out to be fellow progressives, notably the most left wing city administration in the US, Oakland City. While it seems to require hundreds of cops to handle fifty Occupiers, it only takes three rentacops or half a dozen conservatives to handle any number of occupiers. They just take out whichever would be occupier is in front, and when they look around for the next guy in front, no one is in front. Progressives lack cohesion. They have no asabiyyah. Possibly this is a side effect of the progressive strategy of far alliance against near.

If it gets to civil war, progressives will fall like sand before a hose.

Cthulhu for president!

2012-07-19 07:20:55

Romney and Obama are debating capitalism, freedom, and free markets. Which makes it sound as though the election matters. If American people vote for Obama, they will have voted against capitalism, freedom, and free markets, and if they vote for Romney, they will have voted for capitalism, freedom, and free markets.

But no matter what they vote for it will make no difference. Vote Obama, you won't get socialism, but crony capitalism, aka national socialism, vote Romney, you won't get

---

[932]https://blog.reaction.la/culture/murray-on-the-decline-of-marriage.html

freedom and free markets, but crony capitalism, aka national socialism.

Vote Cthulhu!

Not the Jews

2012-07-20 11:15:37

If someone thinks the Jews are behind the collapse of our civilization, he has to think the rot set in after 1950, for in the anglosphere, Jews were substantially excluded from the establishment until after 1954.

Those who can see[933] has a review of the early twentieth century showing rot several decades before that.

I have frequently asserted that everything started to fall apart in the early nineteenth century, and some day I will produce documentation of this charge, that the emancipation of women and extending the vote to the masses had the disastrous consequences that it was predicted to have. Meanwhile, "Those Who Can See" produces documentation for a somewhat later period, though early enough to exculpate the Jews.

---

[933]https://thosewhocansee.blogspot.com.au/2012/07/bcats-against-current.html

It was the Puritans, and their descendent groups, a bunch of people that wore color-less clothes, black or dark brown with a few flashes of white, modeled after the costume of Cromwell, that caused everything to go to hell. When they got on top, re-establishing the puritan theocracy of Cromwell, now known as political correctness, everyone in power started imitating them, resulting in the modern business suit, so that it ceased to be a very reliable indicator. The rot set in when everyone important went monochrome. But to this day, if a businessman wears a bright flash of red and or gold in an otherwise orthodox formal business suit, for example the Koch brothers, it is at least a hint that he is rebelling against the rule of the progressives, whereas a predominantly dark blue tie in an orthodox business suit tends to indicate progressivism, as for example the Google founders. Puritans, now progressives, are near monochrome, avoid sharp color contrasts, tend to dark blue, grey, dark brown, and so forth. Their opponents, even to this day, tend to have a substantial flash of color, often red or gold, though the difference is no longer as reliable, consistent, and striking as it was in the days of roundheads versus cavaliers. Big hats are also a tell. Cowboy hats, top hats, sombreros and so forth, are not progressive and never have been, all the way from 1600 to the present. If anyone unironically puts on a cowboy hat, progressives will spontaneously burst into flames from insane rage - for example Bush derangement syndrome, even if they know or strongly suspect he is only pretending to not be a progressive.

I merely assert this, and in this post am not producing evidence for the claim.

Economic Decline measured by Big Macs per hour

2012-07-21 16:30:35

On the basis of big mac per hour rate, living standards in the US fell 9% between 2007 and 2011, two and half percent a year. This agrees pretty well with cars and meat (two percent fewer cars and two percent less meat per person per year.)

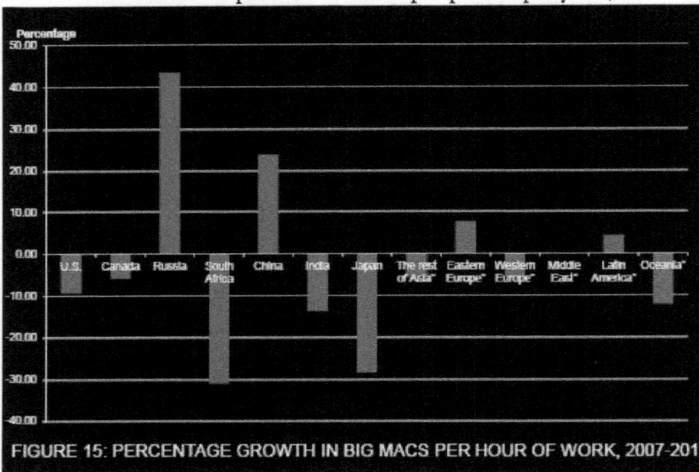

FIGURE 15: PERCENTAGE GROWTH IN BIG MACS PER HOUR OF WORK, 2007-2011

Big mac prices from 2007 to 2011 rose 16%[934], which is suspiciously high since supposedly none of the components went up sixteen percent in the period according to the US official cpi, casting doubt on the official cpi.

Sixteen percent inflation accompanied by a six to nine percent fall in the standard of living is incompatible with Keynesian accounts of the crisis, and indicates a supply side account - that business is being terrorized by regulators.

Big macs are in themselves a broadly based inflation measure, because they are a little bit of everything, bread, meat, manufactured good, and service industry, and are a widely traded good. There is a lot of data suggesting the the big mac index is in fact a pretty good measure of inflation[935], and the cpi not necessarily a very good indicator of inflation. Professor Orely Ashenfelter complains that a lot of cpi prices are not actually measured, but are "imputed" ("Imputed" means that some anonymous government official under pressure to make the numbers come out right makes a guess about how many apples make an orange.)

---

[934]https://www2.lse.ac.uk/assets/richmedia/channels/publicLecturesAndEvents/s-lides/20120228_1830_comparingRealWagesTheMcWageIndex_sl.pdf

[935]https://www2.lse.ac.uk/newsAndMedia/videoAndAudio/channels/publicLecturesAndEvents/-player.aspx?id=1372

It is not hyperinflation but it is substantially higher than official inflation.

The Big mac per hour rate indicates a broad based economic decline across the entire developed world (Western Europe falling at two percent a year, South Africa and Japan collapsing at seven to eight percent a year, see table six below and figure fifteen above.

Interestingly, the big mac per hour rate us that the problem set in long before 2007, it just got a lot worse after 2007. Living standards were disturbingly stagnant for a long time, then started to decline, and now are declining with disturbing speed.

TABLE 6: GROWTH IN McWAGES, BIG MAC PRICES AND BIG MACS PER HOUR OF WORK (BMPH), 2007-2011

	McWage Ratio	Big Mac Price Ratio	BMPH Ratio
U.S.	1.06	1.16	0.91
Canada	1.47	1.56	0.94
Russia	1.78	1.24	1.43
South Africa	0.89	1.29	0.69
China	2.00	1.62	1.24
India	1.36	1.58	0.86
Japan	1.46	2.04	0.72
U.K.	0.86	0.99	0.87
The rest of Asia*	1.34	1.42	0.94
Eastern Europe*	1.31	1.22	1.08
Western Europe*	1.12	1.19	0.95
Middle East*	1.26	1.26	1.00
Latin America*	1.51	1.45	1.04
Oceania*	1.22	1.39	0.88

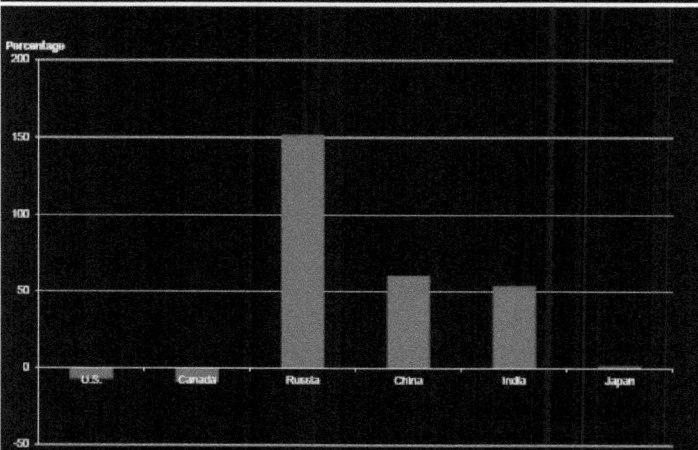

FIGURE 12: PERCENTAGE GROWTH IN BIG MACS PER HOUR OF WORK, 2000-2007

I have long argued that in most economic, technological, and scientific fields, the US peaked in 1972, and has been in decline ever since, though of course progress in the very important field of the ultra small continues rapidly, with the US continuing to lead the world.

There is a lot of ruin in a nation. Looks like we are getting near our total. The overall picture is not "Obama fouled up", or even "Bush fouled up and Obama continued to make it worse", but rather "Western civilization is in decline, condition potentially terminal".

The problem is simple: The moochers have a majority, and we cannot continue with them on the voting rolls. So either the franchise has to be restricted, or democracy ended altogether. The more drastic cure is likely to be the more politically feasible.

Mencius Moldbug suggests a bankruptcy proceeding, in which various financial claims upon the government are turned into shares, and the government reorganized as limited liability corporation, a form of organization that is well known to work effectively. This, however, is only feasible in an environment where people expect contracts to be honored, and debts to be paid, which is not the environment you get when a nation state defaults on its promises. The environment may well more closely resemble anarcho-piratism.

The success of the corporate form of organization rests in substantial part on moral, legal, and social restraints against redistributing wealth from one class of shareholder to another. In a breakup, legality is nonexistent, social constraints destroyed by bitterness and rage. The success of the restoration settlement of 1660 was because the deal, and the official religion that they agreed to impose upon themselves, prohibited redistribution. If everything is up for grabs, conflict will continue till there is nothing left. To actually end the conflict, rather than merely create the sort of "stability" that Diocletian gave the Roman Empire in the west, it will be necessary to create an environment where redistributionists get the same treatment as white supremacists do today, or Puritans got in Restoration England.

The collapse of South Africa and, surprisingly, Japan is proceeding at about the same rate as the growth of China. Russia also shows extraordinary growth, so extraordinary as to suggest measurement error caused by bounceback from ruble crisis of 1998. In Russia, in the years shortly after 1998, big macs may not necessarily have been a broadly based good, due to difficulties in performing international transactions with a collapsed currency. Professor Orely Ashenfelter notes that for big mac based statistics to be meaningful, the economy has to be sufficiently advanced and functional to support reasonable levels of production and consumption of big macs.

Krugman on supply side

2012-07-25 20:53:49

By and large, the elite ignores the argument that our economic crisis is supply side, as if no one could possibly be so crazy, ignorant and stupid as to make such an obviously silly argument.

However, when Professor Pedro Schwartz[936] argued that the problem is supply side, Krugman responded passionately rather than ignoring and mischaracterizing the argument.[937]:

---

[936] https://www.pedroschwartz.com/english/aboutus.asp

[937] https://www.youtube.com/watch?feature=player_embedded&v=N8LmE5cfQKA#!

It has been exceedingly disappointing how many people on one side of this debate have resorted to attempts to pull credentials, to claim that people on my side of the debate don't have the intellectual standing to weigh in on these issues. ... This is not an appropriate way to argue.

This, of course, is total projection. It is Krugman's side that suggests that supply siders are gap toothed gun nuts hoarding beans and bullets and having sex with their sisters. Of course, supply siders sometimes do hoard gold, beans and bullets, but they are not gap toothed, and are considerably less apt to have sex with their sisters than Krugman's side.

At 13:41 in the video Professor Pedro Schwartz protests about this mischaracterization of his argument. Then Krugman starts making a relevant counter argument.

The main thing I would say is, that of the two views, that this is essentially a supply problem versus this is essentially a demand problem ...

This is a big concession, Krugman admitting that there are two views, rather than the official orthodoxy being the self evident, uncontroversial, and uncontested truth. This is not the first time Krugman has wandered off the reservation. Recall when he cheerfully acknowledged that death panels were an essential feature of Obamacare, deviating from the uniform orthodoxy that Sarah Palin's reference to death panels proved that she was a retard whose father was also her grandfather.

In a way Nature had given us an excellent experiment ...at vast human cost...but we have just had an experiment. There were three predictions, three crucial predictions, that differentiated these two views of what the nature of the problem was

One was what would happen to interest rates, where ... and lets leave aside the solvency issue ...

Let us not leave aside the solvency issue, since supply siders are calling the current situation a bubble in taxpayer futures, implying that the demand side prescription is going to render nation states insolvent.

The question was would large scale borrowing on the part of the public sector in the face of a depressed economy. compete with the private sector for funds, and therefore cause interest rates to rise. And there were some very harsh debates about that in early 2009 with many people asserting with great confidence that those US budget deficits would lead to soaring interest rates.

Obviously not, right?

The crisis is precisely that the private sector has not been investing, does not want to use those funds to create wealth. The question then is what is deterring the private sector from building and creating. Lack of demand, or unpredictable regulation and regime uncertainty? Is the lack of private sector investment caused by demand side problems, or supply side problems. Krugman's argument begs the point, assuming that which is to be shown.

There was the question what would large expansion of the monetary base do, to inflation?

And if you had a supply side view you said that there is a certain amount of production, and if we create more money it is going to chase more goods and this is going to lead to vast inflation.

And that has not happened.

Rather, the demand side view was that if we create more money, it is going to chase more goods, and this will elicit more goods, and a corresponding increase in investment and reduction in unemployment.

What in fact happened is that for the most part, it did not chase more goods, but, to the extent that is did chase more goods, more goods were not elicited. We have had a substantial increase in nominal GDP, which is more money chasing more goods, and yet consumption per head of cars, meat, big macs, and electricity has fallen. We don't have *vast* inflation, because expansion of the money supply was far less successful in eliciting demand than anyone expected, but we do have inflation, which, on the demand side view, we should not have. Increasing demand has *not* increased production to meet that demand. This is the big failure of the demand side story, the acid test telling us that the demand side story is false, and the supply side story is true.

> And then there was the question what would happen with governments that for whatever reason did sharp cuts in spending. Would that be expansionary, because it released resources to the private sector, or would it be contractionary?

And unfortunately Europe has given us some clear evidence on all of that.

But no European governments cut spending, except for Estonia, and in Estonia, it was expansionary, and did release resources to the private sector.

In most of Europe, "austerity" has meant increasing expenditure by amounts that were merely extraordinary, astounding, and unprecedented, instead of extraordinary, staggering, stupendous, and astounding, while increasing taxes to levels that were far beyond the Laffer limit on the rich, and often beyond the Laffer limit on the poor. Supply siders point out that raising taxes was contractionary in the past, and predicted that raising taxes would be contractionary, and threatening further tax rises is contractionary, and threatening further taxes on capital is especially contractionary, and so they have proven to be.

Increasing government spending is observed to be contractionary, in that the infamous Keynesian multiplier is observed to be less than unity for spending, while increasing taxes is also contractionary, in that the famous Keynesian multiplier is more than unity for taxing.

Conversely, decreasing government spending is expansionary, even without decreases in taxes, and decreasing taxation is expansionary, because, at the margin, most government spending is destructive and disruptive. The US government would have achieved better results had it spent money bombing its own cities, rather than spending money building housing through HUD projects. No one wants HUD spending money near where they themselves live. The more money the government spends, the harder it is to spend it productively. Even if the first dollar of government spending produces something useful, builds roads, collects garbage, protects people and property, helps widows and orphans, the last dollar of government spending bulldozes neighborhoods, creates garbage, and funds whores and muggers.

The one and only European government to implement austerity for the public sector, rather than the private sector, was Estonia, and in Estonia, austerity worked.

Not the cognitive elite

2012-07-29 22:33:03

Government has accomplished some mighty impressive things, the most impressive being the Manhattan project (nuclear bombs and nuclear energy), and the second most impressive being the landing on the moon.

After Hiroshima, and before the moon landing, people said "Why don't we (meaning government) have a Manhattan project to do X"

After the landing on the moon, people said "If we (meaning government) can put a man on the moon, why cannot we do X"

Well guess what, boys and girls. Today we *can't* put a man on the moon.

Richard Feynman was one of the greatest scientists of all time, in every way a very smart man, and when he was working on the Manhatten project, he was mighty impressed by how smart everyone was.

Let us compare the Manhatten project with the ITER project, (International Thermonuclear Experimental Reactor).

When a group attempts to accomplish any large, complex project, the way to do it is to break it into smaller less complex projects - which requires one to define the interface between the smaller projects and the acceptance criteria for each smaller project. The ITER project was broken into smaller projects *without* defining interface requirements or acceptance criteria. So when the parts were brought together, they simply did not fit, and if they had fitted, would not have worked.

Much comedy ensued, and continues to ensue, with those fouling up being rewarded by larger budgets and more power.

I am pretty sure that if you are not smart enough to accomplish project management, you are not smart enough to accomplish thermonuclear fusion.

Observe that the Manhattan project was done in the bad old days, back when, according to Charles Murray, the elite was selected on the basis of class and race, whereas the ITER project was unsuccessfully attempted by an elite that, Charles Murray assures us, is the cognitive elite.

Even leftists, aka the state, have noticed the declining capability of the state, which they blame on the disturbing lack of faith by Republicans

Allegedly:

> the party of no has made sure that government does not work and will continue to make it impossible for Obama to make good on any cleansing processes he may propose.

Somehow the party of no achieved this remarkable accomplishment even when the president was a democrat, the senate and the house of representatives had Democratic party majorities, and the public service was and is one hundred percent left, far left, and far out left. I suppose it was their evil thought waves that did it.

The state that cannot do project management generates legislation of thousands of pages of entirely opaque prose telling businesses how to do stuff, with the result that business comes to a halt. Hence the economic crisis: Ever greater intrusion, ever less competently done.

The left singularity continues

2012-08-01 09:54:51

Increased repression brings increased leftism, increased leftism brings increased repression, in an ever tighter circle that turns ever faster. This is the left singularity[938]

The increased repression, Chick-fil-A and the Olympic opening ceremony, is not a manifestation of left insecurity, but of the ever accelerating movement left, the left singularity.

Let us compare the arrogant hate filled murderous totalitarianism of the recent British Olympics, with the civilized and sportsmanlike Nazi Olympics of 1936. The British Olympics demonized capitalists as smokestacks, the slave trade, and racism, while celebrating the murderous[939] National Health Service, in which one third of hospital deaths are murder by the state. Imagine if the Nazi Olympics had put on a big show demonizing the Jews and advertizing the benefits of state elimination of lunatics and the feeble-minded. (And, digressing, why does the modern welfare state murder the elderly, while putting the insane and retards on the street? If you are going to murder anyone, murder, or at least lock up, the insane.)

In fact, of course, the Nazi Olympics celebrated the pursuit of excellence by all people and nations. Hitler congratulated Jesse Owens, probably through gritted teeth, but he congratulated him, and the Nazi celebration of the Olympics, the movie Olympia[940], celebrated him, while Voula Papachristou was expelled from today's Olympics.

As Bruce Charleton observes: "Public opinion" has been moved Leftward by truly massive, and now massively-policed, media saturation - and the use of exemplary punishments of public figures for real or imagined violations of the zero-tolerance policy concerning non-PC public (and private)

Leftists are not troubled by the fear that the masses might revolt against the left, but rather each leftist fears he might fail to keep up with the ever changing line, find himself a few years, or weeks, or days behind the current ever changing political correctness, and find himself deemed a rightist.

Which historically halts only in bloodshed. There is no equivalent right singularity, as repressive right wing regimes forbid interest in politics, while repressive left wing regimes

---

[938] https://blog.reaction.la/tag/left-singularity "the left singularity"
[939] https://blog.reaction.la/economics/29-of-british-hospital-deaths-murder-by-the-state.html "29% of British hospital deaths murder by the state"
[940] magnet:?xt=urn:btih:6793045731B794FD08FB63EB618851961C7F2ABF&dn=Olympia.rar&tr= "Olympia"

command interest in politics.

The left singularity is the same each time in its approach to infinite leftism, but differs chaotically and surprisingly each time in its ending short of infinite leftism

If it did not end, the final outcome, infinite leftism in finite time, would be that everyone is tortured to death for insufficient leftism, except the last torturer, who then commits suicide to punish himself for failure to inflict infinitely severe torments, but this does not happen in practice, because always at some point short of infinite leftism, something, or someone, goes boom - though not necessarily very far short of infinite leftism.

The left singularity generally ends when quite a lot of people near the very center of power are terrified that the left singularity, the ever more extreme demand for ever greater purity, has become a threat to at least their property and liberty, and usually to their lives. It ends when the ruling elite become sufficiently frightened of each other that some of them decide to do something drastic - which is to say, it ends after it has gone quite a bit further than it has yet gone. There is a lot of ruin in a nation.

When it ends, things sometimes get a lot better. And sometimes they do not. But things stop getting worse.

Often a left singularity ends when left wing leader, for example Stalin, has everyone to the left of himself shot, or a sufficient number of people to the left of himself shot to halt the singularity, thus conveying, with bullets, the message that the current status quo is left enough. To the right of here you get shot, to the left of here you get shot. The ever leftwards movement has succeeded in bringing us to this glorious utopia, and anyone who wants any more change, rightwards or leftwards, is going to die.

Sometimes the singularity ends in a military coup. This generally results in the message, again conveyed in bullets, that that was wee bit too far left. We are going back a wee bit rightwards - though not necessarily very far rightwards. To get all the way back to before the left singularity set in generally requires armed conflict within the army, with one army faction going to war with another, as in the restoration, or foreign conquest as foreigners take advantage of internal disorder, as in Cambodia, or some event similarly drastic.

The further the reversal goes rightwards, for example the Restoration, the less bloody the reversal is. When you are far left it requires more terror to stabilize the social order, to prevent it from going even further left, than when you are far right, for the order of the restoration rested on the patriarchal authority of heads of households and men of property, while Stalin's order rested on Stalin. Leftist repression makes politics compulsory, while rightist repression makes politics forbidden, which requires a lower level of repression.

In the early days of a left singularity, armed conflicts tend to favor the left, due to greater cohesion, a greater willingness to self sacrifice, and greater willingness to use dreadful means. In the final days of a left singularity, armed conflicts tend to favor the the right, often in a ridiculously one sided way, for reasons not altogether clear to me. Possibly the demand for ever more left wing beliefs selects for people ever more stupid and ever less in contact with reality and undermines military discipline and order. Observe that three rentacops can handle any number of occupiers, though it somehow takes three hundred policemen to handle fifty occupiers. The recent military debacles of the British army suggests that they could similarly handle today's British army. A handful of Blackwater mercenaries can defeat a large horde of Arabs, a handful of Arabs can defeat a horde of British soldiers, which suggests that Blackwater could conquer Britain quite easily if ever the Pentagon were to let them off the leash, or the Pentagon's hand became too feeble to grip the leash. The weakness of Europe makes reversion to seventh century anarcho-piratism a real possibility.

However, whatever is wrong with the military forces of a left singularity near the end, it tends to be decisively remedied after the end, which often gives us a military left force that is potent, and quite left wing, for example Napoleon's army, even though it no longer suffers from the ever leftwards tendency.

Cromwell's army was white, male, and heterosexual, with the death penalty for sodomy. Today's British army is united only by faith, faith in progressivism.

A left singularity ends because of loss of cohesion in the ruling elite, which finds itself having difficulty keeping up with the ever leftwards movement, and because of military weakness, which is perhaps elite incohesion manifested in the army. The worst outcome, and typically the bloodiest outcome, is that further movement leftwards is halted, and military discipline recreated, for example Stalinism. The best outcome, and typically the least bloody outcome, is that the leftists just flat out lose, and are purged from government, academia, and the official Religion, for example the Restoration.

Where the doctrine of equalism comes from
2012-08-07 07:37:05

"View from the right" is Christian rightist, and there they are arguing all men are made in the image of God, and therefore, equally entitled to rights and dignity[941].

Of course, they can argue this without being totally insane since they believe that everyone has an immortal soul inside, regardless of physical and mental inequality and propensity to depraved acts, but when Christians ditched their Christianity, while retaining equalism, thus becoming progressives, which began with the anti slavery movement and was more or less completed in the late 1940s, early 1950s, then, having ditched immortal souls, they then had to argue that men and women, blacks and whites, and so on and so forth were all literally equal in mean and distribution, which position is transparently insane and contrary to casual observation and common sense.

Of course, if you believe in Darwinism, then we are not equal, not individually, nor are the groups to which we belong equal. Further, we are not made in the image of God, but are risen killer apes, and not very far risen at that. Without civilization, custom, culture and such, we would all be back to killing and perhaps eating any stranger or outsider fast enough.

Further, that thin veneer of civilization over our native and natural killer ape tendencies is fragile. To extend it to people far away requires elaborate arrangements, which arrangements have to be maintained and enforced.

This latter fact, that we still are killer apes, and apt to prove it from time to time, provides a Darwinian justification for "hate" laws. Crimes between blacks and whites,

---

[941] https://www.amnation.com/vfr/archives/022977.html

crimes between men and women, crimes between religious sects, and so on and so forth perhaps need to be treated with greater severity because of the propensity for collective conflict. But if that is our justification, then we really need to be cracking down on blacks, who commit the vast majority of race hate crimes, and Muslims, who commit the vast majority of religious hate crimes. And something needs to be done about women, who are usually the ones breaking up families and destroying the lives of their children. In practice "hate" laws are directed against one group, and one group only: White males, primarily working class white males, thus such laws are thus themselves a manifestation of the hatred and intolerance that they supposedly ban, and thus themselves promote the group conflict that they purportedly suppress. It was "Tolerance" that gave us Major Hasan's massacre at Fort Hood.

This was obvious in the recent Chick-fil-A protests. Which side demonstrated hatred, bigotry, and intolerance?

As the state and the laws are undermining, rather than promoting civilization, our killer ape nature is likely to soon be on full display. It is not in our nature to maintain civilized conduct with strangers, with people far away, with people very different from ourselves. Such arrangements have to be built, and have to be maintained, and they are not being maintained.

Most apes seldom kill members of their own species, and never make war. Chimps and men make war. Most apes are vegetarians. Chimps and bonobos are omnivores. Humans are close to being carnivores, in that in the ancestral environment you died if you did not eat some substantial amount of meat, and the stable isotope ratios found in the collagen of ancient bones indicates that primitive humans ate at about the same or higher trophic level as wolves and hyenas– meaning that they ate what wolves and hyenas ate, plus they sometimes ate wolves and hyenas, and, perhaps, sometimes each other. This suggests that humans evolved intelligence largely to facilitate cooperative violence. Humans that cooperated better tended to wipe out humans that cooperated worse. Chances are, our species is what it is because of a persistent inclination to genocide.

The Nazis killing the Jews was a really bad idea. The Nazis should have done what the progressives are doing, and absorbed them. Not only did all the smartest Jews get the hell out of Germany, some of them went to America and set to work on the atom bomb. Hitler did not get the bomb in substantial part because he got rid of "Jewish Science". On the other hand, getting rid of the bushmen, the Amerindians, and the Australian aboriginals worked out fine. It tends to be a seriously bad idea to deliberately pursue conflict with a group that is smarter and better at cooperating than your own group. On the other hand, pursuing conflict with a group that is stupider and less capable of cooperating than your own group usually works out very nicely. Thus the superior group should be more aggressive as a group, recklessly getting close to group conflict, and the inferior group should be more tolerant, seeking to assimilate, and seeking peace. Thus our laws and customs should be less tolerant of black race hate crimes than white race hate crimes, not more tolerant. Similarly, profiling should be encouraged, not only in crime watch, but also as a sanity check on test results and credit ratings. People who race horses do not collect all foals equally, train them equally, race them, then select those who race the best for special training and further racing. They select the foals with the best bloodlines, and give those special training, relying both on test results and ancestry.

A tell revealing central authority over the official line

2012-08-10 07:39:23

The most useful tells are short and sweet– you twit someone with something, and their response reveal their real beliefs and real motivations. This tell is, unfortunately, long, tedious and complex, but it not only reveals an elite that believes or pretends to believe in official truth absolutely regardless of evidence, but reveals that there *is* an official line, and the politically correct know it – reveals that they do not just believe certain improbable things because its is fashionable, or because it is what all the right people believe, they believe in the edicts of a a highly centralized authority, after the fashion of Orwell's Winston Smith, believe because they are damned well told to, fear punishment from on high for heresy, that they are not speaking what they believe, nor what is fashionable to believe, nor what is high status to believe, but what they are damned well told to believe, like communist party members who would spout the official line, and claim to have always spouted that line, and that the line had never changed, even when the line had reversed itself yesterday.

The communist left was infamous for its abrupt reversals on Hitler and Pol Pot, and its confident proclamation, continuing to this day, that the most recent line on these topics had been its line from the beginning. Progressives, unfortunately, do not have anything so spectacular and shameful, but the obscurity of the examples where the line has abruptly changed make their rigid adherence to the line, though less spectacular, all the more revealing of totalitarianism, of highly centralized authority over the line, where a single voice speaks a lie, and every other voice echoes the lie, a million megaphones with one microphone.

A nice short tell, revealing insincerity is to twit a progressive with "Mike's Nature trick … to hide the decline" They will deny that "trick" and "hide" mean what they sound like they mean, but will then explain, not what "trick" and "hide" really mean, but what "decline" really means, implicitly admitting what they explicitly deny, implicitly admitting that they know that "trick" and "hide" mean exactly what they sound like they mean. But they could be doing that because of sincerely held religious convictions about man raping nature or some such, rather than because they are taking orders from someone above them, rather than doing what they are damn well told as Orwell's Winston Smith was told.

This tell, the Lamarck common descent tell, is a tell that justifies a more paranoid and conspiratorial view of disagreements. It reveals that progressives, and anyone employed by the government, media, or a university, are, like communists, faceless minions of higher authority insincerely parroting not merely the fashionable line, the high status line, but the official line, knowing that any deviation is likely to be punished, fearing that they are under continuous scrutiny for any deviation from a ten thousand point official line.

You twit a progressive, or an academic, or a government employee, or a supposedly libertarian and conservative academic, or a supposedly heretical not-all-PC academic, or a government employee, with the fact that history gets rewritten at alarmingly frequent intervals, and everyone important falls into line on the new version, forgetting it was ever different, and failing to notice that no evidence is produced for the new version, while the evidence that supported the older version disappears from newer books, and everyone mysteriously forgets it ever existed.

While all of history is frequently rewritten, I focus on rewrites of science history, because the history of science is the history of what the particular scientists who made history wrote for their colleagues, thus the true version is not in any doubt. Perhaps the latest account of feudalism or colonialism reflects a deeper understanding, rather than barefaced lies, though I doubt it, but the latest version of science history is always barefaced lies, and lies that can be easily checked by reading the works of the scientists that they are lying about.

The revision of history indicates a centralized authority operating Winston Smith style with world wide power, or at least power over the anglosphere, most of europe, and most of the third world, especially Africa.

Your academic, confronted with the evidence that history changed, and that the new version is false, will deny the change, will at first weasel around trying to avoid taking any position on the new version, will sort of change the subject, but will, if pressed, eventually assert the new version is true, and not only true, but was indeed always accepted:

> O'Brien held up his left hand, its back towards Winston, with the thumb hidden and four fingers extended. "How many fingers am I holding up, Winston?"
>
> "Four"
>
> "And if the party says it is not four but five - then how many?"

To which your academic dutifully replies

> "five".

By endorsing a flagrantly false version of history, he reveals that this is not the Zeitgeist, not the climate of opinion, it is people shutting up and saying what they damn well told to say. He reveals that he is afraid.

That the story changed in an abrupt and coherent fashion, with additional details being fabricated to make it all fit together, reveals that the story is decided by centralized authority. Someone must have said to John Painter: "Telling students that Darwin is famous for natural selection focuses undue attention on natural selection. Correct references to Darwin". And so John Painter then fixed it by making Darwin famous for common descent, and then, like Winston Smith inventing comrade Ogilvy to fill the gap, had to adjust Lamarck to fit by denying that Lamarck proposed common descent. Whereupon everyone everywhere was instantly convinced, and instantly forgot that yesterday they had believed that Lamarck, among several others, had proposed common descent, had proposed that groups of species that resemble each other, resemble each other because of physical relationship by blood or sap, because they had a common ancestor, a physical individual, father or mother to both kinds, that similarities between kinds occur because they are chips off the same block.

That if you twit an academic with this, or any other, revision of history, he will go along with the official version and deny that history has been revised shows that the existence of this highly centralized authority is not exactly secret, merely plausibly deniable – and those who most deny it show by their behavior that they most believe it.

On the big issues, official truth tends to be sophisticated and subtle: It is on the minor and obscure issues that the official truth tends to be simplistic, rigid, and absurd, and it is on these obscure minor issues, not the big issues, where one will see O'Brien hold up four fingers and every supposedly high IQ person with tenure swears he is holding up five fingers because the party declares it to be so..

Fraud on Lamarck is a good illustration, because what modern historians of science say is provably false. We may argue about how Harold died at the battle of Hastings, but what Lamarck really said is not in genuine doubt.

Every respectable authority before 1972 that mentions Lamarck's position on common descent says Lamarck proposed common descent, often quoting from Lamarck at length. Every respectable authority after 1972 that mentions his position on common descent says that Lamarck rejected common descent, without, however quoting anything substantial from Lamarck, or mentioning that past authorities disagreed.

Twit an academic with this abrupt change on Lamarck, and he will weasel around, perhaps instead argue that Darwin has legitimately become an unperson because his unspecified theory has been discredited in some unspecified way by new and improved science, but if pressed, will eventually loyally endorse the official line, and deny any rewrite of history,

No one from post 1972 said, "hey, everybody pre 1972 was wrong and here is why they were wrong" Instead, all those writers were flushed down the memory hole. That's not what normally happens when a shift in opinion occurs. When Einstein revised physics, nobody flushed Newton down the memory hole. Everyone said explicitly, "hey, look here everybody, Einstein revised Newton's physics. Turns out that Newton was only accurate for velocities much less than that of light, which of course was all that he could easily observe". But when claims about what Lamarck meant reversed in 1972, nobody said, "hey, look here everybody, the past wrong understanding of Lamarck has been revised." Why the secrecy about the fact of the shift? It's weird. It's significant. It's the same as what's done in the photos that Stalin had his victims airbrushed out of.

If in the Soviet Union you started trying to explain changes in photos, you would be out in the Gulag, and if today you started trying to explain changes in the history books, you would be out of academia. Even if your explanation was politically correct, it would still draw attention to that which you are forbidden to notice.

Even if you wrote "The earlier photograph showing the commissar was in error, and the error happened because Trotskyite wreckers", you would still be in the gulag double plus quick, for drawing attention to the change in photographs.

And so, when you twit an academic with a rewrite of science history, no academic will be able to explain why large numbers of people before 1972 "mistakenly" thought that Lamarck proposed common descent, and why no one doubted that he proposed common descent. Even if the academic was to explain it as evil fabrication by right wing creationist Christian racists, drawing attention to the discrepancy would get him untenured mighty fast. (The commenter Bill, whose knowledge of academia is more current than my own, assures me you would not get untenured, but would merely have eyes rolled at you, and find that your office was eventually transferred to the basement. He knows more than I, but strangely, I see only very mildly heretical documents issuing from offices located in university basements.)

So if your academic or left winger lies on this incredibly obscure and minor point, which he will, he is lying on another ten thousand incredibly obscure and minor points. Your academic will deny that old authorities differ from recent authorities, and claim that the new version is supported in some unspecified way by Lamarck's words. It is just a little lie, but its very unimportance and obscurity implies he lies on everything.

This world wide, or at least anglosphere and academia wide, U turn on the history of science was as abrupt and unexplained as Orwell's hate week, which U turn implies a single command, a decision made by one man, or a group of people small enough to meet around a table and feel each other's breath, a decision made by a few, and imposed on all, to which all academics, major publishers, and so on and so forth, world wide, servilely and abruptly submit, except perhaps for a tiny handful so unimportant and obscure, at such low status universities, that they did not get the message – and thereby demonstrate their low status by having an out of date version of official history.

What happened in or around 1972, that caused this universal 180?

Affirmative action caused it.

I first became interested in this issue when there was a debate on the blogs as to whether Lamarck proposed common descent, and by an interesting coincidence, every blog that claimed Lamarck proposed parallel descent, also took an supporting position on affirmative action. Checking the books, every biology text book that claimed that Lamarck proposed parallel descent, also de-emphasized or denigrated natural selection.

Rewriting Lamarck's position on common descent looks to be a knock on effect of rewriting the history of science to revise Darwin's position on race, much as Bergholz got an invented history as a side effect of revising Beria out of history. When Beria suddenly became an unperson, this left a gap in the Soviet Encyclopedia at Ber, which was filled by an invented history of Bergholz, an event parodied in "1984", when Winston Smith invents Comrade Oglivy to replace the gap created when Comrade Withers becomes an unperson.

Beria became an unperson. Darwin did not become an unperson, but his accomplishments became unfacts, because of the horribly politically incorrect implications of his theory for human races and sexes, implications that he was not shy about mentioning. So just as it became necessary to invent a comrade Bergholz to replace the unperson Beria and a comrade Oglivy to replace the unperson Withers, it became necessary to give a new important accomplishment to Darwin to replace the unfacts for which Darwin had previously been famous. And thus, necessary to take that accomplishment away from Lamarck.

De-emphasizing or denigrating natural selection meant that all these busts of Darwin around the biology department were hard to explain. Students might ask? "Why do we have busts of this obscure little known nineteenth century racist". So it was necessary to give Darwin something else to be famous for. That, or chisel the busts off. So John Painter gave him common descent, which meant that he had to take it away from Lamarck.

And so, whenever you accuse someone who rejects evolutionary psychology of rejecting Darwinism, he will be sincerely puzzled and point out that he believes in common descent, he believes that men and apes had a common ancestor, that he believes that men and monkeys had an earlier common ancestor, and that all mammals had an even earlier common ancestor, that the likenesses between species indicates common descent, descent from a common ancestor, indicate physical relationship by blood or sap, and thinks that this makes him a Darwinist. By and large, those who reject evolutionary psychology associate Darwin with common descent, not with natural selection. And, similarly, if you refer to slavery practiced and still practiced by Arabs and blacks, they will have difficulty comprehending what you could possibly be talking about. To them, it is only slavery if the slaves are owned by white male capitalists.

Which implies that history is being rewritten in an abrupt centralized, conspiratorial, and planned way, after the fashion of Winston Smith in "1984". And we observe that when history changes, it changes everywhere in the world at once, every academy, in every nation, or at least every western nation, and most non western nations.

An individual might misrepresent the facts on his own initiative, or change his mind on the evidence.

When everyone changes their minds at the same time, without explanation, and declines to admit ever holding a different position, they are lying because the official line has been officially imposed.

Science history of the idea of common descent before 1972

1882 Works of Samuel Butler [942]:

> In his preface Lamarck had already declared that "the thread which gives us a clue to the causes of the various phenomena of animal organization, in the manifold diversity of its developments, is to be found in the fact that Nature conserves in offspring all that their life and environments has developed in parents." Heredity "the hidden bond of common descent" tempered with the modifications induced by changed habits which changed habits are due to new conditions and surroundings this with Lamarck, as with Buffon and Dr.Darwin, is the explanation of the diversity of forms which we observe in nature. He now goes on to support this briefly, in accordance with his design but with sufficient detail to prevent all possibility of mistake about his meaning.

1882 Nature, Volume 26[943]

> While he [Lamarck] was engaged in substantially classifying and describing not merely the forms already in existence, but also their extinct ancestors

---

[942] full context available in google books
[943] https://www.google.com/search?tbo=p&tbm=bks&q=%22and+from+this+disclosure+he+inferred+their+common%22&num=10

which he incorporated into his system, there was disclosed to him the inner morphologic connection between the former and the latter, and from this disclosure he inferred their common descent

1895 Geological biology an introduction to the geological history of organisms[944], New York: Henry Holt and Company, pp.158–159[945], (full context in Internet Archive)

> The portion of the theory of Development Evolution which maintains the common descent of all species of animals and plants from the simplest common original forms might, therefore, in honor of its eminent founder, and with full justice, be called Lamarckian ; on the other hand, the theory of Selection, or breeding, might be justly called Darwinism being that portion of the theory of Development Evolution which shows us in what way, and why, the different species of organisms have developed from those simplest primary forms.

1897 The evolution of Man[946] by Ernst Haekel page 58 (Incorrectly dated by Google as 2004, creating the illusion of a break in the pattern wherein everyone before 1972 attributes common descent to Larmarck, and everyone after 1972 denies that Lamarck proposed common descent.)

> Lamarck was the first to formulate as a scientific theory the natural origin of living things, including man ... the rise of the earliest organisms by spontaneous generation, and the descent of man from the nearest related mammal, the ape
>
> ... his theory of the common descent of man and the other animals.

1901 The Century Cyclopedia Volume 4 pp.3334[947] (full context in Internet Archive) Tells us that Lamarckism is:

> the general body of doctrine propounded by the French Naturalist J.B.P.A. de Monet de Lamarck (1744-1829): the theory of evolution as maintained by him at the beginning of the nineteenth century to the effect that all plants and animals are descended from a common primitive form of life. In its fundamental principles and essential features Lamarckism differs from Darwinism in assuming that changes resulted from appetency and the active exertion of the organism.

1914 Scientific American: Supplement: Volume 78[948]

---

[944] https://www.archive.org/details/geologicalbiolo00willgoog

[945] https://archive.org/stream/geologicalbiolo00willgoog#page/n190/mode/2up

[946] https://books.google.com/books?id=2PTIErbazx8C&pg=PA58&lpg=PA58&dq=lamarck+%22Common+descent%22+inauthor:Ernst+inauthor:Haeckel&source=bl&ots=BY4D3IwLok&sigVILYO_tufoGby-WxE4qy_kv1424&hl=en&sa=X&ei=yWsjUKuhNuOVjALtooHABQ

[947] https://archive.org/details/centurydictiona04whit

[948] https://books.google.com/books?id=VwoiAQAAMAAJ&q=%22Lamarck+was+the+first+to+point+this+out+and+plain%22&dq=%22Lamarck+was+the+first+to+point+this+out+and+to+ex-plain%22&source=bl&ots=pfNZlyM36P&sig=OVf-0akcnUYCxPTXJjGlCxdU-daQ&hl=en&sa=X&ei=VOUcUP__G9GuiQeCrIHwCQ&ved=0CC4Q6AEwAA

(quoting or paraphrasing Ernst Haekel above)

> Lamarck was the first to point this out and to explain it by his theory of common descent. But the science of his time did not afford a sufficient body of facts in proof of his conception, and he failed to convince his contemporaries.

Context is that "this" is resemblance, the common characteristics, that group species together. "This" is the "unity of organization" of related life forms.

> ... in order to find a conclusive proof of the idea of Lamarck. Common descent is now acknowledged as the natural cause of the unity of organization.
> ...

1928 Outline and general principles of the history of life[949] By William Diller Matthew, Ayer Publishing, page 52 tells us [950]:

> Lamarck and many others of his time believed that the different species of a genus resembled each other because they were of common descent, and each species had gradually changed in form and become distinct and ceased to interbreed; and in his studies on the fossil mollusks in the Tertiary strata of the Paris basin he believed that he saw the actual record of those changes preserved in the fossils from the successive strata.

Every single relevant pre-1972 book that came up in Google books advanced search told the same story, often, as in the case of Samuel Butler, supporting their account with copious quotes.

One way of rationalizing this away is to claim that rather than history abruptly changing in 1972, the meaning of common descent abruptly changed in 1972, but the 1928 quote from William Mathew above

ceased to interbreed

shows that common descent meant then when what it means now – actual physical ancestry by blood or sap – as indeed would most of the quotes should I give sufficient context. This 1928 quote, like the 1972 quote, makes clear and precisely defines what "common descent" means, so that there is no way you can reconcile the change in the history books by adjusting the meaning of "common descent" between 1928 and 1972.

Science history of the idea of common descent after 1972

1972 Biology Today[951] by John Painter, page 638

---

[949] https://books.google.com/books?idKWNBFhnjgoC&pg=PA52
[950] full context available in google books
[951] https://www.google.com/search?tbo=p&tbm=bks&q=%22can+be+fairly+simply+stated.+According+to+the+Darwinian%22

The central claim of that book The Origin of Species can be fairly simply stated. According to the Darwinian theory, any natural group of similar species-all the mammal species, for instance-owe their common mammalian characteristics to a common descent from a single ancestral mammalian species

Which is of course total bunkum. The central claim of "Origin" is natural selection. And since common descent, rather than natural selection was now supposedly Darwin''s claim to fame, they had to lie about Lamarck: Page 641:

Lamarck's theory is not a hypothesis of common descent, which ascribes the common characteristics of a particular species to their common descent from a single species. He claims that mammals are produced by the gradual complexification of reptiles and that this elevation is going on constantly. Although all mammals are descended from reptiles, they are not descended from the same reptiles.

(Which, oddly, no longer shows up on google book search, though it appears to be the original of the new version of history, of which all subsequent versions are merely repetitions. However I scanned the above from an actual printed book, printed in ink on paper in 1972)

Somehow they neglect to mention that everyone before 1972 thought that Lamarck's theory was a theory of common descent, or explain what caused this change of mind, nor do they mention any authority who made this discovery about Lamarck. Some people cite Ernst Mayer "Lamarck Revisited" as such an authority, but he says nothing of the kind in the original version of his paper. The assertion just appears from nowhere in 1972 as if everyone had always uncontroversially known it and no one had ever doubted it.

This 1972 quote, like the 1928 quote, makes clear and precisely defines what "common descent" means, so no one can weasel out of the abrupt change in history by saying that the meaning of "common descent" changed in 1972

1978: Scientific American: Volume 239

Darwin's two other main postulates were essentially new concepts. One was the postulate of common descent. For Lamarck each organism or group of organisms represented an independent evolutionary line,having had a beginning in spontaneous generation and having constantly striven towards perfection

In context, denies common descent to Lamarck

And what, you might ask was Darwin's other main new postulate? The authors (it is a committee) eventually and reluctantly kind of admit it was natural selection, while doing their best to obfuscate and ignore this inconvenient and embarrassing bastard child of Darwin. They show, however, no similar reluctance in listing all the objections to natural selection.

1981:Environmental ethics: Volume 3

He [Darwin] departed from Lamarck in supposing a common descent.

Departing from Lamarck in supposing natural selection being something to horrible to mention.

1982: The Growth of Biological Thought[952] page 345

Lamarck had no theory of an origin of species nor did he consider common descent.

1999: The Darwinian Revolution: Science red in tooth and claw[953] By Michael Ruse, page 10

Lamarck's theory was in no way a theory of common descent ...

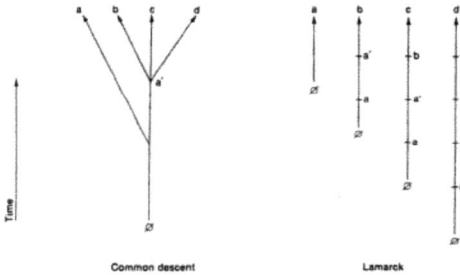

Figure 2. The difference between a theory like Lamarck's and one of common descent. Life is supposed to begin at Ø, and *a*, *b*, *c*, *d*, are kinds of organisms extant today.

Michael Ruse tells us that Lamark's evolutionary diagram looked like the one on the right above. But Lamarck drew an evolutionary diagram of the animals, what we now call the bilaterians

And here is Lamarck's diagram, translated by Elliot, which you will notice is strikingly different from Michael Ruse's account of Lamarck's diagram:

The accompanying text in Elliot's translation of Lamarck can most reasonably be interpreted as showing that Lamarck believed that the common features of worms, flies, men, and seals, what we now call bilaterians, were due to their common descent from an ancient spontaneously generated simple worm, that seals have hands inside their flippers because they share a more recent common ancestor with men, though he thought it likely that jellyfish and such (infusorians, polyps, radiarians) evolved from a separate spontaneously generated ancestor.

And if Michael Ruse wants a different interpretation, he needs to explain away Lamarck's diagram and text instead of making up his own diagram and

[952]https://www.google.com/search?tbo=p&tbm=bks&q=%22origin+of+species+nor+did+he+con-sider+common+descent%22&num=10

[953]https://books.google.com/books?id=B65DBU-vMSoC&pg=PA10&lpg=PA10

confidently attributing it to Lamarck. He needs to acknowledge Lamarck's diagram and explain why his interpretation is better than the interpretation of everyone before 1972

1995:The Spirit *of* System: Lamarck and Evolutionary Biology : Now With ... - Page xxii[954]"

> Lamarck's theory, unlike Darwin's, should not be seen as a theory of common descent. Darwin's emphasis was on common ancestry ...

No, Darwin's emphasis was on natural selection. Again, we see that taking the credit from Lamarck and giving it to Darwin is done to de-emphasize and minimize natural selection.

A 2009 change back?

After I posted this, two of my commenters have drew my attention to a high status post in Nature attributing common descent to Lamarck[955]. Fortunately I had already covered my self against such an embarrassing possibility by writing ...

Not the last rewrite on evolution

Gould's approach to reconciling biology with equalism seems to be out of favor, so tomorrow morning, Lamarck might be reinstated, his arguments for common descent restored to science history. But if he is reinstated, that he was ever removed will be erased. Should science history once again tell the truth on this matter, suddenly no one will remember that it ever lied on this matter. Similarly Hitler went from good guy to bad guy and back again several times amongst the communists, and when he was officially a good guy, no one ever remembered that he had ever been officially a bad guy, and when he was officially a bad guy, no one ever remembered that he had ever been officially a good guy, which Orwell parodied in "1984" as "We've always been at war with Eastasia"

If tomorrow morning, official history once again officially tells us that Lamarck proposed common descent, as well it may, not one academic will remember ever doubting it.

---

[954]https://books.google.com/books?id=JCcTDLgFjzEC&pg=PR22&lpg=PR22&dq=%22unlike+Darwin%27s,+should+not+be+seen+as+a+theory+of+common+descent%22&source=bl&ots=AXgUB3MLUH&sig=lu1s6Ifn2brB0jW-f_JWQLo&hl=en&sa=X&ei=UHgjULyTEsGriAK5v4GoAQ&ved=0CDEQ6AEwAA "The Spirit of System: Lamarck and Evolutionary Biology : Now With "Lamarck in 1995""
[955]https://nsm.uh.edu/~dgraur/ArticlesPDFs/lamarck%20nature%202009.pdf

Why history was adjusted.

The full title of "The Origin" is "The Origin of Species by Means of Natural Selection: The Preservation of Favored Races in the Struggle for Life"

By races, Darwin means both human and non human subspecies. Selection occurs on the level of species, races, and individuals. Races, Darwin tells us, originate by differential selection pressures on populations, and races tend to differentiate into species, eventually becoming so different that crosses have reduced or nonexistent fertility. Races *are* the origin of species. Darwin cheerfully and optimistically tells us:

> At some future period, not very distant as measured by centuries, the civilised races of man will almost certainly exterminate, and replace, the savage races throughout the world. At the same time the anthropomorphous apes, as Professor Schaaffhausen has remarked, will no doubt be exterminated. The break between man and his nearest allies will then be wider, for it will intervene between man in a more civilized state, as we may hope, even than the Caucasian, and some ape as low as a baboon, instead of as now between the negro or Australian and the gorilla.

In short, natural selection is *raaaaciiiiiiist*! That animals are evolving implies that humans are evolving. That humans are evolving implies that human races are unlikely to be equal.

Darwin also concluded that sexual selection means that the differences between the human sexes are likely to be substantial and politically incorrect. In fact, he originated every major way in which biology leads to politically incorrect conclusions. Every politically incorrect fact from evolutionary psychology, you will find foreshadowed in Darwin, plus a pile that no one dares go near any more.

One man, one vote, once

2012-08-14 20:29:59

When you give power to the people, and the people are manifestly incapable of exercising it, power will swiftly wind up in the hands a a man or group of men equally evil and degenerate, but considerably more capable of exercising it.

This process has now completed in Egypt, which has become the simplest form of Islamic Republic, an elective dictatorship.

Ann Coulter goes anti democracy

2012-08-16 06:14:32

Ann Coulter favorably quotes Le Bon

> Mobs, according to Le Bon, have a "fetish-like respect" for tradition, except moral traditions because crowds are too impulsive to be moral. That's why liberals say our Constitution is a "living, breathing" document that sprouts rights to gay marriage and abortion, but the age at which Social Security and Medicare benefits kick in is written in stone.
>
> Le Bon says that it is lucky "for the progress of civilization that the power of crowds only began to exist when the great discoveries of science and industry had already been effected." If "democracies possessed the power they wield today at the time of the invention of mechanical looms or of the introduction of steam-power and of railways, the realization of these inventions would have been impossible."

Ann Coulter says "liberals", but in the context of Le Bon, not to mention an electorate that is majority protected groups, approaching majority underclass, on government handouts, and illegitimate, "liberals" means universal suffrage.

Pussy Riot attacked freedom of speech and freedom of religion

2012-08-18 09:06:36

And the longer they stay in jail, the more secure freedom of speech and freedom of religion is in Russia.

If you desecrate your own altar in your own venue, that is freedom of speech and freedom of religion. If you desecrate someone else's altar in someone else's venue, you are suppressing their freedom of religion, and, in that an altar is symbolic speech, you are silencing their speech.

Pussy Riot have long been exercising their freedom of speech and freedom of religion to attack Putin, the Orthodox Church, Christianity, and public decency. Absolutely no consequences ensued. In Britain, however, you can be jailed for facecrime, or criticizing the presence of immigrants. In the US you cannot be jailed for it, but your business may be suppressed[956], and left wing terrorists may be deniably encouraged to attack you[957].

---

[956] https://www.mediaite.com/tv/chick-fil-a-ban-chicago-the-view/
[957] https://www.mrc.org/press-releases/nbc-and-cbs-aiding-and-abetting-anti-conservative-hatred

The history of Pussy Riot demonstrates that there is more freedom of speech in Russia than in the US, and far more freedom of speech in Russia than in England.

Emboldened by this tolerance, mistaking it for weakness, Pussy Riot then went after other people's freedom of speech and religion, and for that, they were punished.

Allegedly Pussy Riot was a creation of the US manufactured and funded to silence hostile speech in Russia (foreign agents). That they have an English language name, and the mainstream media at their backs, suggests that is true, and, true or not, they have been adopted by the west as a tool to attack freedom of speech and freedom of religion in Russia.

There is less freedom of speech in China. English language blogs located in China seem to be pretty frank about problems in China, but Chinese dissidents in China expressing themselves in Chinese get set to jail – to about the same extent as English dissidents in England expressing themselves in English. Ai Weiwei was recently jailed for criticizing the Chinese regime – after several years of condemning the Chinese regime in a wide variety of media and making lots of money out of dissent.

Freedom of speech in China and Russia is steadily improving, while freedom of speech in the west is steadily diminishing, but, until Chick-a-Fil or the Mormons experience a kristallnacht, there is still some freedom of speech in the US.

We have, however, passed the turning point, where democracies are now generally less free than most other forms of regime, so that whosoever loves freedom should hate democracy.

Western sponsorship of "Russian" protest

2012-08-18 15:02:28

Observe her protest is written on her in English– she is not protesting for the Russian or Ukrainian audience, but for the western audience. This a western propaganda offensive against the last major Church to stick with Christianity.

I am not a Christian, but Christianity is no threat to me, whereas total domination by progressives of all cultural institutions is a threat to me.

Repeating what I said earlier: Progressives have done to Christianity what Christians did to pagans. Christians would convert the elite by some mixture of economic pressure, evangelical persuasion, and, sometimes, the threat or actuality of state violence. The elite ran the pagan religious institutions, and continued to run them. When ordinary lower class pagans showed for the customary pagan festivals, they found that the festival had been Christianized. They continue to do pretty much what they used to do, but now it was Christian, and not only no longer pagan, but gradually came to demonize pagan gods.

Analogously, today a father takes his family to church on Christmas, and instead of hearing what he was expecting, hears that salvation comes from voting for higher taxes and welfare, and that exercising authority over his wife and children is sinful.

And if the Russian Orthodox Church does not get with the program, their stuff is going to continue to be vandalized and desecrated. That this is western state pressure (the left is the state, and the state is the left, the left is the state at prayer) is apparent from the fact that the Orthodox Church in America has gone over to progressivism. The transition from Christianity to progressivism runs on state, rather than Church, boundaries, and the pressure to convert to progressivism is everywhere expressed in English.

Legitimate rape

2012-08-21 05:39:10

Todd is deep trouble for using the phrase "legitimate rape", for implying that a lot of rapes are not legitimate– implying that a lot of rape allegations are false rape allegations, or the post hoc reinterpretation of profoundly ambiguous events as rape.

Evolutionary psychology predicts that women will be far more upset about consenting to sex with someone that they subsequently deem a creep or a loser, than actually being forcibly and unambiguously raped, thus false or delusive rape accusations are likely to be common.

Surveys show that it is very rare for a woman married to the head of her household to be raped, and very common that the rapist is an acquaintance of the woman.

This suggests that most rapes occur under courtship circumstances, where it is apt to be inherently ambiguous whether the women consented or not.

In practice, the only common cases where a woman unambiguously consents to sex is marriage, where she consents verbally in front of witnesses, and prostitution, where she accepts a fee for service. In other cases, consent is seldom verbal, and not merely merely non verbal, but, as in cats, pre verbal, making it genuinely hard to apply our contract based concepts of consent. Illicit sex is usually inherently ambiguous sex. You cannot really say she consented except she comes back or sticks around, she herself cannot really say whether she consented unless she observes herself coming back or sticking around. These days, much, perhaps most, sex outside marriage does not involve people sticking around or coming back.

Observe the courtship of cats. On the one hand the pussy came when the tomcat called her, on the other hand the tomcat beat the hell out of her. If human courtship is usually more subtle and nuanced than that of cats, this makes it harder to interpret in terms of coercion and consent, not easier.

If most rapes are "real", most rapes are nonetheless the result of behavior that a woman married to the head of the household would seldom engage in, presumably immoral behavior by the woman, and thus not sharply distinct, in the women's behavior, in her own mind, and in the kind of evidence available, from "rapes" that are the result of her retroactively changing her mind.

Much, perhaps most, human mating these days occurs on the lek pattern. If you observe animals mating on the lek pattern, the female approaches a male, and then the male has sex with her. There is female choice, in that the female chose to approach one male and not another, but maybe she was just approaching to check him out more carefully, and got done regardless. It is meaningless to attempt to apply the concepts of strict consent applicable in a society of polygyny or monogamy. The concept of rape is difficult to apply to species that practice the lek mating pattern. And humans sometimes, in some societies, particularly our own, mate on the lek mating pattern.

That most rapes involve acquaintances, and that a woman married to the head of her household very seldom reports being raped, indicates that most rapes involve female choice similar to that of leking non human animals, in that the female chose to approach one male and not another. When a woman has promiscuous sex, sex on the lek mating pattern, she in practice usually behaves in way that makes the distinction between consent to sex and consent to be alone with a guy, profoundly unclear. In the lek mating pattern, there is no meaningful distinction between consenting to be with a male and consent to sex.

2005 US Crime victimization survey, Rape/sexual assault rate for wife of male head of household 0.1 per 1000 (which is one in ten thousand, which zero within the margin of error)

Notice how quickly political correctness marches on. Today, using the survey category "wife of male head of household" is apt to cause outrage and indignation. Today, households supposedly have no heads. Indeed, for a household to have a head, and that head be male, is arguably criminal, something that is supposedly only practiced by rare right wing fundamentalist extremists.

(In reality of course, all households have a head. If the head is weak, the household breaks up, and if the head is a woman, the head is apt to be weak and the household apt to break up.)

Rape/sexual assault rate for children over 18 of male head of household 2.3 per thousand

Rape/sexual assault rate for female heads of households 1.6 per thousand.

Which suggest that the overwhelming majority of real or perceived rapes occur in the context of what is politely called courtship behavior by the female, and impolitely called "cruising for some dicking"

Decline of the west

2012-08-22 21:27:48

According to official statistics, living standards are rising, inflation is low, and unemployment is falling.

If living standards are rising, why are people eating less meat and buying fewer cars?

[In the comments Bill makes a telling rebuttal: That people are eating less meat and buying fewer cars because of increasing inequality accurately reported by the official statistics: that the decline in equality renders official statistics compatible with consumption statistics for particular items.]

Freedom in Russia and the US.

2012-08-27 07:21:30

Observe that Brandaun Raub was arrested for calling for the imminent start of Civil War 2, whereas Pussy Riot committed numerous acts of subversion, desecration and obscenity in their own venues without encountering any response, before they were arrested for desecrating someone else's altar in someone else's venue.

So we are moving from the position that subversion in the US is likely to lose you your job, because your employer may be punished for your views, to the position that you yourself may be punished directly by the state. We are, however, not there yet. Brandaun Raub was predictably released[958]. Someone is just trying it on to test the waters, and found that the US is not yet ready for direct repression of dissidents. But then, a couple of years ago, was not yet ready for gay marriage.

Shortly before this happened his facebook page was censored by Facebook, which suggests to me that it was Facebook that asked to have him committed. If so, this is probably a business trying to disassociate itself from politically incorrect views. For a business, it is always safer to err on the side of repression, to get out in front of the movement towards the left singularity, rather than lag behind it. And the faster we move towards the left singularity, the further in front, the further forward towards the singularity you want your business to be. You don't want to find your business, like Chick-fil-A, subject to reprisal for taking the same position as Obama took two years previousy.

Brandon Raub was rightly criticized for engaging in politics while in uniform, which is forbidden for the same excellent reasons as leading assembled troops on the wrong side of the Rubicon was forbidden, to which criticism he responded by engaging in politics in his underwear.

But someone more important than Brandon Raub designed the marine dress uniform to look distinctly reactionary, or chose to retain its reactionary look even though times have changed. The marine dress uniform is itself political, as political as the altar that Pussy Riot desecrated, which may be why

[958]https://communities.washingtontimes.com/neighborhood/citizen-warrior/2012/aug/23/judge-orders-brandon-raub-released-hospital/

they changed their minds about arresting Brandon Raub. I read the marine dress uniform as indicating that, as in past left singularities, the political leadership is getting out ahead of the army.

Dude, where is my flying car?

2012-08-27 14:57:39

The first man on the moon has died, and pretty soon the last men on the moon will be dead also.

where are the space settlements?

By the year 2000, we were supposed to have flying cars, space settlements, and cities that looked like this:

There is no technological obstacle to building big high efficiency free electron lasers that operate in the near infrared. These are the lasers that were supposed to be built for Reagan's star wars initiative. They would be able to push rockets into space as well as blast them out of space. The precision and power you need to destroy a space vehicle at great distance is similar to the precision and power needed to power it from a great distance. A laser rocket can get a person plus some survival equipment into near earth orbit for about the same energy cost as a household uses in year. A laser rocket would be a single stage to orbit, thus would fly back and forth between orbit and the earth's surface like a commercial airliner.

Plasma drives cannot be used to get off earth, but once in orbit, plasma drives could make the entire solar system accessible at reasonable reaction mass cost, and energy in space is nearly free.

So technology that we could have, technology that we know in principle how to build with reasonable amounts of energy and materials, had we the will and competence, could have made entry to space affordable to ordinary individuals and businesses. There is no big technological obstacle to mining the asteroids for precious metals and such like, and then mining the rings of Saturn for volatiles to support the miners mining precious metals with air, water, and reaction mass.

Autogyros are technologically flying cars.

The only problem is that they are not legally flying cars. And if we had the current regulatory regime when people first started building cars, cars would never have become practical either.

You cannot legally put a foldback roof on your garage similar to the foldback door in front, and fly from your house in the suburbs to the parking lot at your place of work, even though physically there is nothing stopping an autogyro from doing that.

Autogyros capable of vertical or nearly vertical landing and takeoff can be built and operated for the price of an expensive car, and would get a whole lot cheaper if lots more people purchased them, but the regulatory burden makes them only useful in the middle of nowhere. There is no technological obstacle to well off people being able to fly to work and shop and visit friends.When the engine fails, or the driver falls asleep, an autogyro goes into a nearly vertical landing slow enough to walk away from. Unlike every other flying vehicle we have built, we can trust the usual idiots to drive and maintain an autogyro. But in practice, the main demand for autogyros is wealthy ranchers who use them to fly around their ranch– since in practice they can only legally fly from the middle of nowhere to the middle of nowhere.

If we are capable of settling space, why have we not already settled Antarctica?

Because we were not *allowed* to settle Antarctica. The antarctic treaty was agreed to because governments feared that the settlement of Antarctica was about to begin, and they decided to put a stop to it, as they similarly put a stop to the settlement of Spitzbergen (the islands of the Arctic), in which settlement had already begun. Settlement of Spitzbergen and Antarctica would have led to the development of environment suits that would have been precursors of space suits, and housing that would have been the precursor of space habitats.

People have stopped settling Spitzbergen, because they cannot buy land, even though it is 99.99% empty. Governments claimed all the land that was as yet unsettled, and refuse to let anyone else have any. Land prices are, therefore, extraordinarily high, despite it being the middle of nowhere. The high price of the tiny amount of land that was settled by pioneers before governments clamped down reveals a large frustrated demand to settle the Spitzbergen islands.

People settled Spitzbergen because there was energy in the form of coal, and food in the form of fish, seals, and whales. Try that today in Antarctica. Governments will not let you.

The reaction to Clint Eastwood's speech

2012-09-02 16:00:22

Every television station, every radio station, every newspaper ...

Every mainstream blog that mentions the topic is being spammed with suspiciously repetitive comments. An abrupt and coordinated attack, endlessly repeating a single message, is like an army, its behavior showing it is thrown into action by a single command, issued by a single commander.

And what is that single message?

That Clint Eastwood is a poopy head.

But it is a stupid command, since of course it generates publicity for Clint Eastwood's message. For actors and directors, any publicity is good publicity, so long as they spell your name right. Even if they successfully convince large numbers of people that Clint Eastwood is an ignorant senile poopy head, it is not Clint Eastwood that is running for President. Attacking Clint Eastwood is a diversion from attacking Mitt Romney.

So what most likely happened, is that Obama was watching, was offended, and reacted exactly like the spoiled angry arrogant petulant child Clint Eastwood depicted him as being: "Call me a poopy head will he", thought Obama, "I will show him! I will have my millions of faithful minions call **him** a poopy head! That will show him!"

But not one of his faithful minions is as funny or entertaining as Clint Eastwood. As Galileo observed, one racehorse can outrun a team of carthorses, no matter how large the team.

Every "um", "err" and "ahh", every rambling change of subject, led into Clint's next punchline with perfect comedic timing, like a clown who trips over his big clown shoes but somehow lands upright without spilling his drink, resulting in mighty gales of laughter exactly at the laughter pauses. Although widely advertised as unscripted and unrehearsed, actor/directors do not do unscripted and unrehearsed in front of an audience of millions.

So what we are getting from Obama's mighty horde of minions is a bunch of childish badly written whines complaining that Clint Eastwood, a great actor and director, who had the convention howling with laughter, delivered a bad act. When Obama's minions can get a big crowd roaring with laughter at their enemies, then they might be able to criticize Clint Eastwood's delivery.

Deregulation

2012-09-10 05:46:17

A lot of people, including pretty much everyone in academia, including supposed libertarians in academia, agree that deregulation has been happening.

Everyone agrees that the US banks were "deregulated" – in that a seventeen page law governing their permitted activities was replaced by three thousand pages of laws governing their activities, which three thousand pages were not so much laws, as headings for regulators to title their decisions. It is impossible to say how many pages of regulations were created, since the extraordinary flood of regulations bypassed the normal mechanisms such as the federal register, and consist of all manner of document categories – not only does no one know how much regulation there is, no one even knows how to find all the regulations that there are.

This was indeed "deregulation" in that activities that banks were previously forbidden to do, were now permitted under the supervision of regulators.

And most of these new activities turned out to be staggeringly costly for taxpayers, and continue to be so.

What happened was not that the government got out of the banking business, but that the government got further into the banking business, making case by case banking decisions on the basis of political considerations, and predictably losing money hand over fist. One such set of decisions, one of many, was case by case approving anything that led to more lending to non Asian minorities – which is how most of the money in the US was lost, though by no means all the money. Most of it was lost in the crisis on loans to non asian minorities, and such little of it as was lost on whites, was lost to whites largely as a result of across the board reductions in credit standards partly motivated by desire to benefit the poor in general, but largely motivated by desire to benefit non Asian minorities in particular.

Government decisions are usually incompetent, and on the rare occasions that they are competent, are competently motivated by short term politics rather than long term profit and loss, so if government increases its decision making burdens, it will reliably lose more money and create more havoc. Deregulation is beneficial if it gets the government out of business activities. It is harmful if it gets the government into business activities, if it substantially increases government decision making and government employment, which banking "deregulation" clearly did. If you wind up with more regulators exercising more power, it is not deregulation, or if, in some sense it is deregulation, in that the banks were doing lots of stuff that was previously forbidden, it is nonetheless apt to be massively damaging, for the new stuff the banks were doing was largely motivated by politics, not profits, as was obvious in the activities of those that lost most of the money: Fannie, Freddy, the FHA, Countrywide, and Washington Mutual.

These highly political banks would make politically motivated decisions that were obviously going to lose a bundle and rationalize them on the basis of incoherent politically correct nonsense and magical thinking. When these decisions started to predictably lose gigantic amounts of money, accounting rules were hastily altered to delay reporting these losses, altered for everyone, not just badly run banks – and remain altered for everyone to this day, even though the losses have become obvious.

That the government agencies, Fannie, Freddy, and the FHA would be badly behaved and politically motivated was inevitable and predictable. If you have government agencies playing with large amounts of money, that the money will disappear is inevitable and predictable. Bernanke, however, was piously puzzled that privately run banks, in particular Countrywide and Washington Mutual, would make decisions that were going to lose colossal amounts of money.

One might suppose that Countrywide and Washington Mutual made million dollar loans to people with no income, no job, no assets, and no credit rating because the government had changed the rules to allow the banks to unload these loans onto some other sucker, that other sucker usually being Fannie or Freddy, but the worst behaved banks, Countrywide and Washington mutual were *not* able to unload all their dud loans onto some other sucker. When the state of the loans could no longer be denied, Countrywide and Washington Mutual, and a great many other banks, went down with their loans.

Rather, it was in large part the other way around. Banks made *politically motivated* dud loans, then begged the government for ways to unload those loans on some other sucker.

And why did they make politically motivated loans? Partly it was that the CRA mandated politically motivated loans. Partly it was political correctness. The regulators demanded not merely politically correct behavior, but also politically correct belief, demanded holy zeal for the true faith, and got it. Partly it was that the leadership of Countrywide and Washington Mutual did not rise to the top by pleasing shareholders, but by pleasing regulators, and in large part, by pleasing regulators with the purity of their political faith. Not only were banks rewarded and punished according to the holiness of their faith, but bankers rose and fell more according to the holiness of their faith, than their ability to make money. Bankers sincerely believed, or sincerely believed that they sincerely believed, that Mexicans and blacks were under served, and therefore that anything that got in the way of serving blacks and Mexicans, such as requiring jobs, income, and a credit rating, was irrational and racist.

The neg in romance stories

2012-09-10 17:27:19

The authors of A Billion Wicked Thoughts: What the Internet Tells Us About Sexual Relationships[959] have surveyed thousands of porn sites and great stinking piles of slash romance fiction. It was a tough job, but someone had to do it.

They tell us that the ideal-looking hero of a romance story has "dark hair," which accents the "white teeth" in his "sensual mouth" curved into a "crooked smile.".

But a crooked smile is an expression of contempt. If the hero is looking at someone with a crooked smile he is laughing *at* them. I checked one romance fiction for a crooked smile, that being all I could stand, and yes, that is what hero was doing, negging the heroine most savagely - no he was not negging, since a neg is back handed compliment, an unsettling comment that *could* be interpreted as insult. He was just insulting her.

So yes, all women are like that.

Religion and reaction.

2012-09-12 07:17:52

Fosetti criticizes Bruce Charlton's claim[960] that

> there are only three sides: Christianity, Islam and secular Leftism[961]

Obviously most Christians *are* secular leftists, in that they have chucked the Gospel overboard because of all those horribly reactionary bits commanding patriarchy and commanding toleration of all sorts of things that progressives are not supposed to tolerate, and in the process they have demoted Christ the redeemer to Jesus the community organizer.

See Dalrock's wonderful blog[962] for its magnificent condemnation of actually existent Christianity. By and large, if we consider the actually existent mainstream churches to be Christian, Christians are leftists. Not only are

[959] https://www.amazon.com/gp/product/0452297877
[960] https://foseti.wordpress.com/2012/09/11/bruce-charltons-christianity/
[961] https://charltonteaching.blogspot.com.au/2012/09/the-necessity-of-picking-sides-pro-or.html
[962] https://dalrock.wordpress.com/

today's militantly atheistic progressives the ideological descendents of the 1940s Christian left, today's Churches are being frog marched along the same path the progressives have already walked. They are just lagging a little, and on the issues that matter most to progressives, such as the destruction the family and fatherhood, they are not lagging in the slightest. Dalrock reports that you will get the same demolition of fathers and fatherhood in the sermons as you get on prime time television.

If we define Christianity by its willingness to socially enforce the politically unacceptable parts of the Gospels, which is most of what Christians were supposed to socially enforce, then Christianity is dead except for a remnant, and heavily outnumbered by Randians, anarcho capitalists, atheistic monarchists in the mold of Moldbug, and the rest.

It is simply ridiculous for churches to oppose abortion and gay marriage, when they have already abandoned fatherhood and traditional heterosexual marriage. Having conceded everything that matters, they will concede on the rest soon enough.

They hate our freedom – and so do Obama and Clinton

2012-09-14 05:46:19

"This video is disgusting and reprehensible," Mrs.Clinton said in remarks at the State Department, broadcast live on CNN.

Maybe she should not be telling people who murder ambassadors that they have perfectly good reasons for doing so, regardless of whether they do or they don't.

Every Muslim believes that a video that depicts Mohammed, let alone a video that depicts him as a the thuggish power drunk mass murdering terrorist that he actually was, must be suppressed, and it is the responsibility of governments to suppress it, and that it is legitimate to wage jihad to suppress it.

When I say that every Muslim believes that, almost everyone who thinks of themselves as a Muslim agrees, and anyone who does not agree is wrong to call himself a Muslim. The number of Muslims, whether heartfelt Muslims or merely nominal Muslims, that disagree on this issue is similar to the number of Americans that doubt that all men were created equal. It is the official government religious belief, and the average man in the street accepts official government religious beliefs without really thinking about them much, whether it is the US government or the Egyptian government.

If you are a sincere Muslim, you should be murdering Americans. Of course most Muslims are not all that sincere, but the ones that are not nonetheless give at least lip service to the rationale that leads to murdering Americans. That is what they learn in school. That is what all the respectable people around them believe, or piously pretend to believe, what all the affluent, urban, well connected people, the ones that had lots of education at the most elite schools believe. It is the high status belief of high status people. If you don't believe it, it is like being a *raaaciiiissst* in America. It is low status. It makes you one of those inbred hicks who lie far out in the wilderness.

The progressives wanted to export democracy because they believed it would lead to rule by people like themselves – urban, privileged, highly educated in all the correct elite schools.

And that is exactly what it did.

They failed, however, to notice that Osama bin Laden and company were urban, privileged, and highly educated in all the elite schools.

Progressives don't recognize that they are a theocracy, or rather an atheocracy, that they are a priesthood. Their belief system is supposedly simply the truth, even though the official truth keeps rapidly moving ever leftwards, so they look at people very similar to themselves, with institutions very similar to their own and are endlessly astonished that these institutions somehow inculcate a truth other than "progressives should rule". They cannot believe it, for in order to believe it, they would have to recognize that they also are a priesthood, a different and competing priesthood.

Theoretically, education is supposed to select the smartest, but the natural state of an education system is to select the obedient, those who will by rote echo back whatever they are told. Smart students are difficult. Teachers don't really like them. Most teachers are not very smart, and find it a lot easier to deal with students less smart than themselves. Thus just as the natural tendency of any bureaucracy is to strangle itself in red tape until all motion stops, the natural tendency of any elite educational institution is to become a religious seminary, churning out docile brainwashed idiots, selecting the most compliant, not the most intelligent.

Hence the stagnation of Muslim countries, and the diminution of technological advance in the west.

The progressives look at people similar themselves, and institutions similar to their own, and cannot believe that it will not produce progressivism.

Because people have no incentive to form true opinions on political questions, the vast majority will vote as directed by religious or quasi religious groups.

If the military are in charge, the influence of religion will be small, soldiers and priests being natural enemies, like doctors and lawyers, and the propensity of theocracies to become ever more extreme will be restrained, perhaps by firing the extremists and blighting their careers, perhaps by shooting them, perhaps, as in Uganda, by chaining them into the shape of suitcases and feeding them to the crocodiles – whatever it takes. But usually making excessive religious purity a poor career move will amply suffice. You don't need to purge the whole board. Just quietly let it be known that the business or institution will not get any government contracts unless it removes one of its more difficult board members, and appoints someone who loudly proclaims more appropriate beliefs as a replacement board member.

Democracy is apt to become theocracy, rule by priests, because religious organizations, especially official religious institutions teaching the official religion (schools and universities) can so easily manipulate the people, because the ordinary person has no incentive to form correct beliefs on these matters, and every reason to form beliefs that associate him with the powerful, the elite.

I repeat: The progressives wanted to export democracy because they believed it would lead to rule by people like themselves - urban, privileged, highly educated in all the right elite schools. And it did. Where formerly we had soldiers ruling, who not only did not take that stuff very seriously, but also seriously disapproved of actually acting on it, we now have priests ruling, and each priest wants to show he more pure than the other priest. Where once excessive faith was a bad career move, now it is a very good career move, and insufficient faith is the bad career move. The guy who was formerly on the board because the government liked him there, is now the guy who is off the board because the government does not like him there.

No prophet mocking

2012-09-18 05:52:57

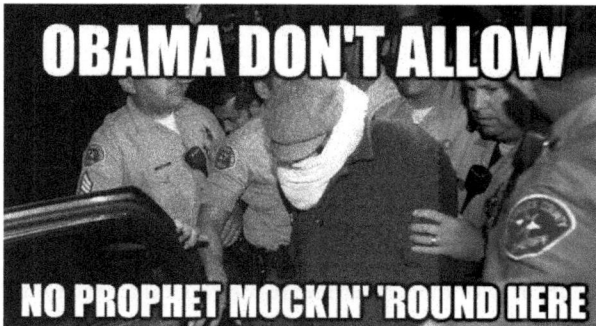

The Dark Enlightenment

2012-09-24 13:03:14

The fundamental realization of the Dark Enlightenment is that all men are *not* created equal, not individual men, nor the various groups and categories of men, nor are women equal to men, that these beliefs and others like them are religious beliefs, that society is just as religious as ever it was, with an official state religion of progressivism, but this is a new religion, an evil religion, and, if you are a Christian, a demonic religion.

The Dark Enlightenment does not propose that leftism went wrong four years ago, or ten years ago, but that it was fundamentally and terribly wrong a couple of centuries ago, and we have been heading to hell in a handbasket ever since at a rapidly increasing rate – that the enlightenment was dangerously optimistic about humans, human nature, and the state, that it is another good news religion, telling us what we wish to hear, but about this world instead of the next.

If authority required me to believe in Leprechauns, and to get along with people that it was important to get along with required me to believe in Leprechauns, I would probably believe in leprechauns, though not in the way that I believe in rabbits, but I can see people not being equal, whereas I cannot see leprechauns not existing.

> "We hold these truths to be self-evident, that all men are created equal, that they are endowed by their Creator with certain unalienable Rights,"

Well obviously if they were not created equal, which plainly they were not, then they were not created with certain inalienable rights either. Rights are quite alienable. If men were created, they were created by a God that wrathfully ordained Monarchy for sinful people who were unwilling or unable to govern themselves (first book of Samuel), a God who similarly also approved slavery. And if instead men are the product of the blind forces of natural selection, are risen killer apes, rights come from fire and steel, or the threat thereof, the second amendment being the father of all of the others, in which case you can rightly be enslaved individually for individual fecklessness, or collectively for collective stubborn but incompetent war making.

Rights and equality sound very nice, but it's all fake, and we are being destroyed.

A lot of people do not want, and cannot competently exercise, real rights. So "equality" means you start giving them such "rights" as "freedom from hunger", meaning that someone more competent and thoughtful than they are has to provide them with food that they are too feckless to obtain for themselves, so the superior person's real rights are destroyed to provide the inferior person with fake "rights", the right to hay and a barn for human cattle – that being the only way that naturally unequal people can be rendered equal.

Rights and equality are fundamentally incompatible. If you want rights, cannot have equality, because some people do not deserve, do not particularly want, and cannot competently exercise, real rights. You are not going to make a below average IQ person with short time preference into a real citizen, independent, free, self sufficient, and property owning. If some people are going to be free, they are going to be more free than such people.

And if you let such people, inferior people, vote, they will always vote against other people's rights and other people's property, being themselves incapable of exercising rights, and themselves too feckless and destructive to have nice things. If they vote, they vote to drag everyone down to their own sub-human level, a desire politicians are eager to fulfill.

And if God created woman, he created woman to be a help meet for man. And if the blind forces of natural selection shaped women, they shaped women to function in a role profoundly unequal to her husband and her father[963], for in the ancestral environment, women were completely dependent upon men, resulting a female psychology that is apt to produce bad results for independent women, as is readily observable as one walks past a fertility clinic and looks at the clientele going in and out.

When the world changed

2012-09-28 11:51:47

A lot of people think the world changed in the 1960s. If the world changed in the 1960s, that would be pretty good evidence that the Jews did it, for the progressive anglophone ruling elite allowed Jews to join them starting 1957. But everything that went wrong in the 1960s was foreshadowed far earlier.

A lot of people think the world changed in 1917[964] - bolshevism and all that, the martyrdom of Saint Czar Nicholas. But Czar Nicholas started the Russian left singularity. His progressivism and idealization of the will of the people did far more to destroy the Monarchy and monarchism than Kerensky or Lenin ever did. Lenin committed multiple crimes for which the death penalty was appropriate, but Saint Tsar Nicholas sent him to a country club prison for the children of the elite, where Lenin did lots of hunting, fishing, horseriding, and conspiring. The ideas that would bring Lenin to power were already so well entrenched by 1917, that the Tsar was their slave. Earlier Tsars would have had Lenin tortured till he named his co-conspirators, then tortured some more to make sure he had not forgotten anything, then

---

[963]https://blog.reaction.la/culture/the-ancestral-environment-of-females
[964]https://charltonteaching.blogspot.com.au/2012/09/why-did-world-change-circa-1917.html

tortured some more, then repeated the process on the co-conspirators, continuing until all the co-conspirators were pretty much in agreement about everything. Tsar Nicholas was so enlightened that he gave Lenin horseback riding.

So where did all that enlightenment come from?

Bastiat, writing before Marx, foresaw the communism that would actually exist, saw in his minds eye the killing fields of Cambodia. Froude, writing in 1888, foresaw decolonization and Zimbabwe. Lord Garnet, the first Viscount Wolseley, in 1875, fighting in what became South Africa, uneasily anticipated that his victories might ultimately lead to black majority rule.

So, doom was already visible on the path the west was walking in 1880.

Unwin, in 1934, predicted death by feminism - not a very prescient prediction, since in retrospect death by feminism was well on the way in the 1870s, but, logically, if the rot set through the state's destruction of the family, patriarchy, and paternity, the state's destruction of the family set in in England with the Matrimonial causes act of 1857. It set in a fair bit earlier in the US, though this is complicated to track, being primarily done in state rather than federal law, with some US states obstinately holding out until the civil war.

The British Matrimonial Causes Act of 1857 meant that a woman who left her husband had the legal status of an independent household, but not a man who left his wife - thus began what in due course became unilateral divorce at female whim, and the requirement for continuing moment to moment consent to sex, rather than consent to sex being formally given once and forever. A woman could wash her hands of her husband, but not a husband of his wife. Hence the 1860s begat the 1960s. Smash monogamy and all that.

So in Britain, did the rot set in 1957?

I don't think so. Why the reforms? Because a woman can be far worse treated in a marriage than a man. So, to counterbalance that, to counterbalance the fact that physical strength, the capacity for violence, and the nature of pregnancy favors the man, they wanted to make the law favor the woman, which point of view is today's celebration of victimhood, with everyone trying to out victim everyone else.

Obamaphone

2012-09-29 19:49:56

This video is racist

Because reality is racist.
> "Everybody in Cleveland got Obamaphone. You minority, you low income, you disability ..."

The obamaphones are not paid by taxes, or printing money, or the US government borrowing from China. The phone companies are required to give obamaphones to people like this woman, so if you pay for your phone, you are also paying for someone like this woman, someone in the 47%, to have a free phone.

And similarly if you pay for a college education, you are paying for someone like this woman to have a free college education, probably in victim studies, which probably gives extra credit for beating up white kids.

And if you pay your medical bills ...

You have probably seen a cascade of spam mail in your inbox announcing that Obama is giving away a great big pile of free stuff. Mostly, it is true, spam mail but not scam mail. He is giving away your stuff to people like this women.

Most of the programs under which the government requires numerous enterprises to give away nice stuff to the supposedly poor long predate Obama, but every year, they get much bigger and give away more stuff. The obamaphone program goes back thirty years or more, but under Obama, has given away far more stuff than under all previous presidents. And I expect that under Bush it probably gave away more stuff than any president previous to Bush, though far less than under Obama.

You are outvoted. Every election from now on is going to be decided by who is going to make people like you give people like this woman more free stuff. Hence Greece, Spain, and most of Europe. And if you don't like it, you are racist.

Time to end democracy.

the gimmedat party

2012-10-05 05:47:54

Today, you can predict pretty accurately how someone will vote from which interest group she belongs to. I say "she", not out of political correctness, but because this is most obvious for females.

The gimmedat party is non whites and single white females. And it has a majority in the US. Thus, Obama and Romney pander to it to precisely equal degrees. This is the end state of democracy, for the politicians seeking votes will steadily increase the gimmedats, until they have a majority, whereupon democracy self destructs.

Even if a Sulla cured the problem by throwing the gimmedats off the voter rolls, this would not be a permanent solution, because it would remain in the interests of politicians to create more gimmedats and put them on the rolls.

The Romney/Obama middle east policy

2012-10-06 20:11:12

The major problem with Obama's policy is that it is a progressive policy. By being nice to our enemies, and hateful to our friends, our enemies will supposedly come to love us. This policy has been tried from time to time over the last several thousand years, particularly by Christians towards Muslims over the last thousand years, with entirely predictable results. Though doubtless sincerely believed, it has in practice a suspicious resemblance to the elite selling out their subjects to their enemies, has a suspicious resemblance to the far against near alliance so characteristic of leftism, wherein the rulers, in pursuit of power over the ruled, destroy the polity that they rule.

In the latter days of the Roman republic, there was a civil war between optimates and populares The populares wanted a democratic Rome, a more democratic Roman empire, and the redistribution of wealth from rich to poor. In the final stages of the war, they allied with the Samnites. The Samnites wanted a permanent and total end to the Roman empire, and proposed to attain it by destroying Rome and killing everyone therein, or perhaps merely all adult males therein, and came mighty close to doing so. I suppose the Samnite cause was just, and most moderns would argue that the cause of the Populares was just, but the Samnite/Populare alliance was a grotesque and extraordinary act of treason by the Populares. The Populares undoubtedly believed that their plans for a more democratic Roman empire ought to be popular with the Samnites, and acted as if their plan was popular with the Samnites but the Samnites did not like the Roman empire and did not care whether it was Optimate or Populare, making the alliance entirely one sided. The Populares were allied with the Samnites, but the Samnites were not really allied with the Populares.

Our elite's foreign policy resembles the Populare foreign policy.

So what is Romney's critique of Obama's foreign policy[965]?

The only point where he has substantial disagreement with Obama is that he promises firm support for Israel.

He tells us:
> The Arab Spring presented an opportunity to help move millions of people from oppression to freedom

equating voting with freedom, and neglecting to wonder if our enemies voting is a good thing.

---

[965] https://online.wsj.com/article/SB10000872396390444712904578024293333633994.html

How to fire big bird

2012-10-09 10:18:56

Romney has promised to defund the Public Broadcasting System.

Reagan promised to defund the left, and did not seriously try it. If Reagan did not, what chance Romney? But if Romney is serious about it, which I doubt, here is how to do it:

The Public Broadcasting System is, in large part, half a billion dollars paying media people to be left wing, which includes paying them to be nasty to Republicans in general and Romney in particular. If you are going to defund the Public Broadcasting System, might as well defund the other key major left wing institutions: the State Department, the Justice Department, the Department of Education, the National Endowment for the Arts, and Harvard. You will have the same sized conflict either way. Theoretically this is a straightforward application of financial power of congress, but in actual practice, will be more like a military coup.

Theoretically money is allocated by Congress in a budget every year, and then spent for the approved purposes by public servants. Theoretically, congress controls the purse strings. That is civics 101. Theoretically, they could simply pass a budget with zero funding for the major centers of the left.

Now if that was the way it actually worked, the budget would be power, and you could not stop congress from passing a budget every year except by cutting off their hands with chainsaws, because getting their hands on the budget would be getting their hands on power.

If the budget had such power, they would hunger and thirst to pass a budget.

They have not bothered to pass a budget in several years, and nothing much has changed as a result, revealing that the budget was an empty ritual, like the Queen of England proceeding to the houses of parliament in a stagecoach. Therefore, passing a budget zeroing out funding allocated to the public broadcasting system, the state department, the justice department, and Harvard would have no effect. The public service would ignore it, the way they have ignored the fact that they have been operating without a budget, the way various laws and plebiscites abolishing affirmative action and so forth have been ignored.

A budget that actually mattered would be an event as extraordinary and dramatic as Meiji Restoration. Sometimes political systems revert to their past, but that is not the way to bet. The Meiji restoration required quite a lot of bloodshed, even though officially nothing happened and it was no change at all.

The Meiji Restoration was the restoration of a simple and workable system which had existed and worked in the remembered past: Monarchy. It is far from clear that US system described by civics 101 has ever worked.

To actually make the system work in accordance with civics 101, there needs to be a credible threat that if it does not function in accordance with civics 101, there will be a pile of dead public servants with bullets in their heads lying by the side of the street outside the Justice Department, and smoke and flames coming out of the Justice Department.

From time to time, State Department proxies kill Pentagon proxies, and vice versa.

For a long time, Australia and Indonesia have been theoretically allied in the war on terror. For a long time, Australia was less than happy with the Indonesian government's performance in this supposed alliance. It came to pass that there were a series of accidental Australian army incursions into Indonesian territory, doubtless due to faulty map reading. Indonesian troops would then accidentally open fire on Australian troops, who would then accidentally fire back, with such accidental effect that Indonesian troops would run away. After several such unfortunate accidents, each followed by pious apologies from both sides, Indonesia developed a somewhat more cooperative policy on suppressing Islamic terror.

I would suggest to Romney, therefore, that should he encounter a lack of cooperation in foreign policy from the state department, a series of unfortunate targeting accidents in which the Pentagon accidentally blows up State Department facilities and personnel. After several such unfortunate accidents, such as perhaps several one ton bombs accidentally landing on 2401 East Street, it might *then* be possible to zero out the budget for the State Department, the Justice Department, Harvard, and, oh yes, also the Public Broadcasting system.

But while I hope for the Public Broadcasting System to be zeroed out as promised, I really do not expect it until after currency collapse and similar dramatic events.

Google is evil

2012-10-10 13:22:41

Google has shut down my gmail, you tube account, google documents, and so on and so forth, until I give them a phone number at which I can be contacted – which is to say, until I give them a provable link to my true name.

This did not come as a total surprise, so I have not lost anything important.

Block google analytics

2012-10-21 05:59:02

Google takes particular and exceptional interest in people with heretical views, as illustrated by the fact that people who post subversive material under their google accounts get special treatment, and special requests for identifying information.

I have reason to believe that google has anomalously little information on me, possibly because of various fairly routine measures I have taken to limit information gathering on me. Perhaps their information collecting tactics are aimed at the low hanging fruit, the ninety nine percent, because gathering information on privacy oriented people is more trouble for less benefit, and likely to produce more bugs, misinformation, and faked identities, relative to the amount of data gathered. When people are so happy to give away their information, it is perhaps more trouble that it is worth to steal it.

Google analytics, however, steals it.

Most sites you go to link to google analytics, so when you look at a web page on, say, naked nine year old girls, or, even worse, differences between the races and the sexes, your browser executes the ga script file, which is three thousand lines of code, eighteen kilobytes, exercising every security flaw and privacy bug to identify you, and then report to google what you have been doing, that you went to this page, that you went to this page from that other page, and so on and so forth.

So even if the web page on gender differences does not link to google analytics, the next web page you go to may well rat you out, telling google not only where you are at, but where you have been. And even if your ideology is as pure from thought crime as the driven snow, executing eighteen kilobytes of javascript code over and over again significantly slows your browser and entire computer.

I use my hosts file to redirect browser requests to google analytics[966] to my local computer, whose local server responds to all such requests with a redirect, that the page has permanently moved to `about:blank`, but of course it does not matter how your local server responds, or whether it responds at all, or whether you have a local server at all. All that matters is that it is redirected to some place that is not google.

I have a very long hosts file, which also blocks most ad related, scam, and tracking sites. Spybot search and Destroy has a long list of tracking sites, and will add its list to your hosts file, but for some reason, does not list Google Analytics as a spy site or tracking site, possibly because it does not

---

[966] https://how-to.wikia.com/wiki/How_to_block_your_browser_from_sending_information_to_Google_Analytics

use a Google analytics tracking cookie as such, that being a fairly blatant privacy violation.

However lots of google services have lots of google tracking cookies, including services you were probably entirely unaware of signing up with, so check your cookies, delete the google cookies, and block their servers if the cookies somehow keep mysteriously re-appearing. They steer mighty close to blatant privacy violation.

If you clear all cookies, and not long thereafter see some mystery sites showing up on your cookies list, the mystery sites are probably up to no good. This happens a lot less if you use spybot's patch to the hosts file.

The Flaw in Moldbug's proposed dictatorship.

2012-10-27 14:42:25

Obviously democracy is not working, is failing catastrophically. The productive are outvoted by the gimmedats, in large part non asian minorities and white sluts. Moldbug's solution is simple: Dictatorship, evolving into Monarchy. The dictator, he hopes and expects, will fire all government employees, except for military, police, and some tax collectors. What use are all the rest of them to a strong dictator?

A good government is a stationary bandit, since a stationary bandit has an incentive to shear the sheep, rather than flay them. A bad government is a mobile bandit, and the government service in democracies increasingly approximate mobile bandits. Each bureaucrat seeks to increase his power and wealth, even if the total burden is well above the Laffer limit.

The trouble is that a dictator is not necessarily a stationary bandit: A *secure* dictator, for example a martial and charismatic monarch of a long established dynasty, is a stationary bandit. Unfortunately, not only are long established dynasties in short supply, but when you have one, the legitimate heir to the throne is seldom martial and charismatic.

Prince Harry, third in line to the British throne, is martial and charismatic, but numbers one and two in line could not get laid if they turned up at a brothel with garbage truck full of money. The reason the British throne is powerless is in substantial part because of a long succession of monarchs incapable of exercising power. Rather than a struggle between King and parliament, it was more the bureaucracy picking up the dangling reins, which is the same problem as afflicts American democracy.

Consider North Korea. It is too soon to tell how bad the new regime will be, but under the old regime:
the people were starving
The technological level of military exports was OK, but the technological

level of other exports was falling from third world to hunter gatherer. Mines were increasingly operated with neolithic technology.

And the new regime looks like it is on the same path.

To which Moldbug replied that the North Korean dictator was insecure. Of course he was insecure– he tried the Chinese style system, economic liberty without political liberty, and it immediately threatened to blow him away. He feared he would be unable to control the forces unleashed. He was weak! He feared that if he allowed capitalists, one of the capitalists would be a George Washington, and another a Sam Adams.

The problem is that most dictators are weak!

If you are a nerd, you are apt to think that dictatorship is easy. Anyone disobeys the dictator, the dictator says

> shoot that man!

And is obeyed.

But that is not really how an army works. An army, like most human institutions, is a thin crust of order floating on a wave tossed sea of chaotic anarchy, the main difference being that the crust in thinner and more brittle than in most institutions, and the anarchy more violent than in most institutions.

A soldier is primarily loyal to the other people in his group, and to his immediate superior officer, and to his commanding officer. If Four Star General Allmighty tells a common grunt:

> "Jump!"

The common grunt, not accustomed to being spoken to by generals, will look at his sergeant, and wait for his sergeant to say "jump!". The sergeant will look at his immediate commanding officer.

And if instead the sergeant says:

> "Grab that general and toss him in the brig!"

The grunt will, without hesitation or a second thought, grab that general and toss him in the brig.

So why is it that sergeants seldom toss generals in the brig?

Mostly because sergeants have trouble organizing pay and logistics. So what tends to happen in military dictatorships is that power winds up in the hands of the lowest ranking officers that have the connections and skills to organize pay and logistics: colonels.

The lower the rank of the dictator or junta, the worse a military dictatorship performs. If you have a junta of colonels the colonels in the junta cannot discipline the other colonels, and all the colonels steal anything not nailed down, and if it is nailed down, they pry it up. They become mobile bandits. And if the dictator is a sergeant, it performs even worse because you have even more mobile bandits with even fewer organizational skills.

Conversely, the higher the rank of the dictator, the better military dictatorship performs, the more military dictatorship is a stationary bandit, a monarch of royal blood being in effect the highest possible rank.

Pinochet's dictatorship worked very well, but military men are never altogether comfortable except they have someone above them. Used to be that military dictators would find a King. Unfortunately we have a King shortage, so now they hold an election.

The Pinochet dictatorship considerably diminished left wing domination of the public service, but he was too wishy washy to do a thorough job. Official history is that Pinochet made a coup against Allende because Allende crushed democracy and destroyed the economy, but in fact Pinochet was in favor of the coup before he was against it, and against the coup before he was in favor of it.

What happened was that parliament, horrified by the ever faster movement left and the associated economic collapse and violence, called upon the army to remove Allende. Allende then appointed Pinochet, as a military leader unlikely to remove Allende, appointed Pinochet as a leftist.

Pinochet was himself a progressive. He was appointed by Salvador Allende who hoped to rule through the army when it became apparent Allende could no longer rule through free elections, nor by the power of the mob.

Six hours before the coup, the rebel officers informed Pinochet that the coup was rolling. They gave Pinochet a piece of paper to sign ordering the army to support the coup, and told him that if he failed to sign it, this would "undermine the unity and discipline of the armed forces", which sounds to me to mean "sign or die". Pinochet signed, then took off. Neither side could find him or contact him. They found him after the coup playing with his grandchildren and hauled him off to the bloodstained and still smoking presidential palace.

Chances are that if the balloon goes up around 2026 or so, the top officer in the Pentagon will be a male to female mestizo transexual claiming to be a lesbian, born male in Mexico.

Western armies are getting visibly weaker as they are politicized. Consider the entirely hopeless performance of the British army, navy, and police force. Thus seems to me that the way out, after the collapse, is anarcho capitalism, neo feudalism, or anarcho piratism. (Anarcho piratism being more or less anarcho capitalism that works out in practice the way that people that fear anarchy imagine it might, and neo feudalism being anarcho capitalism that works out in practice the way that people who fear capitalism imagine that it might)

The weakness of western military forces, and the very impressive performance of private security in dealing with Somali pirates and Occupy Wall Street, makes such an outcome more likely, even though we are more accustomed to republican regimes ending in military dictatorship than general political collapse. On past performance strong dictatorship, Moldbug's bet, is the way to bet, but if the dictator of North Korea feared the capability of capitalism to produce George Washington and Sam Adams, perhaps he had reason to fear. Past performance is not necessarily a guide to future performance.

Moldbug's solution needs a king, even though he calls his hypothetical ruler a CEO, and a monarchy is founded by a general who is bold, martial, and charismatic. Does a military containing ever more officers and ever fewer grunts tolerate such people any more? And if it did contain such a man, would he have any sons?

Origins of Leftism

2012-10-28 08:00:04

Bruce Charlton, who is usually wise except when his religion gets in the way of reality, argues that the origins of the left are not in Christianity, but rather in secularism[967], that Christianity became corrupted into leftism by becoming secular, rather than secular because corrupted into leftism.

He is wrong. Christianity really is to blame. First Christians became leftists, then, being leftists, became secularists.

Christianity became corrupted, then became secular because corrupted. It did not become corrupted because secular. It was corrupt when it opposed New Testament style marriage, slavery, and supported the emancipation of women.

To argue that secularism caused the rot, you have to put the rot beginning around 1950, just as to argue that Jews caused the rot, you have to put the rot beginning around 1950, but the problem set in much earlier. Bruce Charlton wants to argue that secularism set in many centuries ago. It did not. In the early twentieth century, the ruling anglosphere left was still Christian.

Even back in the beginning Christianity was always a little bit leftist relative to the egoistic morality of Aristotle (who argued virtue is cultivation of one's own excellence) and Xenophon (who took for granted that virtue is to be honest and peaceable to those who are willing to be honest and peaceable,

---

[967] https://charltonteaching.blogspot.com.au/2012/10/the-false-christianity-caused-leftism.html

and virtue is to rob, rape, and slaughter in a courageous and manly manner those otherwise inclined)

Thus, when Christians pursued power through being holier than thou, they promptly proceeded to become lefter than thou.

The Puritans, from the execution of the Charles the first to the restoration of Charles the second were Christian, their major defect being that they were holier than thou. They were also leftists and the precursors of twenty first century leftism.

During that period they raised the age of consent, made divorce easier, and prohibited marriage as a sacrament. Marriage became completely secular, resulting in brief and *symmetric* marriage vows. No more did the wife promise to love, honor, and obey, and the husband promise to love, honor, and cherish. No more was marriage accompanied by a long lecture on the New Testament definition of marriage, presented in the presence of all the relatives and friends, including numerous patriarchs and alpha males willing and able to enforce that doctrine. (All this was reversed in the restoration).

The puritans did not like the New Testament doctrine that marriage was an irrevocable commitment to, among other things, sexually gratify one's spouse regardless of whether you felt like it or not. They did not like people having fun, and particularly did not like males having fun, hence did not want a license for men to have fun to be a sacrament, did not want it provided with social enforcement by the congregation and spiritual enforcement by the priest. Puritans wanted to emancipate women because they were never very happy with men humping women.

The puritans were and are leftists, undermining society, killing the King, suppressing the display of excessive wealth, undermining marriage, and being general uptight killjoys who get offended by just about everything. Being offended is a power play. They are holier than me so supposedly I have to do what they say.

The puritans are what you get when people compete for power by competing to be holier than thou.

When priests get the upper hand over nobles and soldiers, they promptly start competing to be holier than thou, and in the process they pervert and corrupt their religion.

Christianity did not become corrupted by secularism. It became secular due to corruption - they pursued supposedly noble goals that were incompatible with the New Testament, in particular the suppression of slavery and the emancipation of women– noble goals that somehow wound up advancing their political power.

Abolishing slavery with fire and sword is arguably a noble cause. Defenses of slavery and justifications of slavery fail in practice to apply to all slaves, though they apply to some slaves. But it is a cause entirely incompatible with the New Testament, which mildly encourages Christians to free their own slaves, and to look the other way when runaway slaves pass by, but forbids slaves to run away, and forbids Christians to interfere with the property of slave owners, even if they do not have to too actively assist in enforcing the property rights of slave owners. The Old Testament prohibits wrongful enslavement, but implies that debt slavery and the enslavement of defeated populations that stubbornly and incorrigibly refuse to surrender is OK.

When Christians adopted the cause of forcibly ending slavery, it was entirely predictable that they would soon demote Christ the Redeemer to Jesus the community organizer. A more martial religion could have adopted the cause of forcibly ending slavery, and still remained true to itself. Christianity could not.

Vote Cthulhu

2012-10-30 07:27:24

Why vote for the lesser evil?

If you vote Democrat, you vote for the branch of the Cathedral's public relations department that specializes in moving the left edge of the Overton window leftwards

If you vote Republican, you vote for the branch of the Cathedral's public relations department that specializes in moving the right edge of the Overton window leftwards.

A vote for Romney will slow the destruction of the private economy, but it means that private health care goes outside the Overton window, that ending population replacement goes outside the Overton window. If Romney gets elected, advocating private health care or border control, or stopping illegals from voting will be as crazy career suicide as advocating white supremacy– as crazy as advocating any non left policy that no longer receives support from the mainstream parties.

The left is the state, and the state is the left. The Republican party is part of the state, and so the range of policies that it is thinkable for republicans to endorse moves ever leftwards. Supposing it matters which party gets elected, the median voter is a gimmiedat, and both parties, in order to win, must appeal to the median voter.

Further, the median voter is a gimmiedat due to policies that used to be unpopular, furtively implemented by both parties, back in the days when the majority of voters were producers and taxpayers, furtively implemented unpopular policies to increase the number of gimmiedat voters and decrease the number of producer voters, steps towards the day when such policies could be openly implemented, as they now are.

The destruction of marriage increases the left vote, as do most government policies. Married women overwhelmingly vote republican, for obvious reasons, single women overwhelmingly vote Democrat, for obvious reasons. Single women expect the government to redistribute wealth from males to them, married women expect their husbands to support them. Thus single women are part of the gimmiedat coalition. One of the big factors destroying marriage is affirmative action accreditation of women and affirmative action employment of women. Give a woman a PhD, and chances are she will wind up a cat lady, because even if her PhD is total rubbish, she will be reluctant to marry a non PhD. Can you imagine a Republican addressing this issue, or any of a thousand other policies to elect a new people? The government encourages and pressures people to move from the producer class to the gimmiedat class by a vast multitude of measures, and no elected republican proposes to end any of these measures.

The damage caused by diversity

2012-11-04 08:32:05

Diversity kills.

Occidentalist has updated his survey of surveys[968]. Despite radical social changes and a wide variety of testing regimes, American black IQ always tests out one standard deviation below American white IQ. Similar differences in character and criminal propensities are obvious.

How big is one standard deviation?

If you take a random black, and a random white, it means that someone's race does not tell you a whole lot about which one is smarter, but, in practice, one seldom meets a *random* black and a *random* white.

If you have additional information, this is apt to make race more informative, more important, rather than less.

Suppose blacks are affirmative actioned into a diverse elite group, police, academia, etc. Then, because IQ variance between academics is lot less than IQ variance between random whites, almost every black academic will be markedly and strikingly dumber than almost every white academic, meaning that few black academics (in a non elite university no black academics whatever) will be capable of doing the kind of academic things that academics traditionally do. Similarly, in a police force, all or almost all black cops will be markedly more criminal than all or almost all white cops.

This leads to the one rotten apple problem. In a diverse police force, being honest is racist and disloyal to you fellow cops. In diverse academia, doing

---

[968] https://occidentalascent.wordpress.com/2012/10/29/secular-change-in-the-bw-iq-gap-in-the-us/

stuff that requires or demonstrates intelligence and ability is racist, anti scientific, anti intellectual, and so on and so forth.

Supposedly by ending all that horrible discrimination, we have a smarter elite. In practice, the opposite is happening, and no one is allowed to notice, because noticing requires horrible racist assumptions and leads to horrible racist conclusions.

We see a similar result when women are affirmative actioned into jobs requiring upper body physical strength: We get the no lift rule. People, both males and females, are forbidden to use upper body strength. In hospitals, when you need a sick patient lifted up, you cannot call a male nurse, because that would be discrimination. This sometimes results in patients dying. Computer science courses are dumbed down so that females can pass them. The removal of certain aspects of computer science on which men tend to perform very differently to women makes both male students and female students ignorant, makes them both worse off. Not only the males, but also the females would be better off covering those areas, even though the women would perform poorly relative to the males.

In general, whenever you mingle two groups, you get a leveling down to the worst characteristics of both groups, so that the diverse group is worse in important ways to at least one of the unmingled groups, and usually worse in important ways to *both* of the unmingled groups, partly because there are few groups so uniformly bad that they do not have at least some virtues, and partly because differences in virtues leads to those virtues being deprecated: The no lift rule denies both men and women the use of their upper body strength, making women effectively weaker than they already are. Similarly, in diverse communities, blacks tend to be more criminal than they already are. If we had all female universities, their computer science classes could do those aspects of computer science that are hard for girls without causing embarrassment.

Notoriously, differences, even innocent differences that really do not constitute being better or worse, reduce trust and cooperation, hence heighten the already alarming tendency to criminality of certain races.

Putnam (Bowling Alone) found that diversity not only made whites distrust everyone, it also made blacks distrust everyone, and made blacks behave worse, perhaps everyone behave worse. (Needless to say, he phrased his findings more piously and evasively than that, but the actual meaning of his findings is impious) Not only is interracial trust lower, not only are people more "racist", but trust and cooperation even within racial groups is also markedly reduced.

It has long been obvious, though strangely unexamined, that the death rate is far higher for whites that live in diverse suburbs. This could, however, be due to factors other than the presence of blacks. Wealthy whites tend to live in suburbs free from diversity. People with dangerous lifestyles are more likely to choose to live in diverse suburbs.

But a recent study reveals that diversity not only kills whites: Diversity may be fatal, says new government health study[969]

Blacks died younger in suburbs where they were a minority, than in suburbs where they were a majority. Similarly for Mestizos. For a given age group, the death rate from cardiovascular disease and so forth was about double. Now one might rationalize this away as a wealth effect. Perhaps more affluent blacks eat more than less affluent blacks, and so die sooner– but then one must argue that in the same suburb, poverty causes the higher death rate among the whites, and affluence the higher death rate among the blacks.

Race segregation is not only good for whites. It is also good for blacks. Gender segregation is not only good for boys, it is good for girls.

I notice that actual busing has been fading away, replaced by teaching students how wonderful busing was and what a gigantic step forward in humanity and civilization it was. It is time for desegregation to get the same treatment. In my own experience, black software engineers educated at traditionally black universities are better than black software engineers educated at white universities.

The Caliphate organized government not by geographic zone, but primarily by race, culture and religion, so that Christians governed Christians, and operated under Christian law, Jews governed Jews, and operated under Jewish law. Homogeneity is efficient, and less stressful to everyone involved.

As I write this, I have just eaten a pineapple I purchased at unmanned stand in the middle of the wilderness. There were pineapples and such on the stand, and a box with a slit in it. I grabbed six pineapples, and put the appropriate amount of money in the box. This is possible, because this is a rural area that is overwhelmingly white, and what few nonwhites are around are Vietnamese or Thai. It is a lot less stressful here. It really is more comfortable and less stressful to not to be around dangerous outgroups. And those that say they are just fine being around dangerous outgroups nonetheless, strangely, have a markedly higher death rate, not only from violence, but from diseases that are arguably stress related.

The left libertarian position is that admission to various select groups should be race and gender blind, based only on test results.

The realist libertarian position is that admission to various select groups should take all evidence into account in a Bayesian manner, considering race, gender, and parental performance as well as test results, since test results do not in fact correlate all that well with performance. A white with the same test results as a black will nonetheless usually perform better at the kind of activities that whites perform better than blacks.

---

[969]https://dailycaller.com/2012/10/27/diversity-may-be-fatal-says-new-government-health-study/?print=1

Even the realist libertarian position, however, overlooks the fact that community is an important source of well being and effective performance. If we took the realist libertarian or left libertarian position on sporting activities, there would be few sporting activities for girls. The left which normally totally rejects all segregation, makes an unprincipled exception for girls' sports.

Let us have, as we had before 1950, a black middle class educated at traditionally black universities to rule the black suburbs, black businessmen protected from white competition by segregation and from the black underclass by black police and black judges backed by white police and white judges, and whites protected from black crime. Segregation worked. Desegregation has been immensely hurtful for everyone, and hurtful most of all for the most able blacks, who instead of getting protected jobs running their fellow blacks, jobs protected from white competition, but nonetheless real jobs producing real value, get affirmative action jobs filling a racial quota while white males do the actual work, which jobs are merely well paid welfare, and have the destructive effects that welfare always does.

The protection of black middle class jobs by segregation produced an important externality. Back in the days of segregation the black middle class kept the black underclass in line. In this, black middle class people were doing a job that white middle class people could not do as effectively. The black universities propagated white values, white discipline, white skills white knowledge into black society via a white created black middle class which intermediated between the white community and the black community.

Maintaining community is hard. Maintaining a mixed race or mixed culture community is considerably harder. Community is a source of value that is hard to incorporate into a strictly individualistic analysis. The left are big fans of communitarianism, but if one wants community, one needs homogeneity. If it takes a village to raise a child, this does not imply that fathers are dispensable and should be ordered out of their homes, which is the conclusion the left expects you to deduce. It implies that everyone in the village should be related, that blood matters, which is the opposite of the meaning that leftists would like. Indeed, if it takes a village to raise a child this has implications so horribly right wing that the likelihood of feuding and genocide worries even me. Perhaps even if it does take a village to raise a child, we should be politically correct and pretend otherwise. Strictly nuclear families are less likely to get people killed.

The end state of democracy

2012-11-06 10:29:50

President Camacho-The Economy[970] from President Camacho[971]
Hat tip Fosetti[972]

America was cooked a long time ago

2012-11-08 05:18:51

A lot of people are saying that this election shows America is cooked.

What this elections shows is that producers are now outvoted by gimmiedats, a change that happened between 2010 and 2012: The gimmiedats are mostly non asian minorities plus white sluts.

Obama's stimulus failed to stimulate, for the same reason as Britain's austerity is not austere. It discouraged people from being producers, while encouraging them to become gimmiedats. While this failed to stimulate the economy, it did a mighty good job of stimulating the left wing vote. The British conservatives, as much as Obama, give economics second place to moving the electorate ever leftwards by making it ever more dysfunctional, and it seems likely that Romney would have at best been no better than British conservatism.

But this outcome was made inevitable a long time back

Obviously politicians want to buy votes, which tends to destroy democracy no matter what the franchise. And they want to buy the cheapest votes going, hence want to expand the franchise and import an underclass, which tends to destroy democracy.

The founders attempted to protect against this tendency, but actively encouraged it by proclaiming that "all men are created equal", and by substituting "pursuit of happiness" for "protection of property and freedom of contract".

America worked when there was a frontier so that people could get away from the establishment, and it worked when there were fifty different establishments in fifty different states, so that there was a high level of competition between state governments, which limited how bad any one state government could get. After the civil war, there was only one establishment, but the constitution limited how much power it could exercise centrally, prohibiting the establishment from cartelizing effectively, so America still

---

[970]https://www.funnyordie.com/videos/d4a8ff5ebe/president-camacho-the-economy "from President Camacho and Mike Judge"
[971]https://www.funnyordie.com/president_camacho
[972]https://foseti.wordpress.com/2012/11/05/democracys-holy-day/

worked – but, inevitably, the establishment set to undermining the constitution from above, and the masses from below. Every barrier to an ever lefter America has been deemed oppressive, and removed or worked around, and this set in immediately. As is apparent when one reads the anti federalist papers, federalism was a leftwards movement, and the bill of rights, and all the features of the constitution that slowed the leftward slide, such as the enumerated powers, were concessions to the anti federalists, which concessions have, predictably, been progressively retracted. The defeat of the Whiskey Rebellion was the initial military victory of progressives, from which followed all their political victories.

Google is evil

2012-11-11 04:46:00

The official story for the shafting of General Petraeus is that:
> Central Intelligence Agency Director David Petraeus resigned after a probe into whether someone else was using his email led to the discovery that he was having an extramarital affair, according to several people briefed on the matter.
>
> A Federal Bureau of Investigation inquiry into use of Mr.Petraeus's Gmail account led agents to believe the woman or someone close to her had sought access to his email, the people said.

All emails directly to and from Google's server are encrypted, unless they pass through a non google server. But they are kept forever in the clear on Google's servers, and searched by the world's greatest AI. So the only entity that could suspect that someone else was using his email is Google, which would normally react by automatically or semi automatically contacting general Petraeus by phone, not the FBI.

So, looks like Google ratted him out

And since when do government officials lose their jobs for extramarital affairs? Looks to me that someone wanted to get rid of General Petreaus, perhaps to replace him with someone even further left, and asked Google for whatever dirt they had on him, and an extramarital affair was the best they could come up with.

Google is evil

2012-11-13 10:54:06

Google tells us[973]
> Like other technology and communications companies, Google regularly receives requests from government agencies and courts around the world to hand over user data.

Note that "*government agencies* and courts". No warrant needed.

> Google ... provides government agencies with e-mail communications, documents, browsing activity, IP addresses used to create an account and other data when asked.

Data from the things you search for, the emails you send, the places you look up on Google Maps, the videos you watch in YouTube, the discussions you have on Google+ are all conveniently collected in one place. It this will particularly affect Android users, whose real-time location (if they are Latitude users), Google Wallet data and much more will be up for grabs. And if you have signed up for Google+, odds are the company even knows your real name, as it still places hurdles in front of using a pseudonym (although it no longer explicitly requires users to go by their real names).

Firefox by default reports your IP and all nearby wifi systems to Google even if you are not using google search nor any google services. Thunderbird reports your IP to Google. It looks like the general was nailed because his location data was the same as one of his girlfriends, rather than the contents of the emails.

All of that data history is explicitly cross-referenced.

Since you must have a Google account for android, separate that account from all your other activities.

Recommended procedure.
1. Turn off Thunderbird and Firefoxs routine tattling.[974]
2. Don't use Google accounts.
3. If you must use Google accounts, for example a google account is mandatory for an android phone, create it using a proxy located in a region of hegemony different from your own, and don't use your android account for anything else.
4. Don't use Google search for anything related to politics or money, since this is sending your searches character by character to Google. Definitely don't use Google search while logged in to your Google account.
5. Don't use chrome, because this reports all browser activity to Google.

[973]https://www.google.com/transparencyreport/userdatarequests/
[974]https://blog.reaction.la/politics/google-is-evil.html

6. Disable all durable cookies for Google
servers.

It sounds like google does not attempt to do anything clever to track you.
They rely on cookies, and they do clever stuff to track the cookies.

State capitalism

2012-11-15 18:57:45

Google and Facebook competing for an Obama cabinet slot
Big corporations get bigger while smaller businesses disappear[975]. Most regulation is impossible to comply with, and is intended to be impossible to
comply with. You "comply" with it by getting favors from the state exempt-
ing you from compliance.

Military incapacity

2012-11-19 07:46:48

When Europe attempted to intervene in the Balkans, the result was shameful and ridiculous. European armies, it seemed, could do nothing.

The ludicrous weakness of Europe is an attractive nuisance. There is a lot of
women and loot sitting around undefended. That cannot continue forever.
It might continue for a very long time, or might end suddenly very soon.

The English speaking countries, particularly American and the Australians,
have remained more effective than most of Europe. Britain, (and perhaps
Canada) not so much. I have seen a few you tube videos of British police
responding to rioting "youths", and rioting Muslims in manner that was
cowardly, ridiculous, and shameful. In Basra and the Persian Gulf, British
forces suffered shameful, ridiculous, and humiliating defeats and surrenders. The British humiliation in Basra was repeated in Helmand province
of Afghanistan, where three thousand British troops were defeated and besieged by what turned out, when the US marines arrived to rescue those girly
men, to be a mere eight hundred Taliban.

The Swiss probably remain effective, though this has yet to be tested, and
the Israelis were effective last time around, though the questionable performance in Lebanon was troubling.

The British were defeated by handful of ignorant savages in Basra and in
Helmand province, though the events in the Balkans suggest that the British

---

[975]https://www.economist.com/news/finance-and-economics/21565609-economies-scale-run-out-certain-
point-largest-firms-america-may-be

could defeat and conquer the rest of Europe with one hand tied behind their backs.

These defeats are all the odder because in modern conflicts, the evidence is that a small group of trained, civilized men, can easily defeat a large group of untrained uncivilized men in a completely one side manner. Private security has a short way with Somali pirates, random criminals, occupy mobs, and left wing terrorists.

A state is near its end, approaching collapse when it is as formidable to its citizens as it is contemptible to its enemies.

It is not clear to me what is causing the weakness of Britain. In one of the you tube videos a substantial proportion of the police were curiously short, presumably females though their sex was invisible due to body armor. The men, however, were no more manly than the women. Perhaps, just as hospitals have a no lift policy, so that the work that female nurses do is equal by decree to the work that male nurses do, thereby justifying equal pay, perhaps British police have a no manliness policy, lest women, gays, and transsexuals be embarrassed. They sent women to do what is the most quintessentially male of all male jobs, and then, on the video, no one, neither male nor female, made any attempt to do the job. If they were serious about getting a man's job done, would not have sent women to do it.

The strongest remaining nation is the US, whose white male army defends a country ever more hostile to the army and its values. Although a large proportion of the US "army" is female, black or Hispanic, these are generally non front line officers, generally the privileged, support and administration. The despised, hated, and neglected low status part of the army, the few people who do the actual shooting and actually get shot at, the grunts, are of course mostly white male, as is apparent from who gets explosion related casualties.

The divorce rate for actual fighting men in the US army is about seventy percent. A soldier has poor prospects of getting his little man wet, and even smaller prospect of retiring in old age surrounded by his biological children.

Part of the reason for this is the low and diminishing status of being a fighting man. Another reason for this is the cash and prizes approach to divorce. If a woman divorces a soldier, she generally does not get an interest in his pension, and in compensation for the lack of long term access to pension, gets his cash and assets up front. Since women tend to focus on the short term at the expense of the long term, this encourages adultery and divorce.

Until 1984, it was illegal for soldiers to commit adultery, but legal, and increasingly financially rewarding, for their wives to commit adultery. Indeed, on paper it is still illegal for soldiers to commit adultery. They stopped enforcing the law against fighting men some time around 1998, shortly after the commander in chief was in an adultery scandal, but as I write this, not yet repealed, and still sometimes enforced against the politically incorrect.

For an effective army, this needs to be reversed. If the wife of a soldier commits adultery, she is undermining national security, but if a soldier commits adultery, he is not undermining national security.

The falling rate of marriage among soldiers suggests that the US army, like everyone else's army, is declining in effectiveness, it is just that everyone else is even weaker than the US. The falling rate of marriage among fighting men is a manifestation of the low and falling status of fighting, fighting men, and general manliness.

Sex and children is not of course the only thing that makes for an effective army, but it is one important thing, and if a society neglects that, it is probably neglecting all the others, probably treating military men as generally expendable and low status. I notice that the only army that routinely fought to the last man, the Japanese imperial army, took extraordinary measures to ensure wifely fidelity and that soldiers routinely got laid, and in the march of the ten thousand, we sometimes read of how they marched with enemies in front, and enemies behind, with shock troops covering the front, then slingers and archers, *then the supplies and the women*, then more slingers and archers, then more shock troops covering the rear, with cavalry shifting position as necessary to keep the enemy from the flanks. In the march of the ten thousand, pretty much everyone acted with extraordinary courage and casual heroism, with one big exception, that sometimes troops would desert their posts *to protect their women*. Xenophon's biggest concern was keeping his troops fed by purchase or pillage of food, but keeping them laid was also pretty high on the list.

As democracy collapses, many conservatives have been hoping for and expecting a military coup, and indeed the only reason that military coups have not taken place in much of Europe is that the Cathedral forbids it.

Lately Obama has been railroading high ranking officers for adultery, adultery which is absolutely routine among upper class males and has been for many years. Women want high status jobs primarily so that they get access to high status males, and when they get those jobs, seldom notice that the job might have any duties or responsibilities other than access to high status males.

Possibly Obama suspects the potential for a coup, or has been spooked by conservatives thinking aloud in that direction, however, declining military capability diminishes the likelihood of a coup, while raising the likelihood of a collapse more drastic and fundamental: Perhaps someone starts helping themselves to women and loot in some decadent state on the periphery of Europe. People stop believing in that state. Intervention is ineffectual, so people also stop believing in nearby states. Anarcho piratism ensues, which then eventually transitions in some places, if we are lucky, to neo feudalism as brigands transition from being mobile brigands to stationary brigands, and, if we are really lucky, to something like anarcho capitalism in other places. Or military regimes under manly commanding officers reappear, which potentially transition into monarchies. Or, likely, all of the above.

Decreasing military capability diminishes the likelihood of a coup, but increases the likelihood of fat tail events, increases the likelihood of the unexpected.

Don't know much about history

2012-11-21 10:31:13

Supposedly we are ruled by the cognitive elite, but, strikingly, when compared to the elite of a century ago, they don't know much about history, don't know much biology, don't know much about a science book, don't know much about the french they took.

The members of the old elite would casually make interlingual puns, erudite references to ancient history and to the latest science of their day. I am not seeing this from our current elite.

I saw on television a US spokesman piously calling for a *cease fire* in Gaza "Israel requires an end to rocket attacks, Hamas requires an end to the state of siege and and end to attacks on Hamas personnel"

"What," I thought, "does the state department hire the mentally retarded?"

The Israelis gave him a flea in his ear. I would hope that that might be because, unlike the Americans, they know some history, but fear it more likely they only know the history they themselves have personally lived through. They used to use the phrase "cease fire" often enough.

The Obama regime abruptly dropped the phrase "cease fire" and started talking about "durable de-escalation" – which unfortunately means much the same thing, if it means anything at all, which I doubt. It is obvious that everyone in the regime has been told not to use the phrase "cease fire". Unfortunately it is equally obvious that they don't know why they should not use that phrase.

John Hubner argues that the rate of innovation has been declining since the 1880s[976], which is roughly the time when I judge the elite to have been smartest - when it was benefiting by recruiting smart people from the lower classes, but had yet not abandoned consideration of parental achievement.

Leftism, based on equalism, leads to systematic discrimination against the dangerously bright[977], which was a problem in the late nineteenth century, and has been getting steadily worse.

Kurzweil and the other futurists of the technological singularity correctly complain that Hubner is focusing only on the initial innovation, neglecting

---

[976]https://accelerating.org/articles/InnovationHuebnerTFSC2005.pdf
[977]https://pjmedia.com/blog/biased-against-the-bright/

the quite large period of development that eventually leads to the innovation becoming an effective improvement in our standard of living or our capability to slay our enemies, but it is reasonable to suppose that the original innovation requires more smarts than perfecting and mass producing it.

Now this sort of fermented mashed bananas, "cease fire", was reasonable enough in the nineteen seventies, when people in the middle east were piously pretending to progressivism, and called themselves anti colonialists and such, but now that they are calling themselves Muslims, there is really no excuse for not cracking open an old, yellowing, dusty history book before calling for a "cease fire".

Like the Obama regime, I am full of good advice for Israelis and for those Muslims who would prefer to postpone receiving their six pack of virgins for as long as possible, but wrestling with a pig only gets one dirty and annoys the pig, so I stick to discussing our "cognitive elite".

Military incapacity illustrated

2012-11-21 13:36:39

Shortly after my post "Military Incapacity", a few hundred Tutsi rebels evicted the "Congolese Army" [978] and seventeen thousand "United Nations International Peace Keepers" equipped with helicopter gunships and suchlike (better equipped and not quite so black Cathedral Armed forces) from the city of Goma in the Congo.

This a straightforward conflict between a minority less inferior black race, and a majority inferior black race, with the Cathedral, naturally, backing the inferiors. The inferiors were in the way of efficient extraction of mineral resources, in that their intolerable crime levels disrupted productivity, hence the need to evict Cathedral forces so that order could be imposed and commerce proceed. This is not the beginning of the end, far from it. The beginning of the end will be when something similar happens a lot closer to the European heartland. I have been expecting anarcho piratism. The rebel takeover in Goma is much more orderly than I expected, imposing the order required by the productive, rather than destroying what little order the Cathedral supported and then stealing whatever is not nailed down, which is a promising portent for the future. The unproductive, living on Cathedral welfare, were evicted, which the Cathedral perceives as disorderly, though I see no reason why the Cathedral should not feed its pet parasites somewhere further away from anything that they can wreck. The rebels are acting like stationary bandits right from the beginning, rather than under-

[978] poorly equipped black Cathedral third world armed forces

going a long, slow and gradual transition from mobile bandits to stationary bandits, which is what I was expecting, and still rather expect.

Puritanism and purity

2012-11-23 14:08:19

As I have said before, the Imperialists were the original anticolonialists, starting out as the British antislavery movement, but, going back further, following the brilliant research of Moldbug, the Puritans were the original leftists. Today's leftists are connected in an unbroken chain of ideology, organizations, and personnel all the way back to the seventeenth century Puritans, with the nineteenth century anti slavery movement and the early twentieth century Christian left connecting them.

This includes the non Anglosphere leftists, in particular the French left. The original French left were descended from Gallicanism, and thus from the Avignon papacy, not puritanism, but outside the Anglosphere, the left repeatedly self destructed in left singularities and was recreated by English speaking leftists backed by English speaking armies, so Gallican descended leftism was replaced by Puritan descended leftism.

(Digressing, the anglosphere left singularity approaches. This will not necessarily be a good thing, since unlike all previous left singularities there is no one outside it and above it to pick up the pieces)

The most infamous characteristics of the Puritans were and are war on Christmas, war on marriage, and war on low status men getting any sex.

Supposedly, now that the left has disowned its Puritan heritage during the mid twentieth century, they have theoretically dropped the third factor, but ever stricter and ever more unreasonable standards of "consent" show they are still at it. When the high school football star bangs the hot high school teacher, supposedly he did not consent, even though he is big enough and strong enough to break her like a twig. The rationalizations shifted swiftly from nominally Christian to nominally anti Christian with no actual change in application.

The Puritans wanted to practice pure Christianity, modeled on the practices of the the early disciples of the new testament. Unfortunately for them, the early disciples tell us in no uncertain terms that such purity is unchristian, for it excludes people from the faith for pleasant, customary, and trivial practices.

Romans 14 verse 10 "why dost thou judge thy brother? or why dost thou set at nought thy brother?"

According to Paul, Romans 14, any unobjectionable ritual, practice, or rule is Christian if done outwardly and inwardly "unto God", and its direct opposite is also equally Christian if done outwardly and inwardly unto God, which directive has been widely and reasonably interpreted as a directive to apply a thin spray of Christian symbolism over any existing practice that promotes family, good conduct, and community (such as the celebration of the unconquered sun, which is to say Christmas) and to welcome all people in such thinly Christian practices (which is to say, promote Christmas to non Christians and celebrate it with them). According to Paul a Christian should never tell someone else that he is unchristian for doing or failing to do some harmless practice, and similarly Jesus said of the obscure, arbitrary, and complicated dietary rules of the Old Testament, that it is not what goes into your mouth that makes you impure, but what comes out of it. Jesus dismissed Jewish purity, and Paul proceeded to dismiss Christian purity. Jesus and Paul were the original latitudinarians.

The Puritans rejected all "invented" ceremonies, such as Christmas, which seems a harmless enough proscription, but becomes dangerously harmful when it becomes grounds for looking down on those that practice invented ceremonies as insufficiently Christian and disrupting their public practice of those ceremonies, becomes harmful when they set at nought their brothers.

The Puritan proscription immediately became a bid for political power, a bid for power in this world. Unsurprisingly, Puritan doctrine immediately started to rapidly mutate into whatever most facilitated the pursuit of power, and continues to mutate to this day. Among most of their successors and ideological descendents, the movement has lost any Christian characteristics. There is no unchanging core of leftism, except power, though force of inertia means that some campaigns, such as war on Christmas, have continued unchanged the whole time since the sixteenth century, even though the rationale for the campaign has changed completely from time to time.

It also became extremely harmful when they rejected the "invented" sacrament of marriage.

The Puritans correctly pointed out that marriage in the time of the early Church was not a christian ceremony, not a sacrament. They therefore proceeded to make marriage not a sacrament, which is to say, proceeded to desecrate it.

Marriage in the time of the early Church was not a sacrament but was a public ceremonial contract between a man, a woman, and the father of the bride, organized and conducted not by the Church, nor by the state, but by the patriarchs of the bride and groom. Paul's prescriptions for marriage (love, honor, cherish, engage in lots of sex, and the wife obeys) correspond to the contract agreed to between the bride and groom in that type of patriarchal marriage that was most honorable and respected in back in the time of the Roman Republic, marriage that was in Paul's time (Early empire, nominally the late Republic) already somewhat old fashioned, conservative, and going out of style among the truly hip high status people.

When the Puritans made marriage not a sacrament, they did not restore the patriarchal marriage of the Old Roman Republic, still less the similar patriarchal marriage of the Jews of the time of Jesus. Instead they had state marriage by a justice of the peace, the hip marriage of hip high status people. No longer did the bride and the groom publicly agree to a contract laying out the duties of marriage, the husband to cherish the bride, worship her with his body, till death do them part, and the wife to cherish, worship, and obey, till death do them part.

Instead, under Puritan rule, the justice of the peace simply announced couple married, without any statement as to what they had agreed to, with neither God nor man informing them of the rights and duties of the contract. The Puritans, in making marriage no longer a sacrament, did not restore it to its original form as it was at the time of the early Church of the New Testament, did not restore the patriarchal marriage ceremonies of the old Roman Republic, conducted by patriarchs of the original families establishing a new patriarchal family and the bride and groom making an irrevocable contract. Instead, they made it state marriage, made it no longer a sacred contract, enforced by community, family, and God, which is to say they desecrated marriage.

That which is enforced merely by the state is not much enforced, and no contract is a contract if one is not informed of what one has agreed to. Seeking state power, the Puritans abandoned the social support and enforcement of marriage, and within a few years after abandoning the sacrament of marriage in the middle of the seventeenth century, legalized divorce (more sex for high status men, less sex for low status men), though that divorce was still very restrictive by today's standards.

The high status man needs no contract and wants no contract because he can get away with stuff. The Puritans obliged, retaining the form of marriage, while emptying out the status of marriage.

And their ideological descendents, having abandoned every doctrine that made them Christian, having changed their stands on just about everything that was supposedly important, have not changed their stands on sex, marriage, and Christmas except to double down even further.

Early Christian Marriage:

The early christian prescriptions on marriage have the effect of maximizing reproductive and sexual activity and maximizing male investment in posterity, thus maximizing the Church's internal biological growth under the conditions prevailing at the time.

Chastity, female subordination, and that there was no divorce except for *female* sexual misconduct maximized male paternal certainty, thus male investment in posterity.

Monogamy and near universal marriage meant that all males invested in posterity, rather than merely the usual third or so of males, and that sexual consent was once and forever maximized sexual activity:.

1:Corinthians 7:

> let every man have his own wife, and let every woman have her own husband.
>
> Let the husband render unto the wife due benevolence: and likewise also the wife unto the husband.
>
> The wife hath not power of her own body, but the husband: and likewise also the husband hath not power of his own body, but the wife.
>
> Defraud ye not one the other, except it be with consent for a time,

One more factor was needed to make this prescription work for maximum male investment. Genetic analysis shows that we have less than half as many distant male ancestor as distant female ancestors, indicating that throughout most of history, a rather small proportion of the males have fathered most of the children, that less than half as many males have been fathers as women have been mothers.

The Victorian take on this problem was that this was caused by evil lustful males oppressing naturally chaste and virtuous females, cruelly ravishing them in spite of their heartfelt desire to be good wives and mothers, but the current state of our campuses and our underclass reveals that the problem is the women, not the men. Women only want to have sex with higher status men. If you doubt what I see, if you say you do not see what I see, download a romance at random.

Hence the low reproduction rate of our smartest and most heavily accredited females. They just don't find males with similar or lower levels of accreditation sexy. They just are not turned on. Eighteenth century patriarchs were worried that their daughters would crawl a hundred miles over broken glass to get impregnated by some bad boy. Female PhD students really are not that interested, finding sex somewhat boring and unhygienic, at least really not that interested in their fellow students.

Monogamy requires higher status for males relative to females, if most females are going to feel motivated to get married in a timely manner.

So, to ensure that every man could have his own wife, and every woman her own husband. Paul proceeded to artificially make all men high status relative to all women. He forbade women to speak in church, and required them to cover their heads, which meant that all the girls in the congregation found all the boys in the congregation sexy, and all wanted to sign up for the Pauline marriage contract as fast as possible, and, the number of males being equal to the number of females, were usually able to do so, and did so, thereby maximizing male investment in posterity and Christian biological expansion.

Puritan and leftist marriage:

The Puritans found it difficult to get away with not making women cover their heads, since they were supposedly being pure and faithful to the bible, but could change the symbolic meaning of the head covering from submission, and they also just plain allowed women to speak in Church, cheerfully violating their pretended purity and supposed fidelity to the practices of the early church. This is not a recent change associated with the left's open abandonment of Christianity. They had female preachers such as Anne Hutchinson early in the seventeenth century, presaging today's university campuses and the hookup culture.

Raising the status of ordinary females to be equal to ordinary males means that the ordinary females will only find high status males attractive. Bingo, more sex for elite males, less reproductive sex, less total sex, less sex for regular males, less male investment in posterity, less total fertility, more deviant sexual activity.

Observe that supermarket checkout girls are undeterred by the risk of gravel rash. They have markedly more enthusiasm than female PhDs. So we still have halfway decent reproduction rates for supermarket checkout girls, but terrible rates of reproduction for high IQ females.

Leftism is, like most human activity, a male plot to get laid. But as the left becomes ever more unequal, as we approach the left singularity of infinite leftism in finite time, the number of leftists for whom it is working diminishes. In the nature of things, Puritanism was bad for most Puritans' chances of having sex, and is worse for most leftists' chances of having sex.

Puritan expansion focused on capture of the organs of state to impose their doctrine on all, rather than on biological expansion.

The first American socialist experiment.

2012-11-23 17:34:35

Doubtless you have all seen this before, but it needs repeating, (and it is free content, being long out of copyright)

Governor Bradford, repeatedly re-elected governor of the Puritan settlement tells us in his journal "Of Plymouth Plantation":

All this while no supply was heard of, neither knew they when they might expect any. So they began to think how they might raise as much corn as they could, and obtain a better crop then they had done, that they might not still thus languish in misery. At length, after much debate of things, the Governor (with the advise of the chiefest amongst them) gave way that they should set corn every man for his own particular, and in that regard trust to them selves ; in all other things to go on in the general way as before. And so assigned to every family a parcel of land, according to the proportion of their number for that end, only for present use (but made no division for inheritance, and ranged all boys & youth under some family. This had very good success ; for it made all hands very industrious, so as much more corn was planted then otherwise would have been by any means the Governor or any other could use, and saved him a great deal of trouble, and gave far better content. The women now went willingly into the field, and took their little ones with them to set corn, which before would allege weakness, and inability; whom to have compelled would have been thought great tyranny and oppression.

The experience that was had in this common course and condition, tried sundry years, and that amongst godly and sober men, may well evince the vanity of that conceit of Plato's and other ancients, applauded by some of later times, that the taking away of property, and bringing in community into a commonwealth, would make them happy and flourishing; as if they were wiser then God. For this community (so far as it was) was found to breed much confusion and discontent, and retard much employment that would have been to their benefit and comfort. For the young men that were most able and fit for labour and service did repine that they should spend their time and strength to work for other men's wives and children, with out any recompense. The strong, or man of parts, had no more in division of victuals & cloths, then he that was weak and not able to do a quarter the other could; this was thought injustice. The aged and graver men to be ranked and [97] equalized in labours, and victuals, clothes, etc, with the meaner and younger sort, thought it some indignity and disrespect unto them. And for men's wives to be commanded to do service for other men, as dressing their meat, washing their clothes, etc, they deemed it a kind of slavery, neither could many husbands well brook it. Upon the point all being to have alike, and all to do alike, they thought them selves in the like condition, and one as good as another; and so, if it did not cut of those relations that God hath set amongst men, yet it did at least much diminish and take of the mutual respects that should be preserved amongst them. And would have been worse if they had been men of another condition. Let none object this is men's corruption, and nothing to the course it self. I answer, seeing all men have this corruption in them, God in his wisdom saw another course fit for them.

So the true lesson of thanksgiving is that socialism leads to famine and slavery.

This, I think, is why anglosphere leftism has lasted considerably longer than the others: Because being Godly men, they were humble, and so eventually realized that leftism really stinks, whereas the usual reaction of leftists to this unwanted discovery is to start executing more people, setting children on fire in front of their mothers to force their mothers to reveal where the seed corn is hidden, crucify starving children for eating grass when they were supposed to be working, and rip the baby out of pregnant woman, pour petrol inside her, and set her on fire in order to punish her husband for thinking dangerous thoughts.

These days, however, they are no longer Godly men. Their response to the crimes of Aristide, and some of their fantasies such as "10:10, no pressure", suggest that a return to form is increasingly probable. Zimbabwe and the Congo show the Cathedral in action in places far from their center of power. In the Congo, Cathedral forces (Forces Armées de la République Démocratique du Congo) are notorious for terrorizing hostile populations by killing women using genital impalement with large objects and sexually mutilating both men and women. That is an army that is 100% armed and paid by the Cathedral, answerable to a government 100% installed by the Cathedral and completely dependent on Cathedral money and UN forces. So far, however, the Cathedral has been pretty civilized, indeed exaggeratedly and absurdly civilized, when operating closer to home.

You can, however, tell that terrorizing hostile populations in the Congo with sexual impalement by large objects is Cathedral policy because the New York Times, when it does not piously avert its eyes, will piously tell you that militia men are the ones doing it, which lie reveals mens rea. Not that the entire Cathedral is going along with this, but those that don't go along are reluctant to fuss overly loudly. More like murmuring quietly.

The median voter

2012-11-25 13:11:55

Heartiste's usually wise, insightful, and excellent blog has a pile of silly advice: What A Future American Right Party Can Do ToWin[979]

---

[979]https://heartiste.wordpress.com/2012/11/23/what-a-future-american-right-party-can-do-to-win/

A future American right party cannot win. You win by winning over the median voter, or, equivalently, the modal swinging voter.

The median voter or modal swinging voter in this election was someone who is single, fatherless, partly on welfare, if female a slut, if male frequently a minor criminal belonging to protected minority. A party that appeals to white sluts on welfare and non white criminals on welfare is not likely to be terribly right wing.

The end state of democracy is that you get 51% of the voters living on their votes and lashing out at the productive more and more cruelly.

The end state of the left wing singularity is infinite leftism in finite time, as an ever more pious priesthood ignores democracy to impose ever more brutally left policies. These two end states are sufficiently similar that even though we could in principle avoid the left wing singularity in the name of democracy using measures somewhat similar to those proposed by Heartiste, there would be small point in doing so.

A non Cathedral government that won an election in the current electorate would be something like La Raza - people that the Cathedral would correctly call Nazis except that most of them are non white.

We need to kick the gimmiedats of the voting rolls before attempting a democratic legitimation of a non cathedral government - which means that a non cathedral government has to get in power without being elected, a project inconceivable under current circumstances. Current circumstances, however, cannot possibly continue.

Further, if a non Cathedral government was to get in power under circumstances strikingly different from current circumstances, democratic legitimation might well be both difficult and of little value.

Leftwards with John Corzine

2012-11-30 09:35:00

Urban Future tells us[980]:

> When the Right attains power, it is by becoming something other than itself, betraying its partisans not only incidentally and peripherally, through timidity or incompetence, but centrally and fundamentally, by practically advancing an agenda that almost perfectly negates its supposed ideological commitments. It builds that which it had promised to destroy, and further enthralls that which it had promised to liberate. Its victories mean ever less, its defeats ever more. To win is at most a lesser evil, whilst to lose

---

[980]https://www.thatsmags.com/shanghai/article/2958/what-we-deserve

opens new, unprecedented horizons of calamity, initiating previously unimagined adventures in horror.

The left theoretically wants equality, but, predictably, its unending victories cause ever more extreme and brutal inequality, as socialism somehow
strangely manifests as crony capitalism. Soak the rich - except, of course, for
friends of Obama. The ensuing social injustice results in louder cries to soak
the rich.

No one could exemplify the evils of Wall Street plutocracy better than Democrat Senator and Democrat Governor John Corzine of MF Global who ro-
tated between looting as a politician, and looting as a financial Chief Executive Officer. He started in finance, went into politics and regulation under Clinton, from regulation back into finance, from finance at Goldman
Sach back into politics as a senator and financial regulator, from politics and
financial regulation back into finance, from finance back into politics as a
Governor, then back again into finance as CEO of MF Global, eventually
committing theft of over a billion dollars, for which there is no prospect that
he will ever be seriously punished, or even forced to disgorge any substantial
part of his ill gotten gains. And, similarly, the Obama cabinet and federal
bureaucracy is full of people who rotate between being regulators, and being the regulated, with the result that regulation works the way that rightists
expect it to, and never the way that leftists piously expect it to.

John Corzine, as well as campaigning for financial regulation and vigorously
implementing it, campaigned for universal health care, universal gun reg-
istration, mandatory public preschool, more taxpayer funding for college
education, affirmative action and same-sex marriage. He is not the one percent, he is the 0.0005%. There are about a thousand similar beneficiaries of
far left economics, many of them vastly richer than he, though he is one of
the most outstandingly criminal of them, and one of the most prominent
in financial regulatory activities.

Human nature means that regulation in practice is John Corzine. For this
reason, we should never regulate anything. If some arguably undesirable
act is not straightforwardly criminal, then any attempt to regulate that act
will result in straightforwardly and uncomplicatedly honest and legitimate
activities such as Intrade being forbidden[981], and straightforwardly and uncomplicatedly criminal activities, such as John Corzine looting MF Global,
being deemed legal.

The only sane solution is unthinkably radical: to end all regulation, and shut
down all regulatory activities. We don't have a political apparatus capable of
wisely and justly regulating, and no society ever has had such an apparatus.
Regulation in practice is always anarcho tyranny: That which is criminal

---

[981]https://main.omanobserver.com/node/131017

is permitted, which is the anarchy, and that which is honest is forbidden, which is the tyranny.

Even if you imposed a hundred percent tax on incomes over a certain level, or a thousand percent tax on incomes over a certain level, it is not going to affect the likes of John Corzine, who seldom pay much taxes, since they get to write the loopholes.

Which result leftists piously pronounce to be deregulation, thus needs to be cured by even more regulation. Regulation, in practice, equals regulators getting very rich indeed.

The theory of Basel II was that wise financial regulators would decide what investments were safe, so financial institutions would only invest in safe things. Predictably, financial institutions only invested in politically correct things, such as million dollar mortgage loans to winos and wetbacks. Financial disaster ensued, for which we got Basel III, which was even more of everything that was horribly wrong with Basel II

As society moves ever leftwards, ever faster, leftists get ever more discontented with the outcome, but of course, the only cure for their discontent that it is permissible to think, is faster and further movement left.

When we were all forced to use the word "gay" in place of "queer", on pain of being fired from our place of employment, or the employer being destroyed by sexual discrimination suits if he did not enforce correct word usage, we all promptly proceeded to use the word "gay" in the same contemptuous and dismissive manner we had previously used "queer". Suddenly the second verse of "Deck the halls" disappeared from the Christmas Carol rotation, and the Flintstones no longer invited their viewers to "Have a gay old time".

This was not at all the intent of the social engineers. Since homosexuality was supposedly a nice fun thing, and supposedly not at all dirty, disgusting, and homosexuals supposedly not in the slightest apt to spread dangerous diseases, we were supposed to keep on singing the second verse of "Deck the halls"

The left did not conclude that efforts to socially engineer the language were counterproductive, but instead escalated the social engineering. In an ever leftwards movement, what else could it do? If people are using "gay" as a slur, the left response was to be twice as determined to make them use the word "gay".

Moldbug's mission completed

2012-12-01 14:43:39

Moldbug has a new post of substance[982], but not a whole lot of substance.

---

[982]https://unqualified-reservations.blogspot.com.au/2012/11/adore-river-of-meat.html

That a significant proportion of votes are fraudulent, disproportionately in the most critical states, such as Ohio, and everyone piously turns a blind eye to voter fraud on a scale that makes the difference between one presidential candidate winning, and another winning, is interesting in that everyone turns a blind eye. Democracy is now so dead that it is impolite to pay attention.

It is not interesting in that even honest elections would not produce results markedly different. OBamacare, Romneycare, who cares? The Democrats move the left hand edge of the Overton window leftwards, the Republicans move the right hand edge of the Overton window leftwards. Bush quietly abolished the difference between Republicanism and the early years of Obamanism, which is to say, he closed the overton window from the right, while Obama now vigorously re-opens it to the left.

Back in 2009 the left won all future elections once and forever in the old fashioned way: By buying the electorate they wanted:

In 2009 the Mises institute pointed out that a Virginian family of three needed to earn sixty thousand dollars to do better than earning nothing - which is why males earning substantially less than sixty thousand generally cannot form families.

What this means is that the class of lesser paid workers has no incentive to become better paid workers, or even to work at all. The women do better off having three children by three thugs, and the men have no prospect of wife or biological descendents. From zero to sixty thousand, no incentive. From sixty thousand to a hundred thousand, low incentives. Normal incentives for a middle class lifestyle, and the normal prospects of normal middle class sort of marriage, set in only with a six figure income.

So if you make a living and support a family and all that, you are outvoted. Outvoted forever. Honest elections would only make some boring minor change in the details.

Hey presto, a majority underclass nation, with the majority living on their votes.

Moldbug's analysis of how our society worked, and how it came to be, was an epochal insight, of enormous importance. We had become uprooted from time, the spin out leftwards had blinded us to the spin out leftwards. Like Winston Smith, we had lost our past. Moldbug reminded us of how the world looks from a viewpoint rooted in deep time, reminded us that that was the way to see what was happening, and understand what was happening, was to see the present from the past.

And then he pretty much shut up, apart from the occasional silly or trivial post. This one is not silly or trivial. It reminds us of how quietly deranged the debate on voter fraud is, how quietly deranged our criminal justice system is, how the progressive religion trumps sanity, but really, all that is a minor corollary of his great insights.

And what, precisely, are his great insights? It is hard to say them briefly. Since he was deliberately verbose, each of his readers is apt to summarize them in a superficially different way.

Viewing the present from the past, the world looks much different from official reality, with a multitude of differences that cannot be briefly described.

China more capitalist than the USA

2012-12-03 19:28:01

With the USA becoming more socialist, and China more capitalist, it was inevitable that they would cross over.

And so today we see that private property rights in China are more secure and respected than in the USA[983].

Which means that in a little while, the average Chinese will be richer than the average North American.

At present, Chinese cars per capita is 21% of the US, electricity per capita is 29% of the US, and most middle class goods are roughly similar, which suggests that Chinese GDP per head is somewhere around a quarter or so of US GDP per head, despite optimistic US figures to the contrary. Since Chinese GDP is rising at about 10% a year, while US GDP per head is probably falling, despite official figures supposedly showing that it is rising, individual Chinese should be richer than individual North Americans after 2026 or so, assuming both countries continue on their current paths for that long, China continuing to head towards capitalism, and the US continuing to abandon it.

As in Britain, maintaining order is being criminalized

2012-12-08 10:16:44

As you know, another photo has come out showing that five foot eleven athlete Trayvon Martin beat the stuffing out of five foot seven overweight George Zimmerman, while Zimmerman never hit back, until he finally shot Martin.

And when I say "come out" I mean that Zimmerman's new lawyers extracted it by a year of litigation. His first set of lawyers were happy to roll over for the state, and help railroad him as a dangerous *raaaaciiiiiist*, hence the

---

[983]https://www.theblaze.com/stories/must-see-pics-home-of-duck-farmer-who-said-no-becomes-symbol-of-chinese-resistance/

widespread accusation that he must have been dangerously insane to fire them and get new lawyers.

As you may also know, the sound on one police call of George Zimmerman getting out of his truck to check out Trayvon Martin happens seven and half minutes before the sound of the gunshot on another police call when he shoots Martin, which means that Martin had ample time to walk to his fathers house, rant to his girlfriend a bit about how horrid Zimmerman was, then turn around and walk back to look for George Zimmerman

That Martin was still walking around in the rain seven minutes after passing Zimmerman's truck implies that he was looking for Zimmerman, or looking for a house to burgle, or both, rather than looking to get home and dry.

Since Zimmerman shot Trayvon Martin a short distance from Zimmerman's truck, and a long distance from Martin's father's house, he had to be returning to his truck or hanging about near his truck at the time of the incident.

If the Zimmerman had "chased down" Martin for seven minutes, they would have had to have been creeping along like snails

Benjamin Crump, an attorney for the Martin family, told NBC News:

> "George Zimmerman profiled and pursued Trayvon," Crump said[984]. "Trayvon had every right to stand his ground."

Whenever someone accuses Zimmerman and defends Martin, they start by accusing Zimmerman of crimethink, and fail to accuse Zimmerman of attacking Martin, which implicitly argues that Martin was justified in attacking Zimmerman, thus implicitly admits that Martin attacked Zimmerman.

This line of argument implies that blacks are entitled to physically attack those that profile them. The scenario Crump implies is that Martin decided not to go home, either hanging around or doubling back, and that Zimmerman either by his behavior or in actual words, demanded that Martin account for himself, and implicitly or explicitly accused him of being a burglar, (which in fact Martin was, though he may not necessarily have been burgling at that particular time, was not necessarily burgling Zimmerman's neighborhood, though he had been burgling in someone's neighborhood to raise funds to buy blunts), and that it is totally and completely unacceptable for whites to accuse blacks of burgling. (Zimmerman being demoted from mestizo to white, for coming in conflict with a black, blacks being more politically correct than mestizos)

Examining the debate, the theory that Zimmerman "chased" Martin has been quietly abandoned, for the theory that Zimmerman "confronted" Martin by asking him what he was up to, or merely by acting as if Martin was

---

[984]https://usnews.nbcnews.com/_news/2012/12/03/15647937-defense-posts-george-zimmerman-photo-from-night-of-trayvon-martin-shooting

a criminal, and that asking blacks who behave suspiciously what they are doing, or even keeping an eye on them, is a completely intolerable and extraordinary act of aggression, that merely by acting as if Martin's behavior was suspicious Zimmerman engaged in aggression against Martin, justifying Martin attacking him.

When I debate people on this topic, the issue rapidly turns to whether it is reasonable for you to ask a seeming outsider what he is doing your neighborhood. When someone argues that this is unreasonable, indeed extraordinary, behavior, he implies that Zimmerman acted wrongfully by watching for crime, and Martin acted rightfully by responding physically to this horrible act of aggression rather than implying that Zimmerman acted wrongfully by attacking Martin.

Whenever you see the words "self appointed neighborhood watch" this implies in the mind of the person using that phrase, *watching* Martin was the original act of aggression that started the fight.

No one doubts that Zimmerman shot Martin, so the question is, who started it? No one can doubt that Martin punched and beat Zimmerman, and Zimmerman did not punch and beat Martin. No one can doubt that Martin was not heading for his father's home at the time of the confrontation, and, given his conversation with his girlfriend, the reason he was out in the rain instead of warm and dry with his dad was that he was looking for Zimmerman. So the real question that no one will quite say out loud is: Is being suspected of being a burglar legitimate grounds for a black man to attack a white man?

Undoubtedly, all the blacks on the jury will vote yes, all the whites on the jury will come under extreme extra social pressure to vote yes. There will probably be a hung jury as one or two whites refuse to accept the social consensus. Blacks will riot, while cops actively make sure that no one does a Zimmerman against rioting blacks.

As a general rule blacks burn down their own neighborhoods, and attack non blacks unfortunate enough to live or work in black majority neighborhoods, but the central key issue in this case is that blacks should be able to attack people in neighborhoods that are not black majority for real and imagined slights, thus the rioting following this case may well intrude on white neighborhoods.

Whenever someone argues against Zimmerman, his arguments make no sense logically, but make sense only as circling around the unstated premise: That black behavior cannot be questioned, and if you question it you deserve what is coming to you. AJStrata's arguments are a good example of this. Zimmerman's Incoherent Statements Destroying His Defense.[985]" " The Nail In George Zimmerman False Claims[986]" "As Details Come Out, George

[985] https://strata-sphere.com/blog/index.php/archives/18492
[986] https://strata-sphere.com/blog/index.php/archives/18526

Zimmerman's Claims Crumble[987]" "Crime Scene Proves Zimmerman Covering Up A Different Story[988]"

For example, one of AJ Strata's purported arguments is that it would be impossible for Zimmerman to pull his gun while Martin was sitting on top of him and restraining Zimmerman's elbow with one hand.

One moment Martin is supposedly a nine year old cherub, and the next he is supposedly superman. Try controlling another man's elbow with just one hand gripping the elbow. It is entirely impossible, and you have to be pretty strong, or have leverage, to do it with two hands. The elbow is much more powerful than the hand. I have not read everything AJ Strata says on the Zimmerman case, because he says a lot, but I read quite a bit, and none of it made any sense whatsoever, except we reinterpret it as "Zimmerman is guilty of crimethink" The general format of all Strata's arguments is "Zimmerman says X, and X is obviously impossible", when X is not merely possible, but overwhelmingly probable, the sort of thing that is bound to happen if we suppose that Zimmerman was an honest peaceable guy watching for crime, and Martin a crazy vicious stupid violent punk criminal looking for trouble. The only reason for supposing X to be impossible is crimestop, that thinking X happened is crimethink. It is not impossible that Zimmerman could draw his gun while Martin incompetently attempts to restrain him. It is politically incorrect to think that Martin would be attacking someone who he knew or should have known was armed, because that would mean that Martin was acting like a dumb nigger. What is impossible is not Zimmerman pulling his gun when a nigger is dumb enough to grab Zimmerman's elbow instead of his wrist. What is crimethink, is that Martin was so stupid and violent as to continue to be violent under those circumstances.

Ostensibly, Strata is saying "This aspect of Zimmerman's story is physically impossible", but none of Strata's arguments that I read made any sense as "This aspect of Zimmerman's story is physically impossible", only as "This aspect of Zimmerman's story is crimethink".

Supporters of Martin believe that it is unthinkable and unspeakable to suggest that Martin behaved as he so obviously did behave, and simultaneously believe that it is perfectly reasonable and entirely appropriate for Martin to behave as he so obviously did behave. When someone says that Zimmerman's story falls apart, he means it is politically unthinkable that Martin attacked Zimmerman, and when he says that Zimmerman profiled Martin, he means it is entirely appropriate, proper, and natural that Martin attacked Zimmerman. Doublethink.

---

[987] https://strata-sphere.com/blog/index.php/archives/18230
[988] https://strata-sphere.com/blog/index.php/archives/18513

Recent posts on Urban Future vanished

2012-12-08 14:03:43

Recent excellent posts on the excellent blog "Urban Future"[989] have mysteriously vanished.

Perhaps the bitbucket ate them, but I suspect the problem was that he said "the Left", instead of saying the US Government.

Edit: In the comments, Nick Land reassures me that they were merely eaten by the bitbucket.

He was discussing the left singularity. He suggests that the left singularity was akin to an alcoholic drinking shoe polish in the gutter, which not only implies that the future of the US government is likely to resemble an alcoholic drinking shoe polish in the gutter, but also inadvertently implies that the Great Leap Forward and the Cultural Revolution resembled an alcoholic drinking shoe polish in the gutter, which of course everyone knows to be true, but is inadvisable to say if your blog is located in China.

Edit: In the comments, Nick Land implies that he is not taking any very great risks when indirectly and inadvertently implying that the Cultural Revolution and Great leap forward resembled an alcoholic drinking shoe polish in the gutter. If so, he is a lot safer in China than in US academia, where it is still inadvisable to be unkind to Mao.

Derivatives did it!

2012-12-12 06:14:44

Bernie Madoff steals from his depositors. An evil Jew did it! Punish the evil Jew Bernie Madoff. Jon Corzine, pillar of the progressive establishment, senior financial regulator, steals from his depositors. Derivatives did it!. Poor Jon Corzine. We must punish derivatives by regulating them further.

When someone says that derivatives caused the financial crisis, he says that everyone did it, so no one more guilty than anyone else – by which he means he is afraid of the people that did do it.

The problem is not derivatives, nor is it evil Jews. The problem is that some people can get away with enormous crimes. While those who commit financial crimes are disproportionately Ashkenazi Jews, the ones that can get away with blatant financial crimes are disproportionately non Jewish. If Jews secretly ruled the world, Jon Corzine would be in jail, and Bernie Madoff would get to keep what he stole. Of course it is quite possible that Jon

---

[989]https://www.thatsmags.com/shanghai/news-features/urban-future-blog

Corzine is secretly Jewish, but if he is, needs to keep it secret. Therefore, Jews do not rule the world. Nor derivatives either.

Blaming Jews is a way of avoiding blaming the powerful. Blaming derivatives is a way of avoiding blaming the powerful while avoiding political incorrectness, at the expense of being obviously absurd. Derivatives cannot steal from people. Only people can steal from people. At least the guy blaming Jews does not sound crazy, whereas the guy blaming derivatives would be viewed as madhouse material, were it not that "derivatives did it" is the official truth.

Derivatives supposedly causing the financial crisis is as stupid as guns supposedly killing people, indeed a lot more stupid, since no one proposes to acquit the killer while convicting his gun.

The Nazi account of the world is incorrect, but it is lot saner, more plausible, and closer to the truth than the official account.

Regulating derivatives is a displacement activity. A displacement activity typically happens when you are too scared, confused, or conflicted to do the sane and necessary thing, so instead you do something irrelevant, which is usually an activity that is crazy or stupid under the circumstances, the circumstances being that it is extraordinarily vital to do something that is actually relevant, such as jailing Jon Corzine and recovering the money he stole, thereby discouraging repetition.

Displacement activity can be a harmless break, a pause to enable one to decide what needs to done. As a permanent alternative to relevant, but scary, action, it is madness and cowardice. Whosoever says "Derivatives did it" is crazy, cowardly, or lying, and if you engage him by naming particular identifiable people who did particular identifiable specific concrete bad things, he will interrupt you to protect himself from hearing such dangerous talk, and will run away for fear he be punished for hearing such disrespectful words, his response revealing his true motives.

They will stand still and listen if you blame Angelo Mozillo, but should you list the people bribed by Angelo Mozillo, they will shout you down or run away, or shout you down and then run away.

You can pretty clearly imply that Angelo Mozillo bribed the management of Freddy and Fannie, and no one reacts, but if you say in plain words that Angelo Mozillo bribed the management of the government sponsored enterprises to take dud mortgages off Countrywide Bank's tab and put them on the taxpayers tab, it is like saying "nigger" in a crowded theater.

You can imply all sorts of terrible things, and progressives will not hear you say them, because crimestop prevents them from registering what you are saying, just as crimestop prevented them from noticing that the movie "District 9" preached that it was the duty of the superior kind to rule over the inferior kind.

Orwell defines crimestop as protective stupidity. A goodthinker makes himself stupid to avoid thoughtcrime

Crimestop is:

> The faculty of stopping short, as though by instinct, at the threshold of any dangerous thought. It includes the power of not grasping analogies, of failing to perceive logical errors, of misunderstanding the simplest arguments if they are inimical to Ingsoc, and of being bored or repelled by any train of thought which is capable of leading in a heretical direction. In short....protective stupidity.

Goodthinker

> One who strongly adheres to all of the principles of Newspeak.

In the discussion of immigration, the financial crisis, and so on and so forth, one can ascertain the principles of Newspeak, the requirements of Goodthink, by observing the outbreaks of selective stupidity. Jon Corzine's crimes induce stupidity. Bernie Madoff's crimes do not.

It is a thoughtcrime to say that black has acted in stereotypically black fashion, for example to say that Trayvon Martin "ducked for cover behind the bushes in the dark", and we can tell it is a thoughtcrime by observing the crimestop that sets in when discussing the movements of Trayvon Martin. But not only blacks are specially protected by goodthink and crimestop. Rich white males in the government are also protected by goodthink and crimestop. Rich white males not in the government are, however, not protected.

.

The left singularity versus the technological singularity

2012-12-14 10:26:58

Lately this blog has largely been about the left singularity: That leftism leads to more leftism, which leads to even more leftism even faster, until everything goes to hell. The best known singularity, however is the information technology singularity, the rapture of the nerds

What of the theory that information technology leads to more information technology?

Well, in a sense, in the long run, looking back over the last several million years, it is obviously true. Problem is that it is far from obvious that dramatic technological change is coming any time soon. We have had quite a few dark ages interrupting the process, and there is what looks like a dark age coming up now.

The distinguishing feature of the technological singularity, what makes it singular, is accelerating progress. Progress has been accelerating from the sixteenth century to the early twentieth, but during the twentieth century, in one field after another, progress has slowed, usually stopping altogether within the west, while continuing at a somewhat slower pace in Asia. Accelerating progress continues in DNA reading, but that is the last place where it is still evident that progress is accelerating. Progress may well have stopped in DNA writing, and any future advances in DNA writing are likely to come from Asia. Rapid progress continues in integrated circuit manufacture, but that progress is not accelerating, and the shrinking number of fabs and increasing cost of fabs threatens to end that progress.

If yet another dark age hits, then when the next civilization rises, the high point of western civilization will be dated precisely to 1972 - last man on the moon, tallest buildings in the west, coolest muscle cars.

Information technology has been growing exponentially - everyone these days has a powerful computer connected to the internet with a lot of storage, giving them instant access to all the information in the world, which they mostly use to download badly made porn and worse written romantic fiction.

The continued advance of computing power, data storage, and internet bandwidth, will likely give us ... lots and lots of 3D computer animated porn taking place in virtual worlds with reasonable physics..

That everyone now has access to all the information in the world has not accelerated the scientific progress that underlies technological progress: Arguably scientific progress was fastest around the 1870s, and it has slowed dramatically after 1942, when peer review was introduced.

DNA, the unification of information technology with biology?

One of the areas of information technology that is progressing rapidly, and the only place where it still accelerating, is DNA reading.

DNA sequencing, protein sequencing, new techniques for revealing the three dimensional structure of proteins, and many other breakthroughs have generated a rapidly increasing flood of data, which is now running into the limits of computers to keep up with it. Back in the 1990s, everyone expected this would result in huge flood of useful biotechnology, that biotechnology would be where fortunes were made, as previously computers were where fortunes were made, that there would be extraordinary and rapid progress in medicine and other practical fields.

Instead, the number of new medical entities has been falling rapidly, with the result that drug companies are facing big troubles as their patents run out.

In the late 2000s, social decay outran information advance.

What is happening with biotechnology is cultural decline, the decline of science, social decay. Biomedical research is rapidly becoming less and less reproducible, so biotech companies cannot use academic research to produce new medical treatments.

Peer Review is science by consensus. Instead of experimentalists telling the scientific community what they see, the scientific community tells experimentalists what they should see. Science ceases to be science, and becomes the consensus of the most holy synod. The academy is generating theology, not biology, and when biotech companies attempt to apply the latest advances in theology to produce actual treatments, the treatments of course do not work. Biotech companies have found that some time in recent years, biomedical scientific research ceased to reproducible. Should a university's biology department try to do biology, it is going to fall short on its goals for affirmative action and number of papers published. Reproducibility seriously slows down the production of papers, and oppresses female ways of knowing.

DNA synthesis

DNA writing may be progressing also, though this is less clear. The high point was Venter synthesizing a functional one million base pair chromosome to create a simple bacterium. It remains to be seen whether this is the start of creating synthetic organisms, or like the landing on the moon, a civilizational high point signalling the beginning of social decay. The next step would be to create synthetic chloroplasts based on blue green algae that can synthesize organic nitrogen from atmospheric nitrogen using sunlight, thus giving bioengineered crop plants a huge advantage over natural weeds, and then, eventually work our way to creating synthetic humans, free from accumulated genetic load.

It is probable that a human free from genetic load would be an all round gold medal Olympic athlete, extremely smart, with a reaction time of less than a hundred milliseconds, rather than the usual three hundred milliseconds. There are large variations in human reaction time and very fast reaction times appear to have no downside - people with very fast reaction times tend to be generally smarter and saner. Reaction time is a good indicator of brain efficiency and effectiveness. People with good reaction times not only make decisions faster, they make better decisions faster.

Since evolution has every reason to select for faster reaction time, and no reason to select for slower, the fact that we have any significant variation in this, that we are not all close to the shortest possible time, suggests that the problem is genetic load.

On average, humans acquire about seventy new single nucleotide variants per genome per generation. This causes genetic load.

The difference between someone whose reaction time is one standard deviation below average, and someone whose reaction time is one standard deviation above average, is apt to be decisive in a fight, overwhelmingly decisive in a fight with deadly weapons, and also quite important when dancing to live music in the presence of members of the opposite sex. These are big differences.

Reaction time is is highly heritable and one would expect it to have a large effect on survival and reproductive success, so, if not already minimized, random mutations must be increasing it as fast as evolution is shortening it.

There is evidence that reaction time has increased by substantially more than a standard deviation since first measured in Victorian times[990], probably due to the relaxation in selection and the resulting accumulation of genetic load due to random mutation.

Silverman IW. Simple reaction time: it is not what it used to be. *American Journal of Psychology*. 2010; 123: 39-50.

Unfortunately, Venter's one million base pair chromosome may turn out to have been the high point of DNA writing, much as 1972 was the last man on the moon. No further functional chromosomes have been synthesized de novo, and plans to create them are slipping further away, not getting closer.

If Moore's law for DNA writing is still on trend, we should be synthesizing human eggs and sperm around 2016 or so. This does not seem at all likely, suggesting that the trend has broken, just as the space travel trend broke in 1972, though it is too early to be sure yet. In the short run, Moore law graphs are bouncy, but this bounce is troublingly large.

DNA Reading is not going to change things in itself:

Reading genomes, DNA sequencing, is still zipping along on a Moore's law curve with a very fast exponential. Pretty soon, it will be reasonable to do a complete high accuracy gene read on every human that shows up for medical treatment. Unfortunately our ability to make sense of gene reads is not improving, so it is far from obvious that this will produce substantial medical benefits. It turns out that most of "non coding" or "junk" DNA is not junk. Instead of coding for proteins, it codes for which proteins will be produced

---

[990]https://charltonteaching.blogspot.com.au/2012/02/convincing-objective-and-direct.html

under what circumstances, and what shall be done with those proteins. Unfortunately it is very hard to make sense of it

We should be able to get a low accuracy read of someone's genome for about a hundred dollars in 2018. Unfortunately a low accuracy read is not particularly useful, because you want to be able to detect rare mutations, since every single person carries thousands of rare mutations. So we should get good information on individual genomes in around 2021, at the present rate of progress. This will provide significant medical benefits, but it is unlikely to be a game changer.

How about artificial intelligence?

Artificial intelligence is doing fine. Unfortunately, artificial consciousness is going absolutely nowhere. Chess playing computers are very impressive, and so is Google translate. Unfortunately, Google translate suffers from the Chinese Room syndrome. If you look at the typical errors that Google makes, it is obviously translating words into the nearest word without knowing what words mean, without even knowing that words have meanings. It is, like the Chinese Room, not conscious, and the lack of consciousness shows.

If you look at the progress we are making towards conscious computers, it is as if we wanted to build a plane, a machine that flies like a bird, but had no idea about aerodynamics, engines, or even that air exists, and so we found ourselves building bigger and better pogo sticks. No matter how big and how good the pogo sticks we build, they are not going to be plane, not getting any closer to being a plane, and no matter how intelligent the computers we program become, they are not getting any closer to being conscious.

Maybe in future we will create artificial consciousness, but at the moment there are no good indications we are headed in that direction, or even know what direction to head. Maybe computer consciousness will quietly appear out of artificial intelligence, but there are no indications that this is likely.

Perhaps the reason we are not making any obvious progress is that we have no clear idea what consciousness is, how it works, or even what it does, as if we were trying to build a plane, but did not realize that air existed.

we cannot design brains, maybe we can copy them:

How about uploads, simulating brains in software and hardware?

The tiny worm caenorhabditis elegans has just three hundred and two neurons, whose connections have been completely mapped. While a lot of its behavior is arguably well described and well explained in terms of those neurons, no one has actually managed to create a simulated worm driven by simulated neurons. Neurons frequently process information in ways that are not altogether obvious, not always easy to explain or describe, and each attempt to upload the worm reveals that we are even further from the capacity to do so than we thought. We are not making progress towards uploading, we are making progress towards realizing how difficult the task is.

Nanotechnology.

When line widths get down to one nanometer, is that not nanotechnology?

Well it is not the nanotechnology that is likely to transform the world. What people are hoping for is nanoassemblers in your laptop, so that you can download a new computer and new nanoassembler, and have your old system make the new one. Laptops could create new laptops as rabbits create new rabbits, except that they could create anything, not just rabbits.

That sort of nanotechnology would mean that everyone would become largely independent of physical trade. The entire economy would move to the internet. We could settle space and inhospitable parts of the earth, because we would not need to do shopping trips every few days. We would only need energy and raw materials, which tend to be abundant in inhospitable unsettled places. It would also mean an end to gun control. The government would find it mighty difficult to stop people from settling the unsettled places.

If we were heading towards nanotechnology in that sense, fabs would be getting smaller and cheaper. Instead, they are getting bigger and more expensive.

If we were using printers, rather photolithography, we could be on that path.

The way we make very small things is that we coat a surface in resist, then we illuminate the resist with an image, so that some parts of the resist are changed by the light, and some parts unchanged by the darkness, which is to say, we create a photo. Chemical processes then transform the surface, so that we get some detailed structure on the surface. Rinse and repeat.

For example, to generate the electrical leads, we coat the entire surface in a very thin layer of conductive metal, then we coat the metal with resist. The resist that is exposed to light becomes non soluble. We dissolve away the unexposed resist, just like developing an old style black and white photo. We then dissolve away the metal except where it is protected by the exposed resist.

Now suppose, instead of using light, we had print heads that made mechanical contact with the surface, laying the resist down, or scraping it off, or transforming it with electrical current. Then the trend would be towards larger and large numbers of smaller and cheaper fabs.

But instead, each generation of fabs is bigger and more expensive than the last one, threatening an end to Moore's law for semiconductors. We are very close to having only one fab in the world, and the next step after that is no fabs.

Even if photolithography can take us all the way down to nanometer scale, which is not clear, as fabs get ever fewer and more expensive, it still not the nanotechnology that is hoped for, the nanotechnology of nanofabs.

The failure.

Continued progress with existing technologies will not get us to the technological singularity. We need some genuinely new technologies to get us there, and the rate at which we have been introducing genuinely new technologies has been slowing down markedly since the nineteen forties, arguably since the eighteen seventies. Biotechnology provides a clear and striking recent illustration of social decay outpacing technological advance.

In 1967, the writers of Startreck assumed that by the 1990s, we would have large nuclear powered orbit to orbit interplanetary craft with large crews. Given the progress that had been happening, that seemed at the time a reasonable expectation. Progress has slowed, slowed strikingly and obviously

No technological singularity is likely until we recover from social decay. Right now we are heading downwards fast, and have no idea how to turn around once we hit bottom, or how deep bottom is going to be. While China and Russia are recovering nicely from their respective left singularities, post Roman Britain tells us that a dark age can be very dark indeed.

Kill their leaders and convert them to … progressivism

2012-12-17 16:28:16

Ann Coulter famously said "Kill their leaders and convert them to Christianity". Regrettably, all the versions of Christianity that once upon a time would have been capable of implementing such a program have replaced the worship of Christ the Redeemer with Jesus the community organizer.

The "Arab Spring" was the Cathedral deluding itself that it was installing progressive "Muslim" regimes in the Middle East – only to discover what was obvious to everyone else, that it was installing "progressive" Muslim regimes in the Middle East.

For a long time the Cathedral has been promoting a transformation of Islam, promoting progressive Islam, which I parody as "There is no God but Allah, and Mohammed is his prophet, and Mohammed, rightly understood, was a feminist and gay rights supporter who only commanded killing Zionists, not killing Jews as such, and furthermore opposed terrorism, except when conservatives and Jews who won't get with the program get terrorized."

They believe they are succeeding, but this belief is deluded. They think that they defeated Christianity by persuasion, by the self evident truth of progressivism, and don't realize that they crushed Christianity by theocratic state power. (Any Christian commenters who think their Church is still doing fine, how is your church treating divorced women who want to remarry? If your church has yielded on several major points, it will soon be yielding on several more, until Christ the Redeemer becomes Jesus the community organizer, and the Father, Son, and Holy Ghost become the spiritual force, so as not to discriminate against parishioners who believe that Jesus gay married Buddha and visits earth from time to time in a flying saucer.)

Progressives gravely underestimate the amount of violence required convert Muslims to progressivism, because they gravely underestimate the amount of violence they used to convert Christians to progressivism.

Progressives think that sincere Muslim believers are rural rednecks, people living in mountain compounds, and that is where they send the drones to blow up terrorists. They think that people like themselves – urban, privileged, affluent, highly educated in all the correct elite schools – must be progressives and cannot possibly be terrorists, cannot possibly take religion seriously, but, in a Muslim country, that is exactly where you find the Muslims, aka "terror". In a theocratic state, belief in the official theocratic beliefs is strongest among the products of the elite schools, and affluent people living close to the center of power, such as, for example, Barack Hussein Obama and Osama bin Laden. We are a progressive atheocracy, the Middle East is full of Muslim theocracies.

The reason that in America, the Christians tend to be in the backwoods and away from the center of power is that the official religion, progressivism, dominates and is more passionately believed, the closer you are to the center of power. Obviously, in a theocracy, faith is centered on the capital, the government bureaucracy, the elite schools, the privileged, the powerful, the wealthy. School attendance is church attendance at the official church.

There are moderate Muslims but there is no such thing as moderate Islam. Moderate Muslims are Muslims who don't take Islam seriously. And you find them in the backwoods and rural areas, in the same sort of places as in America you find Americans who don't take progressivism seriously.

If you want to make war on "terror", you are going to have to make war on Islam, which means you are going to have to start by blowing up the leading schools and think tanks where the children of the privileged hang out. Progressives are losing against Islam because they are blowing up the wrong Muslims.

When Sunni Muslims are in power, they persecute Alawites in the same way they persecute Christians and Jews, since they don't believe the Alawite claim to be Muslim. To avoid persecution, Alawites seized power in Syria. The Cathedral perceived this as soldiers snatching power from priests, or, as they phrased it, "undemocratic", though Alawites are Muslim enough that the distinction between soldiers and priests is small, thus the distinction between democracy and military dictatorship is small. Alawites claim to be Shia Muslims, a claim barely tolerated by Shia Muslims and generally rejected by Sunni Muslims. Alawite ruled Syria allied itself with Shia Iran, allowing Iran to project force against Israel and hostile Sunni Muslim powers, whereupon Iran found it convenient to give credit to the Alawite claim to be Shia Muslims. Because Iranian aid to Hezbollah and such was channeled through Syria, the Cathedral defined the Syrian regime as "terror".

And so, the Cathedral set to overthrowing the Syrian government, intending to replace "terror" with progressive "Islam"

The Alawites fought back with unexpected ferocity, knowing that if the Sunni majority gained power, they would be enslaved, and so the war went on inconclusively.

Syrian Christians support the Alawites, and are fighting beside them, which tells me that Alawites are less dreadful than most Muslims, which is probably the reason that Sunnis don't count them as Muslims.

Indeed, the fact that there are a reasonable number of Syrian Christians still alive tells me that Alawites are less bad than most. America should not be fighting on the other side from middle eastern Christians.

After the murder of America's Libyan ambassador, the Cathedral suddenly realized that in a genuinely free and fair Syrian election, an al-Qaeda franchisee would likely be elected.

Moderate, which is to say insincere, Muslims seem to be in short supply in Syria. So now, in Syria, we have a three cornered war, the Cathedral versus the Alawites versus the Sunnis, the Cathedral versus just about everyone in Syria.

Kissinger said of the Iran Iraq war

> "It's too bad they both can't lose."

Whereupon Reagan proceeded to make sure they both did lose.

I hope that in the Syrian war, all three of them will lose. Indeed, chances are, all three will lose. The Alawites have their backs against the wall, and no alternative but to hang on to power, so in the end, will probably do so, but pay a very high price for doing so. Everyone says that the Assad regime, which is to say Alawites, are on their last legs. Perhaps they are, but they have been on their last legs for a long time. The next most likely outcome is that Al Qaeda gets Syria, while progressives continue to piously pretend that progressivism is winning.

The Syrian government, which is to say the Alawites, agreed to hold free and fair elections, under supervision of China and Russia, but with the Alawites organizing the election. This was of course entirely unacceptable to the Cathedral, which wanted the Alawites to first be thoroughly removed from any power, and then elections held under the supervision of the Cathedral.

The Cathedral proposal resembles the "election" whereby it installed Aristide in Haiti. Not only are the Alawites unlikely to fall for that one, the Sunni majority are not going to fall for it either. If the Sunnis win, there is going to be a genuinely democratic election, one man, one vote, *once*, and then an Al Qaeda franchisee will be in charge, while New York Times optimistically rationalizes that Al Qaeda franchisees contain moderate elements.

The watchmaker is dead

2012-12-24 16:57:51

When the religion dies, so dies the empire. Europe is the faith, the faith is Europe, and the faith is no more.

Everyone who resents the destructive, self indulgent, and self destructive rule of the ever more left wing Cathedral, regrets the passing of Christianity, everyone including the secular right, perhaps especially the secular right, and some of them imagine it could be revived, though the remnant be small as a mustard seed.

Before Darwinism, intelligent Christians believed in a creator God in the same way they believed in Mongolia. Intelligent Christians thought seriously about the implications of theology for the observable world, and the implications of the observable world for theology.

After Darwinism, they did not.

Consider for example CS Lewis. He was an intelligent Christian, familiar with the works of intelligent Christians who wrote before Darwin. But he primarily wrote fantasy and science fantasy, without troubling to make his theology consistent with the observable world, or even with itself. When he discussed the worldview of past Christians, he made no effort to reconcile them with recently discovered facts, treating their theories and analyses the same way he treated his science fantasies, not the way they treated their theories and analyses

Paley argued

> suppose I had found a watch upon the ground, and it should be inquired how the watch happened to be in that place;... There must have existed, at some time, and at some place or other, an artificer or artificers, who formed for the purpose which we find it actually to answer; who comprehended its construction,

and designed its use.... Every indication of contrivance, every manifestation of design, which existed in the watch, exists in the works of nature; with the difference, on the side of nature, of being greater

It was a compelling argument, and those that argued against it, for example proposing that visibly complex well designed organisms such as mice were produced by spontaneous generation were just plain stupid. Spontaneous generation was plausible for creatures such as slimes, that when observed by the means available at the time were seemingly simple, but to propose spontaneous generation for mice, ants, earwigs, and suchlike, was stupidity plain and simple, or clever silliness, intelligent people deliberately making themselves stupid.

Religions based on the worship of a creator God, the worship of Paley's watchmaker, are dead. They just don't know it yet.

Darwinism did not cause progressivism. The Puritans and their successors were already well on the road to apostasy before Darwin, but Darwinism weakened Christian resistance to progressive apostasy. Darwinism may not have necessarily caused the progressive victory, but now that the progressives are victorious, and Christians have for the most part capitulated to apostasy, Darwinism makes it hopeless to appeal to Christianity as a force capable of defending society from progressives.

There is an effort to go back to neopaganism, but paganism is deader than Christianity. In practice, efforts to revive paganism dissolve into Zoism[991] Instead of worshiping the old gods, the neopagans worship themselves and their own irrationality and magical thinking.

The Dharmic religions might have a chance, but Dharmic religions require and endorse social inequality, that some people and entire groups are simply born to an inferior low status role, because of past failure of souls and social groups to perform their duty, thus lack appeal in both progressive societies, which are supposedly egalitarian, and in capitalist societies, in which social mobility occurs in this life, and the self made man, rather than the priest, is the hero. As Judaism and Christianity provide an explanation for nature, the Dharmic religions provide an explanation for an unequal society. (Islam and progressivism do not need to provide explanations for anything, since their method of persuasion is that you had better believe or they will make bad things happen to you)

Dharmic religion adjusted to be compatible with either progressivism or capitalism, let alone both, has no life in it.

What do I believe in?

---

[991] https://blog.reaction.la/tag/zoism

I believe in the economics of "Economics in One Lesson", and in Darwinism. Darwinism and Economics can serve the functions that religion served, a position explained in detail in " Good and Evil from self interest[992]", "Natural Law and Natural Rights[993]", "A short demonstration that morality is objectively knowable.[994]" It is an austere faith, with implications that many find brutal, but has the great advantage of compelling evidence, which worship of a creator God once had, but has no longer.

Christianity was always a bit left wing, so once people started competing for power by being holier than the next guy, was bound to wind up in far left apostasy. Christianity remained sane by being ruled by Kings. If one wanted power, it was inadvisable to advertise that one was holier than the King, and the King was seldom all that holy. Saints were respected, admired, and hidden somewhere out far from the corridors of power, in some safe far away place where the amount of damage they could do and embarrassment they could cause was minimal. But in recent times, in The War Between The States, the saints decided that they would govern. Similarly with Britain's crusade to end slavery.

(You did not know that there was a British crusade to end slavery? Each generation of leftists is apt to demonize the previous generation of leftists as incurably right wing, and the only reason why Lincoln is a progressive hero rather than arch reactionary, is that in the US the war between the states is still a live issue.)

Jesus and Paul's conservative prescription for sex, sex roles, and marriage is of course exactly what civilization needs, what is needed for civilization, since it maximizes male investment in posterity, but you will notice that both Jesus and Paul go gentle on actually enforcing that prescription, *"He that is without sin among you, let him first cast a stone at her"* foreshadowing the Puritans and their successors abandoning Christian sexual morality, at first covertly, then openly, as they headed ever further left, and became ever more hostile to lower status males and male sexuality. Paul's prescriptions for giving males higher status than females consisted entirely of symbolic status, satisfying the female hypergamic impulse, thus making monogamous marriage possible for everyone, even lower class Christians, without imposing any real disadvantages or disabilities on females. A really conservative prescription to enable and enforce monogamous marriage against female hypergamy and male polygyny would impose real disabilities on females, granting them, like children, substantially less sexual and reproductive freedom than males and substantially greater protection than males.

A woman who sleeps with a bad boy, or who refuses to sleep with her husband, creates large harmful externalities for other people. We regulate the

[992]https://reaction.la/constant_on_good_and_evil.htm
[993]https://reaction.la/rights.html
[994]https://reaction.la/moralfac.htm

testicles off people who sell eggs or fermented cabbage. Why do not dishonorable activities that are far more likely to cause harm, and cause far more serious harm, get regulated?

Christian morality, is, as Nietzsche argued, slave morality. Slaves turn the other cheek. The morality burned into our souls by natural selection is that we do good to kin and to those that do good for us, that we do our duty to our friends, associates, and allies, and we destroy our enemies. Far away strangers can look after themselves. One should love oneself, love one's kith and kin, and for the rest of mankind, return good for good, and evil for evil.

There are no utilitarians. Show me a man who would hold a child's face in the fire to find the cure for malaria, and I will show you a man who would hold a child's face in the fire, and forget about trying to cure malaria. It is not in our nature to care about far away outsiders, and those who claim that they care, and that therefore it is their duty to bad things to near people that they may do good things to far people, somehow never get around to doing good things to far people.

Christianity has capitulated to its apostatic spawn, progressivism, because the seeds of progressivism were within it, because it is the nature of Christianity to capitulate, and because the Christian priesthood, like the pagan priesthood in the Roman Empire, does not really believe any more. Read Dalrock's wonderful indictment of actually existent Christianity: Read his reviews of Courageous[995] and Firebomb[996], then read this[997]. People plausibly blame the Jews for affirmative action, but it was Christians transitioning to progressivism that are responsible for the War between the States, the dismantling of marriage, and women's suffrage. Jews pushed the affirmative action bandwagon merely to lefter-than-thou the progressives. A Jewish progressive is a converso, and thus, hates Jews, like Marx and the Trotskyists.

A lot of us are indignant at the progressive complicity in Islamic aggression against infidels, and compare it unfavorably with the heroic battles of Charles the Hammer, the crusaders, and the colonialists. But there is plenty of ancient precedent for turning the other cheek to Islam.

Despite much manufactured guilt about the supposedly horrible crusaders, Christendom has with the utmost regularity met Islamic aggression with a pacific response and extensive concessions. PC history writes up the Barbary wars as US being imperialistic, failing to notice that every Barbary war was started by Muslims taking white Americans as slaves and concluded with a peace in which the US paid Dar al Islam tribute, which peace was promptly broken after the tribute was received, followed by more white Christian Americans being abducted into slavery, and more demands for more tribute from America to Islam.

---

[995] https://dalrock.wordpress.com/2012/05/03/craven/
[996] https://dalrock.wordpress.com/2011/10/30/firebombed/
[997] https://dalrock.wordpress.com/2012/05/11/reframing-christian-marriage/

The Peace of Vasvár resembles the Oslo accords. Christendom won an overwhelming and decisive victory. Christendom sought to make peace on the basis of that victory. Muslims would not make peace. Christendom gave Muslims land for peace, as if Muslims, rather than Christians, had won the war, with entirely predictable results. There has never been an unequal treaty in favor of Christendom and against Dar al Islam except that Christians, after winning a decisive military victory, proceeded to follow up that victory by horribly mistreating Muslims until surviving Muslims agreed to an unequal peace. There has with great regularity been unequal treaties in favor of Dar al Islam and against Christendom, obtained by the stubborn Muslim refusal to make peace despite defeat, treaties that with great regularity Muslims broke. Over the past thousand years Christians have with great regularity turned the other cheek to Muslims, and with great regularity, promptly got slapped on the other cheek. Yes, progressives have been worse than Christians, but Christians were alarmingly and irrationally pacific. Progressives have taken tendencies that were already visible in Christendom to ever greater extremes. While progressives piously complain that Christians were never true to the anti war position of their religion, they were a lot truer to it than was sane or reasonable.

If you win a military victory, and the opposing side declines to make peace, despite defeat, you really should follow up military victory with indiscriminate rape, pillage, arson, and slaughter, until the other side gets the idea that peace might be a good idea. We have had a thousand years where Christians frequently refrained from rape and to some extent refrained from pillage even when rape and pillage would have been militarily advisable. Politically correct history books list those few pages from history when victorious Christians put the boot into defeated Muslims, glibly leaving out all those times, such as the Barbary wars and the Austro-Turkish War when victorious Christians neglected to put the boot in, a restraint never shown by Muslims, and Christians found their restraint rewarded by further attacks.

Mencius on the Fall

2012-12-31 09:15:37

Mencius addresses the question: Does today's US resemble the late Roman Empire in the west, or the late Roman Republic[998], in his usual wonderfully cryptic, long winded, and obscure fashion.

Mencius's proposed solution to our crisis, oligarchy or military dictatorship, assumes that America is analogous to the late Roman Republic. The people have become too degenerate to rule themselves, and so must be ruled by

---

[998] https://unqualified-reservations.blogspot.com.au/2012/12/some-perspectives-from-prudentius_24.html "Some perspectives from Prudentius"

others. In his latest post, however, he considers the possibility that there really is no solution.

Mencius gives us lengthy quotes from Prudentius, 403 AD. Prudentius is confident in the immense military superiority of the US Rome, the pacific nature of Rome's largely Christian enemies, and that the gigantic horde of idlers on welfare is a sign of economic strength.

Mencius neglects to mention, but assumes that we will know, that Rome was sacked, but not raped, in 410AD by Goths. The Goths left after looting the place for three days, but Rome never recovered. Law and order, long declining, collapsed, ending commerce. The state revenues that had supported the idle poor and the decadent rich, long declining, collapsed. Rome's enemies ceased to fear Rome, and over time many of Rome's subjects fled Rome because there was no money, no food, and no way to make a living. In 410 AD, Rome did not fall in the sense that France fell to Germany in 1939. It fell in it that it lost the will and ability to maintain order, and perhaps forgot that order is something that needed to be maintained, forgot what order was.

Prudentius' happy, confident, and blatantly deluded view of enemies and economics is strikingly reminiscent of today's Cathedral, but history does not repeat itself in collapse. Just as all happy families are alike, but each unhappy family is different, or, as we would say today, diverse, each collapse is different. Press hard on a pane of glass till it shatters, and each will shatter differently. The rise of each civilization is much the same as all the others, the fall is always different.

Still, if you walk around with your eyes closed, you are bound to walk into something, and if you have your eyes closed against enemies and economics, you will walk into war and economic collapse. War, lack of cohesion within the army, and economic collapse, are apt to result in shocking and surprising military defeat.

Although the large, overpaid and overpensioned logistic part of the US army is satisfactorily diverse, post Christian, and post marriage, satisfactorily to the Cathedral, the underpaid and shrinking part of the army that actually fights is still white, male, married and Christian. The Cathedral attacks their culture, by such measures as gay rights, which undermines unit cohesion. This may explain the startlingly poor recent performance of European forces.

You could integrate gays into the military by having all hetero units in which sodomy was subject to the death sentence, and lack of traditional masculinity was subject to severe punishment, and having all gay units in which normal sex was subject to the death sentence and the presence of traditional masculinity subject to severe punishment, but integrating gays at the unit level is an attack on unit discipline, morale, and culture.

Multiculturalism and diversity leaves everyone feeling like strangers and out-siders, which is bad for society in general, causing everyone to trash stuff and everyone to prey upon each other, and particularly and extraordinarily bad for unit cohesion. Muslims in Britain are markedly more criminal than in their homeland, and blacks in racially integrated suburbs are markedly more criminal, and suffer higher rates of imprisonment and deaths from tension related diseases, than blacks in all black suburbs – because they feel like out-siders, and view themselves as preying upon outsiders.

Segregation disadvantaged poorer blacks by protecting white working class jobs from black competition, but it advantaged middle class blacks by pro-tecting middle class black jobs from white competition. This created a ho-mogeneous black society dominated by the black middle class, in which the black middle class imposed middle class values, hence less black crime, less black on black crime, less danger, less stress, more black marriage. Integra-tion and multiculturalism is immensely hurtful to everyone, and especially hurtful to the fragile, to members of inferior groups. Nowhere is this dam-age more apparent than in the army. If we are going to have gays fighting, they should be in gay battalions, and if we are going to have blacks fight-ing (which, in practice we mostly do not, they generally wind up doing lo-gistics), they should be in black battalions. Military will comes from unit cohesion, and the more diverse the group, the harder to achieve cohesion.

A different culture, a different kind of society, could have gays integrated in the military and it would be no big deal. The Cathedral is trying to con-vert us into that kind of society, but as with the Arab Spring, they are going about it in entirely the wrong way. Gay Marriage, and teaching gays to hate and that they are hated, is exactly the opposite of the kind of measures that would be effective. Similarly, if you want to integrate Muslims into Britain, you would have to make them believe that they are Englishmen first, and Muslims third or fourth, you would need a self confident culture that pro-ceeds with cultural and social domination – pretty much the way segrega-tion imposed white middle class culture on the black middle class that seg-regation created, who then proceeded to impose it on working class blacks.

Secondly, the elements of the army that do the actual fighting should be the most privileged, the part of the army that has high status. Fighting should be where promotions come from. We need to see a lot fewer high ranking army officers with the "expert infantry man badge", a badge awarded for expertise in keeping oneself out of military activities that might get one shot at. Ac-tual fighting soldiers should have higher legal status than ordinary civilians, whereas at present they have lower legal status. A military husband is at a substantial disadvantage when divorced, compared to a non military hus-band, which contributes the extraordinarily high divorce rate among white fighting men. An ordinary civilian woman is rewarded in the short term with cash and prizes for destroying the life of her husband and the lives of her children, but this goes double if she is married to a military man – which is part of the Cathedral program of destroying the culture that they hate and despise, unfortunately destroying the fighting spirit of the army in the process.

But while the US, and the west generally, is cruising for an extraordinary and startling military defeat, this will not, in itself, cause reformation. It did not cause reformation in Rome.

To reform the US, we need an internal, rather than merely external crisis. The end of the Roman Republic led to a regime that was, for two centuries, pretty good. The fall of Rome led only to chaos and despair. When the Romans fled Britain, the Romano Britons were genocided by the Angles and the Saxons, who in turn were subjugated and raped by the Danes, raped with quite remarkable thoroughness, who in turn were conquered by a remarkably tiny handful of Normans, and only then, after six hundred years of quite extraordinary ruin, did the situation stabilize.

On the mainland of Europe, the situation stabilized rather sooner, under Charles the Hammer, who became a coalition leader among the pirates and brigands that overran the Roman empire, but there were still two centuries of horrifying economic and population decline leading up to Charles the Hammer, so let us hope we repeat the fall of the Roman Republic, rather than the fall of the City of Rome.

It is difficult to say why the failure of Romano-Britain was so stupendously horrible, because its history, buildings, culture and people, were so very thoroughly obliterated. The only significant Romano-British survival was Wales, which was the least Romanized part of Romano-Britain, in that finds of Roman coins have been least in Wales. So there was something about Roman social decay that rendered the Romano British permanently incapable of defending themselves. The legend of King Arthur and the knights of the round table originates from Romano-Britain, though every detail other than that his name was Arthur and the table was round was made up at later times. The table was round, to symbolize equality, that the table had no head, which, on the face of it, seems an obviously disastrous way to run a military organization, or indeed any organization. It sounds like the defense of Romano-Britain was run by the Occupy movement, which if so would explain the near total annihilation of the Romano-British.

Now obviously if America is going to fall to its enemies, imitating the fall of Rome in 410AD, which led to utter ruin lasting centuries, rather than the fall of the Republic in 48 BC, which led to recovery and greatness, Europe will fall before the US does. So how is Europe going?

After Britain's shocking and humiliating defeats in Basra, the Persian Gulf, and Helmand province, Iran did not occupy Britain and take down the British flag, nor was it ever likely that it would, but Britain has subtly and almost imperceptibly changed from indulging its Muslim minority out of political correctness, to privileging its Muslim minority because Britons are scared spitless of them. The British flag is not coming down because Iranian troops took it down, it is coming down because Britons are afraid it might cause offense. If Europe's economy still functions, it is because European assets are still tolerably secure, and they are secure because of US hegemony. If the US should suffer the military defeats that Britain suffered, and these defeats were to cause the loss of spirit, soul, and will that Britain suffered, then there would be no US hegemony, in which case assets would need to be secured by some other means.

In the US, which has cultural and legal tradition allowing property owners to use firm measures against intruders and guests who overstay their welcome, the Occupy movement was decisively smacked down whenever it confronted private owners. It would take one or two generations of victim disarmament before Americans became as passive, helpless, and frightened as today's Britons.

The end of US hegemony would not necessarily mean economic collapse similar to that of Rome, if there was will and ability to maintain a free economy and security of property rights by some other means, but I do not see that will in Britain, so an age as dark as that following the fall of Rome is possible, though by no means inevitable. The end of US hegemony is likely to cause economic collapse in much of Europe because a general lack of will and fighting spirit is evident in much of Europe.. There are parts of America where it might not necessarily cause economic collapse. The problem however might well be that in the US, as in Britain, the government might remain strong enough to stop people from defending what is theirs, but become too weak to defend what is its subjects, as terrible to its subjects as it is becoming contemptible to its enemies.

Milton Keynes UK
Ingram Content Group UK Ltd.
UKHW020703180124
436254UK00017B/969

9 798218 352677